The Investor-State Dispute Settlement System

The Investor-State Dispute Settlement System

Reform, Replace or Status Quo?

Foreword by Annette Magnusson

Edited by
Alan M. Anderson & Ben Beaumont

Wolters Kluwer

Published by:
Kluwer Law International B.V.
PO Box 316
2400 AH Alphen aan den Rijn
The Netherlands
E-mail: international-sales@wolterskluwer.com
Website: lrus.wolterskluwer.com

Sold and distributed by:
Wolters Kluwer Legal & Regulatory U.S.
7201 McKinney Circle
Frederick, MD 21704
United States of America
Email: customer.service@wolterskluwer.com

ISBN 978-94-035-1755-1

e-Book: ISBN 978-94-035-1810-7
web-PDF: ISBN 978-94-035-1854-1

Editors

Alan M. Anderson, PhD, specializes in dispute resolution, particularly international arbitration, both as counsel and as an arbitrator. He received his Master of Business Administration and Doctor of Law (*magna cum laude*) from Cornell University, New York. He received a Master of Laws, with distinction, specializing in international dispute resolution, from the University of London. He earned his PhD in War Studies from King's College London. Dr Anderson is a Fellow of the Chartered Institute of Arbitrators and a Fellow of the Australian Centre for International Commercial Arbitration, where he is in his second term as a member of its Council. He is also a Fellow of the Asian Institute of Alternative Dispute Resolution and an accredited international mediator. A frequent presenter and writer, Dr Anderson is the secretary of the Forum for International Conciliation and Arbitration, an international think-tank. He has participated in the work of UNCITRAL's Working Groups II and III since 2015. He is the President of Alan Anderson Law Firm LLC based in Minneapolis, Minnesota, US and a door tenant with Littleton Chambers in London, where he is a member of its international arbitration practice group.

Ben Beaumont is a barrister and member of Garden Court Chambers in London, England. He is a Chartered Arbitrator, a Fellow of the Chartered Institute of Arbitrators, a Fellow of the Royal Institution of Chartered Surveyors, and a member of the TECBAR and CIArb panels of arbitrators, adjudicators, and dispute board member. Mr Beaumont is a trained mediator. He is the founder and chair of the Forum for International Conciliation and Mediation, an international think-tank, and co-founder of International Dispute Resolution, an international group of dispute resolution specialists. Mr Beaumont is an author of various books on dispute resolution and often speaks on the topic. He has been appointed as arbitrator in more than 300 disputes. He regularly sits as a dispute avoidance board member and as a mediator. He has also been appointed as an adjudicator on more than twenty occasions. He has acted in arbitrations in various locations including UAE, Hong Kong, Singapore, Vietnam, France, United Kingdom and the United States. Mr Beaumont has been active in all five Working Groups of UNCITRAL, particularly Working Group VI, where he was appointed to an expert subgroup drafting the legislative guide to the model law on secured transactions. He also is active on various ICC working groups drafting model contracts.

Contributors

Ahmed Abdel-Hakam is a senior associate in Eversheds Sutherland's International Arbitration and Public International Law practice. He is a Solicitor-Advocate before the Higher Courts of England & Wales and a French Avocat. He represents clients in high-profile cross-border disputes with a multilingual element and legal and procedural issues across civil and common law jurisdictions. He has experience in investment and commercial arbitration proceedings under the rules of all the major arbitral institutions, dealing with disputes covering a broad range of sectors, with a focus on oil and gas. Ahmed is also a member of the Association of International Petroleum Negotiators. He also provides training to governments on investment treaty arbitration and is a contributor to Oxford University Press' online publication 'Investment Claims'. In 2019, Ahmed was selected as a Young Leader by the Franco-British Council, which selects a group of talented French and British individuals under the age of 40 each year, with distinguished careers across a variety of sectors from sciences to arts, politics, law, the military and finance.

Venetia Argyropoulou, PhD, is an Extramural Fellow at Tilburg University, the Netherlands, and Lecturer of Finance Law, at the European University of Cyprus and Hellenic University of Thessaloniki. She is educated in both civil and common law and has actively practised law in Greece and Cyprus. She has worked as a researcher for the University of Cyprus and as a lecturer for the University of West London. She is a member of the Spark Legal Network and the Cyprus Correspondent of the IBFD, Tax Analysts, IBA's Taxes Committee, the World Bank's Women, Business and the Law Initiative, Organisation for Economic Co-operation and Development's (OECD's) Social Institutions and Gender Index and the Observatory for Taxpayers' Rights. She is the correspondent for the Yearbook of International Environmental Law on the International Monetary Fund's (IMF's) Initiatives for Environment, Oxford Publishing. Additionally, she is listed in the European Court of Auditor's list of Experts in Financial Law and she has been selected as the best international law lawyer of Cyprus for 2016 and 2017 by Best 100 and International Advisory Experts. She is the IBA's Individual Tax and Private Client Committee Scholar for 2017.

Fahira Brodlija is the country coordinator for a regional legal reform project in the Western Balkans and an adjunct lecturer at the International University of Sarajevo, Bosnia and Herzegovina. In addition, Ms Brodlija is Director of Research for Arbitrator Intelligence, a global aggregator of data on arbitrations and arbitrators, seeking to enhance the quality and diversity of arbitrator appointments in international arbitration. Since 2016, Ms Brodlija has been coaching Vis Moot teams of the law faculties from Bosnia and Herzegovina. She is also a member of Association ARBITRI, an NGO founded by young attorneys in Bosnia and Herzegovina, seeking to enhance and promote the arbitration system in the country. Ms Brodlija obtained her BA in 2016 from the University of Sarajevo, Faculty of Law and her LLM in 2017 from the University of Pittsburgh, School of Law, Pittsburgh.

Charles H. Camp is an international lawyer with over thirty years of experience representing foreign and domestic clients in international litigation, arbitration, negotiation, and international debt recovery. In 2001, Mr Camp opened the Law Offices of Charles H. Camp, P.C. in Washington, DC to focus on effective, personalized representation in complex, international matters. Mr Camp teaches international negotiations at the George Washington University Law School, Washington, DC.

Kai-chieh Chan holds a Bachelor of Arts in Economics from National Taiwan University, Taiwan,a Master of Laws (*cum laude*) from *Institut d'études politiques de Paris* (Sciences Po Paris), France, a second Master of Laws from the University Paris 2 Panthéon-Assas, France, and is currently pursuing a PhD degree at the University Paris 2 Panthéon-Assas. He has worked as a trainee in several international law firms. His research focuses on international economic law, arbitration, and financial law. His works have been published in the *Revue générale de droit international public*, *Utrecht Journal of International and European Law*, *Journal de l'arbitrage de l'Université de Versailles*, Kluwer Arbitration Blog, and the *Nordic Journal of International Law*.

Anthony R. Daimsis has been teaching at the University of Ottawa, Canada, since 2003 and is the Director of the BiJural (common law/civil law) National Programme. He teaches Contracts Law, International Sales Law, International Commercial Arbitration and supervises the common law Jessup, Vis and FDI moot teams. Professor Daimsis is the lead instructor for the Professional Certificate in International Arbitration, which aims to introduce senior lawyers to the world of international arbitration by covering the process from start to finish. He is a door tenant at Littleton Chambers in London, England, and member of its international arbitration group. His experience includes serving as counsel, arbitrator, and as an expert witness in foreign investment disputes, and in telecommunications, underground resources, international commercial contract and construction disputes. Professor Daimsis appears before Canadian courts, including the Canadian Supreme Court, to set aside arbitral awards and for their recognition and enforcement, as well as in conflict of laws and commercial matters. He has delivered lectures and keynote addresses around the world, including London, New York, Hamburg, Stockholm, Beirut, Tehran, Naypyidaw, and Toronto.

Pallab Das is a research associate and teaching assistant at the National Law University of Odisha (NLUO) in India, where he teaches Maritime Law, Criminal Law and International Commercial Arbitration. He is also in charge of the Centre for Maritime Law at NLUO. He completed his LLM from Swansea University, United Kingdom on an International Excellence Scholarship in 2015, with a specialization in international commercial and maritime law and his BSL-LLB from ILS Law College, Pune, India. He completed Diploma in International Commercial Arbitration from Austrian Arbitration Academy, Vienna in 2018. He has written many articles as well as a book entitled *Justice for Women: Legal Compendium*. He is also the editor of the book on maritime law, *Through the Lens of Maritime Law: A World View*, and the editor of the second edition of the book *Maritime Jurisdiction and Admiralty Law in India*. Prior to joining NLUO, he practised in the High Court of Orissa and worked as a Civil Judge, Odisha Judicial Services. Pallab is a Member of Chartered Institute of Arbitrators and an associate member of Asian Institute of Alternate Dispute Resolution, Malaysia.

Chuanyu Fan has studied at the *Institut d'études politiques de Paris* (Sciences Po Paris), Universidad Pontificia Comillas (Madrid), and Peking University, China. She is currently a PhD candidate at both University Paris-Est and the University of Geneva, Switzerland. Her doctoral thesis concerns the permanent sovereignty of States over their natural resources in international economic law. Her professional experience includes long-term internships in international law firms, multinational corporations, and the Beijing Arbitration Commission. She specializes in project finance and corporate law. Admitted to the Paris Bar School (*Ecole de Formation professionnelle des Barreaux*), she expects to qualify as a French lawyer in late 2020.

Michael R. Garcia is a litigation associate at the Boston office of a global law firm. He is a 2016 graduate of the University of Michigan Law School, where he was a member of the *Michigan Journal of International Law* and an executive board member of the Michigan chapter of the Syrian Accountability Project. While in law school, Mr Garcia was named a 2015 Geneva International Fellow and spent a semester at UNICEF's office in Geneva, Switzerland, advocating for children's rights at the United Nations Human Rights Council. His article entitled, 'Clayton/Bilcon, Investor-State Arbitration and International Approaches to Trade and Investment' was published in volume 13 of the *Manchester Journal of International Economic Law*.

Frank J. Garcia is Professor of Law and Dean's Distinguished Scholar at the Boston College Law School, United States. A Fulbright Scholar, he has lectured widely on globalization and international economic law in Europe, South America and the Asia/Pacific region. He is the author, among other volumes, of *Consent and Trade: Trading Freely in a Global Market* (2019) and *Global Justice and International Economic Law: Three Takes*, both published by Cambridge University Press, and a co-author of *Rethinking International Investment Governance: Principles for the 21st Century* (2018). Professor Garcia is a Senior Fellow of the Columbia Center on Sustainable Investment (CCSI) and a member of the editorial board of the *Oxford Journal of International Economic Law*.

Guillermo Garcia-Perrote is a senior associate with Herbert Smith Freehills in Sydney, Australia. He is an international arbitration lawyer, admitted in England and Wales and Spain. In Sydney, he follows an increasingly active business relationship between Spain, Australia and the APAC region. Mr Garcia-Perrote advises clients on complex cross-border disputes across many sectors and industries, with a particular focus on construction/infrastructure and energy disputes. He speaks at conferences and seminars, and lectures at universities and master's programmes in relation to both arbitration and construction/infrastructure and energy sectors. He regularly publishes on arbitration-related topics. Mr Garcia-Perrote is included in the Arbitrator's List of the Spanish Civil and Commercial Court of Arbitration and is a Member of the Chartered Institute of Arbitrators, the Spanish Arbitration Club, and the Spanish-Australian Chamber of Commerce. In 2008, his team, representing Universidad Carlos III (Madrid), won the Willem C. Vis International Commercial Arbitration Moot, and he also received an honourable mention for the best individual oralist.

Sandeep Golani joined the National Law University Odisha in 2018 after he developed a keen interest in law. Currently, he is pursuing a BBA and an LLB, and is in the second year of law school. He is also pursuing a Company Secretaryship Course (Executive Programme). His interest areas include commercial and investment arbitration, investment law, corporate law, insolvency and bankruptcy laws and securities law. He has written many articles in these areas. Sandeep was also a student editor for the book, *Through the Lens of Maritime Law: A World View*, published by the Centre for Maritime Law, National Law University Odisha, in 2020.

Kiran Nasir Gore focuses her practice on US and transnational dispute resolution. She specializes in complex litigation, international commercial and investment arbitration, and global investigations. Her experience spans a variety of industries, including non-profits, luxury goods, medical devices and pharmaceuticals, natural resources, energy, shipping, and transport. She has previously worked as a senior associate in the Washington, DC office of Three Crowns LLP and as an associate in the New York office of DLA Piper LLP. She currently is Counsel in the Law Offices of Charles H. Camp, PC. Kiran also serves as Associate Editor of the *Kluwer Arbitration Blog* and Associate Editor of the *ICSID Review: Foreign Investment Law Journal*. She draws on her professional experiences as an educator at the George Washington University Law School and New York University's Global Study Center in Washington, DC.

Brooke S. Güven is a senior legal researcher at the Columbia Center on Sustainable Investment at Columbia University (CCSI). Her academic and policy work focuses on analysing the contracts, domestic frameworks and international legal arrangements governing cross-border investments, and the impacts that these frameworks have on sustainable development objectives. Prior to joining CCSI, she was a finance lawyer specializing in cross-border transactions at an international law firm, and also worked as a legal advisor with the Liberian Ministry of Health and Social Welfare. She has an LLM from New York University School of Law, where she was a Human Rights Scholar, a JD and MA from the University of Wisconsin, and a BA from Northwestern University, Illinois.

Margie-Lys Jaime, PhD, FCIArb, is a qualified independent arbitrator and Professor of Law at the University of Panama. She also acts as consultant and expert in commercial, trade and investment matters. Her practice includes international litigation, maritime disputes, commercial arbitration, investor-state dispute settlement, and international trade. Dr Jaime obtained her PhD in Law, with highest honours, and an LLM in International Economic Affairs Law, with honours, both from the University of Paris II (Pantheon-Assas). In addition, she holds an LLM in Arbitration and International Business Law from the University of Versailles (France), and an LLM in International Business and Economic Law with a Certificate in WTO Studies from Georgetown University Law Center, Washington, DC. Dr Jaime is a former trade negotiator for the Republic of Panama, having served as Chief of the Trade in Services and Investments Department at the Ministry of Trade and Industries. She is admitted to practise law in Panama, the State of New York, and holds the Certificate of Aptitude for the legal profession (CAPA) in Paris, France. She is the President of the Mediation and Arbitration Committee of the National Bar Association of Panama (2019–2021).

Marryum Kahloon is an associate in the New York office of Gibson, Dunn & Crutcher LLP, where she is a member of the International Arbitration Practice Group. Ms Kahloon specializes in international arbitration and public international law disputes. She has advised on cases before both the International Court Justice and the European Court of Human Rights. In addition, she has experience advising clients on cases under arbitration rules, including the ICSID, UNCITRAL, SCC, and ICC Rules. Ms Kahloon graduated with an LLM from Columbia Law School in 2018, where she was a James Kent Scholar, a Fulbright Scholar, and recipient of the Edwin Parker Prize for excellence in the study of international law. She earned her Bachelor of Laws degree, *summa cum laude*, from Bond University, Australia, where she was a Vice Chancellor's Scholar. She was also the judicial clerk to the Honorable Margaret McMurdo, AC, President of the Court of Appeal of Queensland. Ms Kahloon is admitted to practise in the State of New York, and in Queensland, Australia.

Karl M.F. Lockhart is an associate specializing in international investigations and disputes at a global law firm. Twice seconded to the firm's Singapore office for matters in South and Southeast Asia, he also has extensive experience in Africa, having worked on development projects in Tanzania, interned at the World Bank in South Africa, and researched human rights issues in Zambia. He was elected to the Order of the Coif at the University of Virginia School of Law, where he received the Monroe Leigh Fellowship in International Law and was a member of the *Virginia Law Review*. His articles have been published in the *Virginia Law Review*, the *Boston College Law Review*, and the *Georgetown Journal of International Law*.

Annette Magnusson is the Secretary General of the Arbitration Institute of the SCC since 2010. She joined the SCC from the law firm Mannheimer Swartling in Stockholm and before that Baker & McKenzie, Sweden. Ms Magnusson is the author or editor of several publications on international arbitration, including *Arbitrating for Peace* (Kluwer, 2017) and *International Arbitration in Sweden* (Kluwer, 2013), and the producer of the documentary *The Quiet Triumph* (2017), a film about interconnection between economic development, arbitration and peace. She is the founder of the Stockholm Treaty Lab, an international crowdsourcing challenge to innovate international law for climate change mitigation and adaptation, and a frequent speaker on sustainability and arbitration, including addressing Climate Change and Arbitration at the 24th ICCA Congress in Sydney in 2018. Ms Magnusson is listed as a Thought Leader and Global Leader in *Who's Who Legal*.

Brian McGarry is Assistant Professor of Public International Law at the Grotius Centre for International Legal Studies, Institute of Public Law, at the Faculty of Law of Leiden University, the Netherlands. He previously was Lecturer in International Dispute Settlement at the Graduate Institute of International and Development Studies, Switzerland. He received his PhD, *summa cum laude*, from the University of Geneva, which awarded him the Prix Bellot for best thesis in law or political economy in December 2019. A member of the New York Bar, he has consulted with States and intergovernmental organizations on a range of legal matters involving international trade and investment. He is a national of Ireland and the United States.

Kinda Mohamadieh is a legal advisor and senior researcher with the Third World Network office in Geneva. Her work covers WTO processes and negotiations, international investment governance and issues pertaining to business and human rights. Previously, she served as senior researcher for seven years with the intergovernmental organization, the South Centre, also based in Geneva. She also worked for nine years with the Arab NGO Network for Development, based in Beirut. Kinda holds an LLM in International Economic Law from the University of Lausanne, Switzerland, a master's in Public Affairs from the University of California in Los Angeles, and an undergraduate degree in Economics. She is currently a PhD candidate at the international law department of the Graduate Institute in Geneva.

Mohamed H. Negm is State Counsel for Arbitration and International Dispute Resolution at the Egyptian State Lawsuits Authority, Ministry of Justice. He represents the interests of Egypt before international courts and arbitral tribunals in international investment arbitrations. He is currently representing the State of Egypt in nine investment arbitration cases before the International Centre for Settlement of Investment Disputes. He has handled many complex, high value, commercial institutional and ad hoc arbitral proceedings involving parties from the Middle East, Europe, Asia, and the United States under the rules of leading arbitral institutions such as the ICC, CRCICA, UNCITRAL, LCIA, and DIAC. Mr Negm has been appointed by the African Union as an Expert Consultant on the Pan African Investment Code. He is the Assistant Editor of Kluwer Arbitration Blog for Middle East and North Africa. He is the Institute for Transnational Arbitration Reporter for Egypt and OHADA. Mr Negm was selected by the Association of Young Arbitrators as one of Africa's fifty Most Promising

Arbitration Practitioners in 2020. He lectures on Arbitration Law and International Dispute Resolution in the American Bar Association Rule of Law Initiative. Mr Negm was the regional representative of LCIA-YIAG for the Middle East and North Africa. He is a founding member of the Steering Committee of the Young Arab Arbitrators Forum. Mr Negm regularly publishes in international journals on issues of international law, international investment and commercial arbitration.

Srilal M. Perera, PhD, is retired Adjunct Professor of Law of the Washington College of Law of the American University, Washington, DC, where he taught a course on International Law of Foreign Investment and conducted an Advanced Research Seminar in International Investment Law from 2000 to 2018. Professor Perera is also a Fulbright Senior Specialist in Law. He served as Chief Counsel of the Multilateral Investment Guarantee Agency of the World Bank Group, until his retirement in 2010. Professor Perera also served as Legal Counsel at the Iran-United States Claims Tribunal in The Hague from 1986 to 1989. He is on the Panel of Arbitrators and Conciliators of the International Centre for the Settlement of Investment Disputes and a member of the Panel of Arbitrators of the Thailand Arbitration Center. Professor Perera holds an LLB from the University of Colombo, Sri Lanka, a JD-equivalent certification from the Sri Lanka Law College and qualified to practise as an attorney-at-law in Sri Lanka, an MA from the School of Advanced International Studies of the Johns Hopkins University, US, and a PhD from Georgetown University in Washington DC. He has several publications to his credit on various subjects directly concerning ISDS.

Relja Radović, PhD, received his PhD in Law from the University of Luxembourg. He also has a LLM (Adv) from Leiden University, the Netherlands and a LLM and a LLB (Hons) from the University of Novi Sad, Serbia. He has assisted with cases before the International Court of Justice, the International Criminal Tribunal for the former Yugoslavia and in international commercial arbitration. His research focus is international adjudication, jurisdiction of international courts and tribunals, investment treaty arbitration, judicial and arbitral law-making, and judicial and arbitral decision-making processes in international law. He has published on these topics in, among others, the *Journal of International Dispute Settlement* and the *Journal of World Investment & Trade*.

Ankita Ritwik is a senior associate in the Washington, DC office of Gibson, Dunn & Crutcher LLP and is a member of the Litigation and International Arbitration Practice Groups. Ms Ritwik has represented individuals and multinational companies with investments in Europe, Latin America, Asia and Africa in the real estate, energy, manufacturing and mining industries in international arbitration and enforcement proceedings. Ms Ritwik earned her Law degree *cum laude* in 2013 from Harvard Law School, Cambridge, US, where she was the Notes Editor for the *Harvard International Law Journal*. She graduated with honours from Yale University, New Haven, US, in 2007.

Victoria Shannon Sahani is Associate Dean of Faculty Development and Professor of Law at Arizona State University Sandra Day O'Connor College of Law in Phoenix, Arizona. She is also Director of the Faculty Inclusion Research for System Transformation, a university-wide initiative at Arizona State University. Prior to academia, she served for five years as Deputy Director of Arbitration and ADR in North America for the International Court of Arbitration of the International Chamber of Commerce (ICC) in New York. She is currently Vice Chair of the Academic Council of the Institute for Transnational Arbitration, Vice Chair of the Academic Subcommittee of the United States Council for International Business Arbitration Committee and a Member of the ICC Commission on Arbitration and ADR. She formerly served as a member of the Executive Council of the American Society of International Law and a member of the ICCA-Queen Mary Task Force on Third-Party Funding in International Arbitration. She also regularly serves as a consultant and an expert witness regarding third-party funding and arbitration issues. In addition to publishing numerous articles, essays and book chapters, Professor Sahani published the second edition of her coauthored book, *Third-Party Funding in International Arbitration* (Kluwer, 2017), with Lisa Bench Nieuwveld. She earned her undergraduate and law degrees from Harvard University and is licensed to practise law in New York and the District of Columbia.

Rose Maria Sebi is currently pursuing BBA and LLB degrees at the National Law University Odisha in India and is in the third year of law school. Her areas of interest include international commercial arbitration law and investment arbitration law. She has authored articles on commercial arbitration in India. She has also participated in moot court competitions, including a competition on international commercial arbitration where her team finished as quarter-finalist and was adjudged the team with the 'best written submissions for the respondent'. She has previously interned with lawyers and at law firms practising domestic and international commercial arbitration.

Ameyavikrama Thanvi is an Indian lawyer who practises at the Supreme Court of India. Her areas of interest include constitution law, public international law and investment treaty arbitration. She has appeared before two separate Constitution Benches of the Supreme Court of India that dealt with interpretation of the provisions concerning trade and commerce in the Constitution of India and the Arbitration and Conciliation Act, 1996. She has also acted as tribunal secretary in a number of domestic commercial arbitrations. In 2019, she received her LLM with distinction and with mention on the Dean's List from Georgetown University Law Center, Washington, DC, where she specialized in international arbitration and dispute resolution, focusing her studies on international investment arbitration. She worked as rapporteur for the white paper submitted by the International Law Institute to UNCITRAL Working Group III, which is mandated to work on reforms in ISDS. She previously has written articles on a variety of issues in domestic as well as international law.

Herman Verbist, PhD, is an attorney at the Ghent and Brussels Bar in Belgium with Everest Attorneys. He is an accredited mediator in civil and commercial matters by the Federal Mediation Commission in Belgium. He worked as counsel at the Secretariat of the International Court of Arbitration of the International Chamber of Commerce in Paris (1988–1996). He has taught, as visitor professor, the course on International Commercial Arbitration at the University of Ghent, Belgium. Since 2016, he is the President of the arbitrators of the Belgian Court of Arbitration for Sport. For many years, he has attended the sessions of UNCITRAL Working Group II. Dr Verbist recently taught a course entitled, 'Case Study Investment Mediation' at the Europa-Institut of Saarland University, Saarbrücken, Germany.

Ella Wisniewski is a senior associate, based in the Perth office of Herbert Smith Freehills. She obtained her Master of Laws in International Dispute Resolution from Humboldt University, Berlin, with a focus on international commercial arbitration, investor-state dispute settlement, and cross-border litigation. She has acted for clients in international commercial arbitrations, both institutional and ad hoc, and in an investor-state arbitration administered by ICSID. She advises clients on the resolution of disputes arising out of major construction and infrastructure projects, as well as within the energy, mining and resources sectors. In 2018, she was awarded third place in the Nappert Prize in International Arbitration, for her paper, which was subsequently published in the *ICC Dispute Resolution Bulletin* (Issue 4, 2018). Ella was also awarded 'best oralist' for defending her paper before a panel of preeminent arbitration practitioners and academics at the Nappert Prize Symposium, hosted by McGill University in Montreal. In 2020, Ella was included in the *Australasian Lawyer* Rising Stars list.

Shahrizal M. Zin, PhD, FCIArb, FAIADR, FMIArb is a legal academic and alternative dispute resolution practitioner. He is an Advocate and Solicitor of the High Court of Malaya. He is an arbitrator and adjudicator empaneled at the Asian International Arbitration Centre. He is a mediator accredited by the Bar Council Malaysian Mediation Centre. His areas of expertise include domestic and international dispute resolution with specific reference to construction law, international commercial arbitration, investment treaty arbitration and international trade matters. He graduated with an LLB (Hons) and LLM from the University of Malaya, Malaysia. He holds a PhD from Monash University, Australia. He was awarded a diploma in International Commercial Arbitration from the Chartered Institute of Arbitrators and admitted as a Fellow since 2016. He is also a Fellow of the Asian Institute of Alternative Dispute Resolution and the Malaysian Institute of Arbitrators. He is currently acting as a senior lecturer at the Faculty of Law, University Technology MARA, Malaysia. He serves as a visiting lecturer of the Faculty of Law, Airlangga University, Surabaya, Indonesia. He sits regularly as an arbitrator and adjudicator in relation to construction disputes pursuant to the Arbitration Act (2005) Malaysia and Construction Industry Payment and Adjudication Act 2012.

Summary of Contents

Table of Contents

Acknowledgements

The genesis of this volume was the editors' participation as representatives of the Forum for International Conciliation and Arbitration at the sessions of UNCITRAL Working Group III in New York City and Vienna, when the Working Group took up the topic of reform of the investor-State dispute settlement (ISDS) system. We were struck by the intensity and diversity of the debates surrounding the issues raised on the fundamental question of whether to reform or replace the ISDS system, and whether any changes practically are feasible, possible or even should be made – hence the title of this book.

We independently reached the same conclusion: that a book that presents a variety of views on the issues regarding the ISDS system would be a welcome and useful contribution to the on-going discussions. The editors at Kluwer Law International welcomed our suggestion and readily accepted our proposal. We were gratified by the number and quality of the proposals received from potential contributors, which made the final selections difficult. We were able to choose contributions addressing most of the key topics regarding ISDS reform, from authors located literally around the world representing diverse points of view drawn from academia, practitioners, government, and those focused on special interest topics.

All the contributors have worked hard to meet the demands we have placed on them, especially in light of the world-wide COVID-19 pandemic. It has been a pleasure working with them, and we thank them for their efforts. The quality and significance of this volume is due to their contributions. We must also extend special thanks to the wise and thoughtful guidance provided by our editors at Kluwer Law International. They have been a pleasure to work with from start to finish. Jonathan Blaney deserves thanks for his assistance in organizing the chapter contributions. Great thanks and appreciation must also be extended to Annette Magnusson, the Secretary General of the Arbitration Institute of the Stockholm Chamber of Commerce, who graciously and immediately agreed to write a foreword to this volume.

This has truly been a team effort by each of us as editors, and despite periodic differences throughout the process, neither of us could have done this alone. Finally, we accept responsibility for any errors or omissions that may inadvertently exist in this volume.

Alan M. Anderson
Ben Beaumont
July 2020

Foreword

On 6 April 2014, at the 23rd biannual Congress of the International Council for Commercial Arbitration (ICCA), Stephen M. Schwebel, former Judge and President of the International Court of Justice, delivered a keynote speech placing international investment arbitration in a historical context. It was an important contribution to the discussion on Investor-State Dispute Settlement (ISDS), adding a big-picture perspective at a time when different views appeared pre-destined to crouch in their respective trenches. But as the saying goes: 'if you do not know where you come from, then you probably don't know where you are going'.

Since 1959, States have entered into over 3,000 bilateral treaties for the purpose of protecting foreign investments. A majority of these treaties provide for arbitration between investors and the State in a situation of potential breach of the investment protection provisions of the treaty. And by the end of 2019, a global total of 1,023 investor-State cases were known to have been filed.[1]

The inclusion of international arbitration in bilateral investment agreements represents what some would call a revolutionary development in international law. Judge Schwebel, in his remarks, referred to it as 'one of the most progressive developments in the procedure of international law of the last fifty years, indeed in the whole history of international law'.[2] Among other things, it confirms that not only States could be the subject of international law, reflecting a general development of international law, as seen also in international human rights.

The inherently evolutionary character of international law has thus brought us ISDS, a relatively young system for resolving disputes. A system (actually a false label as it is rather a collection of separate systems than a single system) which is hailed by some, and heavily criticized by others. Where do we go from here?

In Stockholm, the start of the ISDS engagement was the very first treaty-based investor-State arbitration filed at the Arbitration Institute of the Stockholm Chamber of

1. As at 31 December 2019, UNCTAD Investment Policy Hub (https://investmentpolicy.unctad.org/).
2. The full speech is available in the ICCA Congress Series No. 18, *Legitimacy: Myths, Realities, Challenges*, Wolters Kluwer (2015).

Commerce (SCC) in 1993 under the United Nations Commission on International Trade Law (UNCITRAL) Arbitration Rules. Three years later, the SCC saw the first treaty-based case under the SCC Rules.

At that time, treaty-based investor-State arbitration was a relatively unknown creature in the fauna of international arbitration. Now of course things are different. Since the early cases in the 1990s, the Stockholm trajectory of investor-State arbitration has followed the global trend. With a total of 112 investment arbitration cases[3] and the SCC Rules being the third most commonly used rules in ISDS cases globally, the SCC is an outlier among international arbitral institutions usually administrating primarily commercial arbitration cases.

Against this background, the SCC has closely followed the debate on ISDS – to feed in our practical experience; to contribute to a fact-based discourse; and always to be prepared to contribute to a constructive dialogue on how to develop and, if needed, improve investor-state arbitration.

The proverb alluding to the importance of a historical context has a continuation: 'if you do not know where you are going, then you are probably going wrong'.[4]

Many arguments have been made in recent years that investor-State arbitration has indeed ended up in the wrong place, and that reform is therefore necessary. Some voices assert that this was a futile journey from the very start and that ISDS needs to be replaced with something different. And in parallel to the debate, governments are in the course of negotiating modernized treaties, while new cases are being heard, argued and decided.

It's complicated.

How to address change in a legal universe like that of ISDS? UNCITRAL approached the issue by delegating the task to its Working Group III in 2017. Working Group III was commissioned to start by identifying issues giving rise to concern, and then follow up by working on reform for each of these issues. Working Group III agreed on three main themes around which the work has since been organized: (i) concerns pertaining to consistency, coherence, predictability and correctness of arbitral awards, (ii) concerns pertaining to arbitrators and decision makers, and (iii) concerns pertaining to the cost and duration of ISDS cases.

While UNCITRAL is addressing only procedural aspects of ISDS, the discussion in the Working Group has however illustrated how difficult it can be at times to separate substance from procedure when evaluating and debating ISDS issues. A myriad of issues needs to be addressed. The task has at times appeared Herculean.

The UNCITRAL Member States have had the benefit of working with a large number of observer delegations, along with external experts representing both academia and the private sector. Together everyone is putting in their best effort to answer the question where ISDS needs to be going in the best possible way.

---

3. As at 31 December 2019.
4. A google search on 'if you don't know where you have been how do you know where you are going' gives multiple results and variations. This particular wording is attributed to the author Terry Pratchett. The full quote is 'If you do not know where you come from, then you don't know where you are, and if you don't know where you are, then you don't know where you're going. And if you don't know where you're going, you're probably going wrong.'

It is against this background that a publication like the one you are currently holding in your hands (or perhaps viewing on your screen) is both timely and important. The authors of this book have each contributed to the map going forward. Whether it takes you as a reader to your preferred place of destination – this is up to you. I, for one, am grateful for all our cartography experts offering their advice on the terrain ahead, where some parts are admittedly quite challenging. But just as the historical context matters, so do the chapters of this book in their capacity as building blocks for the better future we need to be ready to build together.

And speaking of building a better future, in the context of ISDS reform there is one question we must not forget to ask: could investment treaty arbitration be 'a force for good' – used to motivate a change of state behaviour to tackle some of our greatest challenges, including climate change? Could ISDS reform potentially pave the way? With global principles for dispute resolution and future investment agreements on the table, adding the perspective of sustainable development could be a tremendous opportunity for governments to contribute to – for example – climate change efforts in a truly meaningful way. Indeed, it is pleasing to see that the perspective is also included in this book.

The debate on ISDS reform needs to continue if we as a global community want to move forward. And move forward we must. Congratulations are therefore due to the authors of this book, who are contributing to the conversation. And I do hope some of its ideas will find a way into the negotiating rooms where the future of ISDS is being carved out.

Annette Magnusson
Secretary General
Arbitration Institute of the Stockholm Chamber of Commerce

Introduction

Alan M. Anderson & Ben Beaumont

The investor-State dispute settlement (ISDS) system has a long and storied history. Some of the earliest, if not arguably the first, ISDS provisions were contained in the 1795 Treaty of Amity, Commerce, and Navigation between Great Britain and the newly-formed United States.[1] Articles VI and VII of that treaty created a commission from which panels of three commissioners were to be drawn, to finally resolve claims by merchants of one country for compensation against the other country following American independence.[2] Approximately 165 years later, what was then West Germany and Pakistan entered into the first bilateral investment treaty (BIT), agreeing not to discriminate against or expropriate investments in one state by nationals of the other.[3] Thereafter, BITs and international investment agreements (IIAs) between States and investors flourished. Thirty years after the first BIT, more than 300 BITs existed around the globe.[4] By 2005, more than 2,500 BITs had been executed.[5] By 2019, more than 3,250 IIAs existed.[6] Multilateral investment treaties, such as the Energy Charter Treaty and geographic free trade agreements, further expanded the scope of protection of foreign investors.[7]

1. Treaty of Amity, Commerce and Navigation, Between His Britannic Majesty and the United States of America, 8 United States Statutes 116 (1794).
2. *Ibid.*, 8 United States Statutes 119–122.
3. Treaty between the Federal Republic of Germany and Pakistan for the Promotion and Protection of Investments (signed 25 November 1959; entered into force 28 April 1962), 457 U.N.T.S. 23, Arts 2, 3.
4. Jeswald W. Salacuse, 'BIT by BIT: The Growth of Bilateral Investment Treaties and Their Impact on Foreign Investment in Developing Countries', 24(3) *The International Lawyer* 655 (1990).
5. *See* Rudolf Dolzer and Christoph Schreuer, *Principles of International Investment Law* (Oxford, 2008), 2; United Nations Conference on Trade and Development (UNCTAD), *World Investment Report 2006: FDI from Developing and Transition Economies: Implications for Development* (United Nations, 2006), 26.
6. UNCTAD, *World Investment Report 2020: International Production Beyond the Pandemic: Key Messages and Overview* (United Nations, 2020), xii.
7. *See* Anders Åslund, 'The World Needs a Multilateral Investment Agreement', *Peterson Institute for International Economics Policy Brief* (January 2013), 5 (available at: http://citeseerx.ist.psu.edu/viewdoc/download?doi=10.1.1.269.6226&rep=rep1&type=pdf).

Not surprisingly, with increased protections against expropriation and discrimination came claims by investors against States that they were being mistreated in violation of treaty or IIA provisions. In August 1961, the general counsel of the International Bank for Reconstruction and Development suggested an international convention to provide a process for resolving disputes between investors and States.[8] By 1965, a text had been developed and agreed, and on 14 October 1966, the Convention on the Settlement of Investment Disputes between States and Nationals of Other States (ICSID Convention) entered into force.[9] Today, more than 160 countries are signatories to the ICSID Convention.[10] The International Centre for Settlement of Investment Disputes (ICSID) administers many investor-State disputes under its arbitration rules, although individual BITs, IIAs or multilateral investment treaties may provide for the use of other administrative facilities, such as the Permanent Court of Arbitration or the Arbitration Institute of the Stockholm Chamber of Commerce, or the use of other arbitration rules, such as the United Nations Model Arbitration Rules. By 2019, more than 1,000 treaty-based ISDS cases were known to have been filed. Fifty-five publicly known cases were filed in 2019, with seventy-one decisions reached that year by arbitral tribunals. Damages awarded against States ranged from a few million to USD 8 billion.[11]

With the increased number of ISDS disputes and the often-significant damages awarded against States, perceptions[12] (at least) arose that the ISDS system was inconsistent, lacked transparency, and was simply unfair.[13] Criticisms on various aspects of the ISDS system mounted,[14] although other commentators came to its defence.[15]

---

8. International Centre for Settlement of Investment Disputes (ICSID), *History of the ICSID Convention*, vol. I (ICSID, 1970), 2–4.
9. *Ibid.*, 8–10.
10. ICSID, 'Database of ICSID Member States' (available at: https://icsid.worldbank.org/en/Pages/about/Database-of-Member-States.aspx).
11. UNCTAD, *World Investment Report 2020, supra* n. 6, at xii.
12. As of the end of 2019, at least 674 ISDS disputes had been concluded. About 37% of the cases were decided in favour of States, roughly 29% were decided in favour of investors with compensation awarded, and approximately 21% of the disputes were settled. UNCTAD, 'IIA Issues Note: Investor-State Dispute Settlement Cases Pass the 1,000 Mark: Cases and Outcomes in 2019', No. 2 (United Nations, July 2020), 5.
13. *See generally* Michael Waibel, Asha Kaushal, Kyo-Hwa Chung and Clair Balchin, *The Backlash Against Investment Arbitration: Perceptions and Reality* (Kluwer Law International 2010).
14. *See*, e.g., Michael Nolan, 'Challenges to the Credibility of the Investor-State Arbitration System', 5(3) *Am. U. Bus. L. Rev.* (2015), 429–445; Raphael Lencucha, 'Is It Time to Say Farewell to the ISDS System?', 6(5) *Int'l J. Health Policy Manag.* (2016), 289–291; Susan Franck, 'The Legitimacy Crisis in Investment Treaty Arbitration: Privatizing Public International Law Through Inconsistent Decisions', 73(4) *Fordham L. Rev.* (2005), 1521–1625; Federico Lavopa, 'Crisis, Emergency Measures and the Failure of the ISDS System: The Case of Argentina', in *Investment Treaties: Views and Experiences from Developing Countries* (South Centre, 2015), 193–214. *See generally* Waibel et al., *The Backlash, supra* n. 13.
15. *See*, e.g., Gloria Maria Alvarez, Blazej Blasikiewicz, Tabe von Hoolwerff, Keoplatra Koutouzi, Nikos Lavranos, Mary Mitsi, Emma Spiteri-Gonzi, Adrian Verdegay Mena and Piotr Willinski, 'A Response to the Criticism against ISDS by EFILA', 33(1) *J. Int'l Arb.* (2016), 1–36; S.W. Schill, 'In Defense of International Investment Law', in M. Bungenberg, C. Herrmann, M. Krajewski and J.P. Terhechte (eds), *European Yearbook of International Economic Law 2016* (Springer, 2016), 2–28.

In light of the mounting criticisms and debate, in 2015, the United Nations Commission on International Trade Law (UNCITRAL) commenced deliberations on whether to take up discussion of possible reform of the ISDS system.[16] At its session in 2017, the Commission decided to assign its Working Group III (WG III) 'with a broad mandate to work on possible reform of ISDS'.[17] WG III was:

> requested to ensure that the deliberations, while benfiting [*sic*] from the widest possible breadth of available expertise from all stakeholders, would be Government-led with high-level input from all Governments, consensus-based and fully transparent. The Working Group would proceed to: (i) first, identify and consider concerns regarding ISDS; (ii) second, consider whether reform was desirable in light of any identified concerns; and (iii) third, if the Working Group were to conclude that reform was desirable, develop any relevant solutions to be recommended to the Commission.[18]

It became apparent very quickly that the discussions and debates in WG III would not be easy or without controversy. Indeed, at the first meeting of WG III in Vienna on 27 November 2017, selection of the session chair required, for the first time in more than forty years, the use of a secret ballot by the UNCITRAL Member States.[19] Interest in the topic of ISDS reform at WG III has been global and ranged well beyond the usual attendees. At its first session in late 2017, representatives from forty-nine Member States, thirty-one observer States, and thirty-five intergovernmental and non-governmental entities were in attendance.[20] With its most recent session that concluded in January 2020, the number of representatives had increased to fifty-five Member States, forty-two observer States, eleven intergovernmental organizations, and fifty-six non-governmental entities.[21] To date, at least thirty-five submissions have been made to WG III by States, intergovernmental entities and non-governmental entities.[22] Inter-sessional meetings have been held in South Korea, the Dominican Republic and the Republic of Guinea.[23] The meeting room has regularly been literally filled to capacity from the beginning of WG III's discussions.

WG III has identified a number of topics for discussion. They include the duration and cost of ISDS; lack of transparency in ISDS proceedings; lack of an early dismissal

16. United Nations Commission on International Trade Law (UNCITRAL), 'Possible future work in the field of dispute settlement: Reforms of investor-State dispute settlement: Note by the Secretariat', A/CN.9/917 (20 April 2017), paras 1–8.
17. UNCITRAL, 'Possible reform of investor-State dispute settlement (ISDS): Note by the Secretariat', A/CN.9/WG.III/W.P.142 (18 September 2017), para. 2.
18. *Ibid.*, para. 3.
19. UNCITRAL, 'Report of Working Group III (Investor-State Dispute Settlement Reform) on the work of its thirty-fourth session' (Vienna, 27 November–1 December 2017), Part I', A/CN.9/930/Rev. 1 (19 December 2017), paras 11–16.
20. *See ibid.*, paras 7–10.
21. *See* UNCITRAL, 'Report of Working Group III (Investor-State Dispute Settlement Reform) on the work of its resumed thirty-eighth session', A/CN.9/1004/Add. 1 (28 January 2020), paras 6–9.
22. *See* UNCITRAL, 'Working Group III: Investor-State Dispute Settlement Reform: Status of preparatory work on reform options and schedule of events: Update as of 20 July 2020' (available at: https://uncitral.un.org/en/working_groups/3/investor-state).
23. *See ibid.*

mechanism to eliminate meritless claims; the lack of a mechanism to address counter-claims by respondent States; the apparent lack of consistency and coherence in ISDS decisions, including review mechanisms; and issues regarding arbitrators, including their appointment and ethical requirements.[24] In four sessions spanning multiple meetings through January 2020, WG III has debated ISDS potential reforms including means of increasing consistency in decisions; creation of a multi-national investment court or court of appeal; creation of an advisory centre similar to the World Trade Organisation's Advisory Centre; means to ensure impartiality and independence of arbitrators; development of a code of conduct for ISDS arbitrators; ways to decrease the costs and duration of ISDS; security for costs; and claims by shareholders for reflective loss.[25] By its sessions in October 2019 and January 2020, WG III was discussing multiple possible reform options.[26] The now-postponed thirty-ninth session, originally scheduled for late March and early April 2020 in New York City, would have continued consideration of possible ISDS reforms.[27] To say that the debates have been wide-ranging, sometimes contentious, but always informative, interesting and useful, would be a considerable understatement.

This book seeks to contribute to the on-going world-wide debate and discussions regarding the ISDS system. Drawing contributors from around the world, it provides insights on many of the critical topics being considered at UNCITRAL's WG III and elsewhere. This book addresses the key question for the ISDS system and the international community it serves: Should the present ISDS system be reformed, replaced, or simply remain as is? In essence, what should be the future character and characteristics of the ISDS system?

The twenty-nine authors of the twenty chapters that follow represent points of view from academia, private practice, non-governmental entities and experiences gained from regional organizations and State governments. This book provides insights and commentary on the myriad proposals of ISDS reform or replacement and their implications, including such topics as the possible consequences of wholesale replacement or elimination of the current ISDS system; the creation of a multi-national investment court or appellate review mechanism; the effects and implications of third-party funding; damages and the ability of tribunals to understand the complexities of damages claims; alternatives to arbitration; and issues relating to post-award enforcement. It further offers insights gleaned from various regional and State-specific

24. UNCITRAL, 'Possible Reform', *supra* n. 17, paras 20–44.
25. *See generally* UNCITRAL, 'Report, thirty-fourth session', *supra* n. 19; UNCITRAL, 'Report of Working Group III (Investor-State Dispute Settlement Reform) on the work of its thirty-fifth session (New York, 23–27 April 2018)', A/CN.9.935 (14 May 2018); UNCITRAL, 'Report of Working Group III (Investor-State Dispute Settlement Reform) on the work of its thirty-sixth session (Vienna, 29 October–2 November 2018)', A/CN.9/964; UNCITRAL, 'Report of Working Group III (Investor-State Dispute Settlement Reform) on the work of its thirty-seventh session (New York, 1–5 April 2019)', A/CN.9.970; UNCITRAL, 'Report of Working Group III (Investor -State Dispute Settlement Reform) on the work of its thirty-eighth session (Vienna, 14–18 October 2019)', A/CN.9/1004; UNCITRAL, 'Report, resumed thirty-eighth session', *supra* n. 21.
26. UNCITRAL, 'Annotated provisional agenda: Thirty-ninth session', A/CN.9/WG.III/WP.189 (16 January 2020), paras 9–10.
27. *Ibid.*, para. 11.

examples of recent efforts at ISDS system reform and replacement, and some of the critical issues that States face in making decisions regarding the ISDS system and its possible revision.

The first chapter introduces the foundational question of how to solve the perceived problem of inconsistency in ISDS arbitration. Written by Ameyavikrama Thanvi, the chapter addresses the essential enquiry of how to address the need for consistency in ISDS decisions. It analyses the concepts of consistency and coherence and discusses different types of inconsistencies that impact the ISDS system and how these issues affect investors and States. Some of the proposed solutions are reviewed. Perhaps not surprisingly, it concludes that none of the options is perfect, and that further discussion and analysis will be necessary to address the issue of consistency.

The next five chapters provide insights into how several geographic regions and economic co-operation areas have sought to address the question of reform of the ISDS system, as well as the different courses of action faced by several States. The European Union's (EU) proposed reform – in many respects a replacement of the existing ISDS system at least within its borders – is considered by Dr Venetia Argyropoulou, focusing of course on the Court of Justice of the European Union's decision in *Slovak Republic v. Achmea BV*.[28] Then, scholars from Bosnia-Herzegovina and India focus on those nations' issues as they consider participation in the ISDS system. Fahira Brodlija looks at the options for ISDS reform from the viewpoint of Bosnia-Herzegovina, a developing State and aspiring EU member in Chapter 3. Rose Maria Sebi, Sandeep Golani and Pallab Das analyse India's 2015 model BIT and consider whether it is really suited to the broader jurisprudence of international arbitration and whether it is the best form for India given its desire to continue to attract and retain foreign direct investment. Mohamed H. Negm then considers the framework of ISDS arbitration under Middle East multilateral and regional agreements. He focuses on the positions expressed by Middle East States and their contributions to ISDS reform. Kiran Nasir Gore and Charles H. Camp analyse the new United States-Mexico-Canada Agreement (USMCA) that replaced the North America Free Trade Agreement, focusing on its ISDS provisions. They conclude that the new agreement is an example of effective ISDS reform. They argue that the USMCA shows that evolution, not an outright replacement, is the best approach to solving any ills in the ISDS system.

After these geographic looks at the ISDS system, the next five chapters focus on some of the particular proposals, issues and considerations of ISDS reform. Professor Margie-Lys Jaime addresses the proposal for the creation of a multilateral court of appeal as a means for ISDS reform. She considers issues such as selection and appointment of the members, as well as the grounds for an appeal and the scope of the power of such a court. In Chapter 8, Dr Relja Radović addresses the law-making function of international tribunals. He argues that the proper application and control of arbitrator-created jurisdictional rules would improve the performance of the ISDS system and advance the goal of greater legal certainty on questions of jurisdiction, and that these improvements could be made within the context of the present ISDS system.

28. Case C-284/16, [2018] ECLI:EU:C:2018:158.

Professor Srilal M. Perera analyses the topic of a State's responsibility for the acts of State-controlled entities in ISDS. He comprehensively reviews tribunal decisions and the various approaches they have taken to resolve this often-critical issue. His chapter endeavours to answer some of the questions presented in deciding whether a State is responsible for the acts of its controlled entity, particularly the approach offered in the 2001 Draft Articles on State Responsibility. Professor Anthony R. Daimsis then presents a cautionary note in Chapter 10, relevant to those States that may decide to terminate existing BITs and investment agreements. Professor Daimsis discusses how investors may retain their right to pursue claims for violation of investment protection following termination of such treaties and agreements. Dr Shahrizal M. Zin follows with an analysis of a State's access to justice in the present ISDS system through recourse to assertion of a counterclaim against the investor-claimant. He identifies a number of key issues that a State often encounters in asserting a counterclaim, and proposes a way forward to enhance a State's ability to present counterclaims and thereby enhance a State's access to justice in the ISDS system.

In Chapter 12, Guillermo Garcia-Perrote and Ella Wisniewski examine the role of ISDS in promoting and protecting renewable energy production, a vital consideration around the world today. They argue that revision of the Energy Charter Treaty would modernize it and ensure that the Treaty's protections cover investments in energy efficiency, storage, transmission and delivery.

Third-party funding and its effects and implications are the subject of the next two chapters. Professor Victoria Shannon Sahani uses third-party funding as the means to analyse the lack of financial access to justice in the ISDS system. She presents possible approaches to address this disparity without requiring renegotiation of existing investment treaties. Brooke S. Güven, Frank J. Garcia, Karl M.F. Lockhart and Michael R. Garcia focus on the role arbitration rules can and should play in regulating third-party funding. They contend that revision of the arbitration rules typically applicable in ISDS could lead to suitable reform of such funding and that this topic should be one of the subjects for discussion as part of ISDS reform.

Chapters 15 and 16 consider alternatives to using arbitration as a means to resolve investor-State disputes. Kinda Mohamadieh discusses mediation and the roles of domestic courts and State-to-State led mechanisms as alternatives to arbitration. She argues that effective integration of such alternatives into the ISDS system would enhance the relevance and legitimacy of possible reforms. Dr Herman Verbist then reviews mediation as a method for resolving investor-State disputes. He examines the available data on the use of mediation in ISDS and reviews the existing international framework, especially the recent Singapore Convention prepared by UNCITRAL Working Group II.

Damages in ISDS presents a thorny issue, especially with stupendously large awards against States that have garnered headlines – awards that seemingly dwarf the State's ability to pay. The question often is whether tribunals in ISDS really understand the complexities and rationalities of the damages claims presented. As an ad hoc annulment committee in an ICSID proceeding stated:

> The Committee takes issue with the complete absence of any discussion of the Parties' expert reports within the Tribunal's analysis of the loss of value claim. While the Committee accepts that a tribunal cannot be required to address within its award each and every piece of evidence in the record, that cannot be construed to mean that a tribunal can simply gloss over evidence upon which the Parties have placed significant emphasis, without any analysis and without explaining why it found that evidence insufficient, unpersuasive or otherwise unsatisfactory.[29]

Kai-chieh Chan and Chuanyu Fan examine the duty to mitigate damages and the present confusion and absence of clear principles to guide ISDS tribunals in applying that duty in investor-State disputes. As a result, they contend that duty is too often minimized by tribunals, thereby permitting excessive damages awards. They argue that ISDS reform should include appropriate clarifications of the duty to mitigate so that it is more frequently, and correctly, applied in ISDS. Ahmed Abdel-Hakam addresses the fundamental question of whether tribunal members are sufficiently qualified to address damages issues. He considers whether new rules, including mandatory tribunal-appointed damages experts, should be part of any ISDS reforms.

The last two chapters examine possible reforms to the post-award processes in the ISDS system. Ankita Ratwik and Marryum Kahloon look at the ICSID annulment process and the increased use of that process as simply a device for delaying enforcement. They present various proposals to enhance post-award efficiency under the ICSID Convention. Professor Brian McGarry explores whether an ISDS award is enforceable as a 'foreign arbitral award' under the 1958 New York Convention on the Recognition and Enforcement of Foreign Arbitral Awards. His chapter links the interim arbitration mechanism recently adopted by some World Trade Organization members to the institutional body that may emerge from the discussions on-going in WG III.

Thus, these twenty chapters provide a broad overview and analysis of many of the issues before WG III and under discussion within the greater ISDS community. The pause in the deliberations of WG III occasioned by the global COVID-19 pandemic has allowed all the participants to catch their breath, and review and meditate on the discussions, proposals and issues that have thus far been raised and debated. The analyses in this volume should be particularly useful now and as the discussions continue. Readers of the chapters should gain a greater understanding of many of the issues, options for reform, and consequences that may result from taking a particular path towards reform or replacement of the ISDS system. The insights achieved can only benefit investors and States in the increasingly complex and inter-connected global community.

29. *TECO Guatemala Holdings LLC v. Republic of Guatemala*, ICSID Case No. ARB/10/23 (Annulment Proceedings), Decision on Annulment (5 April 2016), 36, para. 131.

CHAPTER 1

Bringing Consistency to Investment Arbitration: Challenges and Reform Proposals

Ameyavikrama Thanvi

Investment arbitration has numerous examples where a concept has been given diametrically opposite interpretation by different arbitral tribunals. Limited inconsistency is prevalent in every legal system. However, the inconsistencies in investment arbitration decisions have led to legitimacy concerns. This chapter analyses the concepts of consistency and coherence in Investor-State Dispute Settlement (ISDS) and identifies different types of inconsistencies, both procedural and substantial, that affect the system. The impact of inconsistency in investment arbitration and how it affects the investor as much as it affects the sovereign is explained. Some of the proposals made to address the issue of inconsistency, including tailoring the international investment agreement (IIA), introducing a system of precedent, and prior scrutiny of award, are identified and analysed. While an array of options available to address the issue exists, none is perfect. Nevertheless, the issue of inconsistency ought to be addressed and the options on the table need to be further assessed and experimented upon before a final decision is made.

§1.01 INTRODUCTION

The system of investment arbitration, as we know it, has been under challenge for some time. States have opposed the mechanism more than any other stakeholder, offering a number of reasons for their positions. These reasons include challenges to their sovereignty, inconsistent outcomes, time and money, costs, etc. The concerns raised are neither novel nor raised for the first time. However, for the first time, an all-party effort has been undertaken to address these concerns and identify possible reforms that could improve the system.

The United Nations Commission on International Trade Law (UNCITRAL), at its fiftieth session in 2017, entrusted Working Group III (WG III) with a mandate to: (i) identify and consider concerns regarding ISDS; (ii) consider whether reform was desirable in light of any identified concerns; and (iii) if the working group were to conclude that reform was desirable, develop any relevant solutions to be recommended to UNCITRAL.[1] WG III has, accordingly, identified four core challenges that need to be addressed. Primary among them is the issue of 'consistency, coherence, predictability, and correctness of arbitral decisions by ISDS tribunals'. WG III has observed that in certain cases divergent interpretations of the same treaty standard may be justifiable. Therefore, it is only the 'unjustifiable' inconsistencies that need to be addressed.[2] This chapter addresses the issue of lack of consistency and coherence in ISDS and, like WG III, this chapter's focus will be on unjustified inconsistencies.

At the outset, this chapter examines the premise of the challenge of consistency. This will include instances of divergent interpretations of the same treaty standards and other treaty provisions, which form the basis of the current challenges to ISDS. Second, this chapter will then explain how such divergent interpretations have led to questions on the legitimacy of the mechanism and whether they are justifiable or not. Third, this chapter will examine the proposals made to address the inconsistency and incoherence. Finally, this chapter will conclude by assessing the practicability of the reforms proposed and whether or not scientific consistency can be achieved in investment arbitration where the treaty terms may be identical but the facts and circumstances surrounding every treaty are unique.

§1.02 THE CONSISTENCY AND COHERENCE DEBATE: WHAT IS AT STAKE

The issue identified by WG III regarding consistency is not merely that of uniformity in arbitral decisions but of 'consistency, coherence, predictability and correctness of arbitration decisions'.[3] Thus, before any discussion is undertaken on the need for consistency and the challenges concerning consistency in investment arbitration, an understanding of each of these terms and what they stand for is useful.

1. UNCITRAL, *Report of the United National Commission on International Trade Law Fiftieth* Session, Official Records of Seventy-second Session, Supplement No. 17, ¶264 U.N. Doc A/72/17 (2017), https://undocs.org/A/72/17.
2. UNCITRAL, *Report of Working Group III (Investor-State Dispute Settlement Reform)* on the work of its Thirty-Fifth Session (New York, 23–27 April 2018), ¶25, U.N. Doc A/CN.9/935, https://undocs.org/en/A/CN.9/935.
3. Secretariat, UNCITRAL Working Group III, *Possible Reform of Investor-State Dispute Settlement (ISDS)*, ¶8, U.N. Doc. A/CN.9/WG.III/WP.149 (5 September 2018); *see also* UNCITRAL Working Group III, *Possible Reform of Investor-State Dispute Settlement (ISDS)*, U.N. Doc. A/CN.9/WG.III/WP.150 (28 August 2018).

[A] Consistency

A legal system is consistent if it treats identical or similar situations in the same way and if it gives equal treatment to the participants in the system.[4] The ability of a legal system to maintain stability and consistency in legal situations is decisive in preserving public confidence in the administration of justice.[5] Lack of consistency, on the other hand, prepares a foundation for framing allegations of unfairness, a lack of predictability in operation of law and a general sense of insecurity. The fact that disputing parties can receive diametrically opposite rulings on the same legal question, depending on who leads the decision-making or the personality of each judge, only undermines the credibility of the system.[6] That said, the same rule when applied in different fact situations or even otherwise can often be differently interpreted by different decision-making bodies.[7] Consistency, however, is not an absolute value of the law.[8]

[B] Coherence

Coherence literally means the quality of being logical and consistent.[9] It has been presented as an essential precondition of a legitimate legal system, which makes the system one whole and free from internal contradictions.[10] Legal theorists concur that what constitutes coherence is more than mere logical consistency among propositions, but they are unclear as to what is that something more.[11] Coherence is often confused with consistency, but coherence is a cluster of properties of which consistency is a necessary one and hence a perfectly coherent system will also be perfectly consistent.[12]

---

4. Christoph Schreuer, *Coherence and Consistency in International Law*, in Prospects in International Investment Law and Policy (E. Echnadi and P. Sauve, eds, 2013), https://www.univie.ac.at/intlaw/wordpress/wp-content/uploads/2014/01/Coherence-and-Consistency-in-International-Investment-Law.pdf.
5. *Sahin and Sahin v. Turkey*, Application No. 13279/05 (ECtHR, 20 October 2011), Dissenting Opinion ¶5, https://www.legal-tools.org/doc/d7b771/pdf/.
6. *Ibid.*
7. Christoph Engel, *Inconsistency in the Law: In Search of a Balanced Norm*, Preprints of the Max Planck Institute for Research on Collective Goods, p. 43, No. 2004/16 (December 2004), http://dx.doi.org/10.2139/ssrn.628387.
8. *Ibid.*
9. *Coherence*, Oxford Dictionary, https://www.lexico.com/definition/coherence (last visited: 28 April 2020).
10. Ross Grantham and Darryn Jensen, *Coherence in the Age of Statutes*, 42 Monash U. L. Rev. 360, 363 n.2 (2016), https://papers.ssrn.com/sol3/papers.cfm?abstract_id=2930695.
11. *Interpretation and Coherence in Legal Reasoning*, Stanford Encyclopaedia of Philosophy, https://plato.stanford.edu/entries/legal-reas-interpret/#WhaConCoh (Last visited: 28 April 2020).
12. Luc J. Wintgens, *Coherence of the Law*, 79 Archive for Philosophy of Law and Social Philosophy 483, 484 No. 4 (1993), www.jstor.org/stable/23680253.

[C] Predictability

Legal predictability is a fundamental part of what is meant by the rule of law.[13] Predictability is a dynamic concept that looks at the law in action rather than the law in litigation.[14] In common law, predictability is maintained by adhering to the doctrine of stare decisis, which is supposed to make it easier for people facing a new situation to predict how the courts will deal with it.[15]

In international law, its objects are subject to regulation, which helps ensure predictability when addressing a problem.[16] In fact, the ISDS system was originally created to foster predictability and consistency for the advantage of foreign investors and adherence to the goal of predictability fosters trust in the system.[17]

[D] Correctness of Decision

Decisions delivered by an adjudicating authority in a legal system may be perfectly consistent and therefore coherent and predictable, but that is not a guarantee of their correctness. Emergence of a *jurisprudence constante* based on defective legal reasoning can never be desirable.[18] Broadly, correctness can relate to the quality of reasoning of a decision. Narrowly, it may be understood as a binary assessment by a reviewing authority that separates correct decisions from incorrect ones.[19] In international arbitration, the role of accuracy or correctness of award cannot be downplayed.[20] It is the lodestar without which all other achievements of arbitration process would be an empty prize.[21]

---

13. Stefanie A. Lindquist and Frank C. Cross, *Stability, Predictability and the Rule of Law: Stare Decisis as Reciprocity Norm*, p. 1 (Conference on Measuring the Rule of Law, Austin, March 2010) (transcript at https://law.utexas.edu/conferences/measuring/The%20Papers/Rule%20of%20Law%20Conference.crosslindquist.pdf).
14. Jan H. Dalhuisen, *The Notions of Certainty, Finality and Predictability*, Opinio Juris (4 April 2012), http://opiniojuris.org/2012/04/04/the-notions-of-certainty-finality-and-predictability/.
15. Jeremy Waldron, *Stare Decisis and the Rule of Law: A Layered Approach*, 11 Mich. L.R. 1, 9 Issue 1 (2012), https://repository.law.umich.edu/cgi/viewcontent.cgi?article=1095&context=mlr.
16. Monika Ambrus and Ramses A. Wessel, *Between Pragmatism and Predictability: Temporariness in International Law*, 4 ESIL Reflections 5 Issue 4 (22 June 2015), https://esil-sedi.eu/wp-content/uploads/2015/06/ESIL-Reflection-AMBRUS-WESSEL_0.pdf.
17. Julia Hildebrandt, *Persuasive Authority, Predictability and Consistency in Arbitral Decision Making*, pp. 2–3 (2018), https://eur-int-comp-law.univie.ac.at/fileadmin/user_upload/i_deicl/VR/VR_Personal/Reinisch/Internetpublikationen/hildebrandt.pdf.
18. Anthea Roberts and Zeineb Bouraoui, *UNCITRAL and ISDS Reforms: Concerns about Consistency, Predictability and Correctness*, EJIL Talk! (5 June 2018) https://www.ejiltalk.org/uncitral-and-isds-reforms-concerns-about-consistency-predictability-and-correctness/ (the authors have quoted the submissions made by states to the WG III and attribute this submission to the government of Thailand).
19. Wolfgang Alschner, *Correctness of Investment Awards: Why Wrong Decisions Don't Die*, 18 The Law and Practice of International Courts and Tribunals 345 (2019) https://papers.ssrn.com/sol3/papers.cfm?abstract_id=3429397.
20. William W. Park, *Arbitrators and Accuracy*, 1 Journal of International Dispute Settlement 25, 33 No. 1 (2010), https://10.1093/jnlids/idp004.
21. *Ibid.*, p. 53.

All of these elements together bring about a stable legal system, which is the endeavour behind reforming ISDS. Hence, those undertaking the reform measures intend to attend to each of these aspects, which would ultimately help establish the legitimacy of the ISDS system. This chapter, however, limits itself only to the issue of consistency and coherence in ISDS.

§1.03 INCONSISTENCY AND INCOHERENCE IN INTERNATIONAL INVESTMENT ARBITRATION

International investment arbitration, as it is understood today, is a relatively recently developed mechanism of dispute resolution, which found its first usage in the Bilateral Investment Treaty (BIT) signed between Germany and Pakistan in 1959.[22] The mechanism promptly found favour with its potential users, and through the 1990s, which is often termed the period of 'BIT Bang',[23] proliferated exponentially with BITs numbering 3,317 in 2019.[24] These BITs were entered into with an intent to create a basic legal framework to govern investments by nationals of one country in the territory of another.[25] Most of the BITs consist of a mechanism of dispute resolution between investor and host state through arbitration,[26] the purpose of which is to create an unbiased, objective and impartial dispute settlement mechanism for a foreign investor.

Inconsistency in investment arbitration awards is one of the primary concerns of the ISDS system.[27] Tribunals are free to interpret the agreements before them as they deem fit, following the general rules of treaty interpretation under international law without being subject to any doctrine of precedent.[28] This often leads to inconsistent awards being rendered under the ISDS system. WG III, which is mandated with identifying possible reforms to the dispute resolution process, has also identified this to be as a major concern affecting the system.[29] In the process of looking for possible ways to maintain consistency in the decisions made in ISDS, WG III has identified different kinds of inconsistencies.[30] Notably, as mentioned above, WG III distinguished between divergent decisions that can be justified and those that cannot be justified (e.g., contradictory interpretation of the same substantive standard provided in a treaty or

22. Marc Bungenberg, *A History of Investment Arbitration and Investor-State Dispute Settlement in Germany*, Investor-State Arbitration Series, Paper No. 12 (October 2016), https://www.cigionline.org/sites/default/files/documents/ISA%20Paper%20No.12.pdf.
23. *Ibid.*
24. UNCTAD, *World Investment Report, 2019*, UNCTAD/WIR/2019, p. 99 (2019), https://unctad.org/en/pages/PublicationWebflyer.aspx?publicationid=2460.
25. Esra Yidiz Ustin, *The Development of International Investment Dispute Settlement Systems*, p. 308 (2019), https://dergipark.org.tr/tr/download/article-file/726781.
26. *Ibid.*
27. UNCTAD, *Interpretation of IIAs: What States can Do?*, 3, IIA Issue Note 1 (2011), https://unctad.org/en/Docs/webdiaeia2011d10_en.pdf.
28. UNCTAD, *Investor-State Disputes Arising From Investment Treaties: A Review*, UNCTAD Series on International Investment Policies for Development, UNCTAD/ITE/IIT/2005/4, p. 2 (2005), https://unctad.org/en/Docs/iteiit20054_en.pdf.
29. Working Paper 150, *supra* n. 3, paras 4–8.
30. Working Paper 150, *supra* n. 3, paras 11–18.

the same procedural issue).[31] It also acknowledged that even though lack of consistency is a concern, the ultimate object should be correctness, not uniformity.[32]

[A] Different Kinds of Unjustified Inconsistencies

Given that there are over three thousand treaties governing IIAs,[33] and hundreds of arbitrations going on simultaneously at any given time under ad hoc arbitral tribunals that are independent of each other, unsurprisingly inconsistencies have crept into the ISDS system.[34] These inconsistencies can be broadly identified to include situations such as different tribunals reaching different conclusions about the same standard in the same investment treaty,[35] different tribunals reaching different conclusions about procedural issues in the same investment treaty,[36] different tribunals interpreting same treaty standard differently in resolving disputes under different treaties[37] and different tribunals organized under different investment treaties or the same investment treaty have dealt differently with disputes involving unrelated parties but same fact situation.[38] The following sections consider each of these deviations in arbitral awards with suitable examples to elucidate concerns that have been raised repeatedly by stakeholders.

[1] Varying Interpretations of Provisions of the Same Treaty

Treaty interpretation is the activity through which tribunals give meaning to the terms of a treaty in the context of a given fact pattern. Through this activity, tribunals determine whether or not a party is complying with the treaty.[39] Customary international law concerning the interpretation of a treaty has been codified in the Vienna Convention of Law of Treaties,[40] and like any other treaty, investment treaties are interpreted by tribunals in accordance with the principles laid down therein.[41] While

31. UNCITRAL, *Report of Working Group III (Investor-State Dispute Settlement Reform) on the work of its thirty-fifth session* (51st Session, New York 23–27 April 2018), U.N. Doc. A/CN.9/935, para. 25, https://undocs.org/en/A/CN.9/935.
32. *Ibid.*, para. 26.
33. ICSID, Database of Bilateral Investment Treaties (2019), https://icsid.worldbank.org/en/Pages/resources/Bilateral-Investment-Treaties-Database.aspx.
34. *Possible Improvements of the Framework for ICSID Arbitration*, 15 (ICSID Secretariat Discussion Paper, 22 October 2004), https://icsid.worldbank.org/en/Documents/resources/Possible%20Improvements%20of%20the%20Framework%20of%20ICSID%20Arbitration.pdf.
35. Working Paper 150, *supra* n. 3, para. 11.
36. *Ibid.*
37. *Ibid.*, para. 12.
38. *Ibid.*, para. 13
39. Joost Pauwelyn and Manfred Elsig, *The Politics of Treaty Interpretation: Variations and Explanations Across International Tribunals* (2011), https://papers.ssrn.com/sol3/papers.cfm?abstract_id=1938618.
40. The Territorial Dispute (Libyan Arab Jamahiriya v. Chad), Judgment, 1994 I.C.J. Reports 6, para. 41 (3 February), https://www.icj-cij.org/files/case-related/83/083-19940203-JUD-01-00-EN.pdf.
41. *See*, Andrew D. Mitchell and James Munro, *Someone Else's Deal: Interpreting International Investment Agreements in the Light of Third-Party Agreements*, 28 The Eur. J. Int'l L. 669 Issue

most tribunals adopt uniform principles of treaty interpretation and often even attempt to examine earlier decisions to maintain homogeneity of decision, the sheer number of simultaneous independent parallel proceedings enhances the possibility of conflicting results.[42] Moreover, while each tribunal constituted to resolve a dispute under a treaty is expected to act consistently with other such tribunals, the fact remains that, by their very nature, these tribunals are independent of each other and not bound to maintain any consistency or uniformity in their interpretation of the treaty under consideration.

A prominent example of divergent interpretation of the same treaty provision is the varied interpretation of Article 1105 of North American Free Trade Agreement (NAFTA), which mandates each party to NAFTA to accord to investors of the other party(ies) 'fair and equitable treatment' (FET) and 'full protection and security' (FPS).[43] In *Metalclad*,[44] a claim was raised for violation of FET under Article 1105 of NAFTA against the government of Mexico. Metalclad, a United States (US) corporation, received a permit from the federal government of Mexico and the state government of San Louis Potosi (SLP) to construct and operate a landfill for hazardous waste in Guadalcazar. The corporation was assured that all permits had been granted and the responsibility for obtaining support from local community lay with the federal government. Relying on such assurances, Metalclad began construction at the appointed site. However, within months of starting construction, the municipality of Guadalcazar ordered cessation of all construction due to the absence of a municipal construction permit. Upon enquiry, the corporation was once again assured by the federal government that it had all the necessary permits. At the same time, it was also asked to apply for a municipal permit and assured that it would be granted. Accordingly, Metalclad applied for the municipal permit and resumed construction. However, thirteen months after Metalclad's application was filed, the municipality denied it. In fact, the corporation was not notified of the Town Council meeting where the permit application was discussed and rejected, nor was it given an opportunity to present its case. Moreover, while Metalclad was in negotiation with the state authorities to resolve the issue of permit, the Governor of SLP declared the area surrounding the landfill as a natural area for the protection of a rare cactus. This permanently precluded the operation of the landfill.

In the dispute raised by Metalclad against the government of Mexico, the tribunal concluded that 'Mexico failed to ensure a transparent and predictable framework for Metalclad's business planning and investment. The totality of these circumstances demonstrates a lack of orderly process and timely disposition in relation to an investor of a party acting in the expectation that it would be treated fairly and justly in

3 (2017) http://www.ejil.org/pdfs/28/3/2806.pdf; A.M. Abrishami, *Treaty Interpretation in Investment Arbitration by J. Romesh Weeramantry*, 29 Arb. Int'l 549 Issue 3 (2013), https://doi.org/10.1093/arbitration/29.3.549.

42. Christoph Schreur, *Diversity and Harmonization of Treaty Interpretation in Investment Arbitration* (2006), https://www.univie.ac.at/intlaw/pdf/cspubl_85.pdf.
43. Article 1105, North American Free Trade Agreement [hereinafter 'NAFTA'], https://www.nafta-sec-alena.org/Home/Texts-of-theAgreement/North-American-Free-Trade-Agreement?mvid=1&secid=539c50ef-51c1-489b-808b-9e20c9872d25#A1105.
44. *Metalclad Corporation v. United Mexican States*, ICSID Case No. ARB (AF)/97/1 (Award dated 25 August 2001).

accordance with the NAFTA.'[45] On the other hand, in the case of *Waste Management*,[46] which also concerned a concession agreement granted to a foreign investor, the arbitral tribunal interpreted the FET standard under NAFTA rather narrowly. It set a higher standard for establishing what constituted a breach of FET. Thus, the tribunal held that FET is infringed if the conduct of the state is 'arbitrary, grossly unfair, unjust or idiosyncratic, is discriminatory and exposes the claimant to sectional or racial prejudice, or involves a lack of due process leading to an outcome which offends judicial propriety'.[47]

Divergent opinions abound on the standard of treatment contemplated under NAFTA[48] and also on the definition of investor under the NAFTA.[49] Such divergent opinions are the most concerning because if any kind of perfect consistency can be attained in the extant system of ISDS, it can be achieved only within the universe of a single BIT or a single multilateral investment agreement such as the NAFTA.

[2] Divergent Interpretation of Procedural Issues

Procedural inconsistencies have been found in investment arbitration before, during and after the arbitral proceedings. An extreme example is the case of *Maffezini v. Spain*,[50] a dispute raised under the Spain-Argentina BIT, in which the tribunal interpreted the most-favoured-nation (MFN) clause broadly to extend it to the dispute settlement. The tribunal thus held that where a third-party treaty contains provisions for settlement of disputes that are more favourable to the protection of investor's rights than those in the treaty governing it, then such beneficial provisions may be extended to the beneficiary of the MFN clause. This, it was reasoned, is fully compatible with the *ejusdem generis* principle. Thus, the investor was permitted to forego the requirement under the Argentina-Spain BIT to first approach a Spanish court and in turn was permitted to initiate arbitration in accordance with the procedure contemplated under Chile-Spain BIT.[51] However, in *Plama v. Bulgaria*,[52] the tribunal, after analysing earlier awards, interpreted the MFN clause restrictively so as to not apply it to the dispute

45. *Ibid.*, para. 99.
46. *Waste Management v. United Mexican States*, ICSID Case No. ARB (AF)/00/3 (Award dated 30 April 2004).
47. *Ibid.*, para. 98
48. *See Glamis Gold Ltd v. United States*, UNCITRAL (Award dated 8 June 2009); *Merrill & Ring Forestry L.P. v. Canada*, ICSID Case No. UNCT/071 (Award dated 31 March 2010). These awards take diametrically opposite stands on what constitutes the minimum standard of treatment under customary international law.
49. *See SD Meyers Inc v. Government of Canada*, UNCITRAL (Partial Award dated 13 November 2000); *Pope & Talbot Inc. v. The Government of Canada*, UNCITRAL (Award on Merits of Phase 2 dated 10 April 2001).
50. *Emilio Agustin Maffezini v. Kingdom of Spain*, ICSID Case No. ARB/97/7 (Decision on Objection to Jurisdiction dated 25 January 2000).
51. *Ibid.*, para. 64. A similar stance has been taken by tribunals in *Hochitef AG v. The Republic of Argentine*, ICSID Case No. ARB/07/31, para. 99 (Decision on Jurisdiction dated 24 October 2011). *See also National Grid plc v. The Argentine Republic*, UNCITRAL, paras 92, 93 (Award on Jurisdiction dated 20 June 2006).
52. *See Plama Consortium Limited v. Republic of Bulgaria*, ICSID Case No. ARB/03/24, para. 227.

resolution mechanism, thus creating a dichotomy of opinions. A criticism against *Plama*'s approach was that it abused the MFN clause by attempting to create consent to an International Centre for Settlement of Investment Disputes (ICSID) arbitration when none existed.[53] However, even when such extraordinary attempts were not made and a position similar to *Maffezini* was taken by claimants, tribunals have adopted the position clarified in *Plama*. Thus, the tribunals in *Salini*[54] and *Telenor*[55] ruled that the MFN clause did not apply to dispute settlement.

Similarly, diametrically opposite approaches have been taken by tribunals in the context of a cooling-off/consultation period before initiating arbitration proceedings under an investment treaty. For example, in *SGS v. Pakistan*,[56] even though the Switzerland-Pakistan BIT provided for twelve months for consultation to find a solution before arbitration could be initiated to resolve the dispute, the tribunal held that compliance with such a provision was not a condition precedent for it to exercise jurisdiction.[57] On the other hand, in *Murphy Exploration (I) v. Ecuador*,[58] while adjudicating a dispute pursuant to the Ecuador-US BIT, the tribunal interpreted the requirement to negotiate the dispute for six months very strictly. It held that the requirement to seek to resolve the dispute through consultation and negotiation for a six-month period 'constituted a fundamental requirement that the Claimant must comply with, compulsorily, before submitting a request for arbitration under the ICSID rules'.[59]

While these examples suggest contradictions in arbitral tribunals' position to initiate arbitration, there also have been instances in certain ICSID-administered arbitrations where tribunals have taken divergent stances during the annulment proceedings.[60] Thus, in cases such as *Wena Hotels*[61] and *Vivendi*,[62] the annulment committees were cautious in exercising their power and did not attempt to review the decision of the arbitral tribunal. In contrast, in *Malaysian Historical Salvors, SDN, BHD v. The Government of Malaysia*,[63] the annulment committee practically reviewed the decision of the tribunal and decided to annul the award on the ground of manifest

53. *Ibid.*, para. 209.
54. *Salini Construttori S.p.A. and the Italstrade S.p.A. v. Hashemite Kingdom of Jordan*, ICSID Case No. ARB/02/3, paras 118, 119 (Decision on Jurisdiction dated 9 November 2004).
55. *Telenor Mobile Communications AS v. Hungary*, ICSID Case No. ARB/04/15, ¶100 (Award dated 13 September 2006). *See also ICS Inspection and Control Services v. The Argentine Republic*, PCA Case No. 2010-9, paras 313–317, 326 (Award on Jurisdiction dated 10 February 2012).
56. *SGS Societe Generale de Surveillance S.A. v. Islamic Republic of Pakistan*, ICSID Case No. ARB/01/13 (Decision on Jurisdiction dated 6 August 2003).
57. *Ibid.*, paras 183–184.
58. *Murphy Exploration & Production Company International v. Republic of Ecuador*, ICSID Case No. ARB/08/4 (Award on Jurisdiction dated 15 December 2010).
59. *Ibid.*, para. 149.
60. *See generally* Dohyum Kim, *Multiplying Inconsistency in ICSID Arbitration: The Need to Move away from an Annulment Based System*, 86 NYU L. R. 242 (April 2011).
61. *Wena Hotels Ltd. v. Arab Republic of Egypt*, ICSID Case No ARB/98/4 (Decision on Annulment dated 5 February 2002).
62. *Compania de Aguas del Aconquija S.A. v. Argentine Republic*, ICSID Case No. ARB/97/3 (Decision on Annulment dated 3 July 2002).
63. *Malaysian Historical Salvors, SDN, BHD v. The Government of Malaysia* ICSID Case No. ARB/05/10 (Decision on Annulment dated 16 April 2009).

failure to exercise jurisdiction.[64] The purpose of the annulment procedure within the ICSID framework was to bring about consistency in interpretation and application of international investment law.[65] Such varied decisions continue to contribute to the unjustified inconsistencies in the ISDS system

[3] Varying Interpretations of Substantive Treaty Standards

In recent years, BIT drafting has diversified with countries attempting to broaden the scope of exercising their powers.[66] Nevertheless, a considerable degree of conformity has emerged in terms of the main contents of BITs.[67] Most BITs include the standard of FET, MFN principle, war clause and umbrella clause, among others.[68] A brief analysis reveals how despite being common to most investment treaties, some of these standards of protection have been variably interpreted by tribunals.

[a] Fair and Equitable Treatment

FET is an integral element of most BITs today; however, there is no singular definition of the standard. Vagueness and various formulations in which FET appears in investment treaties is a cause for its divergent interpretation by arbitral tribunals.[69] Nevertheless, tribunals have come to identify certain essential features that may be termed as components of this standard of protection accorded under the BITs.[70] These

64. *Ibid.*, para. 74.
65. Lise Johnson, *Annulment of ICSID Awards: Recent Developments*, p. 4 (IV Annual Forum for Developing Country Investment Negotiators, Background Papers, October 2010), https://www.iisd.org/pdf/2011/dci_2010_annulment_icsid_awards.pdf.
66. Kawaljit Singh and Burghard Ilge, *Rethinking Bilateral Investment Treaties: Critical Issued and Policy Choices* (2016), https://www.somo.nl/wp-content/uploads/2016/03/Rethinking-bilateral-investment-treaties.pdf.
67. UNCTAD, *Bilateral Investment Treaties 1995–2006: Trends in Investment Rulemaking*, p. xi, UNCTAD/ITE/IIT/2006/5 (2007), https://unctad.org/en/Docs/iteiia20065_en.pdf.
68. *Ibid.*, p. xii.
69. UNCTAD, *Fair and Equitable Treatment*, pp. 1–2, UNCTAD Series on Issues in International Investment Agreements II, UNCTAD/DIAE/IA/2011/5 (2012), https://unctad.org/en/Docs/unctaddiaeia2011d5_en.pdf.
70. *See generally supra* (UNCTAD, FET), pp. 17–31, https://unctad.org/en/Docs/unctaddiaeia2011d5_en.pdf. UNCTAD has identified five most widespread approaches to FET standard in treaty practice, which include:

    (i) No FET Obligation – UNCTAD has cited some of the treaties entered into in 1990s and early 2000s to exemplify treaties with no FET clause. However, this is almost unheard of in recent treaties. In fact, even some of the examples cited by the UNCTAD in its report stand repudiated; for instance, the Pakistan-Turkey BIT of 1995, which did not contain any FET clause has been replaced by the Pakistan-Turkey BIT, 2012, which has a rather descriptive FET clause.
    (ii) Unqualified/autonomous FET clause – Many IIAs use a simple unqualified formulation which does no more than state the obligation of a host State to accord fair and equitable treatment to protected investments.
    (iii) FET linked to international law – FET can be linked to international law in two formulations. First, that the state shall accord fair and equitable treatment in

features include legitimate expectations,[71] protection against arbitrariness,[72] consistency and stability in government policies/legislation,[73] transparency,[74] etc. There has

---

accordance with international law and second, a treaty may provide that the state shall accord fair and equitable treatment ... no less than that required by international law.

(iv) FET linked to minimum standard under customary international law - An explicit link between the FET obligation and the minimum standard of treatment is used in these treaties to prevent over-expansive interpretations of the FET standard by arbitral tribunals.

(v) FET with additional substantive content - This has been identified as an emerging trend in international investment agreements, which is a way to bring precision to the content of FET.

71. *Tecnicas Medioambientales Tecmed, S.A. v. The United Mexican* States, ICSID Case No. ARB(AF)/00/2 (Award dated 29 May 2003); *International Thunderbird Gaming Corporation v. United Mexican States* UNCITRAL (Award dated 26 January 2006).
72. *CMS Gas Transmission Company v. The Republic of Argentina,* ICSID Case No. ARB/01/8, para. 290 (Award dated 12 May 2005). The tribunal held that 'The standard of protection against arbitrariness and discrimination is related to that of fair and equitable treatment. Any measure that might involve arbitrariness or discrimination is in itself contrary to fair and equitable treatment.' *Oxus Gold plc v. The Republic of Uzbekistan,* UNCITRAL (Final Award dated 17 December 2015), paras 323, 785 (noting that the arbitrary impairment standard is subsumed within FET).
73. *Crystallex International Corporation v. Bolivarian Republic of Venezuela,* Award, ICSID Case No. ARB(AF)/11/12 (Award dated 4 April 2016), para. 579 and cases cited therein. Consistency and transparency sometimes are linked together. *See Saluka Investments B.V. v. The Czech Republic,* para. 305 (Partial Award dated 17 March 2006); *MTD Equity Sd. Bhd. And MTC Chile S.A. v. Republic of Chile,* ICSID Case No. ARB/01/7, para. 116; *Mr Franck Charles Arif v. Republic Moldova,* ICSID Case No. ARB/11/23, para. 547 (Award dated 8 April 2013). The tribunal held, 'here is a direct inconsistency between the attitudes of different organs of the State to the investment. The Airport State Enterprise and the State Administration of Civil Aviation endorsed and encouraged the investment in the airport premises, while the courts found the same investment to be illegal. This type of direct inconsistency in itself amounts to a breach of the fair and equitable treatment standard'.
74. Some multilateral treaties, such as the Energy Charter Treaty (ECT), contain separate provision on transparency as do certain model BITs such as the US Model BIT 2004. Where it is not explicitly provided for, tribunals have recognized transparency as an integral element of FET. *See Metalclad Corporation v. The United Mexican States,* ICSID Case No. ARB(AF)/97/1, para. 76 (Award dated 30 August 2000) where the tribunal held:

> Prominent in the statement of principles and rules that introduces the Agreement is the reference to 'transparency' (NAFTA Article 102(1)). The Tribunal understands this to include the idea that all relevant legal requirements for the purpose of initiating, completing and successfully operating investments made, or intended to be made, under the Agreement should be capable of being readily known to all affected investors of another Party. There should be no room for doubt or uncertainty on such matters. Once the authorities of the central government of any Party (whose international responsibility in such matters has been identified in the preceding section) become aware of any scope for misunderstanding or confusion in this connection, it is their duty to ensure that the correct position is promptly determined and clearly stated so that investors can proceed with all appropriate expedition in the confident belief that they are acting in accordance with all relevant laws.

See also Tecnicas Medioambientales Tecmed, S.A. v. The United Mexican States, ICSID Case No. ARB (AF)/00/2; *Ioan Micula, Viorel Micula, S.C. European Food S.A., S.C. Starmill S.R.L. and S.C. Multipack S.R.L. v. Romania,* ICSID Case No. ARB/05/20, paras 864–870 (Award dated 11 December 2013).

also been a certain level of comity among tribunals in their approach to the very concept of FET. This can be seen in developments such as abandoning the requirement of bad faith on part of host state to establish a breach of FET,[75] which was earlier a prerequisite to establish a breach of FET[76] under an investment treaty.

Nevertheless, inconsistency in determination of content and level of obligations under the FET clause in an investment treaty continues.[77] These inconsistencies present themselves in a variety of situations, for example whether a breach of legitimate expectation would tantamount to a breach of FET[78] or if denial of justice is a constituted part of FET standard.[79] The variations among tribunals in the interpretation of FET clause have been dramatically different and exhibit a troubling level degree of inconsistency.[80]

[b] Umbrella Clause

The umbrella clause, also labelled as *pacta sunt servanda* clause, mirror effect clause, observation of commitments clause, observance of undertakings clause or sanctity of contract clause, is a provision that appears in most BITs and multilateral investment treaties.[81] It is also one of the biggest contributors to inconsistencies in the ISDS universe. Few interpretations have been as varied as that of the umbrella clause in *SGS v. Pakistan*[82] and *SGS v. Philippines*,[83] two cases with almost similar facts, albeit under

75. *Azurix v. Argentina*, ICSID Case No. ARB/01/12, para. 372 (Final Award dated 14 July 2006). The arbitral tribunal concluded:

> To encourage and protect investment is the purpose of the BIT. It would be incoherent with such purpose and the expectations created by such a document to consider that a party to the BIT has breached the obligation of fair and equitable treatment only when it has acted in bad faith or its conduct can be qualified as outrageous or egregious.

See CMS Gas Transmission Company v. Argentina, ICSID Case No. ARB/01/8, para. 280 (Award dated 25 April 2005).

76. *L. F. H. Neer & Pauline E. Neer v. Mexico* (Opinion rendered on 15 October 1926), 21 AM. J. INT'L L. 555, No. 3 (1927).
77. Working Paper 150, *supra* n. 3, para. 16.
78. *Occidental Petroleum Corporation, Occidental Exploration and Production Company v. The Republic of Ecuador*, ICSID Case No. ARB/06/11, para. 527 (Award dated 5 October 2012).
79. *Hesham Talaat M Al-Warraq v. The Republic of Indonesia*, paras 620–621 (Award dated 15 December 2014). *See also David Aven et al v. The Republic of Costa Rica*, UNCITRAL Case No. UNCT/15/3 (Award dated 18 September 2018).
80. Julian Arato, Chester Brown and Federic Ortino, *Parsing and Managing Inconsistency in Investor-State Dispute Settlement*, 21 JOURNAL OF WORLD INVESTMENT AND TRADE 12 (2010), https://papers.ssrn.com/sol3/papers.cfm?abstract_id=3522483.
81. August Reinich, *Umbrella Clauses*, p. 5 (Seminar on International Investment Protection, 2006-07), https://eur-int-comp-law.univie.ac.at/fileadmin/user_upload/i_deicl/VR/VR_Personal/Reinisch/Internetpublikationen/weissenfels.pdf.
82. *SGS Societe Generale de Surveillance S.A. v. Islamic Republic of Pakistan*, ICSID Case No. ARB/01/13 (Decision on Jurisdiction dated 5 August 2003).
83. *SGS Societe Generale de Surveillance S.A. v. Republic of Philippines*, ICSID Case No. ARB/02/6 (Decision on Jurisdiction dated 29 January 2004).

different BITs.[84] In the first case, the tribunal interpreted the umbrella clause restrictively observing that it had no jurisdiction over the contract claims raised by the parties. In the latter case, the tribunal declared the reasons given by the *SGS v. Pakistan* tribunal unconvincing and went on to hold that it is 'a breach of the BIT for the host State to fail to observe binding commitments, including contractual commitments'.[85] Over time, tribunals have continued to stay divided in their opinion over an umbrella clause.[86] The variations in interpretation of umbrella clauses have been so many that even the tribunal in *BIVAC BC*[87] acknowledged that there is no *jurisprudence constante* on the point.[88]

[c] War Clause

Another example of contradictory treatment of the same treaty standard is interpretation of the war clause, as exemplified in *AAPL v. Sri Lanka*,[89] decided under the UK-Sri Lanka BIT, and *AMT v. Zaire*,[90] decided under the US-Zaire BIT. Even though the scope of the protection under each of the treaties was similar, as was the factual background, the tribunal in the first dispute held a higher threshold of attribution to the state for compensating the claimant under the war clause.[91] In the latter case, however, the tribunal concluded that there was no requirement to establish attribution of destruction to the Zairian armed forces so long as damages were inflicted over the course of prescribed act.[92]

§1.04 IMPACT OF INCONSISTENCY IN INVESTMENT ARBITRATION

Some amount of inconsistency in decision-making is endemic to any legal system, but interpretative inconsistency has been a salient problem for stakeholders in the ISDS

84. Raul Periera de Souza Fleury, *Closing the Umbrella: A Dark Future for Umbrella Clauses?*, Kluwer Arbitration Blog (13 October 2017), http://arbitrationblog.kluwerarbitration.com/2017/10/13/closing-umbrella-dark-future-umbrella-clauses/.
85. *SGS v. Philippines*, *supra* n. 83, para. 128.
86. Tribunals that have followed *SGS Société Générale de Surveillance S.A. v. Islamic Republic of Pakistan*, ICSID Case No. ARB/01.13, include *Salini Construtti S.p.A. and Italstrade S.p.A. v. The Hashemite Kingdom of Jordan*, ICSID Case No. ARB/02/13; *El Paso International Company v. The Republic of Argentina*, ICSID Case No. ARB/03/15; and *Siemens A.G. v. The Argentine Republic*, ICSID Case No. ARB/02/8. Those following *SGS v. Philippines* include *BIVAC BV v. The Republic of Paraguay*, ICSID Case No. ARB/07/9 (Decision on Jurisdiction dated 29 May 2009) and *Bosh International Inc. and B&P Ltd Foreign Investments Enterprise v. Ukraine*, ICSID Case No. ARB/08/11, para. 247 (Award dated 25 October 2012).
87. *BIVAC BV v. The Republic of Paraguay*, ICSID Case No. ARB/07/9 (Decision on Jurisdiction 29 May 2009).
88. *Ibid*, para. 141.
89. *Asian Agricultural Products Ltd. v. Republic of Sri Lanka*, ICSID Case No. ARB/87/3 (Award dated 27 June 1990).
90. *American Manufacturing & Trading Inc. v. Republic of Zaire*, ICSID Case No. ARB/93/1 (Award dated 5 February 1997).
91. *AAPL v. Sri Lanka*, *supra* n. 89, paras 60–64.
92. *AMT v. Zaire*, *supra* n. 90, paras 6.11, 6.13, 6.14.

system.[93] What makes it a greater concern is the fact that investment treaty claims are more than the usual 'bet the company' commercial disputes. They often amount to 'bet the country' disputes,[94] which can impose a huge financial burden on the country-party.[95] The inconsistent decisions rendered by tribunals over time have led to a failure of the establishment of a stable and predictable legal environment.[96] As a result, the impact of inconsistency in outcome of investment arbitration is also grave enough to have raised the spectre of a legitimacy crisis,[97] such that the reliability, effectiveness and, most importantly, credibility of the investment arbitration regime have been negatively affected.[98] The lack of consistency and coherence in investment arbitration has also contributed to creating other challenges to investment arbitration, such as a supposed bias of the arbitrators,[99] along with the issue of neutrality of arbitrators, who often are accused of double-hatting as arbitrators in one dispute and counsel in another.[100]

Inconsistency in investment arbitration jurisprudence is a problem that impacts both the state and the investors alike, who make an informed decision based on regulatory and judicial framework.[101] While inconsistency makes it difficult for states to understand how they must act in order to comply with their legal obligations and contributes to regulatory chill, for investors a predictable dispute settlement environment is a prerequisite to ensure the certainty of protection of their investments.[102]

That said, mechanisms exist to contain the lack of consistency and coherence in investment arbitration, which can broadly be divided into two categories depending on whether the arbitration was under the ICSID framework or non-ICSID rules. In the

93. *Supra* n. 80, p. 1.
94. Susan D. Frank, *The Nature and Enforcement of Investor Rights under Investment Treaties: Do Investment Treaties Have a Bright Future?*, 12 U.C. Davis J. Int'l L. Pol'y 47, 58 (2005).
95. Claire Provost and Matt Kennard, *The Obscure System That Lets Corporations Sue Countries*, The Guardian (10 June 2015), https://www.theguardian.com/business/2015/jun/10/obscure-legal-system-lets-corportations-sue-states-ttip-icsid.
96. Daniel Behn, *Legitimacy, Evolution and Growth in Investment Treaty Arbitration: Empirically Evaluating the State-of-the Art*, 46 Geo. J. Int'l L. 363, 367 (2015).
97. Susan D. Frank, *The Legitimacy Crisis in Investment Arbitration: Privatising Public Law Through Inconsistency decision*, 73 Fordham L. Rev. 1521, 1586 (2005) (the author argues that legitimacy depends in large part on interpretive determinacy of vague treaty standards and coherence, which in turn bring predictability and reliability to the system).
98. Gabrielle Kaufmann-Kohler and Michele Potesta, *Can the Mauritius Convention serve as a model for the Reform of Investor-State Arbitration in Connection with the Introduction of Permanent Investment Tribunal or an Appeal Mechanism*, p. 13 (2016), https://www.uncitral.org/pdf/english/CIDS_Research_Paper_Mauritius.pdf.
99. Giovanni Zarra, *The Issue of Incoherence in Investment Arbitration: Is There as Need for Systemic Reform?*, 17 CJIL 137, 141 Issue 1 (March 2018), https://doi.org/10.1093/chinesejil/jmy005; *see also*, George Kahale III, *Is Investor-State Arbitration Broken?* (October 2012), https://s3.amazonaws.com/cdn.curtis.com/news-attachments/Is-Investor-State-Arbitration-Broken.pdf; Susan D. Frank, *The Legitimacy Crisis in Investment Arbitration: Privatising Public Law Through Inconsistency Decision*, 73 Fordham L. Rev. 1521, 1587 (2005).
100. *See generally* Malcom Langford, Daniel Behn and Runar Hilleren Lie, *The Revolving Door in International Investment Arbitration*, 20 J. Int'l Economic L. 301–332 (2017).
101. *The Role of International Investment Agreements in Attracting Foreign Direct Investment to Developing Countries*, p. 53 (UNCTAD Series on International Policies and Development, 2009), https://unctad.org/en/Docs/diaeia20095_en.pdf.
102. *Supra* n. 2, paras 36–37.

ICSID system, there is a procedure for annulment of an award, while in non-ICSID arbitration, parties have the option to challenge the arbitral award before domestic courts and file an application to set aside the award.[103] WG III, while assessing the extant review mechanisms, concluded that the existing mechanisms address the integrity and fairness of the process rather than consistency, coherence or correctness of the awards.[104]

To address these concerns, various voices have been raised to reform or modify the investment arbitration mechanism as it exists. The United Nations Conference on Trade and Development (UNCTAD), the Organisation for Economic Co-operation and Development (OECD) and several independent academicians have given their opinions to bring about more consistency and coherence in investment arbitration awards.[105] Most importantly, WG III has identified it as the first and foremost concern of IIA and has attempted to address it. This chapter next discusses and analyses some of the suggestions on the table to bring about more consistency in IIA.

§1.05 PROPOSALS TO ADDRESS INCONSISTENCY IN INVESTMENT ARBITRATION

Lack of consistency and the consequent question of legitimacy is one of the biggest criticisms of investor-state arbitration. Stakeholders have been making suggestions to rectify it for some time.[106] In the OECD context, concerns regarding consistency were raised in 2002–2005, leading to discussions within the OECD Investment Committee.[107] Different proposals were made in OECD's working paper to address the issue of inconsistency by the introduction of an appeals mechanism, scrutiny of awards and consolidation of claims to contain multiple parallel proceedings that were adding to the inconsistency in jurisprudence.[108]

Responding to the recurring concerns about systemic deficiencies in the ISDS regime, UNCTAD, in its 2013 World Investment Report, proposed 'five broad paths for reform', which included promoting alternative dispute resolution, tailoring the existing system through individual IIAs, limiting investors' access to ISDS, introducing an

103. *Supra* n. 2, para. 39.
104. *Supra* n. 3, para. 21.
105. Investor-State Dispute Settlement Reform: Online Resources, https://uncitral.un.org/en/library/online_resources/investor-state_dispute.
106. *Supra* n. 96 (the author explains that 'The legitimacy debates in investment treaty arbitration primarily derive from the general anti-globalization movements of the mid-1990s and more specific events, such as the failed Organization for Economic Cooperation and Development (OECD) Draft Multilateral Agreement on Investment (Draft MAI) and resistance to early North American Free Trade Agreement (NAFTA) case against the United States and Canada').
107. Katia Yannaca-Small, *Improving the System of Investor-State Dispute Settlement* (OECD Working Papers on International Investment, No. 01, 2006), https://doi.org/10.1787/631230863687.
108. *Ibid. See also* David Gaukrodger and Kathryn Gordon, *Investor-State Dispute Settlement: A Scoping Paper for the Investment Policy* Community 58 (OECD Working Papers on International Investment, No. 03, 2012), https://www.oecd-ilibrary.org/docserver/5k46b1r85j6f-en.pdf?expires=1582910039&id=id&accname=guest&checksum=A8CF549041726D98562FC743CAB28E68.

appeals facility and creating a standing international investment court.[109] In its World Investment Report 2015, UNCTAD once again sought to address the 'growing unease with the current functioning of the global international investment agreement regime' and offered an 'action menu for IIA reform' building on its earlier suggestions.[110]

ICSID, under whose aegis most of the investment arbitrations are conducted, also initiated a process to amend its rules in 2016[111] and has to that end produced four working papers.[112] To address the issue of consistency,[113] amendments have been proposed to introduce voluntary consolidation of claims.[114] It has been proposed to amend Rule 45 of the ICSID Rules to provide for consolidation or coordination of arbitration.[115] Consolidation would include joining all aspects of the arbitrations sought to be consolidated resulting in a single award. Coordination, on the other hand, would mean aligning specific procedural aspects of each pending arbitration, but the arbitrations would continue as separate proceedings with each having an individual award.

In 2017, UNCITRAL entrusted WG III with a broad mandate to work on possible reform of ISDS.[116] Accordingly, WG III, composed of all state members of the UNCITRAL, held its thirty-fourth session, which was also attended by observers from the European Union (EU), intergovernmental organizations, non-governmental organizations and other observers from the United Nations system,[117] whose numbers over the years have increased. It thus is a truly global endeavour to address reforms in IIA. WG III has since devoted itself to identifying and deliberating over possible reforms to address the concerns of ISDS.[118] To address the issue of lack of consistency and coherence in ISDS, the possible reforms suggested by WG III include introducing a system of precedent; providing guidance to arbitral tribunals; prior scrutiny of arbitral

109. *See generally* UNCTAD, World Investment Report, pp. 110–120, UNCTAD/WIR/2013 (United Nations Publications 2013), https://unctad.org/en/PublicationsLibrary/wir2013_en.pdf.
110. *See generally* UNCTAD, World Investment Report, pp. 119–174 (United Nations Publications 2015), UNCTAD/WIR/2015, https://unctad.org/en/PublicationsLibrary/wir2015_en.pdf.
111. *About ICSID Amendments*, ICSID, https://icsid.worldbank.org/en/amendments/Pages/About/about.aspx.
112. *Ibid.*
113. Rafael Ramos Codeco and Henrique Martins Sachetim, *ICSID Rule Amendment: An Attempt to Remedy Some of the Concerns Regarding ISDS Identified by UNCITRAL WG III*, Investment Treaty News (2 October 2019), https://www.iisd.org/itn/2019/10/02/icsid-rule-amendment-an-attempt-to-remedy-some-of-the-concerns-regarding-isds-identified-by-uncitral-wg-iii-rafael-ramos-codeco-henrique-martins-sachetim/#_ftn3.
114. *Proposals for Amendment of the ICSID* Rules (ICSID Working Paper No. 3, Volume 1, August 2019), https://icsid.worldbank.org/en/Documents/WP_3_VOLUME_1_ENGLISH.pdf.
115. *Ibid.*
116. *Supra* n. 1, para. 264.
117. *Supra*, paras 7–10. UNCITRAL, *Report of Working Group III (Investor State Dispute Settlement) on the work of its thirty-fourth Session*, paras 7–10 (November-December 2017), UN Doc A/CN.9/930/Rev.1, https://undocs.org/en/A/CN.9/930/Add.1/Rev.1.
118. UNCITRAL has thus far conducted five sessions on reforms of ISDS and was going to hold its thirty-ninth session in March-April 2020 (which has now been suspended in the light of the Covid-19 pandemic). In the process, it has invited suggestions and submissions from Member States as well as observer institutions, https://uncitral.un.org/en/working_groups/3/investor-state.

awards; appellate mechanism; introducing a system of preliminary rulings; and setting up an international court system.[119]

While some reform proposals, such as developing an appellate mechanism, have found favour in most reform discussions, there are various ideas on the table for ensuring greater consistency and coherence in investment arbitration awards. The next sections analyse the viability of some of these proposals.

[A] Tailoring Individual IIA

One of the most obvious tools a state has to ensure consistent interpretation is to draft provisions of the treaty to guide its interpretation.[120] As mentioned above, one of the biggest contributory factors towards varied interpretation of treaty standards is their wording, as can be seen from the examples of FET clauses across BITs. Another example has been the divergent interpretation of MFN clause and its applicability to dispute resolution under BITs. The World Investment Report 2013 proposed that to bring about more consistency and coherence in the existing ISDS system, individual treaties could be tailored to increase consistency and coherence of awards.[121] To this end, it suggested inserting provisions for binding joint party interpretations and establishing a mechanism for consolidation of related claims.[122] Moreover, there have been examples of such a provision in the erstwhile NAFTA[123] and more recently the Canada-European Union Comprehensive Economic and Trade Agreement (CETA).[124]

[B] Introducing a System of Precedent

Investment arbitrations are constituted on an ad hoc basis for each arbitration and often operate under confidentiality resulting in their award being unknown to future

119. Working Paper 150, *supra* n. 3, paras 37–47.
120. International Bar Association, *Consistency, Efficiency and Transparency in Investment Treaty Arbitration*, A Report by the Arbitration Subcommittee on Investment Treaty Arbitration (November 2018), https://www.ibanet.org/Document/Default.aspx?DocumentUid = a8d68c6c-120b-4a6a-afd0-4397bc22b569.
121. *Supra* n. 109, p. 113.
122. *Ibid.*
123. Article 2001 of NAFTA established the Free Trade Commission to 'resolve disputes that may arise regarding its interpretation or application', https://www.nafta-sec alena.org/Home/Texts-of-the-Agreement/North-American-Free-Trade-Agreement?mvid = 1&secid = ed3bd8c9-2d73-45fb-9241-d66364f8037a#A2001. *See also* Gabrielle Kaufmann-Kohler, *Interpretative Powers of the Free Trade Commission and the Rule of Law*, FIFTEEN YEARS OF NAFTA CHAPTER 11 ARBITRATION, pp. 175–193, https://www.arbitration-icca.org/media/1/13571335953400/interpretive_powers_of_the_free_trade_commission_and_the_rule_of_law_kaufmann-kohler.pdf (the author argued that even though the FTC used its power only once and tribunals have differed in their opinions despite the authoritative interpretation, existence of such a mechanism is beneficial to rule of law as it increases predictability).
124. Council of the European Union, *Joint Interpretative Instrument on the Comprehensive Economic Trade Agreement (CETA) between Canada and the European Union and its Member States* (27 October 2016), 13541/16, http://data.consilium.europa.eu/doc/document/ST-13541-2016-INIT/en/pdf.

arbitrators in similar situations.[125] This means that every dispute is considered anew even if the exact same issue under the same treaty has already been dealt with one or more times before. Lack of rule of binding precedent is a major contributory factor in lack of predictability in the ISDS system, which in turn adds to the cost and duration of the dispute resolution mechanism.[126] To address this, the WG III recommended introducing a system of precedent to bring about greater consistency, coherence and predictability to the decisions in ISDS.[127] In fact, it previously has been argued that the 'crippling inconsistencies in the jurisprudence of bilateral investment treaty disputes', which seemed 'to be heading for a thrombosis', cannot be cured in the absence of a doctrine of binding precedent.[128]

Although there is no system of stare decisis governing investment arbitration, tribunals often refer to awards previously rendered. In fact, tribunals often have recognized the need to take into account the precedents established by other arbitral tribunals,[129] 'to contribute to harmonious development of investment law and thereby to meet the legitimate expectations of the community of States and investors towards certainty of the rule of law'.[130] And eventually, an accretion of such decisions may, in fact, develop a *jurisprudence constante*.[131] Particularly, in the ICSID framework, it has been extensively argued that there exist fertile conditions to develop a system of precedents, namely: (a) the publication and ready availability of awards and decisions; (b) the development of espirit de corps among the ICSID investment treaty arbitrators who have shown a greater tendency in referring to decisions rendered by each other; and (c) a body of treaties and law that are similar in scope and structure and therefore susceptible to case law development.[132] That said, it must be noted that the value of such references is determined not by their authority but rather by their persuasiveness.[133]

---

125. Gilbert Guillaume, *The Use of Precedent by International Judges and Arbitrators*, 2 J. Int'l Disp. Settlement 5, 14 (2011).
126. UNCITRAL Secretariat, *Possible Reforms of Investor-State Dispute Settlement (ISDS) – cost and duration*, para. 84 (Vienna October-November 2018), A/CN.9/WG.III/W.P.153, https://undocs.org/en/A/CN.9/WG.III/WP.153.
127. Working Paper 150, *supra* n. 3, para. 38.
128. Thomas Roe, *Some Thoughts on Precedent in International Investment Arbitration* citing Foreword to Thomas Roe and Matthew Happold, *Settlement of Investment Disputes under the Energy Charter Treaty* (Cambridge University Press, 2011), xii (a paper delivered at the 18th Commonwealth Law Conference (16 April 2013)), https://www.3harecourt.com/assets/asset-store/file/articles/230413-TR-commonwealth-law-conference-paper-2013-international-investment-arbitration.pdf.
129. *El Paso Energy International Co. v. Argentine Republic*, ICSID Case Arb/03/15, para. 39, Decision on Jurisdiction (Award dated 27 April 2006).
130. *Saipam v. State of Bangladesh*, ICSID Case No. ARB/05/7, para. 90 (Award dated 30 June 2009).
131. Andrea K. Bjorklund, *Investment Treaty Arbitral Decisions as Jurisprudence Constante*, UC Davis Legal Studies Research Paper No. 158, pp. 265–280, https://papers.ssrn.com/sol3/papers.cfm?abstract_id=1319834.
132. Jeffery P. Commission, *Precedent in Investment Treaty Arbitration: A Citation Analysis of a Developing Jurisprudence*, 24 J. Int'l Arb. 129, 136 (2007).
133. Anna De Luca, Mark Fledman, Martins Paparinskis and Catherine Titi, *Responding to Incorrect ISDS Decision-Making: Policy Options*, Academic Forum on ISDS Concept Paper, 2020/1 (21 January 2020), www.jus.uio.no/pluricourts/english/projects/leginvest/academic-forum/.

One of the concerns for introducing precedent in investment arbitration is the lack of legal basis for explaining how over three thousand distinct treaties, each of which is a *lex specialis*, can be bound with each other such that decisions rendered pursuant to one act as a binding precedent for a dispute arising out of another.[134] This has been addressed to some extent by the arbitral tribunal in *Cartube International Oil Company LLP v. Kazakhstan*,[135] in which the tribunal explained that while the arbitrators could not be bound by previous arbitral awards, they could nevertheless be used as supplementary means of interpretation as referred to under Article 32 of the Vienna Convention on Law of Treaties.[136] This interpretation is valid and has been used by many tribunals to refer to external precedents such as decisions of the Permanent Court or the International Court of Arbitration.[137] However, even then it falls short of making such references to previous decisions precedential in nature.

Prima facie, the suggestion of having a binding doctrine of precedent sounds like the perfect pill to cure the ill of inconsistency. Nevertheless, there are concerns that would need to be addressed before this reform measure may be adopted. First, any introduction of the doctrine of precedent will only be prospective in nature and will not be able to cure inconsistencies that have already crept into the system. Second, it is essential for the creation of precedents that all awards be published, which would infringe upon party autonomy in deciding whether or not they want proceedings to be confidential. Third, there is no hierarchy of tribunals in the ISDS system, which leaves a void in determining which decision would in fact be binding and if, when and how can it ever be overruled.

[C] Prior Scrutiny of Award

Another suggestion to bring about greater consistency is to introduce a system of prior scrutiny of draft arbitral awards, akin to the system followed by the International Chamber of Commerce's (ICC's) International Court of Arbitration.[138] Article 34 of the ICC Rules of Arbitration provides for conducting a substantive as well as procedure review of the award before it is finally delivered by the tribunal to the parties.[139]

Notably, in 2017, the Singapore International Arbitration Centre (SIAC) adopted the first Investment Arbitration Rules of the Singapore International Arbitration Centre,

134. *Coherence and Consistency – Is Reform Desirable?*, White Paper by IILC Washington (2019), http://www.ili.org/images/stories/documents/IILC/ILI-UNCITRAL-WG-III-White-Paper-Mar 19.pdf.
135. *Cartube International Oil Company LLP v. The Republic of Kazakhstan*, ICSID Case No. ARB/08/12.
136. Roberto Castro de Figuerdo, *Previous Decisions in Investment Arbitration*, Kluwer Arbitration Blog (23 December 2014), http://arbitrationblog.kluwerarbitration.com/2014/12/23/previous-decisions-in-investment-arbitration/.
137. *Supra* n. 125, p. 21.
138. Working Paper 150, *supra* n. 3, para. 43.
139. Article 34, Scrutiny of the Award by the Court: 'Before signing any award, the arbitral tribunal shall submit it in draft form to the Court. The Court may lay down modifications as to the form of the award and, without affecting the arbitral tribunal's liberty of decision, may also draw its attention to points of substance. No award shall be rendered by the arbitral tribunal until it has been approved by the Court as to its form.'

which also have provisions similar to the ICC Rules of Arbitration for prior scrutiny of an award. Rule 30.3 of these Rules provides that before any award is made, the tribunal is bound to submit the draft award to the registrar, who shall suggest modifications as to the form and substance of the award without affecting the tribunal's liberty to decide the dispute.[140] Similarly, the China International Economic and Trade Arbitration Commission (CIETAC) also introduced a similar provision for prior scrutiny of awards in its International Investment Arbitration Rules, 2017, which it is implementing on an experimental basis.[141]

This suggestion has also found support from the government of Morocco[142] along with Chile, Israel, Japan[143] and the Corporate Counsel International Arbitration Group,[144] all of whom are participants in the ongoing reform deliberations at WG III. The government of Morocco, in its submission to WG III, has also suggested how such scrutiny should be carried out in a time-acknowledged fashion by an independent body under an existing arbitration organization such as ICSID or the Permanent Court of Arbitration (PCA).[145] Morocco's suggestion, to have scrutiny conducted by ICSID or the PCA, is pertinent given most investment arbitrations are administered within the ICSID system. ICSID, like the ICC or the SIAC, has an experienced secretariat. However, it lacks judicial authority to carry out the scrutiny process.[146] Moreover, this mechanism would not be able to cover ad hoc investment arbitration because it is a pre-requirement that there is an institution to conduct the scrutiny of the award.[147] Thus, a systemic change would be necessary to introduce a system of prior scrutiny of investment arbitration award.

Suggestions have also been made about another form of prior scrutiny of award, i.e., by the disputing parties.[148] Such a provision has already been included in some

---

140. Rule 30.3, Investment Arbitration Rules of the Singapore International Arbitration Centre, https://www.siac.org.sg/our-rules/62-our-rules/rules/504-siac-ia-rules-2017.
141. Rule 49, China International Economic and Trade Arbitration Commission International Investment Arbitration Rules (in force from 1 October 2017). http://www.cietac.org/Uploads/201902/5c6148b100105.pdf.
142. Secretariat, *Possible Reform of Investor-State Dispute Settlement*, Submission from the Government of Morocco, A/CN.9/WG.III/WP.161 (March 2019), https://undocs.org/en/A/CN.9/WG.III/WP.161.
143. UNCTIRAL Secretariat, *Submission from the Government of Chile, Israel and Japan*, UNCITRAL Working Group III (Investor-State Dispute Settlement Reform) Thirty-seventh session, A/CN.9/WG.III/WP.163 (1–5 April 2019), https://undocs.org/en/A/CN.9/WG.III/WP.163.
144. *Submission by the Corporate Counsel International Arbitration Group (CCIAC) to UNCITRAL Working Group III* (18 December 2019), https://uncitral.un.org/sites/uncitral.un.org/files/cciag_isds_reform_0.pdf.
145. *Supra* n. 142, paras 23, 25.
146. OECD, *Improving the System of Investor-State Dispute Settlement: An Overview*, pp. 14–16, Making the Most of International Investment Agreements: A Common Agenda (Symposium co-organized by ICSID, OECD and UNCTAD, 2005), https://www.oecd.org/daf/inv/investment-policy/symposiumonmakingthemostofinternationalinvestmentagreementsacommonagenda.htm. *See also* Katia Yannaca-Small, *Improving the System of Investor-State Dispute Settlement* (OECD Working Papers on International Investment, No. 01, 2006), https://www.oecd-ilibrary.org/finance-and-investment/improving-the-system-of-investor-state-dispute-settlement_631230863687.
147. *Ibid.*
148. *Supra* n. 142, para. 24.

treaties, for example, in the Model US BIT 2012[149] and the Trans-Pacific Partnership Agreement.[150] While this process may plausibly lead to fewer challenges, if not restrictive in nature, it also holds the potential to reopen the dispute after a tribunal has declared the proceedings closed.

[D] Appellate Mechanism

The Investment Treaty between the United States of America and Uruguay,[151] the Free Trade Agreement between Chile and the United States of America,[152] the Dominical Republic-Central America Free Trade Agreement 2004,[153] and the CETA[154] all provide for an appellate mechanism. Drawing inspiration from the appeals provision in the extant treaties, members of the WG III have also proposed setting up an appellate mechanism.[155]

As early as 2004, ICSID in its discussion paper assessed the proposal for establishing an appeals facility and even set out its possible features.[156] The very next year, at a symposium organized by ICSID, the OECD and UNCTAD, an appeals mechanism was discussed, which recognized its importance *inter alia* for ensuring consistency in investment arbitration.[157] Again in 2013, the World Investment Report published by UNCTAD suggested the introduction of an appeals facility to improve consistency of case law, correct erroneous decisions of first-level tribunals and enhance the predictability of the law.[158] The recommendation was reiterated in 2015 along with the suggestion that it could be either a standing or an ad hoc body with competence to undertake substantive review and correct an arbitral tribunal's decisions.[159]

While the benefits of having an appellate mechanism to further consistency in the system have been extolled by all its proponents, it is essential to understand its drawbacks. An appeal mechanism is against the principle of finality because the right to appeal represents the recognition that finality may be compromised by infallibility, which may require correction.[160] An appeal mechanism would add to the delays in

149. Article 9(a), MODEL US BIT, 2012, https://ustr.gov/sites/default/files/BIT%20text%20for%20ACIEP%20Meeting.pdf.
150. Article 9.23, Comprehensive and Progressive Agreement for Trans-Pacific Partnership.
151. The Treaty between the United States of America and the Oriental Republic of Uruguay concerning the Encouragement and Reciprocal Protection of Investment, 2005.
152. Free Trade Agreement between the Government of Republic of Chile and the Government of the United States of America, 2003.
153. Dominical Republic-Central America Free Trade Agreement, 2004.
154. Canada-European Union Comprehensive Economic and Trade Agreement (CETA), 2017.
155. Working Paper 150, *supra* n. 3, para. 44, https://undocs.org/en/A/CN.9/WG.III/WP.150.
156. ICSID, *Possible Improvements of the Framework for ICSID Arbitration*, DISCUSSION PAPER (22 October 2004), https://icsid.worldbank.org/en/Documents/resources/Possible%20Improvements%20of%20the%20Framework%20of%20ICSID%20Arbitration.pdf.
157. *Supra* n. 146, pp. 57, 58.
158. *Supra* n. 109, p. 115.
159. *Supra* n. 110, p. 150.
160. Noemi Gal-Or, *The Concept of Appeal in International Dispute Settlement*, 19 EUR. J. INT'L L. 43, 51 (2008).

final decision-making and is therefore bound to increase the cost of arbitration.[161] Moreover, with the uncertain interpretation of the MFN clause and the uncertainty of its extension to a dispute resolution clause, there has also been a concern that it may be used to bring an appeal mechanism into play under a treaty even where it was not contemplated.[162] Apart from this, an appellate mechanism would make the decision-making bodies in investment disputes stronger. With an unbridled mandate to review an arbitral decision, they may undermine the sovereignty of the state party to the dispute.[163] Lastly, a gain in greater consistency brought about by an appellate mechanism will not *ipso facto* guarantee corresponding gains in accuracy of treaty interpretation.[164]

In 2005, ICSID, OECD and UNCTAD could not come to a conclusion about the appeal mechanism and left the option open for ICSID to study further. However, even today the disadvantages of an appellate system weigh heavier than the advantage of ensuring development of a possible uniform jurisprudence.

[E] Creating an International Court System

The CETA,[165] along with other free trade agreements that have been recently negotiated or signed by the EU,[166] provides for the establishment of a multilateral investment court. Creating such a court arguably would replace multiple ad hoc tribunals with a single institution while still retaining investors' right to bring claims against the host states.[167] Proponents especially argue that such a court would contribute towards consistency of investment law because ad hoc tribunals have a natural tendency to diverge as against standing tribunals, which have an inherent element of tradition and continuous collegiality.[168]

Although the idea of a multilateral court has been around for some time, there is no proposed structure. Moreover, the court proposed under CETA is not a permanent standing structure but a two-tier system with ICSID as its secretariat to provide it with appropriate support.[169] CETA provides for a tribunal of first instance, which may decide disputes under any of the rules provided under Article 8.23(2). Under this provision disputes may be resolved using the ICSID Convention and Rules of Procedure for Arbitration Proceedings or the ICSID Additional Facility Rules, if conditions for

161. *Supra* n. 146, p. 194.
162. *Ibid.*, p. 191.
163. Mark Feldman, *Investment Arbitration Appellate Mechanism Options: Consistency, Accuracy and Balance of Power*, 32 ICSID Rev. 520 (2017).
164. *Ibid.*
165. Article 8, Canada-European Union Comprehensive Economic Trade Agreement, https://ec.europa.eu/trade/policy/in-focus/ceta/ceta-chapter-by-chapter/.
166. EU-Singapore FTA, EU-Vietnam FTA, EU-Japan FTA.
167. *Supra* n. 110, p 152.
168. *Supra* n. 98, p. 16.
169. Article 8.27.16, CETA.

proceeding pursuant to the ICSID Convention and Rules do not apply.[170]Parties have also been granted the flexibility to use the UNCITRAL Rules or any other rules that they may agree to. At the same time, the tribunal is also permitted to draw up its own procedure.[171] Until such time that a structure and scope of such a court is fully determined, an ideal and effective solution to most criticisms of ISDS, including consistency, will remain to be seen. Moreover, establishing a court in itself will not ensure consistency or coherence unless it is mandated to follow the doctrine of stare decisis.

Nevertheless, the EU has been pushing the idea of a multilateral court even at WG III[172] meetings. It has proposed developing a standing mechanism for dispute settlement with levels of adjudication, a tribunal of first instance and an appellate tribunal.[173] The proposed mechanism would have permanent adjudicators with fixed salaries subject to ethical requirements.[174] It also suggested that the new mechanism should be transparent and provide access to third parties such as affected communities in the dispute resolution process.[175] The EU has argued that such a mechanism would be an answer to all the identified concerns afflicting present ISDS mechanism.[176]

Simultaneously, it has adopted the policy of introducing a prototype version of this proposed mechanism in its investment agreements with its trading partners. The EU is an important trading partner in global economy and for individual nations to resist its diplomatic might could be challenging. Nevertheless, Japan so far has resisted the idea of an investment court in the ongoing negotiations for the EU-Japan Economic Partnership Agreement (EUJEPA),[177] citing cost issues.[178] It remains to be seen if this dual diplomacy will prevail or fail.

§1.06 CONCLUSION

The lack of consistency and coherence is a challenge for the development of ISDS in its present form, which needs to be addressed. To address this challenge, an array of

170. Article 8.23.4, CETA clarifies that for a claim to be submitted under the ICSID Convention and Rules of Procedure for Arbitration Proceedings, conditions laid down in Art. 25(1) of the ICSID Convention must be satisfied.
171. Article 8.27.10, CETA.
172. UNCTIRAL Secretariat, *Submission from the European Union and Its Member-States*, UNCITRAL Working Group III (Investor-State Dispute Settlement Reform) Thirty-seventh session, A/CN.9/WG.III/WP.159/Add.1 (1–5 April 2019), https://undocs.org/en/A/CN.9/WG.III/WP.159/Add.1.
173. *Ibid.*, paras 3.1–3.2.
174. *Ibid.*, paras 3.4–3.5.
175. *Ibid.*, para. 3.11.
176. *Ibid.*, para. 4.
177. Bilateral Trade Deal with Japan-largest to date for EU, http://www.europarl.europa.eu/RegData/etudes/BRIE/2019/633164/EPRS_BRI(2019)633164_EN.pdf.
178. Trishna Menon and Gladwin Issac, *Developing Country Opposition to Investment Court: Could State-State Dispute Settlement be an Alternative*, Kluwer Arbitration Blog (17 February 2018), http://arbitrationblog.kluwerarbitration.com/2018/02/17/developing-country-opposition-investment-court-state-state-dispute-settlement-alternative/?print=print.

options is available and at the disposal of the states to choose, none of which is perfect but most of which are practicable.

What needs to be appreciated is that to use any of the options, a systemic alteration will be needed along with the political will to make such a systemic change in the ISDS system. This is the real challenge going forward. And even if both of these hurdles are somehow overcome, it must always be borne in mind that no matter what, perfect consistency akin to the pigeon hole theory can never be attained in investment arbitration. Some amount of variation is bound to persist given that every treaty is unique and a *lex specialis* that will have to be interpreted in the light of circumstances in which it was signed and the facts faced by the adjudicating tribunal. For now, the reform measures on the table need to be assessed further and experimented with before the final verdict is rendered on how to achieve consistency and coherence in ISDS.

CHAPTER 2

ISDS Reform in the EU: Are We There Yet?

Venetia Argyropoulou

This chapter critically reviews the recent case law of the European Court of Justice on the question of compatibility of Investor-State Dispute System (ISDS) mechanisms found in intra-European Union (EU) Bilateral Investment Treaties (BITs) as well as Free Trade Agreements (FTAs) entered into, *inter alia*, by the EU itself, within EU law. The aim of the chapter is to present the current situation in investment arbitration and explore the future of investment dispute resolution mechanisms in the EU, be that in a bilateral or multilateral setting.

§2.01 INTRODUCTION

The interplay of international arbitration law and EU law has been in the forefront in the past years following the issuance of the Court of Justice of the European Union's ('CJEU') preliminary ruling in *Slovak Republic v. Achmea BV* ('*Achmea* Ruling').[1] That decision sent shockwaves among practitioners and academic scholars alike, changing the landscape in EU investment arbitration and questioning the compatibility of investment treaties entered into by and/or between EU Member States with EU law. The decision, however, was shortly followed by CJEU's Opinion 1/17[2] ('Opinion 1/17') that seemed to take a different approach, restricting the effect of the *Achmea* Ruling and partly restoring the validity of the Investor-State Dispute Settlement ('ISDS') mechanisms in extra-EU 'BITs'. This chapter will critically explore the interplay between the *Achmea* Ruling and Opinion 1/17 and examine the current status of ISDS in the EU.

1. Case C-284/16 *Slovak Republic v. Achmea BV* [2018], ECLI:EU:C:2018:158 ('Case C-284/16 *Slovak Republic v. Achmea BV*').
2. Opinion 1/17 (Accord ECG UE-Canada) [2019] ECLI:EU:C:2019:72.

This chapter will also examine the European Commission's proposal for the replacement of ISDS with the introduction of a multilateral investment Court.

§2.02 THE *ACHMEA* RULING AND OPINION 1/17

[A] Background of the Cases

The *Achmea* Ruling was issued on 6 March 2018, in response to the request of the German Federal Court of Justice (Bundesgerichtshof) in the case between the Dutch Insurance Company Achmea B.V. (formerly known as Eureko B.V.) and the Slovak Republic. The case related to the measures introduced by Slovakia over the course of 2006 and 2009, changing the legal framework of the health insurance market, whereby the previous open and liberal health insurance market was partly reversed.[3] In particular, the subject of the dispute was the prohibition of the distribution of profits generated by private health insurance activities, introduced by Act. No 530/2007.[4] In this regard, Achmea's Slovak subsidiary was barred from distributing profits to Achmea. Hence in 2008, Achmea instigated arbitration proceedings against Slovakia under the 1991 Agreement on encouragement and reciprocal protection of investments between the Kingdom of the Netherlands and the Czech and Slovak Federative Republic (the 'Achmea BIT') on the grounds of violation of substantive treaty standards.[5] The case was heard by an ad hoc arbitral tribunal constituted under the (United Nations Commission on International Trade Law) UNCITRAL Rules in accordance with the Achmea BIT. The tribunal issued its award in 2012 deciding that Slovakia was in breach of the Achmea BIT and was liable to pay approximately EUR 22.1 million of damages to Achmea.[6] Slovakia filed a petition to set aside the arbitral award claiming the tribunal lacked jurisdiction, as the arbitration clause included in the Achmea BIT was incompatible with EU law and, in particular, with Articles 18, 267 and 344 of the Treaty on the Functioning of the European Union ('TFEU'). This was the question posed to the CJEU by the German Federal Court of Justice, who examined the set-aside proceedings on appeal after the Higher Regional Court of Frankfurt (Oberlandesgericht Frankfurt) had ruled that the ISDS mechanism in the Achmea BIT was not incompatible with the provisions of the TFEU.[7] Hence, the CJEU was called to give a final answer to the question of compatibility.

Opinion 1/17 was requested by Belgium in September 2017 under Article 218(11) of the TFEU, asking the CJEU to advise on the compatibility of the ISDS mechanism provided by the Comprehensive Economic and Trade Agreement between the EU and

3. See C. Greenwood & K. Lee, *International Law Reports* Vol. 178 (Cambridge: Cambridge University Press, 2018), 82, for an analytic review of the measures introduced by the Slovak Government.
4. Case C-284/16 *Slovak Republic v. Achmea BV* [8].
5. *Achmea B.V. v. The Slovak Republic* (formerly *Eureko B.V. v. The Slovak Republic*), UNCITRAL, PCA Case No. 2008-13 (Award on Jurisdiction, Arbitrability and Suspension, 26 October 2010).
6. *Achmea B.V. v. The Slovak Republic* (formerly *Eureko B.V. v. The Slovak Republic*) UNCITRAL, PCA Case No. 2008-13 (Award, 2012) [352].
7. *OLG Frankfurt, Az.:* 26 Sch 3/13.

Canada ('CETA')[8] with EU law, including fundamental rights. In particular, Belgium expressed concern on CETA's ISDS mechanism's compatibility with the general principle of equal treatment and the requirement of effectiveness of EU law and the right of access to an independent tribunal, but most importantly whether the ISDS mechanism infringed the autonomy of the EU legal order by interpreting and applying EU law in a binding manner for the EU and its Member States. Indeed, the autonomy of the EU legal order was the decisive factor in both cases; however, they reached different results.

[B] The Reasoning of the CJEU

In the *Achmea* Ruling, the CJEU concluded that the ISDS mechanism in the Achmea BIT was incompatible with the TFEU, as it had an adverse effect on the autonomy of EU law.[9] The CJEU came to this conclusion by analysing the features of EU legal order, namely its autonomy, stressing that EU Treaties supersede the national law of EU Member States as they constitute an independent source of law, which cannot be interfered and/or affected by international agreements.[10] Furthermore, the CJEU stressed the importance of Member States' courts collaborating with the CJEU, through the referral to the CJEU of questions pertaining to the interpretation of EU law in line with Article 267 of the TFEU. Thus, Member States' courts are responsible for the proper and uniform interpretation of EU law within their jurisdiction, acting as 'guardians'.[11] The CJEU is similarly the 'guardian' of this dialectic system that is required to ensure that EU law operates effectively and uniformly throughout the EU.[12]

Having established the importance of the EU legal order's autonomy, the CJEU noted that investment tribunals, when asked to resolve disputes between investors residing in one Member State and investing in another Member State, can interpret and/or apply EU law.[13] According to the CJEU, in light of the nature and characteristics of EU law, it must be deemed 'both as forming part of the law in force in every Member State and as deriving from an international agreement between the Member States'.[14]

Accordingly, the CJEU found that the qualities of EU law led to the conclusion that investments tribunals, such as the one in the Achmea BIT, will interpret EU law.[15] Thus, the CJEU proceeded to examine whether investment tribunals constitute part of the EU judicial system under the meaning of Article 267 of the TFEU. If the answer to this question was in the affirmative, then such tribunals could make preliminary references to the CJEU and therefore the uniform application of EU law could still be

8. Comprehensive Economic and Trade Agreement (CETA) between Canada and the European Union and its Member States (Brussels, 30 October 2016), OJ L 11, 14.1.2017.
9. Case C-284/16 *Slovak Republic v. Achmea BV* [59].
10. *Ibid.*, [32].
11. *Ibid.*, [33].
12. Venetia Argyropoulou, 'Vattenfall in the Aftermath of *Achmea*: Between a Rock and a Hard Place?', 4 European Investment Law and Arbitration Review Online (2019).
13. Case C-284/16 *Slovak Republic v. Achmea BV* [39].
14. *Ibid.*, [41].
15. *Ibid.*, [42].

upheld. The Advocate General's opinion on this point argued that investment tribunals formed part of the EU judicial system under intra-EU investment treaties and should be deemed as courts or tribunals of the Member States within the meaning of Article 267 TFEU.[16] The Advocate General referred to *Valeri Hariev Belov v. CHEZ Elektro Balgaria AD and Others*[17] and mentioned that it was settled case law that for a 'court or tribunal' for the purposes of Article 267 of the TFEU to exist, several elements should be taken into account. These included, *inter alia*, 'whether the body is established by law, whether it is permanent, whether its jurisdiction is compulsory, whether its procedure is *inter partes*, whether it applies rules of law and whether it is independent'.[18] In addition, it is necessary for a 'case [to be] pending before it and ... it [must be] called upon to give judgment in proceedings intended to lead to a decision of a judicial nature'.[19] The Advocate General examined whether tribunals like the one established under section 8 of the Achmea BIT met each of these criteria and concluded that such tribunals are, in fact, established by law, they are permanent and compulsory, their procedure is *inter partes* and that they are independent. Therefore, they meet all the criteria to be characterised as courts or tribunals under Article 267 of the TFEU.

The CJEU, however, disagreed with this analysis, which was also the case in Opinion 2/13.[20] In fact, it noted that tribunals such as the one created under the Achmea BIT have an exceptional nature which is 'one of the principal reasons for their existence'[21] and therefore such tribunals could not be part of the judicial system of either the Netherlands or Slovakia.[22] Furthermore, arbitral awards are usually final and not subject to review by the courts of EU Member States,[23] while the investment tribunal enjoys the freedom to decide its seat and therefore the applicable law relating to the review of awards. At the case in point, the *Achmea* Arbitral Tribunal was seated in Germany, where, under German law, review of arbitral awards is limited.[24] The CJEU emphasised that this was a material difference between commercial arbitration and investment arbitration. In commercial arbitration, such limited review was acceptable. However, in investment arbitration, which is based on treaties between states, this was not acceptable. This differentiation between investment and commercial arbitration appears to be rooted in the source of consent to arbitration. In the case of commercial arbitration, consent is found in a contract between the parties in dispute. In contrast, in the case of investment arbitration, consent is found in treaties, whereby

16. *Ibid.*, [133].
17. *Valeri Hariev Belov v. CHEZ Elektro Balgaria AD and Others* (Preliminary Ruling, 2013), CJEU, Case C-394/11.
18. Case C-284/16 *Slovak Republic v. Achmea BV* [86].
19. *See* Nils Wahl & Luca Prete, 'The Gatekeepers of Article 267 TFEU: On Jurisdiction and Admissibility of References For Preliminary Rulings', 55 Common Market Law Review (2018).
20. *Opinion pursuant to Article 218(11) TFEU* (Opinion, 2014), CJEU, Opinion No. 2/13 (although in the majority of cases the CJEU adopts the opinion of Advocate Generals). *See* Carlos Arrebola, Ana Júlia Maurício & Héctor Jiménez Portilla, 'An Econometric Analysis of the Influence of the Advocate General on the Court of Justice of the European Union', 5 Cambridge International Law Journal 82–112 (2016).
21. Case C-284/16 *Slovak Republic v. Achmea BV* [45].
22. *Ibid.*, [45].
23. *Ibid.*, [51].
24. *Ibid.*, [52].

EU Member States may consent to the removal of investor-state disputes relating to the application or interpretation of EU law from their national courts, and thus from the system of preliminary references.[25]

On these facts – namely that investment tribunals may interpret EU law although they are not part of the EU judicial order nor are awards subject to review by the courts of Member States – the CJEU came to the conclusion that investment tribunals may prevent disputes 'from being resolved in a manner that ensures the full effectiveness of EU law'.[26] Therefore arbitration clauses, such as clause 8 of the Achmea BIT, are incompatible with EU law and create an adverse effect on the autonomy of EU legal order.[27]

In contrast, in Opinion 1/17, the CJEU decided that the ISDS mechanism in CETA is compatible with EU law. From the Opinion of Advocate General, it had become clear that the approach that would be followed by the CJEU would be different from the *Achmea* Ruling. Indeed, in his opinion, the Advocate General noted that in his view 'the approach adopted by the Court in its judgment in *Achmea* cannot be transposed to the examination of the Investment Court System, because the premises which must guide the line of reasoning are different'.[28] That said, the Advocate General also underlined the importance that 'the establishment of a mechanism to settle disputes between investors and States by means of an agreement between, of the one part, the European Union and its Member States and, of the other part, a third State, must respect the autonomy of the EU legal order'.[29]

Before the CJEU's Ruling in Opinion 1/17 is examined, it should be mentioned that CETA differs from the Achmea BIT. Unlike the Achmea BIT that is a BIT between two EU Member States, CETA is a mixed international agreement,[30][31] i.e., an international agreement including questions which fall both under the EU's competence and under the EU Member States' powers. Such mixed international agreements have been the subject of review of the CJEU in the context of EU autonomy several times before. However, the CJEU had previously adopted a different view than the one expressed in Opinion 1/17. For example, in *Mox Plant*,[32] which related to a dispute between the United Kingdom (UK) and Ireland about the initiation of dispute resolution proceedings under the UN Convention on the Law of the Sea (UNCLOS),[33] the CJEU reached the

25. *Ibid.*, [55].
26. *Ibid.*, [56].
27. *Ibid.*, [58].
28. Opinion 1/17 (Accord ECG UE-Canada) [2019] ECLI:EU:C:2019:72 [106].
29. *Ibid.*, [113].
30. Press corner, European Commission – European Commission (2016), https://ec.europa.eu/commission/presscorner/detail/en/AC_16_3694 (accessed 14 March 2020).
31. But see President Juncker's statement, noting that the Commission is of the view, based on its legal analysis, that the EU-Canada Trade Agreement (CETA) is an 'EU-only' agreement. Press corner, European Commission – European Commission (2016), https://ec.europa.eu/commission/presscorner/detail/en/MEX_16_2357 (accessed 14 March 2020).
32. C-459/03 *Commission v. Ireland* [2006], ECLI:EU:C:2006:345.
33. Although UNCLOS falls within the ambit of authority of the EU, Annex IX Art. 2 contains a subordination clause that stipulates that an international organisation may sign the Convention if its members' majority are signatories to it.

conclusion that the ISDS mechanism in UNCLOS was likely to adversely affect the EU legal order.[34]

Similarly, in its Opinion 1/91 on the Agreement aiming to establish the European Economic Area (EEA)[35] (a mixed agreement concluded between states which were members of the European Free Trade Association and the European Community and its Member States), the CJEU noted that because the EEA Court might interpret and apply EU law in a manner binding for the CJEU,[36] this would 'adversely affect the allocation of responsibilities defined in the Treaties and, hence, the autonomy of the (EU) legal order'.[37] Also in the CJEU's Opinion No. 1/09 on the European and Community Patent Court Agreement,[38] it referred once again to the imperative importance of the judicial dialogue between national courts of the Member States and the CJEU on the interpretation of EU law[39] and concluded that the Patent Courts Agreement would deprive national courts of their power to interpret and apply EU law, something that 'would alter the essential character of the powers conferred on EU institutions'.[40] Lastly, in Opinion 2/13 that was also cited in the *Achmea* Ruling and that related to the European Court of Human Rights (ECtHR), the CJEU again ruled that the binding interpretation of EU law by the ECtHR would affect the allocation of powers set by EU treaties.[41]

In Opinion 1/17, however, the CJEU followed a different approach, noting that the mere fact that the ISDS established under CETA would fall outside the EU's legal order did not necessarily mean that the autonomy of the EU's legal order would be violated.[42] In Opinion 1/17, the CJEU introduced a new notion, namely that of 'reciprocity', to justify the compatibility of CETA with EU law. Particularly, the CJEU noted that in light of the reciprocal nature of international agreements and the EU's need to maintain its power in international relations, the EU should be able to enter such agreements. This would be achieved if the ISDS mechanisms provided for in such international investment agreements had the jurisdiction to interpret their provisions without their interpretation being subject to national courts of the parties to the agreements.[43] This would not mean that the EU's autonomy would be infringed.

For the EU's autonomy to be breached, one of the two following scenarios would have to apply: the CETA ISDS mechanism either would have to interpret and apply EU law or would have the authority to issue awards effecting the operation of EU institutions as set in the EU constitutional framework.[44] Accordingly to the CJEU, none of these conditions were met with the CETA ISDS mechanism. Indeed, unlike intra-EU

34. C-459/03 *Commission v. Ireland* [2006], ECLI:EU:C:2006:345 [154].
35. Opinion 1/91 (Draft agreement between the Community, on the one hand, and the countries of the European Free Trade Association, on the other hand, relating to the creation of the European Economic Area) (1991), ECLI:EU:C:1991:490.
36. *Ibid.*, [39].
37. *Ibid.*, [39].
38. Opinion 1/09 (Draft agreement on the creation of a unified patent litigation system) ECLI: EU:C:2011:123.
39. *Ibid.*, [80–87].
40. *Ibid.*, [89].
41. *Opinion pursuant to Article 218(11) TFEU* (Opinion, 2014), CJEU, Opinion 2/13 [184].
42. Opinion 1/17 (Accord ECG UE-Canada) [2019] ECLI:EU:C:2019:72 [115].
43. *Ibid.*, [117].
44. *Ibid.*, [137].

BITs,[45] the CJEU noted that CETA Article 8.31 paragraphs 1 and 2 provided assurances for the protection of the autonomy of the EU legal order.

Primarily, the tribunals established under CETA could only interpret and apply the provisions of CETA in accordance with international law,[46] including the Vienna Convention on the Law of Treaties. Additionally, CETA tribunals may only examine national law as a matter of fact alone, following the interpretation of national courts on matters of national law. CETA tribunals' examination of EU law would further 'not be binding upon the courts or the authorities of the EU and Member States'.[47] It follows that unlike intra-EU BITs, such as the one examined in the *Achmea* Ruling, in the case of CETA, EU law was not the applicable law and thus the CETA tribunals would not be permitted to interpret and apply EU law.[48] This is in line with the finding of the Permanent Court of International Justice (PCIJ) in previous cases relating to its jurisdiction.[49] Indicatively, in the case concerning certain German interest in Polish Upper Silesia,[50] the PCIJ noted:

> From the standpoint of International Law and the Court, which is its organ, municipal laws are merely procedures which express the will and constitute the activities of States, in the same manner as legal decisions or administrative measures. The Court is certainly not called upon to interpret the Polish law as such; but there is nothing to prevent the Court's giving judgment on the question whether or not, in applying that law, Poland is acting in conformity with its obligations towards Germany under the Geneva Convention.[51]

Similarly, the CJEU noted that that CETA provides sufficient provisions depriving CETA tribunals of the ability to challenge the choices of the democratically elected institutions of the parties because it contains various provisions guaranteeing public interest considerations and the parties' right to regulate.[52] Thus, CETA tribunals could not issue awards effecting the operation of EU institutions in accordance with the EU constitutional framework.[53]

Although this decision has been met with enthusiasm by various scholars, nonetheless the fact that Opinion 1/17 greatly deviates from the previous case law of the CJEU on mixed agreements cannot be overlooked. Of course, the CJEU referred to

---

45. *Ibid.*, [126].
46. *Ibid.*, [121].
47. *Ibid.*, [130].
48. Cristina Contartese, 'Achmea and Opinion 1/17: Why Do Intra and Extra-EU Bilateral Investment Treaties Impact Differently on the EU Legal Order?', 19 ECB Legal Working Paper Series (2019).
49. *See Payment in Gold of Brazilian Federal Loans Contracted in France* Case (1929) P.C.I.J. Series A, No. 20/21.
50. *Certain German Interests in Polish Upper Silesia Case* (1926), P.C.I.J. Series A, No. 7.
51. *Certain German Interest in Polish Upper Silesia Case* (1925) P.C.I.J. Series A, No. 7. Judgment on Jurisdiction of the Court, [19]. *But see* Clarence Wilfred Jenks, 'The Interpretation and Application of Municipal Law by the Permanent Court of International Justice', 67 British Year Book International Law (1938) (Jenks noted that the application of law as a matter of fact bears little importance because in interpreting and applying national law, tribunals are merely treating national law as fact, and this process may not make much difference to the tribunal's reasoning process).
52. Opinion 1/17 (Accord ECG UE-Canada) [2019] ECLI:EU:C:2019:72 [161].
53. *Ibid.*, [137].

this previous case law in explaining the reasons for departure in each case. The CJEU noted that CETA is different from the draft Agreement on the creation of a Unified Patent Litigation System, as in the latter case the CJEU would be bound to follow the interpretation of the Unified Patent Court on matters pertaining to EU law.[54] For the same reason, the CJEU noted that CETA was different from the draft accession agreement to the European Convention on Human Rights (ECHR).[55] The CJEU also referred to another difference between CETA and the draft accession agreement to the ECHR, namely that of the co-respondent mechanism. Indeed, the co-respondent mechanism was considered troublesome under Opinion 2/13, as in such case the ECtHR could invite a High Contracting Party to become a co-respondent to a case, something that was deemed to interfere with the division of powers between the EU and its Member States.[56] CETA, on the other hand, did not interfere with the division of powers between the EU and its Member States.[57] This was the difference between CETA and the draft agreement relating to the creation of the EEA also.[58] However, on 16 May 2017, the CJEU examined another trade agreement, namely the FTA between the EU and the Republic of Singapore. Although the CJEU's examination in Opinion 2/15[59] was limited to the nature of the competence of the EU to sign and conclude this agreement and did not review the compatibility of the agreement's provisions with EU law,[60] the CJEU did mention that ISDS can affect the powers of the courts of the Member States.[61]

The fundamental difference between the *Achmea* Ruling and Opinion 1/17 lies in the notion of mutual trust. Under the notion of mutual trust, only courts and tribunals established within the EU legal system may handle investment disputes involving Member States, because Member States mutually share the common values mentioned in Article 2 of the Treaty of the European Union.[62] It therefore contravenes the notion of mutual trust when disputes on investments performed within the EU are referred to external (outside the EU legal system) ISDS mechanisms. However, while the notion of mutual trust is applicable in disputes relating to intra-EU BITs, as was stated in Opinion 1/17, the notion of mutual trust is not applicable in the relations between EU and third States, including in disputes arising from international investment agreements.[63]

---

54. *Ibid.*, [71].
55. *Ibid.*, [74].
56. *See* Stefan Reitemeyer and Benedikt Pirker, 'Opinion 2/13 of the Court of Justice on Access of the EU to the ECHR – One step ahead and two steps back', European Law Blog (2015), https://europeanlawblog.eu/2015/03/31/opinion-213-of-the-court-of-justice-on-access-of-the-eu-to-the-echr-one-step-ahead-and-two-steps-back/ (accessed 26 March 2020).
57. *Ibid.*, [74].
58. Opinion 1/17 (Accord ECG UE-Canada) [2019] ECLI:EU:C:2019:72 [74].
59. Opinion 2/15 (Division of requisite competences between the Union and its Member States for the conclusion of the EU-Singapore FTA) [2017] EU:C:2017:376.
60. *Ibid.*, [30].
61. *Ibid.*, [290–293].
62. Jens Hillebrand Pohl, 'Intra-EU Investment Arbitration after the *Achmea* Case: Legal Autonomy Bounded by Mutual Trust?', 14 European Constitutional Law Review 767–791 (2018).
63. Opinion 1/17 (Accord ECG UE-Canada) [2019] ECLI:EU:C:2019:72 [74].

[C] Where Do We Stand?

In reviewing these contradicting judgments of the CJEU, the question arises as to what do they mean for ISDS in the EU. To respond to this question, it is necessary to differentiate between intra-EU BITs, extra-EU BITs and FTAs and international investment agreements.

[1] Intra-EU BITs

As to intra-EU BITs and the compatibility of ISDS mechanisms included therein with EU law, the answer is given by the *Achmea* Ruling in a very clear manner. Indeed, although the *Achmea* Ruling examined only the Achmea BIT, nonetheless the findings of the CJEU can be extended to all intra-EU BITs that contain similar ISDS mechanisms.[64] Based on the *Achmea* Ruling, therefore, ISDS mechanisms included in intra-EU BITs are not compatible with EU law, because they may affect the autonomy of the EU's legal order and, possibly, although this was not examined by the CJEU, they might be discriminatory. Such a conclusion, although made clear in the *Achmea* Ruling, has been lingering for quite some time as evident from the stance followed by the European Commission in previous years.

The European Commission first referred to the question of the compatibility of ISDS mechanisms included in intra-EU BITs in *Eastern Sugar B.V. (Netherlands) v. The Czech Republic*[65] in 2006. In that case, the European Commission failed to take a clear stance in favour of either position regarding the compatibility of the ISDS mechanism in question, allowing both disputing parties to use the European Commission's response in their favour.[66] Since then, the European Commission has submitted opinions as amicus curiae in several arbitral cases revolving around the compatibility of ISDS mechanisms found in intra-EU BITs including, *inter alia*, in the cases of *Electrabel v. Hungary*,[67] *AES v. Hungary*,[68] *EURAM v. Slovakia*,[69] *U.S. Steel v. Slovakia*[70] and even the arbitral case of *Achmea*.[71] In these amicus curiae opinions, the European

64. *See* Case C-459/03 *Commission of the European Communities v. Ireland*, ECLI:EU:C:2006:345, where the CJEU noted that it if international arbitral tribunals could find themselves in a position to interpret EU law, this would endanger the CJEU's exclusive jurisdiction and would therefore be incompatible with EU law.
65. *Eastern Sugar B.V. (Netherlands) v. The Czech Republic*, Stockholm Chamber of Commerce, Case No. 088/2004 (Partial Award, 17 March 2007).
66. *Ibid.*, [181].
67. *Electrabel v. Hungary ICSID*, Case No. ARB/07/19 (Decision on Jurisdiction, Applicable Law and Liability, 30 November 2012).
68. *AES Summit Generation Limited and AES-Tisza Erömü Kft v. The Republic of Hungary*, ICSID Case No. ARB/07/22 (Award, 23 September 2010).
69. *European American Investment Bank AG (EURAM) v. Slovak Republic*, PCA Case No. 2008-13 (Award on Jurisdiction, 4 June 2014).
70. *U.S. Steel Global Holdings I B.V. v. The Slovak Republic*, UNCITRAL, PCA Case No. 2013-6 (16 June 2014).
71. *Achmea B.V. v. The Slovak Republic* (formerly *Eureko B.V. v. The Slovak Republic*), UNCITRAL, PCA Case No. 2008-13 (Award on Jurisdiction, Arbitrability and Suspension (26 October 2010)).

Commission strongly opposed the applicability of intra-EU investment treaties on the ground that they are incompatible with EU law.

The EU Commission claims that intra-EU BITs are incompatible with EU law on the following grounds. Primarily, intra-EU BITs allow certain investors – nationals of specific Member States – to claim more protection than investors who are nationals of other Member States, solely on the basis of their nationality and are, therefore, discriminatory. Furthermore, the European Commission argues that such additional protection may hinder the single capital market,[72] because 'all Member States are subject to the same EU rules in the single market, including those on cross-border investments (in particular the freedom of establishment and the free movement of capital)'.[73]

In this respect, since 2014 the European Commission had instigated infringement proceedings against Denmark, Austria, Finland and Sweden.[74] Since 2015 it had instigated infringement proceedings against Austria, the Netherlands, Romania, Slovakia, and Sweden for the abolition of intra-EU BITs.[75] At the same time, with the exception of Ireland and Italy that had already terminated inter-EU BITs, all other Member States were called in for consultation to have intra-EU BITs terminated.[76] Finally, less than a year after the issuance of the *Achmea* Ruling, in January 2019, the EU Member States issued three political declarations announcing their intention to terminate all of their intra-EU BITs by means of a multilateral treaty by the end of 2019 and in particular by 6 December.[77]

To this end, on 24 October 2019, the EU Member States (with the exception of Finland and Sweden),[78] under the supervision of the EU Commission, agreed on a plurilateral treaty for the termination of intra-EU BITs,[79] which was signed on 5 May 2020.[80] This treaty will, once in force,[81] terminate approximately two hundred intra-EU BITs, also eliminating sunset-clauses and deactivating ISDS mechanisms as of the date

See also Venetia Argyropoulou, 'Vattenfall in the Aftermath of Achmea: Between a Rock and a Hard Place?', 4 European Investment Law and Arbitration Review Online (2019).

72. Nikos Lavranos, *Member States' Bilateral Investment Treaties (BITs): Lost in Transition?* 24, Hague Yearbook of International Law (2012).
73. European Commission, Press Release, 'Commission Asks Member States To Terminate Their Intra-EU Bilateral Investment Treaties IP/15/5198' (2015).
74. European Commission, Press Release, 'Free movement of capital: infringement procedures against Denmark, Austria, Finland and Sweden concerning Bilateral Investment Treaties with non-EU countries', IP/04/618 (2004).
75. European Commission, Press Release, 'Commission Asks Member States To Terminate Their Intra-EU Bilateral Investment Treaties IP/15/5198' (2015).
76. *Ibid.*
77. The Governments of the EU Member States, Declaration of the Member States of 15 January 2019 on the legal consequences of the Achmea judgment and on investment protection (2019).
78. Osborne Clarke, *End of the road for intra-EU BITs* (2019), https://www.osborneclarke.com/insights/end-road-intra-eu-bits/ (last accessed 17 May 2020).
79. European Commission, Statement 'EU Member States agree on a plurilateral treaty to terminate bilateral investment treaties' (2019).
80. Agreement for the termination of bilateral investment treaties between the Member States of the European Union (Brussels, 5 May 2020).
81. The treaty enters into force thirty calendar days after the date on which the Secretary General of the Council of the European Union receives the second instrument of ratification, approval or acceptance.

of each Member State's entry into the EU.[82] Thus, it will no longer be possible to instigate investment arbitrations under the terminated BITs.[83] The plurilateral agreement is expected to also affect ongoing disputes that have been commenced before the plurilateral agreement will come into force, something that seems contrary to the principles of legal certainty and *res inter alios acta, aliis nec nocet nec prodest* ('a thing done between others does not harm or benefit others').[84] For such disputes, a settlement mechanism is envisioned that will allow investors to enter into a 'structured dialogue' with the state in dispute within six months from the date of termination of the respective BIT.[85]

The finding that ISDS located in intra-EU BITs is incompatible with EU law is not only important for national courts in EU Member States, where it is settled case law that national courts must set aside and refuse to apply incompatible national and/or international law,[86] but also affects investment tribunals. Indeed, even though the plurilateral agreement has not yet entered into force, nonetheless intra-EU investment disputes that take place outside the International Centre for Settlement of Investment Disputes (ICSID) Convention[87] and are seated within an EU Member State are likely to be annulled by the supervisory Member State court upon application of the losing party.[88] Indicatively, the Dutch companies Airbus Helicopters SAS and Airbus SE proceeded to withdraw the call for arbitration filed against Poland in relation to a cancelled deal for the purchase of helicopters worth USD 3.5 billion, referring to the *Achmea* Ruling, and instead reserved their right to file the claim under national Polish Courts.[89]

Of course, investment tribunals so far have been reluctant to accept the application of the *Achmea* Ruling in their jurisdiction, especially in cases of tribunals

82. Agreement for the termination of bilateral investment treaties between the Member States of the European Union (Brussels, 5 May 2020), Arts 2 and 3. *See also* Nikos Lavranos, 'The EU Plurilateral Draft Termination Agreement for All Intra-EU BITs: An End of the Post-Achmea Saga and the Beginning of a New One', Kluwer Arbitration Blog Kluwer Arbitration Blog (2019), http://arbitrationblog.kluwerarbitration.com/2019/12/01/the-eu-plurilateral-draft-termination-agreement-for-all-intra-eu-bits-an-end-of-the-post-achmea-saga-and-the-beginning-of-a-new-one/ (accessed 28 March 2020).
83. Agreement for the termination of bilateral investment treaties between the Member States of the European Union (Brussels, 5 May 2020), Art. 5.
84. Johannes Tropper, 'The Treaty to End All Investment Treaties', Völkerrechtsblog (2020), https://voelkerrechtsblog.org/the-treaty-to-end-all-investment-treaties/ (accessed 17 May 2020).
85. Agreement for the termination of bilateral investment treaties between the Member States of the European Union (Brussels, 5 May 2020), Art. 9.
86. *See Simmenthal S.p.A. v. Amministrazione Delle Finanze pello Stato*, Case No. 106/77 (Preliminary Ruling, 1978).
87. Convention on the Settlement of Investment Disputes Between States and Nationals of Other States [ICSID Convention] (Washington, 18 March 1965), 575 U.N.T.S. 159; 17 U.S.T. 1270; T.I.A.S. No. 6090, entered into force 14 October 1966.
88. Stephan Schill, 'Slowakische Republik v. Achmea BV – The arbitration clause in the Agreement between the Netherlands and Slovakia on the protection of investments is not compatible with EU law', Email sent to OGEDIM Members, 28 May 2018.
89. S.A. Telewizja, 'Airbus Helicopters To Press Claims Before Polish Courts' (Polandin.com 2018) https://polandin.com/37273654/airbus-helicopters-to-press-claims-before-polish-courts (accessed 27 January 2019).

established under the ICSID Convention.[90] In *UP (formerly Le Chèque Déjeuner) and C.D Holding Internationale v. Hungary*,[91] the tribunal ruled that the *Achmea* Ruling was not relevant to the dispute.[92] In the case of ICSID tribunals, arbitral awards are enforced as final judgments of the jurisdiction where enforcement is sought.[93] Hence, Member States are faced with the dilemma of complying with either EU law, under which ICSID tribunals established through intra-EU BITs are incompatible with EU law for the reasons described in the *Achmea* Ruling and thus refuse enforcement, or the ICSID Convention. Thus far, the UK Supreme Court has responded that Britain's enforcement obligations under the ICSID Convention are not affected by the EU duty of sincere co-operation, refusing to continue the stay of enforcement of an ICSID award that was contradicting EU state aid rules, pending a judgment by the CJEU on the matter.[94] However, this decision was issued after Britain's exit from the EU and, although suggestive of the UK's intention to enforce intra-EU awards, it is not necessarily indicative of the stance that will be followed by other EU Member States that are committed to the primacy of EU law.

The case of *PL Holdings v. Poland*[95] serves as an example of how investment tribunals reacted to the *Achmea* Ruling, in a way that may 'revive' intra-EU BITs. The case related to the Belgium-Luxembourg Economic Union (BLEU)-Poland BIT. Under this BIT, investment disputes are to be resolved by arbitral proceedings in accordance with three different options, including, *inter alia*, the Arbitration Institute of the Stockholm Chamber of Commerce.[96]

The facts of the case are not relevant, but the arbitral tribunal awarded the investor damages for breach of the BIT in an amount of approximately EUR 150 million. Poland proceeded to challenge the arbitral award requesting it be set aside on the basis

90. Although in *Theodoros Adamakopoulos and others v. Republic of Cyprus*, a dispute under the BITs between Cyprus and Greece and between Belgium-Luxembourg and Cyprus, Professor Marcelo Kohen disagreed with the majority judgment on jurisdiction noting the tribunal's competence had to be declined for lack of valid consent to arbitration. *See Theodoros Adamakopoulos and others v. Republic of Cyprus*, ICSID Case No. ARB/15/49 (Statement of Dissent of Professor Marcelo Kohen, 3 February 2020).
91. *UP (formerly Le Chèque Déjeuner) and C.D Holding Internationale v. Hungary*, ICSID Case No. ARB/13/35 (Award, 9 October 2018).
92. The arbitral tribunal found that the *Achmea* Ruling was not relevant to the dispute because: (i) the tribunal was established by the ICSID Convention deciding the case on the basis of international public law and in particular on Art. 52 of the ICSID Convention; (ii) Hungary's accession in the EU was not sufficient to deny the binding nature of the ICSID Convention, including its obligation for enforcement of the award; and (iii) even if Hungary's membership in the EU did somehow deny ICSID Arbitration, the sunset clause in Art. 12(2) of the bilateral investment treaty retained the agreement to arbitrate in force for twenty years, namely until 2024. *See* Venetia Argyropoulou, 'Vattenfall in the Aftermath of Achmea: Between a Rock and a Hard Place?', 4 European Investment Law and Arbitration Review Online (2019).
93. Convention on the Settlement of Investment Disputes Between States and Nationals of Other States (International Centre for Settlement of Investment Disputes [ICSID]) 575 UNTS 159, entered into force 14 October 1966, Art. 53.
94. *Micula and others v. Romania* [2020] UKSC 5.
95. *PL Holdings S.à.r.l. v. Republic of Poland* (Set Aside Proceedings, 2018), CC Case No. V 2014/163.
96. Bilateral Investment Treaty, BLEU (Belgium-Luxembourg Economic Union) – Poland (19 May 1987), entered into force 2 August 1991, Art. 9.

of the *Achmea* Ruling.[97] The request was heard by the Svea Court of Appeal. The Svea Court examined the ISDS mechanism included in the respective BIT and considered that it was different from the one contained in the Achmea BIT.[98] The Svea Court noted that the ISDS mechanism found in the BLEU-Poland BIT resembled that of commercial arbitration in the sense that it allowed investors to enter into arbitration agreements with the state involved, in accordance with the principle of the parties' autonomy.[99] The Svea Court of Appeal concluded that such arbitration agreements are not incompatible with EU law under the *Achmea* Ruling, which aims to preclude ISDS mechanisms that are binding on Member States.[100]

In this regard, the Svea Court of Appeal dismissed Poland's challenge to the award, also emphasising that Poland had omitted to raise the invalidity of the arbitration in a timely manner. Poland challenged this decision before the High Court of Sweden. The High Court stayed the proceedings and requested a preliminary ruling from the CJEU because it considered that it was unclear how EU law would apply to the facts of the case.[101] The ruling of the CJEU in this request for a preliminary ruling is much anticipated because it has the potential to reverse the tendency for the termination of intra-EU BITs and instead introduce new intra-EU BITs that resemble the ISDS mechanism found in the BLEU-Poland BIT.

The request for a preliminary ruling is necessary because it appears equally possible that even if the source for consent to arbitrate a dispute between a Member State and a natural or legal person of another Member State is a contract, the tribunal may interpret and apply EU law. In the *Achmea* Ruling, the CJEU did not successfully explain the differences between commercial and investment arbitration that would allow a different treatment among them. That stated, in light of the political momentum explained previously, a revival of intra-EU BITs is hard to imagine.

[2] Extra-EU BITs

Another question that arises from the *Achmea* Ruling is whether it can also apply to extra-EU BITs, i.e., BITs concluded between one EU Member State and a non-Member State. Currently, there are more than 1,200 extra-EU BITs[102] and one can easily understand the importance of understanding the consequence of the *Achmea* Ruling (if any) on such BITs.

97. *See* Case No. V 2014/163, *PL Holdings S.à.r.l. v. Republic of Poland* (Expert Opinion of Judge Fidelma Macken, Set-aside Proceeding, 22 October 2018).
98. Case No. V 2014/163 *PL Holdings S.à.r.l. v. Republic of Poland* (Judgment of the Svea Court of Appeal on the Set-aside Proceeding, 22 February 2019) [42].
99. *Ibid.*, [43].
100. *Ibid.*, [43].
101. Case No. V 2014/163 *PL Holdings S.à.r.l. v. Republic of Poland* (Decision of the Swedish Supreme Court on referral to the ECJ, 12 December 2019).
102. Rumiana Yotova, 'The New EU Competencies in Foreign Direct Investment and Intra-EU Investment Treaties: Does the Emperor Have New Clothes?', in *Investment Law within International Law: Integrationist Perspectives* (Freya Baetens 2013), [388].

Primarily, the European Commission, in responding to questions posed following its communication on the protection of intra-EU investments,[103] noted that the *Achmea* Ruling 'only concerns intra-EU disputes' and for extra-EU BITs different legal considerations apply.[104] However, the differences between an investment tribunal established under an intra-EU BIT and one established under an extra-EU BIT cannot easily be explained. Similarly, there is no apparent justification of why foreign investors would be granted access to international investment tribunals, while investors from the EU would be deprived of such recourse.

The unqualified wording of the *Achmea* Ruling does not exclude the application of the *Achmea* Ruling to investment agreements entered into between Member States and third-party states. The decisive factor seems to be whether investment tribunals would, in fact, apply EU law and whether such application and interpretation of EU law can be binding on Member States.[105] This is demonstrated by also reviewing the previous case law of the CJEU referred to above. Indicatively, in its Opinion 1/91, the EEA Court's mandate was considered to allow the EEA Court to interpret and apply EU law in a manner binding for the CJEU. Thus, the CJEU found that the jurisdiction conferred to the EEA Court 'is likely to adversely affect the allocation of responsibilities defined in the Treaties and, hence, the autonomy of the (EU) legal order'.[106] Similarly, the fact that the ISDS mechanism under UNCLOS could rule 'on the scope of obligations imposed on the Member States pursuant to Community law'[107] was sufficient for the CJEU to rule that a breach of EU law had occurred.[108] This was also the finding of the CJEU in Opinion No. 1/09 on the European and Community Patent Court Agreement.[109] Lastly, this finding was clearly stipulated in Opinion 2/13, where the CJEU ruled that the binding interpretation of EU law by the ECtHR would affect the allocation of powers set by EU Treaties, something that would not be compatible with the autonomy of the EU legal order.[110]

To decide whether an ISDS tribunal under an extra-EU BIT would in fact interpret and apply EU law, the wording of the respective BIT is of material importance. In particular, the wording that determines the law applicable to the resolution of any dispute arising from the BIT before the tribunal must closely be reviewed. Such wording varies from BIT to BIT,[111] and thus an overall assessment is difficult to make.

---

103. European Commission, Communication on the protection of intra-EU investment COM (2018) [547].
104. European Commission, Fact Sheet, Commission provides guidance on protection border EU investments – Questions and Answers (2018).
105. Case C-284/16 *Slovak Republic v. Achmea BV* [55].
106. Opinion 1/91 (Draft agreement between the Community and the countries of the European Free Trade Association relating to the creation of the European Economic Area) (1991), ECLI: EU:C:1991:490, [39].
107. Case C-459/03 *Commission v. Ireland* [2006], EU:C:2006:345 [177].
108. *Ibid.*, [184].
109. Opinion 1/09 (Draft agreement on the creation of a unified patent litigation system) ECLI: EU:C:2011:123 [80–87].
110. Opinion 2/13 pursuant to Art. 218(11) TFEU [2014] EU:C:2014:2454, [184].
111. Rudolf Dolzer & Christoph Schreuer, *Principles of International Investment Law* (2nd ed. 2012) [288].

However, it is here worth making a brief presentation of possible outcomes based on the wording of the BIT.

Primarily, if the BIT mentions that the applicable law is limited exclusively to the BIT, then the application and interpretation of EU law by the tribunal would be excluded. In such cases, the ISDS mechanism would not be affected by the *Achmea* Ruling, because EU law would not be the subject of review of the tribunal.[112] Similarly, if national law is taken into account only as a set of procedures, as in the case of CETA, based on CJEU's Opinion 1/17, arbitral tribunals established by extra-EU BITs will not be deemed to be incompatible with EU law. Of course, such a position seems to disregard the fact that state laws do not lose their normative value by the mere fact that the state laws are examined as facts of the case.[113] Furthermore, courts when applying national laws in case of divergent interpretations by national laws need to select the most appropriate interpretation, in itself involves interpreting national law.[114]

On the contrary, where a BIT mentions that the applicable law is the national law of the host state, in case the host state is an EU Member State, then, based on the *Achmea* Ruling, the tribunal of such a BIT would in fact interpret and apply EU law. This is in light of the nature and characteristics of EU law, which 'must be regarded both as forming part of the law in force in every Member State and as deriving from an international agreement between the Member States'.[115] Therefore, by interpreting national law, the tribunal would be interpreting EU law as well and if such interpretation would be binding on Member States (as, e.g., if there was no review mechanism, as in ICSID cases), this would be deemed incompatible with EU law.

An interesting question is what happens when the extra-EU BIT is silent on which law is applicable, as is the case with several if not the majority of BITs.[116] In such cases, the arbitral tribunal must apply 'such rules of international law as may be applicable'.[117] Such 'rules of international law' must mean the Vienna Convention on the Law of Treaties[118] and the residual rules provided for in the arbitration rules chosen by the parties.[119] Hence, the outcome of the question of whether the ISDS mechanism contained in the extra-EU BITs is compatible with EU law might be different depending on the arbitration rules chosen by the contracting states. For example, in the event that the extra-EU BIT refers to the ICSID Convention,[120] Article 42, paragraph 1, of the ICSID Convention refers that:

112. Opinion 1/17 *Accord ECG UE-Canada* [2019], ECLI:EU:C:2019:72 [110].
113. Sharif Bhuiyan, *National law in WTO Law* (2011) [42].
114. *Ibid.*, [42].
115. Case C-284/16 *Slovak Republic v. Achmea BV* [41].
116. Lori Fisler Damrosch, Giorgio Sacerdoti & Giorgio Sacerdoti, *Enforcing International Law Through Non-forcible Measures* (1998) [445].
117. Patrick Dumberry, *Formation and Identification of Rules of Customary International Law in International Investment Law* (2019) [380].
118. Vienna Convention on the Law of Treaties (Vienna, 23 May 1969) 1155 U.N.T.S. 331, entered into force 27 January 1980.
119. Quentin Declève, 'Achmea: Consequences on Applicable Law and ISDS Clauses in Extra-EU BITs', 4 European Papers, No. 1, 99–108 (2019).
120. Convention on the Settlement of Investment Disputes Between States and Nationals of Other States [ICSID Convention] (Washington, 18 March 1965), 575 U.N.T.S. 159; 17 U.S.T. 1270; T.I.A.S. No. 6090, entered into force 14 October 1966.

> the Tribunal shall decide a dispute in accordance with such rules of law as may be agreed by the parties. In the absence of such agreement, the Tribunal shall apply the law of the Contracting State party to the dispute (including its rules on the conflict of laws) and such rules of international law as may be applicable.[121]

Thus, in extra-EU BITs where the tribunals are established under the ICSID Convention, if there is no reference to the applicable law, the tribunal may have to apply and interpret national law of the host Member State. This may, inadvertently, include EU law, something that would run foul with the concept of autonomy of the EU legal order, especially since such an interpretation would be binding on the respective EU Member State. Similarly, the relevant UNCITRAL and International Chamber of Commerce (ICC) Rules provide that in the absence of a choice of law designated by the parties, the tribunal must apply the law that it deems most appropriate.[122] This might include the national law of the host state, including, *inter alia*, EU law. Once again, in cases where the extra-EU BIT is silent on the applicable law, the tribunal's compatibility with EU law will vary and will largely depend on what law the tribunal may apply.

Therefore, the impact of the *Achmea* Ruling is not limited to intra-EU BITs but may affect extra-EU BITs as well. Extra-EU BITs' compatibility with EU law will depend on the wording of such BITs vis-à-vis applicable law. In case the wording allows the tribunal to interpret and apply EU law, the question will be if the tribunal's interpretation will have a binding character on the EU Member State(s). If so, then the ISDS mechanism contained in the extra-EU BIT would be incompatible with EU law, in line with the *Achmea* Ruling.

[3] FTAs and International Investments Agreements

FTAs and international investments agreements (IIAs) are unlike extra-EU BITs. In FTAs, the EU is itself a party, either alone or in the case of mixed agreements together with individual Member States. However, despite this difference, the treatment of FTAs in relation to the compatibility of their ISDS mechanisms with EU law should be the same as with extra-EU BITs. This outcome stems from Opinion 1/17, where in order to examine the compatibility of CETA's ISDS mechanism with EU law, the CJEU proceeded to examine the wording of CETA in relation to the applicable law. As indicated previously, the CJEU found that CETA's ISDS mechanism was compatible with EU law because CETA tribunals would not interpret or apply EU law or would apply EU law solely as a matter of fact.

However, the CJEU failed to take into account and respond to important questions, such as what if CETA tribunals do in fact proceed to interpret EU law. This is not impossible because CETA regulates aspects that fall into the ambit of EU law and the competences of the EU, including the free movement of capital. Although CETA

121. *Ibid.*, Art. 42.

122. UNCITRAL Arbitration Rules, GA Res 65/22, UNCITRAL, 2010, Supp. No. 17, UN Doc. A/65/465 (2010), Art. 35(1) and ICC Rules of Arbitration (2012), Art 21(1).

tribunals only interpret national law as a matter of fact, it is questionable how this will work in practice.[123]

The case of mixed agreements, like the Energy Charter Treaty (ECT), should be examined specifically[124] in so far as they apply between EU Member States. Indeed, the ECT is the investment treaty used most often by EU investors against EU Member States.[125] For example, out of the 121 investor-state disputes brought under the ECT until 2019, approximately 78 were disputes between EU investors and Member States.[126] In such cases, the question arises whether the *Achmea* Ruling would bar such disputes from being brought through the arbitration mechanism contained in Article 26 of the ECT.

The EU made no reservations when submitting to the ISDS mechanism of ECT.[127] However, the *Achmea* Ruling casts doubts on the compatibility of intra-EU disputes under the ECT with EU law. Indeed, shortly after the issuance of the *Achmea* Ruling, the European Commission issued a communication noting that the reasoning of the *Achmea* Ruling should equally apply to the intra-EU application of Article 26 of the ECT. According to the European Commission, this clause should not apply to intra-EU disputes, because otherwise this would be incompatible with EU primary law.[128]

Similarly, the governments of the Member States, in their political declaration issued in January 2019 for the termination of intra-EU BITs, also referred to the incompatibility of Article 26 of the ECT with EU law when the ECT is applied in intra-EU disputes.[129] In the declaration, Member States committed to inform tribunals about the application of the *Achmea* Ruling to intra-EU disputes under the ECT and to work together to take steps to address this incompatibility.[130]

That stated, arbitral tribunals established under Article 26 of the ECT have not been eager to accept the effect of the *Achmea* Ruling on their jurisdiction and have to date rejected any claims for lack of jurisdiction.[131] Of course, the enforceability of such

123. Venetia Argyropoulou, 'Vattenfall in the Aftermath of Achmea: Between a Rock and a Hard Place?', 4 European Investment Law and Arbitration Review Online (2019).
124. Energy Charter Treaty [ECT] (Lisbon, 17 December 1994) entered into force 16 April 1998.
125. Nikos Lavranos, 'The Impact of the Achmea Decision', Keynote Speech, First Dispute Resolution Forum Energy Community Secretariat (27 September 2018).
126. April Lacson, *What Happens Now? The Future of Intra-EU Investor-State Dispute Settlement under the Energy Charter Treaty*, 14 New York University Journal of International Law and Politics (2019).
127. Euratom: Council and Commission Decision of 23 September 1997 on the conclusion, by the European Communities, of the Energy Charter Treaty and the Energy Charter Protocol on energy efficiency and related environmental aspects, 98/181/EC, ECSC (2017).
128. European Parliament and European Council, Communication on the Protection of intra-EU investment, COM/2018/547 (2018).
129. Finland, Luxembourg, Malta, Slovenia and Sweden expressed their dissent with this statement, noting that it was 'inappropriate, in the absence of a specific judgment on this matter, to express views as regards the compatibility with Union law of the intra EU application of the Energy Charter Treaty'. *See* Declaration of the Representatives of the Governments of Member States on the enforcement of the Judgement of the Court of Justice in Achmea and on Investment Protection in the European Union (16 January 2019), [3].
130. The Governments of the EU Member States, 'Declaration of the Member States of 15 January 2019 on the legal consequences of the Achmea judgment and on investment protection' (2019).
131. See indicatively, ICSID Case No. ARB/15/50 *Eskosol S.p.A. in liquidazione v. Italian Republic* (Decision on Termination Request and Intra-EU Objection, 7 May 2019), ICSID Case No.

tribunal's awards in the EU would be questionable. In the case of *Novenergia v. Spain*, the Svea Court of Appeal in Stockholm granted Spain's request for a stay of enforcement on the grounds that the tribunal went beyond its jurisdiction in rendering the award in view of the *Achmea* Ruling.[132] Spain requested the Svea Court of Appeal to refer the case to the CJEU by way of a preliminary reference under Article 26 of the TFEU to advise on the compatibility of Article 26 of the ECT with EU law in case of intra-EU disputes. Unfortunately, the Svea Court of Appeal dismissed the request,[133] avoiding the opportunity to give some clarity.

Thus the issue has yet to be clarified by the CJEU. Additionally, despite the political declaration of the governments of the EU Member States, the plurilateral agreement explicitly states that it does not apply to intra-EU ECT disputes, but the Member States will take steps in the future to address this.[134] In this regard, the EU Council granted the European Commission a mandate to initiate negotiations for the modernisation of the ECT, where the ISDS provisions will be revised to reflect the EU approach in its investment protection agreements and the position taken by the EU in ongoing multilateral reforms, which also include the establishment of a future multilateral investment court.[135]

§2.03 MULTILATERAL INVESTMENT COURT

Since 2015, the European Commission has presented the idea for the establishment of a multilateral investment court as part of the negotiations on the Transatlantic Trade and Investment Partnership (TTIP) between the EU and the United States. As part of those negotiations, the European Commission issued a Concept Paper on the path to reform investment in the EU and beyond.[136] The Concept Paper referred to the reform of ISDS and the introduction of an international investment court and appellate mechanism with tenured judges that will aim to replace the bilateral mechanism set in

ARB/07/19 *Vattenfall AB and others v. Federal Republic of Germany* (Decision on the Achmea Issue, 31 August 2018), ICSID Case No. ARB/07/19 *Electrabel S.A. v. Hungary* (Decision on Jurisdiction, Applicable Law and Liability, 30 November 2012), ICSID Case No. ARB/14/3 *Blusun S.A., Jean-Pierre Lecorcier and Michael Stein v. Italian Republic* (Award, 27 December 2016); SCC Case No. 2015/063 *Novenergia II – Energy & Environment (SCA) (Grand Duchy of Luxembourg), SICAR v. The Kingdom of Spain* (Decision of the Svea Court of Appeal 25 April 2019).

132. SCC Case No. 2015/063, *Novenergia II – Energy & Environment (SCA) (Grand Duchy of Luxembourg), SICAR v. The Kingdom of Spain* (Decision of the Svea Court of Appeals Suspending the Enforcement of the Award until Further Notice, 2018) SCC.
133. SCC Case No. 2015/063 *Novenergia II – Energy & Environment (SCA) (Grand Duchy of Luxembourg), SICAR v. The Kingdom of Spain* (Decision of the Svea Court of Appeal 25 April 2019).
134. Agreement for the termination of bilateral investment treaties between the Member States of the European Union (Brussels, 5 May 2020),
135. Council of the EU, Press Release, 'Council adopts negotiation directives for modernisation of Energy Charter Treaty' (15 July 2019).
136. European Commission, Concept Paper, Investment in TTIP and beyond – the path for reform, Enhancing the right to regulate and moving from current ad hoc arbitration towards an Investment Court (2015).

BITs and investment agreements.[137] All the judges would be permanently employed with no possibility to engage in other professional activities. Their mandates would be for a substantial period, but they would not be subject to renewal. The first instance tribunal would be solely responsible for fact-finding, while the appellate tribunal would be responsible for reviewing errors of law or procedure or manifest errors in the appreciation of facts.[138]

The European Parliament also endorsed this proposal, recommending, *inter alia*, to replace the ISDS system with a new system for dispute resolution among investors and states that would ensure transparency, respect of the jurisdiction of courts of the EU and of the Member States, and Member States' authority to set public policy, through publicly appointed, independent professional judges, public hearings and an appellate mechanism.[139] Based on these recommendations, the European Commission presented a proposal for a new investment court system for TTIP, but the negotiations on TTIP did not progress.[140] However, the proposal was not abandoned, but instead served as a basis for various FTAs that the EU later negotiated, like the FTA with Vietnam, the FTA with Mexico, and the revision of CETA.

CETA provides for a permanent tribunal of fifteen members that will be appointed by the EU and Canada, paid monthly retainers and meet other independency requirements, and an appellate tribunal. More importantly, however, CETA aspires to the formation of a permanent multilateral court, noting that Canada and the EU 'shall pursue with other trading partners the establishment of a multilateral investment tribunal and appellate mechanism for the resolution of investment disputes'[141] that will have jurisdiction over disputes arising from CETA, replacing the bilateral ISDS mechanism. Similar wording can be found in the EU-Vietnam Investment Protection Agreement.[142]

Regarding the question of whether such a permanent multilateral court would be compatible with EU law, the CJEU noted in its Opinion 1/17 that EU law does not preclude the establishment of a multilateral investment court so long as it is limited to interpreting and applying the provisions of the relevant investment agreement in line with the rules and principles of international law. Thus, the permanent multilateral court must not interpret and apply provisions of EU law, other than those of the respective investment treaty.[143]

---

137. *Ibid.*, [4].
138. *Ibid.*
139. European Parliament, Resolution of 8 July 2015 containing the European Parliament's recommendations to the European Commission on the negotiations for the Transatlantic Trade and Investment Partnership (TTIP) (2015).
140. Legislative train schedule | European Parliament, European Parliament (2018), https://www.europarl.europa.eu/legislative-train/theme-international-trade-inta/file-ttip-investment-protection-investor-state-dispute-settlement-(isds) (last visited 3 April 2020).
141. Comprehensive Economic and Trade Agreement (CETA) between Canada and the European Union and its Member States (Brussels, 30 October 2016), OJ L 11, 14.1.2017, Art. 8.29.
142. EU-Vietnam Investment Protection Agreement between EU and Vietnam (Brussels, 30 June 2019), Art. 3.41.
143. Opinion 1/17 Accord ECG UE-Canada [2019], ECLI:EU:C:2019:72 [118].

Opinion 1/17, therefore, is not only important for setting CETA as an example for future investment treaties that will be negotiated between the EU and third states, as was already the case with Singapore, Vietnam and Mexico, but is also because it endorses the European Commission's efforts for the establishment of a multilateral investment tribunal. Such a multilateral investment tribunal is proposed not only as way to rectify the EU's investment policy with the findings of the CJEU, but also as a response to the criticism of ISDS worldwide, as a possible solution for reform.[144]

The establishment of such a multilateral goal is promoted also in the international arena. Indeed, in the framework of Working Group III of UNCITRAL, the creation of a permanent multilateral investment court was identified as an 'option for reform' of investor-state dispute settlements.[145] On 18 January 2019, the EU and the Member States submitted two papers to Working Group III describing in more detail the EU's proposal for establishing a multilateral investment court. Although the EU is participating in the negotiations on multilateral reform of ISDS in Working Group III only as an observer, nonetheless the Member States may present such policy reforms. As of the conclusion of the 38th session of UNCITRAL's Working Group III at the end of January 2020, the multilateral investment court clearly forms part of the negotiating considerations, which focuses on structural reform.[146]

§2.04 CONCLUSION

The CJEU has been at the forefront in setting the EU's investment policy vis-à-vis ISDS mechanisms. The CJEU's Opinion 1/17 has provided some clarity to the *Achmea* Ruling that cast doubts about the compatibility of investor-state dispute resolution mechanisms found in investment treaties, intra-EU and extra-EU alike. Although many questions remain unanswered, Opinion 1/17 has clarified that the decisive element for the negotiation of future investment treaties is the law applicable to the investors' state disputes. When an ISDS mechanism may – and the mere possibility here suffices – interpret EU law, including the law of the Member States that inescapably includes EU law, such an ISDS mechanism is not compliant with EU law if its interpretation is binding on the respective Member State. This is because the binding interpretation of EU law by a tribunal that falls outside of the EU legal order infringes the autonomy of

144. Such a proposal has not escaped criticism. For example, in 2016 the American Bar Association Investment Treaty Working Group produced a draft Discussion Paper on the EU's proposal for a permanent investment court system, raising a number of concerns, including independence and impartiality, as well as confusion as to the nature of the systems, as a court or as tribunal, something that would greatly affect the enforcement of its awards. *See* American Bar Association Section on International Law, Investment Treaty Working Group, Task Force Report on the Investment Court System Proposal, Initial Task Force Discussion Paper (14 October 2016).
145. United Nations Commission on International Trade Law, Working Group III, Possible reform of investor-State dispute settlement (ISDS) (Investor-State Dispute Settlement Reform, 2018).
146. United Nations Commission on International Trade Law Working Group III (Investor-State Dispute Settlement Reform), Thirty-eighth session Vienna, 20–24 January 2020, Report of Working Group III (Investor-State Dispute Settlement Reform) on the work of its resumed thirty-eighth session (24 January 2020).

the EU legal order. The EU awards to the CJEU, in collaboration with the national courts of the Member States, exclusive jurisdiction to interpret and apply EU law.

In contrast, in case of investment treaties like CETA, the ISDS mechanism is limited to interpreting and applying only the investment treaty in line with international law. National law of a Member State is only taken into account as a matter of facts. Such an ISDS mechanism would be considered compatible with EU law. This is important because it allows the CETA dispute resolution provisions to be used as 'blueprints' for the negotiation of future investment treaties that will not run afoul with EU law. Importantly, such a principle should also be followed by the multilateral investment court, which is the EU Commission's proposal for the reform of ISDS.

[illegible]

CHAPTER 3

The Path of (Re)volution of the International Investor-State Dispute Settlement Regime: A Case Study of Bosnia and Herzegovina

Fahira Brodlija

The idea of reforming the investor-state dispute settlement (ISDS) system has been simmering at the international level over the past decade. The most prominent proponent of a complete overhaul of the ISDS system has been the European Union (EU), whose voice was amplified after the 2018 *Achmea* decision to the point where they proposed the abandonment of the existing ISDS system and the establishment of a multilateral investment court (MIC), as a standing body dedicated to the resolution of treaty-based disputes. Other countries are more inclined to pursue a gradual, targeted ISDS reform process, building on the existing framework. Bosnia and Herzegovina (BiH), as an aspiring EU Member State and a developing state seeking to attract foreign investments, is caught between these two strong currents. This chapter explores the implications of the ongoing ISDS process and its potential outcome on BiH, by taking a glance into the future of this country as an EU Member State. This chapter addresses the following questions: What reform options are developed and presented at the current stage of ISDS reform? What is the position of the EU and its Member States in the global discussions? How could BiH successfully terminate its intra-EU bilateral investment treaties (BITs) and reform its existing ISDS framework in relations with non-EU states? The chapter concludes with an optimistic view of a possible balanced solution, where BiH would harness its legal and institutional framework to foster dispute prevention and amicable settlement that would be compatible with the approach to ISDS reform in EU and the rest of the world.

§3.01 INTRODUCTION

The reputation of ISDS as the preferred treaty-based mechanism for the resolution of disputes between investors and host states has been under attack over the past decade. ISDS grew in popularity over time as an acceptable compromise and neutral forum that levels the playing field between investors and states as disputing parties.[1] It was a healthy alternative to dispute resolution through diplomatic channels or domestic courts, both of which could raise issues of sovereignty of states, and it offered more procedural flexibility and subject-matter expertise of the decision-makers on the arbitral tribunal.[2] However, with the dramatic increase in the number of ISDS claims and the growing success rate of the investors in arbitration, the voices for systematic reform or total abandonment of ISDS grew louder[3] based on concerns about the predictability, reliability, efficiency and fairness of the process.[4]

In Europe, calls for the abolishment of ISDS escalated after the Court of Justice of the European Union (CJEU) reached its landmark decision in *Achmea*, which declared the ISDS provisions in intra-EU BITs to be contrary to EU law. Soon thereafter, the EU Commission and the EU Member States agreed to embark on the process of terminating intra-EU BITs. Thus, ISDS effectively has no future in the EU.

The discussions on the global stage have been broad and geared at systematic reforms addressing the existing concerns related to ISDS. The most consistent and impactful discussions stem from the United Nations Commission on International Trade Law (UNCITRAL) Working Group III (WG III) on ISDS reform, which has a broad mandate to identify concerns and propose reform options for the existing ISDS system.[5] The discussions and proposals of the WG III are largely government led. The participating states have provided individual and joint submissions on the developed ISDS reform options. An important characteristic of the status quo is the fact that the majority of past ISDS disputes were resolved under the provisions of generation BITs that lack the nuanced regulation of the substantive and procedural issues which are prominent in modern times.[6] The new-generation BITs have incorporated modern provisions on investor protection and ISDS, which may lead to more satisfactory outcomes in the future. Therefore, significant improvements may be attainable through

1. Rachel Wellhausen, *Recent Trends in Investor–State Dispute Settlement*, 7 J. Int'l Dispute Settlement 12 (2016); George Kahale, *Rethinking ISDS*, 44 Brooklyn J. Int'l L. 14 (2018).
2. Tom Ginsburg, *International Substitutes for Domestic Institutions: Bilateral Investment Treaties and Governance*, 25 International Review of Law and Economics 4 (2005).
3. Although investors did indeed start using ISDS more frequently to pursue treaty-based claims with notable success, the notion promoted by some ISDS critics that investors overwhelmingly prevail in ISDS cases is factually incorrect. According to data provided by UNCTAD, out of the 647 cases concluded as of 31 July 2019, states prevailed in 230 and investors prevailed in 190 cases. UNCTAD Investment Settlement Navigator, https://investmentpolicy.unctad.org/investment-dispute-settlement.
4. UNCITRAL Secretariat, Note, 'Possible Reform of Investor-State Dispute Settlement', 6–10, https://undocs.org/en/A/CN.9/WG.III/WP.142.
5. United Nations Commission on International Trade Law Working Group III (ISDS Reform) homepage, https://uncitral.un.org/en/working_groups/3/investor-state.
6. United Nations, *UNCTAD World Investment Report, Key messages and overview*, 7, 2019 https://unctad.org/en/pages/PublicationWebflyer.aspx?publicationid=2460.

the modernization of the existing BITs, without abandoning ISDS as a whole. The EU has taken the opposite position, by strongly promoting the abolition of ISDS and the establishment of a standing MIC.

BiH is currently caught in the cross-fires of these global and regional movements. On the one hand, it is aspiring to EU membership; on the other, it is in dire need of reform in its ISDS structure. Namely, the country has faced (and is currently facing) high-value investor claims in International Centre for Settlement of Investment Disputes (ICSID) and ad hoc arbitration. The country has faced significant losses in the aftermath of the previous cases, and only one of the three pending claims is worth EUR 1.5 billion.[7] Therefore, BiH will certainly have to engage in effective reforms in order to prevent future disputes and to be prepared for proper management of ISDS cases. However, the desire for ISDS reform and its EU aspirations are in tension following the *Achmea* decision of the CJEU,[8] following which the EU Member States agreed to terminate all intra-EU BITs, including the ISDS clauses. In this sense, aside from the mandatory termination of intra-EU BITs which BiH will have to comply with upon accession to the EU, it will also have to deliberate the destiny of its surviving BITs with non-EU states.

This chapter seeks to weigh the best ISDS reform options and their viability in the context of BiH, by providing a glance into its future as an EU Member State. The chapter opens with an overview of the ongoing ISDS reforms on the global stage, mainly under the auspices of WG III. It then explores the post-*Achmea* stance against ISDS in the EU. This chapter then turns to BiH and its existing ISDS system based on its BIT framework. Next, insights into the possible future of BiH as an EU Member State regarding the termination of intra-EU BITs are considered, followed by the reform of the ISDS clauses in the surviving BITs. The conclusion weighs the advantages and disadvantages of the proposed ISDS reform options and their viability in BiH.

§3.02 ISDS REFORM AT THE GLOBAL LEVEL: UNCITRAL WG III

ISDS has been subject to significant criticism and debate during the past decade, which intensified with the increased success rate of investor's claims against states.[9] Although there was no proven correlation with the nature of ISDS and a state's unfavourable outcomes, it was deemed to favour investors and to preclude states from fully defending themselves and presenting their case.[10] The comprehensive study and analysis conducted by the United Nations Conference on Trade and Development (UNCTAD) showed that various countries are taking different approaches in ISDS

7. *Elektrogospodarstvo Slovenije – razvoj ininzeniring d.o.o. v. Bosnia and Herzegovina* (ICSID Case No. ARB/14/13).
8. *Slovak Republic v. Achmea B.V.*, ECJ 20, Case C-284/16) EU C 2018 158 (April 2018).
9. UNCTAD Investment Settlement Navigator, https://investmentpolicy.unctad.org/investment-dispute-settlement.
10. Alan Redfern, *Law and Practice of International Commercial Arbitration* (Oxford Law, 4th ed. 2004), 486.

reform, primarily through treaty renegotiation.[11] The study showed the diverse ISDS models adopted in the investment treaties concluded in 2018, which ranged from no ISDS provision, reformed ISDS procedure, to a standing investment tribunal.[12]

Amid the widespread call for a reform of the existing ISDS system, the Secretariat of UNCITRAL tasked WG III with a broad mandate to: (1) identify the most prominent ISDS concerns; (2) determine the need for reform in such areas; and (3) propose viable reform options.[13] WG III is currently at the third stage, where it is developing and proposing reform options for the identified areas of concern. The entire process is government led, with delegations from all over the world gathering twice a year in Vienna and New York to discuss and propose various options. Between sessions, there are regional and bilateral meetings, where delegations exchange their views and positions.[14] It is a gradual and systematic process, which is focused on the procedural aspects of ISDS, while the substantive matters remain outside of its scope.

WG III has grouped the major concerns related to ISDS into three main categories:

(1) Consistency, coherence, predictability and correctness of arbitral awards.
(2) Arbitrators and decision-makers.
(3) Cost and duration of ISDS cases (with focus on arbitration proceedings).[15]

The global ISDS reform discussions within the framework of WG III reflect the diversity and specificity of issues which concern individual nations. The numerous submissions[16] to the UNCITRAL Secretariat provided by governments reflect their positions on the identified concerns and the reform options which would meet their needs. With the exception of the EU Member States supporting the replacement of the ISDS system with a MIC, most countries favour a pragmatic, targeted approach to ISDS reform, based on the outlined reform framework.

[A] Reform Options for Consistency, Correctness and Predictability of the Interpretation of Treaties and Principles of International Law

The existing ISDS system has been widely criticized for its lack of consistency and predictability because of diverging decisions in concurrent proceedings in which the

11. UNCTAD, *Reforming Investment Dispute Settlement: A Stocktaking*, International Investment Agreements Issues Note, 2, https://unctad.org/en/PublicationsLibrary/diaepcbinf2019d3_en.pdf.
12. *Ibid.*
13. United Nations Commission on International Trade Law Working Group III (ISDS Reform) homepage, https://uncitral.un.org/en/working_groups/3/investor-state.
14. An overview of the official WG III sessions, inter-sessional meetings and government submissions can be found on the official website of WG III, https://uncitral.un.org/en/working_groups/3/investor-state.
15. Chartered Institute of Arbitrators, Discussion Paper, 'Efficiency, Decisions and Decision-Makers', https://www.ciarb.org/media/6286/february-ciarb-isds_discussion-papers.pdf.
16. The list of country submissions provided to date can be found on the official website of WG III, https://uncitral.un.org/en/working_groups/3/investor-state.

facts, parties, treaty provisions and applicable arbitration rules were identical.[17] This is attributed to expansionistic interpretations that are considered to disproportionately favour foreign investors to the detriment of the host states. The critics state that arbitral tribunals do not feel any sense of accountability for the effects of their awards, because they are appointed on an ad hoc basis.[18] Furthermore, the lack of transparency of arbitral proceedings prevents the creation of a body of case law that would be a reliable resource for arbitral tribunals in the establishment of a credible and legitimate investment arbitration system.[19]

The EU holds the position that this issue can only be resolved in a systematic manner through the establishment of a MIC. In this standing dispute resolution mechanism, with public proceedings and published awards, the judges would be able to draw from the body of previous decisions of the court in order to maintain a consistent line of interpretation of the most complex international treaties. In addition, the MIC is designed as a two-instance court, which is supposed to create an incentive for the judges to act with care and due diligence in their deliberations and conclusions, in order to avoid having their decisions overturned or remanded on appeal.

However, the issue of inconsistency and unpredictability of arbitral awards can be effectively addressed with targeted reform of the existing ISDS system. One of the most practical reform options is the addition of a mechanism for the exchange of binding treaty interpretations by the treaty parties.[20] This mechanism is also recognized under the provisions of the Vienna Convention on Vienna Convention on the Law of Treaties.[21] The availability of treaty interpretation notes provided by the treaty parties would assist the arbitral tribunal in reaching the right conclusions regarding the treaty text, and enhance the consistency and predictability of arbitral awards.[22]

Another proposal comes from country submissions to WG III,[23] in the form of an advisory centre for the parties in investment disputes, following the model of the

---

17. UNCTAD, IIA Issues Note No.2, *Reform of investor-state dispute settlement*, https://unctad.org/en/Pages/Publications/Intl-Investment-Agreements--Issues-Note.aspx.
18. Gus Van Harten, *Investment Arbitrators' Evident Lack of Restraint*, 5 J. Int'l Dispute Settlement 1-4 (March 2014).
19. Chartered Institute of Arbitrators, Discussion Paper, 'Efficiency, Decisions and Decision-Makers', 15, https://www.ciarb.org/media/6286/february-ciarb-isds_discussion-papers.pdf.
20. UNCITRAL Secretariat, Note, A/CN.9/930/Add.1/Rev.1, para. 34; A/CN.9/935, para. 43.
21. Article 31(3)(a) of the Vienna Convention on the Law of Treaties (VCLT) expressly requires that interpreters of a treaty 'take[] into account ... any subsequent agreement ... [between the treaty parties] regarding the interpretation of the treaty or the application of its provisions'.
22. David Gaukrodger, *The legal framework applicable to joint interpretive agreements of investment treaties*, OECD Working Papers on International Investment (2016/01), https://www.oecdilibrary.org/docserver/5jm3xgt6f29wen.pdf?expires=1588353194&id=id&accname=guest&checksum=04061FBEA4E44D3637B725E7E35EDF17.
23. Submission from the Government of Brazil, State-to-State mechanisms, paras 33-36; A/CN.9/WG.III/WP.176, Submission from the Government of South Africa (raising the question whether ISDS mechanisms are desirable or necessary in the first place). *See* General Assembly resolution 70/1 of 25 September 2015, Transforming our world: the 2030 Agenda for Sustainable Development; A/CN.9/WG.III/WP.176, Submission from the Government of South Africa; A/CN.9/WG.III/WP.161, Submission from the Government of Morocco; A/CN.9/WG.III/WP.162, Submission from the Government of Thailand; A/CN.9/WG.III/WP.164 and A/CN.9/WG.III/WP.178, Submissions from the Government of Costa Rica; A/CN.9/WG.III/

Advisory Centre on World Trade Organization Law (ACWL).[24] This proposal was also supported by the community of investors' counsel in their submission to WG III.[25] The advisory centre, as proposed, could certainly help increase the clarity, consistency and predictability of the ISDS system, providing states (especially least developed states) to prepare for and anticipate potential claims from investors, which will allow them to react in a timely and effective manner. In addition, the advisory role of the centre in any cooling-off period could help mitigate the tensions and provide grounds for early settlement, once the State has a clear picture of the claim and its likelihood of success. The clarity and consistency of treaty interpretation in ISDS could be ensured through a neutral advisory body.

The development of a body of case law in investment arbitration could be accomplished by the adoption of the international standards for transparency in investment. The United Nations Convention on Transparency in Treaty-Based Investor-State Arbitration[26] (Mauritius Convention) entered into force in 2017. It aims to promote the more widespread application of the UNCITRAL Rules on Transparency in Treaty-Based Investor-State Arbitration.[27] Under these rules, the submissions, hearings and awards are made available to the public with some exceptions.[28] The widespread ratification of the Mauritius Convention would turn transparency from an exception to the rule in ISDS proceedings.

Thus far, the Mauritius Convention has been signed by twenty-three states,[29] and ratified by five. BiH is not among the signatory states of the Mauritius Convention, but the competent ministries are conducting an analysis of its implications to determine the best path forward in this regard.[30] The lack of guidance in treaty interpretation and inconsistencies in arbitral awards could be overcome through the reform of the existing ISDS framework. Through the application of the Transparency Rules, arbitral tribunals in ISDS proceedings could get useful guidance from previous decisions, and they would be careful in their deliberations with the public eye awaiting their awards. However, the establishment of a precedent system in ISDS would be counterproductive due to the

WP.174, Submission from the Government of Turkey; A/CN.9/WG.III/WP.179, Submission from the Government of the Republic of Korea.

24. UNCITRAL Secretariat, Note, *Possible Reform of Investor-State Dispute Settlement* 5–6, https://undocs.org/en/A/CN.9/WG.III/WP.166.
25. Submission by the Corporate Counsel International Arbitration Group (CCIAG) to UNCITRAL Working Group III – Investor-State Dispute Settlement (ISDS) Reform, 14 (18 December 2019).
26. United Nations Convention on Transparency in Treaty-based Investor-State Arbitration, https://www.uncitral.org/pdf/english/texts/arbitration/transparency-convention/Transparency-Convention-e.pdf.
27. UNCITRAL Rules on Transparency in Treaty-based Investor-State Arbitration, https://www.uncitral.org/pdf/english/texts/arbitration/rules-on-transparency/Rules-on-Transparency-E.pdf.
28. UNCITRAL Rules on Transparency in Treaty-based Investor-State Arbitration, Art. 7, https://www.uncitral.org/pdf/english/texts/arbitration/rules-on-transparency/Rules-on-Transparency-E.pdf.
29. The status of the Mauritius Convention is available on the UNCITRAL website, https://uncitral.un.org/en/texts/arbitration/conventions/transparency/status.
30. Thus far, the Mauritius Convention has been signed by Cameroon, Canada, Gambia, Mauritius, Switzerland.

sui generis nature of the subject matter of each dispute and the applicable law.[31] The fragmented nature of the sources of law underlying each ISDS case, the decentralized regulation, and the complex fact patterns in each dispute are not a formula for the creation of consistent and coherent case law in ISDS.[32] A system of binding precedent in ISDS would force arbitral tribunals to apply the same reasoning to diverging legal issues, thus forcing a one-size-fits-all solution to otherwise irreconcilable issues. The arbitral tribunals should refer to previous cases to seek common patterns which may lead to the establishment of standards and interpretative tools, which would improve the consistency and coherence of ISDS decisions.[33] This may be accomplished in the near future, with a more forceful and universal application of the existing framework for transparency in ISDS.

[B] Reform Options for Independence and Impartiality of the Arbitrators and Decision-Makers, Diversity and Transparency in ISDS

The second universally recognized concern is closely connected to the confidentiality of the arbitral proceedings. The criticism is primarily aimed at the lack of information on the appointed arbitrators, disclosure obligations and their potential conflicts of interest, the unspecified terms of challenge procedures and the lack of diversity in arbitral tribunals. Another major concern is the practice of 'double-hatting' where a single person may act as party counsel in one case and then be appointed by them as an arbitrator in other proceedings.[34]

Once again, the EU promotes the MIC as a panacea that can resolve all concerns related to independence and impartiality of the arbitrators and the transparency of the proceedings. The State would appoint the MIC, and once appointed, they would serve nine-year terms. The judges would have a fixed remuneration and would be assigned to cases at random case, which should reduce the concerns of bias towards the parties.[35] The judges would not be allowed to hold any other position during their tenure at the MIC, and they could not act as counsel or arbitrators in investment disputes for a certain period of time after their term.[36] The hearings and the awards would be available to the public, and the participation of interested third parties would be enabled, especially in relation to sensitive cases with public health and environmental implications.[37]

31. Note by the UNCITRAL Secretariat, Possible reform of investor-State dispute settlement (ISDS): Consistency and related matters, 15 (28 August 2018), https://undocs.org/en/A/CN.9/WG.III/WP.150.
32. *Ibid.*
33. Gabrielle Kaufmann-Kohler, *Arbitral Precedent: Dream, Necessity or Excuse? (The 2006 Freshfields Lecture)*, Arbitration International, Volume 23, Issue 3, LCIA (2007) https://www.arbitration-icca.org/media/4/77507134886347/media012319143087130009500001.pdf.
34. UNCITRAL Secretariat, Note, *Possible reform of investor-State dispute settlement (ISDS), Background information on a code of conduct* 3, https://undocs.org/A/CN.9/WG.III/WP.167.
35. UNCITRAL Working Group III (ISDS Reform), Note by the Secretariat, *Possible reform of investor-State dispute settlement (ISDS)* 7, https://undocs.org/en/A/CN.9/WG.III/WP.166.
36. *Ibid.*
37. *Ibid.*

The WG III proposed a pragmatic solution for the achievement of the independence and impartiality of the arbitrators and the transparency of ISDS proceedings, which can be implemented in the existing framework. On 1 May 2020, the UNCITRAL Secretariat and ICSID published the Draft Code of Conduct for Adjudicators (Draft Code). The Draft Code resulted from a joint effort by UNCITRAL and ICSID to develop a set of universal standards which would address the existing concerns about the independence, impartiality and accountability of the decision-makers in ISDS.[38]

The definition of 'adjudicators' in the Draft Code covers a wide range of decision-makers in ISDS, including arbitrators, ad hoc committee members, candidate adjudicators, appeal judges, and judges in permanent bodies.[39] The Draft Code provides the general rules of independence and impartiality of adjudicators, along with a broad and ongoing disclosure obligation.[40] The extensive disclosure obligations also address the key issues specific to ISDS: repeat appointments, issue conflicts and double-hatting.

Repeat appointments of adjudicators by the same party in ISDS (as counsel, arbitrators, experts, advisors) have been widely criticized for their potential negative effect on the integrity of the process.[41] The Draft Code does not prohibit repeat appointments, but it creates a broad disclosure obligation that can be modified by lawmakers in the manner they deem appropriate.[42] The adjudicators will have to disclose all past and present appointments that may give rise to doubts about their independence and impartiality.[43] The broad disclosure obligation in the Draft Code also includes the duty to disclose any publications or speeches which reflect any established position of the adjudicator on legal matters relevant to the dispute, which could raise doubts of existing issue conflicts.[44]

'Double-hatting' has been criticized in the ongoing ISDS reform process as one of the main flaws of the existing system. It is the practice of ISDS adjudicators simultaneously acting as counsel, experts, adjudicators, or taking other roles in multiple ongoing ISDS proceedings. The Draft Code provides policymakers the ability to choose the appropriate approach to this issue, ranging from a complete ban to a robust disclosure obligation (which can be time-phased or related to specific parties, facts or treaties).[45]

The enforcement of the rules provided in the Draft Code would be primarily based on voluntary compliance, but they can also be considered in the challenge proceedings. Other sanctions can be defined by policymakers, including monetary, disciplinary and reputational measures. The Draft Code is open for comments, and it will be discussed by the WG III in its regular sessions, but it is already a significant step

38. UNCITRAL Secretariat, Note, *Possible reform of investor-State dispute settlement (ISDS), Background information on a code of conduct* 3, https://undocs.org/A/CN.9/WG.III/WP.167.
39. Draft Code of Conduct for Adjudicators in Investor-State Dispute Settlement, Art. 2.
40. *Ibid.*, Art. 4.
41. *Ibid.*, Art. 5.
42. *Ibid.*
43. *Ibid.*
44. *Ibid.*
45. *Ibid.*, Art. 6.

forward in the creation of universal standards for the conduct for ISDS adjudicators, which could enhance their perceived neutrality and independence.

The issue of transparency in ISDS can be addressed by the application of the UNCITRAL Transparency Rules.[46] The Transparency Rules comprise a set of procedural rules dealing with, among other things, the disclosure of case-related documents, public access to hearings, and submissions by amici curiae and non-disputing state parties. The Transparency Convention could extend the application of the Transparency Rules to the entire treaty-based international investment regime as it stood on 1 April 2014, including all the old-generation treaties, regardless of the applicable arbitration rules.[47] Its wide adoption would generate the systematic reform without complex multilateral or bilateral renegotiations of treaties.

Therefore, the desired reform effects, including those pursued by the EU in its MIC proposal, could be accomplished through one legal instrument applied to the existing ISDS framework, based on international consensus.[48] The provisions of the Transparency Rules envision the same level of transparency as desired by the EU in their proposal for the MIC. The Transparency Convention also allows for reservations in relation to a specific treaty or investment, which will allow for flexibility in relation to certain treaty partners.[49]

[C] Reform Options for Cost and Duration of ISDS Proceedings

ISDS proceedings have become lengthier and more burdensome for the states, which is another point of criticism raised at the WG III. ISDS has been criticized for the increasing length of the proceedings.[50] There is dissatisfaction with the lack of predictable rules on cost allocation and the issue of security for costs, and the fact that arbitral tribunals often make cost orders which are in favour of the investors.[51] The complaints are also aimed at the dilatory tactics which are sometimes employed by the investors, which impede the efficiency of the proceedings and contribute to the accumulation of costs.[52]

---

46. UNCITRAL Rules on Transparency in Treaty-based Investor-State Arbitration, https://www.uncitral.org/pdf/english/texts/arbitration/rules-on-transparency/Rules-on-Transparency-E.pdf.
47. United Nations Convention on Transparency in Treaty-based Investor-State Arbitration, https://www.uncitral.org/pdf/english/texts/arbitration/transparency-convention/Transparency-Convention-e.pdf.
48. *Ibid.*
49. *Ibid.*
50. UNCITRAL Secretariat, Note, *Possible reform of investor-State dispute settlement (ISDS) – cost and duration* (31 August 2018) 3, https://undocs.org/en/A/CN.9/WG.III/WP.153.
51. Article 47 of the ICSID Convention provides a basis for respondent states to request security for costs as a provisional matter in cases where the claimant is likely unwilling or unable to pay the costs of the responding state. This was exercised in practice, including the decision 13 August 2014, where an ICSID tribunal ordered security for costs and sanctioned the claimant's failure to comply with the order on security for costs. *RSM Production Corporation v. Saint Lucia*, ICSID Case No. ARB/12/10.
52. UNCITRAL Secretariat, Note, *Possible reform of investor-State dispute settlement (ISDS) – cost and duration* (31 August 2018) 4–5, https://undocs.org/en/A/CN.9/WG.III/WP.153.

In any deliberation about the balance of the costs and duration of ISDS proceedings, there must be a distinction between 'excessive' or 'unjustified' time and costs, on the one hand, and 'necessary' or 'justified' time and costs on the other.[53] In cases with multiple parties arising out of complex legal relations and dealing with industry-specific standards and regulations, efficiency has to be sacrificed for precision and accuracy. Therefore, the quality of outcomes should be balanced with the desire to reduce cost and duration.[54] Furthermore, there is a lack of consistency in the basis for the calculation of the duration of ISDS proceedings because it also includes the period after the award, enforcement and challenge proceedings.[55]

The main concerns related to the cost and duration of ISDS proceedings could be addressed by reforms and amendments of the existing framework, through some reform options by the WG III. These reform options include a more serious approach to alternative dispute resolution (ADR), strict procedural timetables and securities for costs, as well as the use of videoconferencing and other technical tools for time and cost-efficiency.[56] These specific considerations either can be addressed in the form of universally applicable rules of procedure or they can be developed for each treaty on a case-by-case basis.

§3.03 ISDS AT THE REGIONAL LEVEL: EU PERSPECTIVE POST-*ACHMEA*

Although the concerns regarding ISDS at the international level were not raised only by the EU, the viability of the existing ISDS system has been under unrelenting scrutiny ever since the highly anticipated judgment in *Slovak Republic v. Achmea B.V*. This was a case brought before the CJEU based on the dispute between the Dutch insurer Achmea B.V. (formerly known as Eureko B.V.) and Slovakia. The *Achmea* decision was the death sentence for ISDS among EU Member States, but it was also the dawn of the idea of the MIC and its global promotion as an alternative for ISDS.

Achmea brought a claim against Slovakia in 2008 after the State reversed its policy of liberalization of the health market in 2006. This move by the Slovak Government prohibited the distribution of the profits obtained by Achmea through its insurance activities in Slovakia. Therefore, Achmea initiated arbitral proceedings against Slovakia on the grounds of substantive treaty violations of the Slovakia-Netherlands BIT. The dispute was decided by an arbitral tribunal seated in Frankfurt under the UNCITRAL Rules. The arbitral tribunal ruled in favour of Achmea in 2012, finding that Slovakia violated its obligations under the BIT and ordered a payment of damages in the amount of approximately EUR 22.1 million.

This award was followed by setting-aside proceedings brought by Slovakia before German higher courts.[57] Ultimately, the German Federal Court of Justice referred

53. *Ibid.*
54. *Ibid.*
55. *Ibid.*
56. *Ibid.*
57. *Bundesgerichtshof* (German Federal Court of Justice) Decision of 3 March 2016, Case I ZB 2/15.

questions on the compatibility with EU law to the CJEU for a preliminary ruling, stating its position that the clause was not contrary to EU law. The CJEU held that the dispute resolution clause in the Netherlands-Slovakia BIT was contrary to the provisions of the Treaty of the Functioning of the EU (TFEU), which provide the CJEU as the exclusive jurisdiction to give preliminary rulings concerning the interpretation of EU treaties[58] and to decide disputes related to the interpretation of the EU treaties.[59] Thus, the CJEU ruled in favour of Slovakia, effectively declaring ISDS provisions of intra-EU BITs 'incompatible with EU law'.[60]

The EU Member States swiftly moved to enforce the CJEU ruling, negotiating in bilateral and multilateral settings to create an appropriate mechanism for the termination of the existing intra-EU BITs. Interestingly, the UK was also among the states which declared their willingness to join the movement, despite the fact that they are on the verge of leaving the EU, after which they will no longer be bound by EU law.[61]

On 15 January 2019, twenty-one Member States (including the UK) issued a declaration committing to the termination of their intra-EU BITs by 6 December 2019.[62] On 16 January 2019, Finland, Luxembourg, Malta, Slovenia and Sweden adopted a largely similar declaration, with the addition of provisions connected to the ECT.[63] Following these declarations, the EU Member States reached an agreement on a plurilateral treaty for the termination of intra-EU BITs on 24 October 2019.[64] This agreement solidified the decision of the EU and its Member States to terminate all intra-EU BITs in a plurilateral manner, rather than bilaterally. This clearly enforced the determination of the EU to eliminate ISDS and to create the conditions for the establishment of a MIC, which it has been promoting intensively in international circles, including in the WG III meetings.[65]

Thus, the EU and the rest of the world are on parallel tracks in the process of overcoming existing ISDS concerns. At the global level, WG III is pursuing a more gradual approach, starting with the drafting of ISDS clauses in investment treaties and a case-by-case approach to the internationally accepted reform options for ISDS. In

58. Treaty of the Functioning of the EU (TFEU), Art. 267.
59. *Ibid.*, Art. 344.
60. Jens Hillebrand Pohl, *Intra-EU Investment Arbitration after the Achmea Case: Legal Autonomy Bounded by Mutual Trust?* 14 European Constitutional L. Rev. 77 (2018).
61. Harkiran Hothi, Chiraag Shah and Philipp Kurek, *EU Member States Agree to Terminate Their Intra-EU BITs: Is This the End of Intra-EU BIT Arbitrations and What about Brexit?* Practical Law Arbitration Blog (8 February 2019) http://arbitrationblog.practicallaw.com/eu-member-states-agree-to-terminate-their-intra-eu-bits-is-this-the-end-of-intra-eu-bit-arbitrations-and-what-about-brexit/.
62. Declaration of the Member States of 15 January 2019 on the legal consequences of the *Achmea* judgement and on investment protection, https://ec.europa.eu/info/publications/190117-bilateral-investment-treaties_en.
63. Declaration of the representatives of the governments of the Member States, of 16 January 2019 on the legal consequences of the judgment of the court of justice in *Achmea* and on investment protection in the European Union, https://www.kormany.hu/download/5/1b/81000/Hungarys%20Declaration%20on%20Achmea.pdf.
64. Statement: EU Member States agree on a plurilateral treaty to terminate bilateral investment treaties (24 October 2019) https://ec.europa.eu/info/publications/191024-bilateral-investment-treaties_en.
65. *Ibid.*

contrast, the EU is pursuing a systematic overhaul of the investment dispute resolution system through a rigid, institutional system which prefers adherence to its formalities over the proposed practical solutions.[66]

§3.04 ISDS REFORM AT THE NATIONAL LEVEL: THE CASE OF BiH

As an aspiring EU Member State, BiH is caught between the progressive flow of global ISDS reform discussions and the unequivocal intent of the EU to eliminate intra-EU BITs and the ISDS system, replacing them with a standing MIC. Considering that BiH has almost an equal number of intra-EU and non-EU BITs,[67] it will soon find itself in a two-track reform process. On the one hand, it will have to find the most favourable method of termination of its intra-EU BITs. Once the BITs are terminated, the investment protection provisions under EU law will govern its relations with foreign investors, including dispute resolution before the MIC or otherwise. On the other hand, BiH can benefit from the global ISDS movement to reform the ISDS clauses in the non-EU BITs in order to enable a more effective management of investor claims, primarily through dispute prevention and ADR.

BiH has been exposed to several high-value claims by investors recently, which have ended up in significant financial losses, and currently faces three pending cases.[68] The value of just one of these claims is around EUR 1.5 billion.[69] The institutional ISDS structure in BiH is complex and the existing ISDS provisions originate from old-generation BITs, which cannot adequately protect the State nor the investors. Therefore, BiH would certainly benefit from effective ISDS reform.

[A] The Existing ISDS Framework in BiH

The current ISDS system in BiH consists of a network of BITs whose ISDS clauses provide for various dispute resolution mechanisms. BiH is a party to thirty-seven BITs, twenty of which are with EU Member States. In addition, BiH has BITs with four countries that are aspiring for EU membership, all of which are old-generation BITs.[70]

The ISDS mechanisms in BiH BITs mostly consist of three elements: an attempt to resolve the dispute amicably, followed by a 'fork in the road' provision, allowing the investor to choose to submit its claim before the national courts or administrative

66. Discussion papers – *CIArb at UNCITRAL Working Group III on ISDS Reform: Efficiency, Decisions and Decision-Makers* https://www.ciarb.org/media/6286/february-ciarb-isds_discussion-papers.pdf.
67. UNCTAD Investment Policy Hub, Country Navigator – Bosnia and Herzegovina https://investmentpolicy.unctad.org/country-navigator/28/bosnia-and-herzegovina.
68. Information provided by the State Attorney's Office of Bosnia and Herzegovina.
69. *Elektrogospodarstvo Slovenije – razvoj ininzeniring d.o.o. v. Bosnia and Herzegovina*, ICSID Case No. ARB/14/13.
70. Analysis of the applicable BiH BITs conducted by the author, based on the treaty texts available in the UNCTAD Country Navigator, https://investmentpolicy.unctad.org/country-navigator/28/bosnia-and-herzegovina.

tribunals of the host state, or to submit to institutional or ad hoc arbitration.[71] The nature of the fork-in-the-road provisions is such that once a party chooses a dispute resolution mechanism, they automatically waive the possibility of referring to another court or institution.[72] The purpose of such provisions is to prevent the duplicity of proceedings over the same claim.[73] The fact that an investor submits a claim before a national court does not fully preclude arbitration, as long as the investor terminates the court proceedings and initiates arbitration before the conclusion of the judicial proceedings. None of the BiH BITs contain a mandatory exhaustion of domestic remedies as a precondition for arbitration.[74]

All BiH BITs provide for ICSID arbitration as an option, while some also refer to conciliation or proceedings under the Additional Facility Rules of ICSID.[75] The other most common arbitral institution provided in BiH BITs is the ICC in Paris.[76] Some of the BITs also refer to arbitral institutions of the home state, in addition to the international arbitral institutions and ad hoc arbitration.[77] The most common form of ad hoc arbitration provided in BiH BITs is arbitration under the UNCITRAL Rules, which are modified directly in the BIT in certain cases, including the modification of the default appointing authority.[78]

[B] The Future of ISDS in BiH as an EU Member State

Based on the recent developments in the EU, BiH as a new Member State will have to terminate all of its BITs with other EU Member States. There is no longer a question of 'if', but only 'when' and 'how'. The answers to the latter questions may have gotten their contours with the Agreement for the Termination of Bilateral Investment Treaties Between the Member States of the European Union (Agreement), which was signed by twenty-three EU Member States on 5 May 2020. The Agreement implemented the

71. *Ibid.*
72. Johan Billet, Maria Elenora Benini, Cari-Dee Lee and Cecile Oosterveen, *International Investment Arbitration -Practical Handbook* 188 (Maklu Publishers 2016).
73. *Ibid.*
74. Analysis of the applicable BiH BITs conducted by the author, based on the treaty texts available in the UNCTAD Country Navigator, https://investmentpolicy.unctad.org/country-navigator/28/bosnia-and-herzegovina.
75. Agreement on encouragement and reciprocal protection of investments between Bosnia and Herzegovina and the Kingdom of the Netherlands (2002).
76. Contained in five BITs, two of which are intra-EU BITs: Agreement Between the Belgo-Luxembourg Economic Union and Bosnia and Herzegovina on the Reciprocal Promotion and Protection of Investments (2010); Agreement Between the United Kingdom of Great Britain and Northern Ireland and Bosnia and Herzegovina on the Promotion and Protection of Investments (2003); Agreement Between the Ukraine and Bosnia and Herzegovina on the Promotion and Reciprocal Protection of Investments (2004); Agreement Between the Republic of Austria and Bosnia and Herzegovina on the Promotion and Protection of Investments (2002); Agreement Between the Republic of Turkey and the Council of Ministers of Bosnia and Herzegovina Concerning the Reciprocal Promotion and Protection of Investments (2009).
77. An example of such a BIT is the Agreement Between the Belgo-Luxembourg Economic Union and Bosnia and Herzegovina on the Reciprocal Promotion and Protection of Investments (2010).
78. Agreement Between Bosnia and Herzegovina and the Government of the Italian Republic on the Promotion and Protection of Investments (2005) and Agreement on the Promotion and Protection of Investments Between Sweden and Bosnia and Herzegovina (2002).

Achmea decision of the CJEU and sealed the fate of intra-EU BITs and ISDS within the EU.[79] Upon its entry into force, the Agreement will terminate all the existing BITs among EU Member States, which includes their sunset clauses – the clauses that would grant the investors the right to bring claims against the host state for a specified period of time after the termination of the BIT.[80] The BITs will be considered null and void as of the date of the *Achmea*[81] decision, 6 March 2018. The Agreement does not foresee any effect on arbitral proceedings that were previously concluded under the BITs,[82] but it certainly creates a disruption for the cases which remain unresolved.

A review of the Agreement shows that the EU is proposing internal solutions with the same effect as those it so vocally opposing at the global stage, while at the same time offering some solutions which it otherwise finds concerning in the existing ISDS system. The Agreement provides that pending arbitration proceedings which were commenced prior to the *Achmea* decision will be discontinued and replaced by 'structured dialogue' that must be initiated within six months from the termination of the BIT.[83] Prior to the initiation of 'structured dialogue', the investor must terminate pending arbitral proceedings and court proceedings for the recognition and enforcement of arbitral awards.[84]

The settlement proceedings through structured dialogue can only be initiated if the CJEU or a national court finds that the contested state measure is a violation of EU law.[85] Otherwise, the Agreement leaves investors without any recourse for their investment claims that were previously based on provisions of the BIT. Structured dialogue is described as a proceeding before an impartial facilitator 'with a view of finding between the parties an amicable, lawful and fair out-of-court and out-of-arbitration settlement'.[86] This individual should be appointed by mutual agreement of the investor and the Member State involved, or alternatively by an appointing authority, which is yet to be determined.[87] This provision opens many questions and creates uncertainties for both the investor and host state, which could have been avoided in the normal course of the arbitral proceedings.

The facilitator's role seems largely similar to the role of a sole arbitrator, not only in the nature of their position but also in the manner of appointment. Therefore,

79. EU Commission Press Release: *EU Member States sign an agreement for the termination of intra-EU bilateral investment treaties*, 5 May 2020, https://ec.europa.eu/info/files/200505-bilateral-investment-treaties-agreement_en. The signatories of the Agreement are Belgium, Bulgaria, Croatia, Republic of Cyprus, the Czech Republic, Denmark, Estonia, France, Germany, Greece, Hungary, Italy, Latvia, Lithuania, Luxembourg, Malta, the Netherlands, Poland, Portugal, Romania, Slovakia, Slovenia and Spain.
80. Articles 2–4 of the Agreement for the termination of bilateral investment treaties between the Member States of the European Union.
81. *Slowakische Republik v. Achmea, BV*, Case C-2-84/16, http://curia.europa.eu/juris/document/document.jsf;jsessionid=CD386D75A08C38C220B01D933C8D059D?text=&docid=205702&pageIndex=0&doclang=EN&mode=req&dir=&occ=first&part=1&cid=4089282.
82. Agreement for the termination of bilateral investment treaties between the Member States of the European Union, Art. 6.
83. *Ibid.*, Art. 8.
84. *Ibid.*, Art. 9.
85. *Ibid.*
86. *Ibid.*
87. *Ibid.*

'structured dialogue' will be nothing but displaced ad hoc arbitration before a sole arbitrator, conducted under the conditions put forth by the EU. The difference is the smaller likelihood of the parties agreeing to the sole facilitator than to a panel of arbitrators, which can lead to additional delays and uncertainty. This is already an echo of the complaints the EU had voiced against the existing ISDS system.

Furthermore, there is no requirement of subject-matter expertise or knowledge in investment arbitration on the side of the facilitators, but they are required to have expertise in EU law.[88] In addition, the Agreement provides that the facilitator should base their decision on the jurisprudence of the CJEU and the national courts, as well as the decisions of the EU Commission.[89] This undermines one of the main interests of parties who engage in ISDS before arbitral tribunals: the possibility of appointing arbitrators with the required expertise that is crucial for the case at hand. Once again, the complaint of the EU about the ad hoc selection of the arbitrators by the parties can easily be applied to the 'structured dialogue' proposal.

The facilitation proceedings are also meant to be confidential,[90] just like arbitral proceedings. There is no visible advantage in the replacement of arbitral proceedings with 'structured dialogue' in this respect. The investors would still be able to seek recourse with the courts of the EU Member States within six months from the termination of the BITs, regardless of the statute of limitations.[91] Therefore, if the Agreement was supposed to be a first glance at the world without ISDS in the EU, the transition period still strongly resembles ISDS as we know it.

In the context of BiH, this primarily means that it would have to ratify the Agreement upon accession into the EU, thereby automatically terminating its existing intra-EU BITs, including the sunset clauses. The most significant consequences will be felt by the investors who have pending arbitration cases against BiH under intra-EU BITs, most notably in *EGS v. Bosnia and Herzegovina*,[92] which is also the highest valued claim ever brought against the country in ISDS (appx. EUR 1.5 billion). This case was brought under the ECT and the Slovenia-BiH BIT.[93]

At the outset of this case, the competent BiH court declined jurisdiction and amicable settlement attempts were unsuccessful. Therefore, if EGS is forced to engage in 'structured dialogue' as another attempt of peaceful settlement or instead to refer the case to a domestic court, BiH may effectively get a 'second bite of the apple'. The dispute which was elevated to the neutral forum of the ISDS arbitral tribunal would once again be brought to the 'home court' of the respondent host state. If the CJEU or a national court finds that the contested measure of the State was not contrary to EU law, the investor may be denied even the chance to reach a settlement agreement in the new framework of structured dialogue. Thus, it seems that the EU is using the

88. *Ibid.*
89. *Ibid.*
90. *Ibid.*
91. *Ibid.*, Art. 10.
92. *Elektrogospodarstvo Slovenije – razvoj ininzeniring d.o.o. v. Bosnia and Herzegovina* (ICSID Case No. ARB/14/13).
93. Agreement Between Bosnia and Herzegovina and the Republic of Slovenia for the Reciprocal Promotion and Protection of Investments (2002).

transition period between the ISDS system and its proposed MIC to refer some of the arbitral cases back to the domestic forum or at least to alternative dispute settlement under EU law.

This brief overview of the text of the draft Agreement shows that the EU has made a sweeping decision to terminate intra-EU BITs quickly, and now it must retrofit the mode of implementation to match their desired outcome. Without discussing the *pro futuro* effects of the termination of intra-EU BITs and their ISDS clauses, it seems counterproductive and disruptive to force parties in pending arbitration cases to transplant their dispute into a provisional forum which brings no visible improvement to the existing ISDS system. However, BiH as a Member State will not have any choice but to follow suite and ratify the Agreement with all its implications. It may even have a second chance to settle its ongoing ISDS cases with investors from EU Member States if the proceedings are not concluded before its accession to the EU.

[C] ISDS Reform Options for the Surviving BiH BITs

BiH is a country with an abundance of natural resources that are ripe for exploitation and which can be harnessed for long-term economic development.[94] Due to the limited capacities within the country itself, such goals can effectively be accomplished only with the engagement of serious foreign investors.[95] Therefore, in its pursuit of ISDS reform, BiH should take the interests of such existing and future investors into account.

Investors closely follow and have expressed their support for the proposals set forth by some governments in their submissions to WG III.[96] From their perspective, the main advantages of ISDS are in the balance of the positions of the disputing parties, the balance between the consistency, correctness and finality of the arbitral award, and the enforceability regime of arbitral awards.[97] The submission of the Corporate Counsel International Arbitration Group makes clear that the investor community is in favour of gradual ISDS reform and that they will not support reform options which endanger their interests.[98] Therefore, BiH should consider the reform options embraced by the community of investors and their legal representatives which were outlined in their submissions to the WG III.

Once BiH becomes an EU Member State, the surviving BITs with non-EU states should be reformed and modernized in accordance with international standards. This can be accomplished by treaty amendments in the spirit of the global ISDS reforms. Although the ISDS reform discussions cover a broad range of topics, one of the most important reform areas for BiH is the prevention and peaceful settlement of disputes. The significance of robust dispute prevention and ADR mechanisms for BiH cannot be overstated due to the fact that amicable settlement was not pursued effectively in the

94. The World Bank in Bosnia and Herzegovina, Country Context Overview, https://www.worldbank.org/en/country/bosniaandherzegovina/overview.
95. *Ibid.*
96. Submission by the Corporate Counsel International Arbitration Group (CCIAG) to UNCITRAL Working Group III – ISDS Reform (18 December 2019).
97. *Ibid.*
98. *Ibid.*

ISDS cases BiH recently lost.[99] This stage of dispute resolution is very rarely pursued in a structured and genuine manner, but it usually amounts to a formal meeting or exchange of correspondence documenting the failure to find common ground.[100] An effective reform in this area, followed by treaty amendments, should enhance the position of BiH as a respondent state and prevent investor claims from escalating into lengthy disputes.

[D] ISDS Reform in BiH: Spotlight on Dispute Prevention and ADR

The amicable settlement provisions in BiH BITs appear in several variations, but in essence they are all broad, vague and do not contain any guidance for their actual application.[101] The only parameter that appears in these provisions is the duration of amicable settlement attempts, although in some cases, even the duration of amicable settlement proceedings is left open.[102] Amicable settlement in BiH BITs refers to either consultations and/or negotiations or, in the cases of Egypt and Kuwait, recourse to diplomatic channels.[103] The terms negotiation, conciliation and consultations are mostly used interchangeably, and it does not seem like they were meant to be interpreted narrowly.

More than 21% of BiH BITs only provide for an attempt of amicable settlement, without any further specifications (none of the non-EU BITs fall into this category). The remaining amicable settlement provisions are distributed as follows:

- consultations (5.4% of total BiH BITs/14.3% of non-EU BITs);
- negotiations (10.8% of total BiH BITs/7.1% of non-EU BIT);
- consultations and negotiations (45.9% of total BiH BITs/64.3% of non-EU BITs).[104]

The amicable settlement provisions in BiH BITs are placed within a frame of six months (in 51.7% of the total BiH BITs and 42.8% of the non-EU BITs) or three months (29.7% of total BiH BITs and 42.8% of non-EU BITs).[105] During this time, the parties should attempt conciliation, settlement or negotiations, and in some cases even diplomatic channels. In several cases recourse to diplomatic channels is explicitly

99. The Ministry of Foreign Trade and Economic Relations BiH, Information on the trends and current global reform activities in the field of international investment disputes, 12 (June 2019).
100. *Ibid.*
101. *Ibid.*
102. BITs with Sweden, https://investmentpolicy.unctad.org/international-investment-agreements/treaty-files/483/download; Austria, https://investmentpolicy.unctad.org/international-investment-agreements/treaty-files/174/download; and The Netherlands https://investmentpolicy.unctad.org/international-investment-agreements/treaty-files/495/download.
103. Agreement Between Bosnia and Herzegovina and the Arab Republic of Egypt Concerning the Promotion and Reciprocal Protection of Investments (2001); Agreement Between Bosnia and Herzegovina and the State of Kuwait for the Encouragement and Reciprocal Protection of Investments (2002).
104. Information provided by the State Attorney's Office in Bosnia and Herzegovina.
105. *Ibid.*

excluded.[106] The potential reform solutions can be tailor-made for each BIT, guided by the reform options developed through the work of WG III.

[E] Structured and Effective Amicable Settlement Provisions (Consultations, Negotiations, Mediation)

Among the variety of reform options for dispute prevention, the use of ADR mechanisms, such as mediation, has been strongly endorsed by the Secretariat of UNCITRAL.[107] There has been a series of significant developments in the field of mediation, especially in the context of international arbitration. The most notable instrument is the United Nations Convention on International Settlement Agreements Resulting from Mediation (Singapore Convention on Mediation).[108] The Singapore Convention will play a valuable role in allowing the parties to enforce post-mediation settlement agreements internationally in a similar manner as arbitral awards. ICSID is also currently preparing mediation rules as part of the proposed amendments to the ICSID Rules aimed at streamlining the dispute resolution process and reducing the time and cost of proceedings.[109] The proposed mediation rules would apply in ISDS cases, regardless of the existence of a previous agreement to mediate.[110]

Therefore, mediation can become a powerful tool for amicable settlement of investor-state claims based on internationally accepted standards. BiH could propose a model mediation clause that could be adjusted for each BIT or adopted in a unified manner. The ratification of the UNCITRAL Mediation Convention would add clarity, structure and legitimacy to amicable settlement through mediation between investors and states. Mediation is also endorsed in twelve submissions to WG III, including the submission by the EU and its Member States.[111] None of the dispute resolution clauses in BiH BITs provide for mediation because the amicable settlement provisions in BiH BITs stem from old-generation treaties that predated the modern developments in ADR.[112] Mediation could become the default amicable settlement mechanism in BiH BITs with the benefit of international enforcement through the Singapore Convention.

Another potential solution is consultations and exchange of information between the State and the investor. Such a provision already exists in the BiH-Serbia BIT, but it

---

106. Unless if the Secretary General of the ICSID declares that the dispute cannot be resolved under the auspices of ICSID, or if one of the parties is withholding the performance of a final award.
107. UNCITRAL Secretariat, Note, https://undocs.org/en/A/CN.9/WG.III/WP.166.
108. *See* information on the website of UNCITRAL, https://uncitral.un.org/en/texts/mediation.
109. The ICSID Mediation Rules are expected to be offered to a vote to the ICSID Membership in the second half of 2020. ICSID, *Updated Backgrounder on Proposals for Amendment of the ICSID Rules* (28 February 2020). https://icsid.worldbank.org/en/Documents/WP_4_Backgrounder_EN.pdf.
110. *Ibid.*
111. Submissions from the governments of Indonesia, the EU and its Member States, Morocco, Thailand, Chile, Ireland, Japan (joint submission), Costa Rica, Turkey, Brazil, South Africa, China, the Republic of Korea, UNCITRAL Secretariat, Note, https://undocs.org/en/A/CN.9/WG.III/WP.166.
112. Analysis of the applicable BiH BITs conducted by the author, based on the treaty texts available in the UNCTAD Country Navigator, https://investmentpolicy.unctad.org/country-navigator/28/bosnia-and-herzegovina.

applies only to the contracting parties (i.e., the states themselves).[113] Provisions of this kind serve to help the contracting parties arrive at a common understanding on potentially unclear treaty provisions to avoid disputes. This is an important tool available at the government level for the avoidance of State-to-State disputes, but it could also be used in the context of investor-state disputes. Many ISDS claims are based on claims of indirect expropriation, violations of fair and equitable treatment (FET) clauses and most-favoured-nation (MFN) treatment due to the harmful effect of legislative changes.

Thus, the ability of the investor to approach the host state with a request for information or clarification of the relevant norms could significantly de-escalate the tensions between the parties and potentially serve as a dispute avoidance tool. This also applies in cases where investors have an erroneous or diverging interpretation of their rights and duties under the applicable BIT.

[F] Institutional Framework for Amicable Settlement Proceedings: Best Practices from Brazil and BiH

The key factor in the success and effectiveness of any amicable settlement mechanism is a strong, dedicated institutional framework. There are many examples of different standing or ad hoc bodies established by governments around the world mandated to carry out work on dispute prevention and amicable settlement on behalf of the government. These bodies and agencies aim to ensure a timely response to potential investor claims and the prevention of the escalation of the disputes where possible.[114] Two examples are the institutional frameworks established in Brazil and BiH.

[1] Cooperation and Facilitation Investment Agreement in Brazil

One example of a potentially beneficial and effective mechanism for dispute prevention and amicable settlement was established in Brazil, whose government adopted the Brazilian Cooperation and Facilitation Investment Agreement (CFIA) in an attempt to overcome the growing concerns regarding the existing ISDS framework.[115] The CFIA provides for a twofold dispute prevention mechanism:

113. Agreement on the Promotion and Protection of Investments between Bosnia and Herzegovina and the Federal Republic of Yugoslavia, Art. 9, https://investmentpolicy.unctad.org/international-investment-agreements/treaty-files/490/download.
114. Submissions from the governments of Indonesia, the EU and its Member States, Morocco, Thailand, Chile, Ireland, Japan (joint submission), Costa Rica, Turkey, Brazil, South Africa, China, the Republic of Korea, UNCITRAL Secretariat, Note, https://undocs.org/en/A/CN.9/WG.III/WP.166.
115. Felipe Hees, Pedro Mendonça Cavalcante and Pedro Paranhos, *The Cooperation and Facilitation Investment Agreement (CFIA) in the context of the discussions on the reform of the ISDS system*, Investment Policy Brief (May 2018).

- An ombudsperson is appointed to facilitate the communication between the host state and the foreign investor on any existing concerns, with the aim to prevent disputes from arising.
- A joint committee, which is composed of government representatives of both treaty parties, acts as a collaborative body for all matters regarding bilateral investments between the parties, and especially in preventing disputes and ensuring amicable settlement.[116]

In case an investor raises a complaint, the ombudsperson proactively assesses the complaints received from the other party or investors of the other party and recommends adequate actions to resolve it.[117] The joint committee operates the second phase, reactively, whenever it receives a written request enquiring about the incompatibility of a specific measure and the Agreement. The joint committee deliberates and issues a report on the issue at hand, regarding the specific measure for which the investor is complaining.[118] In its report, the joint committee will try to find an amicable solution to the measure in question, which can encompass, for example, a recommendation to the relevant government agency to bring the measure in conformity with the CFIA. Only after the complaining party has exhausted the dispute prevention procedure without a satisfactory resolution, can the parties initiate arbitral proceedings between states or ad hoc arbitration between the investor and the State.[119]

[2] Permanent Negotiating Body for the Peaceful Settlement of International Investment Disputes in BiH

In an effort to improve the management of investor claims, the Council of Ministers of BiH has recently established a 'task force' for international investment disputes. Namely, the Permanent Negotiating Body in BiH for the Peaceful Settlement of International Investment Disputes (the Permanent Body) was established by the Decision of the Council of Ministers on 24 November 2017, with the mandate to 'ensure a timely, coordinated and efficient performance of the competent institutions in the representation and protection of the interests of Bosnia and Herzegovina in the process of the peaceful settlement of international investment disputes, in cases which are initiated against Bosnia and Herzegovina'.[120]

The Permanent Body consists of representatives of the:

- Ministry of Foreign Trade and Economic Relations;

116. UNCITRAL Secretariat, Note, *Possible reform of investor-State dispute settlement (ISDS), Submission from the Government of Brazil* 3 (11 June 2019), https://undocs.org/en/A/CN.9/WG.III/WP.171.
117. *Ibid.*
118. UNCITRAL Secretariat, Note, *Possible reform of investor-State dispute settlement (ISDS), Submission from the Government of Brazil* 3 (11 June 2019), https://undocs.org/en/A/CN.9/WG.III/WP.171.
119. *Ibid.*
120. Press Release of the Council of Ministers 27 November 2019 http://www.vijeceministara.gov.ba/saopstenja/sjednice/saopstenja_sa_sjednica/default.aspx?id=26838&langTag=bs-BA.

- Ministry of Justice;
- Ministry of Finance;
- Ministry of Foreign Affairs;
- State Attorney's Office;
- Ad hoc members from the legal entity, which is involved in the dispute, the competent ministries and institutions of the entities and the State Attorney's Office.[121]

The Permanent Body coordinates and assists the State Attorney's Office in the attempted peaceful settlement, and the State Attorney's Office (with the approval of the Council of Ministers) takes over all the activities if the negotiations fail and the investor initiates arbitration.[122] The Permanent Body has the potential to be a valuable asset for BiH in the process of developing and implementing effective amicable settlement mechanisms for ISDS in BiH BITs. As a party at the negotiating table, the Permanent Body can bring not only the legitimacy of the government but also the cooperative spirit and fairness which comes from its mandate.

Thus, the tools for effective ISDS reform in BiH already are in place in the existing BIT framework. However, these tools need to be modernized and fine-tuned to meet the challenges of the contemporary standards in investment protection. A significant first step would be to harness the potential of the amicable settlement mechanisms, which could help prevent the escalation of disputes and retain valuable investments in the country.

§3.05 CONCLUSION

This chapter has reviewed the colourful spectrum of ISDS reform options that are taking shape at the global, regional and national level. WG III has become the global forum for high-level discussions on the various potential directions of ISDS reform, ranging from its complete abandonment to gradual and targeted reform. The EU and its Member States are on the verge of the complete abandonment of ISDS in its current form and the establishment of a standing MIC in its stead. Other regions of the world and investors have submitted proposals for specific, gradual reforms to be implemented through international instruments and treaty amendments.

The concerns identified through the discussions at WG III are universally accepted and are grouped into three main areas of intervention: consistency and predictability of the ISDS proceedings, arbitrators and decision-makers, and the cost and efficiency of ISDS proceedings. Although the concerns are universal, the proposed solutions differ significantly between the EU and the rest of the world. While most of the participating countries propose specific reforms that can be implemented in the

121. The Decision on the Establishment of the Permanent Negotiating Body of Bosnia and Herzegovina for the Peaceful Settlement of International Investment Disputes (Official Gazette BiH, no. 17/18).
122. Decision on the Establishment of the Permanent Negotiating Body of Bosnia and Herzegovina for the Peaceful Settlement of International Investment Disputes, Art. 6 (Official Gazette BiH, no. 17/18).

existing ISDS framework, the EU and its Member States are insisting on the MIC as the only systematic solution that would resolve all the identified concerns in one package. The discussions are still ongoing, and whether the support for the MIC will spread to the international level remains to be seen. Within the EU itself, the EU Commission has laid down the groundwork for the termination of all intra-EU BITs. There clearly will no longer be a place for ISDS in the EU.

BiH, the small, complex transitioning country in the heart of Europe, which is still progressing towards EU membership, is caught in the whirlwind of diverging reform options. On the one hand, it will have to terminate intra-EU BITs and refer investor disputes to dispute resolution mechanisms compliant with EU law. On the other hand, the non-EU BITs should be reformed to enhance the dispute prevention and ADR mechanisms to avoid the escalation of disputes with investors. Although BiH has its hands tied in relation to intra-EU BITs, this chapter's analysis has shown that the ISDS mechanisms in the surviving BITs could be successfully reformed and that no need exists to abandon ISDS as we know it to address the present concerns.

The most promising starting point for ISDS reform for BiH is in the field of dispute prevention and amicable settlement, which could bring long-term benefits to the country and its investors. An effective modernization of the existing BITs with non-EU states may be sufficient to overcome the existing concerns and improve the ISDS system in the future.

Whether the new EU investment protection landscape and a reformed ISDS system can coexist in a single EU Member State is difficult to determine. Therefore, BiH could serve as a case study for the viability of such a framework. The next chapter of this story will depend on the success of ISDS reform in the upcoming years. Although the calls for revolution coming from the EU are compelling, the BiH ISDS system may achieve its desired results through a steady evolution.

CHAPTER 4

The 2015 India Model BIT and Its Suitability under ISDS

Rose Maria Sebi, Sandeep Golani & Pallab Das

The Government of India redrafted its Model Bilateral Investment Treaty (Model BIT) in 2015. In the context of the Model BIT, this chapter studies the Indian approach towards BITs, the scope of the Investor-State Dispute Settlement (ISDS) system in the Model BIT and the inherent lacunae in it. The chapter then considers the extent to which the relevant clauses (particularly, the exhaustion of local remedies requirement and the most-favoured-nation (MFN) clause of the Model BIT) are in consonance with the jurisprudence on international arbitration. While discussing the inherent commonalities and differences in domestic and international arbitration rules and policies, this chapter examines how the Indian Model BIT and ISDS can still survive despite the inconsistencies. Lastly, this chapter considers whether being a member of international arbitration institutions is a suitable option for India.

§4.01 INTRODUCTION

A BIT is an agreement between two countries regarding the mutual promotion and protection of private investment made by individuals and businesses in each other's territories.[1] The existence of a BIT often provides investors from other countries protection which would not have been otherwise readily available in contracts entered into by the host state and investor, or in other agreements entered into by their respective states. Every investment treaty is unique and is specific to the two countries that are parties to it. However, some aspects are common throughout. These include

1. Lauren Corbett, *Application of Contract Law in BG Group v. Argentina*, 34(81) Boston University Int'l L. J. 184.

national treatment, fair and equitable treatment, protection from expropriation and performance requirements for investments, and access to a neutral dispute settlement. For foreign investors, the BIT assures that their investment will enjoy such protection. For the host states, BITs serve the purpose of attracting and increasing foreign investment by providing investment security. Additionally, since BITs provide a combination of national treatment, fair and equitable treatment and MFN treatment, they contribute greatly to maintaining the rule of law.

Most states have a model BIT based on which they enter into BITs with several states. A model BIT aids in the promotion of efficiency and consistency in the BITs a state might enter into, and it is supposed to help states with unequal bargaining power negotiate the best deal for themselves. Irrespective of having a model BIT, most BITs are made on a case-by-case basis, taking into consideration the parties' circumstances. Nonetheless, a model BIT does foster uniformity to some extent and more importantly reflects the foreign investment regime and policies of a state and the extent of protection it may be willing to provide to its investors.

This chapter initially examines the causes for a regime change in investment arbitration in India and discusses the provisions of the 2015 India Model BIT (2015 India BIT) that mandates exhaustion of local remedies prior to submission of claims before an arbitral tribunal. It describes how the provision is not the best suited for India because it is anti-arbitration and, therefore, anti-investor. Next, this chapter assesses how MFN clauses have been used by investors to import elements of a dispute resolution clause and whether the complete exclusion of an MFN clause in the revised model BIT is consistent with India's aspiration of attracting foreign direct investment (FDI). Finally, this chapter examines India's position as a non-member of International Centre for Settlement of Investment Disputes (ICSID) and whether India should consider becoming a member. India can balance interests of the host state as well as that of an investor if it designates a more reasonable period for the exhaustion of local remedies and if it incorporates a fair MFN clause. Further, India needs to secure investors' interests by being pro-enforcement and becoming a member of the ICSID will be a step in that direction.

§4.02 DISPUTE RESOLUTION AND EXHAUSTION OF LOCAL REMEDIES

[A] Investment Arbitration in India under the 2003 India Model BIT

Until the 1990s, India was an isolated economy. However, Indian policymakers opened its economy in that decade to foreign trade as it adopted new policies of liberalization and globalization. India started encouraging foreign investment and established a fast-track process for investment approval. Soon, India became one of the most attractive emerging markets globally and FDI in India saw an eleven-fold growth in two decades, from USD 4 billion in 1990 to USD 44.8 billion in 2010.[2] The gross FDI received

2. Shikha Singh, *Foreign Direct Investment (FDI) Inflows in India A Review*, 6 J. of General Management Research, 42–50 (January 2019).

in India from April 2000 to June 2018 was USD 563.32 trillion.[3] As a result, FDI has been a major driver of economic growth in India.[4] India was among the top ten recipients of FDI in 2019, attracting USD 49 billion in capital inflows.[5]

Its frequent capital imports resulted in India entering into BITs with various nations, most of which were developed economies. India's initial BITs, including its first BIT with the United Kingdom, were based on the 1993 India Model BIT,[6] which was modelled on the Organisation for Economic Co-operation and Development's (OECD) Draft Convention for Protection of Foreign Property of 1967[7] (Draft Convention of 1967).[8] The Draft Convention of 1967 was based on a model created by developed countries which prioritized protection of foreign investment, rather than protecting the exercise of regulatory powers of the state.[9] Even the 2003 India Model BIT[10] (2003 India BIT) was strikingly similar to the 1993 Model.

Pursuant to Article 9 of the 2003 India BIT,[11] an investor could initiate an arbitral proceeding for a dispute which could not be amicably settled by the parties within six months. There was no requirement in this model BIT to exhaust local remedies. Thus, parties could opt for arbitration without approaching the local courts of the relevant jurisdiction.[12] Barring a few exceptions, almost all BITs to which India was a signatory did not require exhaustion of local remedies. The 1997 India-Switzerland BIT[13] and the

3. Quarterly Fact Sheet, Fact Sheet on Foreign Direct Investment (FDI) from April 2000 to June 2018 https://dipp.gov.in/sites/default/files/FDI_FactSheet_23August2018.pdf.
4. *Ibid.*
5. PTI United States, *India among top 10 FDI recipients, attracts $49 billion inflows in 2019: UN report*, Business Line (20 January 2020), thehindubusinessline.com/economy/india-among-top-10-fdi-recipients-attracts-49-billion-inflows-in-2019-un-report/article30608178.ece.
6. Agreement between the Government of the Republic of India and the Government of the United Kingdom of Great Britain and Northern Ireland for the Promotion and protection of Investments, signed on 14 March 1994. https://dea.gov.in/sites/default/files/United%20Kingdom.pdf.
7. Draft Convention on the Protection of Foreign Property 1967, https://investmentpolicy.unctad.org/international-investment-agreements/treaty-files/2812/download.
8. Saurabh Garg et al., *The Indian Model Bilateral Investment Treaty: Continuity and Change*, Rethinking Bilateral Investment Treaties: Critical Issues and Policy Choices 69, 82 (Kavaljit Singh and Burghard Ilge, eds, 2016).
9. Rashmi Banga, *Impact of Government Policies and Investment Agreements on FDI Inflows* (Indian Council for Research on Int'l Econ. Relations, Working Paper No. 116, 2003), http://www.icrier.org/pdf/WP116.PDF.
10. Indian Model Text of Bilateral Investment and Protection Agreement 2003, https://www.italaw.com/sites/default/files/archive/ita1026.pdf.
11. *Ibid.*, Art. 9.
12. *Ibid.*, Art. 9. (3)(a), states:

> If the Contracting Party of the Investor and the other Contracting Party are both parties to the convention on the Settlement of Investment Disputes between States and nationals of other States, 1965 and the investor consents in writing to submit the dispute to the International Centre for the Settlement of Investment Disputes such a dispute shall be referred to the Centre.

13. Agreement Between the Government of the Republic of India and the Swiss Confederation for the promotion and protection of investments, signed on 4 April 1997, https://dea.gov.in/sites/default/files/Switzerland.pdf.

2007 India-Libya BIT[14] were two international investment agreements that required the investor to exhaust local remedies when a dispute arose. Apart from these exceptions, all BITs allowed for a claim to be submitted to an international tribunal. This investor-centric approach on dispute resolution in BITs was one of the reasons why India became one of the most frequent respondent states in investor-state arbitrations.

The first of these cases was *Dabhol*[15] which, until now, was India's largest investment project to date with an anticipated cost of USD 2.9 billion.[16] In this case, Dabhol Power Corporation (DPC), a local corporation owned by General Electric, Bechtel, and Enron, entered into an agreement with the Maharashtra State Electricity Board (MSEB) for a project for the construction of distillate fuel power plant. MSEB agreed to buy 90% of the power generated by the project regardless of market demand for electricity and at a cost well above that of other available energy sources. This deal, from its very inception, was contentious as being impractical and highly unfavourable to India's national energy policy and its taxpayers, who would ultimately bear the cost of the project.[17] Amidst public opposition, alleged irregularities and the high contract value, MSEB cancelled the contract. Subsequently, DPC sued MSEB in India and submitted claims before international tribunals whose authority was derived from the various contracts and BITs concluded by India.[18] General Electric (GE) and Bechtel invoked the 1998 India-Mauritius BIT[19] through their subsidiaries in Mauritius and challenged measures adopted by India as constituting expropriation and claimed compensation. Eventually, for multiple reasons, the case was closed and it ended in an out of court settlement,[20] pursuant to which India heavily compensated the claimants. Reportedly, GE received USD 145 million in compensation, while Bechtel settled for USD 160 million.[21] Nonetheless, this experience alerted India to its obligations under a BIT, because the claims raised against it were based on its obligations under a BIT it had signed with Mauritius.

A series of investment disputes against India occasioned a change in India's take on its investment dispute settlement policy and consequently in its model BIT. The decisive moment, however, was *White Industries*,[22] in which a three-member ad hoc

14. Agreement Between the Republic of Indian and the Great Socialist People's Libyan Arab Jamahiriya for the promotion and protection of investments, signed on 26 May 2007, https://dea.gov.in/sites/default/files/Libya.pdf.
15. *Offshore Power Production C.V. & Others v. Republic of India* UNCTAD, Investment Policy Hub, 'India-as Respondent State', https://investmentpolicy.unctad.org/investment-dispute-settlement/cases/139/offshore-power-v-india.
16. Parikh, *Thinking through the Enron Issue*, 36 (17) Econ. & Pol. Wkly. 1463 (28 April 2001), https://dea.gov.in/sites/default/files/Libya.pdf; *see also* John J. Kerr and Janet Whittaker, 'Dabhol Dispute', Construction Law International 1, 17–20 (March 2006).
17. Girish Sant et al., *Dabhol Project PPA – Structure and Techno-Economic Implications*, 30(24) Econ. & Pol. Wkly. 1449, 1455 (17 June 1995).
18. *Supra* n. 16, John J. Kerr and Janet Whittaker 17.
19. *Ibid.*
20. *Maharashtra Power Development Corpn. Ltd. v. Dabhol Power Co.* (2005) 11 SCC 207.
21. V. Sridhar, *Reviving Dabhol Frontline* (22 May 2020), https://frontline.thehindu.com/the-nation/article30205826.ece.
22. *White Industries Australia Limited v. Republic of India*, UNCITRAL, Final Award (30 November 2011) https://investmentpolicy.unctad.org/investment-dispute-settlement/cases/378/white-industries-v-india.

arbitral tribunal unanimously held that India's inordinate delay in enforcing an arbitral award violated the 'effective means' standard incorporated by an MFN provision. In 1989, an Australian mining company called White Industries had entered into a long-term mining contract with Coal India Limited (Coal India) which was a state-owned Indian company. When a dispute regarding the quality of coal and the payment of penalties arose between the two parties, White Industries commenced arbitral proceedings under the International Chamber of Commerce (ICC) Arbitration Rules in 1999. The outcome of the case in May 2002 was a majority decision in favour of the claimants, and the ICC tribunal awarded USD 4.08 million to White Industries.[23]

In September 2002, under section 34 of the Indian Arbitration and Conciliation Act, 1996 (Arbitration Act), Coal India applied to the Calcutta High Court to set aside the ICC Award.[24] At the same time, White Industries applied to the High Court of New Delhi to enforce the same award under section 48 of the Arbitration Act and applied for an interim stay on the Calcutta proceedings.[25] Both proceedings were significantly delayed as each party tried to have the case transferred to the court to which they had initially applied. Ultimately, White Industries withdrew its transfer petition. However, instead of arguing on the merits in the Calcutta High Court, it challenged Coal India's application to set aside the award on the grounds that the court did not have jurisdiction. At the same time, it filed an application in the Supreme Court of India to transfer Coal India's application from the Calcutta High Court to the Delhi High Court.[26] The Calcutta High Court rejected the argument that the court did not have jurisdiction.[27] While the matter was still pending in the Supreme Court, White Industries invoked arbitration under the India-Australia BIT and initiated arbitral proceedings under the United Nations Commission on International Trade Law (UNCITRAL) Rules. That tribunal awarded White Industries USD 4.08 million as compensation because it found that there was an unjustifiable delay by the Indian courts in dealing with the jurisdictional issues and India had violated its obligation to provide to the investor 'effective means' of asserting claims and enforcing rights.[28] This provision was borrowed from the 1996 India-Kuwait BIT[29] by way of an MFN clause in the 2009 India-Australia BIT.[30]

The award granted in *White Industries* and other cases challenging regulatory measures, such as cancellation of telecom licences and the imposition of retrospective taxes, made India rethink clauses such as MFN and the dispute settlement clause in its BITs. Post-2011, after *White Industries*, India adopted a less investor-friendly approach

23. *Ibid.*
24. *Ibid.*, para. 3.2.35.
25. *Ibid.*, para. 3.2.36.
26. *Ibid.*, para. 3.2.40.
27. *White Industries Australia Limited v. Coal India Limited*; (2004) 2 Cal LJ 197.
28. *Supra* n. 22, para. 11.4.19.
29. Agreement between the State of Kuwait and the Republic of India for the encouragement and reciprocal protection of investment, signed on 27 November 2001, https://dea.gov.in/sites/default/files/Kuwait.pdf.
30. Agreement between the Government of the Republic of India and the Government of Australia on the promotion and protection of investments, signed on 26 February 1999, https://dea.gov.in/sites/default/files/Australia.pdf.

to protect its interests as a host nation. The complete exclusion of taxation measures from the ambit of BITs as provided for in Article 2.4(ii) of the 2015 India BIT[31] is arguably a reaction to the ISDS claims brought in *Cairn Energy*.[32] In that case, the Indian government had amended its taxation law and made it retrospectively applicable. Under the amended law, Cairn Energy was required to pay INR 10,247 more in taxes. In 2015, the company initiated an arbitration under the India-United Kingdom BIT (1994) and challenged the retrospective legislation, seeking full restitution of losses caused by the Government's expropriation of its investments in India. The arbitral tribunal is expected to issue the award in mid-2020.[33]

The Central Government Working Group began a review process in 2012 aimed at creating an investor-state dispute resolution regime that would balance investor rights with state regulatory obligations. As a result, the 2015 India BIT was drafted and fifty-eight of the eighty-four BITs that India had entered into were terminated unilaterally by India with the intention to renegotiate future BITs, free trade agreements and other multilateral trade arrangements based on the 2015 India BIT.[34] To protect the host state's interest, the 2015 India BIT introduced the mandatory requirement of exhausting local remedies. It also removed the MFN clause that was present in the 2003 India BIT.

[B] Investment Regime Change in India

The dispute resolution clause in a BIT can be broad by providing an option to the investors to either litigate a dispute in the local courts of the host state or submit their claims before an international arbitral tribunal. A narrow dispute resolution clause entails a mandatory requirement to exhaust local remedies before an arbitration proceeding can be initiated.[35] Since a wider clause is more investor-friendly, most BITs allow foreign investors to bring claims without exhausting local remedies. However,

31. Article 2.4(ii), Model Text for the Bilateral Investment Treaty 2015, states:

> This Treaty shall not apply to: (i) any measure by a local government; (ii) any law or measure regarding taxation, including measures taken to enforce taxation obligations. For greater certainty, it is clarified that where the State in which investment is made decides that conduct alleged to be a breach of its obligations under this Treaty is a subject matter of taxation, such decision of that State, whether before or after the commencement of arbitral proceedings, shall be nonjusticiable and it shall not be open to any arbitration tribunal to review such decision.

https://dea.gov.in/sites/default/files/ModelBIT_Annex_0.pdf.

32. *Cairn Energy PLC and Cairn UK Holdings Limited v. The Republic of India* (PCA Case No. 2016-7).
33. Press Trust of India, *Cairn India Tax Case: Arbitration Tribunal Delays Award of Rs 10,247 Crore to Mid-2020*, Bloomberg Quint (28 October 2019, 7:02 PM), https://www.bloombergquint.com/business/arbitration-tribunal-delays-award-in-rs-10-247-cr-cairn-retro-tax-case-to-mid-2020.
34. Nicholas Peacock and Nihal Joseph, *Mixed Messages to Investors as India Quietly Terminates Bilateral Investment Treaties with 58 Countries* (16 March 2017), https://hsfnotes.com/arbitration/2017/03/16/mixed-messages-to-investors-as-india-quietly-terminates-bilateral-investment-treaties-with-58-countries/.
35. August Reinisch, *How Narrow Are Narrow Dispute Settlement Clauses in Investment Treaties?* 2(1) J. of Int'l Dispute Settlement, 115–174 (2011).

some BITs have mandated the exhaustion of local remedies. For instance, the agreement on economic cooperation between the Government of the Kingdom of the Netherlands and the Government of the Republic of Singapore,[36] under Article XI, mandates foreign investors to exhaust all local administrative and judicial remedies for the settlement of investment disputes between host states and investors.

In the 2003 India BIT, India had a broad dispute resolution clause because there was no requirement to exhaust local remedies.[37] Thus, an investor could negotiate with the host state and amicably settle the issue, approach local courts, seek diplomatic protection or it could submit its claims to an arbitral tribunal. The only mandatory requirement under this model was that the investor and the host state were required to attempt to settle disputes through negotiation. In the event that they were not able to reach a resolution after six months, they could submit their claims to an arbitral tribunal.[38]

In contrast to the 2003 India BIT, the 2015 India BIT has a narrower and a more restricted dispute resolution clause. First, its jurisdiction is limited to claims bought under Chapter II of the 2015 India BIT, excluding obligations arising out of Article 9 and Article 10.[39] This means that the dispute resolution clause does not extend to any claims arising out of a separate contract between the investor and the host state. Any disputes arising from such a contract must be resolved according to the dispute resolution clause provided in the concerned contract.[40] Second, the exhaustion of local remedies is a mandatory requirement. The dispute resolution clause in the 2015 India BIT is multi-tiered and intricate. Article 15.1[41] and

36. Agreement on economic cooperation between the Government of the Kingdom of the Netherlands and the Government of the Republic of Singapore, signed on 9 August 1965, https://arbitrationlaw.com/sites/default/files/free_pdfs/netherlands-singapore_bit.pdf.
37. *Supra* n. 10, Art. 9.
38. *Ibid.*
39. Articles 9 & 10, Model Text for the Bilateral Investment Treaty 2015 https://dea.gov.in/sites/default/files/ModelBIT_Annex_0.pdf.
40. *Ibid.*, Art. 13.2.
41. *Ibid.*, Art. 15.1. This article states:

> In respect of a claim that the Defending Party has breached an obligation under Chapter II, other than an obligation under Article 9 or 10, a disputing investor must first submit its claim before the relevant domestic courts or administrative bodies of the Defending Party for the purpose of pursuing domestic remedies in respect of the same measure or similar factual matters for which a breach of this Treaty is claimed. Such claim before the relevant domestic courts or administrative bodies of the Defending Party must be submitted within one (1) year from the date on which the investor first acquired, or should have first acquired, knowledge of the measure in question and knowledge that the investment, or the investor with respect to its investment, had incurred loss or damage as a result. For greater certainty, in demonstrating compliance with the obligation to exhaust local remedies, the investor shall not assert that the obligation to exhaust local remedies does not apply or has been met on the basis that the claim under this Treaty is by a different party or in respect of a different cause of action. Provided, however, that the requirement to exhaust local remedies shall not be applicable if the investor or the locally established enterprise can demonstrate that there are no available domestic legal remedies capable of reasonably providing any relief in respect of the same measure or similar factual matters for which a breach of this Treaty is claimed by the investor.

Article 15.2[42] of this model require that an investor must first exhaust local remedies for at least five years from the date on which the investor first acquired knowledge of the action in question or when the investor should have acquired knowledge of it. Moreover, the limitation for submitting such a claim in the local courts is one year.[43]

Article 15.4[44] provides that after exhausting local remedies and spending five years in the local courts, the investor then must enter into negotiations for not less than six months. It is only after the completion of these six months that an investor can initiate arbitration by providing the host state a notice of arbitration. Additionally, Article 15.5(v)[45] states that an arbitration can commence only after three months have passed after issuance of the notice of arbitration.

When the article on conditions precedent to the submission of a claim to arbitration[46] is read as a whole, it is evident that it takes five years and nine months from the date on which the investor acquired knowledge of the act in question to submit a claim to international investment arbitration. At the same time, not more than six years should have passed before the claim is brought before an arbitral tribunal. This gives investors a period of only three months to successfully submit their claims to arbitration, thus making it very difficult for a foreign investor to have access to

---

42. *Ibid.*, Art. 15.2, which states:

> Where applicable, if, after exhausting all judicial and administrative remedies relating to the measure underlying the claim for at least a period of five years from the date on which the investor first acquired knowledge of the measure in question, no resolution has been reached satisfactory to the investor, the investor may commence a proceeding under this chapter by transmitting a notice of dispute ('notice of dispute') to the Defending Party.

43. *Supra* n. 41.
44. *Ibid.*, Art. 15.4. This article states:

> For no less than six (6) months after receipt of the notice of dispute, the disputing parties shall use their best efforts to try to resolve the dispute amicably through meaningful consultation, negotiation or other third party procedures. In all such cases, the place of such consultation or negotiation or settlement shall be the capital city of the Defending Party.

45. *Ibid.*, Art. 15.5(v). Art. 15.5(v) provides:

> In the event that the disputing parties cannot settle the dispute amicably, a disputing investor may submit a claim to arbitration pursuant to this Treaty, but only if the following additional conditions are satisfied: (v) At least 90 days before submitting any claim to arbitration, the disputing investor has transmitted to the Defending Party a written notice of its intention to submit the claim to arbitration ('notice of arbitration'). The notice of arbitration shall: a. attach the notice of dispute and the record of its transmission to the Defending Party with the details thereof; b. provide the consent to arbitration by the disputing investor, or where applicable, by the locally established enterprise, in accordance with the procedures set out in this Treaty; c. provide the waiver as required under Article 15.5 (iii) or (iv), as applicable; provided that a waiver from the enterprise under Article 15.5 (iii) or (iv) shall not be required only where the Defending Party has deprived the disputing investor of control of an enterprise; d. specify the name of the arbitrator appointed by the disputing investor.

46. *Ibid.*, Art. 15.

international investment arbitration. Instead of attracting more investment, the 2015 India BIT upsets prospective investors. Moreover, the mandatory requirement to enter into negotiations after having spent five years in local courts is most likely to be fruitless, because an adversarial action has already been initiated before the negotiations started. This adversarial system is likely to antagonize negotiations and render them unsuccessful.

Thus, the mandatory requirement in the Model BIT potentially hampers FDI capital inflows because it provides little for the protection of the investor's rights in ISDS. Further, it undermines India's potential as a capital-exporting nation. India is now an economy that not only imports capital but has also seen a significant increase in its capital exports. With investments of USD 2.6 billion in 2017–2018, India was ranked 20th among the top capital-importing countries globally.[47] Thus, the requirement to exhaust local remedies in the host state is an obligation that can incur detriment to Indian investors in a foreign country with which India has signed a BIT modelled on the 2015 India BIT. Thus, the 2015 India BIT protects the interest of the host state but does not provide leeway for dispute resolution to Indian investors in foreign countries.

[C] Response to 2015 India Model BIT

Following the revision of the 2003 India BIT with the 2015 India BIT and the subsequent termination of BITs, not many states have entered into new BITs with India. However, there are a few states that have signed BITs or Joint Interpretative Notes (JIN)[48] with India.[49] Some of these agreements have followed the 2015 India BIT. For example, on 24 September 2018, Belarus entered into a new BIT with India.[50] This BIT is yet to be enforced, but is modelled on the 2015 India BIT. Article 13.2 of this BIT requires an alleged breach of a contract to be resolved by the domestic courts only. The limitation period for filing a claim against India before the relevant domestic courts is two years (unlike the one year in the 2015 India BIT). Similarly, the limitation period to initiate an arbitration has been increased to seven years (unlike six years provided for in the 2015 India BIT). Similarly, on 4 October 2018, India entered in a Joint

47. Press Trust of India, *India among top 10 FDI recipients, attracts $49 billion inflows in 2019: UN report*, Money Control (17 June 2019) https://www.thehindubusinessline.com/economy/india-among-top-10-fdi-recipients-attracts-49-billion-inflows-in-2019-un-report/article30608178.ece.
48. JINs are agreements entered into by states after having entered into a BIT. These notes clarify the interpretation of various clauses in the treaty.
49. Countries that have renewed their investment regime with India include Bangladesh, Belarus, Columbia, Brazil and India Taipei Association (ITA) in Taipei and Taipei Cultural & Economic Centre (TECC) which is the representative office of the Republic of China (Taiwan) and is responsible for promoting bilateral relations between Taiwan and India.
50. Treaty Between the Republic of Belarus and the Republic of India of Investments, signed on 24 September 2018 https://dea.gov.in/sites/default/files/BIT%20with%20Belarus.pdf.

Interpretative Declaration with Colombia.[51] This was almost identical to the India-Bangladesh JIS, with an added provision on denial of benefits.

Further, India entered into a Bilateral Investment Agreement (BIA) with the India Taipei Association in Taipei (ITA) and the Taipei Economic and Cultural Center in India (TECC).[52] In this BIA, the dispute resolution clause provides a limitation period of one year and six months (unlike the one year in the 2015 India BIT) to the investor to file its claim against India before the relevant domestic courts. Additionally, the period for the exhaustion of local remedies has been relaxed to four years (unlike the five years provided for in the 2015 India BIT).

On a different note, on 4 October 2017, India executed a JIN with Bangladesh[53] keeping India's 2012 BIT with Bangladesh alive. The JIN attempts to match the 2015 India BIT but does not specifically require the exhaustion of local remedies. Instead, it uses the doctrine of 'ripeness' in Article 9, where it requires that for a dispute to be bought by a claimant, the claims must be ripe for adjudication under the agreement.[54]

The latest advance in this area has been the Investment Cooperation and Facilitation Treaty between Brazil and India,[55] which contains a dispute prevention clause providing for a joint committee, comprised of a government representative of both parties. Pursuant to Article 19 of the BIA, a dispute that has not been settled by the dispute prevention procedure can be submitted to an ad hoc arbitral tribunal or arbitration institution. There is no mention of a limitation period for submitting such claims.

As a result of the recent agreements, it is evident that very few states are willing to enter into a BIT that mirrors the 2015 India BIT. The terms of any BITs or JINs that India might enter into would be largely based on the bargaining positions of the two states. To make a BIT workable and agreeable to both parties, India would have to open itself to the ISDS mechanism. Even if India wants to preserve the requirement to exhaust local remedies, it might have to adopt a period less than five years, because it likely will face claims for compensation of losses that an investor might incur when the dispute was in court, similar to *White Industries*,[56] where India had to pay compensation due to inordinate delay in its judicial proceedings. A more appropriate duration for

51. Joint Interpretative Declaration between the Republic of India and the Republic of Columbia regarding the agreement for the promotion and protection of investments between India and Columbia, signed on 4 October 2018, https://dea.gov.in/sites/default/files/JID%20with%20Colombia.pdf.
52. Bilateral Investment Treaty between The India Taipei Association in Taipei and the Taipei Economic and Cultural Centre in India, signed on 18 December 2018, https://dea.gov.in/sites/default/files/BIA%20between%20ITA%20and%20TECC.pdf.
53. Joint Interpretative Notes on the Agreement between the Government of the Republic of India and the Government of the People's Republic of Bangladesh for the Promotion and Protection of Investments, signed on 4 October 2017, https://dea.gov.in/sites/default/files/Signed%20Copy%20of%20JIN.pdf.
54. *Ibid.*, Art. 9. The ripeness of claims accesses if the claims are fit for review.
55. Investment Cooperation and Facilitation Treaty between the Federative Republic of Brazil and the Republic of India, signed on 25 January 2020, https://dea.gov.in/sites/default/files/Investment%20Cooperation%20and%20Facilitation%20Treaty%20with%20Brazil%20-%20English_0.pdf.
56. *Supra* n. 22.

exhaustion of local remedies is the eighteen-month period that is widely used in several BITs.[57] However, this period is commonly seen in BITs entered into by developed nations whose courts have a much faster disposal rate than India and far lower number of pending cases. Thus, the specific period for which India should mandate exhaustion of local remedies should not be as long as five years. It cannot be merely eighteen months because that would be unrealistic in India's case. Therefore, a middle ground needs to be achieved and a more appropriate time period adopted. At the same time, India will have to strengthen its courts to be able to handle a large number of pending cases and work on having a better disposal rate.

§4.03 EXCLUSION OF MFN CLAUSE FROM THE 2015 INDIA MODEL BIT

[A] Importation of MFN Clauses for Dispute Resolution

According to the International Law Commission (ILC), an MFN clause is defined as 'a treaty provision whereby a State undertakes an obligation towards another State to accord most-favoured-nation treatment in an agreed sphere of relations'.[58] For example, assume there is an agreement containing an MFN clause between A, the host state, and B, the investor. C is another investor with whom A also signs an agreement similar to that of B containing an MFN clause. In this case, C by virtue of the MFN clause enshrined in the agreement between C and A can claim its rights according to the clauses or provisions mentioned in the agreement between A and B. An MFN clause is important because it aims to guarantee non-discrimination by granting equality of competitive opportunities to all foreign investors with whom the host state has an MFN obligation. Further, it is important from the perspective of investor protection, which is the primary objective of the ISDS system. These clauses[59] in a BIT have been used in most of the treaties dating back to the seventeenth century, thus marking an impressive

57. Treaty between the Federal Republic of Germany and the Argentine Republic on the Encouragement and Reciprocal Protection of Investments, signed on 9 April 1991, https://jusmundi.com/en/document/treaty/en-treaty-between-the-federal-republic-of-germany-and-the-argentine-republic-on-the-encouragement-and-reciprocal-protection-of-investments-argentina-germany-bit-1991-tuesday-9th-april-1991; Agreement between the Republic of Turkey and Turkmenistan concerning the Reciprocal Promotion and Protection of Investments, signed on 2 May 1992, https://jusmundi.com/en/document/treaty/en-agreement-between-the-republic-of-turkey-and-turkmenistan-concerning-the-reciprocal-promotion-and-protection-of-investments-turkey-turkmenistan-bit-1992-saturday-2nd-may-1992; Agreement between the Government of the United Kingdom of Great Britain and Northern Ireland and the Government of the Republic of Argentina for the Promotion and Protection of Investments, signed on 11 December 1990, https://jusmundi.com/en/document/treaty/en-agreement-between-the-government-of-the-united-kingdom-of-great-britain-and-northern-ireland-and-the-government-of-the-republic-of-argentina-for-the-promotion-and-protection-of-investments-argentina-united-kingdom-bit-1990-tuesday-11th-december-1990.
58. 2 Final Draft Articles on Most Favoured Nation Clauses, Y.B. of Int'l Comm'n, pt. 2, 30th session n. 16 Art. 4 (1978).
59. Committee of Experts for the progressive Codification of Int'l Law, Rep. of the Sub-Comm., *The Most-Favoured-Nation-Clause*, League of Nations Doc.C.205.M.79 1927 V (1927), reprinted in 22 Am. J. Int'l L. (Special Supplement) 137 (1928).

lineage.[60] ILC's draft Article 7[61] underlines the conventional status of MFN treatment, which indicates its wide usage in BITs.

With respect to the interpretation of an MFN clause, there is no bright-line rule applicable. The subject matter of a treaty also plays a pivotal role when it comes to the application of MFN clause because the investors usually choose only those provisions by way of an MFN clause that pertain to the same subject matter.[62] In other words, an MFN clause will operate only to the extent that the provision in the other treaty is compatible, in principle, with the scheme negotiated by the parties in a treaty and the objectives of the concerned treaty. For example, in *MTD Equity v. Chile*,[63] the state did not allow for zoning changes for a land development project to the investors from Malaysia. Consequently, the investors under the Malaysia-Chile BIT argued that the MFN clause should be used to import a provision concerning the granting of necessary permits or licences from the Croatia-Chile BIT and the Denmark-Chile BIT. The tribunal allowed importation because it considered it consistent with the treaty's objective.[64] Importation helps to avoid the unpredictable consequences (like vitiating the intent of the contracting parties) resulting from the application of the clause in relation to all other areas of a treaty or a broad range of circumstances. Thus, an MFN clause requires careful and precise drafting by states.

With regard to the importation of an MFN clause for the application of the dispute resolution clauses, decisions by tribunals under ICSID are very inconsistent. MFN clauses have been applied differently on a case-to-case basis. For example, in *White Industries*, the India-Australia treaty, which had incorporated the MFN clause, was in dispute and the claimant imported the 'effective means of asserting claims and enforcing rights' provision of the India-Kuwait BIT to bypass the exhaustion of local remedies requirement. The result was a fiasco for India because the MFN clause was successfully imported and the Indian government had to pay USD 4.10 million.[65] To ensure there is no repeat of a *White Industries* situation, the Model BIT does not include an MFN provision.

Similarly, in *Maffezini v. Spain*,[66] an Argentine investor initiated an ICSID arbitration against Spain under the Spain-Argentina BIT, which mandated exhaustion of remedies in local courts for a period of eighteen months before international arbitration. Maffezini submitted that because the Spain-Chile BIT did not contain an exhaustion of local remedies clause. Thus, by virtue of the MFN clause in the Spain-Argentina BIT, Maffezini could directly initiate the proceeding before international arbitration institutions. As a result, ICSID allowed Maffezini to file his claim directly to the tribunal, superseding the local courts' requirement.[67] The usage of an

60. 5 J.H.W. Verzijl, *International Law in Historical Perspective*, 429–438 (1972).
61. 2, *Draft Articles on most-favored-nation clauses with commentaries*, Y.B. of the Int'l. L. Comm'n, pt. 2, Art. 7 (1978).
62. *United Kingdom v. Iran*, I.C.J. Reports 1952 p. 93.
63. *MTD Equity Sdn Bhd and MTD Chile SA v. Republic of Chile*, ICSID Case No. ARB/01/7 (25 May 2004).
64. *Emilio Agustin Maffezini v. The Kingdom of Spain*, ICSID Case No ARB/97/7 (25 January 2000).
65. *Supra* n. 22, 137.
66. *Supra* n. 64.
67. *Ibid.*, 8.

MFN clause for importing the 'effective means' provision is so widely accepted that tribunals have termed it *lex specialis* in customary international law.[68]

In contrast, multiple cases exist where the tribunal has refused to allow the claimants to import dispute resolution provisions from other treaties.[69] One such case is *Plama Consortium Ltd v. Republic of Bulgaria,*[70] where Bulgaria and Cyprus had signed a BIT providing for international arbitration in its dispute settlement clause. Although the investor referred to other BITs in which Bulgaria had allowed for international arbitration directly, the tribunal rejected the investor's argument. The tribunal deciphered from the wording of the MFN clause that it could apply with respect to all matters dealt with by the basic treaty. But the tribunal decided that the dispute settlement provision could not be assumed in an MFN clause without it being explicitly specified.

Telenor v. Hungary[71] reached a similar result. In that case, the tribunal stated that it was the commercial intent of the contracting parties that matters most.[72] Always claiming a wider interpretation of an MFN clause by investors would require tribunals to ignore the general policy considerations concerning investor protection and the dispute resolution mechanism specifically negotiated by the parties.[73] An investor cannot always argue a wider interpretation of an MFN clause. An MFN clause in the basic investment treaty does not incorporate by reference, in whole or in part, provisions relating to the jurisdiction of the arbitral tribunal set forth in another investment treaty, unless there is an unequivocal provision to that effect in the basic investment treaty.[74] Further, the tribunal held that contracting states cannot be presumed to have agreed that those provisions can be enlarged by incorporating dispute resolution provisions from other treaties negotiated in an entirely different context.[75]

These cases holistically discuss the interpretation of the MFN clause by various tribunals across the world. There is no uniformity in precedents about allowing the importation of the clause.

[B] Suitability of MFN Clause in India's Current Investment Regime

A discussion of the Indian law in this regard and the specificity that India should consider when drafting an MFN clause is now necessary. A BIT with an MFN clause is preferred by investors because it entitles them to import the substantive and procedural

68. *Legal Authority CLA-60, Chevron Corporation (USA) v. The Republic of Ecuador*, UNCITRAL, PCA Case No. 34877, para. 242 (30 March 2010).
69. *Salini Costruttori SpA and Italstrade SpA v. Jordan*, ICSID Case No ARB/02/13, 118–119 (9 November 2004).
70. *Plama Consortium Limited v. Republic of Bulgaria*, ICSID Case No. ARB/03/24 (27 August 2018).
71. *Telenor Mobile Communications A.S. v. The Republic of Hungary*, ICSID Case No. ARB/04/15 49–54 (13 September 2006).
72. *Ibid.*
73. *Ibid.*
74. *Supra* n. 41, para. 223.
75. *Ibid.*, para. 207.

clauses provided in another treaty by the host state.[76] For this reason, emerging and developing nations such as India had provided for it in order to attract FDI. An MFN clause was previously present in Article 4(1) & (2) of the 2003 India BIT, which stated:

> Each Contracting Party shall accord to investments of investors of the other Contracting Party, treatment which shall not be less favourable than that accorded either to investments of its own or investments of investors of any third state. Further, each contracting party shall accord to investors of the other contracting party, including in respect of returns on their investments, treatment which shall not be less favourable than that accorded to investors of any third state.[77]

This provision does not exist in the 2015 India BIT. Thus, an MFN clause does not exist in India's BIA with ITA[78] and TECC, the Investment Cooperation and Facilitation Treaty signed between Brazil[79] and India or in the India-Belarus BIT.[80]

The drastic change of removing the MFN clause from the 2015 India BIT might prevent investors from treaty-shopping, but it will also be unappealing to the investors who could have used it appropriately and for legitimate reasons. Additionally, as pointed out in the Law Commission of India in its 260th report,[81] the absence of an MFN clause is not a welcome change because it does not provide protection against the discriminatory treatment of foreign investors. Although the 2015 India BIT does not include an MFN clause, it can be stipulated in the Model BIT for the benefit of investors. There can be two approaches in this regard, viz. the restricted approach and the prospective approach. Under the restricted approach, certain substantive or procedural clauses are culled out from an MFN clause as exceptions so that the intent of the contracting parties in a BIT is not affected. As discussed earlier, in *White Industries*, the investors had used an MFN clause in a way that was fundamentally in contradiction with the basic intention of the contracting parties or in a manner that could affect the substantive content of the BIT significantly. Under the restrictive approach, specific articles to which an MFN clause may not apply must be mentioned in the model as exceptions. This approach is reflected in the Joint Interpretation Notes on the Agreement between the Government of the Republic of India and the Government of the People's Republic of Bangladesh for the Promotion and Protection of Investments (JIN).[82] The note on the interpretation of national treatment and MFN under the JIN states:

---

76. *Maffezini v. Spain* (2000) 5 ICSID Reports 396; (2004) 40 ILM 1129.
77. *Supra* n. 10, Art. 4(1) & (2).
78. Bilateral Investment Treaty between the India Taipei Association in Taipei and the Taipei Economic and Cultural Centre in India, signed on 18 December 2018, https://dea.gov.in/sites/default/files/BIA%20between%20ITA%20and%20TECC.pdf.
79. Investment Cooperation and Facilitation Treaty between the Federative Republic of Brazil and the Republic of India signed on 25 January 2020, https://dea.gov.in/sites/default/files/Investment%20Cooperation%20and%20Facilitation%20Treaty%20with%20Brazil%20-%20English_0.pdf.
80. Treaty between the Republic of Belarus and the Republic of India of Investments, signed on 24 September 2018, https://dea.gov.in/sites/default/files/BIT%20with%20Belarus.pdf.
81. Government of India, Law Commission of India, Report No. 260 *Analysis of the 2015 Draft Model Indian Bilateral Investment Treaty* (August 2015).
82. *Supra* n. 53, Art. 4.

The MFN and national treatment provisions under Article 4 are designed to protect against illegitimate and intentional discrimination against an investment, or investor with respect to its investment, on the basis of nationality.

a) The Contracting Parties further affirm that MFN obligation is not intended to alter the Agreement's substantive content by, for example, permitting piece-meal incorporation of and reliance on provisions found in other treaties, investment or otherwise;
b) For greater certainty, the Contracting Parties note their agreement that MFN obligation provided under Article 4 does not apply to the mechanism for settlement of investment disputes contained in this Agreement or to other procedural and jurisdictional issues under any circumstance.

India can use this restrictive approach when it comes to the drafting of an MFN clause that plays an imperative role in persuading the foreign investors towards FDI. Additionally, because periodic reviews[83] of the BITs are possible even after signing a BIT under Article 36[84] of the 2015 India BIT, India can still look to rely on an MFN clause through the incorporation of the post-establishment exception.

Apart from having a restrictive approach, India should have a prospective approach as well in its MFN clauses. In this approach, the usage of an MFN clause will be applicable from a point in time (a designated date/event), and the BITs signed before such a designated date/event cannot be used for importing a provision by virtue of an MFN clause. This application of the clause is limited to investment treaties and other agreements entered into by India. Usually, an MFN clause is used by an investor to bring to a tribunal any provision of any previous BIT signed by the host state with any other investor. Instead of following the usual approach, if the 2015 India BIT had included a prospective MFN clause and followed it in its future BITs and other agreements, the clause would be available in a limited manner.

The wording of such a proposed clause could be:

Investments made by investors of either Contracting Party in the territory of the other Contracting Party shall receive treatment which is fair and equitable, and not less favourable than that accorded to investments made by investors of any third state post the bringing into force of the 2015 India Model BIT.

Pursuant to such a provision, an investor would not be allowed to use the provisions or rights granted to investors in the treaties signed before 2016 with India. The reason for making the clause prospective and asserting the designated date to be the date on which the Model BIT was revised is because since that date only two agreements containing a restricted MFN clause were entered into by India. This limitation protects the host state (India) from investors using the wider MFN clauses that were entered into by India prior to the revision of the Model BIT. Therefore, this approach gives India an opportunity to carefully determine the usage of an MFN clause in the future and limit the extent to which the clause can be used.

83. *Supra* n. 31, Art. 36.3.
84. *Ibid.*, Art. 36.

It is our suggestion that India should consider having a prospective and restrictive MFN clause that excludes its importation from previously signed BITs and also prohibits its application to dispute resolution retrospectively. This would ensure that investors do not incorrectly use an MFN clause for dispute resolution, but at the same time, they are not devoid of the benefits of using MFN clauses for other valid claims (such as expropriation). Consequently, foreign investors would not indulge in treaty-shopping and also would be treated in a non-discriminatory manner.[85] Moreover, following this concept would facilitate the country in its development and the promotion of FDI.

§4.04 SHOULD INDIA BE A MEMBER OF THE ICSID?

Developing and developed nations are interdependent for the benefit of investment and trade. Despite having plenty of natural resources, developing nations are often dependent on the capital contribution by foreign investors (mostly from developed nations) to boost their economic performance and growth. Concurrently, it is financially prudent for a developed nation to invest in a developing nation because costs incurred in these destinations are lower. As a result of such intermingling of developed and developing nations, disputes naturally may arise between them. While arbitration is the preferred choice for most investors, they might find it difficult to enforce awards.

In India, the law governing the enforcement of both domestic and international arbitral awards is the Arbitration Act. However, Indian courts have had differing opinions regarding the applicability of the Arbitration Act in the enforcement of investment arbitration awards. While the Calcutta High Court in *Louis Dreyfus Armatures*[86] allowed the application of the Arbitration Act to investment arbitration awards, the Delhi High Court in *Vodafone*[87] and *Khaitan Holdings*[88] held that the Arbitration Act cannot be applied to investment arbitration awards because they are not commercial in nature. Thus, investors are not guaranteed that they will be able to enforce an award under the Indian law. This jeopardizes enforcement of awards even under the New York Convention,[89] despite India being a signatory. For an obligation to arise under the New York Convention, it may require statutory implementation by the state that is required to enforce the award. While India has adopted the New York Convention in Part II of the Arbitration Act, in keeping with the Delhi Court judgment, it cannot be applied to investment arbitration awards. Even though this judgment is not binding on other courts, it is persuasive. Besides, India has adopted a commercial reservation under Article I.3 of the New York Convention, by virtue of which enforcement can be sought only for commercial disputes.[90]

---

85. UNCTAD, Most Favoured Nation Treatment, *UNCTAD Series on Issues in International Investment Agreements* II, 60, 111 (2010).
86. *Board of Trustees of the Port of Kolkata v. Louis Dreyfus Armatures*, 2014 SCC Online Cal 17695.
87. *Union of India v. Vodafone Group PLC United Kingdom & Anr.*, 2017 SCC Online Del 9930.
88. *Union of India v. Khaitan Holdings (Mauritius) Ltd & Ors*, 2019 SCC Online Del 6755.
89. Convention on the Recognition and Enforcement of Arbitral Awards, 1958.
90. s. 44, Arbitration and Conciliation Act 1996.

Because the enforcement of investment arbitration awards under Indian law and the New York Convention can be problematic, India could look to the ICSID. Currently, India is not a member of ICSID and has not ratified the ICSID Convention. But ICSID inevitably has a prominent role in the ISDS system. The growth of investment treaty arbitrations has surged in the last decade, as can be seen in the statistics highlighting the number of ICSID cases. The latest *ICSID Caseload – Statistics* indicates that the number of cases registered from 2000 to 2019 under the ICSID Convention and Additional Facility Rules is 676,[91] which shows the importance of ICSID. Thus, ICSID is one of the preferred destinations for foreign investors. It would be consistent with India's aspirations as a capital-importing state to be a member of ICSID.

In any case, under Article 16.1[92] of the 2015 India BIT, an investor having exhausted local remedies may submit a claim to arbitration under the Additional Facility Rules of ICSID. Even though India is not a member of the ICSID, a dispute can be raised against India by a foreign investor that is a member of the ICSID under the Additional Facility Rules of ICSID. This shows India's willingness to utilize ICSID's facilities. However, because India is not a signatory to the ICSID Convention, it is not bound by Article 54(1)[93] of the ICSID Convention that requires states to recognize the award as binding.

Thus, foreign investors will find enforcement of international investment arbitration claims difficult in India. India can make enforcement of such awards investor-friendly if: (a) the Supreme Court of India decides that the term 'award' under the Arbitration Act includes international investment arbitration awards; (b) the Government of India amends the Arbitration Act to make it applicable to the enforcement of investment arbitration awards; or (c) India ratifies the ICSID Convention and implements it through national legislation so that investors can enforce awards under the

91. *The ICSID Caseload – Statistics Issue 2020-1*, International Centre for Settlement of Investment Disputes https://icsid.worldbank.org/en/Documents/resources/The%20ICSID%20Caseload%20Statistics%202020-1%20Edition-ENG.pdf.
92. *Supra* n. 31, Art. 16.1, states:

> A disputing investor who meets the conditions precedent provided for in Article 15 may submit the claim to arbitration under:
>
> (a) the ICSID Convention, provided that both the Parties full members of the Convention;
> (b) the Additional Facility Rules of ICSID, provided that either Party, but not both, is a member of the ICSID Convention; or
> (c) the UNCITRAL Arbitration Rules.

93. Article 54(1) of the ICSID Convention, International Centre for Settlement of Investment Disputes, 2003, states:

> Each Contracting State shall recognize an award rendered pursuant to this Convention as binding and enforce the pecuniary obligations imposed by that award within its territories as if it were a final judgment of a court in that State. A Contracting State with a federal constitution may enforce such an award in or through its federal courts and may provide that such courts shall treat the award as if it were a final judgment of the courts of a constituent state.

convention. While Indian courts have had a pro-arbitration approach in the enforcement of international commercial arbitration awards, its approach towards the enforcement of investment arbitration awards is not the same. Therefore, India should either bring about a change in its arbitration law or become a member of ICSID and provide for the implementation of the ICSID Convention under its national legislation.

§4.05 CONCLUSION

Until 2015, India did not mandate the exhaustion of local remedies before a claim could be submitted before an arbitral tribunal. Because of a broad dispute resolution clause and an MFN clause, India faced adverse decisions and this resulted in a change in India's investment policies. This change is reflected in the 2015 India BIT and in investment agreements entered into post-2015.

After the revision of its model BIT, India started requiring investors to exhaust local remedies. It even terminated BITs that included a broad dispute resolution clause. The problem does not lie in mandating the exhaustion of local remedies. What is problematic is the complex, multi-tiered dispute resolution provision in the 2015 India BIT that requires the investor to first spend five years in the domestic courts of the host state and then another six months in negotiation, at which stage negotiations are likely to fail. The five-and-a-half-year period before an arbitration proceeding can begin is far too long and will not be commercially viable for both parties. Accordingly, even if India wants to mandate exhaustion of local remedies, the specified period should be closer to the eighteen-month period that is generally followed. India must also ensure that its judicial system is equipped to deal with such high-value cases and that there is no inordinate delay in the delivery of justice.

Regarding the MFN clause in the 2015 India BIT, there is an international inconsistency in the application of the clause in dispute resolution. Host states could argue that the importation of a dispute resolution clause by an MFN clause defeats the objective of the treaty and the commercial intent of the parties. Nevertheless, for India, the MFN clause need not be done away with completely. India can adopt a restrictive and prospective MFN clause, to protect the interest of host states and at the same time extend equitable treatment to investors in its territory.

Thus, the duration for which India mandates the exhaustion of local remedies should not be as long as five years. A shorter, more reasonable period is preferable. If Indian courts are not able to resolve disputes within the specified time, investors should have the option of commencing arbitration. An investor should not be able to bypass the requirement to exhaust local remedies by importing an arbitration clause of an older BIT under the MFN clause. A restrictive and prospective MFN clause will ensure that such an importation cannot occur, thus ensuring that India is able to balance the interests of the host state and the investor without compromising its sovereignty or being anti-arbitration.

CHAPTER 5

Chronicles of Middle East in Investor-State Arbitration: Autopsy of Prevalent Practice Trends and Future Epidemic Challenges

Mohamed H. Negm

Middle East States have had an active participation in investor-State dispute settlement (ISDS) over the past three decades. New investment treaties have been negotiated and grand plans for reform have been deliberated. This chapter provides an overview of Middle East States' investment treaty practice and experience with ISDS thus far. Before turning to the kernel of the subject, the chapter starts by recapping the rights and guarantees Middle Eastern States have traditionally agreed to accord foreign investors, which form the bases of those claims brought against host States. The chapter then discusses the framework of investor-State arbitration and analyses investment arbitration under Middle East multilateral and regional treaties. Finally, the chapter addresses the debate surrounding the future of ISDS by focusing in particular on the positions expressed by Middle East States and their contributions to ISDS reform.

§5.01 INTRODUCTION

International investment law's origins and purpose have generated divisive opinions. Some argue it developed as a method to protect colonial interests in the wealth of States emerging from colonialism.[1] An 1864 arbitration between the Suez Canal Company

1. D. Schniederman, *The Global Regime of Investor Rights: Return to standards of Civilised Justice?* (2014) 5(1) *Transnational Legal Theory* 60, in K. Miles (ed.), The Origins of International Investment Law: Empire, Environment, and the Safeguarding of Capital (Cambridge University Press, 2013).

and the Khedivate State of Egypt is considered by some as one of the first investor-State arbitrations.[2] Others argue that international investment law emanates from fundamental principles of diplomatic protection and good faith in commercial contracts (*pacta sunt servanda*).[3] Some dismiss the interpretation of the system as protecting the interests of the Global North at the expense of the Global South as illusory. Instead, they highlight the important role international investment law plays in economic growth, particularly for developing States, thus equalizing global economic and power structures.[4] With all that being said, on any view, international investment law is now a firmly established and burgeoning international legal regime.

The first investment arbitral award issued under a bilateral investment treaty (BIT) and the Washington Convention was in *AAPL v. Sri Lanka* in 1990.[5] A large number of claims – 983 – as of February 2020, have been brought since then.[6] The most prominent of these claims have historically coincided with often cataclysmic, sociopolitical and economic fluctuations. Today, the very existence of an international investment arbitration regime is the subject of a multifaceted polemic, involving practitioners, academics, politicians and civil society.

Predominantly composed of capital-importing States, the Middle East region has attracted a significant number of claims where host States' conduct vis-à-vis investors from capital-exporting home countries was scrutinized before international arbitral tribunals. The recent political upheaval that swept through the region brought a fresh wave of cases, which most notably shed light on an increasingly burgeoning practice of intra-Middle East ISDS. This highlights its importance for the protection of intra-Middle East investments and, by the same token, debunks the North-South divide so often associated with ISDS. To that effect, several cases have been brought by Middle Eastern investors against Middle East States (Egypt, Jordan, Sudan and Yemen) on the basis of BITs. The existence of such intra-Middle East disputes signals that investors have come to realize that they too can rely on BITs to protect their investments abroad.

This chapter explores Middle East States' investment treaty practice and experience with ISDS thus far. It provides an analysis of the rights and guarantees accorded to foreign investors by Middle Eastern States. The chapter also discusses the framework of investor-State arbitration and analyses investment arbitration under Middle East multilateral and regional treaties. It further addresses the debate surrounding the future

2. The arbitration related to various issues surrounding the construction of the Suez Canal, which was completed in 1869, including most notably Egypt's decision to suspend the project's forced labour regime. *See* J. Web Yackee, *The First Investor-State Arbitration: The Suez Canal Company v. Egypt (1864)*, 17 J. World Investment & Trade 401 (2016).
3. For example, G. van Harten, *Investment Treaty Arbitration and Public Law* (Oxford University Press, 2007); Z. Douglas, *The Hybrid Foundations of Investment Treaty Arbitration*, 74 Brit. YB Int'l L. 151 (2004).
4. R. Dolzer and C. Schreuer, *Principles of International Investment Law* (Oxford University Press, 2nd ed., 2012).
5. *Asian Agricultural Products Ltd v. Republic of Sri Lanka*, ICSID Case No. ARB/87/3, Award 27 June 1990. The esteemed Egyptian Prof. Ahmad Sadek El-Kosheri presided over the tribunal.
6. UNCTAD, *Investment Dispute Settlement Navigator*, accessible at: http://investmentpolicyhub.unctad.org/ISDS.

of ISDS by focusing in particular on the positions expressed by Middle East States and their contributions to ISDS reform.

§5.02 EVOLUTION OF INVESTMENT TREATIES AND ISDS PROVISIONS IN THE MIDDLE EAST

International investment law seeks to protect foreign investors while taking due regard of host States' police powers to act in the public interest. The historic aim of that protection was to provide a minimum standard of treatment in accordance with international, as opposed to domestic, standards. This aim has been criticized on several grounds, including its unequal protection of traditionally capital-exporting States to the detriment of traditionally capital-importing States, particularly on the basis that it effectively guarantees more robust protections to foreign investments than it does to local investments.[7]

The countries of the Middle East region have been taking part for many years in the global trend of concluding BITs. Indeed, Egypt is the fifth most prolific State worldwide for concluding such treaties, with over one hundred BITs signed. Other Middle East countries that have been in the forefront of concluding BITs include Jordan, Morocco and Kuwait. Traditionally, the Gulf Cooperation Council (GCC) countries, with the exception of Kuwait, have relied less heavily on BITs. This may reflect the fact that as resource-rich countries, these States felt less compelled to enter into such binding agreements. Nevertheless, the interest of GCC countries in securing the investments of their nationals in different parts of the world has given these countries a strong incentive to conclude BITs. It may also not be a complete coincidence that Kuwait, which has the largest number of BITs from among Gulf States, is also the largest capital exporter in this region. Interestingly, the BITs concluded between Arab Middle Eastern countries in Arabic contain provisions similar to those concluded between countries from other regions of the world in other languages. These typically include provisions on non-discrimination, fair and equitable treatment (FET), full protection and security (FPS), and compensation in case of expropriation. They also contain provisions on ISDS.

[A] First Generation Treaties: A Perilous Path to Pass

Generally, international investment agreements offer two types of protection; substantive and procedural. Substantive rights refer to the standards and principles pursuant to which contracting States must comply when dealing with foreign investments or investors. Through procedural rights, investors of the contracting parties can access international ISDS mechanisms to resolve disputes with the contracting State hosting their investment(s). This subsection outlines the parameters of these substantive and procedural rights and provide a brief insight into their content.

7. This is epitomized by the BIT claims brought by dual nationals against one of their home States.

[1] Substantive Rights and Guarantees

Substantive rights provided in international investment agreements are often considered indeterminate and vague. Their content is therefore the subject of extensive debate.[8] A cornerstone of international investment law is the protection against nationalization or expropriation. A typical example of this right appears in the BIT between Bahrain and Yemen, which provides as follows:

> Investments of nationals or companies of either Contracting Party shall not be nationalised, expropriated or subjected to measures having effect equivalent to nationalisation or expropriation in the territory of the other Contracting Party except for a public purpose in accordance with law on a non-discriminatory basis and with adequate, effective and prompt compensation. Such compensation shall amount to the genuine value of the investment expropriated immediately before the expropriation or before the impending expropriation became public knowledge, whichever is the earlier, and such compensation shall be paid without unreasonable delay, be effectively realisable and freely transferable.[9]

The FET standard is considered one of the most important rights in international investment law. It is the right most frequently invoked in ISDS by investors, although the content of this right may vary significantly from one treaty to the next. For example, the BIT between Egypt and Oman provides that 'Each Contracting Party shall accord fair and equitable treatment to the investments of the investors of the other Contracting Party.'[10] In contrast, the BIT between Oman and Morocco states that 'Each Contracting Party, in accordance with the principles of international law, shall provide fair and equitable treatment to the investment of investors of the other Contracting Party within its territory.'[11]

The content of FET is considered by some as notoriously indeterminate,[12] and a large number of cases have grappled with its meaning and scope and its relationship with the minimum standard of treatment under customary international law. In this regard, not every act of State or governmental measure with an adverse impact on the investor will constitute a violation of FET. This is especially true where the validity of the procedure or measure in question is upheld before the local courts. For example, the tribunal in *Fouad Alghanim v. Jordan* stated that 'A governmental authority cannot

8. Farouk El-Hosseny and Ruba Ghandour, *Investor-State Dispute-Settlement in the Arab World: Is There a Clear Path For*, 10 Int'l J. Arab Arb. 8 (2018).
9. The Agreement between the Government of Bahrain and the Republic of Yemen for the Promotion and Protection of Investments, signed on 28 December 2002, and entered into force on 2 June 2004, Art. 4(1).
10. The Agreement between the Arab Republic of Egypt and Sultanate of Oman for the Promotion and Protection of Investments, signed on 25 February 1998 and entered into force on 25 March 1998, Art. 3(2).
11. The Agreement between the Sultanate of Oman and the Government of the Kingdom of Morocco for the Reciprocal Promotion and Protection of Investments, signed on 8 May 2001, and entered into force on 3 March 2003, Art. 2(1).
12. With the European Parliament being particularly vocal in its criticism of this use of vague language, *see* European Parliament Resolution of 6 April 2011 on the Future European International Investment Policy.

be faulted for acting in a manner validated by its courts, unless the conduct of the courts themselves constitutes a breach of treaty.'[13]

The investor in that case was unable to establish any violations of the Jordan-Kuwait BIT[14] primarily, though not exclusively, because of its inability to substantiate a claim for a denial of justice perpetrated by the Jordanian courts. The FET standard encompasses the international law concept of denial of justice. The tribunal in this dispute found that the Jordanian Court of Cassation did not act in an arbitrary manner such that its decision was one 'that no reasonably competent tribunal could reach'.[15] The tribunal also found that the Court of Cassation was not politically motivated in coming to its decision, nor did it act in bad faith, thereby undermining a claim for a violation of FET.

Despite attempts to narrow the scope and application of FET, the expansive interpretation applied by several tribunals to the content of FET remains controversial. Some argue that this approach would restrict the host State's ability to enact policies necessary to protect the public interest, specifically as it relates to environmental protection, public health, and human rights. This has prompted some States to carefully define the scope of FET in more recently concluded investment treaties (second-generation treaties).[16]

Another common standard of protection is the FPS standard.[17] Its content is often derived from general principles of international law. For example, the BIT between the United Arab Emirates (UAE) and Sudan provides that 'Investments of investors of each of the Contracting Parties shall enjoy full protection and security in the territory of the other Contracting Party in a manner consistent with the recognised principles of international law and those of this treaty.'[18] The traditional understanding of the scope of FPS is physical protection or the protection of an investor's person or property.[19] While some have extended the scope of this protection to also encompass legal protection, this has been criticized by a number of tribunals.[20] Some States have

13. *Fouad Alghanim & Sons Co. for General Trading & Contracting, W.L.L. and Fouad Mohammed Thunyan Alghanim v. Hashemite Kingdom of Jordan*, ICSID Case No. ARB/13/38, Award of the Tribunal, 14 December 2017, para. 318; *See also Robert Azinian, Kenneth Davitian, & Ellen Baca v. The United Mexican States*, ICSID Case No. ARB (AF)/97/2, para. 98.
14. The Agreement between the Government of the Hashemite Kingdom of Jordan and the Government of the State of Kuwait for the Encouragement and Protection of Investments, signed on 21 May 2001 and entered into force on 19 March 2004.
15. *Fouad Alghanim & Sons Co. for General Trading & Contracting, W.L.L. and Fouad Mohammed Thunyan Alghanim v. Hashemite Kingdom of Jordan*, ICSID Case No. ARB/13/38, Award of the Tribunal, 14 December 2017, para. 479.
16. M. Sornarajah, *The International Law on Foreign Investment* 109–1101 (Cambridge University Press, 3d ed., 2010); *Bilcon of Delaware Inc., et al. v. Government of Canada* (UNCITRAL), Dissenting Opinion of Prof. Donald McRae, 10 March 2015, paras 48, 51.
17. For more information on the content and application of the principle of FPS, *see* C. Schreuer, *Full Protection and Security*, 1 J. Int'l Dispute Settlement 353 (2010).
18. The Agreement between the UAE and the Republic of Sudan for the Reciprocal Promotion and Protection of Investments, signed on 18 February 2001 and entered into force on 3 April 2002, Art. 3(1).
19. *Asian Agricultural Products Ltd. v. Republic of Sri Lanka*, ICSID Case No. ARB/87/3, Award, 27 June 1990, para. 67.
20. *Saluka Investments B.V. v. The Czech Republic (UNCITRAL)*, Partial Award, dated 17 March 2006, paras 483–484.

clarified and defined the scope of FPS in second-generation treaties, limiting it to physical protection only.[21]

Most Middle East treaties provide for a most-favoured-nation (MFN) clause, through which a contracting State accords the investors of the other contracting State treatment no less favourable than that accorded to investors of a third State.[22] Seeing as an investor can rely on any provision in any other treaty concluded by the host State through the MFN clause (including the dispute resolution clause), some States have begun clarifying the scope of this clause in more recently concluded treaties.

Some treaties also enshrine other substantive protections such as the host State's duty to respect and observe commitments made or obligations assumed in relation to an investment protected under treaty. These include contractual, legislative, or regulatory commitments (the so-called umbrella clause).[23] Another substantive right is the free transfer of capital, profit, dividends, fees and salaries.[24]

[2] Procedural Rights and Guarantees

Procedural rights in international investment law refer primarily to dispute resolution. International investment agreements generally guarantee foreign investors access to local courts or to international arbitration in order to resolve their disputes with host States.[25] The arbitration procedure takes place without interference from an investor's home State and without recourse to the international law of diplomatic protection (which often led to the abuses of 'Gunboat diplomacy'), because it is an individual investor's *direct* right. For this reason, international arbitration is widely perceived as an effective method for resolving such disputes, one that accounts for modern developments in international dispute resolution.

Generally, international investment agreements provide for the right of an investor to resort to arbitration by accepting the State's standing offer to arbitrate contained in the dispute resolution clause in the applicable treaty. The Tunisia-Lebanon BIT contains a standard dispute resolution clause:

21. G. Foster, *Recovering 'Protection and Security': The Treaty standard's Obscure Origins, Forgotten Meaning, and Key Current Significance*, 45 Vanderbilt J. Trans. L. 1095, 1099 (2012).
22. *See*, for example, the Agreement on the Reciprocal Promotion and Protection of Investments between the Lebanese Republic and the Sultanate of Oman, signed on 11 April 2006 and entered into force on 20 October 2008, Art. 3(2).
23. *See*, for example, the Agreement between the Government of the UAE and the Government of the Kingdom of Morocco on the Reciprocal Promotion and Protection of Investments, signed on 24 April 2001 and entered into force on 1 June 1998, Art. 6.
24. *See*, for example, the Agreement between the Arab Republic of Egypt and the Government of the Kingdom of Morocco for the Promotion and Protection of Investments, signed on 14 May 1997 and entered into force on 1 June 1998, Art. 6.
25. A number of investment agreements provide for the possibility of resorting to conciliation or to the creation of an institutional court, such as the Arab Court for Investment that was created pursuant to the Unified Arab Investment Agreement. For more information on the Arab Investment Court, *see* Mohamed S. Abdel Wahab, *A Study of the Arab Investment Agreement*, 19 J. Int'l Arb. 60–72 (2013).

1. Disputes relating to investments between a Contracting Party and an investor of the other Contracting Party shall, so far as possible, be settled through negotiations between the two concerned parties with a view to resolving the dispute amicably.
2. If such negotiations fail to resolve the dispute within six months from the date at which a written request for settlement, the investor may submit the dispute, upon his/her discretion, to:
   a. the competent court of the Contracting State in whose territory the investment is made; or
   b. in accordance with the special chapter on the resolution of disputes under the Unified Agreement for the Investment of Arab capital in the Arab States of 1980; or
   c. ICSID, as created under the Washington Convention, in the event that both parties become contracting States/members to this agreement; or
   d. the ICSID Additional Facility rules, subject to the disputing Contracting Party, or the Contracting Party to which the investor belongs, is party to the Washington Convention (and not both); or
   e. an ad hoc tribunal constituted for this purpose in accordance with the UNCITRAL arbitration rules.[26]

While most international investment agreements contain a dispute resolution clause referring to international arbitration, its formulation is far from uniform. Further, most treaties provide for some form of institutional arbitral proceedings. The most popular has been the International Centre for Settlement of Investment Disputes (ICSID) as an administering authority. Almost 55% of investment treaty disputes are resolved through ICSID arbitration, with 31% through ad hoc arbitration under the United Nations Commission for International Trade Law (UNCITRAL) arbitration rules,[27] which can be administered by the Permanent Court of Arbitration (PCA) in The Hague. International investment arbitrations proceed in accordance with the recognized principles of international commercial arbitration, including the freedom to appoint the arbitrators, with the attendant right to object to their appointment on the basis of independence and impartiality.

Traditionally, arbitral proceedings are conducted in private, which has made arbitration the preferred method of dispute resolution for parties wary of disclosing sensitive information in investment and commercial disputes. Indeed, several international treaty arbitrations proceed entirely in private, without any public awareness as to the existence of a dispute, save in the event of the occasional leak. This has given rise to questions of legitimacy in the ISDS regime, which has been criticized as a system of

26. The Agreement between the Lebanese Republic and the Government of the Republic of Tunisia on the Reciprocal Promotion and Protection of Investments, signed on 24 June 1998 and entered into force on 4 June 2000, Art. 7.
27. The remaining cases are conducted pursuant to the ICSID Additional Facility Rules (6%), the Stockholm Chamber of Commerce (SCC) (5%), and, finally, the International Chamber of Commerce (ICC) (2%), *see* UNCTAD, IIA Issues Note: Special Update on Investor-State Dispute Settlement: Facts and Figures, November 2017, p. 5, accessible at: http://unctad.org/en/PublicationsLibrary/diaepcb2017d7_en.pdf.

justice administered 'behind closed doors'.[28] This criticism has been fuelled by the fact that investment arbitrations often involve matters of public concern, not only in terms of the application of substantive principles and its effect on regulatory powers but also in terms of the investments themselves, which often relate to life-sustaining resources such as water or electricity. Some have criticized this form of dispute resolution as effectively a 'method of public law adjudication' conflicting with 'cherished principles of judicial accountability and independence in democratic societies'. This view outlines investment treaty arbitration as a public law system that goes beyond all other forms of international adjudication in giving arbitrators a comprehensive jurisdiction to determine the legality of sovereign acts and to award public funds to businesses that sustain alleged loss as a result of government regulation. The system allows public law to be interpreted by arbitrators in private as a matter of course with limited scope for judicial review.[29]

[B] Transformation of the Treaties Signed by Middle East States

Treaties signed by States in recent years have undergone a notable transformation. Changes have been made to both substantive and procedural provisions. In terms of substantive rights, States are capable of directly amending the content of their provisions, often on a bilateral basis, subject only to bargaining power and diminishing inequities in international legal sophistication. Procedural rights, on the other hand, have attracted broader institutional interest, and consequently require a multilateral, consensus-led campaign.

In theory, a host State will not be responsible for any measures taken in good faith in the public interest, pursuant to its police powers, so long as such measures are proportionate to that aim, are applied without discrimination and without violating any specific undertakings accorded to or agreed with a foreign investor.[30] Nonetheless, the imprecise drafting of some substantive standards has led to expansive interpretations that, at times, have been criticized as unjustifiably disciplining States and unduly restricting their exercise of public powers. It has also led to arbitral tribunals interpreting these provisions inconsistently.[31] Many States have been careful to include discreet content in substantive protections in more recently concluded treaties in order to avoid

28. G. Kaufmann-Kohler and M. Potestà, *Can the Mauritius Convention Serve as a Model for the Reform of Investor-State Arbitration in Connection with the Introduction of a Permanent Investment Tribunal or an Appeal Mechanism?*, Geneva Centre for International Dispute Settlement, 14 (2016). *See generally*, D. Euler et al. (eds), *Transparency in International Investment Arbitration: A Guide to the UNCITRAL Rules on Transparency in Treaty-Based Investor-State Arbitration* (Cambridge University Press, 2015).
29. *See* Gus Van Harten, *Investment Treaty Arbitration and Public Law* (Oxford University Press, 2008).
30. Newcombe, Andrew and Lius Paradell, *Law and Practice of Investment Treaties: standards of Treatment* (Kluwer Law International, 2009), 358; *Saluka Investments BV v. The Czech Republic* (UNCITRAL), Partial Award, 17 March 2006, para. 255.
31. A. Martinez, *Invoking State Defences in Investment Treaty Arbitration*, in M. Waibel et al. (eds), The Backlash against Investment Arbitration (Wolters Kluwer, 2010), 326.

such inconsistencies, increase the predictability and coherence of ISDS and international investment law, and reduce any potential encroachment on public powers.

For example, the BIT between Iraq and Kuwait, signed in 2013, provides for 'Exceptions' to substantive protections, clarifying that 'Each Contracting party may take any necessary measures to protect its national security, including ... arrangements [measures] necessary to protect the environment from pollution.'[32] In the same vein, the BIT between Egypt and Mauritius, signed in 2014, provides under the title 'Security Exceptions' as follows:

> Subject to the requirement that such measures are not applied in an arbitrary or discriminatory manner or constitute a disguised restriction on investors and investments, nothing in this Agreement shall be construed to prevent either Contracting Party from taking measures to fulfil its obligations with respect to the protection of its essential security interests, the protection of public health or the prevention of diseases and pests in animals or plants.[33]

In another example, the BIT between Kuwait and Canada, signed in 2011, provides the following under its Article on 'General Exceptions':

> Subject to the requirement that such measures are not applied in a manner that would constitute arbitrary or unjustifiable discrimination between investments or between investors, or a disguised restriction on international trade or investment, nothing in this Agreement shall be construed to prevent a Party from adopting or enforcing measures necessary: (a) to protect human, animal or plant life or health; (b) to ensure compliance with laws and regulations that are not inconsistent with this Agreement; or (c) for the conservation of living or non-living exhaustible natural resources.[34]

Thus, many States – including Middle East States – have carefully preserved their ability to take measures in the public interest within their respective territories. The historic goal of international investment law has been the reciprocal protection and encouragement of investment along with providing States with the incentive to attract foreign investment inwards and ensure the protection of its outward investment. Nonetheless, international investment law has been criticized as demoting essential public functions in favour of foreign investor protection.[35] Today, given the scope and influence of such agreements, there has been a notable trend in second-generation treaties to rebalance government power and regulatory space to act in the public interest.

32. The Agreement between the Government of Iraq and the Government of Kuwait for the Reciprocal Promotion and Protection of Investments, signed on 6 December 2012, entered into force on 4 February 2015, Art. 13(7).
33. The Agreement between the Government of the Arab Republic of Egypt and the Government of the Republic of Mauritius on the Reciprocal Promotion and Protection of Investments, signed on 25 June 2014 and entered into force on 17 October 2014, Art. 13.
34. The Agreement between the State of Kuwait and Canada for the Promotion and Protection of Investments, signed on 26 September 2011 and entered into force on 19 February 2014, Art. 17(1).
35. *See generally* K. Vandevelde, *A Brief History of International Investment Agreements*, 12 UC Davis J. Int'l L. & Policy 157 (2005).

Further, as regards procedural rights and guarantees, greater focus has been placed on transparency in ISDS, starting with the 2006 amendment of the ICSID Arbitration Rules. Transparency can be manifested through public hearings, the publication of case files and the opportunity for third parties with a significant interest in the arbitration to participate in the proceedings as 'friends of the tribunal' (amicus curiae).[36] Since 2006, proceedings before ICSID take place with relative transparency where cases, names of arbitrators, and details of the procedure, at a *minimum*, are published on the ICSID website. The public also has the opportunity to attend hearings in a large number of cases. Further, ICSID intends to further enhance transparency through newly proposed rules, which are likely to be issued in 2020.[37] This surge in interest in transparency has also spread to other international institutions such as UNCITRAL, which released the UNCITRAL Rules on Transparency in Treaty-Based Investor-State Arbitration in 2014.[38] These Rules provide for transparency and accessibility to the public of treaty-based investor-State arbitration. It is also increasingly common to find procedural rules promoting transparency in new international investment agreements.

For example, the BIT between Oman and Japan includes many provisions aimed at enhancing the transparency of arbitral proceedings. For instance, it allows the disputing parties to publish all the files and exhibits in the case, including the arbitral award. In this regard, it is possible to redact confidential trade information or information that is legally privileged.[39] Notably, the same agreement clarifies that MFN does not apply as regards ISDS, such that an investor cannot rely on the dispute settlement clause in a third treaty in proceedings against the host State.[40] The BIT between Kuwait and Canada provides that the arbitral hearings must be open to the public (subject to tribunal discretion to hold in camera hearings if confidential information is to be discussed) and provides for the publication of case files and exhibits in their entirety.[41] It also allows third parties with a significant interest in the arbitration to participate in proceedings as amicus curiae.[42]

36. For more details regarding third-party interventions in international arbitration, *see* F. El-Hosseny, *Civil Society in Investment Treaty Arbitration: Status and Prospects* (Brill Nijhoff, 2018).
37. ICSID, *Backgrounder on Proposals for Amendment of the ICSID Rules*, 3 August 2018, accessible at: https://icsid.worldbank.org/en/Documents/Amendment_Backgrounder.pdf.
38. These rules apply to all ISDS governed by the UNCITRAL Rules brought under BITs signed after 1 April 2014. *See* UNCITRAL Rules on Transparency, Art. 1(1).
39. The Agreement between the Sultanate of Oman and Japan for the Reciprocal Promotion and Protection of Investment, signed on 19 June 2015 and entered into force on 21 January 2017, Art. 15(12).
40. *Ibid.*, Art. 4(1).
41. The Agreement between the State of Kuwait and Canada for the Promotion and Protection of Investments, signed on 26 September 2011 and entered into force on 19 February 2014, Art. 30.
42. *Ibid.*, Art. 31.

§5.03 FRAMEWORK OF INVESTOR-STATE ARBITRATION IN THE MIDDLE EAST

The Middle East States are parties to a growing number of 'South-South' BITs that in fact outnumber their 'North-South' ones.[43] Some of the BITs that have been entered into by Middle Eastern States refer to ICSID procedures. ICSID clauses may be found in BITs concluded by Middle East countries not only with developed countries but also with other developing countries, including Middle East countries. Indeed, in *Desert Line Projects LLC v. Republic of Yemen*,[44] which involved an Omani company, the basis of jurisdiction was an ICSID clause in the Oman-Yemen BIT 1998, which had been concluded in the Arabic language. In that case, the ICSID Tribunal held that the conduct of Yemen in pressuring the Omani investor to accept and execute a settlement agreement, instead of a final and binding Yemeni award, amounted to a breach of a provision of the Oman-Yemen BIT. The said provision imposed on both Oman and Yemen a duty to ensure 'fair and equitable treatment' for the investments of the other contracting State's investors, and to eschew 'legally unjustified measures'. *Desert Line v. Yemen* was not the first case submitted to ICSID involving a Middle Eastern State and a Middle Eastern investor. The first such case, and indeed the first 'South-South' ICSID arbitration, was *Ghaith Pharaon v. Republic of Tunisia*.[45] Unlike *Desert Line*, however, consent to ICSID jurisdiction in *Ghaith Pharaon* was based on an arbitration clause contained in an investment agreement concluded between the Saudi investor and Tunisia. The case ultimately was discontinued as a result of a settlement reached between the parties during the proceedings.

[A] Impact of the Arab Spring on Investment Arbitration Landscape

The Arab Spring erupted in Tunisia in December 2010 and quickly spread to Egypt, Libya, Yemen, Bahrain, and other countries of the Arab World in 2011 and 2012. The uprisings of the Arab Spring and the political changes resulting therefrom have had a quantifiable and significant impact on the international investment arbitration landscape with a surge of new investment cases filed against Arab States.[46] The number of newly filed ICSID cases from the Middle East did indeed rise sharply in the period from 2011 to 2019. While the respondent States from the region have become increasingly diverse, Egypt has remained the most frequent respondent State with twenty-two new cases filed against it between 2011 and 2019. Behind Egypt, Algeria was confronted with five new cases in the 2011–2019 period. Morocco was faced with four cases, while Jordan had three new cases.

43. Nassib G. Ziadé, *Arbitration Under MENA Regional Investment Treaties*, Chartered Institute of Arbitrators, No.1 (2017).
44. *Desert Line Projects LLC v. Republic of Yemen*, ICSID Case No. ARB/05/17.
45. *Ghaith Pharaon v. Republic of Tunisia*, ICSID Case No. ARB/86/1.
46. Cherine Foty, *Impact of the Arab Spring on the International Arbitration Landscape*, Kluwer Arbitration Blog (2019).

Despite the increasing number of new cases filed against Middle Eastern respondent States, the outcomes have not always been favourable for investors. A number of cases brought by investors have been dismissed on jurisdictional grounds[47] or resulted in liability decisions in favour of the respondent State.[48] An even larger number of cases have settled,[49] at least twelve since 2011, which leads to the question whether investment arbitration may have been increasingly employed during this period as a tactical mechanism for obtaining amicable settlement.

[B] Investment Arbitration under Middle East Multilateral Treaties

In addition to the Middle East region BITs, which typically have been relied upon soon after their conclusion, investors from the region have come to realize at rather a late stage that they also have regional venues to which they can submit their disputes with other States from the Middle East region. Principally, two regional multilateral investment treaties have recently gained prominence, the Unified Agreement for the Investment of Arab Capital in the Arab Countries and Agreement on Promotion, Protection and Guarantee of Investments among Member States of the Organization of the Islamic Conference.

[1] Unified Agreement for the Investment of Arab Capital in the Arab Countries

The first treaty is the Unified Agreement for the Investment of Arab Capital in the Arab Countries 1980 (the Unified Arab Investment Agreement). It initially lacked political commitment, which is changing now because of the increase in investment disputes within the region. The Unified Arab Investment Agreement came into force in 1981 and was ratified by all Member States of the Arab League, with the exception of Algeria and the Comoros. It covers the regulation of inter-Arab investments and aims to facilitate the free movement of Arab capital within Arab States. Pursuant to the Unified Arab Investment Agreement, investor-State disputes may be settled by ad hoc conciliation or arbitration procedures detailed in the agreement, or by the Arab Investment Court (AIC), a judicial body established by the agreement. The AIC was established in 1985. It remained dormant for a further nineteen years until it issued its first judgment in 2004 in a case involving a Saudi company and Tunisia. The Court has issued only a few

47. *See*, e.g., *National Gas S.A.E. v. Arab Republic of Egypt*, ICSID Case No. ARB/11/7, Award dated 3 April 2014.
48. *See Veolia Propreté v. Arab Republic of Egypt*, ICSID Case No. ARB/12/15, Award dated 25 May 2018; *Adel A Hamadi Al Tamimi v. Sultanate of Oman*, ICSID Case No. ARB/11/33, Award dated 3 November 2015.
49. *Bawabet Al Kuwait Holding Company v. Arab Republic of Egypt*, ICSID Case No. ARB/11/6; *Hussain Sajwani, Damac Park Avenue for Real EState Development S.A.E., and Damac Gamsha Bay for Development S.A.E. v. Arab Republic of Egypt*, ICSID Case No. ARB/11/16; *Indorama International Finance Limited v. Arab Republic of Egypt*, ICSID Case No. ARB/11/32; *LP Egypt Holdings I, LLC, Fund III Egypt, LLC and OMLP Egypt Holdings I, LLC v. Arab Republic of Egypt*, ICSID Case No. ARB/16/37.

judgments since then. All judgments rendered thus far by the AIC have been in favour of Arab host countries.

The AIC may hear more cases in the future because several BITs concluded between Arab countries (such as the Oman-Yemen BIT 1998, Bahrain-Jordan BIT 2000, Bahrain-Syria BIT 2000, Jordan-Kuwait BIT 2001, Jordan-Syria BIT 2001 and Bahrain-Lebanon BIT 2003) refer to the Court among the various dispute settlement options they provide. Also, the laws of several Arab countries refer to the AIC as an available venue for the resolution of investment disputes brought by nationals of other Arab States against those countries.

[a] *Ad Hoc Arbitration:* Al Kharafi v. Libya

Under ad hoc arbitration, the parties are allowed to tailor the arbitration process to the specific circumstances of their dispute. With respect to ad hoc arbitration under the Unified Arab Investment Agreement, the first case, brought in 2012 by Kuwaiti investors, *Al Kharafi and sons v. Libya*, resulted in 2013 in an award in favour of the investors. The arbitration, governed by the Unified Arab Investment Agreement and Libyan law, took place in Cairo in the premises of the Cairo Regional Centre for International Commercial Arbitration (CRCICA). The tribunal upheld jurisdiction over the dispute, finding that the relevant contract established the parties' consent to arbitration under the Arab Investment Agreement when it provided that disputes 'arising from the interpretation or performance of the present contract during its validity period ... shall be settled amicably', failing which 'the dispute shall be referred to arbitration pursuant to the provisions of the Unified Agreement for the Investment of Arab Capital in the Arab States'. The tribunal awarded an unusually high amount of moral damages as part of the overall award. The tribunal held that the arbitrary cancellation of the investment project based on the decision of the Minister of Economy was a decision that violated the Unified Agreement for the Investment of Arab Capital in the Arab States. The tribunal further noted that the Unified Agreement for the Investment of Arab Capital in the Arab States was an integral part of the Libyan law and its provisions prevailed over other Libyan laws. The award won notoriety both for its USD 935 million award to the Kuwaiti investors for a cancelled tourism project – the second largest investment treaty award at the time – and for its award of USD 30 million in moral damages against the respondent State.[50]

Rejecting Libya's jurisdictional objection that it had not consented to arbitration in accordance with Article 2 of the Annex to the Unified Arab Investment Agreement, the tribunal found express consent in the provisions of the investment contract between the claimant and the Libyan Tourism Development Authority. On the merits, the tribunal found that, by failing to hand over land necessary for the claimant's investment and by cancelling the underlying contract, the State had breached Article 9 of the Arab Investment Agreement. With respect to damages, the tribunal took account

50. *Mohamed Abdulmohsen Al-Kharafi & Sons Co. v. Libya and others*, Final Award (22 March 2013), p. 6.

of the amount of just over USD 2 billion reported by the claimant's expert in its final calculation of lost profit, but used 'its discretionary power to estimate compensation at its minimum' and reduced lost profit damages to USD 900 million.[51] The tribunal justified its award of moral damages by referring to the Libyan Civil Code, rather than applicable principles of international law. Libya's appointee to the tribunal refused to sign the award.[52]

Libya brought an action for annulment of the award before the courts in Egypt, the seat of the arbitration. The Cairo Court of Appeal rejected Libya's application and decided that it has no jurisdiction to rule on the action for annulment under the Unified Arab Investment Agreement. The award was subsequently granted leave for enforcement by the Paris Court of Appeal on 28 October 2014. However, on 4 November 2015, the Egyptian Court of Cassation overturned the decision of the Cairo Court of Appeal and referred the case to another circuit of the Cairo Court of Appeal. Most recently, on 3 June 2020, the Cairo Court of Appeal found that it has jurisdiction and that the award shall be annulled. In the meantime, the Libyan parties tried to obtain an annulment decision from the AIC which held that it had no jurisdiction.

There are in fact two ICSID precedents in which moral damages have been awarded, *Benvenuti & Bonfant v. Congo*,[53] in 1980, and more recently *Desert Lines v. Yemen*.[54] But neither award was of a similar magnitude to the sum awarded against Libya. Had a decision on moral damages of that magnitude been awarded in an international context, it could have received critical disapproval. In this respect, the ICSID award in *Rompetrol v. Romania* stated that 'The Tribunal is firmly of the view that "moral damages" cannot be admitted as a proxy for the inability to prove actual economic damage.'[55]

[b] The AIC

Chapter VI of the Unified Arab Investment Agreement created the AIC for the settlement of investment disputes.[56] The statutes of the AIC came into force on 22 February 1988. The AIC heard its first case brought under the Arab Investment Agreement, *Tanmiah Co. v. Tunisia*, in 2003. The Court rendered its first decision on 12 October 2004.[57] The Arab Investment Agreement provides the framework for the

51. *Ibid.*, p. 380.
52. Abdel Hamid El Ahdab sat as chairman of the tribunal, with Ibrahim Fawzi and Mohamed El-Kamoudi El-Hafi acting as co-arbitrators.
53. *S.A.R.L. Benvenuti & Bonfant v. People's Republic of the Congo*, ICSID Case No. ARB/77/2, Award dated 8 August 1980.
54. *Desert Line Projects LLC v. The Republic of Yemen*, ICSID Case No. ARB/05/17, Award dated 6 February 2008.
55. *The Rompetrol Group N.V. v. Romania*, ICSID Case No. ARB/06/3, Award dated 6 May 2013, at [293].
56. Unified Arab Investment Agreement, Ch. VI.
57. The decision is available in Arabic on the website of the League of Arab States at: http://www.lasportal.org/en/legalnetwork/Pages/Investment_CourtRulings.aspx (last accessed in March 2020).

AIC until an Arab Court of Justice is established and its jurisdiction is determined.[58] First referred to in Article 19 of the Charter of the Arab League, the Arab Court of Justice has yet to see the light of day, despite numerous attempts by Member States to set it up. In the meantime, the AIC remains the proper forum for disputes arising under the Unified Arab Investment Agreement. Several intra-Arab BITs also refer arbitration disputes to the AIC.[59] It is noteworthy that *Desert Lines v. Yemen* was the first investment dispute between an Arab investor and an Arab host State which have led to a final award by an ICSID tribunal. It was brought under the Oman-Yemen BIT and the claimant's choice of forum may be partially explained by the fact that, at the time, the AIC had yet to hear its first case.[60]

The AIC is seated at the permanent headquarters of the League of Arab States in Cairo and is composed of at least five serving judges and several reserve judges, each of a different Arab nationality, chosen by the Economic Council of the Arab League from a list of Arab legal specialists drawn up specifically for that purpose.[61] Each State proposes two candidates for the list. The Economic Council appoints the Chairman of the Court from among the members of the Court. The judges serve on the Court for a renewable three-year term. According to Article 29 of the Unified Arab Investment Agreement, the AIC has broad jurisdiction over disputes: (i) '[b]etween any State party and another State party or between a State party and the public institutions and organizations of the other parties or between the public institutions and organizations of more than one State Party'; (ii) between a State Party, or a public institution or organization of a party and an Arab investor; and (iii) between a State Party, a public entity or an Arab investor and the State agencies providing investment guarantees in accordance with the Unified Arab Investment Agreement.[62]

The Unified Arab Investment Agreement underwent substantial amendment in 2013, namely enhancing its investment protections. Among its many innovations, the amended agreement expands the scope of the investors that it covers (i.e., the Arab investor should hold at least 51% of the capital of the juridical person); introduces a MFN clause; includes an unqualified FET standard; recognizes the right to transfer capital in the original investment currency or in a convertible currency recognized by the International Monetary Fund; and calls on host States to exert their utmost efforts to ensure that their domestic laws do not hinder the development of the investments.

---

58. Unified Arab Investment Agreement, Art. 28.1 ('Until such time as the Arab Court of Justice is established and its jurisdiction determined, the Arab Investment Court shall be established').
59. *See*, e.g., Agreement between the Government of the Arab Egyptian Republic and the Syrian Arab Republic for the Promotion and Protection of Investment (providing for the resolution of disputes by 'conciliation, arbitration, in the host State or by recourse to the Arab Investment Court in accordance with the provisions of Article 6 of the Unified Agreement for the Investment of Arab Capital in the Arab States'); Agreement for the Mutual Promotion and Protection of Investments between the Government of the Sultanate of Oman and the Government of the Republic of Yemen, Art. 11(2) (allowing investors to resort to the following fora for the resolution of disputes: (i) domestic courts of the host State; (ii) ad hoc arbitration according to the arbitration law of the host State; (iii) the Arab Investment Court; or (iv) ICSID arbitration).
60. *See Desert Line Projects LLC v. The Republic of Yemen*, ICSID Case No. ARB/05/17, Award dated 6 February 2008.
61. No judge may be of the same nationality as any party to the proceedings.
62. Unified Arab Investment Agreement, Art. 29.

It is too early to tell whether the amended agreement will present the Middle East with a viable alternative to traditional ISDS facilities.

[2] Agreement on Promotion, Protection and Guarantee of Investments Among Member States of the Organization of the Islamic Conference

The second important regional investment treaty that has been activated only recently is the Agreement on Promotion, Protection and Guarantee of Investments among Member States of the Organization of the Islamic Conference 1981 (the OIC Agreement). This agreement has been signed by thirty-six States that are members of the OIC, and twenty-eight have ratified it.[63] The OIC Agreement was dormant for decades but recently has been the basis for several ad hoc arbitration claims. In one of these claims, brought by a Saudi investor Hesham Talaat M. Al-Warraq against Indonesia, the tribunal assumed jurisdiction.[64] It determined in a decision of 21 June 2012 that States parties to the OIC Agreement are deemed to have expressed prior consent to arbitration in relation to future disputes with investors in a way similar to traditional BITs. In the merits phase, however, the tribunal determined in an award rendered on 15 December 2014 that although Indonesia had breached the FET standard in dealing with the Saudi investor, the investor was prevented, as a result of his own wrongdoing, from pursuing his claim, and that the doctrine of 'clean hands' precluded the awarding of damages to him.

A second award under the OIC Agreement was rendered recently in an arbitration brought by Tunisian investor in *Kontinental Conseil Ingénierie SARL v. Gabon*, concerning the alleged destruction of a social housing construction investment. Although the award remains confidential, the tribunal reportedly affirmed its jurisdiction to hear the investor's claims, found Gabon liable for unfair treatment, but rejected the bulk of the compensation claimed.[65]

The OIC Agreement envisaged arbitration as a temporary way of resolving investment disputes pending the creation of an Islamic International Court of Justice in Kuwait. Although more than thirty years have elapsed since the creation of the OIC Agreement, the Court has yet to be established. There is thus much uncertainty remaining in this respect.

63. To date, the following countries have ratified the OIC Agreement: Burkina Faso, Cameroon, Egypt, Gabon, Gambia, Guinea, Indonesia, Iran, Iraq, Jordan, Kuwait, Lebanon, Libya, Mali, Morocco, Oman, Pakistan, Palestine, Qatar, Saudi Arabia, Senegal, Somalia, Sudan, Syria, Tajikistan, Tunisia, Turkey, Uganda, and the UAE.
64. *Hesham T. M. Al-Warraq v. Republic of Indonesia* ('*Al-Warraq*'). The case was conducted as an ad hoc arbitration under the UNCITRAL Arbitration Rules (the 'UNCITRAL Rules') and was seated in Singapore. Bernardo M. Cremades (Spain) presided over the tribunal, with Michael Hwang S.C. (Singapore) and Fali S. Nariman S.C. (India) sitting as co-arbitrators.
65. *See* Luke Eric Peterson, *Investigation: New Developments in Investor-State Arbitration Claims under the OIC Investment Agreement*, IA Reporter (10 August 2017), available at: https://www.iareporter.com/articles/investigation-new-developments-in-investor-Statearbitration-cla. Pierre Mayer presided over the tribunal, with Nassib Ziadé and Mathias Audit sitting as co-arbitrators.

If investment arbitration is to take place within the region, it should be administered by one of the existing regional arbitration institutions instead of being conducted ad hoc. The involvement of an institution would give the arbitration a public perception of legitimacy, not to mention administrative efficiency and support. The institutions can also handle the delicate issue of transparency sensitively, and they have the potential to develop mechanisms to deal with the publicity surrounding high-profile cases. For its part, the CRCICA has administered an investment arbitration. The request for arbitration was filed pursuant to the Libya-Morocco BIT 2000 providing for the CRCICA among the options offered to investors. Egypt has concluded a number of BITs, such as the ones with Chad, Cyprus, Switzerland and Zambia, which all include the CRCICA as one possible option available to investors.

[C] Prevalent Issues of ISDS Claims in the Middle East

[1] Interest and Lost Profits under the Laws of Middle Eastern States

States in the Middle East region are predominantly Muslim, Islamic law or *sharia* thus finding application in several matters. While *sharia* is not uniform, certain fundamental principles are recognized by all *sharia* schools[66] and jurisdictions. As far as principles of compensation for damages are concerned, the discussion has revolved around the concepts of interest (*riba*) and valuation taking into account lost profits (*gharar*). In general, public policy under *sharia* prohibits *riba* and *gharar*.[67] That is so because findings on interest and lost profits are based on speculation, and guarantee gain without hard work and personal activity.[68]

Despite the dictates of *sharia* and its strict interpretation by some courts, lost profits and interest are either partially or fully permitted in most Islamic Middle East States. As one commentator notes, 'be it through pragmatism, evasion, or the principle that agreements must be observed, arbitration agreements are, in fact, sprinkled with Western style provisions in a number of parts of the Islamic Middle East'.[69] Accordingly, an arbitral award granting 'Western' style remedies should in principle be

66. Different interpretations on what Islamic law should be are reflected in the diverse range of schools of thought or ways of studying and practising Islam. The common factor among the different groups is the Quran and the recorded sayings and actions of the Prophet (peace and blessings upon him) – Sunnah – as sources of information and guidance. Within Sunni and Shi'a Islam, there are six main schools of Islamic law: Hanbali School, Hanafi School, Shafi' School, Maliki School, Zaydi School and Ja'fari School.
67. Abdel Hamid El Ahdab and Jalal El Ahdab, *Arbitration with the Arab Countries* (Kluwer Law International, 2011), 22.
68. O.M.H. Aljazy, *Jurisdiction of Arbitral Tribunals in Islamic Law (Shari'a)*, in M.A. Fernández Ballesteros and D. Arias (eds), Liber Amicorum Bernardo Cremades (Kluwer Law International, 2010), 79.
69. A.J. Gemmell, *Commercial Arbitration in the Islamic Middle East*, 5 Santa Clara J. Int'l L. 169, 181 (2006).

recognized and enforced in most *sharia* jurisdictions.[70] Some States have in fact enacted laws expressly recognizing the validity of lost profits and interest, while others have legalized them 'in some very unconventional ways'.[71]

More specifically, one commentator has observed that parties have often introduced claims equivalent to interest in the form of alternative remedies, consisting of 'proven financial damages resulting from late payment or late performance or claims for sharing or disgorging profits made by the defaulting party, as well as various other forms of penalty that can be provided by contract or recognized by custom'.[72] Further, parties have included, and courts have enforced, clauses providing for liquidated damages, i.e., the payment of a predetermined sum additional to the damages awarded for the breach of contract.[73] Such alternative remedies may, in fact, even exceed, compound, let alone simple interest.

[2] Consolidation and Consistency: **Orascom** *and* **OTH** *Cases Against Algeria*

The case law in the Middle East region is extensive, rich and provides interesting analysis of salient procedural issues in investment arbitration. Examples of such procedural issues could be found in the *Orascom* and *OTH* cases filed against Algeria. In these particular cases, the investors issued three notices of arbitration based on the same facts each based on a different agreement (Algeria-Egypt BIT, Algeria-Belgium BIT, and Algeria-Italy BIT). Two proceedings were registered: (i) *Orascom v. Algeria* before ICSID based on Algeria-Belgium BIT; and (ii) *OTH v. Algeria* before PCA based on Algeria-Egypt BIT.

The *Orascom* case tribunal found that 'while the parties to the dispute and the legal bases for the claims (the BITs) are different, the dispute being notified in the three notices is effectively one and the same'. The tribunal further indicated that 'the existence of several legal foundations for arbitration does not necessarily mean that the various entities in the shareholder chain could make use of the existing arbitration clauses to assail the same measures and to recover the same economic loss under any circumstances'.[74] The case was settled in favour of Algeria.

None of the BITs included clauses for consolidation of proceedings. However, if the parties had reached an agreement on this issue, a single tribunal could have

70. H. Arfazadeh, *A Practitioner's Approach to Interest Claims under Sharia Law in International Arbitration*, in F. de Ly and L. Lévy (eds), *Interest, Auxiliary and Alternative Remedies in International Arbitration*, Dossier V of the ICC Institute of World Business Law (ICC, 2008) 211, 213.
71. Abdel Hamid El Ahdab and Jalal El Ahdab, *Arbitration with the Arab Countries* (Kluwer Law International, 2011), 22.
72. H. Arfazadeh, *A Practitioner's Approach to Interest Claims under Sharia Law in International Arbitration*, in F. de Ly and L. Lévy (eds), *Interest, Auxiliary and Alternative Remedies in International Arbitration*, Dossier V of the ICC Institute of World Business Law (ICC, 2008), 211, 212.
73. T. Badawy, *The General Principles of Islamic Law as the Law Governing Investment Disputes in the Middle East*, 29 J. Int'l Arb. 255, 264 (2012).
74. *Orascom v. Algeria*, ICSID Case No. ARB/12/35, Award dated 31 May 2017, paras 488, 495, 518.

analysed all three claims and determined to which extent each of the claimants was due compensation.[75] The fact that the PCA rendered an award detailing the settlement between the parties in *OTH* was key in helping Algeria to win *Orascom*. This case reveals that it is advisable that any settlement reached with a claimant be formalized through institutional channels.

[3] Enforcement of Investment Arbitration Awards

Awards rendered in investment disputes may be ICSID awards or non-ICSID awards. From a purely legal standpoint, should an investor seek enforcement of an ICSID award, the ICSID Convention Articles 53–55 would apply. Article 53 of the ICSID Convention requires each party to ICSID arbitration to abide by the award and comply with its terms,[76] subject to remedies provided under Articles 50–52.

Meanwhile, arbitral awards rendered under the OIC Agreement or the Unified Arab Investment Agreement are enforceable as though they were final decisions of national courts of the State in which enforcement is sought. To that effect, Article 34(3) of the Unified Arab Investment Agreement provides that 'A judgment delivered by the Court shall be enforceable in the States Parties, where they shall be immediately enforceable in the same manner as a final enforceable judgment delivered by their own competent courts.' The statutes of the AIC confirm that its decisions shall be enforceable in the Member States of the Unified Arab Investment Agreement in the same manner as a final enforceable judgment delivered by their own competent courts.[77] Its decisions are final and not subject to appeal.[78]

Similarly, under the OIC Agreement, the arbitral decisions have the force of judicial decisions. The contracting parties are under an obligation to implement them in their territory, no matter whether it be a party to the dispute or not and irrespective of whether the investor against whom the decision was passed is one of its nationals or residents or not, as if it were a final and enforceable decision of its national courts.[79]

75. *Border Timbers v. Zimbabwe*, ICSID Case No. ARB/10/25, and *Von Pelzold v. Zimbabwe*, ICSID Case No. ARB/10/15, were two cases by investors of different nationality based on the same facts. The cases were consolidated under the ICSID Rules and single tribunal headed both cases issuing two separate awards, one for each BIT.
76. *See* the ICSID Convention Art. 53, which provides:

> (1) The award shall be binding on the parties and shall not be subject to any appeal or to any other remedy except those provided for in this Convention. Each party shall abide by and comply with the terms of the award except to the extent that enforcement shall have been stayed pursuant to the relevant provisions of this Convention. (2) For the purposes of this Section, 'award' shall include any decision interpreting, revising or annulling such award pursuant to Articles 50, 51 or 52.

77. *See* AIC statutes, Art. 46.
78. *Ibid.*, Art. 33(2).
79. *See* OIC Agreement, Art. 17.2(d).

§5.04 POSITIONS AND CONTRIBUTIONS OF MIDDLE EAST STATES FOR ISDS REFORM

Middle East economies follow the international trends in the evolution of international investment agreements and their implementation. The number of BITs signed by Middle East economies is increasing. Some countries have revised their investment agreement policies or are in the process of elaborating new model BITs, in order to reflect recent treaty practice.

[A] Investment Disputes Prevention Policies

Dispute prevention policies are a set of policies, measures and concrete procedures aimed at avoiding disputes between foreign investors and the authorities of the host State, addressing and solving problems encountered by foreign investors at an early stage to the extent possible, ensure compliance by foreign investors with clear, transparent and predictable procedures with a view to ensuring long-lasting investment relationship and retaining foreign investment within the host economy.

Egypt presents an interesting case study in this regard. Since the inception of the revolution in January 2011, the State has engaged in a full-fledged legal audit of existing investment treaties in an attempt to curb and prevent any disputes with investors while maintaining an investor-friendly approach and climate. In Tunisia and Libya, similar initiatives have been implemented to promote investment under the new paradigms. Following the 14 January 2011 revolution, the Organisation for Economic Co-operation and Development (OECD) and the Government of Tunisia have started a joint review of Tunisia's investment policies. The review aimed at charting the country's progress in developing an effective policy framework to promote investment for development and suggest ways to further improve the climate for both domestic and foreign investment.

Further, Morocco has recently prepared a new model BIT that strikes a balance between rights and obligations, both those of investors and those of the host State, and in which it has opted to maintain the existing ISDS system while updating relevant provisions. The main innovations introduced by the new model treaty in respect of ISDS are aimed at: (i) establishing an institutional framework for dispute prevention with an important role in avoiding disputes between foreign investors and the authorities of the host State; (ii) limiting the types of disputes that may be submitted under the ISDS mechanism and setting a time limit for the submission of claims in order to prevent old claims from being submitted; and (iii) ensuring that domestic remedies are exhausted before a dispute is submitted to international arbitration.

[B] Contributions of Middle East States to ISDS Reform

Beside adopting dispute prevention policies, Middle East States have addressed multiple options to reform ISDS system. For example, in its submission to UNCITRAL

Working Group III,[80] Bahrain proposed that arbitral institutions should take the lead in creating binding codes of conduct.[81] Such codes should address all aspects of conflicts of interest, including the selection of arbitrators, arbitrators' ethical duties, arbitrator challenges, and the ethical conduct of counsel and institutional staff. Moreover, Bahrain suggested that when it comes to challenges, the code of conduct should contain clear and enforceable guidelines on what is and what is not permissible behaviour. The various 'multiple-hatting' scenarios should be covered. Consideration should also be given to creating a truly independent body within an arbitral institution specifically to handle challenge applications. This would put an end to the ICSID practice of a challenged arbitrator's fate being decided by the other members of the tribunal or, if those arbitrators take different positions, by the President of the World Bank.

Additionally, efforts to ensure greater diversity must also focus on widening the pool of arbitrators to include members from developing countries, so that 'all legal systems of the world are fairly and inclusively represented on the arbitration tribunals that shape [ISDS] jurisprudence'.[82] Other proposals include establishing joint interpretative committees, rather than an appeals mechanism, alongside arbitral tribunals which might be a better way to harmonize the interpretation of treaty provisions. Arbitral tribunals would continue to determine issues of fact and consider matters of law, while a parallel permanent interpretative body would provide guidance on jurisprudence.

Bahrain further declared that ICSID should create a diverse pool of arbitrators dedicated to handling annulment proceedings. This would help to ensure consistency in the application of the ICSID Convention and Rules by annulment committees. Working Group III may also consider drafting model clauses providing additional grounds for annulment, which would be available for States to insert in new or existing international investment treaties. This would answer the criticism that the ICSID system permits annulment only on limited grounds.

On the other hand, Morocco highlighted the importance of achieving consensus on reform of the ISDS regime.[83] This reform should be comprehensive and should take into account the concerns raised by various States with a view to achieving a fair and equitable ISDS system that all countries, in particular, developing countries, can rely upon. Morocco proposed to establish a mechanism for supporting and assisting developing countries in dealing with ISDS cases so as to enable them to better prepare for, handle and manage disputes relating to international investment. Moreover, it is vital to identify the best options for reducing arbitration costs and saving time.

Morocco also noted the importance of establishing a procedure for the prior scrutiny of arbitral awards, similar to the procedure used by the International Court of

80. In 2017, the United Nations Commission on International Trade Law (UNCITRAL) entrusted its Working Group III with a mandate to work on the reform of ISDS.
81. *See* Submission from the Government of Bahrain to the UNCITRAL Working Group III, Thirty-eighth session, 29 August 2019.
82. *See* Nassib G. Ziadé, *Is ICSID Heading in the Wrong Direction?*, Global Arbitration Review (2015).
83. *See* Submission from the Government of Morocco to the UNCITRAL Working Group III, Thirty-seventh session, 4 March 2019.

Arbitration of the International Chamber of Commerce. Such prior scrutiny, which should be carried out within a short period of time, would ensure that each award complied with all formalities, addressed all claims and set out the grounds on which it was based. Furthermore, it has been emphasized that third-party funding cannot play a constructive role in ISDS unless it is regulated. In this regard, rules and procedures should be established to regulate such funding so that it cannot be used in a speculative or abusive manner by investors. Those rules and procedures could provide for disclosure of the third-party funder's identity, the amount of funding and the terms of the funding contract, including the existence or otherwise of an irrevocable commitment by the third-party funder to bear any legal costs that the claimant investor may be ordered to pay, given that investors that seek third-party funding are usually in a difficult financial situation that prevents them from complying with orders to pay legal costs, such non-compliance representing a risk to the host State.

Nonetheless, Morocco supports the establishment of a standing appellate mechanism for arbitral awards which would be regarded as a higher judicial authority to ensure consistency in the interpretation of the provisions of BITs, especially the substantive clauses of such treaties, in order to avoid arbitral tribunals reaching different conclusions with respect to the same facts and thus develop homogeneous case law that promotes legal certainty. Such a mechanism would rectify errors in awards that could have a significant impact on public funds, particularly since investment arbitration often relates to matters of public interest.

Meanwhile, Kuwait considers that the development of a code of conduct could aim at providing a uniform approach to requirements applicable to ISDS tribunal members and to give more concrete content to broad ethical notions and standards used in the applicable instruments, including the ICSID Convention, investment treaties, applicable laws and applicable rules. This would be in line with the preference expressed by Working Group III that one general code is preferable to numerous institution-specific codes. In particular, a code of conduct could aim at: (i) clarifying the content of the standards, thereby furthering harmonization and clarification of the different existing requirements; (ii) ensuring that all stakeholders understand the thresholds for when independence, impartiality and integrity would be impaired; (iii) developing requirements for qualification; (iv) determining the mechanisms for disclosure, and the sanctions in case of non-compliance; and (v) as far as arbitrators are concerned, providing clarity on their roles, in particular regarding the question of double-hatting and repeat appointments.[84]

Accordingly, it is vital that any reform proposals do not sacrifice the benefits of the existing ISDS system. Reform should not only maintain the advantages of ISDS but also substantially improve upon them. Most importantly, any reform should not risk further fragmentation of ISDS system. These objectives have guided Middle East States in their observations and contributions to ISDS reform.

84. *See* Submission from the Government of Kuwait to the UNCITRAL Working Group III, Thirty-ninth session, 30 December 2019.

§5.05 CONCLUSION

Middle East States have positively contributed to investment promotion and have likewise concluded many BITs and engaged in investment disputes under the auspices of diverse fora. Over the last two decades, States in the region have positively contributed to intra-regional investments and have notably boosted their share of investments. Nevertheless, investment in the Middle East entered a new paradigm during the Arab Spring.[85] The unprecedented revolutionary tidal wave sweeping across the region and aimed at promoting the rule of law in a corruption-free political and economic environment has, so far, been successful.

Prior to this revolutionary tsunami sweeping the Middle East, the economic and legal crises suffered by some States striving to join the developed world were not purely a manifestation of the inadequacy of the regulatory and legal framework. These crises were also a manifestation of the catastrophic lack of well-structured institutions, as well as the lack of sustainable implementation of the rule of law. Predominantly, a distorted image and erratic enforcement of the rule of law prevailed. Nevertheless, the revolutionary spark that lit the candle of democracy and freedom in the region has certainly impacted traditional perceptions of States and governments. Today, the 'rule of law' serves as a recipe for an effective long-term solution to the most pressing challenges and ails in the Middle East, including despotism, poverty, conflict, endemic corruption, and disregard for human rights. In such tumultuous times, people are torn between contradictory centrifugal and centripetal forces. As long as the desire for security, prosperity, stability, and true democracy remains unfulfilled, people's aching hearts and throbbing minds will reject and continue in utter denial of corruption, despotism, oppression, and poverty. This has generated a colossal sense of optimism and a belief that the future must hold a myriad of better opportunities, which mitigates the looming scepticism, fear, and uncertainty. With such mixed feelings of hope and fear, the proper utilization and implementation of the rule of law hopefully will bring about an eternal season of light, hope, wisdom, freedom, and productivity. This will ultimately have a profound positive impact on the prevailing investment climate and available investment opportunities.

Based on this review of many BITs and investment decisions involving Middle East States, it is essential that: (a) States should reconsider their BITs in light of the prevailing investment case law; (b) States should reconsider the relationship between BITs and the promotion of investment; (c) States should engage in a proper assessment of their investment policies to attract foreign investment and should administer processes and schemes that are consistent with international investment-friendly approaches; (d) States should administer proper schemes for the amicable settlement of investment disputes and avert any risk of legal proceedings that could be detrimental to their image and investment standing; (e) States should avert abusive, discriminatory, and illicit behaviour that could trigger international liability; (f) international arbitrators should carefully consider the behaviour of host States and should also

85. Mohamed S. Abdel Wahab, *Investment Protection and Arbitration in the Arab Mediterranean Area: The Arab Spring of Hope*, Economy and Territory Commercial Relations, 2012.

consider investors' conduct in order to dispense with any possible abuse of process; (g) States should encourage the building of competent legal teams of experts that are well versed in principles of investment and international arbitration to ensure adequate representation in disputes if needed; and (h) States should discern their competitive investment advantage by determining the sectors and projects that are most appealing to investors.

On the other hand, ICSID procedures need to be revisited in a number of respects. ICSID should take measures that would bolster confidence in the Middle East region. First, there should be a better appreciation and understanding by ICSID of the political conditions within the countries concerned. As States in the Middle East continue their difficult transitions, ICSID must remain attentive to their special needs and circumstances, for example, by recognizing in procedural matters that the strictness of timelines in registering a case or appointing a tribunal may be problematic. Second, when called upon to appoint arbitrators, ICSID should appoint individuals who, if not from the region, at least have a deep understanding of the region and of its present problems. The number of arbitrators originating from the Middle East region is lamentably low, and the serious implications of these numbers affect the legitimacy of ICSID arbitration.

Finally, ICSID should embark on internal reforms that seek to eliminate legitimate concerns raised by certain Member States with respect to arbitrators' real or apparent conflicts of interest. These conflicts remain unregulated by any internal code of conduct or authoritative guidelines. Such a code of conduct should address a diverse range of issues, such as that presented when a person simultaneously holds counsel and arbitrator roles in cases featuring the same legal issues. Addressing such problematic relationships would assuage the concerns of Member States, provide clear guidelines to parties and arbitrators alike, bring predictability and consistency to the smooth conduct of arbitration proceedings and help to maintain trust, especially in regions undergoing major transitions such as the Middle East.

CHAPTER 6

The Rise of NAFTA 2.0: A Case Study in Effective ISDS Reform

Kiran Nasir Gore & Charles H. Camp

From 1994 to 2020, the North American Free Trade Agreement (NAFTA) enabled a free trade zone in the region. Its early days were undoubtedly successful. NAFTA was credited with stimulating trade, economic growth, and cooperation among Canada, Mexico, and the US. Yet, NAFTA was not without controversy. Its Chapter 11 offered an Investor-State Dispute Settlement (ISDS) mechanism that American and Canadian trade negotiators anticipated would protect their investors from risks posed by Mexico's legal system. They did not expect ISDS claims against their own governments, which they perceived as a threat to their sovereignty. NAFTA's successor, the US–Mexico–Canada Agreement (USMCA), entered into force on 1 July 2020 and adopts a new approach to ISDS in its Chapter 14. As the existing ISDS system faces increasing criticism and scrutiny, much of the debate centres on whether the ISDS system remains fit for its purpose. This chapter examines the social, political, and experiential circumstances which led to the rise of USMCA. It concludes that USMCA is a practical example of effective ISDS reform. In sum, the story of USMCA demonstrates that evolution, and not death, is the answer to the modern ISDS debate.

§6.01 INTRODUCTION

As the ISDS system faces increasing criticism and scrutiny, much of the debate centres on whether the ISDS system remains fit for its purpose. The most common criticisms involve fundamental disagreement with both the system and its mechanisms. Some opponents of ISDS argue that foreign investors should not be permitted to challenge possibly legitimate domestic regulations, that arbitrators are inherently biased in claimant investors' favour and therefore ill-equipped to render important decisions concerning use of public funds, or that the lack of consistency among ISDS decisions undermines the system as a whole. These aspects are fundamental to the system and difficult to tackle. Meanwhile, other concerns, regarding transparency, cost and time associated with arbitral proceedings, or the need for an appellate review mechanism perhaps can be remedied through digestible and piecemeal reform.

Many of these criticisms are actively under debate at the International Centre for Settlement of Investment Disputes (ICSID) as part of its ICSID Rule Amendment Project, aiming to 'modernize, simplify, and streamline the rules, while also leveraging information technology to reduce the environmental footprint of ICSID proceedings'.[1] A parallel and broader initiative for modernization and reform is underway through the United Nations Commission on International Trade Law (UNCITRAL) Working Group III.[2] Both initiatives begin with the premise that modernization of the ISDS system generally, and reform of specific ISDS mechanisms, can address stakeholders' concerns. They also draw on the experiential reality of ISDS as the number of investor-State arbitrations has exponentially increased over the past two decades.

Fundamentally, a State's decision to include an ISDS mechanism in its international investment agreements (IIAs) reflects its decision to accede a piece of its sovereignty to attract foreign investment and increase global trade. This is the starting point for the best responses to most criticisms of ISDS. During the past few years, proponents of the ISDS system have methodically dispelled myths with statistics. For example, in 2015, the International Bar Association (IBA) published a short factsheet that sought to clarify misinformation.[3] It explained that over time, States have won a higher percentage of cases than investors, investors rarely recover windfall damages, and in all events, States retain the right to regulate in the public interest.[4]

Within this context, NAFTA's rise and fall over a quarter of a century makes more sense. Since 1994, NAFTA enabled a free trade zone between the economies of the US, Canada, and Mexico.[5] NAFTA's Preamble reflected its intent to 'establish clear and mutually advantageous rules governing ... trade' and 'ensure a predictable commercial framework for business planning and investment'.[6] Legal scholars heralded it as an 'unprecedented' multilateral agreement that represented a 'model for similar arrangements in other contexts'.[7] NAFTA's early success went beyond mere positive

1. *See* ICSID Rules and Regulations Amendment Process website, https://icsid.worldbank.org/en/amendments.
2. For the latest information concerning the progress of UNICTRAL Working Group III, *see* https://uncitral.un.org/en/working_groups/3/investor-state.
3. *Investor-state dispute settlement: the importance of an informed, fact-based debate*, International Bar Association (IBA) (20 April 2015), https://www.ibanet.org/Article/NewDetail.aspx?ArticleUid=1dff6284-e074-40ea-bf0c-f19949340b2f.
4. *Ibid.*
5. North American Free Trade Agreement (1 January 1994), https://www.nafta-sec-alena.org/Home/Texts-of-the-Agreement/North-American-Free-Trade-Agreement (NAFTA).
6. *Ibid.*, Preamble, cls 5 and 6.
7. David A. Gantz, *Resolution of Investment Disputes under the North American Free Trade Agreement*, 10 Ariz. J. Int'l & Comp. L. 335, 348 (1993).

assessment by legal scholars. It was credited with stimulating trade development, economic growth, and cooperation among its Member States.[8]

Yet, NAFTA was accompanied by controversy. Its Chapter 11 provided an ISDS mechanism with protections comparable to those in many 1990s-era IIAs.[9] American and Canadian trade negotiators anticipated that the ISDS mechanism would protect their investors from risks posed by Mexico's legal system.[10] They did not expect ISDS claims against their own governments, concerning everything from their environmental legislation to their national judicial processes.[11]

This background information places into context Donald Trump's presidential campaign focus on renegotiating NAFTA and his swift actions to implement changes to NAFTA. In January 2017, only weeks into his presidential term, Trump announced that he would renegotiate NAFTA.[12] By May 2017, his Administration formally launched the clock on a ninety-day waiting period, after which renegotiations with Canadian and Mexican counterparts could officially begin.[13] In the following months, the Trump Administration applied aggressive import tariffs on both Canadian and Mexican goods to influence renegotiation.[14]

In October 2018, Trump, alongside his Mexican and Canadian counterparts, delivered 'NAFTA 2.0'. But the USMCA adopts not only a new name but also a new approach to ISDS within its Chapter 14.[15] On 30 November 2018, leaders of all three

---

8. *See, e.g.*, *NAFTA: A Decade of Success*, Office of the United States Trade Representative (July 2004), https://ustr.gov/about-us/policy-offices/press-office/fact-sheets/archives/2004/july/nafta-decade-success; Daniel Griswold, *The Success of NAFTA*, CATO Institute (originally appearing on freetrade.org) (1 July 1998), https://www.cato.org/publications/commentary/success-nafta.
9. Charles N. Brower and Lee A. Steven, *Who Then Should Judge: Developing the International Rule of Law under NAFTA Chapter 11*, 2 Chi. J. Int'l L. 193, 193–194 (2001). *See also* Fredrick M. Abbott, Max Planck Encyclopaedia of Public International Law: North American Free Trade Agreement, Dispute Settlement (Oxford University Press, 2014), para. 18.
10. *Ibid. See also* Ian A. Laird, *NAFTA Chapter 11 Meets Chicken Little*, 2 Chi. J. Int'l L. 223, 230 (2001); Laurence Hecht and Peter Morici, *Managing Risks in Mexico*, Harvard Business Review (July-August 1993), https://hbr.org/1993/07/managing-risks-in-mexico ('In fact, many businesspeople still question how adequately Mexico's legal system will support a market economy or ensure the security of foreign businesses'). *See generally* James F. Smith and Aureliano Gonzalez-Baz, *Confronting Differences in the United States and Mexican Legal Systems in the Era of NAFTA*, 1 U.S.-Mex. L.J. 85 (1993).
11. Abbott, *supra* n. 9, para. 18; Gantz, *supra* n. 7, at 1302.
12. *USTR: Trump Administration Announces Intent to Renegotiate the North American Free Trade Agreement*, Office of the United States Trade Representative (18 May 2017), https://ustr.gov/about-us/policy-offices/press-office/press-releases/2017/may/ustr-trump-administration-announces.
13. Megan Cassella, *Trump Launches NAFTA Renegotiation*, Politico (18 May 2017), https://www.politico.com/story/2017/05/18/trump-administration-formally-kicks-off-renegotiation-of-nafta-238552.
14. Max Bouchet and Joseph Parilla, *How Trump's Steel and Aluminium Tariffs Could Affect State Economies*, The Brookings Institute Blog (6 March 2018), https://www.brookings.edu/blog/the-avenue/2018/03/06/how-trumps-steel-and-aluminum-tariffs-could-affect-state-economies/.
15. *See generally* Robert Landicho and Andrea Cohen, *What's in a Name Change? For Investment Claims under the New USMCA Instead of NAFTA (Nearly) Everything*, Kluwer Arbitration Blog (5 October 2018), http://arbitrationblog.kluwerarbitration.com/2018/10/05/whats-in-a-name-change-for-investment-claims-under-the-new-usmca-instead-of-nafta-nearly-everything/.

Member States signed the USMCA.[16] One year later, on 10 December 2019, they executed a 'Protocol of Amendment' (USMCA Amendment), which impacted a variety of provisions in USMCA, but did not change Chapter 14.[17] With this final revision, USMCA was quickly ratified through each of its Member States' domestic processes.[18] USMCA entered into force on 1 July 2020.[19] On this same date, NAFTA, including its procedural and substantive protections, was officially terminated.[20]

This chapter considers the social, political, and experiential circumstances that led to the rise of USMCA. Section 6.02 examines NAFTA and provides an overview of Chapter 11, including its history, substantive features, and key criticisms. Section 6.03 provides context for the rise of USMCA and key features of its Chapter 14. Finally, §6.04 frames USMCA as a practical example of effective ISDS reform. In sum, the story of USMCA demonstrates that evolution, and not death, is the answer to the modern ISDS debate. The differences between NAFTA's Chapter 11 and USMCA's Chapter 14 reflect concrete 'evolution' for regional ISDS and perhaps USMCA offers a template for future global trends.

§6.02 NAFTA: HISTORIC CONTEXT AND FEATURES OF ITS CHAPTER 11 ISDS MECHANISM

This section first provides an overview of NAFTA's Chapter 11, including context for its development and objectives. Next, it sets out the protections and means for investors to pursue claims against host States. Then, it summarizes key criticisms of Chapter 11 based on the experiences of Member States and investors. Finally, it provides the experiential reality element and discusses several investor-State arbitrations that exemplify NAFTA's challenges.

16. Bill Chappell, *USMCA: Trump Signs New Trade Agreement with Mexico and Canada to Replace NAFTA*, NPR (30 November 2018), https://www.npr.org/2018/11/30/672150010/usmca-trump-signs-new-trade-agreement-with-mexico-and-canada. *See generally* Agreement between the United States of America, the United Mexican States, and Canada (signed 30 November 2018), https://ustr.gov/sites/default/files/files/agreements/FTA/USMCA/Text/14_Investment.pdf (USMCA).
17. Protocol of Amendment to the USMCA (10 December 2019), https://ustr.gov/sites/default/files/files/agreements/FTA/USMCA/Protocol-of-Amendments-to-the-United-States-Mexico-Canada-Agreement.pdf.
18. David Ljunggren, *Canadian Parliament Rushes Through Ratification of USMCA Trade Pact*, Reuters (13 March 2020), https://www.reuters.com/article/us-usa-trade-usmca-canada/canadian-parliament-rushes-through-ratification-of-usmca-trade-pact-idUSKBN2102I5.
19. *USMCA to Enter into Force July 1 after United States Takes Final Procedural Steps for Implementation*, Office of the United States Trade Representative (14 April 2020) https://ustr.gov/about-us/policy-offices/press-office/press-releases/2020/april/usmca-enter-force-july-1-after-united-states-takes-final-procedural-steps-implementation.
20. As discussed later in this chapter, USMCA's Annex 14-C provides that ISDS under NAFTA's Chapter 11 remains available for legacy investments (i.e., investments established or acquired between 1 January 1994 and termination of NAFTA), provided that any arbitration proceeding against a Member State is commenced within three years of NAFTA's termination on 1 July 2020. These claims will remain subject to all procedural requirements in NAFTA's Chapter 11. This does not cleanly resolve how a potential investor claimant would choose between pursuing claims under NAFTA or USMCA where the procedural and standing prerequisites of both free trade agreements are met.

[A] NAFTA's Context and Objectives

When launched, NAFTA and its Chapter 11 ISDS framework were historic for two reasons: the balanced approach among and towards NAFTA Parties and the immense economic impact on the region. First, through NAFTA, the US and Canada submitted themselves to binding arbitration to resolve foreign investment claims in a forum other than their own domestic courts.[21] In the 1990s, this was unprecedented. As explained by Judge Charles N. Brower and Lee A. Steven in 2001:

> The only potentially unique aspect of NAFTA Chapter 11 is that the governments of two nations with developed economies agreed to enter into an investment protection treaty between themselves. The overwhelming majority of BITs to date have been North to South, between capital-exporting countries and capital-importing countries, and the private investors who actually have benefited from such treaties have been those from the North.[22]

Second, the trade and economic opportunities created by NAFTA were immense. As explained in 1998 by economic commentator Daniel Griswold:

> Despite what opponents of trade liberalization such as Pat Buchanan contend, the North American Free Trade Agreement has been a success by any measure. Trade among the United States, Canada, and Mexico has flourished since the passage of NAFTA, benefiting American consumers and exporters. Since 1993, two-way trade with our NAFTA partners has increased by 44 percent, to $421 billion in 1996. That compares with a 33 percent increase in American trade with all other countries. Mexico has now become America's second largest market for exports, just ahead of Japan and behind only Canada.[23]

In 2015, Congressman William L. Owens of New York and R. Andrew Fitzpatrick (legislative director to Congressman Owens) explained that Chapter 11 was a key element of NAFTA's success:

> NAFTA's Chapter 11 aims to create a fair and predictable framework to allow for expanded flows of cross-border investment, which in turn can generate greater economic growth across North America. Improving the efficiency of capital allocation is meant to enable each signatory nation to benefit from the corresponding growth in cross-border investment associated with freer trade in goods and services. 'Since NAFTA came into force in 1994, foreign direct investment in North America has risen from $110 billion per year in 1992 to $650 billion per year in 2010, a 490% increase.'[24]

21. Gantz, *supra* n. 7, at 1302.
22. Brower and Steven, *supra* n. 9, at 193–194.
23. Daniel Griswold, *The Success of NAFTA*, CATO Institute (originally appearing on freetrade.org) (1 July 1998), https://www.cato.org/publications/commentary/success-nafta.
24. William L. Owen, *Investment Arbitration under NAFTA Chapter 11: A Threat to Sovereignty of Member States?* 39 Can.-U.S. L.J. 55, 56 (2015), https://scholarlycommons.law.case.edu/cuslj/vol39/iss/4 (quoting Diana Villiers Negroponte, *North American Leaders Meet in Toluca, Mexico: What Can We Hope For?* Brookings Blog (18 February 2014), http://www.brookings.edu/blogs/upfront/posts/2014/02/18-north-american-leaders-toluca-negroponte).

In sum, NAFTA's Chapter 11 facilitated the free trade agreement's main objectives: breaking down barriers to foreign investment; instilling investor confidence throughout the region with clear, balanced, and fair rules; and eliminating political elements which might hinder success.[25]

[B] NAFTA's Chapter 11 ISDS Mechanism

Structurally, NAFTA's Chapter 11 was divided into two parts. Section A outlined the substantive protections available to investors from host States.[26] In summary:

- Investors were entitled to three types of treatment: (1) national treatment (NT); (2) most-favoured-nation (MFN) treatment; and (3) treatment meeting minimum standards of international law in the event that local treatment (particularly in the event of expropriation) does not meet such standards (MST).[27] In effect, an aggrieved investor could pursue a claim against a host State based on the standard most favourable, given its particular circumstances.
- Direct or indirect expropriation of an investor's property was prohibited, except when undertaken for a public purpose, on a non-discriminatory basis and in accordance with due process and MST. In all cases of expropriation, compensation equivalent to fair market value based on the value prior to the date of the expropriation was required 'without delay' and in 'fully realizable' convertible currency.[28]
- Performance requirements, such as requiring the export of a minimum percentage of production or achieving a specific level of local content, were prohibited.[29]
- Investors were free to select senior management without regard to nationality (subject to certain exceptions regarding numerical majorities on the board of directors) and could transfer or repatriate profits or investment proceeds in freely convertible currency.[30]

Various Annexes to NAFTA outlined exceptions and reservations to these general protections.[31]

NAFTA's section B reinforced these protections with a dispute resolution framework. Following a conciliation and negotiation period, investors could pursue arbitration against host States for breach of the substantive protections available in section A pursuant to the Arbitration (Additional Facility) Rules of ICSID or the UNCITRAL

25. Brower and Steven, *supra* n. 9, at 195.
26. NAFTA, *supra* n. 5, Chapter 11 (Investment), section A (Investment), Arts 1101–1114.
27. *Ibid.*, Chapter 11 (Investment), section A (Investment), Arts 1102–1104.
28. *Ibid.*, Chapter 11 (Investment), section A (Investment), Art. 1110.
29. *Ibid.*, Chapter 11 (Investment), section A (Investment), Art. 1106.
30. *Ibid.*, Chapter 11 (Investment), section A (Investment), Arts 1107 and 1109.
31. *See*, e.g., *ibid.*, Chapter 11 (Investment), section A (Investment), Annex IV (Exceptions from Most-Favored-Nation Treatment).

Arbitration Rules.[32] Allowing investors to directly bring claims against host States was not the only way to resolve investment disputes, but without a doubt it provided investors with heightened confidence in the system.

At the time of negotiation, nothing about NAFTA's Chapter 11 (procedural or substantive) was remarkable. It was consistent with many other IIAs negotiated by NAFTA Parties during the 1990s. As explained by Brower and Steven in 2001:

> In the last decade the BIT has become the predominant method by which States regulate investment on the international plane and it should come as no surprise that NAFTA's investment protection scheme, including provision for the arbitration of investor-State disputes, is essentially identical to that of the vast majority of BITs concluded since 1990. The NAFTA Parties themselves have negotiated no less than eighty-six BITs with other States and Chapter 11 closely follows the US Model BIT.[33]

[C] NAFTA: General Experiences under and Criticisms of Chapter 11

During its twenty-seven-year tenure, NAFTA's Chapter 11 was put to the test. Dozens of investor claims were brought against each of the host States. This was unexpected for the American and Canadian governments. Both, as discussed previously, expected NAFTA to protect investors from their own countries, rather than trigger claims that they would have to defend.[34] This is the experiential reality of NAFTA. Investor protections, which may have worked in theory, proved to be very challenging to manage after less than ten years of implementation. As explained by Professor Ian Laird in 2001:

> The main response of government officials who negotiated Chapter 11, or act on the government side of disputes, is that 'we did not intend NAFTA to mean that.' What they are really saying is that Chapter 11 was intended to protect Canadian and US investments from arbitrary or discriminatory conduct of the Mexican government, and that Canada and the US should never attract claims. They never thought that their own governments might violate international treatment obligations.[35]

The sentiment is reflected in a law journal article authored by David A. Gantz that same year:

> The focus on litigation between Canada and the United States was probably not anticipated by the Canadian and American negotiators of Chapter 11, although perhaps it should have been. It is only as [both the American and Canadian

32. *Ibid.*, Chapter 11, section B (Settlement of Disputes between a Party and an Investor of Another Party), Arts 1115–1138.
33. Brower and Steven, *supra* n. 9, at 193–194. *See also* David A. Gantz, *Resolution of Investment Disputes under the North American Free Trade Agreement*, 10 ARIZ. J. INT'L & COMP. L. 335, 341–342 (1993).
34. *See* Abbott, *supra* n. 9, para. 18; Gantz, *supra* n. 7, at 1302.
35. Ian A. Laird, *NAFTA Chapter 11 Meets Chicken Little*, 2 CHI. J. INT'L L. 223, 230 (2001).

governments] gain experience in defending their respective governments that the magnitude of the potential problems become clear.[36]

Much ink has been spilled analysing two specific Chapter 11 protections: the standard for investor treatment and the meaning of indirect expropriation.[37] While the precise contours of criticisms vary based on the identity of the critic, all share a common theme: providing an aggrieved investor with the right to assert a claim directly against a national government may unduly infringe on the sovereign's right to legislate, enforce, and adjudicate according to its own laws.[38] Some commentators have astutely observed that these criticisms are primarily rooted in the concern that private arbitral tribunals may not reach 'correct' decisions, rather than concern about the substance of these protections.[39]

Public Citizen, a non-profit consumer advocacy organization based in Washington, DC, was at the forefront of NAFTA criticism for many years. In 2004, Public Citizen published a leaflet on NAFTA's ten-year track record.[40] It voiced sovereignty-based criticisms of NAFTA, including the precise trade opportunities it created.[41] On the ISDS front, Public Citizen suggested that NAFTA undercut the American federalist system, offered disproportionate protections to foreign investors, and put the American 'civil justice system[]' in the hands of 'special closed-door trade tribunals for cash compensation'.[42]

To those well versed with ISDS and recent discussions about its merits and future viability, these concerns are familiar, well worn, and likely alone not enough to signal the end of NAFTA, especially considering NAFTA's successful and reliable stimulation of North American trade and economic development. However, as discussed below, another more nuanced layer of criticism developed through the NAFTA Parties' experience in various arbitrations.

[D] Experiential Reality: NAFTA Claims Pursued Against the US and Canada

Key challenges of NAFTA's Chapter 11 emerged only through experience as host States defended against various investor claims. This section does not chronicle the dozens of cases arbitrated under Chapter 11. It only highlights a few examples as illustrations of the American and Canadian host State experience,[43] with the aim of contextualizing the rise of USMCA's Chapter 14 as a reformed and revised approach to regional ISDS.

36. Gantz, *supra* n. 7, at 1302.
37. *See generally* Robert Meltz, *Foreign Investor Protection under NAFTA Chapter 11*, U.S. Congressional Research Service Report for Congress (29 September 2003).
38. Zachary M. Eastman, *NAFTA's Chapter 11 – For Whose Benefit*, 16 J. INT'L ARB. 105, 112 (1999).
39. Brower and Steven, *supra* n. 9, at 199–200.
40. Public Citizen NAFTA at Ten Series: *The Ten Year Track Record of the North American Free Trade Agreement: Undermining Sovereignty and Democracy*, https://www.citizen.org/wp-content/uploads/nafta_10_democracy.pdf.
41. *Ibid.*, at 3–4.
42. *Ibid.*, at 2–3.
43. Years ago, a law journal article by the late Professor Guillermo Aguilar Alvarez and Professor William W. Park similarly sought to draw conclusions regarding NAFTA's Chapter 11 based on

[1] Loewen Group, Inc. et al. v. United States[44]

In 1994, a Mississippi businessman sued Loewen, a Canada-based funeral home conglomerate, for anticompetitive and predatory acts. The claim asserted USD 105 million in damages. Following a jury trial, the plaintiff was awarded USD 500 million, including USD 400 million in punitive damages, the largest punitive damages award in Mississippi's history. Loewen settled the claim with the businessman for approximately USD 150 million rather than appeal the case to a higher court, which would have required posting a bond worth 125% of the damages owed (USD 625 million) in order to obtain a stay of execution, which it viewed as a prohibitively expensive undertaking.[45]

Loewen then filed a NAFTA Chapter 11 claim against the US for USD 725 million. It alleged that the Mississippi trial was biased against Loewen as a foreign entity, resulting in procedural denial of justice. It further alleged that the Mississippi court's final disposition of the case deprived it of NT and fair and equitable treatment (FET) (i.e., violations of NAFTA Articles 1102 and 1105) and that the excessive jury verdict amount, the effective denial of right of appeal, and related coerced settlement were equivalent to an uncompensated expropriation (i.e., violation of NAFTA Article 1110).

The tribunal's 2003 final award concluded that the Mississippi trial's mismanagement resulted in a lack of due process and amounted to a failure by the US under principles of international law.[46] However, the tribunal found that Loewen should have exhausted its domestic remedies and appealed the trial court's decision to a higher Mississippi court, notwithstanding the very high financial cost associated with posting the 125% bond.[47] Moreover, the tribunal determined that it lacked jurisdiction to adjudicate the claim on its merits because Loewen lost its status as a qualified investor under NAFTA's Chapter 11 when it undertook corporate restructuring under US bankruptcy laws.[48]

Loewen's arbitration claim became the source of many NAFTA criticisms.[49] It brought to the forefront whether domestic civil judicial proceedings may be reexamined by international tribunals.[50] It also served as ammunition for NAFTA opponents to claim that NAFTA afforded foreign investors with an unfair advantage over domestic entities, who would not have standing to pursue a NAFTA claim against the US government. Public Citizen, the American non-profit consumer advocacy

---

exemplar ISDS claims arbitrated between American and Canadian parties. *See generally* Guillermo Aguilar Alvarez and William W. Park, *The New Face of Investment Arbitration: NAFTA Chapter 11*, 28 YALE J. INT'L L. 365 (2003).

44. *Loewen Group, Inc. et al. v. United States*, ICSID Case No. ARB(AF)/98/3, https://www.italaw.com/cases/632.
45. For a full chronicle of the Mississippi litigation *see* Lucien J. Dhooge, *The Loewen Group v. United States: Punitive Damages and the Foreign Investment Provisions of the North American Free Trade Agreement*, 19 CONN. J. INT'L L. 495 (2004).
46. *Loewen Group, Inc. et al. v. United States*, ICSID Case No. ARB(AF)/98/3, Award (26 June 2003), at paras 122–123.
47. *Ibid.*, at paras 184–188.
48. *Ibid.*, at para. 238.
49. *Ibid.*, at para. 497.
50. *Ibid.*

organization discussed earlier in this chapter, issued a seven-page leaflet concerning *Loewen* and referred to Loewen's right to ISDS as a 'special privilege' that provided a means 'to attack domestic public interest, land use, regulatory, and other laws if they feel that a domestic policy or government decision as undermined the firms' new trade pact privileged, such as threatening their "expected future profits"'.[51] Other critics perceived NAFTA Chapter 11 arbitration as a threat to the American civil jury system's legitimacy.[52]

[2] Methanex Corporation v. United States[53]

In the late 1990s, California banned a methanol-based gasoline additive known as MBTE based on concerns about its leakage from underground fuel storage tanks and possible contamination of the State's drinking water supply. Methanex, a Canadian corporation with interests in the MBTE industry, filed a claim under NAFTA's Chapter 11 against the US. Methanex alleged discrimination, denial of MST, and expropriation of its investment (i.e., violations of NAFTA Articles 1102, 1105, and 1110). Methanex described its damages as loss of 'a substantial portion of their customer base, goodwill, and market for methanol in California'.[54] The tribunal's 2005 final award concluded that there was no 'legally significant connection' between the US regulatory measures and Methanex's US investments and therefore the tribunal lacked jurisdiction to decide Methanex's claims.[55]

Environmentalists and the US Environmental Protection Agency (EPA) protested upon the claim's filing and amicus submissions were accepted by the tribunal.[56] Critics claimed that NAFTA afforded foreign corporations favouritism by allowing their private corporate interests to trump exercise of legitimate sovereignty by the California state government, at great risk to the American public. The tribunal was further attacked at an existential level and many criticisms echoed the sentiments present in modern debates. Chief among these concerns was that private tribunals could not

51. Public Citizen, *Trade Pacts' 'Investor-State' Systems: Private Corporate Tribunals Used to Attack Countries' Courts* (16 April 2012), https://www.citizen.org/article/loewen-funeral-home-conglomerate-unhappy-with-domestic-jury-awards-in-private-contract-disputes-demands-bailout-from-taxpayers/.
52. Dhooge, *supra* n. 45, at 497–498 and sources cited therein.
53. *Methanex Corporation v. United States of America*, UNCITRAL, https://www.italaw.com/cases/683. *See generally* Marisa Yee, *The Future of Environmental Regulation after Article 1110 of NAFTA: A Look at the Methanex and Metalclad Cases*, 9 Hastings West Northwest J. of Envtl. L. & Pol'y 85 (2003).
54. Methanex's Second Amended Claim, at para. 322 (as cited in *Methanex Corporation v. United States of America*, UNCITRAL, Final Award of the Tribunal on Jurisdiction and Merits (3 August 2005), Part IV, para. 2.
55. *Ibid.*, Part IV, para. 22.
56. For a survey of the criticisms of NAFTA provoked by Methanex, *see* Lucien J. Dhooge, *The Revenge of the Trail Smelter: Environmental Regulation as Expropriation Pursuant to the North American Free Trade Agreement*, 38 Am. Bus. L.J. 475, 478–479 (2001). For details on amicus submissions, *see Methanex Corporation v. United States of America*, UNCITRAL, Final Award of the Tribunal on Jurisdiction and Merits (3 August 2005), Part II, paras 26–30.

legitimately adjudicate corporate claims that might have a lasting impact on domestic environmental law and procedure.

[3] Eli Lilly and Company v. Canada[57]

Eli Lilly, a US-based global pharmaceutical company, sought to market proprietary pharmaceutical products in Canada. Under Canadian patent law, those products could only be patented if the underlying invention was new, non-obvious, and had utility. To determine 'utility', Canadian courts increasingly made use of the 'promise of the patent' doctrine in their analysis. If a product does not meet its intended utility the patent was void. After two patent applications by Eli Lilly were invalidated by Canadian courts, Eli Lilly filed a claim against Canada under NAFTA's Chapter 11.[58] Eli Lilly alleged it was deprived of MST (i.e., violation of NAFTA Article 1105) and invalidation of the patent constituted an unlawful expropriation (i.e., violation of NAFTA Article 1110). Canada's defence was four-pronged: (1) the sole legal basis on which a national court decision could result in a breach of NAFTA's Chapter 11 was a denial of justice, which was not alleged; (2) the tribunal lacked jurisdiction *ratione temporis* because Eli Lilly's claim was time-barred; (3) there had been no dramatic change in Canadian courts' interpretation of the requirement under the Canadian patent law that an invention be 'useful'; and (4) the invalidation of Eli Lilly's patents was not a breach of NAFTA's Chapter 11 or any other international obligation.[59]

In its 2017 final award, the tribunal rejected Canada's jurisdictional objections and focused on Eli Lilly's argument that the promise doctrine constituted a 'dramatic change' to Canadian patent law.[60] The tribunal disagreed with Eli Lilly, observing that the relevant Canadian court decisions were decided over a period time.[61] Moreover, the tribunal's analysis of the promise doctrine, coupled with the judiciary's role, confirmed that no dramatic change took place, but rather an evolution of legal approach to a sphere of domestic regulation.[62] Eli Lilly's claim was accordingly dismissed on its merits.[63]

[4] Relevant Observations

While each of these illustrative arbitrations involved unique facts and different claims, they exemplify themes found in many NAFTA arbitrations. The tribunal in each of

57. *Eli Lilly and Company v. The Government of Canada*, ICSID Case No. UNCT/14/2, https://www.italaw.com/cases/1625.
58. *Eli Lilly and Company v. The Government of Canada*, ICSID Case No. UNCT/14/2, Final Award (16 March 2017), at para. 5.
59. *Ibid.*, at para. 6.
60. *Ibid.*, at para. 171.
61. *Ibid.*, at paras 309-325.
62. *Ibid.*
63. *Ibid.*, at XII (Award).

these arbitrations found in favour of the host State based on fine factual and evidentiary distinctions. Moreover, none of the tribunals challenged the legitimacy of a challenged government regulation or policy. Broader empirical studies of NAFTA arbitrations have not identified any landmark case in which an American or Canadian government policy was effectively overturned due to a tribunal's ruling in favour of a claimant investor pursuant to a Chapter 11 claim.[64] Nor have such empirical studies found evidence that NAFTA Parties were prevented or deterred from adopting new or updated regulations in the interest of legitimate public interests because of the risk of exposure to Chapter 11 claims.[65] Where NAFTA tribunals have decided in favour of an investor, the host States have only been compelled to pay 'fair, monetary compensation to the aggrieved investor rather than actually punish or otherwise compel a member state to reverse the policy in question'.[66]

However, the American and Canadian host State experiences revealed the true challenge of managing risks and confirmed the potential that such claims could be asserted against them. This does not necessarily mean NAFTA's Chapter 11 failed. Over time, host States must actively reconsider their model IIAs, including whether ISDS should be included in future trade deals. In making these decisions, trade negotiators must consider past experiences, including past allegations and evidence that foreign investors may have experienced disparate treatment meriting damages. This analytical approach allows negotiators to clarify concepts and implement appropriate lessons to strengthen trade, globalization, and ISDS. Indeed, as noted by Professor Frederick Mayer in 2017:

> NAFTA was always far from perfect and there is a need to update it – not surprising for an agreement negotiated a quarter century ago. But just as NAFTA did not cause inequality, killing NAFTA would do nothing to address it. The danger is that the demonization of NAFTA will distract from the much harder work of figuring out how to make economic globalization more equitable, more inclusive and more sustainable.[67]

§6.03 THE RISE OF USMCA AND KEY REVISIONS WITHIN ITS CHAPTER 14

This section first provides social, economic, and political context for the rise of USMCA. It then identifies key changes in USMCA's Chapter 14 ISDS mechanism.

64. Owen, *supra* n. 24, at 64.
65. *Ibid.*, at 65.
66. *Ibid.*
67. *See*, e.g., Frederick Mayer, *The Politics of NAFTA Have Been Driven More by Story Than by Fact*, The Hill (18 August 2017), https://thehill.com/blogs/pundits-blog/international/347078-the-politics-of-nafta-have-been-driven-more-by-story-than-by.

[A] Social, Economic, and Political Context for USMCA's Development

Donald Trump's presidential campaign hinged on an economic plan that would 'make America great again'.[68] This 'America First' ideology captured the concerns of many American workers - social inequality and economic stagnation - and campaign rhetoric focused on creating more jobs for American workers.[69] NAFTA became a symbolic target under this agenda and has been characterized by many commentators as a 'scapegoat' for Trump's economic plan.[70]

Immediately upon entering office, President Trump took two steps to put this plan into action: withdrawing from further negotiations on the Trans-Pacific Partnership (TPP) and announcing his intent to renegotiate NAFTA.[71] Both decisions reflected economic nationalism and deployed protectionist trade policies to defend US industries from foreign competition, the wisdom of which is subject to great debate.

[B] USMCA's Chapter 14 and Noteworthy Shifts

Since the release of USMCA's text in September 2018, many commentators have undertaken side-by-side comparisons of NAFTA and USMCA. From a trade and economic perspective, the resounding view is that not much has changed.[72] From an ISDS perspective, USMCA's Chapter 14 reflects some noteworthy shifts. Several revisions tie rights to the identity of individual investors and host States. This approach contrasts starkly from NAFTA's approach, which generally provided mirrored rights to support balance among all three NAFTA Parties.

Notably, Canada has withdrawn from Chapter 14. Its consent for legacy claims expires three years after 1 July 2020, NAFTA's termination date.[73] It is not clear what this means in practice. 'Termination' is a vague concept and the concurrent existence of NAFTA and USMCA could lead to confusing interpretations and adjudications by investors, host States, and tribunals. ISDS survives for the benefit of American and Mexican investors, but as discussed below, the types of disputes investors may pursue

68. Kimberly Amadeo, *President Donald Trump's Economic Plan*, The Balance (25 June 2019), https://www.thebalance.com/donald-trump-economic-plan-3994106; *Trade Wars, Trump Tariffs and Protectionism Explained*, BBC (10 May 2019), https://www.bbc.com/news/world-43512098.
69. Daniel J. Ikenson, *USMCA: A Marginal NAFTA Upgrade at a High Cost*, Cato Institute (10 April 2019), https://www.cato.org/publications/commentary/usmca-marginal-nafta-upgrade-high-cost.
70. *See*, e.g., Mayer, *supra* n. 67.
71. Catherine Rampell, *Trump's 'Historic' Trade Deal Doesn't Look So Historic after All*, The Washington Post (1 October 2018), https://www.washingtonpost.com/opinions/trump-didnt-blow-up-our-trade-system-whoop-de-doo/2018/10/01/2137be18-c5b7-11e8-9b1c-a90f1daae309_story.html?utm_term=.e3cdfefe98ef.
72. *See*, e.g., Ikenson, *supra* n. 69; Gwynn Guilford, *The Net Impact of Trump's New NAFTA Is Probably Nothing*, Quartz (22 April 2019), https://qz.com/1600240/the-net-impact-of-trumps-new-nafta-is-probably-nothing/.
73. A 'legacy investment' is defined as 'an investment of an investor of another Party in the territory of the Party established or acquired between January 1, 1994, and the date of termination of NAFTA 1994, and in existence on the date of entry of force of this agreement'. USMCA, *supra* n. 16, Annex 14-C (Legacy Investment Claims and Pending Claims), Art. 6(a).

(and the procedural means to do so) have been realigned and no longer mirror each other.

Investor-claimants are now required to litigate claims 'before a competent court or administrative tribunal of the respondent'.[74] Claimants must litigate until a 'final decision from a court of last resort', or, alternatively, thirty months have elapsed since local court proceedings were initiated.[75] There is an exception to this local litigation requirement 'to the extent recourse to domestic remedies was obviously futile or manifestly ineffective'.[76] This scheme is accompanied by a four-year concurrent statute of limitations for asserting any claim under USMCA.[77]

In a departure from NAFTA, USMCA provides an 'asymmetrical' fork-in-the-road provision.[78] If, during local court proceedings, an American investor alleges a breach of USMCA itself (as opposed to a breach of Mexican law), this will bar any right to arbitration under USMCA.[79] USMCA does not contain a parallel provision for Mexican investors, thereby altering dispute resolution procedures and the scope of investor rights based solely on nationality.

Under USMCA, investors may seek arbitration of claims involving the following:

- Direct expropriation (but not indirect expropriation).[80] 'Direct expropriation' occurs when 'an investment is nationalized or otherwise directly expropriated through formal transfer of title or outright seizure'.[81]
- Violations of NT, which means 'treatment no less favorable than that it accords, in like circumstances, to its own investors with respect to the establishment, acquisition, expansion, management, conduct, operation, and sale or other disposition of investments in its territory'.[82]
- Violations of MFN, which arises when a State's treatment of an investor is 'less favorable than the treatment it accords, in like circumstances, to investors of any other Party or of any non-Party with respect to the establishment, acquisition, expansion, management, conduct, operation, and sale or other disposition of investments in its territory'.[83]

74. *Ibid.*, Annex 14-D (Mexico-United States Investment Disputes), Art. 14.D.5 (Conditions and Limitations on Consent).
75. *Ibid.*, Annex 14-D (Mexico-United States Investment Disputes), Art. 14.D.5 (Conditions and Limitations on Consent).
76. *Ibid.*, Annex 14-D, n. 24.
77. *Ibid.*, Art. 14.D.5 (Conditions and Limitations on Consent).
78. For an in-depth discussion, *see* Alexander Bedrosyan, *The Asymmetrical Fork-in-the-Road Clause in the USMCA: Helpful and Unique*, Kluwer Arbitration Blog (29 October 2018), http://arbitrationblog.kluwerarbitration.com/2018/10/29/usmca/.
79. USMCA, *supra* n. 16, Annex 14-D (Mexico-United States Investment Disputes), Appendix 3.
80. *Ibid.*, Annex 14-B (Expropriation), Art. 2.
81. *Ibid.*
82. *Ibid.*, Art. 14.4.1 (National Treatment).
83. *Ibid.*, Art. 14.5.1 (Most-Favoured-Nation Treatment).

There is a carve-out for NT or MFN claims 'with respect to the establishment or acquisition of an investment'.[84] Notably, footnote 22, which accompanies the MFN provision, provides that 'treatment':

> *excludes provisions in other international trade or investment agreements that establish international dispute resolution procedures or impose substantive obligations*; rather, 'treatment' only includes measures adopted or maintained by the other Annex Party, which may include measures adopted or maintained pursuant to or consistent with substantive obligations in other international trade or investment agreements.[85]

Overall, this reflects a departure from the language of similar provisions in other IIAs.

Additional ISDS rights are available for investors who are parties to government contracts in identified 'covered sectors', which include oil and natural gas, power generation, telecommunications, transportation, and infrastructure, each a highly regulated industry involving significant government involvement.[86] These additional rights include the option to assert claims for violations of the minimum standard of treatment under customary international law, claims of indirect expropriation, or claims about the establishment or acquisition of an investment.[87]

Finally, provisions to promote transparency and ethical conduct have been added. With respect to transparency, specific articles now support the publication of documents concerning arbitral proceedings, access to hearings, and the possibility of amicus participation.[88] With respect to ethical conduct, arbitrators must now adhere to the IBA's Guidelines on Conflicts of Interest in International Arbitration and refrain from acting as arbitrator in one USMCA proceeding while acting as party representative in another (e.g., as counsel, party-appointed expert, or witness).[89] These revisions reflect current debates in the field and aim to promote public confidence in the ISDS system and its legitimacy.

As discussed above in §6.01, on 10 December 2019, all three Member States executed the USMCA Amendment, providing twenty-six pages of modifications.[90] The covered topics include dispute settlement, labour and environmental provisions, intellectual property rights, and steel and aluminium requirements in the rules of origin for automobiles.[91] The Amendment does not make any changes to Chapter 14. However, it introduces novel concepts for international dispute resolution, including evidentiary guidelines for any tribunal empanelled to hear a State-to-State dispute

84. *Ibid.*, Annex 14-D (Mexico-United States Investment Disputes), Art. 14.D.3 (Submission of a Claim to Arbitration).
85. *Ibid.*, Annex 14-D (Mexico-United States Investment Disputes), Art. 14.D.3 (Submission of a Claim to Arbitration), n. 22 (emphasis added).
86. *Ibid.*, Annex 14-E (Mexico-United States Investment Disputes Related to Covered Government Contracts), Art. 6.
87. *Ibid.*
88. *Ibid.*, Annex 14-D, Art. 14.D.8 (Transparency of Arbitral Proceedings), Annex 14-D, Art. 14.D.7 (Conduct of the Arbitration), cl. 3.
89. *Ibid.*, Annex 14-D, Art. 14.D.6 (Selection of Arbitrators), cl. 5.
90. Protocol of Amendment to the USMCA, *supra* n. 17.
91. *Ibid.*

under USMCA's Chapter 31. This is not directly relevant for ISDS disputes, but it is interesting nonetheless because international investors and global businesses may be impacted by State-to-State disputes arising from the Trump Administration's legacy of protectionist policies.

§6.04 CONCLUSION: FRAMING USMCA'S DEVELOPMENT WITHIN THE GLOBAL ISDS DEBATE

Only time will tell how the transition from NAFTA to USMCA will impact the North American trade and investment environment and the benefits derived by each State. After the 30 November 2018 signing ceremony at the G-20 Summit in Buenos Aires, President Trump tweeted that USMCA represents 'one of the most important, and largest, Trade Deals in U.S. and World History'.[92] This is likely true. USMCA is expected to account for more than USD 1.2 trillion in trade in one of the world's largest free trade zones.[93]

Many commentators (including the authors of this chapter) have written elsewhere that USMCA's origins in 'America First' protectionist policies challenge post-World War II multilateral institutions and risk the stability of the transnational legal system.[94] However, from an ISDS perspective, a crystallized evolution is palpable. The transition from NAFTA's Chapter 11 to USMCA's Chapter 14 is a practical example of effective ISDS reform.

A State's decision to include an ISDS mechanism in its IIAs reflects its decision to accede a piece of its sovereignty to benefit from foreign investment. NAFTA's Chapter 11 reflected an approach to these choices that sought to stimulate unprecedented trade advantages. USMCA's Chapter 14 takes a more nuanced approach. Rightly referred to by many as 'NAFTA 2.0', USMCA's Chapter 14 is informed by more than twenty-five years of trade and ISDS dispute resolution experience. Each State's approach presumably benefits from a greater understanding of its sovereignty and the challenges and risks it is willing to accept.

Canada, for its part, has determined to continue to participate in USMCA for economic and trade reasons. However, it has expressly withdrawn from Chapter 14 and will not offer ISDS benefits to any prospective American or Mexican investors.[95]

---

92. *See* Donald Trump (@RealDonaldTrump), Twitter (30 November 2018, 6:45 AM) https://twitter.com/realDonaldTrump/status/1068516326010830849 [https://perma.cc/A5ZB-K6BJ].
93. Heather Long, *The USMCA Is Finally Done. Here's What Is in It*, The Wash. Post (10 December 2019), https://www.washingtonpost.com/business/2019/12/10/usmca-is-finally-done-deal-after-democrats-sign-off-heres-what-is-it/.
94. Kiran Nasir Gore and Charles Camp, *2019 Scorecard: The Trump Effect on Future International Business Disputes*, The World Financial Review (22 January 2020), https://worldfinancialreview.com/2019-scorecard-the-trump-effect-on-future-international-business-disputes/; Kiran Nasir Gore, *From NAFTA to USMCA: Providing Context for a New Era of Regional Investor-State Dispute Settlement*, Young Arbitration Review (Vol. 8, ed. 34, July 2019), available at: https://ssrn.com/abstract=3412709.
95. For many commentators, this is surprising: Canada remains committed to multilateral trade deals and continues to participate in ISDS through other trade agreements. Some speculate that Canada's opt-out may reflect Canada's mixed success with arbitrations involving American

The US and Mexico continue to offer ISDS protection to prospective investors through their participation in Chapter 14. However, the balanced and equitable playing field that previously was a lynchpin of NAFTA has been lost. This is inherent in the loss of American and Mexican investors' ISDS rights against Canada.[96] It is further reinforced by the fact that possible claims and associated remedies available to American and Mexican investors are now driven by national identity.

The differences between NAFTA's Chapter 11 and USMCA's Chapter 14 reflect the concrete ISDS 'evolution' for regional ISDS, and perhaps offers a template for future global trends. Optimistically speaking, the story of USMCA may demonstrate that evolution, and not death, is the answer to the modern ISDS debate.

---

investors under NAFTA. Others cite Canada's perceived lack of bargaining power during USMCA negotiations and an ultimate decision simply to abstain. *See* Kiran Nasir Gore and Esmé Shirlow, *The USMCA/CUSMA/T-MEC's Entry into Force: Introducing a New Era in Regional ISDS with NAFTA 2.0*, Kluwer Arbitration Blog (22 June 2020), http://arbitrationblog.kluwerarbitration.com/2020/06/22/the-usmca-cusma-t-mecs-entry-into-force-introducing-a-new-era-in-regional-isds-with-nafta-2-0/.

96. Canada and Mexico have an alternate path for resolution of ISDS disputes through the Comprehensive and Progressive Agreement for Trans-Pacific Partnership (CPTPP), to which both are parties. *See* Comprehensive and Progressive Agreement for Trans-Pacific Partnership (CPTPP) (30 December 2018), https://www.international.gc.ca/trade-commerce/trade-agreements-accords-commerciaux/agr-acc/tpp-ptp/text-texte/toc-tdm.aspx?lang=eng.

CHAPTER 7

Reshaping Investor-State Dispute Settlement Through an Appellate Review Mechanism

Margie-Lys Jaime

Over the past fifteen years, the lack of consistency and predictability in arbitral awards, the absence of a review mechanism, and questions surrounding the independence and impartiality of party-appointed arbitrators have all challenged the legitimacy of Investor-State Dispute Settlement (ISDS). Under the aegis of the United Nations Commission on International Trade Law (UNCITRAL), recent ISDS reform discussions revived the debate to find possible solutions that states may adopt to address their concerns about the current system. The chapter focuses on the establishment of a multilateral 'Court of Appeal' as a way to reshape ISDS. In this context, the chapter addresses important issues such as the selection, appointment, and remuneration of the adjudicators, as well as the scope of their power, and grounds for appeal. The analysis of these issues could contribute to the ongoing discussions at UNCITRAL and finally the adoption of an appeal review mechanism by the Commission.

§7.01 INTRODUCTION

The analysis of investor-state cases illustrates that arbitral tribunals have arrived at different interpretations even when the terms of the treaty are the same. Divergent legal interpretations of the same treaty provisions may harm the legitimate expectations of both investors and sovereigns. In the same vein, inconsistent decisions involving the same facts and issues create uncertainty, producing disconformity with respect to the role of arbitrators.[1] Additionally, repeat appointments have raised awareness about the lack of independence and impartiality of arbitrators, and the existence of a small 'elite' group of arbitrators handling most arbitrations.[2] The limited number of individuals repeatedly appointed as arbitrators in ISDS cases, and the fact that some act both as counsel and as arbitrators in different ISDS proceedings, has undermined the perception of legitimacy of the ISDS system.[3] As a result, some countries have withdrawn from the International Centre for Settlement of Investment Dispute (ICSID), and a number of others have terminated their investment treaties.[4] Simultaneously, several initiatives have looked to reform or even replace the current system.

By way of example, it may suffice to refer to the failed attempt by Union of South American Nations (UNASUR, by its acronym in Spanish) to establish a centre for the settlement of investment disputes,[5] or by Brazil and the Southern Common Market (MERCOSUR, by its acronym in Spanish) to encourage the adoption of cooperation and investment facilitation agreements,[6] as breaking with the traditional bilateral investment treaty mould. More recently, the proposal of the European Union (EU) for a permanent investment court system moves away from the rules of investment arbitration towards a new paradigm for ISDS.[7] These attempts, however, remain dead in the water if the proposed reforms or 'replacements' do not achieve a critical mass to be multilaterally implemented.

Section §7.02 will discuss the advantages and disadvantages of creating an appellate review mechanism. Section §7.03 will examine the nature and scope of an ISDS Court of Appeal, analysing the issues that might be subject to appeal and the grounds for appeal. Section §7.04 will focus on the composition and structure of an appellate body, the selection, appointment, and remuneration of its members. Finally, section §7.05 will analyse options for creating an appellate review mechanism.

---

1. Susan Franck, *The Legitimacy Crisis in Investment Treaty Arbitration: Privatizing Public International Law Through Inconsistent Decisions*, 73 Fordham L. Rev. 1521, 1558–1582 (2005).
2. European Federation for Investment Law and Arbitration, *A response to the Criticism Against ISDS* 21–23 (17 May 2015), https://efila.org/wp-content/uploads/2015/05/EFILA_in_response_to_the-criticism_of_ISDS_final_draft.pdf.
3. Gabrielle Kaufmann-Kohler and Michele Potestà, *Can the Mauritius Convention Serve as a Model for the Reform of Investor-State Arbitration in Connection with the Introduction of a Permanent Investment Tribunal or an Appeal Mechanism? Analysis and Roadmap*, para. 21 (3 June 2016) (hereinafter 'CIDS Report'). *See also* Margie-Lys Jaime, *Shifting Sands: New Trends on Ethics Regulation of Arbitrators in Investor-State Dispute Settlement*, 10 World Arb. & Med. Rev. 383, 394, n. 3 (2016) (commenting on case law involving the double-hatting phenomenon).
4. UNCTAD, *International Investment Policymaking in Transition: Challenges and Opportunities of Treaty Renewal*, IIA Issues Note No. 4, UNCTAD/WEB/DIAE/PCB/2013/9 (21 June 2013).
5. Silvia Karina Fiezzoni, *The Challenge of UNASUR Members Countries to Replace ICSID Arbitration*, 2 Beijing L. Rev. 134 (2011); Daniela Páez-Salgado, *New Investment Arbitration Center in Latin America: UNASUR, a Hybrid Example of Success or Failure?* Kluwer Arbitration Blog (27 May 2016), http://arbitrationblog.kluwerarbitration.com/2016/05/27/unasur/; Katia Fach Gómez and Catharine Titi, *UNASUR Centre for the Settlement of Investment Disputes: Comments on the Draft Consecutive Agreement*, Investment Treaty News (10 August 2016).
6. José Henrique Vieira Martins, *Brazil's Cooperation and Facilitation Investment Agreements (CFIA) and Recent Developments*, Investment Treaty News (12 June 2017).
7. Council of the European Union, *Multilateral Investment Court: Council Gives Mandate to the Commission to Open Negotiations*, EU News 55/2018 (20 March 2018).

§7.02 ADVANTAGES AND DISADVANTAGES OF AN APPELLATE REVIEW MECHANISM

The availability of appeals mechanisms in investment arbitration is not new,[8] but it was not until the early 2000s that countries like the United States started to incorporate provisions regarding the establishment (although programmatic) of a bilateral appellate body in their investment treaties.[9] In 2004, the ICSID Secretariat, noting that at least twenty countries may have signed treaties with provisions on an appeal mechanism for investment awards, explored the possibility to establish an appeals facility.[10] ICSID did not go forward with this initiative, considering it was 'premature'.[11] Sixteen years later, ICSID decided not to include the creation of an appellate body under the current reform process.[12] Still, the establishment of an appeal mechanism is a 'recurrent feature' in the debate about ISDS.[13] One possible reason for not including an appeals facility is that the ICSID reform process is not intended to amend the ICSID Convention but to improve the ICSID rules and regulations, within the framework of the ICSID Convention. Indeed, amendment of the ICSID Convention requires the unanimous ratification of the contracting states, which could be difficult to achieve.[14] This section analyses the advantages and disadvantages of establishing an appeal mechanism vis-à-vis the current annulment system and the multilateral investment court.

[A] Advantages Vis-à-Vis Annulment

An appellate body focuses on the substantive correctness of the decision, being able to modify or reverse the legal findings and conclusions of the first tribunal.[15] By contrast, annulment is concerned with the legitimacy of the process, voiding the award, in total

8. Gabriel Bottini, *Reform of the Investor-State Arbitration Regime: The Appeal Proposal*, in *Reshaping the Investor-State Dispute Settlement*, 456–457 (Jean E. Kalicki and Anna Joubin-Bret eds, 2015).
9. An appeals mechanism appears formally in the Trade Promotion Authority provisions of the Trade Act of 2002, which was included in the 2004 US Model BIT. *See* generally UNCTAD, *Bilateral investment treaties 1995–2006: Trends in investment rulemaking*, 123–124 (2007), https://unctad.org/en/Docs/iteiia20065_en.pdf.
10. ICSID Secretariat, *Possible Improvements of the Framework for ICSID Arbitration* Discussion Paper, para. 20 (22 October 2004).
11. Elsa Sardinha, *The Impetus for the Creation of an Appellate Mechanism*, 32 ICSID Rev. - FILJ 503, 508, n. 3 (2017).
12. ICSID Secretariat, *Proposals for Amendment of the ICSID Rules – Synopsis*, Vol. 1 (2 August 2018).
13. *See* Christoph Schreuer and Andrea de la Brena, *Does ISDS Need an Appeals Mechanism?* 17 TDM Journal 1, n. 2 (February 2020), https://www.transnational-dispute-management.com/article.asp?Key=2719.
14. Pursuant to Art. 53(1) of the ICSID Convention, awards rendered in accordance to the Convention 'shall not be subject to any appeal or to any other remedy except those provided to the Convention'. *Cf.* ICSID Convention, Art. 66.
15. While consistency is a systemic notion, correctness is about the substantive quality of a specific decision. Thus, correctness in the current debate has become related to the question when different treaties justify different interpretations. *See* Wolfgang Alschner, *Ensuring Correctness or Promoting Consistency? Tracking Policy Priorities in Investment Arbitration Through Large-Scale*

or in part, without substituting the decision.[16] Indeed, the result of a successful appeal is the correction of the arbitral award, while the result of a successful annulment is the invalidation of the original decision.

Article 52 of the ICSID Convention constitutes the exclusive and limited means to annul an ICSID award.[17] The intention of the drafters of the ICSID Convention was to exclude any possibility of appeal and to establish 'rigidly fixed limits' for challenging the validity of an award.[18] In other words, it was designed as an exceptional and narrowly circumscribed remedy where the ad hoc committee cannot substitute the tribunal's determination on the merits for its own.[19] In this sense, the ad hoc Committee in *Victor Pey Casado* noted that Chile was seeking to appeal the tribunal's decision by asking the Committee to substitute its decision for that of the tribunal, which was not the purpose of an annulment committee.[20] This reflects the will of the drafters of the Convention to ensure finality of awards.

Under the current system, finality has taken precedence over the principle of correctness.[21] As a result, parties may not seek a remedy on the same dispute in another forum. In other words, the res judicata effect applies in relation to other arbitration tribunals, including ICSID tribunals and domestic courts. Yet, the applicability of the doctrine of binding precedent for subsequent cases is excluded.[22] This means that tribunals are all at the same level and there is no review for error law similar to that performed by national courts of appeal or supreme courts.

The annulment process under ICSID was primarily designed for contractual disputes and not for disputes under a myriad of international investment agreements (IIAs). Yet, as of 1 January 2019, the total number of known ISDS cases pursuant to IIAs had reached 942, most of which were under the ICSID Convention.[23] Furthermore, 87% of ICSID cases have been brought under IIAs.[24] Most IIAs provide the option between an arbitration under the ICSID Convention or the ICSID Additional Facility

---

Citation Analysis, in *Legitimacy of Investment Arbitration: Empirical Perspectives* (Daniel Behn, Ole Kristian Fauchald and Malcolm Langford eds, 2020).

16. Christoph H. Schreuer, Loretta Malintoppi, August Reinisch and Anthony Sinclair, *The ICSID Convention: A Commentary* 901 (2d ed. 2009) (distinguishing between annulment and appeal).
17. Ian Laird and Rebecca Aske, *Finality Versus Consistency: Does Investor-State Arbitration Need an Appellate System?*, 7 J. App. Prac. & Process 285, 290 (2005) (analysing the possible conflicts between finality, on the one side, and consistency and correctness, on the other side).
18. United Nations, *Documents of the Fifth Session Including the Report of the Commission to the General Assembly*, 2 Yearbook of the International Law Commission 211 (1953) U.N. Doc. A/CN.4/SER.A/1953/Add.1.
19. ICSID, *Updated Background Paper on Annulment for the Administrative Council of ICSID* (5 May 2016). *See also* David Caron, *Reputation and Reality in the ICSID Annulment Process: Understanding the Distinction Between Annulment and Appeal* (1992) 7 ICSID Rev. 21.
20. *Víctor Pey Casado and Foundation (Presidente Allende) v. Republic of Chile*, ICSID Case No. ARB/98/2, Decision on the Application for Annulment of the Republic of Chile, para. 129 (18 December 2012).
21. Schreuer, Malintoppi, Reinisch and Sinclair, *supra* n. 16, at 903.
22. *See AES Corporation v. The Argentine Republic*, ICSID Case No. ARB/02/17, Decision on Jurisdiction, para. 30 (26 April 2005) (stating that each tribunal remains sovereign to retain a different solution for resolving the same problem).
23. UNCTAD, *Fact Sheet on Investor-State Dispute Settlement Cases in 2018*, IIA Issues Note (May 2019), https://unctad.org/en/PublicationsLibrary/diaepcbinf2019d4_en.pdf.
24. ICSID, The ICSID Caseload-statistics 23 (Issue 2020-1).

Rules and an ad hoc arbitration under the UNCITRAL Arbitration Rules.[25] Some IIAs may also include the possibility to choose between other institutional arbitrations (e.g., the Arbitration Institution of the Stockholm Chamber of Commerce or the International Court of Arbitration of the International Chamber of Commerce). Thus, investors may choose a non-ICSID forum.

Beyond the self-contained ICSID Convention system, international arbitral awards could be challenged before domestic courts. In most countries, at least those that follow the UNCITRAL Model Law, setting aside is the exclusive recourse against arbitral awards.[26] Furthermore, the exhaustive list of grounds on which an award may be set aside under UNCITRAL Model Law mirrors Article V of the New York Convention.[27] This looks for a uniform treatment of international awards irrespective of the country of origin. Thus, the grounds relating to public policy and non-arbitrability may vary in substance depending on the law applied by the competent court in the state for setting aside or the state of enforcement.

An appeals mechanism will exclude any other existing recourse at the place of arbitration against awards. In particular, it would avoid the risk of attacking the award under the guise of public policy. More importantly, an appeals mechanism would allow the adjudicators to correct erroneous decisions.

The ad hoc Committee in *CMS v. Argentine Republic* pointed out that an ad hoc committee is not a court of appeal and its competence extends only to the annulment based on one or other of the grounds expressly set out in Article 52 of the ICSID Convention, notwithstanding the error of law made by the arbitral tribunal.[28] Specifically, the tribunal erred in analysing the requirements of the US-Argentina investment treaty Article XI[29] and the Draft Articles on the Responsibility of States for Wrongful Acts Article 25.[30] According to the ad hoc Committee, the errors made by the tribunal could have had a 'decisive impact on the operative part of the Award', and yet, the award could not be annulled based on those errors.[31] In two other cases involving similar issues of interpretation (*Enron* and *Sempra*), the ad hoc Committee also recognized the exceptional nature of Article 52. However, in both cases, the ad hoc

25. United Nations Commission on International Trade Law (UNCITRAL) Arbitration Rules (as revised in 2010).
26. Article 34 for UNCITRAL Model Law on International Commercial Arbitration 1985 (with amendments as adopted in 2006).
27. Convention on the Recognition and Enforcement of Foreign Arbitral Awards (New York 1958).
28. *CMS Gas Transmission Company v. Argentine Republic*, ICSID Case No. ARB/01/8, Decision of the ad hoc Committee on the Application for Annulment of the Argentine Republic, para. 43 (25 September 2007).
29. Treaty between United States of American and the Argentine Republic concerning the reciprocal encouragement and protection of investment (in force since 20 October 1994).
30. International Law Commission, *Draft Articles on Responsibility of States for International Wrongful Acts*, Annex to General Assembly Resolution 56/83 of 12 December 2001. Yearbook of the International Law Commission, Vol II (2001).
31. The ad hoc Committee partially annulled the award based on the failure to state reasons for arriving at its conclusion regarding the umbrella clause. *CMS Gas Transmission Company v. Argentine Republic*, *supra* n. 28, paras 96-97.

Committee annulled the award based on tribunal's manifest excess of power.[32] These contradictions show systemic failures of the current annulment system.

As one commentator has stated, 'there are no set criteria that would assist in determining which fundamental issues or rules will emerge and shape how investment arbitration law will evolve'.[33] Without a formal system of precedents, it would be difficult to achieve the goal of consistency. An appellate body could achieve consistency by introducing the concept of binding precedent. Furthermore, because decisions by the appellate body will be binding to first-instance tribunals, it would enhance the predictability of the decisions.

[B] Advantages Vis-à-Vis a Multilateral Investment Court

The EU Commission has recently received the mandate to negotiate a convention for the establishment of a multilateral investment court.[34] This approach would solve the problem of fragmentation and would allow the establishment of a system of precedents. Specifically, the EU's proposal includes a first-instance tribunal that would hear the disputes and conduct the arbitration as arbitral tribunals do today, and an appellate tribunal that would hear appeals from the tribunal of first instance, having the power to correct errors of law and manifest errors in the appreciation of facts.[35] The EU proposes full-time adjudicators at both levels. Thus, investors would not be involved in the selection process. In other words, a multilateral investment court eliminates party autonomy in the selection of arbitrators.[36] The preselection of adjudicators may create an appearance of bias in favour of the respondent states, which could undermine the authority of the investment court system.[37]

The establishment of an appeal mechanism does not raise the same concerns than a permanent investment court would regarding the selection and appointment of the decision-makers, as parties to the dispute may continue to appoint the decision-makers of the first-instance tribunal. In fact, parties do not make the appointments at the review level. Indeed, set-aside of arbitral awards is decided by judges at the seat of

32. *Enron Creditors Recovery Corporation (formerly Enron Corporation) and Ponderosa Assets, L.P. v. Argentine Republic*, ICSID Case No. ARB/01/3, Decision on the Application for Annulment of the Argentine Republic, para. 237 (30 July 2010); *Sempra Energy International v. Argentine Republic*, ICSID Case No. ARB/02/16, Decision on the Argentine Republic's Request for Annulment of the Award, paras 73, 78–79 (29 June 2010).
33. Andreas Bucher, *Is There a Beed to Establish a Permanent Reviewing Body?*, in *The Review of International Arbitral Awards* 285, 286–287 (Emmanuel Gaillard ed., 2008).
34. Council of the European Union, Multilateral Investment Court: Council Gives Mandate to the Commission to Open Negotiations, EU News 55/2018 (20 March 2018).
35. UNCITRAL Working Group III, *Submission from the European Union and its Member States*, A/CN.9/WG.III/WP.159/Add.1 (24 January 2019) (hereinafter 'EU Submission').
36. *See* Corporate Counsel International Arbitration Group, *Submission by the Corporate Counsel International Arbitration Group to UNCITRAL Working Group III* (18 December 2019) (hereinafter, 'CCIAG submission'), https://uncitral.un.org/sites/uncitral.un.org/files/cciag_isds_reform_0.pdf.
37. European Federation for Investment Law and Arbitration, *Task Force Paper regarding the proposed International Court System (ICS)* 15 (Draft dated 1 February 2016), https://efila.org/wp-content/uploads/2016/02/EFILA_TASK_FORCE_on_ICS_proposal_1-2-2016.pdf.

arbitration. Likewise, members of the ad hoc committees under the ICSID self-contained regime are appointed from a roster of arbitrators by the Chairman of the Administrative Council.[38]

According to the EU, a two-tier mechanism would be more effective than an appeal mechanism because there will be a greater degree of deference towards appeal decisions as compared to that likely to be displayed by ad hoc tribunals.[39] Furthermore, according to the EU, a two-tier mechanism would allow the appeal body to send cases back to the first-instance tribunal in order to complete the resolution of the dispute.[40] The EU asserts that it could be problematic to operate remand with ad hoc first-instance tribunals because they will be already extinct.

However, unlike in the domestic context where the remand of the issue to the lower instance is the rule, an appeal tribunal in the arbitration context should be able to modify or reverse the legal findings and conclusions of the first tribunal without the need to remand the issue to a new tribunal.[41] This is particularly true where the appellate body is limited to correcting errors of law, and the facts established by the first-instance tribunal allow the appeal tribunal to render a final decision. Accordingly, an appeal mechanism would avoid the resubmission of the dispute to a new tribunal whenever the arbitral award has been set aside or annulled.

An appeal mechanism would allow the parties to continue selecting the decision-makers at a first level, and, at the same time, would set a higher level of continuity in the composition of adjudicators at a second level, which is key to achieve consistency and predictability. Furthermore, it could avoid review by domestic courts, without overly disturbing the current system.[42] This is a clear advantage of a hybrid procedure with an ad hoc first-instance tribunal (preserving the party-appointment principle), and an appeal mechanism for treaty-based arbitration, regardless of the institution or arbitration rules under which the arbitration is conducted.

Regarding the costs of the procedure, an appeal mechanism with a standing or quasi-standing body would also present several advantages compared to a multilateral investment court. In the case of a permanent investment court, it is uncertain how dispute settlement proceedings will be funded and maintained over time.[43] While it is true that financing contributions could be made by the contracting parties, in accordance with their respective level of development,[44] it could represent a heavy burden on the public finances of some developing countries.

38. Article 52(3) of the ICSID Convention.
39. EU Submission, *supra* n. 35.
40. *Ibid.*
41. Margie-Lys Jaime, *A New Legal Framework for Improving Investor-State Dispute Settlement*, in *Privatizing Dispute Resolution and Its Limits* 485 (Loic Cadiet, Burkhard Hess and Marta Requejo eds, 2019).
42. *Ibid.*
43. CCIAG Submission, *supra* n. 36.
44. EU Submission, *supra* n. 35, at 8.

[C] Disadvantages of a Multilateral Court of Appeal

According to some commentators, the appellate mechanism 'tilts the balance of the dispute settlement system against investors', in the same or similar manner as the multilateral investment court, allegedly because states are likely to appoint adjudicators that would be inclined to rule in favour of states.[45] As discussed above, an appeal mechanism does not raise the same concerns as a permanent investment court because parties to the dispute may continue to appoint the decision-makers of the first-instance tribunal, regardless of the applicable arbitration rules or the arbitration centre managing the procedure.

Commentators have contended that an appeal mechanism may add an additional layer to the process, compromising the finality of the system.[46] For others, an appellate mechanism increases the cost and duration of the proceedings, because it would require more time and cost than other review mechanisms.[47] Furthermore, challenges may be even more frequent as all three adjudicators would be prone to challenges by both sides.[48] As a practical matter, however, it is hard to believe that parties to the dispute will be inclined to challenge adjudicators just because they have not been included in the appointment process.

Moreover, the appellate mechanism could make erroneous decisions permanent.[49] This does not have to be the case. Certainly, an appellate mechanism will look to create consistent case law across the myriad of investment treaties. However, this does not mean that the appellate body will take the interpretation of a provision in one agreement and 'misapply' this interpretation to interpret another agreement inconsistently.

Each treaty should be interpreted under the limits of the Vienna Convention on the Law of the Treaties (VCLT).[50] Although no tribunal is free from erroneous interpretation, an appellate mechanism could provide more consistency and correctness than the current system where there is no binding precedent. The appellate body, as the Supreme Court in a common law country, may overturn its own precedent, under certain circumstances.[51]

§7.03 NATURE AND SCOPE OF AN ISDS APPELLATE BODY

The appellate review mechanism has two basic functions: (i) correct errors of law or fact as needed in a particular litigation; and (ii) declare a legal principle by creation,

45. CCIAG Submission, *supra* n. 36.
46. *See* Doak Bishop, *The Case for an Appellate Panel and the Scope of Review*, in *Appeals and Challenges to Investment Treaty Awards: It Is Time for an International Appellate System?* (Audley Sheppard and Hugo Warner eds, April 2005); Mark B. Feldman, *The Annulment Proceedings and the Finality of ICSID Arbitral Awards*, 2 ICSID Rev. – FILJ 85, 103, n.1 (1987); Laird and Aske, *supra* n. 17.
47. CCIAG Submission, *supra* n. 36.
48. *Ibid.*, 15.
49. *Ibid.*
50. Vienna Convention on the Law of the Treaties, Arts 31–33, 1155 UNTS 331 (27 January 1980).
51. William N. Eskridge, Jr., *Overruling Statutory Precedents*, 76 Georgetown L.J. 1361 (1987–1988).

clarification, extension or overruling.[52] This section studies the nature of an appellate tribunal, distinguishing this mechanism from the current system. Additionally, this section examines the grounds for appeal.

[A] Nature of the Appeal Mechanism

As a general matter, review of arbitral awards is intended to preserve the interests of the parties to the dispute. No one other than the parties to the dispute is entitled to initiate a review proceeding ex officio, even in the 'perceived presence of a ground for annulment' or review.[53]

Before national courts, actions or omissions are subject to review on a given appeal. As pointed out above in section §7.02, an appellate tribunal focuses on the correctness of the decision. More precisely, an appellate tribunal would have the function to correct the errors of the first-instance tribunal. This is not possible in the current system, because the judicial review of an international award may not engage in a de novo review. Likewise, a set-aside or annulment tribunal may not amend or replace the award by its own decision on the merits.[54] In *MCI v. Ecuador*, the ad hoc Committee emphasized the fact that the annulment mechanism is not designed to bring consistency in the interpretation and application of international law,[55] and even though the parties have relied on the arbitral 'jurisprudence' of ICSID and other investment tribunals, the award does not constitute a binding precedent on other tribunals.[56] An appellate tribunal, unlike a national court at the place of the arbitration or an ad hoc Committee in an ICSID arbitration, could be able to avoid unjust results in a particular case, and may well clarify a legal principle, either for guidance in the same case or for general precedential purposes.

Regarding the issue of correctness and the quality of the decisions, an appeal mechanism could avoid decisions where treaty provisions have been improperly interpreted by tribunals, not reflecting the intent of the parties to the treaty, or contrary to the applicable rules of interpretation.[57] Similarly, an appeal mechanism could correct manifest errors of law, for which there is a lack of mechanism to rectify the

52. J. Dickson Phillips, Jr., *The Appellate Review Function: Scope of Review*, 47 Law and Contemporary Problems, 2 n. 2 (1984).
53. Schreuer, Malintoppi, Reinisch and Sinclair, *supra* n. 16, at 904.
54. In *Industria Nacional de Alimentos, S.A. and Indalsa Perú, S.A.* (formerly *Empresas Lucchetti, S.A. and Lucchetti Perú, S.A.*) *v. Republic of Peru*, the tribunal stated: '... it is no part of the Committee's function to review the decision itself which the Tribunal arrive at, still less to substitute its own views for those of the Tribunal, but merely to pass judgment on whether the manner in which the Tribunal carried out its functions met the requirements of the ICSID Convention'. ICSID Case No. ARB/03/4, Decision on Annulment, para. 97 (5 September 2007).
55. *MCI Power Group LC and New Turbine Inc. v. Republic of Ecuador*, ICSID Case No. ARB/03/6, Decision on Annulment, para. 24 (19 October 2009).
56. The reasoning and conclusions developed by ad hoc committees may in practice provide guidance to the Committee in settling similar issues, and help to ensure consistency and legal certainty.
57. UNCITRAL, *Report of Working Group III (Investor-State Dispute Settlement Reform) on the Work of its Thirty-sixth Session I.* A/CN.9/964 para. 57 (6 November 2018).

error. Moreover, ensuring correctness might generally assist in obtaining consistency of decisions as well.

Substantive correctness of the decision may involve additional time and effort which could have an impact on the principle of finality. However, an appeal tribunal should not imply an additional layer of control. An appeal proceeding should be intended to replace the current annulment system for treaty-based investment arbitration cases. While the proceedings may take additional time and costs for hearings, particularly if the appeal involves an alleged error in the appreciation of facts (as allowed by the EU-Singapore and the EU-Vietnam Free Trade Agreements), the appeal mechanism could be introduced as a substitute to the annulment/set-aside proceedings for treaty-based arbitrations, without adding an additional layer to the process.

Furthermore, unlike in the domestic context where the remand of the issue to the lower instance is the rule,[58] an appeal tribunal in the arbitration context should be able to modify or reverse the legal findings and conclusions of the first tribunal, without the need to remand the issue to a new tribunal. This would avoid extra costs produced by a second arbitration.

[B] Grounds for Appeal

Regarding the grounds for appeal, the EU has included in its trade agreements (e.g., EU-Canada Comprehensive Economic and Trade Agreement (CETA) and EU-Singapore) the following options for the competence of the appellate tribunal: (i) the first-instance tribunal has erred in the interpretation or application of the applicable law; (ii) the first-instance tribunal has manifestly erred in the appreciation of the facts, including the appreciation of relevant domestic law; or (iii) the first-instance tribunal has erred in one of the grounds provided for in Article 52 of the ICSID Convention,[59] in so far as they are not covered by the other two grounds.

The appeal tribunal may still grant or deny the appeal based on the annulment grounds of the ICSID Convention. The introduction of an appeal mechanism would not allow for review of award before national courts at the seat of arbitration based on applicable domestic law. In particular, parties would not be allowed to challenge an arbitral award based on the ground that enforcing the award would be inconsistent with the public policy of the place of the enforcement.[60]

The omission of any reference to an award being contrary to 'public policy' should be highlighted. There is not a precise definition of public policy and it can never

58. *See*, e.g., Michael A. Berch, *We've Only Just Begun: The Impact of Remand Orders from Higher to Lower Courts on American Jurisprudence*, 36 Ariz. St. L.J. 493 (2004).

59. Pursuant to Art. 52 of the ICSID Convention, the grounds for annulment are that: (a) the tribunal was not properly constituted; (b) the tribunal has manifestly exceeded its powers; (c) there was corruption on the part of a member of the tribunal; (d) there has been a serious departure from a fundamental rule of procedure; or (e) the award has failed to state the reasons on which it is based.

60. *Cf.* Art. 34(b)(ii) (application for setting aside as exclusive recourse against arbitral award) of the UNCITRAL Model Law on International Commercial Arbitration of 1985 with amendments as adopted in 2006; Art. V(2)(b) of the New York Convention.

be exhaustively defined. But some jurisdictions have interpreted the public policy exception under the New York Convention to mean the fundamental principles on which the legal order to which the enforcement court belongs is based. In this sense, the public policy exception has been used as a 'safety valve' whenever it is impossible for a legal system to recognize an award and enforce it without violating the forum state's 'most basic notions of morality and justice'.[61]

A careful distinction must be made between the failure to apply the proper law, which may amount to an excess of powers, and an incorrect or erroneous application of the law, which is not a ground for annulment under the ICSID Convention. In *Amco v. Indonesia*, the ad hoc Committee clarified its role in the examination of the law applied by the tribunal, stating that this examination was not for the purpose of 'scrutinizing whether the Tribunal committed errors in the interpretation of the requirements of applicable law or in the ascertainment or evaluation of the relevant facts to which such law has been applied'.[62] The contrary would be the task of an appellate body. Regarding the interpretation of Articles 52 and 53 of the ICSID Convention, the ad hoc Committee in *AES v. Hungary* highlighted the need to consider the object and purpose of these provisions and avoid qualifying a tribunal reasoning as 'deficient, superficial, sub-standard, wrong, bad or otherwise faulty'.[63] Indeed, a reassessment of the merits would be typical for an appeal. Conversely, an obvious transgression of a tribunal's mandate or its obvious non-execution would constitute a manifest excess of power, penalized by the ICSID Convention.

The approach taken by the EU free trade agreements differs from other international tribunals like the appellate review mechanism of the World Trade Organization (WTO). The WTO Appellate Body can 'uphold, modify or reverse' the legal findings and conclusions of the panel, but it cannot address the facts upon which a panel report is based.[64] Furthermore, the WTO system does not contemplate the possibility of remanding the case to the panel.[65] The WTO Appellate Body may, however, complete the panel's legal analysis if a legal provision that has not been examined by the panel

61. *Parsons & Whittemore Overseas v. Societe Generale de L'Industrie du Papier (RAKTA)*, Court of Appeals, Second Circuit, United States of America, 508 F.2d 969, 974 (1974). *See also Ameropa A.G. v. Havi Ocean Co. LLC*, District Court, Southern District of New York, United States of America, 2011 WL 570130 (16 February 2011) (concerning an award whose recognition and enforcement was alleged to violate the United States sanctions against Iran).
62. *Amco v. Indonesia*, Decision on Annulment, 1 ICSID Reports 515 (16 May 1986). *See also Daimler Financial Services A.G. v. Republic of Argentina*, ICSID Case No. ARB/05/1, Decision on Annulment, para. 189 (7 January 2015) (emphasizing the role of an ad hoc Committee was not to verify whether the interpretation of the law by the tribunal was correct or whether it correctly ascertained the facts or whether it correctly appreciated the evidence).
63. *AES Summit Generation Limited and AES-Tisza Erömü Kft. v. Hungary*, ICSID Case No. ARB/07/22, Decision of the ad hoc committee on the application for annulment, para. 17 (29 June 2012).
64. Pursuant to Art. 17.6 of the Understanding on Rules and Procedures Governing the Settlement of Disputes (DSU), the appellate tribunal has the authority to review 'issues of law covered in the panel report and legal interpretations developed by the panel'.
65. WTO, *A Handbook on the WTO Dispute Settlement System* 119–121 (2d ed. 2017) (discussing about the mandate of the appellate body).

is 'closely related to a legal provision that a panel has examined', provided that the parties' due process rights are not compromised.[66]

The distinction between questions of law and questions of fact is essential to define the scope and powers of the appellate tribunal. When an appeal tribunal is vested with the right to review the facts by examining new factual evidence or by re-examining existing evidence, certain delays as well as an increase in the costs of the proceedings may occur. While errors of fact are an inherent risk in judicial decisions, the problem that is crucial to address in the current ISDS regime relates to errors of treaty interpretation rather than an inaccurate appreciation of the facts.[67]

The main concern for vesting the appeal tribunal with the power of revising findings of fact is a possible error in the appreciation of the relevant domestic law. If this is the intention, then the scope of the grounds for appeal should be limited to errors in the interpretation of domestic law and not to any error in the appreciation of the facts, even if this error was manifest. But, if the correction of flagrant errors in the interpretation of facts is considered among the powers of the appellate body, then such a provision needs to be carefully drafted. For instance, under the ICSID framework, the revision of the award is allowed on the ground of discovery of new facts that may decisively affect the award.[68] Revision may involve substantive modification of the award, but the fundamental basis of such review is not simply factual. The legal nature of revision is similar to a decision on interpretation and it could be argued that the award had never been final due to the incomplete representation of the facts upon which the decision was taken.[69]

§7.04 COMPOSITION AND STRUCTURE OF AN ISDS APPELLATE BODY

The long-term success of an appellate mechanism depends in part on the structure of the mechanism itself. The process by which selection and appointment take place is the legitimizing factor that provides the credibility of every tribunal or court.[70] As a general matter, 'selection' refers to how adjudicators are chosen. Selection implies the assessment of qualified independent and impartial arbitrators and differs from the 'appointment' made by an appointing authority with the authority to do so.[71]

Arbitrations under the UNCITRAL Arbitration Rules provide for recourse to an appointing authority, including the Secretary General of the Permanent Court of Arbitration at The Hague.[72] In the case of an ICSID arbitration, party-appointment is

66. *Ibid.*, 120.
67. Margie-Lys Jaime, *An Appellate Body in Treaty-based Investment Arbitration: Redefining the Investor-state Dispute Settlement Mechanism*, 21 Spanish Arb. Rev. 101 (2014).
68. ICSID Convention, Art. 51(1).
69. European Federation for Investment Law and Arbitration, *supra* n. 37.
70. Andrea K. Bjorklund, Marc Bungenberg, Manjiao Chi and Catharine Titi, *Selection and Appointment of International Adjudicators: Structural Options for ISDS Reform, Academic Forum on ISDS, Concept Paper 2019/11* (17 September 2019).
71. *Ibid.*, 2.
72. *See* UNCITRAL Arbitration Rules, Arts 6, 8.

also the rule.[73] The Chairman of the Administrative Council shall appoint the arbitrators or arbitrators not yet appointed only when the tribunal has not been constituted within the required period of time.[74] The Chairman is also the competent authority to appoint the ad hoc committee of three persons in an annulment proceeding from the Panel of Arbitrators. The appointment of members of ad hoc committees differs substantially from the appointment of arbitrators. Likewise, the selection and appointment of members of the appellate tribunal would imply a redefinition of the process to adapt it to the new structure.

[A] Re-edifying the Selection and Appointment Process: Roster Versus Standing Body

The lack of capacity of the disputing parties to appoint the members of the arbitral tribunal is one of the main criticisms against the establishment of a permanent investment court. An appellate mechanism should not necessarily affect the selection and appointment process of the first-instance tribunal. In this sense, parties may continue to select the adjudicators under the different arbitration rules, including the UNCITRAL Arbitration Rules for ad hoc arbitrations and the ICSID Convention, rules and regulations. Furthermore, in treaty-based arbitrations, investors would continue to have the right to choose among several arbitration proceedings, as provided by the treaty.

Regarding the selection and appointment of the appellate body, there are two main possibilities: either a permanent standing body or a quasi-standing body by recourse to a roster or panel of arbitrators. However, the distinction between a standing-body model and a roster model appears less relevant in the appellate mechanism situation than in the multilateral investment court scenario.[75]

[1] Standing or Permanent Appellate Body

In 2004, the study made by ICSID Secretariat regarding the possible features of an ICSID appeals facility included the establishment of an appeals panel composed of fifteen persons elected in a staggered manner by the Administrative Council of ICSID on the nomination of the Secretary General of the Centre.[76] This slightly differs from the WTO Appellate Body, which is composed of seven members appointed by the dispute settlement body.[77] Other possibilities have been proposed, taking into consideration the practice of different international organizations.[78] In any event, costs should be

73. ICSID Convention, Art. 37(2).
74. ICSID Convention, Art. 38.
75. CIDS Report, *supra* n. 3, para. 203.
76. ICSID Secretariat, *Possible Improvements of the Framework for ICSID Arbitration*, Discussion Paper, Annex para. 5 (22 October 2004).
77. Donald McRae, *The WTO Appellate Body: A Model for an ICSID Appeals Facility*, 1 J. Int'l Disp. Settlement 371, 383 n. 2 (2010) (highlighting the difference among both systems).
78. For example, the International Court of Justice has fifteen judges and the International Tribunal for the Law of the Sea has twenty-one judges. *See* Jaime, *supra* n. 67, at 100.

considered when determining the number of members of a standing appellate body. Indeed, a permanent standing body with a high number of members may be expensive. Therefore, a selective representation should be preferred to a 'full representation' body.

The option of a stand-alone appeal mechanism has been the object of study.[79] Under this model, there could be a general plenary body, similar to the Dispute Settlement Body of the WTO, whose main role would be to appoint the permanent members of the appellate body.[80] Presumably, a secretariat to administrate the appeal proceedings would be required.

In principle, candidates for the standing mechanism could be proposed by the contracting states. Ideally, the contracting states should appoint neutral and impartial adjudicators, rather than those perceived as 'pro-investors' or 'pro-states' arbitrators.[81] Unfortunately, there is no certainty that appointees to the standing tribunal would comply with all the necessary criteria, particularly if, as in the case of ICSID arbitration, the designation of individuals to the panel of arbitrators is not subject to any challenge or scrutiny.[82] Thus, a member of the standing appellate body may still be challenged and disqualified at the moment of the actual appointment in a particular case.

Under this model, disputing parties have no say in the selection of the panel hearing of a specific dispute, whose members are likely to be appointed by the president of the appellate body. Some restrictions, particularly regarding the nationality of the members hearing the dispute, may apply.[83] In this regard, the ICSID Convention precludes the appointment of arbitrators having the same nationality as the parties in the case to avoid any bias or conflict of interest. Other restrictions could include not having other remunerated activities such as serving as arbitrators and/or counsel in ISDS.

[2] Semi-Standing or Roster Model

The choice between a roster and a permanent appellate body is a policy choice.[84] There are several types of rosters, depending on what the conditions for nomination to a particular list will be, what institution, if any, will host the list, and how the parties will

79. Marc Bungenberg and August Reinisch, *From Bilateral Arbitral Tribunals and Investment Courts to a Multilateral Investment Court: Options Regarding the Institutionalization of Investor-State Dispute Settlement* ch. 9 (2d ed. 2020).
80. *Ibid.*, 198.
81. *See* Anthea Roberts, *Would a Multilateral Investment Court be Biased? Shifting to a Treaty Party Framework of Analysis*, EJIL: Talk! (27 April 2017), https://www.ejiltalk.org/would-a-multilateral-investment-court-be-biased-shifting-to-a-treaty-party-framework-of-analysis/.
82. Some commentators have argued that in certain cases contracting parties have appointed members of the panel not having the necessary qualifications for appointments. Christoph H. Schreuer, *The ICSID Convention: A Commentary* para. 6 (2001).
83. *See* Art. 52(3) of the ICSID Convention.
84. Gabrielle Kaufmann-Kohler and Michele Potestà, *The Composition of a Multilateral Investment Court and of an Appeal Mechanism for Investment Awards* (hereinafter 'CIDS Supplemental Report') para. 169 (15 November 2017), http://www.uncitral.org/pdf/english/workinggroups/wg_3/CIDS_Supplemental_Report.pdf.

select arbitrators from the list.[85] A single mandatory list would be preferred over multiple lists or rosters. The selection of the chairperson might be done by the institution administrating the proceedings, subject to the applicable administrative fees. In the case of ad hoc arbitrations, like those under UNCITRAL Arbitration Rules, parties would need the assistance of an appointing authority. Administrative costs will be substantially reduced considering the absence of a plenary body and/or a permanent secretariat.

Under a roster model, the assignment of an actual case coincides with the constitution of the tribunal. In practice, parties to the dispute could select the individuals to constitute the tribunal or panel. This may strengthen the idea that the appeal is an arbitration and that decisions from the appellate body should be viewed as arbitral awards under the New York Convention for enforcement purposes. For some, however, a roster model would not address disputing party-appointment concerns, because adjudicator bias in favour of the appointing disputing party may exist.[86] This would be a pessimistic assumption and there are several tools that can be put in place to secure arbitrators' impartiality and independence, and to avoid some of the 'dangers' of having party-appointments.[87] Another option could be having the arbitral institution select the two co-arbitrators and the chairperson, either directly through an internal selection process or permitting the input of the disputing parties.[88]

Under the ICSID system, where members of the ad hoc committees are chosen by the Chairman, contracting states exercise a limited indirect influence on the composition of the ad hoc Committee.[89] Indeed, pursuant to Article 13 of the ICSID Convention, each contracting state may designate four persons to the Panel of Arbitrators who may but not be its nationals.[90] As in the case of ICSID, any roster of arbitrators shall, as much as possible, guarantee a balanced representation of the different legal systems.

[B] Qualifications, Diversity, Independence and Impartiality

Qualifications of adjudicators are, without doubt, an essential element for the success of an arbitration. For instance, under ICSID arbitration, there are attributes deemed to be highly desirable for the Panel of Arbitrators, including the knowledge of and

---

85. Malcom Langford, Daniel Behem and Maria Chiara Malaguti, *The Quadrilemma: Appointing adjudicators in future Investor-State Dispute Settlement, Academic Forum on ISDS*, Concept Paper 2019/12 (13 October 2019).
86. CIDS Supplemental Report, *supra* n. 84, para. 173.
87. *See* History of the ICSID Convention, Vol. II-1, 40 (commenting that the manner to appoint the members of the arbitral tribunal was probably 'the most usual method for the constitution of an arbitral tribunal', although it could 'be argued that it is the least desirable method because of the danger that each party will look upon the arbitrator to be appointed by it as an advocate').
88. For instance, the institution could circulate a list of potential co-arbitrators to each of the parties and the parties could rank their preference of the list. The same could apply for the appointment of the chairperson, or the two co-arbitrators could appoint the Chairman from the list. Langford, Behem and Malaguti, *supra* n. 85.
89. Schreuer, *supra* n. 82, para. 346.
90. The Chairman may designate ten persons to the Panel of Arbitrators. Art. 13 of the ICSID Convention.

experience with international investment law, public international law, and international arbitration or conciliation.[91] The creation of an appellate body should consider specific qualifications and high ethical standards for adjudicators.

UNCITRAL Working Group III has noted the lack of diversity in terms of gender, geographical distribution, ethnicity and age in the practice of investment arbitration.[92] Therefore, states may wish to have an appellate body that reflects a certain balance with respect to geographical distribution, legal systems representation, nationality or gender, among other factors.

Two key elements of any system of justice that need to be regulated by a code of ethics for adjudicators acting in ISDS are the independence and impartiality of members of the appellate body.[93] In this sense, Working Group III has stated that a multilateral code of ethics should be comprehensive, encompassing all issues related to decision-makers.[94] In particular, the issue of 'double hatting' has raised particular concerns in ISDS.[95]

Even if the number of arbitrators who no longer act as counsel in arbitrations has increased over time, this phenomenon takes renewed importance in the context of investment arbitration where cases often involve similar legal issues.[96] As a result, members of the appellate body could be forbidden to act as counsel or as party-appointed expert or witness in any pending or new treaty-based ISDS. For some, however, this prohibition 'may hinder entrance of new players in the arbitration system, and thus be an obstacle to increase diversity'.[97] This does not necessarily need to be the case in a system where adjudicators are selected and appointed in a manner that guarantees their diversity, independence and impartiality. In any event, ISDS reform should consider the strong interaction between the need for enhancing and the role of arbitrators in treaty-based arbitration.

[C] Remuneration

Remuneration of adjudicators is an important element to the independence of the judiciary.[98] Yet, party remuneration of arbitrators has been considered, for some, as a

91. *See* Art. 14 of the ICSID Convention regarding qualifications. Relevant knowledge as well as availability and other qualifications to handle the case are also considered in the WTO system. *See* ICSID Convention, Art. 17(3) ('Understanding on Rules and Procedures Governing the Settlement of Disputes').
92. *Ibid.*, para. 70.
93. While independence usually relates to the lack of conflict of interests between an arbitrator and a party to the arbitration, impartiality is a subjective element implying the absence of bias or predisposition of the decision-maker towards a party.
94. UNCITRAL, *supra* n. 57.
95. *See* Langford, Behem and Malaguti, *supra* n. 85.
96. Jaime, *supra* n. 3, 383, 393 n. 3 (2016).
97. Chiara Giorgetti and Mohammed Abdel Wahab, *A Code of Conduct for Arbitrators and Judges, Academic Forum on ISDS. Concept Paper 2019/12*, para. 20 (13 October 2019). *See also*, John Crook, *Dual Hats and Arbitrator Diversity: Goals in Tension*, 113 AJIL Unbound 284, 287 (2019).
98. According to the UN Basic Principles on Independence of the Judiciary, states have the duty to guarantee the conditions of service and tenure in their legislation, including their independence, security and adequate remuneration. UN, *Basic Principles on Independence of the Judiciary*,

possible reason of why co-arbitrators might support the position of their appointing party.[99] Dissenting opinions made by the arbitrator appointed by the losing party may also contribute to the overall perception of bias.[100] In the same vein, the lack of transparency on the remuneration of arbitrators by the disputing parties may create a perception about the lack of independence and impartiality.

If the path of a standing appeal body is followed, the manner in which the decision-makers are appointed and remunerated must guarantee their structural independence.[101] Thus, adequate remuneration should be taken into consideration while structuring an appellate review mechanism. According to the EU's proposal for the creation of a multilateral investment court, adjudicators should be employed full-time and should not have any outside activities.[102] Pursuant to this proposal, adjudicators would be paid salaries comparable to those of other international courts.[103] Furthermore, the appointment process proposed by the EU in their own investment treaties[104] is similar to the structure of the Iran-United States Claims Tribunal.[105] However, under this structure where the states - and not the disputing parties - select the adjudicators and bear the expenses of the arbitration, one can argue that the purpose of the tribunal was to favour state parties rather than finding a fair judgment.

The establishment of a permanent court, unlike an appeal mechanism, should consider not only adjudicators' salaries but also staff salaries, and the costs of funding and maintaining permanent facilities.[106] This could be very expensive and sensitive for

---

https://www.ohchr.org/en/professionalinterest/pages/independencejudiciary.aspx. *See generally* Dominik Zimmermann, *The Independence of International Courts: The Adherence of the International Judiciary to a Fundamental Value of the Administration of Justice* 75–77 (2014) (referring to concerns related to how a court is financed as an example of an institutional aspect of independence).

99. Under arbitration rules of main arbitral institutions, each party shall bear the fees of co-arbitrators and share equally the fees of the presiding arbitrator. *See* UNCITRAL, *Ensuring independence and impartiality on the part of arbitrators and decision makers in ISDS, Note by the Secretariat*, A/CN.9/WG.III/WP.151 para. 41 (30 August 2018).
100. There is no explanation or consensus on why dissenting opinions are usually made by arbitrators appointed by the losing parties. While the level of dissents is not itself indicative of bias, it might create the perception that arbitrators feel themselves under a duty to their appointing parties or counsel. *Ibid.*, para. 42.
101. Structural or institutional independence refers to the 'absence of external influence on the institution or dispute settlement body' and it is generally distinguished from individual or personal independence. CIDS *Supplemental Report*, *supra* n. 84.
102. UNCITRAL Working Group III, *Submission from the European Union and its Member States*, 5 A/CN.9/WG.III/WP.159/Add.1 (24 January 2019).
103. *See* David Gaukrodger, *Adjudicator Compensation Systems and Investor-State Dispute Settlement, OECD Working Papers on International Investment 2017/05*.
104. *See*, e.g., CETA Art. 8.27 (Constitution of the Tribunal), http://trade.ec.europa.eu/doclib/docs/2016/february/tradoc_154329.pdf.
105. The Iran-United States Claims Tribunal was established following the Declaration of the Government of the Democratic and Popular Republic of Algeria of 19 January 1981, http://iusct.net/general%20documents/2-claims%20settlement%20declaration.pdf.
106. Corporate Counsel International Arbitration Group (CCIAG), *Submission by the Corporate Counsel International Arbitration Group to UNCITRAL Working Group III* (18 December 2019), https://uncitral.un.org/sites/uncitral.un.org/files/cciag_isds_reform_0.pdf.

certain developing countries. Rights and duties resulting from this asymmetrical financing contribution could also be a concern for developing countries.

Where an appeal mechanism is established without the existence of a permanent body, parties to the dispute will continue to use the current mechanisms to deal with ISDS, in particular ICSID arbitration. Furthermore, no salaries would be needed, and disputing parties would have to bear the fees of the appellate proceedings, reducing perception of bias in favour of states.

Regarding the term of office, a longer term may present several advantages if the chosen path is a standing appellate body, as it may secure independence and reduce concerns of adjudicators over having to secure another job after a short tenure.[107] However, longer terms may reduce the pool of qualified appeal arbitrators and discourage the entry of new actors. If a roster model is followed, it could be more beneficial to have a shorter (and renewable) term of office (e.g., four to six years), as is the case for the WTO Appellate Body or the ICSID Panel.

§7.05 OPTIONS FOR ESTABLISHING AN APPELLATE REVIEW MECHANISM

According to some commentators, the establishment of a multilateral appellate body seems illusory due to political and practical hurdles that would need to be overcome in order to amend the ICSID Convention.[108] This might have been the case fifteen years ago. However, the situation has changed and the UNCITRAL forum opens a door for the materialization of a multilateral appellate body (for ICSID and non-ICSID arbitrations). Several structural options could be considered for ISDS reform and in particular for the establishment of an appellate review mechanism. Yet any solution should avoid politicization because the depoliticization of ISDS was a primary benefit of the current system.

[A] The Treaty-Specific Approach

As mentioned, the EU – just as the United States in the early 2000s introduced the negotiation of appellate bodies – has introduced the establishment of a permanent

107. CIDS Supplemental Report, *supra* n. 84, paras 162–163.

108. Nikolaos Tsalokidis, *ICSID Annulment Standard: Who Has Finally Won the Reisman v. Broches Debate of Two Decades Ago?* in *Reshaping the Investor-State Dispute Settlement System* 828, 851 (Jean E Kalicki and Anna Joubin-Bret eds, 2015); *See also* N. Jansen Calamita, *The (In)Compatibility of Appellate Mechanisms with Existing Instruments of the Investment Treaty Regime*, Journal World Investment & Trade, 585–627 (2017); Christian J. Tams, *Is There a Need for an ICSID Appellate Structure?*, in *The International Convention on the Settlement of Investment Disputes (ICSID): Taking Stock after 40 Years*, 223, 250 (Rainer Hofmann, Christian J. Tams eds, 2007) (concluding that there are no compelling reasons to move towards an investment appellate structure).

investment court in their investment treaty negotiations.[109] As the ICSID Secretariat has noted, a plurality of appeals mechanisms could create fragmentation and provide space for more inconsistencies.[110] Indeed, there would be as many permanent tribunals as there would be treaties incorporating the creation of such a standing body. Thus, each tribunal would be competent only with respect to the treaty concerned, without creating a binding precedent for other courts and tribunals. This situation explains the EU Commission's new mandate to negotiate a multilateral investment court.

An unexplored option of reform might be the design of a model agreement on ISDS that could be adopted by the parties to an investment treaty. The model would have to reflect the worldwide consensus of key aspects of investment law practice and policies, in the quest of an effective, transparent and accountable regime. Although this option cannot avoid fragmentation, it may achieve a certain level of harmonization and predictability in the system.

[B] The Multilateral Alternative

In 2016, the CIDS Report on the reform of ISDS explored the possibility of an opt-in convention modelled on the Mauritius Convention.[111] An opt-in convention can be defined as 'an instrument by which the Parties to IIAs express their consent to submit disputes arising under their existing IIAs' to the multilateral appellate body.[112]

A convention creating an appellate body could be created as a flexible instrument by which parties may formulate reservations, thereby excluding from the application of the convention a specific investment treaty or a specific set of arbitration rules other than the UNCITRAL Arbitration Rules (negative-list approach), or to declare that it will not provide a unilateral offer of application.[113] In any event, the convention would have to establish its relationship with current and future IIAs, particularly with respect to the existing IIAs' procedural rules.

Ideally, both the disputing state and the investor's home state should be part of the convention establishing the appeal mechanism. This may not, however, always be the case. Other scenarios may involve the host state's unilateral consent to the convention. Where the dispute is between an investor whose home state is party to the convention, but the host state is not, the investor may not be able to appeal the decision

109. *See*, for example, CETA, the TTIP, the EU-Vietnam and EU-Singapore Free Trade Agreements, and the EU-Japan Economic Partnership Agreement. Texts available at European Commission website http://ec.europa.eu/trade/policy/countries-and-regions/negotiations-and-agreements/.
110. ICSID Secretariat, *Possible Improvements of the Framework for ICSID Arbitration*, Discussion Paper, 15-16 (22 October 2004).
111. CIDS Report, *supra* n. 3. The Mauritius Convention was conceived as an instrument by which parties express their consent to apply the UNCITRAL Rules on Transparency to investment treaties concluded before its adoption (1 April 2014). The UNCITRAL Rules on Transparency in Treaty-Based Investor-State Arbitration came into effect on 1 April 2014. Resolution adopted by the General Assembly on 16 December 2013, 68/109 Report of the Sixth Committee (A/68/4 62).
112. CIDS Report, *supra* n. 3, at 75.
113. Jaime, *supra* n. 41, at 529-530.

unless the host state decides to become part of the convention or accept the jurisdiction of the appellate body on a case-by-case basis. By contrast, if only the disputing party state is party to the convention, the investor may initiate the appeal without affecting its home state.[114] That is to say, the investor would be accepting the unilateral offer of the host state to file an appeal in case of disagreement with tribunal's decision.

§7.06 CONCLUSION

The practice of ISDS has evolved over time. The question is no longer whether the ISDS regime should be improved but rather how and to what extent the structure of investment arbitration needs to be reformed. This chapter proposes the establishment of an appeal review mechanism – likely under a roster model – as a way to reshape ISDS, rather than to replace the current system.

The overarching purpose behind a second degree of review for treaty-based arbitral awards is to enhance coherence and consistency in the ISDS system by a body able to review manifest errors in the interpretation and application of treaty law. Because of its purpose and its nature, a multilateral appeal mechanism is expected to apply the same principles to any award that is appealed, moving towards a precedent-based system. This is a clear solution to the current system, where there is no hierarchy between awards that would ensure effectiveness and predictability of decisions.

The absence of party-appointed arbitrators may make a standing or quasi-standing appellate body less attractive to the parties to the dispute. However, such an appellate body could address several concerns of the current system, including the lack of independence and the perceived impartiality of arbitral tribunals. While independence usually relates to the lack of conflict of interests between an arbitrator and a party to the arbitration, impartiality is a subjective element implying the absence of bias or predisposition of the decision-maker towards a party.

More generally, the introduction of an appeal system should favour a balance between the finality and the correctness of arbitral awards. In other words, correctness and consistency of arbitral awards should not unnecessarily undermine the finality of arbitral awards by increasing the cost and duration of the proceedings.

Finally, the establishment of an appellate body would allow the ISDS regime to keep its main features while being complemented by an appeal mechanism. Parties to the dispute would continue to use the administration services of ICSID and other arbitral institutions as deemed appropriate. In fact, with the opt-in convention option, the ICSID Convention would not need to be amended. In the same vein, states would not need to renegotiate the underlying IIAs to implement the appellate review mechanism. ISDS might never be the same as it was at its inception because of the establishment of a multilateral appeal mechanism, but the system needs to continue evolving to reflect lessons learned by states, investors, and other stakeholders from the past fifty-plus years of practice.

114. Jaime, *supra* n. 67, 101.

CHAPTER 8

Arbitrator-Made (Jurisdictional) Law in Investment Treaty Arbitration: Application, Creation and Control

Relja Radović

The lawmaking function of international courts and tribunals is well known in both theory and practice, including that function of arbitral tribunals in the field of investment treaty arbitration. However, no clear guidance exists regarding the conduct of arbitrators in their decision-making and lawmaking. This chapter offers such guidance in respect of one peculiar lawmaking activity of arbitral tribunals, namely their regulatory function regarding their own jurisdiction, and to that end discusses the proper application, creation and control of arbitrator-made jurisdictional rules. Such guidance is warranted because arbitral jurisdictional regulation has so far remained unrecognized, usually disguised as varieties in treaty interpretations, due to the consensual foundations of the process of jurisdictional regulation. The chapter argues that the recognition of the arbitral jurisdictional regulation, by employing the discussed methods of application, creation and control of arbitrator-made rules in practice, would provide conditions for a better performance of the system of investor-State dispute settlement, including the advancement of legal certainty regarding questions of jurisdiction. Such recognition can be implemented within the existing framework of investment arbitration, but the implementation would be particularly fertile in the context of institutionalized adjudicatory mechanisms. While these recommendations are made in the context of arbitral jurisdictional regulation, this can be a starting point for similar considerations in the sphere of substantive law.

§8.01 INTRODUCTION

International legal scholarship theorizes extensively about judicial and arbitral lawmaking,[1] and the same trend has also affected the field of investment treaty arbitration.[2] While the role of arbitrators in the clarification and development of international investment law is widely acknowledged, the reflections of this role of arbitrators on their conduct are not the focus of academic attention. The same applies to treaty practice, particularly regarding the reformist actions establishing court-like adjudicatory mechanisms. They recognize the role insofar as they attempt to tame the interpretative freedom of arbitrators substantively[3] and establish their control procedurally.[4] However, treaties and other rules stop short of giving any guidance regarding arbitral decision-making and lawmaking, and they do not address questions such as whether arbitrators are required to follow precedents and in what cases it is possible to depart from them.[5]

Be that as it may, arbitral lawmaking is here to stay, and therefore requires stronger recognition. One way to initiate such stronger recognition is to open a debate about the norms of arbitral decision-making and lawmaking. This is not a procedural law topic in the strict sense, although it touches upon certain procedural questions such as how decisions should be motivated.[6] The real effect of this topic will be experienced in the substantive work of arbitrators and members of control mechanisms. Should tribunals follow previous decisions and apply arbitrator-made rules, and if so, how should that be reflected in decisions? In what cases should arbitrators create new rules and how should they do so? And how should the arbitral application and creation of rules be controlled?

This chapter discusses these questions in the context of one peculiar lawmaking activity of arbitral tribunals, namely the creation of the rules governing their own

1. *See, e.g.*, *International Judicial Lawmaking: On Public Authority and Democratic Legitimation in Global Governance* (Armin von Bogdandy and Ingo Venzke eds, Springer 2012); Alan Boyle and Christine Chinkin, *The Making of International Law* Ch. 6 (Oxford Univ. Press 2007).
2. *See, e.g.*, Catharine Titi, *The Arbitrator as a Lawmaker: Jurisgenerative Processes in Investment Arbitration,* 14 J. World Inv. & Trade 829 (2013); Stephan W. Schill, *System-Building in Investment Treaty Arbitration and Lawmaking,* in *International Judicial Lawmaking: On Public Authority and Democratic Legitimation in Global Governance* 133 (Armin von Bogdandy and Ingo Venzke eds, Springer 2012); Eric De Brabandere, *Arbitral Decisions as a Source of International Investment Law,* in *International Investment Law: The Sources of Rights and Obligations* 245 (Tarcisio Gazzini and Eric De Brabandere eds, Brill 2012).
3. Through the system of binding interpretations. *See, e.g.*, Comprehensive Economic and Trade Agreement between Canada and the European Union, Art. 8.31(3), 30 October 2016 (hereinafter 'CETA'); EU-Vietnam Investment Protection Agreement, Art. 3.42(5), 30 June 2019 (hereinafter 'EU-Vietnam IPA'); EU-Singapore Investment Protection Agreement, Art. 3.13(3), 19 October 2018 (hereinafter 'EU-Singapore IPA').
4. Through appellate mechanisms. *See, e.g.*, CETA, *supra* n. 3, Art. 8.28; EU-Vietnam IPA, *supra* n. 3, Arts 3.39, 3.54; EU-Singapore IPA, *supra* n. 3, Arts 3.10, 3.19.
5. Cf. the instruction to observe interpretations of the World Trade Organization Dispute Settlement Body in the context of inter-State arbitration: CETA, *supra* n. 3, Art. 29.17; EU-Vietnam IPA, *supra* n. 3, Art. 3.21; EU-Singapore IPA, *supra* n. 3, Art. 3.42.
6. Other procedural questions relevant for this topic include, among others, the application of the principle *jura novit curia,* the power or duty to raise legal questions *proprio motu* or ex officio, and the observance of the arguments and sources other than those advanced by disputing parties.

jurisdiction, which can be called 'arbitral jurisdictional regulation'. The emphasis is not on the content of such rules, but on the approaches taken by tribunals in their application and creation, and by annulment committees and courts exercising control. To that end, the chapter takes a practical approach and offers examples of negative and positive practices in the application, creation and control of arbitrator-made jurisdictional rules. Naturally, the decisions addressed here are those which have either relied on the existing arbitrator-made law or attempted to create new law, and for the same reasons, the chosen decisions are well known to the investment law readership. The chapter also enquires what aspects of practice should be encouraged and what should be improved. For the sake of clarity, this chapter focuses on investment *treaty* arbitration.

This chapter argues that the arbitral jurisdictional regulation should be recognized by employing the discussed methods of application, creation and control of arbitrator-made rules in practice. This would provide conditions for a better performance of the system of investor-State dispute settlement, most importantly advancing the legal certainty regarding the questions of jurisdiction. While the suggestions of this chapter can be implemented within the existing framework of investment arbitration, that would be especially possible in the context of institutionalized adjudicatory mechanisms. Furthermore, because arbitral jurisdictional regulation is discussed here as an example of arbitral lawmaking, the employment of the same methods in relation to the substantive law would also be advantageous, although a definite answer to that question requires further examination.

Section §8.02 introduces the concept of arbitral jurisdictional regulation. Section §8.03 discusses the proper application of arbitrator-made jurisdictional rules. Section §8.04 examines their proper creation, while section §8.05 analyses the proper control of the application and creation of arbitrator-made jurisdictional rules. Finally, section §8.06 draws conclusions from the analysis.

§8.02 ARBITRATOR-MADE JURISDICTIONAL RULES

Arbitral practice in the field of investment treaty arbitration has developed the regulatory function of arbitral tribunals regarding their own jurisdiction. This argument relates to a broader work and it will not be pursued here extensively.[7] For the sake of context, this is a curious development for several reasons. First, the process of jurisdictional regulation in international law is generally based on party consent, which in essence means that the authority of an investment arbitral tribunal to adjudicate, as of every other international court or tribunal, is defined by disputing parties.[8] Second, the notion of jurisdiction implies clearly defined limits of the authority to adjudicate,

7. Arbitral jurisdictional regulation and its effects on the process of jurisdictional regulation are addressed in detail in the author's work in progress *Beyond Consent: Revisiting Jurisdiction in Investment Treaty Arbitration.*
8. This is the basic premise of the principle of consensualism which governs the process of jurisdictional regulation in international law due to the lack of a central legislative authority.

eliminating the flexibility that is necessary for the exercise of the judicial lawmaking function.[9]

Arbitrator-made jurisdictional rules can be provisionally classified as presumptions, default rules and standards.[10] While such rules are indeed numerous, only several prominent examples will be given here, which are also relevant for the following discussion. The practice analysed in this chapter is intentionally well known in the literature. The focus is on the qualification of the products of such practice as rules of law, rather than on its content.

Presumptions instruct the interpretation of party-provided jurisdictional rules. The best known example is the attempt of tribunals to create presumptions regarding the applicability of most-favoured-nation (MFN) clauses to dispute settlement clauses, although without consensus. Some tribunals have considered that the applicability of MFN clauses to dispute resolution provisions should be presumed, unless there are indicators to the contrary in the relevant treaty.[11] Other have considered that such clauses should be presumed inapplicable to dispute settlement provisions, unless there are indicators to the contrary.[12] While practice has not established one firm jurisdictional rule, it is striking how clearly the issue has been seen by arbitrators as a question of regulation.[13] Another notable example, where consensus arguably has been reached, concerns the protection of indirect investments. Arguably, a presumption in favour of the protection of indirect investments exists, which can be rebutted by some indicators to the contrary in the relevant treaty.[14]

Default rules fill gaps in party-provided jurisdictional rules. The best example concerns legality requirements. While many investment treaties limit the scope of their protection, and therefore the access to international arbitration, with the requirement that investments must be made in compliance with the law of the host State, some treaties do not. This was perceived as a regulatory gap, and tribunals have created a

9. One theory is that the opportunity of international courts and tribunals to engage in lawmaking arises from the vagueness and ambiguity of the treaty provisions that they are asked to apply. *See* Andreas Kulick, *From Problem to Opportunity? An Analytical Framework for Vagueness and Ambiguity in International Law*, in *German Yearbook of International Law* vol. 59, 274–275 (Andreas von Arnauld and Kerstin von der Decken ed., Duncker & Humblot 2016).
10. This is not an exhaustive list and it is meant to describe the function of the arbitrator-made rules analysed in this chapter. New examples of arbitrator-made rules, which could require a new classification, can be found in the future.
11. *See*, e.g., *Gas Natural SDG, S.A. v. The Argentine Republic*, ICSID Case No. ARB/03/10, Decision of the Tribunal on Preliminary Questions on Jurisdiction, para. 49 (17 June 2005) ('Unless it appears clearly that the state parties to a BIT [i.e. bilateral investment treaty] or the parties to a particular investment agreement settled on a different method for resolution of disputes that may arise, most-favored-nation provisions in BITs should be understood to be applicable to dispute settlement').
12. *See*, e.g., *Vladimir Berschader & Moïse Berschader v. The Russian Federation*, SCC Case No. 80/2004, Award, para. 181 (21 April 2006) ('Instead, the present Tribunal will apply the principle that an MFN provision in a BIT will only incorporate by reference an arbitration clause from another BIT where the terms of the original BIT clearly and unambiguously so provide or where it can otherwise be clearly inferred that this was the intention of the contracting parties').
13. *See* quotations in *supra* nn. 11 and 12 and *infra* n. 52.
14. *See*, e.g., *Señor Tza Yap Shum v. The Republic of Peru*, ICSID Case No. ARB/07/6, Decision on Jurisdiction and Competence, para. 111 (19 June 2009).

default legality requirement that must be fulfilled regardless of treaty texts.[15] Another example concerns umbrella clauses, i.e., clauses guaranteeing the observance of commitments towards investors. Considering that such clauses lack sufficient instruction, tribunals have created a default privity requirement, according to which umbrella clauses cover only contracts in respect of which there is privity between the investor and the State.[16]

Standards define the criteria for the implementation of party-provided jurisdictional rules. The best known example is the *Salini* test setting the criteria of the objective definition of 'investment' under the Convention on the Settlement of Investment Disputes between States and Nationals of Other States (ICSID Convention),[17] but also outside that framework in conjunction with a default rule that investments must satisfy an objective definition in addition to that under the relevant treaty.[18] Another example concerns fork-in-the-road clauses, i.e., clauses making the choice between domestic courts and international arbitration final. Lacking any criteria regarding their triggering, tribunals have preferred the 'triple identity' test, which observes the identity of parties, objects and causes of action.[19]

What makes an arbitrator-made jurisdictional rule? Admittedly, the arbitral function to determine jurisdiction primarily consists of the interpretation of the given jurisdictional rules defined by disputing parties and their application to jurisdictional facts. Yet, when it comes to the arbitral task to discover the meaning of concrete jurisdictional rules, arbitrators may perceive the given set of jurisdictional rules as simply insufficient to determine how it regulates certain jurisdictional questions. In that scenario, arbitrators can be inclined to add independent input in terms of a general and prescriptive premise, inspired by some external sources, to assist the resolution of the jurisdictional question. But the arbitral production of jurisdictional rules is not a question of creativity. An arbitral interpretation of the law can be more creative, just as arbitral lawmaking can be less creative.

The main features of arbitrator-made jurisdictional rules are, therefore, their general and prescriptive terms and their external origins, unrelated to the will of disputing parties. Furthermore, their character as jurisdictional rules cannot be ignored for both practical and theoretical reasons. First, as these are not incidental considerations along treaty interpretations, but premises of general and prescriptive terms, they must be rules when followed by tribunals due to the belief that they should be

15. *See, e.g., Gustav F W Hamester GmbH & Co KG v. Republic of Ghana*, ICSID Case No. ARB/07/24, Award, paras 123–124 (18 June 2010).
16. *See, e.g., Burlington Resources Inc. v. Republic of Ecuador*, ICSID Case No. ARB/08/5, Decision on Liability, paras 214–215 (14 December 2012).
17. *See, e.g., Mr. Saba Fakes v. Republic of Turkey*, ICSID Case No. ARB/07/20, Award, paras 110–111 (14 July 2010).
18. *See, e.g., Isolux Infrastructure Netherlands, B.V. v. Kingdom of Spain*, SCC Case No. V2013/153, Award, paras 683–685 (12 July 2016).
19. *See, e.g., Mobil Exploration and Development Argentina Inc. Suc. Argentina and Mobil Argentina Sociedad Anónima v. The Argentine Republic*, ICSID Case No. ARB/04/16, Decision on Jurisdiction and Liability, para. 139 (10 April 2013).

followed.[20] Second, these rules are jurisdictional, because they contribute to the definition of the authority to adjudicate, and they qualify as Hart's 'rules of adjudication'.[21] Regarding their function in the definition of the authority to adjudicate, arbitrator-made jurisdictional rules can both direct the interpretation and application of party-provided jurisdictional rules and impose independent jurisdictional limits. Regarding their function in relation to party-provided jurisdictional rules, arbitrator-made jurisdictional rules can roughly be classified as presumptions, default rules and standards, as discussed above.

This type of the arbitral regulatory activity can be labelled 'arbitral jurisdictional regulation', in contrast to the consensual jurisdictional regulation, which is exercised by disputing parties. While the consensual jurisdictional regulation asserts the authority of its rules in the will of disputing parties, the arbitral jurisdictional regulation does not, and lacking a clear source of authority, the normativity of the rules it creates is factual, appearing in the practical function and application of such rules.

§8.03 APPLICATION

That arbitral decisions are being followed in subsequent decisions as precedents was admitted in the scholarship relatively early.[22] The problem is that this frequently presents cherry-picking of decisions that are favourable to the acting tribunal's approach to the issue at hand. In such a scenario, precedents appear to have a justificatory, rather than regulatory function. This supports the theory that decisions in international investment law cannot be binding but only 'persuasive' precedents.[23] It is true that previous decisions are sometimes 'only consulted' to verify otherwise-made conclusions, and tribunals tend to insist that they are not bound by them.[24] However, it would be an exaggeration to say that prior decisions *always* play a justificatory or verifying role. In fact, arguments developed in previous decisions are often used as legal premises by subsequent tribunals, rather than as justifications for resolutions of jurisdictional questions.

Problems in arbitral reasoning begin with the failure to identify particulars of the applied rule. For example, applying the arbitrator-made default rule which imposes the legality requirement independently of the applicable treaty, the Tribunal in *Cortec*

20. *See*, among other decisions containing the same statement, *Cargill, Incorporated (United States of America) v. Republic of Poland*, UNCITRAL arbitration, Final Award, para. 224 (29 February 2008) ('It [the Tribunal] believes that, subject to compelling contrary grounds, it has a duty to adopt solutions established in a series of consistent cases'); and, for practical examples of the reliance on jurisprudence, the text accompanying *infra* nn. 25 and 28.
21. According to Hart, 'rules of adjudication' are the type of secondary rules that confer the power to make authoritative determinations of breaches of primary rules. H.L.A. Hart, *The Concept of Law* 96–97 (Oxford Univ. Press 3d ed. 2012).
22. Jeffery P. Commission, *Precedent in Investment Treaty Arbitration: A Citation Analysis of a Developing Jurisprudence*, 24 J. Int'l Arb. 129 (2007).
23. Frédéric G. Sourgens, *Law's Laboratory: Developing International Law on Investment Protection as Common Law*, 34 Northwestern J. Int'l L. & Business 181, 239–246 (2014).
24. *See*, for example, the approach taken by the Tribunal in *Burlington Resources Inc. v. Ecuador*, *infra* n. 81 and the accompanying text.

Mining Kenya Limited et al. v. Kenya simply noted that '[i]t is accepted jurisprudence that in order to be protected an investment has to be in accordance with the laws of the host State and made in good faith'.[25] The Tribunal referred to *Phoenix* to support its statement,[26] but otherwise did not address the extensive jurisprudence on the matter. While the Tribunal was right in noting that an independent legality requirement can now be considered accepted in jurisprudence, the practice is not unanimous and it required more exhaustive analysis.[27] The superficiality of the Tribunal's reasoning is also visible where it noted that '[i]t is well established in arbitral law that the "origin of funds" issue is not a valid objection',[28] without mentioning any authority. The Tribunal therefore adopted premises developed in practice, but without validating their source and content.

If previous decisions are given such a significant function, they require a more rigorous scrutiny. A thorough analysis of the previous practice on the issue, militating in favour of one or another premise as a jurisdictional rule, is often absent in practice, at times even suggesting intentional negligence of certain prior decisions. This becomes especially problematic when a tribunal applies a rule that stems from sharply divided practice or, in a more extreme example, which deviates from the dominant practice. The Tribunal in *H&H Enterprises Investments, Inc. v. Egypt* adopted the presumption created in *Plama* that MFN clauses do not cover dispute settlement clauses unless there are indicators to the contrary.[29] The Tribunal did not discuss different approaches to the issue appearing in the extensive case law, which by no means can be considered settled.[30] The same Tribunal rejected the 'triple identity' test as the relevant standard in the application of fork-in-the-road clauses and applied the 'fundamental basis of the claim' test.[31] While acknowledging the origins of the former in the jurisprudence, the Tribunal did not address any decision setting out the rationale behind that test and the reasons for its acceptance in prior practice.[32]

The Tribunal in *Le Chèque Déjeuner and CD Holding Internationale v. Hungary* supported the application of MFN clauses to dispute settlement clauses in principle and extended its substantive jurisdiction on that basis.[33] Verifying its interpretative conclusions, the Tribunal dedicated a section to 'Relevant jurisprudence of other tribunals', where it found sufficient only to refer to the International Law Commission's

25. *Cortec Mining Kenya Limited, Cortec (Pty) Limited and Stirling Capital Limited v. Republic of Kenya*, ICSID Case No. ARB/15/29, Award, para. 260 (22 October 2018).
26. *Ibid.*, para. 261.
27. *See*, e.g., *Bear Creek Mining Corporation v. Republic of Perú*, ICSID Case No. ARB/14/21, Award, para. 320 (30 November 2017). In fact, this decision was invoked by the Claimants in *Cortec: Cortec Mining Kenya Limited, Cortec (Pty) Limited and Stirling Capital Limited v. Kenya, supra* n. 25, at para. 314.
28. *Cortec Mining Kenya Limited, Cortec (Pty) Limited and Stirling Capital Limited v. Kenya, supra* n. 25, at para. 271.
29. *H&H Enterprises Investments, Inc. v. The Arab Republic of Egypt*, ICSID Case No. ARB/09/15, Award, para. 358 (6 May 2014).
30. Cf. the two streams of jurisprudence at *supra* nn. 11 and 12 and the accompanying text.
31. *H&H Enterprises Investments, Inc. v. Egypt, supra* n. 29, at paras 363–269.
32. *Ibid.*, para. 364.
33. *Le Chèque Déjeuner and CD Holding Internationale v. Hungary*, ICSID Case No. ARB/13/35, Decision on Preliminary Issues of Jurisdiction, paras 135–222 (3 March 2016).

summaries of the case law.[34] The Tribunal directly addressed only the *RosInvest* decision on jurisdiction, which also extended substantive jurisdiction via an MFN clause and which tribunal was chaired by the same arbitrator.[35] The Tribunal dismissed the relevance of other decisions.[36]

While the decisions addressed so far present examples of insufficient reasoning in the application of arbitrator-made jurisdictional rules, more extreme examples are those where such rules were entirely ignored. For instance, despite the extensive arguments made by the Respondent about the existence of an independent legality requirement stemming from practice and limiting the jurisdiction of arbitral tribunals,[37] the Tribunal in *Bear Creek Mining Corporation v. Peru* simply noted that it could not draw additional jurisdictional limits.[38] And despite the long and established practice creating the objective definition of 'investment' under the ICSID Convention, some tribunals have refused to apply it, either by considering it non-mandatory[39] or by deferring to definitions in investment treaties.[40]

Proper application of arbitrator-made jurisdictional rules therefore requires a comprehensive analysis of the case law on the issue, and in the case that the practice offers multiple competitor rules, a justified and reasoned choice. The Tribunal in *Impregilo S.p.A. v. Argentina*, for example, recognized the extensive case law on the applicability of MFN clauses to dispute settlement clauses, and found that there was support for the applicability where MFN clauses referred to 'all matters', but also in some other instances.[41] The Tribunal noted that the case law was not uniform and acknowledged a decision favouring the non-applicability of an MFN clause although it referred to 'all matters', but did not follow that decision noting that one arbitrator 'strongly dissented' and 'that there were also some special elements'.[42] Furthermore, the Tribunal distinguished other decisions favouring the non-applicability on the ground that the MFN clauses concerned did not refer to 'all matters'.[43] The Tribunal noted that the practice was not settled as this other group of decisions expressed doubts about the applicability of MFN clauses to dispute settlement clauses in general, but decided to take the reference to 'all matters' as the common denominator of the decisions supporting the applicability and militating in favour of accepting the same solution.[44]

Another positive instance of the application of arbitrator-made jurisdictional rules can be found in the example of the privity requirement in the application of

34. *Ibid.*, para. 209.
35. *Ibid.*, para. 213.
36. *Ibid.*, para. 214.
37. *Bear Creek Mining Corporation v. Perú*, *supra* n. 27, at paras 299–307.
38. *Ibid.*, para. 320.
39. *M.C.I. Power Group L.C. and New Turbine, Inc. v. Republic of Ecuador*, ICSID Case No. ARB/03/6, Award, paras 159, 165 (31 July 2007).
40. *Alpha Projektholding GmbH v. Ukraine*, ICSID Case No. ARB/07/16, Award, para. 314 (8 November 2010).
41. *Impregilo S.p.A. v. Argentine Republic*, ICSID Case No. ARB/07/17, Award, paras 104–105 (21 June 2011).
42. *Ibid.*, para. 106.
43. *Ibid.*, para. 107.
44. *Ibid.*, paras 107–108.

umbrella clauses. The Tribunal in *WNC Factoring Ltd v. Czechia* found an explicit privity requirement in the applicable umbrella clause.[45] The Tribunal then addressed the case law on the issue,[46] recognizing that '[t]here is no consensus, but the dominant view is that in respect of contractual obligations, only parties entitled to enforce the obligation under the proper law of the contract may sue'.[47] The analysis of the case law led the Tribunal to state that it 'would uphold the requirement of privity even for generally worded umbrella clauses, which are intended to give effect to legal commitments entered into by the host state with regard to investments, not to change their scope or content'.[48] A careful analysis of the practice encouraged the Tribunal's recognition of the privity requirement as an arbitrator-made default rule in the application of umbrella clauses, although that default rule was not necessary in the given case due to the specific wording of the treaty.

§8.04 CREATION

The dynamic nature of legal practice will always allow for the emergence of new jurisdictional questions that reveal regulatory space to be filled by arbitrators. An example is the *Maffezini* case, where an attempt at applying an MFN clause to dispute settlement provisions was made for the first time. Although the Tribunal did not express any surprise,[49] it addressed the issue as a new regulatory question, which is visible in its definition of a general rule with a set of exceptions.[50] Yet, although possible, and although arbitrators have some discretion in framing issues as new,[51] such scenarios are rather rare, and more often arbitrators wish to substitute an existing rule with a new one, or at least to deviate from the existing practice. *Maffezini* was thus rebutted in *Plama*, and the Tribunal in the latter case clearly saw the question before it

45. *WNC Factoring Ltd (United Kingdom) v. The Czech Republic,* PCA Case No. 2014-34, Award, para. 320 (22 February 2017).
46. *Ibid.*, paras 325–340.
47. *Ibid.*, para. 325.
48. *Ibid.*, para. 335.
49. *Emilio Agustín Maffezini v. The Kingdom of Spain,* ICSID Case No. ARB/97/7, Decision of the Tribunal on Objections to Jurisdiction, para. 43 (25 January 2000) ('The arguments outlined above are familiar to international lawyers and scholars. Indeed, many of the issues mentioned have been addressed in the *Anglo-Iranian Oil Company Case (Jurisdiction)*, in the *Case concerning the rights of nationals of the United States of America in Morocco* and in the *Ambatielos Case (merits: obligation to arbitrate)*, as well as in the proceedings of the *Ambatielos case* before a Commission of Arbitration' [references omitted]).
50. *Ibid.*, paras 56, 62–63.
51. *See*, e.g., *Vladimir Berschader & Moïse Berschader v. Russia, supra* n. 12, at para. 135 ('Indeed, it would seem that this is the first case in which the sole claimants are foreign shareholders in a foreign incorporated company seeking to rely upon the terms of a BIT without having made any direct investment on their own part. In the absence of any authority on the point, the Tribunal believes that there can be no presumption that the wording of Article 1.2 encompasses the kind of indirect investment relied upon in the instant case'). The same question could have been framed as concerning the protection of indirect investments in principle, which was not new.

as the one of regulation.[52] The crucial question, therefore, is how tribunals should engage in the creation of new jurisdictional rules, even where a relevant arbitrator-made rule is already in place.

Being in the domain of regulation, tribunals must first identify a regulatory space. When a rule is already in place, tribunals must find such a regulatory space either in the fact that the existing rule is wrong or in the fact that the conditions in the international community have changed, thereby requiring new solutions.[53] This has not been the practice of arbitral tribunals. The first error often encountered is that tribunals wishing to disregard previous rules tend to distinguish cases, even if on very loose grounds. The Tribunal in *Bear Creek Mining Corporation v. Peru* distinguished that case from the decisions cited by the Respondent in support of the existence of an independent legality requirement. The Tribunal held that the applicable treaty did not contain an explicit legality requirement, whereas the treaties in the cited decisions did.[54] The Tribunal considered this sufficient for avoiding the application of the independent legality requirement, ignoring the fact that precisely such a requirement was addressed – and enforced – in the cited decisions.[55]

Another notable error is that some tribunals, even without distinguishing cases, engage in an impulsive creation of rules. In 2009, the Sole Arbitrator in *Pantechniki S.A. Contractors & Engineers v. Albania* held that the relevant standard in the application of fork-in-the-road clauses was the 'foundational basis of a claim', that 'it is no longer sufficient merely to assert that a claim is founded on the Treaty' and that treaty claims must have 'an autonomous existence' from the contract.[56] The Sole Arbitrator did so despite the established practice in favour of the 'triple identity' test and its elements.[57] The Sole Arbitrator did not address that practice either to distinguish its relevance or to identify a regulatory space for a new rule. He went straightforward into defining a new standard.

52. *Plama Consortium Limited v. Republic of Bulgaria,* ICSID Case No. ARB/03/24, Decision on Jurisdiction, para. 223 (8 February 2005) ('the principle with multiple exceptions as stated by the tribunal in the *Maffezini* case should instead be a different principle with one, single exception: an MFN provision in a basic treaty does not incorporate by reference dispute settlement provisions in whole or in part set forth in another treaty, unless the MFN provision in the basic treaty leaves no doubt that the Contracting Parties intended to incorporate them').
53. This is not a novel proposition. According to Shahabuddeen, the International Court of Justice follows its previous decisions, 'unless they can be distinguished on valid grounds or shown to be clearly wrong, or, possibly, where they no longer meet the new conditions of the evolving international community'. Mohamed Shahabuddeen, *Precedent in the World Court* 12 (Cambridge Univ. Press 1996).
54. *Bear Creek Mining Corporation v. Perú, supra* n. 27, at para. 320 ('Indeed, the above considerations distinguish the FTA from the treaties applicable in *Flughafen Zurich, Hamester, Inceysa,* and *Phoenix Action,* which expressly required compliance with the host State's law').
55. *See,* e.g., *Phoenix Action, Ltd. v. The Czech Republic,* ICSID Case No. ARB/06/5, Award, para. 116 (15 April 2009) ('It is the Tribunal's view that in referring expressly to the necessity to invest "in connection with economic activities" and to make the investment "in accordance with the laws and regulations" of the host State, the BIT does not modify in any way the ICSID notion, but only explicitly expresses two necessary elements of the test – 4 and 5 – implicit in the rules of interpretation').
56. *Pantechniki S.A. Contractors & Engineers (Greece) v. The Republic of Albania,* ICSID Case No. ARB/07/21, Award, para. 64 (30 July 2009).
57. For an example of such practice, *see supra* n. 19.

In contrast, the Tribunal in *Georg Gavrilović and Gavrilović d.o.o. v. Croatia* acknowledged the practice establishing the *Salini* criteria and the objective definition of 'investment'.[58] However, the Tribunal then took 'a different view, and consider[ed] it appropriate to defer to the State parties' articulation of the meaning of "investment" in their instrument of consent to arbitration, namely, the BIT'.[59] Although conceding that the *Salini* test could be 'useful',[60] and although analysing the fulfilment of some of its elements,[61] the Tribunal challenged the objective definition of 'investment' in principle. It therefore needed to address the weaknesses of such definition to a greater extent in search for a regulatory space, and not merely to take 'a different view' from the previous practice.

Once a regulatory space is identified, tribunals can formulate a new rule, but in doing so they must justify its substance. Justification is crucial because it provides conditions for and increases the likelihood of the acceptance of the new rule by subsequent tribunals. The Tribunal in *H&H Enterprises Investments, Inc. v. Egypt* attempted to find some regulatory space regarding the relevant standard in the application of fork-in-the-road clauses, by briefly discussing what it saw as the deficiencies of the 'triple identity' test (although, as argued above, the analysis of that test was insufficient).[62] The Tribunal then opted for the 'foundational basis of the claim' test and cited the *Pantechniki* decision in support.[63] However, excerpts from the latter case were quoted only to enquire about the application of the test.[64] The Tribunal did not address any advantages and disadvantages of the 'foundational basis of the claim' test that would justify its broader acceptance.

The Tribunal in *United Parcel Service of America Inc v. Canada* held that a continued act renewed a time bar, thus effectively extending the validity of consent.[65] Justifying its regulatory action, the Tribunal said this was 'true generally in the law' and invoked an interim decision in *Marvin Roy Feldman Karpa v. Mexico* in support,[66] even though the latter decision did not address continuing acts as the means of extending the validity of consent.[67] The poor justification of the proposed rule did not provide conditions for its broader acceptance, and it is not surprising that other tribunals have rebutted it.[68]

58. *Georg Gavrilović and Gavrilović d.o.o. v. Republic of Croatia*, ICSID Case No. ARB/12/39, Award, para. 191 (26 July 2018).
59. *Ibid.*, para. 192.
60. *Ibid.*, para. 193.
61. *Ibid.*, paras 195–218.
62. *H&H Enterprises Investments, Inc. v. Egypt, supra* n. 29, at para. 367.
63. *Ibid.*, paras 368–370.
64. *Ibid.*, paras 370, 377.
65. *United Parcel Service of America Inc v. Government of Canada*, ICSID Case No. UNCT/02/1, Award on the Merits, para. 28 (24 May 2007).
66. *Ibid.*
67. *See Marvin Roy Feldman Karpa v. United Mexican States*, ICSID Case No. ARB(AF)/99/1, Interim Decision on Preliminary Jurisdictional Issues (6 December 2000); and Sadie Blanchard, *State Consent, Temporal Jurisdiction, and the Importation of Continuing Circumstances Analysis into International Investment Arbitration*, 10 Washington Univ. Global Studies L. Rev. 419, 466–467 (2011).
68. *Spence International Investments, LLC, Berkowitz, et al. v. Republic of Costa Rica*, ICSID Case No. UNCT/13/2, Interim Award, para. 208 (25 October 2016).

A positive example of engagement in the creation of jurisdictional rules can be seen in *Plama Consortium Limited v. Bulgaria* regarding the MFN-dispute settlement conjunction. The Tribunal clearly considered the rule established in *Maffezini* wrong,[69] questioning its reasoning extensively,[70] and criticizing its effect on practice.[71] Having found a regulatory space for a different rule, the Tribunal did not frame its examination narrowly as that of treaty interpretation with the additions of its own beliefs. The Tribunal, among others, discussed the formation of arbitration agreements by reference,[72] noted a (negative) State reaction to *Maffezini* in treaty practice,[73] noted an example of explicit inclusion of dispute settlement provisions within the reach of an MFN clause,[74] and revisited the older International Court of Justice (ICJ) and arbitration jurisprudence that inspired *Maffezini*.[75] Of course, the Tribunal was still able to permeate the reasoning with its own considerations for presuming the inapplicability of MFN clauses to dispute settlement provisions.[76] The crucial point here is that regardless of one's opinion about the soundness of the rule advanced in *Plama*, the Tribunal in that case fully engaged in the discourse on the proper rule governing the MFN-dispute settlement conjunction.

For better or for worse, much of arbitral approaches to the creation of new rules depends on individual attitudes and activism. The Tribunal in *Burlington Resources Inc. v. Ecuador* expressed the view that 'subject to compelling contrary grounds, it ha[d] a duty to adopt solutions established in a series of consistent cases' and that 'it ha[d] a duty to seek to contribute to the harmonious development of investment law'.[77] The Tribunal then declined to follow an annulment decision as establishing a general condition of privity in the application of umbrella clauses,[78] and it did so on rather technical grounds,[79] although in the end it took the same route and reached the same conclusion.[80] Finally, the Tribunal found support for the condition of privity in different ICSID decisions, including the said annulment decision.[81] The Tribunal thus chose not to give precedential value to another decision, but to build reasoning potentially gaining precedential status on its own. Certainly, the Tribunal promised allegiance to 'a series of consistent cases' and not precedents, but it also could have

69. *See supra* n. 52.
70. *Plama Consortium Limited v. Bulgaria, supra* n. 52, at paras 216–224.
71. *Ibid.*, para. 226.
72. *Ibid.*, paras 198–200.
73. *Ibid.*, para. 202.
74. *Ibid.*, para. 204.
75. *Ibid.*, paras 213–215.
76. *See*, e.g., *ibid.*, paras 206–212 (on specificities of dispute settlement arrangements); and particularly *ibid.*, para. 212 (advancing the argument about the separability of arbitration clauses).
77. *Burlington Resources Inc. v. Republic of Ecuador*, ICSID Case No. ARB/08/5, Decision on Jurisdiction, para. 100 (2 June 2010).
78. *Ibid.*, para. 195.
79. *Ibid.*, para. 196 (noting that the annulment decision dealt with the failure to state the reasons, not with a manifest excess of powers).
80. *Burlington Resources Inc. v. Ecuador, supra* n. 16, at paras 214–215.
81. *Ibid.*, paras 221–233.

motivated the decision as building on previous practice instead of lawmaking from scratch.

Similarly, the Tribunal in *Phoenix Action, Ltd. v. Czechia* chose to make law where it did not need to do so. The applicable treaty contained an explicit legality requirement,[82] but the decision has become famous for its creation of a default legality requirement that exists independently of treaty texts.[83] The Tribunal did well insofar as it recognized the regulatory space prompted by earlier tribunals' recognition of the issue as concerning international public policy.[84] The use of that regulatory space created conditions for the later conferral on that precedent the status of law.

§8.05 CONTROL

The most drastic improvements suggested by this chapter concern control mechanisms. Improvements are necessary to secure their more active engagement in the process of arbitral lawmaking and its control. Such improvements are achievable in the existing system of investment arbitration, but the investment court system will provide even more fertile conditions for them.

The practice of control mechanisms in relation to arbitral jurisdictional regulation has been ambivalent. On the one hand, ICSID annulment committees have maintained that their task is not to correct errors made by tribunals.[85] That attitude has led some tribunals to decline to examine the substance of arbitrator-made rules. For example, committees have held that they could not examine whether the interpretation of MFN clauses in respect of dispute settlement clauses conducted by tribunals was correct and refused to address the question of the applicability of MFN clauses to dispute settlement clauses in principle.[86]

---

82. *Phoenix Action, Ltd. v. Czechia, supra* n. 55, at para. 56.
83. *Ibid.*, paras 101–105, 114.
84. *See ibid.*, para. 101 (referring to the merits decision in *Plama,* where a legality requirement was found implicit in the Energy Charter Treaty); *Plama Consortium Limited v. Republic of Bulgaria,* ICSID Case No. ARB/03/24, Award, paras 141–142 (27 August 2008) (reviewing previous decisions linking the issues of legality to the international public policy); and *ibid.*, para. 143 ('The Tribunal is of the view that granting the ECT's protections to Claimant's investment would be contrary to the principle *nemo auditur propriam turpitudinem allegans* invoked above. It would also be contrary to the basic notion of international public policy – that a contract obtained by wrongful means (fraudulent misrepresentation) should not be enforced by a tribunal').
85. *Hussein Nuaman Soufraki v. The United Arab Emirates,* ICSID Case No. ARB/02/7, Decision of the ad hoc Committee on the Application for Annulment of Mr. Soufraki, para. 116 (5 June 2007).
86. *Impregilo S.p.A. v. Argentine Republic,* ICSID Case No. ARB/07/17, Decision of the ad hoc Committee on the Application for Annulment, paras 140–141 (24 January 2014); *Suez, Sociedad General de Aguas de Barcelona S.A. and Interagua Servicios Integrales de Agua S.A. v. Argentine Republic,* ICSID Case No. ARB/03/17, Decision on Argentina's Application for Annulment, paras 173–180 (14 December 2018).

On the other hand, some committees have indeed addressed the issues of the arbitral jurisdictional regulation. For example, the contribution of annulment committees to the debate about the objective definition of 'investment' is significant.[87] The means of engagement are plural: committees can analyse both whether tribunals have manifestly exceeded their powers[88] and whether they have failed to properly reason their awards.[89] In doing so, committees have not challenged the lawmaking function of tribunals, but the substance of arbitrator-made jurisdictional rules. This means that committees have on some occasions engaged substantively in the lawmaking process.[90] The precedential value of annulment decisions, however, remains uncertain, given that tribunals can dismiss their relevance for different factors, such as the addressed grounds of annulment and their pertinence to jurisdictional matters.[91]

The same applies to domestic courts in the non-ICSID context. Their practice is complex, insofar as the scope and standard of review applied by domestic courts are regulated differently from country to country. In principle, however, domestic courts have more opportunities to examine arbitral jurisdictional determinations than ICSID committees. International standards do not require the excess of powers to be manifest to succeed in setting aside[92] and refusal of recognition/enforcement.[93] Domestic courts thus usually conduct a de novo examination of jurisdiction[94] and have the possibility to conduct the same type of jurisdictional analysis as arbitral tribunals. Similarly to ICSID committees, domestic courts have not contested the lawmaking activity of arbitral tribunals regarding their jurisdiction and occasionally have even engaged in it

---

87. Cf. *Mr. Patrick Mitchell v. The Democratic Republic of Congo*, ICSID Case No. ARB/99/7, Decision on the Application for Annulment of the Award, paras 27–33 (1 November 2006) (the contribution to the development of the host State is relevant) *with Malaysian Historical Salvors Sdn Bhd v. The Government of Malaysia*, ICSID Case No. ARB/05/10, Decision on the Application for Annulment, paras 75–81 (16 April 2009) (the contribution to the development of the host State is not relevant).
88. *Malaysian Historical Salvors Sdn Bhd v. Malaysia, supra* n. 87, at para. 80.
89. *Mr. Patrick Mitchell v. DRC, supra* n. 87, at para. 41.
90. Note that the Annulment Committee in *Malaysian Historical Salvors* criticized the Sole Arbitrator because 'its analysis of these [*Salini*] criteria elevated them to jurisdictional conditions'. *Malaysian Historical Salvors Sdn Bhd v. Malaysia, supra* n. 87, at para. 80(b). But the Committee was not really criticizing the exercise of the lawmaking function by the Sole Arbitrator, but rather supporting the stream of practice opposed to that of *Salini*, which holds that there are no hard, objective requirements of an investment. *Ibid.*, para. 79. Therefore, this was a critique of the substance of arbitrator-made rules, not of their existence as such.
91. The Tribunal in *Burlington* denied precedential value to an annulment decision, because the latter addressed the relevant jurisdictional issue through the lens of the failure to state the reasons, not manifest excess of powers. *See supra* n. 79.
92. UNCITRAL Model Law on International Commercial Arbitration of 1985, with amendments as adopted in 2006, Art. 34(2)(a)(iii), http://www.uncitral.org/pdf/english/texts/arbitration/ml-arb/07-86998_Ebook.pdf.
93. Convention on the Recognition and Enforcement of Foreign Arbitral Awards, Art. V(1)(c), 10 June 1958, 330 U.N.T.S. 38.
94. *See, e.g.*, *The Republic of Ecuador v. Occidental Exploration & Production Co* [2006] EWHC 345 (Comm), para. 7 ('The test for the court is: was the Tribunal correct in its decision on jurisdiction? The test is not: was the Tribunal entitled to reach the decision that it did').

substantively.[95] For example, after the Tribunal in *Renta 4 S.V.S.A. et al. v. Russia* held that MFN clauses can be applicable to dispute settlement clauses in principle, but found indicators of exclusion of that conjunction (the limitation of the MFN clause to fair and equitable treatment),[96] the Svea Court of Appeal repeated the same interpretative trajectory implying the same presumption.[97] On some occasions domestic courts have disagreed with tribunals, as French and English courts have done regarding the objective definition of 'investment' outside the ICSID Convention.[98] These were not occasional challenges of the arbitral regulatory function and of arbitrator-made jurisdictional rules, but engagements in their substantive making.

However, the non-contestation of arbitral jurisdictional regulation by control mechanisms does not in reality ensure its proper functioning. ICSID annulment committees and domestic courts must assume a controlling role in respect of the application and creation of arbitrator-made jurisdictional rules. This means that controlling bodies should first review the reasoning of arbitral tribunals and enquire whether they have addressed the case law on the issue comprehensively and distilled the applicable jurisdictional rule correctly. If a tribunal has decided to create a new rule, the controlling body should consider if the tribunal has identified a regulatory space and justified the substance of the proposed rule. Second, controlling bodies can contribute to the content of such rules by determining whether tribunals have applied proper rules, clarifying the current state of practice, and even advancing their own lawmaking arguments, if the regulatory space makes it appropriate.

The crucial issue here is that the ICSID Convention requires the excess of powers to be 'manifest' for annulment.[99] This issue can be overcome by treating arbitrator-made jurisdictional rules as proper law. Their disregard, improper application or creation should be sanctioned. If arbitrator-made jurisdictional rules continue to be treated as only details in treaty interpretations, their improper application and creation will remain outside the reach of annulment committees. But if they are accepted as law, their improper application and creation must constitute a 'manifest' excess of powers. In addition, as seen above, annulment committees have already been willing to address the questions of arbitral jurisdictional regulation through the lens of the failure to state the reasons. Bearing in mind that their controlling role in this context should be focused on the reasoning of arbitral decisions, this is another important avenue for implementing the understanding of arbitrator-made jurisdictional rules as proper law.

---

95. The treatment of the arbitral jurisdictional regulation before domestic courts is the subject of the author's work in progress entitled 'Arbitral Jurisdictional Regulation in Investment Treaty Arbitration and Domestic Courts'.
96. *Renta 4 S.V.S.A. et al. v. The Russian Federation*, SCC Case No. 24/2007, Award on Preliminary Objections, paras 100–120 (20 March 2009).
97. *The Russian Federation v. GBI 9000 SICAV S.A. et al.* [2016] Svea Court of Appeal T 9128-14, 8–10.
98. Arrêt du 25 septembre 2008, Cour d'Appel de Paris, 1ère Chambre – Section C (France) 07/04675, 5; *The Republic of Korea v. Mohammad Reza Dayyani et al.* [2019] EWHC 3580 (Comm) [57]–[59].
99. Convention on the Settlement of Investment Disputes Between States and Nationals of Other States, Art. 52(1)(b), 18 March 1965, 575 U.N.T.S. 159.

These suggestions can be implemented in the existing system of investment arbitration, but institutionalized dispute settlement bodies will likely provide additional conditions for their successful implementation.[100] The existing treaty texts reveal that the control mechanism in particular will provide better conditions for the exercise of the arbitral lawmaking function. For now, ICSID annulment committees can only annul awards, and they cannot correct jurisdictional determinations made by tribunals.[101] This fact constrains the ability of annulment committees to engage more actively in the process of creating jurisdictional rules, especially when arbitrator-made jurisdictional rules are framed as mere details in treaty interpretations. The investment court system advanced by the European Union allows appellate tribunals to modify or reverse arbitral awards for the manifest excess of powers.[102] This model will allow appellate tribunals to engage more directly in the arbitral jurisdictional regulation because through its power to modify or reverse awards it will be able to express its views on the correct arbitrator-made rule. However, the crucial condition remains that only accepting arbitrator-made jurisdictional rules as proper law will allow qualifying their improper application or creation as a 'manifest' excess of powers. Without that change, appellate tribunals might remain inactive when it comes to arbitral jurisdictional regulation, ignoring its existence and treating its products as mere details of treaty interpretations. Of course, the fact that first-instance and appellate tribunals will deal with only one treaty text (or several, if similar mega-regionals are taken into account together) will be another incentive for uniform approaches to jurisdictional determinations, including arbitrator-made rules that now form their inevitable part.

§8.06 CONCLUSION

Improvements are necessary when it comes to all three issues discussed in this chapter, namely the application, creation and control of arbitrator-made jurisdictional rules, although to different degrees. Such improvements are necessary in the sphere of arbitral decision-making and reasoning. In short, tribunals must address previous decisions comprehensively and distil the applicable arbitrator-made rule for the jurisdictional question they are facing. If they wish to create a new jurisdictional rule, they should first identify a regulatory space and then justify the newly formulated rule. These processes must be controlled by ICSID annulment committees and domestic courts outside that framework, and by appellate tribunals within investment court mechanisms. A crucial factor, enabling such control, is the recognition of arbitrator-made jurisdictional rules as proper law. Such recognition would seek the sanctioning of improper application or creation of arbitrator-made jurisdictional rules, and would

100. For example, the institutionalization of the system and narrowing down the circle of decision-makers will contribute to the consolidation of practice and encourage the reliance on previous decisions.
101. *See supra* nn. 85 and 99.
102. CETA, *supra* n. 3, Art. 8.28(2)(c); EU-Vietnam IPA, *supra* n. 3, Art. 3.54(1)(c); EU-Singapore IPA, *supra* n. 3, Art. 3.19(1)(c).

overcome current obstacles in their control, such as the need for an excess of powers to be 'manifest' under the ICSID Convention.

The implementation of these recommendations would secure the recognition of the arbitral jurisdictional regulation as a pertinent part of the jurisdictional structure of investor-State dispute settlement. This would ultimately provide conditions for a better performance of the system of investor-State dispute settlement, including most importantly the advancement of legal certainty when it comes to the questions of jurisdiction. While this can be done within the existing framework of investment arbitration, institutionalized dispute settlement mechanisms will provide particularly fertile conditions. The recommendations of this chapter are made in the context of arbitral jurisdictional regulation, but they can also be useful regarding the arbitral making of substantive law, although that is a separate topic requiring further examination.

CHAPTER 9

State Responsibility for Acts of State-Controlled Entities in Investor-State Dispute Settlement

Srilal M. Perera[*]

A continuing challenge in Investor-State Dispute Settlement (ISDS) concerns the determination by arbitral tribunals of a State's responsibility for acts of its State Controlled Entities (SCEs). Since the 1970s, the decisions of arbitral tribunals considering this important issue have been inconsistent for the most part. Resulting investment disputes, characterized as treaty breaches, have forced ISDS tribunals to determine the preliminary question of whether the alleged wrongful act of the SCE carries the responsibility of the State under established principles of international law. Tribunals have had to determine, through an examination of the relevant municipal law, the structure and functions of an SCE and the degree and extent to which it is linked to the State, because international law is silent on the matter. The 2001 Draft Articles on Responsibility of States for Internationally Wrongful Acts (2001 DARSIWA) attempted in many ways to present in key articles the principles for the methodical application of both, implicitly municipal law and international law, to assist in the determination of responsibility of States for acts of SCEs. The central problem with the 2001 DARSIWA, however, is that it is not binding. The relevant articles also present serious interpretational issues. Problems of consistency in application of the principles in ISDS abound, sometimes raising more questions than answers. This chapter endeavours to raise some of the many complex issues that were confronted by adjudicatory bodies to decide on State responsibility for acts of SCEs and the disparate methods by which they were disposed of.

* The author is grateful to Alex Levin Canal, JD, for his research assistance in preparing this chapter.

§9.01 INTRODUCTION

One of the most important subjects to yield innumerable inconsistent arbitral decisions in ISDS concerns attribution to the State for acts of its State-Owned Entities. These inconsistencies have emerged in decisions at both the jurisdiction and merits stages of arbitral proceedings in ISDS. This trend has continued despite guidance offered under principles of public international law and the 2001 DARSIWA[1] that includes generally accepted principles of State responsibility under international law. Some arbitral decisions have also yielded pragmatic methodologies to assist in the decision-making process.

The principles of State responsibility that apply in relation to State persons or entities acting directly with foreign investors, or when allegedly wrongful acts are committed by persons or entities of one of its 'sub-sovereigns' (such as states in a federal system, the state's provincial governments, municipalities, etc.) are clear. At those levels the State bears the responsibility for such wrongful acts.[2] Inconsistencies in ISDS have all concerned disputes that have arisen from investment relations, often contractual, between an investor and a State Controlled Entity (SCE).[3] In such circumstances adjudicatory bodies have had to resolve three preliminary questions. First, it had to resolve the question of jurisdictional objections raised by the State that it is not the proper party to the dispute, because the dispute, de jure, is one with a separate legal entity in the form of an SCE. Second, if the position of a claimant is that the SCE acted as an alter ego of the State, then under what circumstances and what law should a piercing of the corporate veil be warranted to find the State responsible? Third, even if the conclusion is that the SCE is an alter ego of the State, should the adjudicatory body go further to determine whether the specific act that caused the loss was an internationally wrongful act that invokes the responsibility of the State (*acta iure imperii*) under an applicable treaty, or whether the act was undertaken in pursuit of a

1. International Law Commission, Draft Articles on Responsibility of States for Internationally Wrongful Acts, UN Doc A/56/83, 3 August 2001 (hereinafter 2001 DARSIWA).
2. *Ibid.*, Art. 4; *see* Srilal Perera, *State Responsibility – Ascertaining the Liability of States in Foreign Investment Disputes*, 6 J. World Investment and Trade 499–511 (2005). *See also EDF(Services) Limited v. Romania*, ICSID Case No. ARB/05/13, Award, (8 October 2009); *Kristian Almas and Geir Almas v. Republic of Poland*, PCA Case No. 2015-13 (27 June 2016).
3. Preference is given to the term State Controlled Entities (SCE) rather than the commonly used term State Owned Entities (SOEs), because it covers a wider array of entities. Besides, 'ownership' is not the only criterion for determining attribution. SCE's here refer to various categories of State controlled or directed entities. Some have been established by statute, e.g., Millennium Challenge Corporation (MCC) or the Overseas Private Investment Corporation (OPIC) in the USA, or the Electricity Generating Authority of Thailand (EGAT), which all have distinct legal status, can enter into agreements in their corporate name and often operate on a commercial basis. These statutory bodies are often called 'para-statals'. Some entities have also been created as private companies under the company laws of the State, where the State holds the shares in their entirety or some, e.g., the Kenya Power and Lighting Company (KPLC) engaged in generating and distribution of electricity in Kenya. Others could be entirely private entities acting as agents for the government or government entities, or have contracts to perform specific functions on behalf of the government and or are acting under the directions and instructions of the Government or Government entity.

commercial transaction (*acta iure gestionis*) for which a State will not be responsible under international law.

Linking actions of an SCE to the State has essentially forced adjudicatory bodies to review municipal legislation of the State in which the SCE is incorporated. Primarily, it necessitated a piercing of the corporate veil; an exercise which required a review of municipal law principles to reveal the structure and functions of the entity, similar to the methodology applied by municipal courts. Conclusions drawn from this exercise must then be aligned with established principles of public international law to attribute the wrongful act of the SCE to the State under international law. Often it is the insufficiency of and inconsistency in the application and consideration of principles drawn, from both municipal law and international law, that has contributed significantly to the inconsistent decisions in cases of State responsibility for acts of SCEs in ISDS.

§9.02 ANTECEDENTS TO THE 2001 DARSIWA

The 2001 DARSIWA includes the guiding principles under international law that can be applied to investor-State disputes, to determine whether or not wrongful acts can be attributed to the State. However, prior to 2001, certain legal principles on State responsibility were also generated in ISDS. Indeed, important principles were developed, if not highlighted, by international adjudicatory bodies, as well as municipal courts at the highest level, to resolve the problems of attribution to the State for acts of SCEs. Extremely pragmatic principles on State responsibility and methodologies that can be applied even contemporaneously were enunciated in the International Court of Justice (ICJ) cases of *Belgium v. Spain*[4] (also known as *Barcelona Traction*), *Trendtex Trading Corporation v. Central Bank of Nigeria,*[5] the jurisprudence of the Iran-United States Claims Tribunal, and *Emilio Maffezini v. The Kingdom of Spain.*[6]

[A] *Belgium v. Spain (Barcelona Traction)*

The central issue considered by the ICJ in *Barcelona Traction* was whether Belgium had *jus standi* before the ICJ to provide diplomatic protection for Belgian shareholders of the Barcelona Traction Company, a limited liability company (LLC) incorporated under the company law of Canada. Belgium, on behalf of the shareholders who were nationals of Belgium, sought reparations from Spain for allegedly wrongful acts caused to the company that had an investment in Spain. Implicitly, the question revolved around the circumstances and conditions under which shareholders could assert a

4. *Barcelona Traction, Light and Power Company, Limited (New Application 1962) (Belgium v. Spain)*, Judgment, I.C.J Rep. 1970 (5 February 1970) (hereafter '*Barcelona Traction Case*').
5. *Trendtex Trading Corporation v. Central Bank of Nigeria*, Court of Appeal, QBD [1975] T. No. 3663 (1977).
6. *Emilio Maffezini v. The Kingdom of Spain*, ICSID Case No. ARB/97/7, Decision on Objections to Jurisdiction (January 2000), and Award (November 2000). (Also posted in 16 ICSID Rev-F.I.L.J. 248 (2001)).

right for reparations for injuries caused to their company. The ICJ concluded that in such situations, international law requires recognition of 'institutions of municipal law that have an important and extensive role in the international field'.[7] In determining the rights of shareholders, the ICJ ruled that when it is the company which had been wronged, it was municipal law of the State of incorporation of the company that should apply.[8]

The ICJ found that the company and its shareholders were legally distinct: 'Separated from the company by numerous barriers, the shareholder cannot be identified with it.'[9] Their legal rights were similarly distinct and separate and 'the shareholders' right in relation to the company and its assets remain limited, this being, moreover, a corollary of the limited nature of their liability'.[10] The ICJ proceeded to deny *jus standi* to Belgium and commented that while international law may not provide specific principles to guide particular situations, in this instance 'the company against which allegedly unlawful acts were directed is expressly vested with a right, whereas no such right is specifically provided for the shareholder in respect of those acts'.[11]

Thus, where a wrongful act is committed against a company, only the company has the right of claims for redress and not the shareholders. Conversely, where it is the company that has committed the wrongful act, logically, it is the company that is responsible and not the shareholders. This fundamental principle reinforces the limited liability nature of a company, albeit there can be exceptions to the rules, as will be discussed subsequently.

[B] *Trendtex Trading Corporation v. Central Bank of Nigeria*

Trendtex Trading Corporation before the Court of Appeal in the UK is instructive of the problems of attribution to the State of Nigeria, of allegedly wrongful acts of the Central Bank of Nigeria. The key issue was whether, in light of the Central Bank being a statutory body created under a Nigerian federal statute, it enjoyed immunity from suit in the courts of England. The facts of the case were that the Central Bank of Nigeria issued an irrevocable letter of credit to Trendtex, the plaintiff, to pay for a consignment of cement. The cement was to be shipped to Nigeria where it was to be used for construction of barracks in Nigeria. The plaintiff shipped the cement to Nigeria, but the Central Bank declined to honour the letter of credit posted in a UK Bank.

Trendtex then brought a claim against the Central Bank in a Court of First Instance in England and Wales, based on wrongful repudiation of the letter of credit and sought an injunction ordering the Central Bank to retain specific sums within the UK jurisdiction until trial. This injunction was granted. But at trial, Justice Donaldson agreed with the Central Bank's application to set aside the injunction, based on the

7. *Barcelona Traction Case*, ICJ, *supra* n. 4, para. 38.
8. *Ibid.*, para. 41.
9. *Ibid.*
10. *Ibid.*, para. 42; *see also ibid.*, para. 50.
11. *Ibid.*, para. 52.

reasoning that the Central Bank of Nigeria was a 'department of the State of Nigeria and was therefore immune from suit'.[12] Trendtex appealed the decision.

After an extensive survey of precedents, authoritative sources and references to international law, the Court of Appeal overturned the decision of the lower court and concluded that the Central Bank of Nigeria 'which had been created as a separate legal entity with no clear expression of intent that it should have governmental status, was not an emanation, arm, alter ego or department of the State of Nigeria and was therefore not entitled to immunity from suit'.[13]

The Court of Appeal did a two-pronged investigation. First, it considered whether the Central Bank of Nigeria was an integral part of the Government of Nigeria. Second, the Court examined whether, even if it were to be deemed as such, the Central Bank was engaged in sovereign acts binding the Government of Nigeria or whether it was engaged in commercial acts.

The Court of Appeal concluded that the Act of 1958, which created the Bank of Nigeria, established it as a separate legal entity, but recognized that it was vested with powers to issue 'legal tender and acted as banker and financial adviser to the Government of Nigeria. It also acted as banker for other banks and its affairs were under considerable governmental control'.[14] Considering these powers, Lord Denning opined that he found it difficult to decide whether the Central Bank was a department of the Federation of Nigeria, even though it was a separate legal entity.[15] He surmised that the Central Bank, 'on the whole' should not be considered as a department of the Federation of Nigeria.[16] Even if that were the case – that the Central Bank was not a department of the Federation of Nigeria – Lord Denning concluded that he would prefer to rest his decision based 'on the ground that there is no immunity in respect of commercial transactions, even for a government department'.[17] This latter conclusion was buttressed by a particularly important pronouncement from Lord Denning:

> In the last fifty years, there has been a complete transformation in the functions of a sovereign state. Nearly every country now engages in commercial activities. It has its departments of state – or creates its own legal entities – which go into market places of the world. They charter ships. They buy commodities. They issue letters of credit. This transformation has changed the rules of international law relating to sovereign immunity. Many countries have now departed from the rule of absolute immunity. It has been replaced by a doctrine of restrictive immunity. This doctrine gives immunity to acts of a governmental nature, described in Latin as *jure imperii*, but no immunity to acts of a commercial nature, *jure gestionis*.[18]

Lord Justice Stephenson concurred with the conclusions of Lord Denning (as did Lord Justice Shaw) but added an important corollary to determining the separateness of the Central Bank from the Government of Nigeria. He pronounced that the latter did

12. *Trendtex v. Nigeria*, *supra* n. 5, s. 529.
13. *Ibid.*
14. *Ibid.*
15. *Ibid.*, s. 560.
16. *Ibid.*
17. *Ibid.*
18. *Ibid.*, s. 555.

not create a department of the State under the 1958 Statute establishing the Central Bank but a 'government bank and a prime Bank' 'with no declaration of government status' that was not 'immune from suit internally or externally' and was capable of suing or be sued in its own name 'under Section 3(2) of the Central Bank of Nigeria Act 1958'.[19]

Broadly, *Trendtex* illustrates the importance of considering both international law with municipal law to unravel difficult problems of attributing to governments the acts of its statutory bodies and by extension whether or not to extend sovereign immunity. More specifically, it highlights the importance not only of investigating the historical structure of statutory bodies such as the Central Bank of Nigeria but also of their specific functions through application of municipal law. *Trendtex* is atypical of a claim before ISDS, because the facts relate to a trade dispute than an investment dispute, but the fundamental principles enunciated are equally applicable to investment disputes with States.

[C] Jurisprudence of the Iran–United States Claims Tribunal[20]

Many contending principles of attribution to the State for acts of its SCEs emerged from the adjudication of claims before the Iran–United States Claims Tribunal that had jurisdiction to decide on claims under Article II of the Claims Settlement Declaration (CSD) that states in relevant part: 'An international tribunal (the Iran–United States Claims Tribunal) is hereby established for the purpose of deciding claims of nationals of the United States against Iran and claims of nationals of Iran against the United States.'[21] Giving context to the issue of attribution, the CSD in Article VII(3) defined 'Iran' to mean 'the Government of Iran, and any agency, instrumentality, or entity controlled by the Government of Iran or any political sub-division thereof'.[22] Emphasis on the word 'controlled' is important. How was the tribunal going to test 'control'? Determining 'control' would inevitably lead to a 'piercing of the corporate veil' or similar investigation.

From the vantage point of attribution, the importance of *Economy Forms*[23] is not so much in the decision of the majority of the tribunal, which had very little hesitation in finding that the acts of the SCEs in this case could be attributed to the Government of the Islamic Republic of Iran (GOI) but in the very strong dissent by Judge Mahmoud

19. *Ibid.*, s. 563.
20. The Iran-United States Claims Tribunal was established in 1981 pursuant to the Algiers Accords concluded between the United States of America and the Islamic Republic of Iran, which also included the Declaration of the Government of the Democratic Popular Republic of Algeria Concerning the Settlement of Claims by the Government of the United States of America and the Government of the Islamic Republic of Iran Declaration (19 January 1981) (reprinted in 1 Iran – U.S. C.T.R. 9 (1983)).
21. *Ibid.*
22. *Ibid.*
23. *Economy Forms Corporation, Claimant v. The Government of the Islamic Republic of Iran et.al (Economy Forms)* Award No. 55-165-1, 42 Iran-U.S.C.T.R. 1. (15 June 1983).

Kashani. Economy Forms, a US company, contracted to provide certain construction materials with two private Iranian construction companies, Sabir and Mana, which were totally owned by Iranian government entities, including the Ministry of Energy of Iran. The construction materials were supplied but not paid for under the letters of credit.

Consequently, Economy Forms filed a claim against GOI, Sabir, Mana and Bank Mellat, the issuer of the letters of credit. The claimant argued that GOI was responsible for the losses, since it controlled Sabir and Mana. GOI argued that the shares of the two companies were only indirectly owned by it and that in any event Sabir and Mana were never controlled by GOI. After reviewing the evidence, the tribunal's majority conclusion was decisive. It stated that the 'separate juridical status of an entity two or more levels removed from the government itself is not a sufficient basis from which to conclude that the entity conducts its operations free of the control of the government'.[24]

The majority decision elicited a very detailed dissent from Judge Kashani, who stated that the definition of 'Iran' in the CSD must be appropriately applied to every situation. He argued that there is no question about responsibility of Iran for acts of the Government and its political sub-divisions, but that careful scrutiny must be exercised when dealing with agencies or instrumentalities controlled by GOI.[25] While Judge Kashani stated that there are some agencies that are government agencies that carried out public services throughout Iran, it was nevertheless imperative to examine Iranian municipal law to determine whether these agencies were, in fact, and in law, controlled by GOI.

In this regard, Judge Kashani recommended a three-pronged test. First, he advocated for a review of the applicable Iranian law to determine whether the agency or control relationship existed. Second, he stated that even though there was a control relationship shown under the law, it must still be established that the relationship was entirely under the supervision of and dependent on some central organ of the government. Most importantly, Judge Kashani pronounced that the functions of the entity must be governmental as distinguished from commercial or private activity.[26] Since Sabir and Mana were private joint stock companies established under Iranian law for commercial purposes, Judge Kashani concluded that they should be excluded from the tribunal's jurisdiction as not meeting the definition of 'Iran', and furthermore, on the basis of international law.[27] Judge Kashani's dissent in *Economy Forms* is, of course, reflective of the reasoning of the unanimous decision in *Trendtex*, particularly in relation to the distinction drawn there between commercial and sovereign acts of the State. Although Judge Kashani's propositions did not prevail in *Economy Forms*, his dissent influenced a number of subsequent claims before the tribunal, namely

24. *Ibid.*, at 47.
25. *Ibid.*, dissenting opinion of Judge Kashani, 5 Iran-U.S.C.T.R. 1, 8 February 1984, at 1.
26. *Ibid.*, at 4–5.
27. *Ibid.*, at 2.

Sea-Land Services,[28] *Oil Field of Texas,*[29] *Flexi-Van Leasing*[30] and *Schering Corporation,*[31] among others.

The *Oil Field of Texas* award is particularly pertinent. There, the central issue revolved around the status of an entirely private joint stock company registered under the Company Law of Iran, called the Oil Services Company of Iran ('OSCO'). The National Iranian Oil Company ('NIOC'), a joint stock company, entirely owned by the GOI and with the entire responsibility for the operations and management of the oil sector in Iran on behalf of GOI, concluded several agreements with OSCO to conduct specific operations in the oil sector. The performance of services by OSCO was completely funded by NIOC. OSCO, under NIOC's instructions, in turn, concluded a number of contracts, one of which was a contract with Oil Field for the lease of equipment needed to prevent oil-well blow-outs. With the Iranian Revolution, OSCO was apparently liquidated and ceased to exist. Consequently, lease payments ceased and the leased equipment sequestered. No direct assertion was ever made or denied about NIOC's status as a GOI entity.

Oil Field of Texas argued that OSCO was an agent of NIOC and under general principles of commercial law, NIOC as the principal, was responsible for all unpaid lease amounts. NIOC countered that whether or not an agency relationship existed between itself and OSCO had to be determined under Iranian law. NIOC further asserted that the agreement with OSCO could only be characterized as one between an employer and contractor and not as between principal and agent. GOI was made a respondent by Oil Field based on an ostensible link theory. GOI directly controlled NIOC, NIOC controlled OSCO and, therefore, GOI indirectly controlled OSCO. The tribunal reviewed the municipal law of Iran and concluded that there was no agency relationship and that OSCO had acted as an independent contractor when it entered into the lease agreement with Oil Field.[32] The tribunal decided, therefore, that GOI could not be held responsible for the acts of OSCO.

The fact pattern examined in *Sea-Land* regarding the characteristics of ILB, an Iranian transportation company as an agent of the Port Shipping Organization (PSO), an Iranian government instrumentality, yielded the same result as in *Oil Field:* that GOI was not responsible for the acts of ILB.[33] In *Sedco*, the tribunal concluded that an alleged de facto taking of property by NIOC could not be attributed to Iran, where there

28. *Sea-Land Services, Inc. v. The Islamic Republic of Iran, Ports and Shipping Organization of Iran,* Award No. 135-33-1, 6 Iran-US C.T.R. 149, 217 (22 June 1984).
29. *Oil Field of Texas, Inc. v. The Islamic Republic of Iran,* Award No. 258-43-1, 12 Iran-US C.T.R. 308 (8 October 1986).
30. *Flexi-Van Leasing v. The Government of the Islamic Republic of Iran,* Award No. 259-36-1, 12 Iran-US C.T.R.335 (13 October 1986).
31. *Schering Corporation v. The Islamic Republic of Iran,* Award No. 122-38-3, 5 Iran-US C.T.R. 361 (16 April 1984).
32. *Oil Field, supra* n. 29, at 311–313.
33. *Sea-land Services, supra* n. 28, at 149, 217. The Tribunal here concluded that Iranian law did not recognize an agency or third-party relationship.

was no evidence to demonstrate that Iran used its ownership interest in NIOC to direct the taking.[34]

One of the key awards concerning attribution to Iran for acts of allegedly government-controlled entities is *Flexi-Van Leasing*. Flexi-Van, a US company, entered into two lease agreements dealing with leasing marine transport equipment with two private Iranian companies, Star Line Iran and Iran Express Lines Co. Flexi-Van lodged its claim against GOI, arguing that with the beginning of the Iranian Revolution, Star Line and Iran Express ceased to make lease payments sometime in 1978 and onwards and that GOI had effectively taken control of Star Line and Iran Express through its agents, such as the Foundation for the Oppressed. Consequently, Flexi-Van argued that the lease agreements had been effectively expropriated by GOI. The tribunal concluded first, that 'Expropriation of the Claimant's contract rights can only be found in case of interference with these contract rights themselves, and a basic condition for such a finding is that such interference be attributable to the Government.'[35] Further, addressing the alleged breach of contractual obligations by the government, the tribunal asserted that 'the Government would only be liable for damages arising out of breaches of the lease agreements if it had caused the two companies to breach these agreements or prevented them from fulfilling them'.[36]

Applying this causal test, the tribunal concluded that Flexi-Van failed to present proof of any action of the Government that caused Star Line and Iran Express to breach the lease agreements.[37] Characterizing both Star Lines and Iran Express as commercial entities, although probably being controlled by the Government after the Revolution, the tribunal concluded that both entities still had autonomy in making day-to-day decisions about their commercial dealings and that there was no evidence that GOI interfered with that autonomy.[38] Whether the tribunal over extended itself in introducing a commercial actions test in *Flexi-Van*, in light of evidence of control by GOI of the two entities, is a fair question to ask. It is particularly pertinent in light of the definitional requirement of evidence only of 'control' by the government.

The tribunal in *Cal-Maine Foods, Inc.* evaluated and then came to a different conclusion about the issue of 'control', which differed from the previous decisions.[39] Cal-Maine had concluded contracts with a private Iranian joint-stock company called Seamurgh to develop a poultry enterprise by forming a joint enterprise called Sea-Cal. The claimant argued that Seamourgh's actions, after the Iranian Revolution, had deprived it of its property rights, thereby causing loss. Its principal contention was based on the fact that Seamourgh, and indirectly, one of its subsidiaries, Shargh (that had been contractually assigned but had not paid for Cal-Maine's shares under a

34. *SEDCO, Inc. v. National Iranian Oil Co. and The Islamic Republic of Iran*, 15 Iran-U.S.C.T.R. (1987).
35. *Flexi-Van Leasing, supra* n. 30, at 349.
36. *Ibid.*, at 351–352.
37. *Ibid.*
38. *Ibid.*
39. *Cal-Maine Foods, Inc. v. Government of the Islamic Republic of Iran and Sherkat Seamourgh Company, Inc.*, Award No. 133-340-3, 6 Iran-U.S. C.T.R. 52 (11 June 1984).

'put-option',), had come under the control of the State of Iran during the time of the loss.

Cal-Maine admitted that Seamourgh was a private entity, but at the time of the loss had come under the control of an Iranian state entity called the Iranian National Industrial Organization (INIO), which assumed control under an Iranian state law in force, called the Protection Law of Iran. Cal-Maine alleged that under the authority of Iranian Legal Bill No. 6738, INIO first advised and then appointed an Iranian government official to the Board of Directors of Seamourgh. Cal-Maine sought outstanding payments for its shares based on the premise that GOI controlled Seamourgh, which in turn controlled Shargh. Reviewing the evidence, the tribunal concluded that 'Government officials had taken over the control of the Company.'[40] It rejected the Respondent's contention that Seamourgh had not been and was not owned by the Government and stated that 'lack of formal changes in the status of a company is immaterial once it is established that the Government of Iran exercises actual control over the management of the company as has occurred in this case'.[41] The tribunal also saw support for its conclusion in the *Raygo Wagner* and *Rexnord* awards.[42] Here, the link theory appears to have been effectively used, in that the State controlled an entity, which entity then controlled a third entity, and by extension, the State is held responsible for wrongful acts of the third entity.

Some important principles have emerged from the jurisprudence of the Iran–United States Claims Tribunal about State responsibility, despite many inconsistencies in the decisions. First, the later tribunals' decisions (after the *Economy Forms* award) appear to be consistent about the need to review municipal law to establish the status of a particular SCE as a State entity or not. In that exercise, the tribunal also engaged in determining the structure and functions of the concerned SCE to determine the degree of control by the State. Second, the tribunal concluded that ownership of an entity is not conclusive of control. Third, the tribunal, on a majority of the occasions, distinguishes between SCEs that engaged in commercial activities and those engaged in governmental activities. Fourth, in *Flexi-Van,* the tribunal implicitly adopted the approach taken in *Trendtex* by concluding that even if a particular SCE is controlled by the State, the State would not be responsible for commercial acts of the SCE. Finally, the burden of proving attribution to the government for the act of an SCE, particularly where it has been deemed a private company under the municipal law, appears to have been with the claimant.

40. *Ibid.*
41. *Ibid.*
42. *Ibid.*; *Raygo Wagner Equipment Company v. Star Line Iran Company,* Award No. 20-17-3; *Rexnord Inc. v. Government Islamic Republic of Iran, Tchacosh Company and Iran Siponex Industrial and Manufacturing Works Limited,* Award No. 21-132-3.

[D] *Emilio Maffezini v. Kingdom of Spain*[43]

The crucial importance of the *Maffezini* award is in the International Centre for the Settlement of Investment Disputes (ICSID) Tribunal's efforts to apply structural and functional tests to determine whether a particular SCE was in fact a governmental entity engaged in carrying out governmental functions. Emilio Maffezini, an Argentine national, owned 70% of a Spanish incorporated company called Emilio A. Maffezini, S.A. (EAMSA). The other 30% of EAMSA was owned by a Spanish State-owned entity called Sociedad para el Desarrollo Industrial de Galicia, Sociedad Anónima (SODIGA S.A.). This joint venture was created for the construction of a plant that would produce and distribute chemical products. Using SODIGA's status as a State-owned entity, EAMSA was able to obtain a number of concessionary loans to capitalize the project. Another loan was extended to EAMSA from the personal funds of Maffezini by a director nominated by SODIGA. Nonetheless, EAMSA remained under-capitalized and was not able to effectively implement the project, and it then stalled. Maffezini sought damages against the Kingdom of Spain for his losses caused by SODIGA. Maffezini based his claims on the principal fact that SODIGA's actions were attributable to Spain, since SODIGA was owned and controlled by Spain. He also claimed that the losses were caused by SODIGA's wrong advice based on a poor business plan and feasibility study provided by SODIGA; that the personal loan extended to EAMSA was not authorized; and the additional costs incurred for an environmental assessment impact study had to be reimbursed.

The Government of Spain objected to the tribunal's jurisdiction on the ground that it was not the right party to the proceedings, arguing that SODIGA was a private Spanish company that had engaged in a private contractual association with the claimant.[44] In addition, Spain argued that SODIGA and its activities were outside of the scope of the activities of entities that properly came within the 1992 Law 30/92. Therefore, SODIGA was not an entity that came within the Spanish public administration system. Having that status, SODIGA's actions could not be attributed to the Government of Spain.[45]

The tribunal initially reviewed objections to its jurisdiction and directly addressed the question of attributing the actions of SODIGA to Spain. The tribunal then sought to apply what it termed a structural test and a functional test to evaluate the status of SODIGA. The tribunal stated, 'a finding that the entity is owned by the State, directly or indirectly, gives rise to a rebuttable presumption that it is a State entity'.[46] Similarly, the tribunal advised that the same presumption applies when reviewing the functions of the State 'if an entity's purpose or objective is the carrying out of functions which are governmental in nature or which are otherwise normally reserved to the State, or which by their nature are not usually carried out by private businesses or

43. *Emilio Maffezini, supra* n. 6.
44. *Ibid.*, Objections to jurisdiction, para. 71.
45. *Ibid.*
46. *Ibid.*, para. 77.

individuals'.[47] After evaluating all the evidence before it, the tribunal concluded that on applying the structural test, SODIGA 'could not at the period relevant to the present dispute be held to fall entirely outside the overall scheme of public administration'.[48]

The tribunal pointed out further that the creation of SODIGA as an entity dedicated to carrying out governmental functions for regional industrial development had involved the Government of Spain at the highest levels.[49] With reference to SODIGA's functions, the tribunal concluded that even if it was created as an independent corporate entity, since its functions were delegated by the State, its functions could still be considered 'government functions in the light of international law'.[50] Applying the structural and functional tests cumulatively, the tribunal concluded that structurally SODIGA was a State creation with State ownership of its capital and that in terms of its functions, it performed activities of a public nature. Therefore, the tribunal concluded that SODIGA 'is a State entity acting on behalf of the Kingdom of Spain'.[51] However, the tribunal held that this conclusion was limited to whether the tribunal had jurisdiction to find that SODIGA was a State entity carrying out government functions.

During the merits stage of *Maffezini*, the tribunal explained that whether all the acts and omissions allegedly committed by SODIGA were governmental, rather than commercial, needed to be determined on the merits, fully cognizant that Spain would only be responsible for acts of SODIGA if those acts were governmental, but not commercial.[52] Applying the functional test once again, in context of the specific acts causing loss, the tribunal stated:

> While originally a number of SODIGA's functions were closer to being governmental in nature, they must today be considered commercial in nature. But at the time of transition, there was in fact a combination of both, some to be regarded as functions essentially governmental in nature and others essentially commercial in character.[53]

On evaluating each of the causes of action to determine whether they were commercial or governmental activities, the tribunal concluded that alleged losses caused by the poor business plan and the feasibility study, and the consequent cost over-runs, were caused by actions of EAMSA and not by SODIGA alone and that poor business decisions for which the claimant itself was responsible could not be attributable to SODIGA and, therefore, to Spain.[54] On the matter of one of SODIGA's directors extending a loan from the personal account of Maffezini to EAMSA, the tribunal concluded that the official was acting in his official capacity, and therefore was exercising a governmental function that by extension was attributable to Spain. Similarly, on additional costs incurred by the claimant to provide an Environmental

47. *Ibid.* The Tribunal also cited Art. 7 of a previous version of the DARSIWA to support its analysis, para. 78.
48. *Ibid.*
49. *Ibid.*, para. 85.
50. *Ibid.*, para. 87.
51. *Ibid.*, para. 89.
52. *Ibid.*, Award, paras 51--52.
53. *Ibid.*, para. 57.
54. *Ibid.*

Impact Assessment (EIA), the tribunal concluded that the production of an EIA was a requirement not only under the Bilateral Investment Treaty between Argentina and Spain but it was also under Spanish law. Therefore, neither SODIGA nor Spain was responsible for such costs.[55]

Maffezini is instructive of an almost meticulous exercise of the tribunal, through the introduction of a structural and functional test, to evaluate and determine whether a particular SCE was governmental in nature and whether its activities were equally governmental in nature. Second, as in a majority of the previously discussed cases, the *Maffezini* tribunal confirmed the importance of reviewing the municipal law of the State in applying the structural and functional tests and equally emphasized the distinction between commercial acts and governmental acts of a State.

However, the tribunal's acceptance of a rebuttable presumption that a particular SCE must be deemed prima facie governmental if such entity was 'owned' by the government and its activities are governmental rather than private can be troublesome.[56] Such a presumption can be particularly problematic where the SCE is a *Société Anonyme* (SA) or a LLC. If the SCEs are private entities by nature or are carrying out commercial activities, should they not be presumed to be private rather than governmental entities unless rebutted by evidence to the contrary, by applying the structural and functional tests? And should the responsibility of rebutting that presumption be on the claimant?

§9.03 THE 2001 DARSIWA

The 2001 DARSIWA[57] is a watershed in encompassing a comprehensive set of principles to determine a State's responsibility for wrongful acts under international law. Chapter 2, 'Attribution of Conduct to a State',[58] is directly relevant to this subject. More specifically, Article 5 and Article 8 carry the substantive principles that apply to SCEs.[59] Article 5 states as follows:

> The conduct of a person or entity which is not an organ of the State under Article 4 but which is empowered by the law of that State to exercise elements of the governmental authority shall be considered an act of State under international law, provided the person or entity is acting in that capacity in the particular instance.[60]

55. *Ibid.*, paras 65–72.
56. *Ibid.*, *supra* n. 47.
57. *2001 Draft Articles, supra* n. 1.
58. *Ibid.*, Arts 4–15.
59. *Ibid.*
60. *Ibid.*, Art. 5. The reference to Art. 4, is to organs of the State that are integral entities or persons of the executive, legislative or judicial branches of government at the central or territorial subdivisions of the State. The actions of these government organs or persons acting in such capacities are deemed 'Acts of State'.

Article 5 addresses what are commonly deemed 'parastatals'.[61] However, it seems to encapsulate within it several entities like statutory bodies, corporations, cooperatives and similar bodies that have been empowered to exercise governmental authority. The text does not specify whether these entities are separate legal entities and can act and contract in their own name.

Article 5 has several important factors that need to be taken into account, other than the type of entity that it includes. The first important factor is the emphasis on 'conduct' or actions of the entity or person. It does not emphasize the structure of the entity, but rather its functions. This review of acts corresponds to the Act of State doctrine under international law, in that the actions of the entity must be deemed acts of the State to engage the responsibility of the State. James Crawford, the ILC Rapporteur of the 2001 DARSIWA, states that whether an entity can be classified:

> as public or private according to the criteria of a given legal system, the existence of a greater or lesser State participation in contributing to its capital, or more generally in the ownership of the assets, the fact that it is not subject to executive control – these are not decisive criteria for the purpose of attribution of the entity's conduct to the State.[62]

This commentary somewhat departs from the emphasis placed on the structural test in the *Maffezini* decision.

The second factor is that the acts of the entity must have been empowered under the municipal law of the State. Here the text is consistent with the need to evaluate the functions of an entity in accordance with municipal law. More specifically, the entity must be empowered by municipal law to exercise 'governmental authority', and by extension engaged in governmental activity as opposed to commercial acts.[63] The phrase 'governmental authority' itself cannot be precisely defined and is rather ambiguous. Therefore, what is 'governmental' may have to be determined in relation to each instance, the time of the acts and applicable characterizations given to such acts under a given municipal system.[64]

The third is the inclusion of an apparent caveat, 'provided the person or entity is acting in that capacity in the particular instance', included at the end of Article 5.[65] Here, the text apparently acknowledges the importance of evaluating each act to determine whether it was indeed an exercise of governmental authority. The caveat seems to acknowledge implicitly that the entities may at times not be exercising governmental authority, and in those instances, such acts could not be deemed an act of State for which the State can be held responsible. Such a possible interpretation also leads to the same conclusion as the *Trendtex* judgment, of the dichotomy between *acta*

61. James Crawford, *The International Law Commission's Articles on State Responsibility; Introduction Text and Commentaries* (Cambridge University Press 2002), 100–102. Prof. James Crawford was the Special Rapporteur State Responsibility to the International Law Commission (1998–2001).
62. *Ibid.*, at 100.
63. *Ibid.*, para. 5, at 101.
64. *Ibid.*, para. 6.
65. 2001 DARSIWA, *supra* n. 1, Art. 5.

iure imperii and *acta iure gestionis*, and that only the former acts will engage the State's responsibility.

Article 8 of the 2001 DARSIWA brings within its scope a very broad category of persons and entities. The text of Article 8 states: 'The conduct of a person or group of persons shall be considered an act of State under international law if the person or group of persons is in fact acting on the instructions of, or under the direction or control of, the State in carrying out the conduct.'[66] Article 8 is extremely wide in its breadth and scope. It obviously includes private persons who are either directed, instructed or controlled by the State to commit what may be deemed an internationally wrongful act.[67] Crawford, however, elaborates on the presumptions and limits of the Article's application to 'controlled persons':

> In discussing this issue, it is necessary to recall that international law acknowledges the general separateness of corporate entities at the national level, except in those cases where the 'corporate veil' is a mere device or a vehicle for fraud or evasion. The fact that the State initially establishes a corporate entity, whether by a special law or otherwise, is not a sufficient basis for the attribution to the State of the subsequent conduct of that entity. Since corporate entities, although owned by and in that sense subject to the control of the State, are considered to be separate, *prima facie* their conduct in carrying out their activities is not attributable to the State ... .[68]

These interpretations identify four very important factors. The first refers to a key principle discussed in *Barcelona Traction*, that the corporate veil can only be pierced under extraordinary circumstances and the significance is to maintain the legal separateness of the owners and the corporate entity. The second factor is that when the legal entity is separate from the State, the presumption, *ab initio*, is that the entity's activities are not attributable to the State unless the activity was performed in the exercise of governmental authority. This view contrasts with the principle established in *Maffezini*, where the tribunal concluded that the State's ownership of an entity carries the rebuttable presumption that its activities are governmental. Third, ownership of an entity by the State does not, *ipso facto*, suggest that it is controlled by the State. Fourth, as with Article 5, Article 8 also emphasizes the pre-eminence of the functions or acts of the SCE, rather than the structure of the entity.

Articles 5 and 8 of the 2001 DARSIWA reflect the present position of international law on State responsibility for wrongful acts of SCEs. Although the 2001 DARSIWA is not a treaty and therefore not binding, it provides a very useful and persuasive framework within which to address investor-State disputes that confronts problems of State responsibility, at both the jurisdiction and merits stages of adjudication.

66. *Ibid.*, Art. 8.
67. *Ibid.* But note that unlike in Art. 5, the reference to 'entity' has been dropped. It would seem, however, that the word 'person' used here can be deemed to refer both to a natural person, including non-governmental organizations or a corporate person. Nevertheless, the dropping of the word 'entity' seems to be inadvertent.
68. Crawford, *supra* n. 61, at 112.

§9.04 POST-2001 DARSIWA ADJUDICATION IN ISDS: SELECTED DECISIONS

Prior to an evaluation of the post-2001 DARSIWA adjudication of issues concerning State responsibility in ISDS, an established fundamental premise is that the State's responsibility for acts of SCEs is restricted to internationally wrongful acts. International law has long recognized that a State will not be responsible, for example, for breach of a contractual obligation[69] except under specified circumstances, such as consideration of contractual breaches under an 'umbrella clause' of a treaty. In this latter case, a tribunal's consideration of the act would be for a breach of a treaty clause rather than the breach of the contract. But the State will be responsible under international law if it expropriates property, directly or indirectly. Similarly, the State would be responsible for any treaty breach by the State. That the alleged act must be a wrongful act under international law is, therefore, a pre-requisite for proceeding to engage the State's responsibility for such act. Adjudging the State's responsibility, thus, becomes complicated if the alleged internationally wrongful act is actually committed by an SCE. The other difficulty concerns the starting point of how a State is defined in the specific treaty that undergirds the dispute in question. For instance, the 1966 Convention on the Settlement of Investment Disputes between States and Nationals of Other States[70] that established the ICSID states in Article 25(1): 'The jurisdiction of the Centre shall extend to any legal dispute arising directly out of an investment, between a Contracting State (or any constituent subdivision or agency of a Contracting State designated to the Centre by that State) and a national of another Contracting State.'[71] A 'Contracting State' is otherwise not defined. A significant number of disputes concerning State responsibility have been addressed under the ICSID Convention.

Equally important are the bilateral investment treaties or free trade agreements under which ICSID arbitration is convened, and how State parties therein are defined. While many of these agreements do not define 'Parties' some do refer to 'Enterprise of a Party'.[72] For example, in the North American Free Trade Agreement (NAFTA)[73] 'Enterprise of a Party' is defined as 'an enterprise constituted or organized under the (municipal) laws of that Party'.[74] Importantly, 'enterprise' is defined as 'an entity constituted or organized under applicable law, whether or not for profit, and whether

69. *See* Michael Feit, *Responsibility of the State under International Law for the Breach of Contract Committed by a State Owned Entity*, 28 Berkeley J. Int'l L. 142–176 (2010).
70. Convention on the Settlement of Investment Disputes between States and Nationals of Other States [ICSID Convention] (Washington DC 18 March 1965), 575 U.N.T.S. 159, *entered into force* 14 October 1966 (otherwise commonly known as the ICSID Convention).
71. *Ibid*., Art. 25(1). Art. 25(3) further states that 'Consent by a constituent subdivision or agency of a Contracting State shall require the approval of the State unless that State notifies the Centre that no such approval is required.'
72. North American Free Trade Agreement (Washington D.C., 17 December 1992), U.S.-Can-Mex U.S. Gov't Printing Office (1992), *entered into force* 1 January 1994 (NAFTA). (As of 1 February 2020, has been replaced by Mexico, Canada Agreement (US-MCA).)
73. *Ibid.*
74. *Ibid*., Art. 201.

privately owned or governmentally owned, including any corporation, trust, partnership, sole partnership, joint venture or other association'.[75]

For purposes of binding the State, the specific transaction documents between the investor and the State party that is at the heart of the dispute must be examined. For example, in a dispute surrounding a power purchase agreement for non-payment of contractually agreed tariffs, it must be determined whether the specific SCE that executed the agreement was acting in its own name and as a separate legal entity, or whether it is clearly stated in the agreement that the SCE was acting on behalf of the State. In each of the following selected tribunal decisions, the presumption was that an alleged internationally wrongful act had occurred. It is under this presumption that tribunals have proceeded to review issues of State responsibility at both the jurisdictional and merits phases.

Two early awards set the stage for determination of attributing acts of an SCE to the State. They both applied the structural and functional tests employed by the *Maffezini* tribunal, rather than place reliance on the 2001 DARSIWA. In *Salini v. Morocco,*[76] the claimants, which were two Italian construction companies, concluded contracts with a private company named Société Nationale des Autoroutes du Maroc (ADM) to construct specified highways in Morocco. ADM was a *SA*, or a LLC, incorporated under the company law of Morocco. The Moroccan Treasury and other governmental entities owned 89% of the shares of ADM. After construction was completed, Salini filed claims due to cost-overruns, first with ADM, and then with the Minister of Infrastructure, who was also concurrently ex officio chairman of the board of directors of ADM. The claims for payment were denied.

The tribunal was confronted with the question of whether acts of ADM and its officials could be attributed to the Government of Morocco. The tribunal reviewed the structure of ADM and noted that the majority of seats on the board of directors were held by State officials and, ex officio, chaired by the Minister of Infrastructure. The tribunal, therefore, concluded that structurally ADM could be deemed a State entity.[77] Examining its functions, the tribunal noted that ADM's Articles of Association obligated it with 'the construction, maintenance and operation of the highways and communication routes of a large dimension, granted by the State'.[78] Thus, functionally the tribunal concluded that ADM was carrying out State functions. The tribunal pronounced that ADM's separate legal entity status was not important when structurally and functionally, it could be characterized as a State entity.[79] The tribunal concluded that 'ADM is a State Company, acting in the name of the Kingdom of Morocco.'[80] Therefore, ADM's actions were attributable to the Kingdom of Morocco.

75. *Ibid.*
76. *Salini Costruttori S.P.A. and Italstrade S.P.A. v. Kingdom of Morocco*, ICSID Case No. ARB/00/4. Decision on Jurisdiction (23 July 2001) (*Salini v. Morocco*).
77. *Ibid.*, para. 32.
78. *Ibid.*, para. 33.
79. *Ibid.*
80. *Ibid.*, para. 35.

A similar decision was reached in *Salini v. Jordan*.[81] Salini concluded a contract with the Jordan Valley Authority (JVA) for the construction of a dam. After the construction, Salini claimed for additional costs incurred during the construction. The tribunal reviewed Article 9(2) of the applicable Bilateral Investment Treaty between Italy and Jordan,[82] under which Salini made the claim, to determine whether the JVA was an 'entity' of the Kingdom of Jordan. The tribunal then reviewed the applicable law of Jordan. The JVA was a statutory body created under Jordan law No. 19 of 1998 entitled 'Jordan Valley Development Law'.[83] Reviewing the scope and structure of the JVA, the tribunal concluded that 'although the Government exercises a strict control over the JVA, this Authority is an autonomous corporate body, distinct legally and financially from the State of Jordan. It must thus be considered as an "entity" of the Kingdom of Jordan ... '.[84] While the tribunal did not conclude whether the specific acts of the JVA were attributable to Jordan, it found that for purposes of jurisdiction the JVA was a State entity.

One of the first cases that applied the 2001 DARSIWA was *Noble Ventures v. Romania*.[85] In that case, Noble Ventures, a US incorporated company, came to an agreement with a State entity named the State Ownership Fund (SOF), authorized to privatize Romanian State-owned enterprises. Noble Ventures invested in a steel mill with associated other assets previously owned by the State. Due to acts and omissions of SOF and its successor agency, the Authority for the Privatization and Management of State Ownership (APAPS), the claimant alleged that it had been deprived of the beneficial interests of ownership of the steel mill and therefore, had been expropriated by Romania. The claimant argued that acts and omissions of SOF and APAPS were attributable to Romania.[86] Romania argued that the acts of SOF and APAPS could not be attributable to it, since they were separate legal entities.[87]

The tribunal concluded that with regard to attribution to States for actions of State entities, the 2001 DARSIWA should be referenced. The tribunal considered whether SOF and APAPS could be considered as de jure organs of the State under Article 4 of the 2001 DARSIWA. It concluded that because 'SOF and APAPS were legal entities separate from the Respondent, it is not possible to regard them as de jure organs' of the State.[88] Examining the competencies of the Romanian law that enabled SOF and APAPS to privatize and engage in transactions with investors, the tribunal concluded that 'SOF as well as APAPS were at all relevant times acting on the basis of Romanian law which defined their competence.' Thus, the tribunal determined that their actions came well within the scope of Article 5 of the 2001 DARSIWA.[89] The tribunal concluded:

81. *Salini Costruttori S.P.A. and Italstrade S.P.A. v. Hashemite Kingdom of Jordan*, ICSID Case No. ARB/02/13, Decision on Jurisdiction (9 November 2004).
82. Agreement between the Government of the Italian Republic and the Government of the Hashemite Kingdom of Jordan on the Promotion and Protection of Investments (2 July 1999).
83. *Salini et.al, supra* n. 81, paras 81–82.
84. *Ibid.*, para. 84.
85. *Noble Ventures Inc. v. Romania*, ICSID Case No. Arb/01/1 (12 October 2005).
86. *Ibid.*, paras 2–24.
87. *Ibid.*, para. 66.
88. *Ibid.*, para. 69.
89. *Ibid.*, para. 70.

> The Tribunal deduces from the foregoing that it was not only within the competence of SOF - and APAPS, which replaced SOF at the end of 2000 - when acting as the empowered public institution under the Privatization Law, to conclude agreements with investors but also, acting as a *governmental agency*, to manage the whole legal relationship with them, including all acts concerned with the implementation of a specific investment. In the judgment of the Tribunal, no relevant legal distinction is to be drawn between SOF/APAPS, on the one hand, and a government ministry, on the other hand, when one or the other acted as the empowered public institution under the Privatization Law.[90]

The tribunal further ruled that for purposes of attribution the distinction between *acta iure imperii* and *acta iure gestionis* need not be maintained, stating that it was 'difficult to see' the reasons for such a distinction.[91] Therefore, the tribunal concluded that 'the acts of SOF and APAPS which were of relevance in the present case are attributable to the Respondent'[92] The tribunal's decision of the implied irrelevance of the distinction between the commercial acts and sovereign acts of the State for purposes of attribution seems to have been unnecessary, because the alleged internationally wrongful act was one of expropriation in breach of the applicable United States–Romania Bilateral Investment Treaty. The distinction, however, between governmental acts and commercial acts bears significant relevance in enforcement of arbitral awards and to those commercial acts that are not internationally wrongful acts, such as a breach of a contract. Especially in the latter case, the remedies are limited to the contract terms. In addition, the tribunal's examination of the structure and activities of the two entities closely resembled an implicit piercing of the corporate veil, to conclude that both SOF and APAPS were 'alter egos' of the State.

In a factually similar situation, the tribunal in *Bayindir v. Pakistan*[93] reviewed the acts of a Pakistani State entity called the National Highway Authority (NHA) specifically in the context of 2001 DARSIWA. Unlike any other previous case, the tribunal went to great lengths to evaluate the structure of NHA. It determined that the NHA was statutorily created under the laws of Pakistan to perform distinct functions. The tribunal concluded that the NHA was a separate legal entity and therefore was not an organ of the State under Article 4.[94] With reference to Article 5, the tribunal concluded that NHA, in general, was created to exercise elements of governmental authority, but this was a prima facie empowerment under the statute creating the NHA. However, this general empowerment to exercise elements of governmental authority was not sufficient to determine whether the specific conduct of NHA fell within the scope of Article 5 of the 2001 DARSIWA.[95] Finally, in relation to the specific conduct of NHA, the tribunal concluded that NHA had acted under the instructions or directions and control

90. *Ibid.*, para. 79.
91. *Ibid.*, para. 82.
92. *Ibid.*, para. 83.
93. *Bayindir Insaat Turizm Ticaret VE Sanay A.S v. Islamic Republic of Pakistan*, Award, ICSID Case No. ARB/03/29 (26 August 2009) in particular paras 117–130.
94. *Ibid.*, para. 119.
95. *Ibid.*, para. 123.

of the Government of Pakistan, and therefore its conduct was attributable to Pakistan under Article 8 of the 2001 DARSIWA.[96]

In the earlier case of *Jan de Nul v. Egypt*,[97] an ICSID tribunal came to a different conclusion in interpreting the 2001 DARSIWA concerning the conduct of an Egyptian State entity, the Suez Canal Authority (SCA). Through a previous decision on objections to jurisdiction, the tribunal had remitted the matter of attribution to the State for acts of the SCA to the merits stage of the case.[98] The claims related to contracts that the claimants had with the SCA for dredging the Suez Canal.

The significant difference in the approach that the *Jan de Nul* Tribunal took is that it focused more on the specific acts or omissions of the SCA that needed to be evaluated in context of the 2001 DARSIWA to determine attribution to the State. Based on the fact that the SCA had been created under Egyptian Law No. 30/1975, the tribunal saw no difficulty in identifying SCA as a separate legal entity that enjoyed an 'independent juristic personality'.[99] Further, the tribunal cited Articles 4, 5 and 10 of Egyptian Law No. 30/1975 and found that structurally, the SCA was created akin to a business enterprise with an independent budget and with rules adopted in business enterprises, but within the overall supervision of the Central Auditing Department. The funds of the SCA were also considered private funds.[100] Therefore, the tribunal rejected the claimant's position that the SCA was an organ of the Government, which came within the scope of Article 4 of the 2001 DARSIWA. SCA's acts could not be attributed to the State, under Article 4.[101]

Considering whether the SCA as an entity that exercised elements of Government authority for purposes of attribution under Article 5 of the DARSIWA, the tribunal once again examined the Egyptian Law 30/175. Here, the tribunal concluded that the SCA, in terms of the Respondent's own admission and Article 6 of the Law, exercised elements of governmental authority. Thus, the SCA was deemed as coming within the scope of Article 5 of the 2001 DARSIWA.[102]

While this was the prima facie characterization of the SCA's structure and functions, the tribunal proceeded to evaluate whether the specific actions or omissions of the SCA were an exercise of governmental authority. After reviewing the SCA's conduct in the tender process that adversely affected the claimants, the tribunal concluded that the SCA had not exercised governmental authority. The tribunal pointed out that '[a]ny private contract partner could have acted in a similar manner'.[103] On this basis, the tribunal concluded:

> [A]lthough the SCA is a public entity empowered to exercise elements of governmental authority, the acts of the SCA vis à vis the Claimants are not attributable to

96. *Ibid.*, para. 129.
97. *Jan de Nul N.V. and Dredging International N.V. v. Arab Republic of Egypt*, Award ICSID Case No. ARB/04/13 (6 November 2008).
98. *Ibid.*, para. 142.
99. *Ibid.*, para. 160.
100. *Ibid.*, para. 161.
101. *Ibid.*, para. 162.
102. *Ibid.*
103. *Ibid.*, para. 170.

the Respondent in this arbitration on the basis of Article 5 of the ILC Articles, as they were not performed pursuant to the exercise of governmental authority.[104]

Finally, the tribunal examined whether the specific acts of the SCA were either undertaken at the instruction or direction of the Government or were undertaken pursuant to the Government's control of the SCA. The tribunal concluded that there was no evidence 'of any instructions that the State would have given to the SCA in regard to the very specific acts and omissions of the SCA that are complained of in this arbitration'.[105] With regard to 'control', the tribunal, citing the ICJ *Decision in the Case concerning Military and Paramilitary activities in and against Nicaragua,*[106] concluded that 'effective control' must be shown; and that mere general g control is insufficient.[107] For these reasons, the tribunal concluded that the conduct of the SCA could not be attributed to Egypt under Article 8 of the 2001 DARSIWA.[108] The tribunal did not, however, proceed to explain what 'effective control' meant in the context of attribution.

The methodology for attribution used in *Hamester GmbH & Co KG v. Republic of Ghana*[109] mirrors that of the tribunal in *Jan de Nul.* Here, too, the tribunal focused its review of attribution to Ghana entirely on the specific acts of the Ghana Cocoa Board (Cocobod) that allegedly caused loss to the claimants. The tribunal observed that the Cocobod was created by a special Ghanaian statute as a 'corporate body' that could be 'sued in its corporate name'.[110]

Reviewing the law, the tribunal concluded that the Cocobod was a commercial corporation, and that for purposes of Article 4 of the 2001 DARSIWA, 'it could not be considered an organ of the Ghanaian State, de jure or de facto'.[111] Similarly, the tribunal concluded that the Cocobod was endowed with some elements of governmental authority under the Ghanaian law.[112] But the tribunal concluded that 'for an act of a separate entity exercising elements of governmental authority to be attributed to the State, it must be shown that the precise act in question was an exercise of such governmental authority and not merely an act that could be performed by a commercial entity'.[113] The tribunal observed that the specific acts of Cocobod were acts *iure gestionis* and not acts that could be characterized as an exercise of elements of governmental authority to be considered under Article 5 of the 2001 DARSIWA. Yet, the tribunal required an examination of whether the specific acts fell within Article 8 of the 2001 DARSIWA.[114] The tribunal came to a preliminary conclusion that Cocobod

104. *Ibid.*, para. 171.
105. *Ibid.*, para. 173.
106. *Ibid. Military and Paramilitary Activities in and against Nicaragua (Nicaragua v. United States of America,* Merits, Judgment, I.C.J. Rep. 1986 (27 June 1986).
107. *Jan de Nul*, para. 173.
108. *Ibid.*
109. *Gustav F W Hamester Gmbh & Co KG v. Republic of Ghana*, Award ICSID Case No. ARB/07/24 (18 June 2010).
110. *Ibid.*, para. 184.
111. *Ibid.*, paras 184–188.
112. *Ibid.*, para. 190.
113. *Ibid.*, para. 193.
114. *Ibid.*

was neither effectively controlled nor was it under the 'direct command' of the Government of Ghana, to justify a conclusion that Cocobod's acts in this case could be attributed to the government.[115] It proceeded to review the acts of Cocobod vis-à-vis the claimant with great specificity and detail, but justified its preliminary findings that the acts of Cocobod could not be attributable to the Government of Ghana under Article 5 or Article 8 of the 2001 DARSIWA.[116] Importantly, in the subsequent case of *Almas v. Poland*, the tribunal concurred with the *Hamester* Tribunal that 'For purposes of attribution under Article 5, the *Hamester* tribunal correctly insisted that it had to be shown "that the precise act in question was an exercise of such governmental authority."'[117]

The detailed analysis of the structure and functions of a State entity and the conclusion drawn therefrom in *Trendtex* was mirrored in an important judgment of the Privy Council in *La Générale des Carrières et des Mines v. Hemisphere.*[118] The Privy Council concluded that GECAMINES, a wholly State-owned corporation, was a separate legal entity from the Democratic Republic of Congo (DRC). GECAMINES appealed to the Privy Council to vacate an attempt by the Respondent to attach the assets of GECAMINES, to enforce two earlier ICC awards against the DRC. The Privy Council concluded that GECAMINES' assets were private and not owned by the State, that they did not enjoy the immunity of the State and therefore, enforcement of the ICC awards against those assets of GECAMINES could not proceed.[119] The important distinction in this case, in contrast with *Trendtex*, is that the Privy Council also considered the relevance of Articles 4 and 5 of the 2001 DARSIWA to determine attribution.[120]

Finally, in *Ortiz v. Algeria*,[121] one of the most recent cases directly related to State responsibility for acts of SCEs, the tribunal went to great lengths to determine whether Algeria was responsible for the allegedly wrongful acts of three state-owned corporations by applying Articles 4, 5 and 8 of the 2001 DARSIWA. In contrast to the *Noble v. Romania* tribunal's conclusions, and aligning mainly with the approach taken by the *Jan de Nul* and *Hamester* tribunals, the tribunal directed that attribution for acts of the three State entities must be determined through a review of their functions, both *acta iure gestionis* and *acta iure imperii*. The tribunal reviewed the SCEs' functions from within the framework of Algeria's municipal law, while also citing the Commentary to the 2001 DARSIWA. In doing so, the tribunal examined the functions performed by the entities from the manner by which the SCEs received State authorization, the purposes for which they were established by the State and their responsibilities towards the State.[122]

115. *Ibid.*, paras 199–200.
116. *Ibid.*, paras 202–268.
117. *Almas v. Poland, supra* n. 2, para. 216.
118. *La Générale des Carrières et des Mines v. F.G. Hemisphere Associates LLC*, Judgment Privy Council Appeal No. 0061 of 2011 (2012) UKPC 27.
119. *Ibid.*, paras 67–78.
120. *Ibid.*, paras 15–18.
121. *Ortiz Construcciones y Proyectos, S.A. v. Algeria*, ICSID Case No. Arb/17/1 (29 April 2020).
122. *Ibid.*, para. 204.

On reviewing the specific acts of the three SCEs, the tribunal concluded that they had not exercised any 'elements of governmental authority' in accordance with Article 5 of the 2001 DARSIWA.[123] Further, in conformity with the 2001 DARSIWA, the tribunal, in examining the very specific acts that allegedly caused loss to the claimant, separated out the acts of the State itself from the acts of the three SCEs. The tribunal concluded that all alleged actions, omissions and commissions by the Ministry of Housing and Algeria's Council of Participation (CPE) were directly attributable to the State of Algeria, because these two entities were integral parts of the State and thus came within the scope of the acts contemplated in Article 4 of the DARSIWA. Applying Article 8 of the 2001 DARSIWA, the tribunal concluded that with the exception of a single act of one of the three SCEs of relocating a manufacturing plant that was 'directed' by the Ministry of Housing and, therefore, attributable to the State, the rest of the alleged acts of the three SCEs were not attributable to the State.[124] These post-2001 DARSIWA decisions[125] illustrate the different methodologies adopted and diverse conclusions reached by tribunals and adjudicatory bodies to assign responsibility of States for the acts of SCEs.

§9.05 CONCLUSION

Since the decades following the 1970s, States have significantly altered the ways in which they have concluded investment transactions with investors. One of the key ways of how States engaged investors is by creating SCEs, which then fronted and executed investment contracts with investors for their investments in various sectors of the State's economy. The proliferation of these SCEs, in their various forms, was described well by Lord Justice Denning in *Trendtex*.[126] As a consequence, an investor confronting an investment dispute with an SCE faces challenging problems. It had to determine *ab initio* whether to proceed against the particular SCE with which it had contracted based on the specific contract terms, or alternatively to proceed against the State in which the SCE had been incorporated. In the latter case, filing a claim cannot be based on a pure contract breach because the State has no contractual privity with the investor unless proceedings were initiated under the breach of an 'umbrella clause' in a treaty. Such a claim must be based on an indirect commission of an internationally wrongful act that can be attributed to the State for which the State could be made responsible under the applicable treaty.

123. *Ibid.*, paras 219, 227, 234.
124. *Ibid.*, 194. Note, however, the Tribunal concluded that even those acts that were attributable to the State, the claimant ultimately failed to prove that breaches of the Fair and Equitable Treatment Standard clause or the Umbrella Clause of the applicable bilateral investment treaty between Spain and Algeria had occurred.
125. Also note two other relevant cases on the subject of State responsibility: *AMTO LLC v. Ukraine*, Decision Arbitration No. 080/2005, Arbitration Institution the Stockholm Chamber of Commerce (26 March 2008) that concerned the acts of Energoatom a State-owned entity; and *Deutsche Bank AG v. Democratic Socialist Republic of Sri Lanka*, Award, ICSID Case No. ARB/09/02 (31 October 2012).
126. *See Trendtex, supra* n. 5.

A decision to pursue ISDS through reference to principles of State responsibility in these situations has generated challenging legal problems at the jurisdiction level, with adjudicatory forums having to decide on the proper party to the arbitration (*ratione personae*) and whether the claim arose out of a material breach of a treaty (*ratione materiae*).[127] Similarly, questions also arise at the merits stage, where tribunals have to decide whether the specific act that caused the loss was a commercial act (*acta iure gestionis*) or a sovereign act (*acta iure imperii*).

Adjudicatory bodies have struggled with the question of determining State responsibility for acts of SCEs. Principally, they encounter difficulties with determining the degree and extent of control by the State of SCEs. Application of standard principles of customary international law to determine a State's responsibility that concern acts of SCEs was wholly inadequate to determine the question, forcing adjudicatory bodies to resort to municipal law to finally resolve the issue. Many tribunals arrived at different conclusions on the matter of a State's 'control' over an SCE even after consideration of municipal law. The jurisprudence of the Iran-United States Claims Tribunal demonstrates the challenges involved and the inconsistent conclusions reached, often, based on similar factual circumstances. However, there seems to be a consensus that fundamentally, the controlling law for determination of whether acts of SCEs can be finally attributed to a State is through an examination municipal law. Municipal law that must be examined to determine attribution seems now to have been developed into a general principle of law. The declaration by the *Almas* Tribunal that '"domestic law is the starting point" for the determination of the status of an entity as a State organ'[128] appears to be dispositive for this proposition.

The Structural and Functional Tests applied by the *Maffezini* Tribunal were important developments to systematically examine the nature and characteristics of an SCE created under municipal law. Ultimately, application of these tests can reveal whether the acts of an SCE can be attributable to the State. The Functional Test is particularly crucial to examine, not only with regard to deciding subject matter jurisdiction but also to determine whether an SCE was acting in a commercial or sovereign capacity. Equally, the Structural Test is important to decide the personal jurisdiction issue. However, a review of decisions shows that the tests were either inconsistently or insufficiently applied. In particular, investigation was rarely made with regard to ownership of assets of the SCE and under which particular municipal law and under what circumstances an SCE could be liquidated. These are crucial issues that need to be resolved to determine whether the entity was acting in a private capacity or as a sovereign entity carrying out governmental functions, because the fundamental premise in ISDS is that the State has engaged ultimately in an internationally wrongful act. Equally, final determinations of the structure and functions of an SCE and its links with the State impact enforcement of final awards.

The problems associated with applying Articles 5 and 8 of the 2001 DARSIWA are many. First, the 2001 DARSIWA is not binding. It is merely 'Draft Articles'. The articles are, however, instructive of the status of international law on the issues of State

127. *See Salini v. Morocco, supra* n.76.
128. *Almas v. Republic of Poland, supra* n. 2, para. 207.

responsibility, and therefore are persuasive. Second, some of its operational phrases and words are fairly challenging to apply. What does exercise of elements of 'governmental authority' by an SCE mean, when it has been created, for example, as a trading corporation? In rapidly evolving economic environments driven by market forces, can State acts be deemed more commercial than sovereign, forcing adjudicatory bodies to evaluate the distinct roles? What is 'control' of an entity? Is ownership the only and decisive criterion? Third, the emphasis on functions and not the structure eludes the application of a comprehensive key test that would assist a tribunal to determine whether the acts of an SCE can be attributed to the State, and therefore, to determine the State's responsibility for such acts. These difficult interpretational issues in the 2001 DARSIWA will continue to challenge adjudicatory bodies as they consider the application of Articles 5 and 8.

Thus, ISDS, in this important area of determining State responsibility for wrongful acts of SCEs, is unpredictable, inconsistent, and often lacks comprehensive analysis of the factual data in each case and their alignment with principles and tests of and for State responsibility that have evolved over time.

CHAPTER 10

Striking Back: An Investor's Right to Confront Its Home State's Decision to Terminate Investment Protection Agreements

Anthony R. Daimsis

As Canada, the United States (US), and Mexico move to terminate the North American Free Trade Agreement (NAFTA) and replace it with a new agreement (United States-Mexico-Canada Agreement (CUSMA)), investors, particularly Canadian ones, will lose one of the International Investment Agreements (IIAs) defining rights: the right to arbitrate alleged investment protection breaches. This chapter proposes how these investors may very well retain their rights by reconsidering the nature of this right to arbitrate and eschewing the distinction made in cases and academic writing that treat distinctions between procedural and substantive rights as meaningful distinctions.

§10.01 INTRODUCTION

The nature and character of rights enjoyed by investors under IIAs is not a new question. Those who have tackled the issue have approached the topic from different angles. Broadly, the conclusions reached in these writings and awards come down to investors enjoying derivative rights, direct rights, and rights as third-party beneficiaries.[1] Why then, write again on the topic? The papers referenced have all approached

1. Anthea Roberts, *Clash of Paradigms: Actors and Analogies Shaping the Investment Treaty System*, 107 Am. J. Int'l L. 45 (2013); Zachary Douglas, *The Hybrid Foundations of Investment Treaty Arbitration*, 74 Brit. Y.B. Int'l L. 151-289 (2003) ('Douglas'); Preeti Bhagnani, *Revisiting the Countermeasures Defense in Investor-State Disputes: Approach and Analogies*, IC-JA 124 (2015) ('Bhagnami').

the topic from a rather theoretical perspective. That is not a criticism, but the reality of the time when they were penned. For example, some followed on the outcome of three NAFTA Chapter 11 cases, known as the Sugar Cases.[2] Moreover, one early paper addressing the character and nature of investor rights under investment agreements, which other writers have cited over 300 times, is Jan Paulsson's *Arbitration Without Privity*, written only one year after the NAFTA[3] came online.[4]

This chapter's addition to the topic comes on the heels of a watershed moment in the life (and death) of one of the best-known trade zone regimes: NAFTA, in particular its Chapter 11.[5] The three State parties have agreed to replace NAFTA with the new agreement known as the CUSMA.[6] One of the many changes CUSMA brings to NAFTA is Canada's decision to pull out of the investor-State arbitration mechanism. Knowledgeable arbitration practitioners point out that Canada may have calculated it had much to gain, and its investors little to lose, by withdrawing from the investor-State dispute settlement (ISDS) provisions in CUSMA given Canadian investors' track record against the US and Canada's track record against US investors.[7] Nevertheless, Canadians who invest in the US will no longer enjoy the benefit of using arbitration as a means to resolve their investment disputes. It also means that US and Mexican investors in Canada will no longer enjoy a right to sue Canada in arbitration for alleged investment protection breaches.[8] Naturally, investors who currently hold investments in the US, Mexico, and Canada have had no say in Canada's decision. To mollify concerns that current investments and investors might be caught off guard by Canada's decision, the States have introduced what they term 'Legacy investment claims'. These legacy investments, however, expire three years after NAFTA's termination.

2. *Archer Daniels Midland and Tate & Lyle Ingredients Americas, Inc. v. United Mexican States*, ICSID Case No. ARB(A.F.)/04/5 ('*ADM*'); *Corn Products International, Inc. v. United Mexican States*, ICSID Case No. ARB (A.F.)/04/1 ('*CPI*'); *Cargill, Incorporated v. United Mexican States*, ICSID Case No. ARB(A.F.)/05/2 ('*Cargill*').
3. North American Free Trade Agreement Between the Government of Canada, the Government of Mexico and the Government of the United States, 17 December 1992, Can. T.S. 1994, No. 2 ('NAFTA').
4. Jan Paulsson, *Arbitration Without Privity*, 10 ICSID Review – Foreign Investment Law Journal 232–257 (1995).
5. Done 17 December 1992, reprinted in (1993) 32 I.L.M. 605.
6. The Canadian government refers to it as the Canada-United States-Mexico Agreement (CUSMA). It entered into force 1 July 2020. *See* Protocol Replacing the North American Free Trade Agreement with the Agreement between Canada, the United States of America, and the United Mexican States, 1 July 2020, Can. T.S., No. 5.
7. *See* Martin J. Valasek, Alison G. FitzGerald and Jenna Anne de Jong, *Major Changes for Investor-State Dispute Settlement in New United States-Mexico-Canada Agreement*, available at https://tinyurl.com/vqx5u4u.
8. CUSMA will not include a trilateral ISDS mechanism. Under CUSMA, the United States and Mexico have agreed to maintain a bilateral ISDS mechanism for a narrow set of disciplines and sectors. The State parties have agreed to a transitional period of three years, during which ISDS under the original NAFTA will continue to apply only for investments made prior to the entry into force of CUSMA. *See* Global Affairs Canada, available at: https://www.international.gc.ca/trade-commerce/trade-agreements-accords-commerciaux/agr-acc/cusma-aceum/investment-investissement.aspx?lang=eng.

This chapter questions what happens after the three-year expiry date. Are Canadian investors unable to use arbitration if they find their investments interfered with one day after the three-year expiration date? In particular, in the context of Canadian investment in the US, a Canadian investor apparently must go before US courts to vindicate its rights. The Comprehensive and Progressive Agreement for Trans-Pacific Partnership (CPTPP)[9] may offer Canadian investors with investments in Mexico another option, but rights under the CPTPP are different from current rights Canadian investors enjoy under NAFTA's Chapter 11.

Clarity surrounding the nature of investor rights under the NAFTA is even more critical now because it will help those investors who will lose their Chapter 11 protections, by offering them a view on how to forge a direct right of action, using arbitration, to maintain the promises made to them under Chapter 11. Naturally, although this chapter focuses mostly on NAFTA's Chapter 11, it can apply to similar IIAs.

Do investors enjoy direct rights under IIAs? The classic answer is 'not quite'. Traditional thinking imagines that because investment treaties are only between States, non-State parties are merely incidental to treaties. At most then, investor rights are derivative,[10] or that of a third-party beneficiary of the right enjoyed by the investor's home State. Under this view, investors' 'rights' are beholden to their home State. The home State may alter these rights as it pleases, even, for example, choosing to pull out of a treaty and thereby eliminating investor rights, whatever their nature.[11] Under this orthodoxy, investors enjoy no rights. At most, what they possess are privileges, which a State fully controls.[12]

This chapter argues that this view ignores the economic reality and nature of investments under IIAs, in particular, that they are intended and understood as long-term capital outlays (greenfield investments) induced by direct promises given to investors. These promises, like an investor's investment, are understood and expected to remain stable, long-term promises. Although this chapter focuses on protections under the NAFTA and USMCA, the reasoning applies to all IIAs, and any investment treaty implicating investors as the *promisees* of promises given by both their home States and host States, as *promisors*. Consequently, when State-promisors decide between themselves to end their relationship, mutually or unilaterally by way of rescission or denouncement, this chapter will show how these decisions should not affect vested rights enjoyed by the promisee-investors. Furthermore, and of particular focus, when these direct promises contain the right to use arbitration - a neutral

9. Signed 8 March 2018.
10. Derivative rights are often conceived as diplomatic protection. One reason to question whether this dichotomy should hold in the investor-State model is that, as ICSID Art. 27 explains, once an investor makes use of arbitration, it foregoes its right to diplomatic protection. Consequently, an investor who commences arbitration loses its right to rely on its home state for protection - a catch-22.
11. States may pull out from treaties either under the treaty's own terms or via public international law principles enshrined under the Vienna Convention on the Law of Treaties ('VCLT') ss 3, 4, and 5.
12. Wesley Newcomb Hohfeld, *Some Fundamental Legal Conception as Applied in Judicial Reasoning*, 23 Yale L.J. 16 (1913–1914) ('Hohfeld').

dispute resolution method to resolve disputes – investors may rely on arbitration to hold States to their promises.

This chapter will endeavour to prove that investors have direct rights against their home State. It begins by setting the stage of what IIAs seek to achieve, focusing on how these treaties craft relationships between States and investors. Next, this chapter will examine the nature of investor rights by examining three cases under NAFTA that addressed the question. This chapter will then briefly address the history of third-party rights under both common law and civil law, and finally conclude that investors are owed duties, which translate into direct rights.

§10.02 SETTING THE STAGE

Today, over 3,300 treaties deal with investment matters, in particular through Bilateral Investment Treaties (BITs) and Multilateral Investment Treaties (MITs).[13] These treaties use investor-State arbitration as the primary method to resolve investment disputes caught by these treaties. In its purest form, an investment treaty, IIAs are contracts between BIT and among MIT States. In these contracts, one State promises to another State, or States, that nationals of the other contracting State will receive protection for any investments made in the territory of the promising State, provided the alleged investment meets the definition of investment defined in the relevant treaty. Because the purpose of these treaties is to entice private players to act in a way that benefits public players, these agreements are legal estuaries where public and private law meet.[14]

Generally, to take advantage of these promises (1) an investor must come from a State that has entered into one of these treaties with another State; (2) the investment must meet the definition of investment defined in the relevant treaty; and (3) the investor must have invested in the territory of the promising State to which the investor is not a national. Finally, if the treaty contains the promise that an investor may avail itself of arbitration to resolve disputes, then the investor may commence an arbitration to receive compensation where a dispute arises.

Quite importantly, under this system, an investor controls whether it will bring a claim, and once brought, it is the investor's right to revoke its claim. Furthermore, investors finance their own claims (or enter agreements with third-party funders) and it is the investor who directly receives any monetary vindication.[15] This lies in stark contrast to a State espousing its national's claim. When a State presents a claim of its national, the national is beholden to the whims of its master State. If the State deems it politically injudicious to pursue its national's claim, the national has nothing to say.

13. Taking Stock of IIA Reform: Recent Developments [IIA Issues Note, No. 3, 2019] (UNCTAD/DIAE/PCB/INF/2019/5), 7 June 2019.
14. Tania Voon and Andrew D. Mitchell, *Denunciation, Termination and Survival: The Interplay of Treaty Law and International Investment Law* 31 ICSID Review (2016), 413–433, 413 (2016).
15. Douglas, *supra* n. 1, at 170.

This distinction responds quite well to the view that State obligations towards investors are merely derivative rights that are held and owed to the State.[16]

Writers have spilled much ink proclaiming how unique the investor-State template is in contrast to the archetypal view maintained under public international law, which considered individuals as, at their highest, merely objects of public international law.[17] The actual subjects (and therefore holders of the entirety of rights) are States.

[A] State Obligations Intended to Induce Investment

What is an investment? Although these treaties take the time to define what is meant by 'investment', investment generally, requires long-term commitments, with sunken costs aimed at creating long-term relationships with host States. In brief, investors take on significant risks by investing capital in a foreign country in exchange for protection. These investments are not the kind of investments that are easily moved from place to place. Often, they include physical plants, machinery, and other infrastructure paid for by the investor. Included among the many benefits host States enjoy are new industry, or more competitive industries, job creation, and skilled labourers.

Attracting this type of investment is ideal for States. Consequently, their specific promises serve to allay an investor's fears that it might waste its investments, or worse still, see their investment taken by the very State in which the investor has selected to invest. These promises can take many forms, but usually include promises not to treat investors or their investments differently than local investors or investments, not to treat investors arbitrarily and not to take their investments, without prompt and proper compensation.[18]

[B] The Promise to Arbitrate

A critical promise included in a vast number of these treaties is the promise that an investor may use arbitration as the method to resolve an alleged breach of a State promise made to the investor. Arbitration is a valuable method of dispute resolution because it offers the investor a neutral forum in which to resolve its dispute with the host State. Investors who wish to sue a host State are understandably hesitant to commence court actions inside the very State it is accusing of foul play.

Orthodoxy, however, treats all promises contained within BITs and MITs as promises made exclusively between and among States as 'States only and exclusively are subjects of the Law of Nations.'[19] Seen through the lens of public international law,

16. *Ibid.*, at 169–170.
17. Anthony Aust, *Handbook of international law*, 2nd ed, (Cambridge University Press, 2010), 12, 345. ('Aust').
18. Marina Pavlović, and Anthony Daimsis, *Arbitration*, in John C. Kleefeld, et al., eds., Dispute Resolution: Readings and Case Studies, 4th ed. (Toronto: Emond Montgomery, 2016), 630.
19. Lassa Oppenheim, *International Law: A Treatise* vol. 1 (2nd ed., Longmans, Green & Co 1912), 362–64, s. 289 (citations omitted).

wherein private players like investors have no direct rights, this position is plausible. After all, BITs and MITs are treaties. Furthermore, treaties are agreements between States. Generally, they are not agreements between States and private parties.

[C] IIA Building Blocks

In an investment treaty, State A promises to offer protection to investors from State B in exchange for State B's promise to offer the same protections to investors from State A. From a contract standpoint, both States A and B benefit from these reciprocal promises because they will attract investors from each other's State. Investors, in turn, benefit by receiving these protections and promises in exchange for their investment with the expectation of a stable investment climate. Simply put, any right A may have against State B is simply a product of the promises exchanged (and thereby created) between A and B. What this orthodoxy is trying to describe, quite clumsily, is not a right at all. Instead, it is properly termed a privilege. Moreover, this privilege vests upon the investor, making its investment.

Returning to the agreements at play in these IIAs, what exists is a cluster of contracts. There is a contract between States A and B (the investment treaty), contracts between investors from State A and State B (investment into B), and contracts from investors from State B with State A (investment into A). The following diagram offers a visual:

Figure 10.1 The Cluster of Agreements Formed in the Investor-State Model

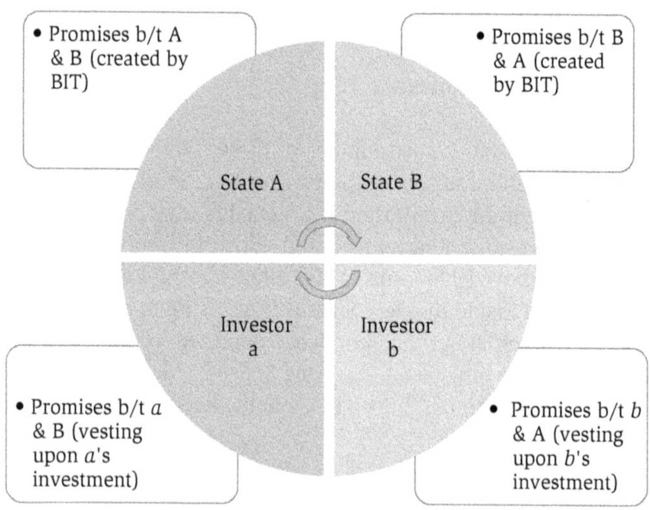

§10.03 DO INVESTORS BENEFIT FROM RIGHTS OR MERELY PRIVILEGES?

[A] The Sugar Cases

Arbitral tribunals empanelled under NAFTA's Chapter 11 have weighed in on the topic of investor rights, albeit indirectly, within the context of countermeasures. Three tribunals, in particular, have tackled the topic. Although the three awards examined in this section are not the only awards to have touched on the idea of the nature and characteristics of investor rights, they are the three awards most often looked to as denoting some formal pronouncement on the subject. Consequently, this contribution will focus on them. These three awards, however, offer little more than an introduction on the subject. Nevertheless, writings abound citing to these three decisions, *ADM*, *CPI*, and *Cargill*, as a near exhaustive discussion of the subject of investor rights.[20] As this section will show, the reasoning in these awards rely on unsupported assumptions to reach conclusions that make these cases a weak launching point for the discussion of the nature and character of investor rights. Most notably, these three awards adopt a form of reasoning that does little more than restating their conclusion. What these awards lack is cogent reasoning.

[1] ADM

In *ADM*, the investor sued Mexico, alleging Mexico's breach of NAFTA's Chapter 11.[21] In the tribunal's discussion on whether investors enjoy individual rights, the tribunal sided with Mexico, holding that under NAFTA's Chapter 11, investors enjoy secondary procedural rights to bring a dispute against a host State, but that investors possess no individual substantive rights; they merely step into the shoes of the home State. In the words of the tribunal:

> Different doctrinal theories coexist regarding the nature of investors' rights under international investment agreements. The derivative theory, briefly described above, supports the proposition that investment treaties provide a set of obligations which require the state to treat investments of qualified investors in accordance with the standards of the treaty; but these obligations are only owed to the state of the investor's nationality. If a breach of any of these standards occurs, the investor may bring the host State to an international arbitration in order to request compensation, but the investor will be in reality stepping into the shoes and asserting the rights of the home State.[22]

20. Douglas, *supra* n. 1, at 151–289; Bhagnani, *supra* n. 1, at 124; Inna Uchkunova, *In Someone Else's Shoes: Are the Investor's Rights His Own or Those of the Home State?*, Kluwer Arbitration Blog, 15 April 2013, http://arbitrationblog.kluwerarbitration.com/2013/04/15/in-someone-elses-shoes-are-the-investors-rights-his-own-or-those-of-the-home-state/.
21. The alleged breaches were brought as breaches of Arts 1102 (National treatment), 1106 (Performance requirements), and 1110 (Expropriation).
22. *ADM*, para. 169.

> The procedural obligation under Section B of Chapter Eleven to submit the investment dispute to arbitration – which may arise from the breach of the primary obligations of the host State addressed in Section A – is owed directly to the beneficiary of the obligation, in this case the investors, who have opted in the present case, as a secondary right holder, to commence international arbitration proceedings under Chapter Eleven. The power to bring international arbitral proceeding under Section B, makes the investor the holder of a procedural right, irrespective of whether this right may be suspended by the NAFTA Parties.[23]

The tribunal did not define or distinguish between substantive and procedural rights, let alone *secondary* procedural rights. Perhaps more concerning was that the tribunal did not explain why distinguishing between process and substance bears on rights at all.

The concurring opinion[24] questions the veracity of the award by pointing out, 'The ILC articles do not distinguish between procedural rights that may be superseded by countermeasures, and substantive rights that may not.'[25] The concurring arbitrator goes on to say:

> Unless the provisions of Chapter Eleven create obligations owed to investors, to be enforced by investors, they have no meaning, even if the enforcement rights are 'procedural' and 'derivative'. It is not correct to posit that the States Parties to NAFTA have national treatment obligations, for example, as Article 1102 provides, but investors in those countries have no corresponding individual rights of national treatment owed to them by the States Parties. As Claimants pointed out at the hearing 'Nowhere in the case law of *Chapter* Eleven or of BITs will you find the suggestion that claimants are enforcing the rights of the State. Nowhere do you find the suggestion that somehow investors are just deputized to enforce the rights of the state.' And Respondent has acknowledged, as noted, that investors have 'rights' to file claims and to collect damages for breach, and that these are 'significant' rights.[26]

[2] CPI

In *CPI* the tribunal decided that because NAFTA's Chapter 11 confers procedural rights to investors, it follows that substantive rights are also conferred. The tribunal acknowledged, without explaining, that a difference between substance and process exists, but seemingly concluded that this difference is immaterial in terms of rights. The tribunal found it unnecessary to distinguish between procedural and substantive rights, preferring instead to assume that because procedural rights exist, so too must substantive rights. In the tribunal's words:

> In the case of Chapter XI of the NAFTA, the tribunal considers that the intention of the Parties was to confer substantive rights directly upon investors. That follows

23. *ADM*, para. 177.
24. *ADM*, concurring opinion of Arthur W. Rovine. Issues of Independent Investor Rights, Diplomatic Protection and Countermeasures.
25. *Ibid.*, para. 4.
26. *Ibid.*, para. 45 (internal footnote omitted).

> from the language used and is confirmed by the fact that Chapter XI confers procedural rights upon them. The notion that Chapter XI conferred upon investors a right, in their own name and for their own benefit, to institute proceedings to enforce rights which were not theirs but were solely the property of the state of their nationality is counterintuitive.[27]

Even if the tribunal's view is correct that it seems counterintuitive for a State to provide procedural rights but not substantive rights to investors, merely saying so is hardly sufficient to explain why it is counterintuitive. It would have been far more helpful to provide a cogent reason for future tribunals to rely on. For example, pointing out that a procedural right absent a substantive right is akin to a remedy without a right.[28]

[3] Cargill

The tribunal in *Cargill*, similar to the *CPI* tribunal, differed from the *ADM* tribunal in holding that investors do possess more than just procedural rights. The tribunal, despite acknowledging that these rights originate in the NAFTA and that the NAFTA is an agreement among States, nevertheless concluded that the NAFTA confers rights onto investors. Again, the tribunal did not distinguish between procedural and substantive rights and saw no need to explain why such a distinction would matter. Worse still, the tribunal did not explain why investors enjoy rights; the tribunal merely offered its conclusion. In the tribunal's words:

> With due respect to the majority in ADM and Respondent in this case, the tribunal does not agree that investors under Chapter 11 are granted mere procedural rights of access. The tribunal agrees with Respondent that if a State, through diplomatic protection, were to espouse the claims of its nationals damaged by a legitimate countermeasure, then that countermeasure would preclude the wrongfulness of the act that otherwise would have entailed State responsibility and the claims would be denied.
>
> ...
>
> This is not the situation under Chapter 11 of the NAFTA. Article 1116(1) provides that it is the investor that 'may submit to arbitration under this Section a claim;' not the state of that investor. Likewise, it is the investor, and not the state of that investor, that is the named party to the proceedings. Similarly, it is the investor that is named in the operating paragraph or 'dispositive' of the award.[29]

27. *CPI*, para. 169.
28. In his terse separate opinion, Andreas F. Lowenfeld, seems equally troubled by how his co-arbitrators have obscured the decision and possibly set the discussion back by introducing ideas that would appear to breathe life into Mexico's *unjustified argument*. *See* Separate Opinion of Andreas F. Lowenfeld, para. 6.
29. *Cargill*, paras 424 & 425.

[B] Evaluating the Sugar Cases

It would be easy to rely on *Cargill* and *CPI* to reason that investors enjoy rights under the NAFTA and, accordingly, investors in all IIAs enjoy direct rights. The distinguished tribunals in both decisions decided their cases after *ADM*, and thus had the benefit of the *ADM* tribunal's reasoning, and disagreed with it. However, this chapter argues further that investors enjoy unfettered rights to use arbitration to remedy wrongs resulting from the obligations undertaken by the State parties to the NAFTA. Unlike the reasoning in *Cargill* and *CPI*, this chapter does not tether an investor's direct rights to any granting, by States, of procedural rights of action but instead will explore how the nature of the rights held by investors is different and more expansive than what these tribunals found. This chapter offers a better justification than what the Sugar Cases concluded.

[C] Rights and Duties

Black's Law Dictionary defines duty as 'a legal obligation that is owed or due to another and that needs to be satisfied; an obligation for which somebody else has a corresponding right'.[30] Importantly, this basic definition defines the correspondence between rights and duties. In its purest sense, a duty can exist only where a corresponding right also exists.[31]

So what is the nature of Chapter 11 obligations? All three 'sugar' tribunals consider the obligations found in Chapter 11, specifically Articles 1102–1114, are duties that have corresponding rights. The *ADM* tribunal differed, however, in that it considered these rights were held not by investors but by the other State parties. Consequently, according to the *ADM* tribunal, the only 'right' investors enjoy under Chapter 11 is the right to invoke the responsibility of the host State in investor-State arbitration. Much discussion has taken place both academically and in cases about whether or not these rights are derivative or direct rights.[32] The notion that these rights are derivative is a reversion to a time when States could extend only diplomatic protection to their nationals and, in so doing, the State espoused claims on its nationals' behalf.

With the advent of IIAs, this reasoning is antiquated and problematic. Diplomatic protection is not a right; it is a privilege a national could request but one that a State could refuse. If IIAs offer nothing more than diplomatic protection, then many

30. *Black's Law Dictionary*, 8th ed, *sub verbo*, 'duty'.
31. Hohfeld, *supra* n. 12, at 30.
32. The debate around whether these rights are properly derivative or direct may appear superficially pedantic but upon closer examination it is a necessary debate to establish not only the nature of investor rights but also their breadth and available remedies. Those favouring the direct rights theory include Campbell McLachlan, Laurence Shore and Matthew Weiniger, *International Investment Arbitration: Substantive Principles* (Oxford University Press, 2007), 61–2. Opposing this view is James Crawford, *Treaty and Contract in Investment Arbitration*, 356. For an early use of the term derivative *see* Maximilian Koessler, *Government Espousal of Private Claims before International Tribunals*, 14 U. Chicago L. Rev. 189 (1945).

esteemed writers have wasted much ink suggesting otherwise.[33] Either a right exists, or it does not. Furthermore, without investor rights, no corresponding duties on the host State exist. However, even the *ADM* tribunal did not go this far. It conceded that investors have rights to make a claim in investment arbitration and States have a right to benefit of the investor protection obligations for their investors.

The tribunals in *ADM*, *CPI*, and *Cargill* seem to share a common belief that NAFTA's Chapter 11 sections A and B neatly divide substantive and procedural rights, with the former falling under section A, and the latter falling under section B. These tribunals can be excused because, as a heuristic, it is helpful to conceive of Chapter 11 in this way. After all, Articles 1102–1114 set down what the respective State's promise not to do to investments and investors, and Articles 1115–1138 provides the mechanism investors may use to address State-breaches of their section A promises. This structuring, however, does not lead to the conclusion that section A contains substantive rights, while section B only contains procedural rights. The reason not to conflate procedural and substantive rights this way is that it may lead to the same unhelpful reasoning the *ADM* tribunal reached that investors enjoy a right to use arbitration (found in section B of Chapter 11), but that it is the States that enjoy the section A, substantive protection. But arbitration is not merely a procedural right.

[D] Substantive Versus Procedural Rights: A False Dichotomy

Chapter 11 makes no reference to 'substantive' rights. It speaks only of obligations. It does use the term 'procedures', but only in the context of explaining how an investor may use its right to arbitrate. This right to use arbitration to resolve an investment dispute arises out of the obligation undertaken by the host State. In this sense, Chapter 11 concerns obligations and rights. Nowhere does Chapter 11 distinguish between substantive obligations and procedural ones.

Is there a difference? Legal systems tend to divide, albeit unevenly, substance from procedure. Rules in court are often termed procedural, whereas rules that govern relationships, like contract law, are spoken of in terms of substance. Hence, the substantive contract law of New York may govern a contract, but if the parties are before courts in England, it is English procedural law that governs the hearing. Arbitration, however, is another legal estuary that synthesizes elements of jurisdiction and contract. Jurisdictionally, an arbitration agreement, by naming a particular juridical seat where the arbitration takes place, is arbitration's jurisdictional aspect. In international arbitration, this concept is often referred to as *lex arbitri*. The arbitration agreement is, itself, the substantive contract and hence the substantive aspect of the right.

33. Aust, 445–447; Malcolm Shaw, *International Law*, 6th ed. (Cambridge University Press, 2008), 838 et seq.; Andreas Lowenfeld, *International Economic Law*, 2nd ed. 554, et seq.

[E] *Lex Arbitri*

What is the *lex arbitri*? Simply put, it is the supervisory law governing the 'external' relationship between the State (usually via national courts) and the arbitration, as well as the 'internal' regulations of the arbitration itself.[34] So how is the *lex arbitri* determined? It helps to understand the constructs of an arbitration agreement, or at least the process through which parties wind up with an applicable arbitration law. In drafting an arbitration agreement, parties may decide on a place to hold the arbitration hearings, such as London, New York, or Paris, and generally, the arbitration law in force in London, New York, or Paris is the law that governs the arbitration - the *lex arbitri* - where such law uses a territorial approach. For example, the Model Arbitration Law explains in relevant part that 'the provisions of this [Model] Law ... apply only if the place of arbitration is in the territory of this [Model Law] State'.[35] What this provision reveals is that where parties name a Model Law jurisdiction as its place of arbitration, the Model Law will apply to their arbitration and is the *lex arbitri*.

Another expression often used in place of *lex arbitri* is *lex loci arbitri*. While *lex* denotes 'law' and *arbitri* denotes 'arbitration', the additional term *loci* stands in for 'place'. Taken together, the literal translation of *lex loci arbitri* is 'law at the place of arbitration'. These terms are often used interchangeably in practice and even in academic writing.[36] The reason for this is the underlying assumption that the arbitration law at the place of arbitration is the *applicable* arbitration law for the conduct of the dispute, as is the result of Article 1(2) of the Model Law. This assumption is the foundation of what is known as the 'seat' theory. The seat theory posits that because a party may not avoid the arbitration law in force at the seat, this law is the applicable arbitration law to the dispute.[37]

34. The classic explanation of the 'internal/external' dichotomy is found in *Union of India v. McDonnell Douglas Corp.* [1993] 2 Lloyd's Rep 48, where the House of Lords, in finding that the *lex arbitri* was the law of the seat of the arbitration (England) and therefore governed the proceedings, the Indian Arbitration Act as chosen by the parties to govern their arbitration's procedure was limited to the 'internal' conduct of the arbitration to the extent it is not inconsistent with English arbitration law.
35. United Nations Commission on International Trade Law, *UNCITRAL Model Law on International Commercial Arbitration 1985, with Amendments as Adopted in 2008* (Vienna: United Nations, 2008), ('Model Law') Art. 1(2).
36. Mauro Rubino-Sammartano, *International Arbitration Law and Practice*, 3rd ed. (2014), 157 (where the author refers to lex arbitri as 'venue of the proceedings'); William W. Park, *The Lex Loci Arbitri and International Commercial Arbitration*, 32 Int'l & Comp. L.Q. 21 (January 1983) (where the author uses *lex loci arbitri* to denote mandatory curial laws of where the award is rendered); Roy Goode, *The Role of the Lex Loci Arbitri in International Commercial Arbitration*, (2001) 17 Arb. Int'l 19–40 (where the author defines *lex loci arbitri* as the law of the procedure where the arbitration takes place but then also uses *lex arbitri* to mean the same).
37. Synonyms for the seat of arbitration include place, locale, location, forum, venue, or *locus arbitri*.

[F] Seat Theory

The seat theory is not a universal rule, and so caution is necessary when using these terms interchangeably. Parties are free, although not advised, to adopt an arbitration law that is different from the arbitration law at the place of arbitration.[38] Nevertheless, even where parties select an arbitration law different from the arbitration law at the place of arbitration, the latter law is usually unavoidable.[39] This territorial approach, which endorses the general principle of public international law that a State is sovereign within its borders, confirms that States control and regulate acts made within their territory.[40]

Investment arbitration is not so different from international commercial arbitration. NAFTA's Chapter 11, section 1130, unless the disputing parties agree otherwise, requires tribunals to hold arbitrations in the territory of a NAFTA 'Party' who is a party to the United Nations Convention on the Recognition and Enforcement of Foreign Arbitral Awards (New York Convention).[41]

The seat theory's effect is a bit different when an investor under the NAFTA selects the International Centre for Settlement of Investment Disputes (ICSID) Rules of arbitration to govern their dispute.[42] Commentators suggest that ICSID represents a 'de-nationalized' or 'a-national' arbitration and consequently idiosyncratic rules of the seat should not bear on the arbitration.[43] However, an ICSID tribunal's seat is quite relevant in terms of party representation, to cite just one example. Jurisdictions, like Canada,[44] that only permit licensed lawyers (members of the Bar) to act as legal representatives in an ICSID arbitration would find the romanticized view that an ICSID arbitration is de-nationalized quite unconvincing. Consequently, any non-member of the local Bar who represents a party in an ICSID arbitration, where that arbitration takes place within a particular law society's territorial jurisdiction, risks practising law

38. *Union of India* is a classic example of why parties should avoid doing this. While often thought of as merely an academic curiosity (*cf.* Albert Jan van den Berg, *The New York Arbitration Convention of 1958. Towards a Uniform Judicial Interpretation*, (The Hague: Kluwer Law International, 1981), 350), a few cases of some import have tested this curiosity in practice. *See generally Karaha Bodas Co. v. Perusahaan Pertambangan Minyak Dan Gas Bumi Negara*, 364 F.3d 274, 291 (5th Cir. 2004); *Yusuf Ahmed Alghanim & Sons v. Toys 'R' Us, Inc.*, 126 F.3d 15, 21 & n. 3 (2d Cir. 1997) (cited in Matthew Slater, *On Annulled Arbitral Awards and the Death of Chromalloy*, 25 Arb. Int'l n. 6, 273 (2009).
39. For example, *a contrario*, Model Law Art. 1(2) explains that the Model Law applies when an arbitration takes place in the territory of a State that has adopted the Model Law.
40. For an extensive discussion on this and other elements of the nationality and territoriality approach generally, *see International Law*, 2 ed. 345 et seq. (Evans, M. D. ed).
41. Done at New York 10 June 1958, U. N. Doc. No. E/Conf. 26/9 Rev. 1; 330 U.N.T.S. 3.
42. The ICSID Arbitration Rules are contained in the *ICSID Convention* (*Convention on the Settlement of Investment Disputes between States and Nationals of Other States*, done at Washington, 18 March 1965, 575 U.N.T.S. 159, reprinted in 4 I.L.M. 532 (1965).
43. Aron Broches, *Awards Rendered Pursuant to the ICSID Convention: Binding Force, Finality, Recognition, Enforcement, Execution*, 2 ICSID Rev.: Foreign Investment L.J. 287 (1987).
44. *See* Law Society of Ontario By law 4, part VI, available at: https://lawsocietyontario.azureedge.net/media/lso/media/legacy/pdf/b/by/by-law-4.pdf. Of note, section 35 provides a carve out only to those foreign lawyers conducting arbitrations under the Ontario statute that adopts the Model Law. Investor-State arbitrations, when they are against Canada, are conducted under the federal statute.

illegally. Therefore, ICSID Arbitration Rule 18, which allows for anyone (licensed attorney or not) to represent a party in ICSID arbitrations, would have to yield to a domestic rule (applicable via seat theory) that restricts who may represent a party. Party representation is just one example of how the seat matters, even in ICSID arbitrations.

[G] Contractual Aspect of Arbitration Agreements

In addition to its jurisdictional nature, an agreement to arbitrate is a contract. As a contract it must satisfy the legal requirements applicable to any contract made under the law to which the parties have, by design or by implication, subjected their arbitration agreement. Under common law, the usual rules of contract formation apply to arbitration agreements requiring an offer, an acceptance and consideration, in circumstances where the parties are *ad idem,*[45] or more simply, that the parties all understand the terms and promises made to each other. In these agreements, the consideration is the mutual covenant to submit disputes to arbitration, and more precisely, the forbearance of their right to go before national courts.

French civil law has a distinctive philosophy concerning contract law that shapes the rules relating, in particular, to the formation of arbitration agreements. Under French civil law (and the family of French civil laws), consideration is not a necessary element to contract formation. Consequently, while the absence of consideration is fatal to the formation of arbitration agreements under the common law, it is inconsequential under civil law. Still, French civil law relies on the *causa*, an idea that is perhaps best summarized: 'To use a much-repeated aphorism, whereas *objet* provides an answer to the question *quid debetur?* (what is owing?), *cause* answers the question why it is owing (*cur debetir?*).'[46]

Forming arbitration agreements under IIAs remains somewhat murky. The competing theories, which to examine exhaustively is beyond this chapter, essentially fall into one of the three categories:

(1) the classic common law approach described above whereby the offer is a standing offer to arbitrate perfected upon an investor notifying its intent to arbitrate a claim. Under this model a State may revoke its offer before an investor substantially performs;
(2) an irrevocable offer, similar to a firm offer, whereby the State may not revoke its offer; and

45. J. Brian Casey, *Arbitration Law of Canada: Practice and Procedure*, 3rd ed. 64 (Huntington, New York: Juris, 2017).
46. Barry Nicholas, *The French Law of Contract* 118 (2nd ed. Clarendon 1992).

(3) an act of State binding at international law. Here the theory tracks public international law obligations arising from the law of treaties and the law of unilateral declarations.[47]

Of the three models, option 3 seems most appropriate for NAFTA's Chapter 11 arbitrations.[48] NAFTA Article 1131 (governing law) found in section B explains, 'A Tribunal established under this Section shall decide the issues in dispute in accordance with this Agreement and applicable rules of international law.'[49] As a treaty, the NAFTA Agreement is governed by the Vienna Convention on the Law of Treaties (VCLT).[50] What is more, Article 1131 directs decision makers to rely on rules of international law.[51] Consequently, the offer to arbitrate under Chapter 11 binds all three State parties once the act of ratification occurred.[52]

§10.04 THIRD-PARTY RIGHTS

Although investors may enjoy direct rights under the NAFTA, even under the view that investors only enjoy third-party rights, a direct right to use arbitration still inures to investors as third-party beneficiaries. Courts in many jurisdictions commonly allow parties, who were otherwise not involved in a contract's negotiation or agreement, to enforce one of the contracting party's duties as a third party. However, it is not every third party who enjoys this right. To the common law lawyer, the doctrine of privity of contract describes a situation where a stranger to the contract, not being privy to the contract, has no rights under it. In the context of NAFTA, one could easily analogize investors to third parties to NAFTA, because none of the investors negotiated or signed NAFTA. But, by analogy to third-party beneficiaries under both common law and civil law theories, investors under NAFTA enjoy direct rights as third-party intended beneficiaries. The principle on third-party beneficiaries exists in both common law and civil law. According to Article 38 of the Statute of the International Court of Justice (ICJ),[53] once identified, these principles may be accepted as a general principle of law.[54]

---

47. Michael D. Nolan and Freddy G. Sourgens, *Limits of Consent – Arbitration Without Privity and Beyond* Liber Amicorum Bernardo Cremades (Kluwer, 2010), 9, available at: https://ssrn.com/abstract=2180302.
48. Earlier writers suggested it was a standing offer to arbitrate, but with respect to those writers, their viewpoint was skewed by the paucity of cases and writers giving this topic serious thought. *See* Alan Redfern and Martin Hunter, *Law & Practice of International Commercial Arbitration* (Sweet & Maxwell, 4th ed. 2004), 1-142.
49. NAFTA Art. 1131.
50. Done at Vienna, 23 May 1969, entered into force 27 January 1980, 1155 U.N.T.S. 331, reprinted in 8 I.L.M. 679 (1969).
51. *Cargill*, paras 131-134.
52. Naturally jurisdictional conditions remain that an investor must meet, for example in NAFTA Art. 1121, et seq.
53. 33 UNTS 993.
54. In particular, ICJ Statute Art. 38(1)(c), which reads:

    1. The Court, whose function is to decide in accordance with international law such disputes as are submitted to it, shall apply:

[A] Third-Party Beneficiaries under the Common Law and Civil Law

In the US, third parties traditionally had no rights in other people's contracts. However, in 1859, *Lawrence v. Fox*[55] allowed a third-party creditor to sue on a contract to which he was not a party. In that case, Fox had borrowed money from another party (Holly) and, as payment for the loan, agreed to repay Lawrence, to whom Holly owed a debt. When Fox did not pay Lawrence, Lawrence sued Fox for the promise Fox had made with Holly. The New York court found in favour of Lawrence and created what became known as 'creditor beneficiaries' who could enforce contracts to which they were not a party.[56] Of course, Lawrence retained its right to sue Holly should Lawrence not recover from Fox.[57]

[B] The Second Restatement of the Law of Contracts

Section 302 of the Restatement (Second) of Contracts[58] simplified matters somewhat, by creating what it termed 'intended or incidental' beneficiaries. The distinction is simple. Intended beneficiaries may sue to enforce the promisor's obligations, whereas incidental beneficiaries may not. The reasoning is sound. Arguably, almost anyone could deem themselves incidental beneficiaries. Using investors under NAFTA as an example, only the investor would meet the intended beneficiary definition. In contrast, the investor's employees, who would undoubtedly feel the effects of a State's interference with the investor's investment, could not benefit from State promises under the NAFTA as the employees, unless particular facts exist, are merely incidental beneficiaries.

[C] Third-Party Beneficiaries under Civil Law

Much like the Second Restatement, French civil law accepts that intended beneficiaries acquire rights under contracts. Incidental beneficiaries do not.[59] The civil law sees no difficulty in allowing parties to create direct rights to third parties for a variety of reasons. For one, contractual relationships in the civil law are guided by obligations, in contrast to the common law that sees the contract as the source of rights. Indeed, those who study contracts in civil law traditions take courses called *Obligations*. Another reason the civil law is untroubled with third parties enjoying direct rights is that the

---

(c) the general principles of law recognized by civilized nations;

Is one of the sources of international law for the ICJ.

55. 20 N.Y. 268 (1859).
56. The rule further expanded in *Seaver v. Ransom*, 224 N.Y. 233, 120 N.E. 639 (1918), to allow what US law described as *donee beneficiaries* and formally codified in The First Restatement of Contracts (US).
57. The classic case known to those jurisdictions who continue to follow, more closely, England's common law is *Tweddle v. Atkinson* (1861), 1 B. & S. 393, 121 E.R. 762 (Q.B.).
58. Restatement (Second) of Contracts § 302 (1981).
59. Tadas Klimas, *Comparative Contract Law, A Transystemic Approach with an Emphasis on the Continental Law: Cases, Text and Materials*, 420 (Carolina Academic Press, Durham, 2006).

civil law never fell into common law's *consideration* straightjacket. Although it is questionable whether any substantial connection should exist between the common law's obsession with consideration and its adherence to the doctrine of privity.[60]

Quebec's civil code sets down quite neatly the traditional civil law view on third-party beneficiaries in the following articles (provisions):

> 1444. A person may, in a contract, stipulate for the benefit of a third person.
>
> The stipulation gives the third person beneficiary the right to exact performance of the promised obligation directly from the promisor.[61]
>
> ...
>
> 1445. A third person beneficiary need not exist nor be determinate when the stipulation is made; he need only be determinable at that time and exist when the promisor is to perform the obligation for his benefit.[62]

[D] Third-Party Beneficiaries as General Principles of Law

Patrick Dumberry distills the process of identifying a General Principle of Law and transposing them on the international law plane into three stages.[63] The first requires identifying a principle that is common to domestic orders. The second requires distilling the essence of the principle while discarding domestic idiosyncrasies, while the third step, arguably the more difficult one, requires transposing or adapting the principle to the international legal order. Below is a brief overview of each stage but the reader is directed to many more works on the topic.[64]

Stage 1: Identifying a principle

Although no definitive methodology to identify a principle emerges as the leading contender, a comparative approach, coupled with positive law enactments, as well as cases and doctrinal writing, is a safe way to identify a principle. Therefore, where one can identify rule shared throughout nations, this common thread is a reliable candidate to serve as a principle. A rule about third-party beneficiaries meets this first stage, because the rule exists in common law jurisdictions, as well as civil law jurisdictions,

60. Bruce MacDougall, *Introduction to Contracts*, 4th ed., 92 (Lexis Nexis, Toronto, 2019).
61. 1991, c. 64, art. 1444; I.N. 2014-05-01. As long ago as 1979, Canada's Supreme Court recognized this principle, albeit in a sale of goods transaction. *See General Motors Products of Canada v. Kravitz*, [1979] S.C.J. No. 9, 93 D.L.R. (3d) 481 (S.C.C.).
62. 1991, c. 64, art. 1445.
63. Patrick Dumberry, *A Guide to General Principles of Law in International Investment Arbitration* (Oxford: Oxford University Press, 2020) ('Dumberry').
64. M. C. Bassiouni, *A Functional Approach to 'General Principles of International Law'*, 11 Michigan J. Int'l L. 809 (1990). *See also* Fabián Raimondo, 'General Principles of Law in the Decisions of International Criminal Courts and Tribunals', Unpublished Ph.D. Thesis, Amsterdam Center for International Law, 2007; J. Ellis, *General Principles and Comparative Law*, 11 European J. Int'l L. 950 (2011); Bassiouni, *A Functional Approach*, 809, n. 1; ILC, *First Report on General Principles of Law*, by Marcelo Vázquez-Bermúdez, Special Rapporteur, ILC, Seventy-first session Geneva, 29 April–7 June and 8 July–9 August 2019, UN Doc. A/CN.4/732, 5 April 2019, para. 166 (noted in Dumberry, *supra* n. 63).

including those civil law jurisdictions that have seen their socialist modifications to their civil codes, for example, in Russia. Estonia and Lithuania.

Stage 2: Distilling the Principle's Essence

If stage one is a horizontal survey,[65] stage two is decisively vertical.[66] It requires a form of comparing and contrasting different jurisdictions' rules on the principle with the goal of discarding idiosyncratic rules or exceptional rules that do not affect the overarching idea. For example, the interplay between consideration and third-party beneficiaries under common law is not relevant to the principle that under the common law, a third party named in a contract has rights. Similarly, the distinction between intended and incidental beneficiaries found under US law is irrelevant to the horizontal third-party beneficiary principle.

Stage 3: Adapting and Transposing the Principle into the International Legal Order

Not all principles are appropriate to adapt to international law.[67] The reasons are varied and relate to the subjects of international law and the topics that concern them. For example, rules about divorce find no application in international law because States, as usual subjects of international law, neither marry nor divorce one another. On the other hand, reparation for damages caused applies both to natural persons as well as States. However, particular rules surrounding how to pay out damages may not adapt well to international law. One example of this is the notion of a court supervising monthly payments from the breaching party to the injured party. The ICJ, for example, is well within its right to award a sum of damages in the form of a judgment, but it is in no position to administer the execution of payments.[68]

65. So described by Anthea Roberts, Paul B. Stephan, Pierre-Hugues Verdier and Mila Versteeg, *Comparative International Law: Framing the Field* 109 Am. J. Int'l L. 471–2 (2015) (noted in Dumberry, *supra* n. 63, at 136).
66. Dumberry, *supra* n. 63, at 136.
67. E. Voyiakis, *Do General Principles Fill 'Gaps' in International Law?*, 14 Austrian RIEL 245 (2009).
68. Chapter 2 of the ICJ Statute, particularly Arts 34–36, set down the Court's competence. However, for enforcement of the Court's judgments, one must turn to Art. 94 of the UN Charter which explains:

    > (1) Each Member of the United Nations undertakes to comply with the decision of the International Court of Justice in any case to which it is a party.
    > (2) If any party to a case fails to perform the obligations incumbent upon it under a judgment rendered by the Court, the other party may have recourse to the Security Council, which may, if it deems necessary, make recommendations or decide upon measures to be taken to give effect to the judgment.

    This provision seems to allow only for the Security Council to enforce decisions of the ICJ. *But see* Abiodun Sani Amuda-Kannike and Sylvanus Abila, *A Critical Examination of the Enforcement of ICJ Decisions through the Organs of the United Nations*, 6 J. L. & Criminal Justice, 22 (June 2018), who argue that in addition to the Security Council, the Secretary General and the UN General Assembly also enjoy a form of enforcement power.

[E] Transposing the General Principle of Third-Party Beneficiaries to IIAs

IIAs can be envisaged as providing investors in IIAs a direct right to use arbitration by grafting the original reasoning in *Lawrence v. Fox* and later modernized in the Restatement (Second) of Contracts, as well as Commonwealth views on third-party beneficiaries.[69] For simplicity's sake, this analysis will use NAFTA's Chapter 11 inter-State promises in one context, here between the US and Canada. Of course, under NAFTA the same would work with US and Mexican investors. Furthermore, this analysis will consider this transposition in two ways. The first, less controversial, allows investors to directly arbitrate claims against the host State, even after termination of the treaty containing the arbitration promise. The second, admittedly more controversial consequence of the third-party beneficiary principle transposed into international law, leads to investors enjoying a right to sue their home States, using arbitration, as a consequence of the home State receiving a benefit from the IIA.

The US promises Canada that it will protect Canadian investors' investments in the US. This protection promise is intended to benefit the investor and is enforceable by the investor under Chapter 11. This is Contract 1, and this is the contract with a third-party beneficiary, here a Canadian investor. A Canadian investor's right to use arbitration (for this example, the investor is a creditor beneficiary) vests in Contract 1 upon providing value to the US by investing. Assume that the value of an investment by a Canadian investor is USD 10,000,000 and that the investment is lost as a result of a US action that breaches an investor protection obligation in Chapter 11. In this example, the US is the promisor because it is promising to perform in a way that benefits the third-party beneficiary, the Canadian investor. Canada is the promisee, because Canada intended to make a promise to the US to benefit US investors (the NAFTA) in return for benefitting the third-party Canadian investor, by causing a return promise from the US.

The Canadian investor, the creditor beneficiary to Contract 1, has two choices. It can assert its Chapter 11 rights to recover its USD 0,000,000 against the US or, alternatively, the investor can assert its right as a creditor beneficiary of Contract 1 to recover USD 10,000,000 from Canada if the US refuses to honour its arbitration promise. Naturally, the investor cannot sue twice as this would lead to double recovery.

Finally, there is the matter of vesting. Under US law, Canada and the US may modify their NAFTA's Chapter 11 obligations as owed to investors but only if the investor's rights have not yet vested. The thorny question under Chapter 11 is when do investor rights vest? This chapter concludes that the offer of arbitration in Chapter 11 is less a standing offer, and more an irrevocable offer, or acts of States. But even as a

69. Although England only formally arrived at the conclusion that third parties enjoyed rights in 1999 through the passing of its Contracts (Rights of Third Parties) Act 1999, Lord Denning planted earlier seeds in his decision in *Beswick v. Beswick*, [1967] UKHL 2 [1968] AC 58. New Zealand was well ahead of England having passed the New Zealand Contracts (Privity) Act 1982. Canada's common law jurisdictions, with the exception of the Province of New Brunswick, remain in the dark ages on this front, holding strong to the doctrine of privity.

standing offer (to the common law mind, a unilateral offer) the offer is irrevocable once performance has commenced,[70] which is the moment an investor accepts to invest in the relevant country. Under any of these scenarios, therefore, the investor's rights vest upon making an investment that meets the definition of an investment in the territory of the State. This vesting period is critical. To believe that the investor's right vests only upon commencing arbitration would allow States to breach their investment protection promises an hour before treaty termination. In the case of NAFTA, this is particularly wicked given that NAFTA has no survival period clause (sunset clause), which would extend protections to investors, often in the range of ten to fifteen years. And while the parties to NAFTA are free to terminate the treaty by agreement consistent with the VCLT provisions on termination,[71] where third-party rights have vested, the effect of termination should not affect these third parties. This point can be further supported by relying on an accepted general principle of international law, that of estoppel.[72] As one researcher has explained, investment arbitration tribunals have referred to estoppel in fifty-three cases.[73] Numerous academics have also identified estoppel as a general principle of international law.[74] Given that contemplated investments under IIAs are intended as long-term investments (like greenfield investments) States who terminate their IIAs, where these IIAs do not contain survival clauses, may be estopped from denying such protections to long-term investments where the investments are made just before termination. This should remain so even in the fact of the CUSMA's three-year transition period given that, as indicated earlier, investments contemplated in the ISD system may not ripen into claims until well past three years.

70. This assumes that one accepts Lord Denning's reasoning and ultimate holding in *Errington v. Wood*, [1952] 1 KB 290, [1952] 1 All ER 149, which this writer does.
71. *VCLT* Art. 54 provides for the mutual termination on consent.
72. Dumberry, *supra* n. 63, at 342 et seq.
73. Andreas Kulick, *About the Order of Cart and Horse, Among Other Things: Estoppel in the Jurisprudence of International Investment Arbitration Tribunals*, 27 European J. Int'l L. 110ff. (2016) (noted in Dumberry, *supra* n. 63, at 342.
74. *See* numerous authors mentioned in Antoine Martin, *L'estoppel en droit international public: Précède d'un aperçu de la théorie de l'estoppel en droit anglais* (Pedone 1979) 229; I.C. MacGibbon, *Estoppel in International Law*, 7 ICLQ 468, 470 (1958); E. Gaillard, *L'Interdiction de se Contredire au Détriment d'Autrui comme Principe Général du Droit du Commerce International*, Rev. Arb. 250 (1985); Hersch Lauterpacht, Private Law Sources and Analogies of International Law (With Special Reference to International Arbitration) (Longman, Green and Co., 1927), 204; H. Lauterpacht, The Development of International Law by the International Court (Stevens, 1958), 169–172; Megan L. Wagner, *Jurisdiction by Estoppel in the International Court of Justice*, 74 Cal. L. Rev. 1777–1779 (1986); Christian Dominicé, *A propos du principe de l'estoppel en droit des gens*, in M. Battelli et al. (eds) Recueil d'études de droit international en hommage à Paul Guggenheim (Institut Universitaire de Hautes Études Internationales, 1968); Ian Brownlie, *Principles of Public International Law* (6th ed., Oxford University Press, 2003), 616; G. Fitzmaurice, *The Law and Procedure of the International Court of Justice: General Principles and Sources of Law*, 30 British Yearbook Int'l L. 1–38 (1958); Schreuer, et al., *The ICSID Convention* 608; Stephan W. Schill, *General Principles of International Law and International Investment Law*, in T. Gazzini and E. De Brabandere (eds), International Investment Law. The Sources of Rights and Obligations (Brill, 2012) 143 (all of the above noted in Dumberry, *supra* n. 63, at 342).

§10.05 INVESTORS ARE OWED DUTIES, WHICH TRANSLATE INTO RIGHTS

If investors enjoy direct rights, the matter becomes even more pressing now that the State parties to NAFTA have agreed to affect investors' rights by altering and eliminating them. The USMCA does precisely this. In it, the US, Mexico, and Canada seek to replace the rights found under NAFTA, particularly in Chapter 11, with lesser rights housed in Chapter 14 of the USMCA.

A pertinent example of how USMCA reduces protections for investors is its severe curtailing of expropriation protection. Whereas under NAFTA, an investor could claim indirect expropriation of its investment, under USMCA investors may only claim direct expropriation, and even this is subject to a qualified understanding of what expropriation means. From a timeliness perspective, under NAFTA, investors were required to wait for six months following the events giving rise to the claim (NAFTA Article 1120). Now this period is increased five-fold to thirty months and requires investors to pursue a remedy first in domestic courts. This change is significant. A waiting period of two and half years after the event giving rise to a claim will surely put even robust companies in a precarious State and, likely, its intended purpose is to press investors to settle.

Whatever may be thought about the new agreement, investors from the US, Mexico, and Canada will witness their previous NAFTA rights severely truncated under USMCA. However, if investors possess direct rights under NAFTA they may push back against this unilateral attempt to interfere with their NAFTA protections. Thus, even after the NAFTA is officially terminated, under the theory of separability, right holders may use the arbitration mechanism found in NAFTA to protect their rights.

[A] Separability

Although arbitration agreements are in a practical sense inextricably linked to the legal relationships to which they relate, their continued existence does not rely on these underlying relationships. Arbitration agreements are notionally separate, independent agreements by which the parties agree to resolve disputes using arbitration. Such disputes include how the parties terminated their underlying agreements. The autonomous nature of arbitration agreements remains a hallmark of arbitration and is essential. In a world where arbitration agreements are not independent of the contracts to which they relate, their legal fate would remain tied to the related contract. Moreover, without separability, where the overriding contract is deemed void or voidable, or is terminated, the arbitration agreement risks suffering from the overriding contract's fate.[75] This would allow a party to circumvent the arbitral process by

75. The distinction between contracts that are *void* and contracts that are *voidable* was important in earlier cases mainly from the United States that posited void contracts could not lead to enforceable agreements to arbitrate, whereas contracts that were merely *voidable*, could. *See* W. Park, *An Arbitrator's Jurisdiction to Determine Jurisdiction*, 13 ICCA Congress Series 55 (2006).

establishing invalidity grounds of the main contract as a means to invalidate the arbitration agreement.

To guard against this unsatisfactory result, the independence of the arbitration agreement theory emerged. While the theory of independence goes by various names, its substance is the same. English law refers to the theory as the separation doctrine or doctrine of separability, whereas US law speaks of severability.[76] The separability doctrine applies equally, with full force, in the treaty context. Indeed, the VCLT codifies the concept of separability in Article 44, a provision contemplating State parties withdrawing from treaties (like the NAFTA parties). VCLT Article 44 permits the survival, by way of separability, of certain provisions found in the treaty from which the State parties seek to withdraw, under the specified conditions. Furthermore, VCLT Article 70, which is customary international law, encompasses the view that while States may withdraw from or terminate treaties, the effects are inter-State. Article 70 does not speak to third parties affected by the decision to withdraw or terminate treaties. Nevertheless, as Article 70 speaks only of future rights and obligations[77] and not acquired or vested rights. Consequently, terminating NAFTA does not affect investors' acquired arbitration rights.

Of note, in his dissenting opinion in the *Fisheries* case,[78] ICJ Judge Bedjaoui connected VCLT Article 44 to arbitration when he wrote: 'it should also be observed that the principle of separability is fully accepted in international commercial arbitration, in so far as treatment of the arbitration clause is deemed to be independent of that of the other provisions in the agreement'.[79] Courts have long accepted that a contract's termination,[80] invalidity,[81] and even fraud[82] do not terminate the existence of the arbitration agreement, which formed an element of the contract.

What this means is, notwithstanding Canada's decision to eliminate the right for Canadian investors to use arbitration to resolve their disputes by terminating NAFTA and replacing it with USMCA, a Canadian investor who believes this decision to unilaterally alter the investor's substantive right to arbitrate harms its investment, retains the right, applying the separability of arbitration agreements, to use arbitration to remedy this wrong, even against Canada. The ability to do this is particularly pertinent under NAFTA because under Article 2021, no State party 'may provide for a right of action under its domestic law against another [State] Party on the ground that

76. The civil law, most notably France, discusses this theory under the heading *autonomie de la clause compromissoire* (and *compromis*). French law emphasizes the independence of the arbitration agreement where English and US law emphasize the agreement's separateness from the underlying contract. *See* J.D.M. Lew, L. Mistelis and S. Kröll, *Comparative International Commercial Arbitration* (Kluwer Law International, 2003), 102, n. 10.
77. Christian Tams, Antonios Tzanakopoulos, Andreas Zimmermann, *Research Handbook on the Law of Treaties* (Edward Elgar Publishing Ltd., 2014), 337.
78. *Fisheries Jurisdiction Case (Spain v. Canada)* Jurisdiction of the Court Judgment of 4 December 1998.
79. *Ibid.*, at 539 (English translation).
80. *Harper v. Kvaerner Fjeellstrand Shipping A.S.*, 1991 CanLII 1735 (B.C. S.C.).
81. *Sojuznefteexport v. JOC Oil Co.*, 4 Mealey Int'l Arb. Rep. B1 (1989) (Court of Appeal of Bermuda 1989).
82. *Prima Paint v. Flood & Conklin*, 388 U.S. 395 (1967).

a measure of another [State] Party is inconsistent with this Agreement'.[83] The USMCA contains a similar provision.[84] Consequently, the effect of terminating NAFTA, for a Canadian investor at least, means it may only go before US courts. Closing off the arbitration venue and forcing an investor into the host State's home court contradicts one of the main reasons an investor may have chosen to invest in the host State.[85] In real terms, treating rights under the entirety of Chapter 11 as rights owed to investors and given that arbitration agreements survive even the termination of treaties like NAFTA, an investor may, by way of arbitration, seek redress for injuries it sustains as a consequence of any promise made to it in section A of Chapter 11.

§10.06 CONCLUSION

Treating promises made to investors under IIAs as creating rights and not merely incidental privileges challenges the prevailing attitude. However, if investors do not possess direct rights, the obligations found under agreements like NAFTA, indeed any IIA, are nothing more than a recycling of the incomplete privileges nationals enjoy under diplomatic protection. In short, the right to direct action against a State is an illusion.[86] And the many who claimed that investment protections found under IIAs were revolutionary were wrong. Holding that investors, in fact, enjoy no direct rights sets international economic law back sixty years before the advent of modern IIAs. This is not a welcome future.

83. NAFTA Art. 2021.
84. USMCA Art. 31.21.
85. Jan Paulsson, *International Arbitration is not Arbitration*, 2 Stockholm Int'l Arb. Rev. 1-3 (2008).
86. To be fair, while the treaty is in force, investors may protect against breaches, but to interpret this protection as available only until the States wish to terminate it, is hardly an independent right because it is tied to the states forbearing their independent right to terminate the treaty.

CHAPTER 11

Reappraising Access to Justice in ISDS: A Critical Review on State Recourse to Counterclaim

Shahrizal M. Zin

Investor-State arbitration has been under relentless attacks since the 1990s. Its opponents have argued that Investor-State Dispute Settlement (ISDS) tends to favour the investor in a claim brought against State. The ISDS regime features a selected few individuals who review and evaluate a State's action, although they are largely unaccountable to the constituencies that their decisions affect. Lately, the large amounts of damages awarded by Investor-State arbitral tribunals to investors have come under great scrutiny. In view of this, ISDS has been perceived by many as giving too much leeway to the investor, due to the one-sided nature of the claims. Thus, the absence of counterclaims has become one of the main deficiencies of ISDS. A State is unable to hold a transgressing investor accountable in the quest to seek redress on behalf of its effected community. Questions abound, therefore, with regard to a State's access to justice when an investor is found to be in breach of its legal obligations. Despite a clear indication on equality of access between State and investor pursuant to Article 46 of the International Centre for Settlement of Investment Disputes (ICSID) Convention, there are challenges that restrict a State from accessing justice in the present ISDS system. In light of these considerations, this chapter reappraises access to justice through a State's recourse to asserting a counterclaim. This chapter identifies five key issues that a State frequently encounters when presenting a counterclaim against an investor and proposes a way forward to enhance a State's access to justice in the ISDS system.

§11.01 INTRODUCTION

Typically, an investment treaty only allows claims that arise directly out of a 'protected investment'[1] to be brought before an arbitral tribunal. In other words, a claim is not arbitrable unless it is closely connected with the investment dispute. In addition, it is also subject to the parties' consent to submit to the jurisdiction of the arbitral tribunal. Over the years, arbitral tribunals have been struggling to determine whether or not counterclaims should be admissible in the same proceedings with the claims brought by the investor. This is particularly disputed in cases where counterclaims are not directly related to the investor's claims. In most cases, the tribunal declines jurisdiction to entertain a counterclaim. Even if counterclaims pass the jurisdictional hurdle, this is only the first step. The party asserting a counterclaim still must prove its case to succeed on the merits.

This chapter highlights five key challenges that restrict a State's access to justice within the context of presenting a counterclaim against the investor. These challenges consist of: (1) extending a tribunal's jurisdiction to admit a counterclaim; (2) the lack of express consent which allows a counterclaim; (3) the unilateral character of a bilateral investment treaty (BIT) that seeks to protect the investor; (4) the sources of an investor's obligations either arising from general obligation under the host State's law or investment agreement; and (5) a State's non-compliance with the substantive and procedural requirement of arbitration rules. In the course of the discussion, this chapter examines several cases that shape the jurisprudence of investment treaty counterclaim. Finally, the chapter explores a way forward to enhance a State's access to justice through assertion of counterclaim.

§11.02 WHAT DOES A COUNTERCLAIM PROMOTE?

Proponents of the counterclaim concept have argued that the exercise of jurisdiction by the tribunal over the respondent's counterclaim would advance the goals of economy and efficiency in international dispute resolution. The rationale is that if the tribunal extends its jurisdiction to entertain a counterclaim, the respondent would not have to pursue its claim elsewhere. This is the argument that the respondent in *Saluka v. Czech*

---

1. *See* a definition of 'investment' in the UK-Malaysia BIT, signed on 21 May 1981 (entered into force on 21 October 1988). Art. 1(1)(a) provides that 'investment' means *every kind of asset* and in particular, though not exclusively, includes:

   (i) movable and immovable property and any other property rights such as mortgages, liens or pledges;
   (ii) shares, stock and debentures of companies or interests in the property of such companies;
   (iii) claims to money or to any performance under contract having a financial value;
   (iv) intellectual property rights and goodwill;
   (v) business concessions conferred by law or under contract, including concessions to search for, cultivate, extract or exploit natural resources.

Republic[2] made to support the possibility of a host State bringing a counterclaim based on the treaty language that purported to cover 'all disputes'. Until recently, the same argument was adopted in *Aven v. Costa Rica*,[3] in which the respondent argued on procedural economy and efficiency grounds that the tribunal had jurisdiction to resolve both the investor's and the State's claims in the same proceedings. In addition, a counterclaim also promotes equality between the parties to bring a claim against each other. This will enhance neutrality and fairness in the ISDS system where both parties will have an equal opportunity to present their claims before the tribunal. In the same vein, a counterclaim will serve as a deterrence to a frivolous claim which lacks merits in commencing arbitration.

§11.03 A LEGAL BASIS FOR A STATE TO ASSERT COUNTERCLAIMS

The competence of an ICSID tribunal to hear the investment claim is anchored in Article 25(1) of the ICSID Convention. In terms of a counterclaim, the competence of the ICSID tribunal stems from Article 25(1) in conjunction with Article 46 of the ICSID Convention. Article 25(1) provides that the 'jurisdiction of the Centre shall extend to any legal dispute arising directly out of an investment between a Contracting State … and a national of another Contracting State, which the parties to the dispute consent in writing to submit to the Centre'. Article 46 provides that an ICSID tribunal has jurisdiction to 'determine any identical claims or counterclaims arising directly out of the subject-matter of the dispute provided that they are within the scope of the consent of the parties and are otherwise within the jurisdiction of the Centre'. Notwithstanding Articles 25(1) and 46 of the ICSID Convention, the jurisdiction of an arbitral tribunal over a State party counterclaim under an investment treaty depends upon the terms of the dispute resolution provisions of the treaty, the nature of the counterclaim and the relationship of the counterclaims with the claims in the arbitration.[4]

§11.04 EXTENDING TRIBUNAL'S JURISDICTION: A CLOSE CONNECTION TEST FOR ADMISSIBILITY OF A COUNTERCLAIM

The first requirement that a State would have to establish is the 'connectedness' between counterclaim and the primary claim. A State's asserted counterclaims in the investment treaty arbitration came into a spotlight in the early 1980s. An ICSID tribunal was first tested with the issue of a counterclaim in *Klockner v. Cameroon*.[5] The *Klockner*

2. *Saluka Investments BV v. The Czech Republic*, UNCITRAL, Decision on Jurisdiction Over the Czech Republic's Counterclaim, 7 May 2004.
3. *David R. Aven and others v. The Republic of Costa Rica*, ICSID Case No. UNCT/15/3, 18 September 2018.
4. *Limited Liability Company Amto v. Ukraine*, SCC Case No. 080/2005, Final Award, 28 March 2008.
5. *Klockner Company v. Republic of Cameroon*, ICSID Case No. ARB/81/2, Decision, 21 October 1982. *See also* earlier cases with respect to State's asserted counterclaim in *Maritime International Nominees Establishment (MINE) v. Government of Guinea*, ICSID, Decision, 6 January 1988 and *Atlantic Triton v. Government of Guinea*, ICSID, Award, 21 April 1986.

Tribunal was seized of a dispute submitted by an investor in respect of its investment pursuant to a supply contract for a fertilizer factory concluded in 1972. The parties also had concluded, in the context of the supply contract in issue, a Protocol of Agreement in 1971 and an Establishment Agreement in 1973. During the course of the proceedings, the tribunal was called upon to consider whether its jurisdiction extended to a counterclaim by Cameroon based on alleged shortcomings in the management of that factory and involving those three instruments and not just the supply contract. The tribunal concluded that it 'has jurisdiction to rule both on the claim and the counterclaim, while taking into account the Establishment which, together with the Protocol of Agreement and the Supply Contract, constitute an indivisible whole'.[6] At a later point the tribunal said:

> This case involves one and the same bilateral relationship, because the three instruments are bound together by a close connecting factor: agreement was reached for the supply of a fertilizer factory, and its technical and commercial management, in return for payment of a price and for certain investment guarantees. The reciprocal obligations had a common origin, identical sources and an operational unity. They were assumed for the accomplishment of a single goal, and are thus interdependent.[7]

Thus, the tribunal's decision in *Klockner* emphasized the need for the subject matter of the counterclaim to be intimately connected with the subject matter of the primary claim. They were, as the tribunal put it, 'indivisible' and 'interdependent'.[8]

The competence of arbitral tribunal to hear a counterclaim resurfaced in *Saluka.*[9] The *Saluka* Tribunal took painstaking efforts to examine the jurisprudence of the Iran-US Claims Tribunal to determine the proper test in relation to the admissibility of a counterclaim. After noting that there were no previous decisions on a counterclaim in an arbitration involving both the United Nations Commission on International Trade Law (UNCITRAL) Rules and a BIT, the *Saluka* Tribunal reviewed a few ICSID and Iran-US Claims Tribunal decisions dealing with a similar issue. The tribunal concluded that it was:

> satisfied that those provisions (of the ICSID Rules and of Iran-US Claims Settlement Declaration) as interpreted and applied by the decision which have been referred to, reflect a general principle as to the nature of the close connection which a counterclaim must have with the primary claim if a tribunal with jurisdiction over the primary claim is to have jurisdiction over the counterclaim.[10]

Having concluded that the respondent was trying to bring a third party into the proceedings, with which *Saluka* had a close relationship through a share purchase

6. *Klockner Company v. Republic of Cameroon*, Award, 21 October 1983: ICSID Reports, vol. 2, at 17.
7. *Ibid.*, 65.
8. *Ibid.*, 9.
9. *Saluka, supra* n. 2.
10. *Ibid.*, 17.

agreement, the tribunal decided that it did not have jurisdiction to hear the counterclaims as there was not enough of a close connection between them and the primary claim.[11]

In *American Bell International Inc. v. The Government of the Islamic Republic of Iran, et al.*,[12] the primary claim was based on two counts. The respondent presented counterclaims based on a different contract between the parties. The tribunal upheld its jurisdiction over the counterclaims. It found that all the contracts involved the same project, and the linkage between them was sufficiently strong to make them from one single transaction. A similar conclusion was reached in *Westinghouse Electric Corp v. The Islamic Republic of Iran, et al.*[13]

The interdependent and essential unity of the instruments on which the original claim and counterclaim were based in those cases resulted in the tribunals holding that they had jurisdiction over the counterclaims. This may be contrasted with other cases in which tribunals have found that there was no sufficient connection between the claims and the counterclaims to justify it having jurisdiction over the counterclaims. In *Owens Corning Fiberglass Corp v. The Government of Iran, et al.*,[14] the primary claim was based on a licensing agreement between the parties. A counterclaim was submitted based on a separate licensing agreement. The Iran-US Claims Tribunal declined jurisdiction over the counterclaim because each licensing agreement was stated to constitute the entire transaction to which it related, from which the tribunal concluded that they could not be treated as together constituting the 'same transaction' over which the tribunal would have had jurisdiction. In *Morrison-Knudsen Pacific Ltd v. The Ministry of Roads and Transportation, et al.*,[15] the US-Iran Claims Tribunal reached a similar conclusion in relation to three contracts between the parties because, although they related to a single motorway project, they could not be viewed as a single transaction since they were executed on different dates and involved different services to be performed on different dates, and where findings made with respect to claims and defences raised in connection with one contract would have no effect on claims and defences on the other contracts.

The tribunal in *Saluka* found that Article 19.3 of the UNCITRAL Rules, Articles 25(1) and 46 of the ICSID Convention and Article II(1) of the US-Iran Claims Settlement Declaration all reflect essentially the same requirement. Further, the tribunal observed that the claim must arise out of the 'same contract' (UNCITRAL Rules 19.3) or must arise 'directly out of an investment' (ICSID Article 25(1)) and 'directly out of the subject matter of the dispute' (ICSID Article 46) or must arise 'out of the same contract,

11. *Ibid.*, 18.
12. *American Bell International Inc. v. The Government of the Islamic Republic of Iran*, Interlocutory Award No. ITL 41-48-3, 11 June 1984, 6 Iran-US CTR 74 at 83–84.
13. *Westinghouse Electric Corp v. The Islamic Republic of Iran et al.*, Interlocutory Award No. ITL 67-389-2, 12 February 1987, 14 Iran-US CTR 104.
14. *Owens Corning Fiberglass Corp v. The Government of Iran et al.*, Interlocutory Award No. ITL 18-113-2, 13 May 1983, 2 Iran-US CTR 322 at 324.
15. *Morrison-Knudsen Pacific Ltd v. The Ministry of Roads and Transportation et al.*, Award No. 143-127-3, 13 July 1984, 7 Iran-US CTR 54 at 82–84.

transaction or occurrence that constitute the subject matter of [the primary] claims' (Article II(1) of the Claims Settlement Declaration).[16]

These provisions and application of the decisions of the Iran-US Claims Tribunal reflect a general legal principle of the close connection test. The tribunal noted that there must be a close connection between the counterclaim and the primary claim if it ever has a jurisdiction over the counterclaim.

The tribunal in *Saluka* found that the respondent's counterclaim involved non-compliance with the general law of the Czech Republic. Therefore, it could not be regarded as constituting an indivisible whole with the primary claim. Consequently, the disputes underlying counterclaim fell within the ambit of the Czech law rather than the investment protection procedures under the treaty. On this basis, the tribunal concluded that it had no jurisdiction to hear the respondent's counterclaim due to the lack of a sufficiently close connection between the counterclaim and the subject matter of the original claim.

In *Paushok v. Mongolia,*[17] the respondent asserted several counterclaims in relation to the claimants' gold mining operation in Mongolia. First, the claimants allegedly had violated their obligation under licence agreement to extract gold in an efficient and effective manner. This caused a loss in Mongolia's tax revenue, loss of employment of its nationals and other benefits. Second, the claimants allegedly violated their environmental obligations towards Mongolia. Third, the claimants owed damages for gold smuggling. In response to the counterclaims, the claimant argued that the UNCITRAL Tribunal lacked jurisdiction *rationae materiae* because Mongolia's counterclaims were not sufficiently connected to the claimant's claims because these counterclaims arose under the municipal laws of Mongolia and from different occurrences than the claimant's claims.[18] Through the counterclaims the respondent sought to extend the extraterritorial application and enforcement of its public laws, and in particular its tax law, to individuals or entities not subject to, and not having accepted to submit to, Mongolian public law and its courts. Thus, if the arbitral tribunal extended its jurisdiction to the counterclaims, it would be acquiescing to a possible exorbitant extension of Mongolia's legislative jurisdiction without any legal basis under international law to do so, because the generally accepted principle is the non-extraterritorial enforceability of national public laws and specifically of national tax laws.[19]

For these reasons, the tribunal found that the respondent's counterclaims lacked a close connection with the primary claim. Therefore, the counterclaims failed to be decided according to the Mongolian legislation and regulation than the Mongolia-Russia BIT.[20] In short, the tribunal decided that it had no jurisdiction over any of the respondent's counterclaims.

16. *Saluka, supra* n. 2, at 17.
17. *Sergei Paushok et al v. The Government of Mongolia*, UNCITRAL, Award, 28 April 2011.
18. *Ibid.*, 163.
19. *Ibid.*, 166.
20. Agreement on Encouragement and Reciprocal Protection of Investments between the Government of Russian Federation and the Government of Mongolia, signed on 29 November 1995 (entered into force on 26 January 2006) ('Mongolia-Russia BIT').

In *Urbaser v. Argentina*,[21] the respondent based its counterclaim on the ground that the Argentine Republic had suffered damages as a result of the claimant's administration of the concession for water and sewage services to be provided in the province of Buenos Aries. The counterclaim rested on the assertion that the claimant failed to make the investment it had agreed to make, which was to provide drinking water and sewage services. The claimant submitted that the counterclaim had no basis in the Spain-Argentine BIT and therefore did not relate to a 'dispute in connection with an investment within the meaning of the BIT' as required in Article X(1) of the BIT. Further, the claimant argued that all of the respondent's claims were based on Argentine domestic law and related to the Regulatory Framework and the Concession Contract.

Regarding the interconnectedness requirement, the tribunal observed that the factual link between the counterclaim and the principal claim was manifest under the BIT. This was because both the principal claim and counterclaim were based on the same investment. Since the counterclaim was not subject to the domestic law of Argentina, the tribunal was satisfied that it had jurisdiction over the counterclaim. The tribunal accepted the respondent's submission that the claimant's failure to provide the necessary investment caused a violation of the fundamental right for access to water. Therefore, the claimant's failure to provide access to water defeated the purpose of the investment agreed upon in the Regulatory Framework and the Concession Contract. In the words of the tribunal:

> It would be wholly inconsistent to rule on Claimant's claim in relation to their investment in one sense and to have a separate proceeding where compliance with the commitment for funding may be ruled upon in a different way. Reasonable administration of justice cannot tolerate such a potential inconsistent outcome ... Article X of the BIT provides for a possibility of a host State submitting a claim or a counterclaim to international arbitration. Therefore, when seized with such a claim, the Tribunal must assume its competence provided that Respondent submits a claim based *prima facie* on a dispute relating to an investment covered by the BIT and to facts that if established as alleged may constitute violations of rights and obligations that are within the scope of the arbitration agreement governed by Article X.[22]

The tribunal concluded that it has jurisdiction to deal with the respondent's counterclaim in accordance with Articles 25 and 46 of the ICSID Convention. The tribunal's finding was fortified through Article X of the BIT, which allows the respondent to raise a counterclaim. Neutral language encompassed in Article X of the BIT clearly allows 'either party' to submit a dispute in connection with an investment to arbitration. Unless the arbitration clause is drafted in a more narrow manner, Article X of the BIT did not restrict the respondent from submitting a counterclaim as long as a dispute submitted was connected to the investment within the meaning of the BIT.

21. *Urbaser SA v. The Argentine Republic*, ICSID Case No. ARB/07/26, Award, 8 December 2016.
22. *Ibid.*, 307.

§11.05 THE REQUIREMENT OF EXPRESS CONSENT IN THE BIT

Traditionally, unless the parties provide express consent in the BIT, the tribunal will not exercise jurisdiction to hear counterclaims. In this regard, consent by both parties is an indispensable condition for the exercise of the tribunal's jurisdiction. In *Saluka*,[23] the claimant argued that the respondent's counterclaim was directed against Nomura, which was a legal entity incorporated in the UK that had not consented to be a party to the arbitration. The claimant placed primary reliance on the fact that while the tribunal had jurisdiction over Saluka, which was constituted under the law of the Netherlands, it had no jurisdiction *ratione personae* over Nomura. The claimants argued that the tribunal, being established under a Czech-Netherland treaty, did not have jurisdiction over entities of a third nationality without the express consent of all parties.

The claimant also denied the tribunal's jurisdiction over the counterclaim *rationae materiae*. In the claimant's view, the UNCITRAL Rules did not allow counterclaims because Article 19.3 only allowed counterclaims arising out of the same legal instrument containing the reference to arbitration. In contrast, the respondent's counterclaim was not based on the treaty provisions which formed the basis of the claimant's claims. Furthermore, the treaty could not be assimilated to the 'contract' referenced in Article 19.3. The law required the presence of symmetry between a primary claim and the counterclaim, which must be grounded in the same legal instrument. The respondent's offer of arbitration, contained in Article 8 of the treaty, was only accepted by the claimant in respect of the claims based on the treaty, which limited the parties' mutual consent to arbitration. In any event, the respondent had failed to establish the necessary close connection between its counterclaim and the primary investment dispute before the tribunal. Policy considerations concerning the alleged advantages of economy and efficiency being best served by allowing the respondent's counterclaim were insufficient to override the principle that the scope of the tribunal's jurisdiction is determined by the scope of the parties' consent.

In *Spyridon Roussalis v. Romania*,[24] the respondent argued that when the claimant resorted to ICSID arbitration for the settlement of his claims, he agreed to settle all disputes relating to his investment, including the counterclaim. By submitting his claim to ICSID, he accepted Romania's offer to arbitrate contained in the BIT in accordance with the ICSID Convention and Rules, which included the possibility that he would be required to arbitrate the closely related counterclaims. Moreover, after urging that the respondent to terminate the two cases pending before the Romanian court and rely instead on ICSID to resolve the share pledge and nullification disputes, the claimant could not dispute that he had consented to arbitration of the disputes in question.[25]

The *Roussalis* Tribunal held that under the system created by the ICSID Convention, consent by both parties was an indispensable condition for the exercise of the Centre's jurisdiction. The Convention only requires that consent be in writing, leaving

23. *Saluka*, *supra* n. 2.
24. *Spyridon Roussalis v. Romania*, ICSID Case No. ARB 06/1, 7 December 2011.
25. *Ibid.*, 127.

the parties otherwise free to choose the manner in which to express their consent. The investor's consent to the BIT's arbitration clause could only exist in relation to counterclaims if such counterclaims came within the consent of the host State as expressed in the BIT.

In *Urbaser*,[26] the claimants submitted that the Argentine Republic did not have a right to submit a claim under the BIT for the additional reason that the claimants did not consent to such an extension of the arbitral proceedings. Accordingly, the scope of the consent expressed by the investor became an essential element, because it determined whether the counterclaim was within the scope of the tribunal's competence. Neither the request for arbitration nor its registration within ICSID was proof of the claimant's consent concerning a counterclaim. As decided in *Roussalis*,[27] the existence of the parties' consent must be determined on the basis of instruments other than the ICSID Convention itself, Article 46 of the Convention not being sufficient.

In *Antoine Goetz and others v. Republic of Burundi*,[28] the tribunal took a different approach from the *Roussalis* Tribunal, which required the existence of express consent by the parties to establish the tribunal's jurisdiction in respect of counterclaims. The dispute in *Goetz* arose out of an order through which the commercial activities of the claimants were stopped, leading to the closure of several locally incorporated companies. The respondent sought by counterclaim USD 1 million from the claimants for their banks' failure to honour the terms of a free-zone certificate. The claim and counterclaim were based on the convention between the Belgium-Luxembourg Economic Union and the Republic of Burundi regarding the reciprocal encouragement and protection of investments dated 13 April 1989. The claimants contested the competence of the tribunal by submitting that the treaty did not establish the right of a State to assert counterclaims. It is also contended, based on *jurisprudence constante*, that counterclaims could not be based on BITs. The respondent replied that it had the right to assert a counterclaim if it fulfilled the conditions pursuant to Article 40 of the ICSID Arbitration Rule. The respondent also submitted that the jurisprudence confirmed the competence of the tribunal and the admissibility of the counterclaim.

The *Goetz* Tribunal held that it was not relevant that the treaty did not contain any provision giving competence to the tribunal to hear counterclaim. It concluded that because the disputing parties had consented to arbitrate any kind of dispute related to an investment, the tribunal was competent to hear the counterclaim. The *Goetz* Tribunal focused its analysis on the wording of the dispute resolution provision in Article 8(1)(b)[29] of the treaty and on the fact that the counterclaim was related to an investment. Article 8(1)(b) provided that 'a dispute related to an investment is defined as a dispute concerning', among others, 'the interpretation or the application of

26. *Urbaser, supra* n. 21.
27. *Roussalis, supra* n. 24.
28. *Antione Goetz and others v. Republic of Burundi*, ICSID Case No. ARB/01/02, Award (21 June 2012). *See also* Andrea Marco Steingruber, '*Antoine Goetz and others v. Republic of Burundi:* Consent and Arbitral Competence to Hear Counterclaims in Treaty-based ICSID Arbitrations', 28 *ICSID Review*, 291–300 (2013).
29. Belgium-Luxembourg Economic Union and the Republic of Burundi, dated 13 April 1989.

investment authorisations granted by host State authorities that govern foreign investments'. The tribunal's decision in *Goetz* made it possible for the counterclaim to be based on the treaty without being expressly mentioned therein because the general consent of the host State to arbitrate was sufficient. Accordingly, the requirement that the treaty shall contain express consent to submit counterclaim was less relevant because the applicable rules allowed assertion of a counterclaim.

§11.06 SOURCES OF THE INVESTOR'S OBLIGATIONS

Tribunals in the past have distinguished the investor's obligations in terms of a general obligation under the host-State law and obligations arising out of an investment agreement. In essence, the tribunal's competence *rationae materiae* is only applicable to the sources of an investor's obligations that derive from the investment treaty. The *Saluka* Tribunal cited approvingly, for example, the Iran-US Claims Tribunal decision:

> When claims are based on contracts the Tribunal has consistently held that it has no jurisdiction over counterclaims seeking Iranian taxes or social security premiums allegedly owed by the claimant and attributable to the performance of those contracts. The reason is that such counterclaims arise from provision of Iranian law, not from the contracts. Even when the contract contained clauses requiring the claimant to comply with Iranian tax and social security laws, it was the law, not the contract that was the source of the obligations.[30]

Another case is *Amco v. Indonesia*,[31] decided by the ICSID tribunal, to whose decision Articles 25(1) and 46 of the ICSID Convention were relevant. Amco made an investment in Indonesia relating to its development of a hotel and office block on a site in Indonesia. Problems arose and Amco initiated an ICSID arbitration claiming damages arising from the seizure of its investment and the cancellation by Indonesia of the associated investment licence. After the first award on the merits had been annulled, the case was resubmitted to a new ICSID tribunal. In those new proceedings, Indonesia asserted a counterclaim based on alleged tax fraud by Amco. While both parties and the tribunal agreed that tax claims might be within its jurisdiction, the tribunal observed that the immediate issue was:

> whether this particular claim falls within Article 25(1) of the ICSID Convention. In answering this question, the Tribunal believes that it is correct to distinguish between rights and obligations that are applicable to legal or natural persons who are within the reach of a host State's jurisdiction, as a matter of general law; and rights and obligations that are applicable to an investor as a consequence of an investment agreement entered into with that host state. Legal disputes relating to the latter will fall under Article 25(1) of the Convention. Legal disputes concerning the former in principle fall to be decided by the appropriate procedures in the relevant jurisdiction unless the general law generates an investment dispute under the Convention.

30. G.H. Aldrich, *The Jurisprudence of the Iran-United States Claims Tribunal* (Clarendon Press, 1996) at 166.
31. *Amco Asia Corporation and others v. Republic of Indonesia*, Resubmitted Case, Decision on Jurisdiction, 10 May 1988; ICSID Reports, vol. 132, 543.

> The Tribunal held that the obligation not to engage in tax fraud is clearly a general obligation of law in Indonesia. It was not specially contracted for in the investment agreement and does not arise directly out of the investment. For these reasons the Tribunal finds the claim of tax fraud beyond its competence *rationae materiae.*[32]

In *Paushok,*[33] the tribunal examined Article 19(3) of the UNCITRAL Arbitration Rules, which states that 'the respondent may make a counterclaim arising out of the same contracts or rely on a claim arising out of the same contract for the purpose of a set off'.[34] Article 19(3) states the right to assert a counterclaim in the context of a contractual relationship, which is not the situation in *Paushok*, where the relationship was based upon a treaty between two States. For the tribunal to consider its jurisdiction over the counterclaim, it depended on whether there was a close connection between the counterclaims and the primary claim or whether the counterclaims were covered by the general law of the respondent. If the respondent's counterclaim was closely connected with the primary claim, then it established the tribunal's jurisdiction over the counterclaims. However, the tribunal lacked jurisdiction if the counterclaims fell within the ambit of the host State's general law.

Unlike the situation expressly covered by the wording of Article 19(3) of the UNCITRAL Arbitration Rules, the respondent's counterclaims alleging the claimants' unpaid tax and fees did not arise out of an investment contract or other contract to which the foreign investor was a party. More importantly, the counterclaims arose out of Mongolian public law and exclusively raised issues of non-compliance with Mongolian public law, including the tax laws of Mongolia. All these issues squarely fell within the scope of the exclusive jurisdiction of Mongolian courts and therefore were governed by Mongolian public law. Accordingly, the respondent's counterclaims did not constitute an indivisible part of the claimant's claims based on the BIT and international law. Neither had it shown a reasonable nexus between the claimant's claims and the counterclaims to justify the exercise of the tribunal's jurisdiction established under the BIT over the counterclaims. Based on the foregoing reasons, the *Paushok* Tribunal declined to exercise its jurisdiction over any of the respondent's counterclaims.

§11.07 UNILATERAL CHARACTER OF BITs

Another stumbling block to a counterclaim is associated with a unilateral character of the BIT itself. It is often argued that because the object and purpose of the BIT seeks to protect the investment, it provides no basis whatsoever for the host State to assert counterclaims. In other words, the BIT is not designed for the host State to present its counterclaims against the investor. Traditionally, a BIT imposes no obligation on the investors, only on the host State. Therefore, while the BIT does specify that the applicable law is the BIT itself, counterclaims fall outside the tribunal's jurisdiction.

32. *Ibid.*, 565.
33. *Paushok, supra* n. 17.
34. *Ibid.*, 164.

In *Roussalis*, the dispute arose out of the Greece-Romania BIT. The respondent asserted counterclaims against the claimant and his companies, Continent SRL and Continent SA, arising out of the failure of the claimant and Continent SRL to make the USD 1.4 million investment on which the claimant based his investment claim. The central factual issue related to this counterclaim was whether Continent SRL failed to invest USD 1.4 million in Continent SA. In addition, the respondent sought an order from the tribunal requiring Continent SRL to pay damages in a sum representing the value of all funds and assets of Continent SA that were misappropriated by Continent SRL and/or the claimant after privatization. The respondent asked the tribunal to hold Continent SRL jointly and severely liable for those damages.

According to the respondent, Article 46 of the ICSID Convention guaranteed Romania's right to arbitrate a closely related counterclaim. Indeed, once an investment dispute was submitted to ICSID, Article 9(4) of the BIT required that all aspects of the dispute be decided in accordance 'with the provision of this Agreement [BIT] and the applicable rules and principles of international law'.[35] The applicable rules and principles of international law necessarily included the Convention in its entirety, including Article 46 which governed relations between Romania and Greece and their respective nationals with respect to BIT arbitrations. The respondent argued that because there was no explicit exclusion of counterclaims in the treaty, the claimant failed to establish that respondent was precluded from asserting a counterclaim. Indeed, there was no ICSID precedent requiring an explicit authorization in the BIT as a precondition for asserting a counterclaim. In reply, the claimant argued that the treaty provided obligations owed by its contracting States to an investor and not the other way round. Accordingly, the treaty restricted the ability of the State to file a counterclaim.

In light of these submissions, the Greece-Romania BIT in *Roussalis* provided in Article 9 that 'disputes between an investor ... and the other Contracting Party concerning *an obligation of the latter* under this Agreement, in relation to *an investment of the former*, shall if possible be settled', or '*the investor concerned* may submit the dispute' to arbitration.[36] The majority of the *Roussalis* Tribunal found this was a narrow offer to arbitrate relating only to investor claims, not a consent to arbitrate State counterclaims. Therefore, it covered only obligations 'under this Agreement' (i.e., those imposed on States), but not obligations imposed on investors under local law or contract. In reaching its decision, the tribunal was guided by Article 31 of the Vienna Convention on the Law of Treaty 1969 and the ICSID decisions quoted in *Amco v. Indonesia*.[37] The wording of Article 9(1) of the BIT to 'disputes ... concerning an obligation of the latter' undoubtedly limits jurisdiction to claims brought by investors

35. *Roussalis, supra* n. 24 at 123–124.
36. *Ibid.*, 142 (emphasis added).
37. *See also Amco Asia et al v. Indonesia*, Decision on Jurisdiction, 25 September 1983, 23 I.L.M. 359 (1984). The *Amco* Tribunal held that:

> A convention to arbitrate is not to be construed restrictively, nor as a matter of fact, broadly or liberally. It is to be construed in a way which leads to find out and to respect the common will of the parties ... Moreover, ... any convention, including conventions

about obligations of the host State. Accordingly, the BIT did not provide for counterclaims to be introduced by the host State in relation to obligations of the investor. The meaning of the 'dispute' was confined to the scope of compliance by the State with its obligations under the BIT. Hence, the BIT imposed no obligations on investors, only on contracting States. The *Roussalis* Tribunal concluded that a claimant's mere filing at ICSID was insufficient in and of itself to create consent to counterclaims. The tribunal's reason was that 'the scope of the consent' of the parties in Article 46 must be determined by reference to instruments external to the Convention, such as by the dispute resolution clause contained in the BIT.

A shift is beginning to take place where the tribunal has found its jurisdiction over the counterclaim based on a much broader treaty language. Therefore, the unilateral character of a BIT, which earlier favoured the investor, is now gradually being interpreted in a more neutral fashion. This different approach is illustrated in *Urbaser*,[38] where the respondent's counterclaim was based on the damage suffered by the Argentine Republic as a result of the claimant's failure to make the investment concerning water and sewage services.

In response to the counterclaim, the claimant submitted that the asymmetric nature of BITs prevents a State from invoking any right based on such a treaty, not even a right to submit a counterclaim against an investor. In support of its submission, the claimant relied on the general proposition that the aim of the BIT was to protect the investor, but it was never intended to allow the host State to submit counterclaims. The claimant further submitted that investment treaties do not impose obligations upon investors and accordingly, host States cannot rely on the violation of the provision of any such treaty as the basis to sue an investor. Such a right would run counter to the object and purpose of treaty arbitration, which is to grant the investors a one-sided right of quasi-judicial review of national regulatory system.

The *Urbaser* Tribunal dismissed the claimant's argument as to the asymmetric nature of the BIT. The tribunal found that Article X of the BIT contains a simply worded dispute resolution provision, which is completely neutral as to the identity of the parties who can submit an investment dispute. This view found support in Article X(2), which states that when no settlement had been reached within six months from the date 'on which *one of the parties* to the dispute' instigated it, 'it has, at the request of the other party', to be submitted to the competent tribunals to the host State. Moreover, Article X(3) states that in certain circumstances, the dispute may be submitted to an international arbitral tribunal 'at the request of *either party* to the dispute'. Looking at the language of Article X in its entirety, the BIT does not differentiate between the claimant and the respondent. Consequently, either the investor or the host State can be a party by submitting a dispute in connection with an investment to arbitration. The neutrality of these provisions prompted the tribunal to accept the possibility that the respondent may raise a counterclaim under the BIT. The tribunal in *Urbaser* found that

to arbitrate, should be construed in good faith, that is to say by taking into account the consequences of the commitments the parties may be considered as having reasonably and legitimately envisaged.

38. *Urbaser, supra* n. 21.

because Argentina's counterclaim was related to the investment and the same concession, there was enough support to establish a connection between the investor's claim and the counterclaim. The tribunal concluded that it had jurisdiction to consider the respondent's counterclaim in accordance with Articles 25 and 46 of the ICSID Convention and Article X of the BIT.

In all of these cases, none of the counterclaims succeeded on the merits. However, the case of *Burlington v. Ecuador*[39] broke the tradition of failure. There, the tribunal ruled in favour of the host State on its counterclaims. In *Burlington*, the tribunal admitted it had jurisdiction to hear the counterclaims brought by the State for violation of human rights and environmental damage. The *Burlington* Tribunal awarded USD 39.2 million against the investor for environmental damage.[40] Another recent case which the tribunal allowed the respondent's counterclaim is *Perenco v. Ecuador*.[41] In that case, Ecuador presented the environmental counterclaim on the existence of an 'environmental catastrophe' in the two oil blocks situated in the country's Amazonian rainforest that had been worked by the consortium under Parenco's operatorship. Ecuador presented counterclaims against Burlington and Perenco, who were the joint and several contractors for both blocks. They were referred to as 'the Consortium' and Perenco managed the blocks on behalf of the consortium. In each of the arbitrations, Ecuador filed counterclaims seeking substantial compensation for environmental damage part of the Amazon rainforest affected by the work of Perenco, as well damages for the alleged failure to return the blocks' infrastructure in reasonable condition as required by the Participation Contracts. Ecuador raised its counterclaims against Burlington on 17 January 2011, and on 5 December 2011 raised the same counterclaims against Perenco. The tribunal awarded Perenco damages of approximately USD 449 million in respect of Ecuador's interference with its interests in the two Amazonian oil blocks. At the same time, it awarded Ecuador damages of USD 54 million pursuant to its counterclaim for environmental remediation. This trend is likely to continue and shows that investment tribunals are ready and willing to hear a counterclaim when dealing with investor wrongdoing.

Most international investment tribunals have not recognized jurisdiction over counterclaims introduced before them in the absence of an explicit agreement between the parties to submit the counterclaim. However, some tribunals recently have asserted jurisdiction over a counterclaim, in particular the tribunals in *Urbaser v. Argentina*, *Burlington v. Ecuador* and *Perenco v. Ecuador*, all within the framework of the ICSID Convention and the three BITs (Spain-Argentina, USA-Ecuador and France-Ecuador, respectively).

In *Burlington* and *Perenco*, jurisdiction was not at issue because the parties reached an agreement that the arbitration was 'the appropriate forum for the final resolution of the counterclaims arising out of the investment made by Burlington Resources and its affiliates in Blocks 7 and 21, so as to ensure maximum judicial

39. *Burlington Resources Inc. v. Republic of Ecuador*, ICSID Case No. ARB/08/05, 7 February 2017.
40. *Ibid.*, 462.
41. *Perenco Ecuador Limited v. The Republic of Ecuador*, ICSID Case No. ARB/08/6. The Award on Quantum dated 27 September 2019.

economy and consistency'.[42] Consequently, the investor did not challenge the tribunal's jurisdiction to decide the counterclaim. Additionally, the tribunal mentioned Article 46 of the ICSID Convention, which empowers ICSID tribunals to decide 'counterclaims arising directly out of the subject matter of the dispute provided they are within the scope of the consent of the parties and are otherwise within the jurisdiction of the Centre'. Thus, the consent of the parties was explicit and unambiguous.

§11.08 SUBSTANTIVE AND PROCEDURAL NON-COMPLIANCE

Recently, the host State's counterclaims have been challenged on the basis of pleading deficiencies. In some cases, the claimant has argued that the counterclaim should be dismissed due to non-compliance with substantive and procedural requirements contained in the applicable arbitration rules. The argument related to substantive and procedural non-compliance was invoked in *Paushok*.[43] With respect to the standard of pleadings, the claimant in *Paushok* put forward two submissions. First, Articles 18(2) and 19(4) of the UNCITRAL Rules require that each counterclaim be specific enough to enable the claimants to provide a reply in their statement of defence against counterclaims. Second, the respondent's statement of counterclaim did not allow the claimant to adequately reply because the respondent had failed to explain its legal arguments and proposed evidentiary support.[44] In addition, the claimant submitted that the tribunal did not have jurisdiction to hear any of the counterclaims. Moreover, the claimant argued that all the counterclaims were undeveloped and poorly drafted to such an extent that they did not meet the basic pleading requirement in Articles 18(2) and 19(4) of the UNCITRAL Rules.

In the recent case of *Aven*,[45] the respondent's counterclaim is based on the damages suffered by Costa Rica as a result of the claimants' operation of the Las Olas Project. The respondent argued that the claimants undertook works that adversely impacted the Las Olas Project Site, affecting the environment. The respondent argued that the tribunal had jurisdiction over the counterclaim on two grounds. First, the text of the Dominican Republic-Central American Free Trade Agreement (DR-CAFTA)[46] envisaged the possibility for respondent States to bring counterclaims against investors for misconduct for which they are liable. Second, reasons of procedural economy and efficiency justified that the claim and its counterclaim should be resolved in the same proceeding.

The respondent argued that Article 10.16 of the DR-CAFTA was completely neutral as to the identity of the claimant or the respondent in an investment dispute arising between the parties, thereby allowing a State party to sue an investor in relation to a dispute concerning an investment in that country. Accordingly, the respondent

42. *Burlington, supra* n. 39 at 462.
43. *Paushok, supra* n. 17.
44. *Ibid.*, 163.
45. *Aven, supra* n. 3 at 230.
46. The Dominican Republic-Central American Free Trade Agreement (DR-CAFTA), signed on 5 August 2004 (entered into force for Costa Rica on 1 January 2009).

believed that the text of the DR-CAFTA encompassed counterclaims by respondent States within the jurisdiction of the tribunal. Despite concluding that it had prima facie jurisdiction over the counterclaim, the tribunal decided to dismiss the respondent's counterclaim due to a failure to satisfy the procedural requirements in Articles 20 and 21 of the UNCITRAL Arbitration Rules. Similarly, the tribunal in *Hamester v. Ghana*[47] found that although the treaty provided consent to arbitrate counterclaims, the respondent failed to particularize its counterclaims in an adequate manner.

§11.09 ENHANCING THE STATE'S ACCESS TO JUSTICE: A WAY FORWARD

Having discussed the legal impediments that impair State's access to justice, it is time to chart the way forward. There are certain approaches that a State could take to improve the standing of its counterclaim assertion. First, the right of a State to bring a counterclaim arises from a broad and clear language of BIT.[48] Hence, any BIT should expressly preserve the State's right to bring a counterclaim against the investor. Despite the existence of treaties that provide broadly for arbitration of 'all' or 'any' investment disputes, it often leads to confusion when there is distinguishing between 'claim' and 'counterclaim'. Therefore, a question arises regarding the intention of the drafters: Whether they intended to consent to arbitrate their claims as well as counterclaims. One way of circumventing this interpretation problem is to provide an express provision in the BIT that allows a State to assert counterclaims. By inserting an express provision on counterclaims, it will provide a legal certainty that affirms the State's right to bring a counterclaim. By the same token, express provision for a counterclaim will ease the admissibility question during the jurisdiction phase of an arbitration. In this regard, the express provision will provide a legal basis for the tribunal to exercise its jurisdiction over a counterclaim. Therefore, the counterclaim will be heard at the merits stage without going through complicated arguments on its admissibility. It will potentially be a deterrent for an investor to challenge the State-asserted counterclaim on jurisdictional grounds, knowing that the tribunal will eventually derive its jurisdiction from the express provision in the treaty. In the end, it will enhance the efficiency of the process and provide cost-effective arbitration to the parties.

Second, the parties may incorporate 'express consent' to arbitrate a counterclaim in the BIT from the outset. Once express consent is incorporated in the BIT, it will overcome the tribunal's jurisdictional barrier over counterclaim caused by the lack of express consent. As illustrated by the ICSID tribunal's awards in cases such as *Saluka, Roussalis* and *Urbaser*, the issue of consent has been a significant barrier for a State to assert a counterclaim. This is due to the unilateral character of a BIT that seeks to protect the investor and thus provide a remedy in cases where the host State is found to be in violation of its obligations. However, a trend is emerging in which express

47. *Gustav F W Hamester GmbH & Co KG v. Republic of Ghana*, ICSID Case No. ARB/07/24, 18 June 2012.
48. On the new Indian model BIT, *see* G. Hanessian and K. Duggal, 'The Final India Model BIT: Is This the Change the World Wishes to See?' 32 *ICSID Review-FILJ*, 216–226 (2017).

consent is incorporated in the new generation of BITs. Although limited in scope, the incorporation of express consent in the treaty language at least acknowledges that the State has a legitimate right to assert counterclaims except for any explicitly excluded circumstances. The tribunal in *Aven* found that the language of the DR-CAFTA[49] fell within the scope of parties' consent to arbitrate a counterclaim. In the words of the tribunal:

> It follows that, except for a counterclaim by a Respondent State alleging that 'Claimant has received or will receive indemnification or other compensation for all or part of the alleged damages pursuant to an insurance or guarantee contract,' Respondent's right to counterclaim under the Treaty is contemplated and falls within the scope of jurisdiction of a tribunal constituted under the Treaty.[50]

Such a model clause has its origin in North American Free Trade Agreement (NAFTA)[51] and was adopted in treaties concluded in the 1990s. The trade negotiators continued to apply similar or identical provisions in the new generation of BITs. For instance, nearly similar language with the DR-CAFTA was identified in Argentina-Japan BIT concluded in 2018.[52] Another treaty, the Kuwait-Singapore BIT, contains the same prohibition, but articulates it in a more permissive manner.[53] This provision appears to allow a State to assert a counterclaim provided that it is not based on the investor's right to receive indemnification from an insurance contract. The broad language of this provision affirms a State's right to assert a counterclaim, which negates the issue of the parties' consent. Article 9.19 of the Comprehensive and

49. *Aven*, *supra* n. 3, para. 693. Art. 10.20.7 of DR-CAFTA provides that 'A Respondent may not assert as a defense, counterclaim, right of set-off, or for any other reason that the Claimant has received or will received indemnification or other compensation for all or part of the alleged damages pursuant to an insurance or guarantee contract.'
50. *Ibid.*, para. 694.
51. Similar provisions prohibiting State defences or counterclaims based on insurance or guarantee contracts appeared in NAFTA (entered into force on 1 January 1994). Art. 1137.3 provides, 'In an arbitration under this Section, a Party shall not assert, as a defence, counterclaim, right of set off or otherwise, that the disputing investor has received or will receive, pursuant to an insurance or guarantee contract, indemnification or other compensation for all or part of its alleged damages.' *See also* the new United States-Mexico-Canada Free Trade Agreement (USMCA), signed on 30 November 2018. It appears that USMCA has retained the language of Art. 1137.3 of NAFTA. Art. 14.D.7 (Conduct of the Arbitration), clause 8 of USMCA provides that 'a respondent may not assert as a defence, counterclaim, right to set-off, or for any other reason, that the claimant has received or will receive indemnification or other compensation for all or part of the alleged damages pursuant to an insurance or guarantee contract'.
52. Agreement between the Argentine Republic and Japan for the Promotion and Protection of Investment, signed on 1 December 2018 (not yet in force). Art. 25.14 states that 'the Respondent shall not assert, as a defence, counterclaim, right to set off or otherwise, that the Claimant has received or will receive indemnification or other compensation for all or part of the alleged damages pursuant to an insurance or guarantee contract'.
53. Kuwait-Singapore BIT, signed on 5 November 2009 (entered into force on 15 April 2013). Art. 9.6 provides:

    > In any proceeding under this Article, any counterclaim or right of set-off may not be based on the fact that the investor concerned has received or will receive, pursuant to an insurance contract, indemnification or other compensation for all or part of its alleged damages from any third party whomsoever, whether public or private, including such other Contract party and its subdivisions, agencies or instrumentalities.

Progressive Agreement for Trans-Pacific Partnership (CPTPP), for example, provides that 'the Respondent may make a counterclaim in connection with the factual and legal basis of the claim or rely on a claim for the purpose of a set off against the Claimant'.[54]

Some recent treaties not only include an express consent to assertion of a counterclaim but also incorporate a connectedness requirement into that consent. An example is Article 28(4) of the Argentine-UAE BIT, which provides that 'the Respondent may submit a *counter-claim* directly related with the dispute'.[55] Another example is Article 17 of the Slovak Republic-Iran BIT, which provides that 'the Host State may pursue any defense, *counterclaim*, right of set off or other similar claim pursuant to Article 14 of this Agreement in arbitration under this Section'. Further, Article 14(3) of the Slovak Republic-Iran BIT provides that 'the respondent may assert as a defense, *counterclaim*, right of set off or other similar claim that the claimant has not fulfilled its obligations under this Agreement to comply with the Host State law or that it has not taken all reasonable steps to mitigate possible damages'.[56] This treaty language expressly provides for a counterclaim that is directly related to the investment dispute. In this sense, it ties the connectedness requirement to the issue of consent to arbitrate. Thus, it becomes a question of jurisdiction rather than one of admissibility.[57] In terms of the parties' consent to arbitrate, these treaties have made an inroad for a State to assert counterclaims. Through incorporation of express consent in the BIT, a State will be able to avoid the situation of lacking 'mutual consent' previously faced in *Saluka*, *Roussalis* and *Urbaser*.

Third, the State's right to regulate deserves recognition in the BIT. There has been an emerging trend in the new generation of BITs that saw the inclusion of a provision recognizing a State's right to regulate particularly in areas related to public interest. The tribunal in *Aven* acknowledged the treaty language that sought to protect the State's right to regulate and enforce measures that imposed environmental obligation on the investor.[58] The investment chapter in the DR-CAFTA provides that 'nothing in this Chapter shall be construed to prevent a Party from adopting, maintaining or enforcing any measure otherwise consistent with this Chapter that it considers appropriate to ensure that investment activity in its territory is undertaken in manner sensitive to environmental concerns'.[59]

54. The CPTPP, which followed the Trans-Pacific Partnership Agreement (TPP12) after the withdrawal of the United States, was signed on 8 March 2018 in Santiago, Chile, by eleven participating countries: Australia, Brunei Darussalam, Canada, Chile, Japan, Malaysia, Mexico, New Zealand, Peru, Singapore and Vietnam.
55. The Agreement for the Reciprocal Promotion and Protection of Investments between the Argentine Republic and the UAE, signed on 16 April 2018 (not in force).
56. The Agreement between the Slovak Republic and the Islamic Republic of Iran for the Promotion and Reciprocal Protection of Investments, signed on 19 January 2016 (entered into force on 30 August 2018).
57. Yasmine Lahlou, Rainbow Willard and Meredith Craven, 'The Rise of Environmental Counterclaim in Mining Arbitration', *Global Arbitration Review, The Guide to Mining Arbitration-First Edition* 2019.
58. *Aven, supra* n. 3. The tribunal observed at para. 739 that 'under Article 10, Section A of DR-CAFTA, foreign investors have the obligation to abide and comply with the measures taken by the host State to protect the environment'.
59. *See* Art. 10.11 of DR-CAFTA, *supra* n. 46.

The *Aven* Tribunal took the view that this treaty language incorporated the State's domestic environmental measures into the treaty. It determined that the investor who had breached the State's environmental measures was in violation of both domestic and international law. While the treaty did not expressly impose obligations on the investor to protect the host-State environment, the tribunal assimilated the breach of host-State environmental regulation as a breach of the treaty obligation triggering a cause of action for a counterclaim. Similar treaty language also appears in other recent BITs. For example, paragraph 9 of the CPTPP Preamble provides:

> the Parties to this Agreement, resolving to recognise their *inherent right to regulate* and resolve to preserve the flexibility of the Parties to set legislative and regulatory priorities, safeguard public welfare, and protect legitimate public welfare objectives, such as public health, safety, the environment, the conservation of living or non-living exhaustible natural resources, the integrity and stability of the financial system and public morals.[60]

Another example is illustrated in Article 6.3 of the Comprehensive Economic Partnership Agreement between the European Free Trade Association (EFTA) States and the Republic of Ecuador, which provides that 'nothing in this Chapter shall be construed to prevent a party from imposing, maintaining or enforcing measures … necessary to protect human, animal or plant life or health'.[61] Likewise, the Chile-Hong Kong BIT reflects similar phrases giving effect to the State's right to regulate.[62] In short, these new generations of BITs provide an explicit provision, which recognizes the right of State to regulate in areas related to environmental concerns. As a result, it imposes an obligation on the investor to comply with the host State's environmental regulations. In the event of non-compliance, it will give rise to form a legitimate cause of action to assert counterclaim.

Fourth, the BIT has to incorporate a condition relating to the investor's compliance with the domestic law of the host State. In a number of cases, a State relied on a violation of domestic law as a basis for the counterclaims. The tribunals in *Saluka*, *Paushok*, *Spyridon* and *Rusoro v. Venezuela*[63] all dealt with the issue of the investor's

60. Also *see* Art. 9.16 of the CPTPP: Investment and environmental, health and other regulatory objectives, which states:

> Nothing in this Chapter shall be construed to prevent a party from adopting, maintaining or enforcing any measure otherwise consistent with this Chapter that it considers appropriate to ensure that investment activity in its territory is undertaken in a manner sensitive to environmental, health or other regulatory objectives.

61. Comprehensive Economic Partnership Agreement between the EFTA States and the Republic of Ecuador, signed on 25 June 2018.
62. Hong Kong-Chile BIT, signed on 18 November 2016 (entered into force on 14 July 2019). Art. 15.1 provides that 'nothing in this Agreement shall be construed to prevent party from adopting, maintaining or enforcing measure otherwise consistent with this Agreement that it considers appropriate to ensure that investment activity in its area is undertaken in a manner sensitive to environmental, health or other regulatory objectives'.
63. *Rosuro Mining Limited v. The Bolivarian Republic of Venezuela*, ICSID Case No. ARB(AF)/12/5, Award 22 August 2016.

non-compliance with domestic laws, which were the basis for the host State's counterclaims. In all these cases, the tribunals dismissed the counterclaims on the ground that the obligation to comply with domestic law did not arise from the BIT, but rather from the host State's law itself. Because the BIT does not clothe the tribunal with jurisdiction to arbitrate a cause of action arising under domestic law, such counterclaims are not permitted.

Traditionally, the idea has been that 'the arbitration agreement should refer to disputes that can also be brought under domestic law for counterclaims to be within the tribunal's jurisdiction'.[64] In response to this issue, the treaty language should capture the cause of action that is triggered by the investor's violation of domestic law of the host State. This could be done by incorporating the investor's obligation to comply with domestic law into the treaty. The drafters of the recent treaty between the Slovak Republic and Iran have attempted to address this issue by incorporating a provision that expressly allows the State to assert a counterclaim based on a violation of the investor's obligations under the Agreement to comply with host-State law.[65] While the treaty does not impose an explicit obligation on the investor to comply with domestic law, its counterclaim provision at least paves the way for a cause of action once the investor violates the host State's law.

Fifth, the State has to ensure that it complies with the substantive and procedural requirements of the relevant arbitration rules. On several occasions, the tribunal has dismissed counterclaims due to a failure by the respondent to comply with applicable arbitration rules when presenting their pleadings. As discussed above, tribunals in *Paushok*, *Hamester* and *Aven* have dismissed counterclaims on the ground of pleading deficiencies despite finding the admissibility of counterclaims in the first place. This issue has not gone unnoticed among the treaty drafters. For example, the recent Argentine-UAE BIT addressed this issue by expressly providing a pleading standard. In particular, it requires that 'the disputing party shall specify precisely the basis for the counterclaims'.[66] Although it may be a vague and generic requirement, it serves as a reminder that a party should not overlook the importance of preparing specific and explicit counterclaims to meet the standard set out by the arbitration rules. This will reduce the risk of the counterclaims being challenged on the substantive and procedural irregularity grounds.

§11.10 CONCLUSION

After years of failure, a change in the landscape of investment treaty arbitration has occurred. A tribunal now may be prepared to consider counterclaims. In this regard, it is safe to expect a departure from the traditional approach due to the arrival of the new generation of BITs that seek to balance the interests between the host State and the investor. The drafters of recent BITs have learned the lessons of the past and attempted

64. P. Lalive and L. Hanolen, 'On the Availability of Counterclaims in Investment Treaty Arbitration', *Czech Yearbook of International Law*, 41 (2011).
65. *See* Art. 14(3) of the Slovak Republic-the Islamic Republic of Iran, *supra* n. 56.
66. Article 28.4 of the Argentine-UAE BIT, *supra* n. 55.

to bridge the gap in the current BITs. Moreover, the broad language of the new generation of BITs will improve the standing of States to have recourse to counterclaims in ISDS. As a result, it will enhance a State's access to justice while correcting the misconception that ISDS is biased towards the investor. In recent years, there also has been a rise of human rights and environmental counterclaims in cases such as *Urbaser*, *Burlington*, *Perenco* and *Aven*. This trend is likely to continue through substantive reform in the manner BITs are drafted. In the end, all of these developments will contribute to a more predictable and consistent ISDS jurisprudence on counterclaims.

In summary, a way forward for access to justice in ISDS requires the enhancement of a State's right to assert counterclaims through several ways. First, the language of the BITs needs to be expressed in a broad and clear manner to empower a State's assertion of a counterclaim against the investor. As long as the counterclaim is closely connected with the primary claim, the tribunal should find it has jurisdiction because the BIT recognizes the State's right to assert such a counterclaim. Second, an incorporation of express consent to arbitrate counterclaims in the BIT will enable the tribunal to extend its jurisdiction to hear the State's counterclaim in the same proceedings with the investor's claim. Third, increased recognition of a State's right to regulate in areas related to public interest will oblige the investor to comply with the host State's law. In that case, the investor can no longer argue that the sources of its obligations only arise out of the investment agreement but not under host-State law. Hence, the tribunal's jurisdiction is wider where a breach of the host State's law is arbitrable through a counterclaim than merely a submission for a hearing in the domestic courts. Fourth, the BIT has to contain provisions requiring the investor to comply with the host State's laws. This will strike a balance to ensure that a BIT is no longer unilateral towards the protection of an investment, but also reserves the host State's right to assert a counterclaim against the investor. A breach of this obligation gives rise to a counterclaim under the BIT. Finally, a State cannot overlook the importance of compliance with the substantive and procedural requirements of the applicable arbitration rules. Strict compliance with the rules of pleadings set out by the arbitration rules will enhance the prospect of a counterclaim's success.

CHAPTER 12

Time for a Clean Energy Charter Treaty? Examining the Role of ISDS in Promoting and Protecting Renewable Energy Investments

Guillermo Garcia-Perrote & Ella Wisniewski[*]

A pressing need exists for a global reallocation of capital away from high-carbon energy and into low-carbon (primarily, renewable) energy investment to keep global climate and sustainable development goals within reach. This chapter explores the role of the Investor-State Dispute Settlement system, as provided for under the Energy Charter Treaty (ECT), as a means of promoting and protecting investment in the renewable energy sector, by offering investors a viable means to redress regulatory or political risk. While the increased significance of global climate goals arguably requires the adaptation of the ECT, this should not be a 'whole-cloth' reinvention, but rather a modification and supplementation of existing definitions, rules and procedures. Such changes, though having the effect of modernizing the ECT (by reference to the context in which it was originally drafted), would be neutral in nature, and therefore, more likely to be achievable. In particular, it will be important to ensure that ECT protections extend to investments at the forefront of the regulatory and technological landscape, including developments in energy efficiency, storage, transmission and delivery.

* The authors wish to acknowledge the research assistance provided by Jake Lowther, LL.M (Berlin), an Australian-qualified lawyer currently based in Stockholm at Nordic-Baltic law firm, Magnusson.

§12.01 INTRODUCTION

In order to meet the targets set out in the Paris Agreement, as well as future climate and environment protection goals, governments will likely need to implement increasingly dramatic and disruptive measures to reduce carbon emissions. Concerns have been raised that foreign investors in the traditional energy sector will institute Investor-State Dispute Settlement (ISDS) claims to challenge such measures, and that the cumulative effect of such claims will be to deter governments from implementing meaningful political and regulatory reforms. This is the essential premise of the 'regulatory chill' thesis.

However, under the ECT, ISDS is not only available to investors in the traditional energy industry but is also available to investors in the 'clean' (i.e., low-carbon or renewable) energy industry. This chapter examines a proposition which is essentially the inverse of the 'regulatory chill' thesis, at least so far as energy investment is concerned: that the availability of ISDS under the ECT has an important role to play in promoting and protecting investments in the renewable energy sector.[1] This proposition is founded on a number of assumptions, which are explored throughout the chapter, including:

- regulatory and political risk continues to impact the inflow of foreign capital and technology in the renewable energy sector – as discussed in §12.03; and
- the ECT offers an effective means of protecting investments in renewable energy from the impact of adverse regulatory and political change – as discussed in §12.04.

Whether the availability of ISDS under the ECT actually *attracts* investment in the renewable or low-carbon energy sector, in addition to its role in protecting existing investments, is more difficult to assess. This is discussed in §12.05. Finally, this chapter explores:

- in §12.06, whether the ECT could (and indeed, should) be modernized to better protect investments at the forefront of developments in clean energy; and
- in §12.07, whether the relative success of renewable energy investors in enforcing protections under the ECT may cause states to withdraw from the system of ISDS altogether.

1. References to the 'renewable energy sector' are references to the capturing of energy from sources that are naturally replenished on a human timescale, such as sunlight, wind, rain, tides, waves and geothermal heat (and not to other sources of non-fossil fuel energy, such as nuclear). Omar Ellabban, et al., *Renewable energy resources: Current status, future prospects and their enabling technology*, 39 Renewable and Sustainable Energy Reviews 748, 749 (2014).

§12.02 CONTEXT

The discourse surrounding regulatory chill is typically premised on the simplistic assumption that foreign investors are in the business of damaging the environment, and domestic governments are in the business of protecting it.[2] When posited in this way, ISDS is viewed as an impediment to the implementation of environmental policies that would benefit the public interest. There are certainly examples of ISDS cases having arisen in response to environmental protection measures. For example, in 2017, a claim was made (and is presently pending) against Italy under the ECT in relation to the re-introduction of a general ban on oil and gas exploration and production activity within the 12-mile limit of the Italian coastline.[3] However, in recent cases which have involved public interest measures in sensitive policy areas, the deferential approach taken by tribunals indicates that states will be well placed to defend such claims. Indeed, much has been written to rebut the assumptions underlying the notion of regulatory chill, by examining 'state-friendly' readings of various treaty protections, and canvassing the numerous arguments available to governments in order to successfully defend measures implemented to achieve a clear and rational public interest objective.[4]

Moreover, foreign investors do not invariably invoke treaty protections to safeguard environmentally destructive investments. The legislative and regularly measures which host states must defend, in the face of ISDS claims, are not always measures designed to protect the environment. On the contrary, a significant percentage of ISDS claimants in recent years have been renewable energy investors, seeking compensation in response to the scaling back of incentive schemes by European states. In addition to the curbing of carbon emissions from traditional sources of energy (i.e., coal, oil and gas), the achievement of far-reaching climate goals will require governments to promote and facilitate the development of low-carbon energy infrastructure. The International Energy Agency (IEA) has identified an unprecedented need for a

2. *See*, for example, the public statement circulated by civil society groups in opposition to ISDS in CETA, *Stop the Corporate Giveaway* (November 2013), https://www.epsu.org/sites/default/files/article/files/Stop_the_Corporate_Giveaway_-_A_transatlantic_plea_for_sanity_in_the_EU-Canada_CETA_negotiations.pdf; Petition to the European Parliament, European Commission and Member States, *EU: Stop Letting Corporations Trample Our Laws for Profit. End ISDS Now.*, SumOfUs (2019), https://actions.sumofus.org/a/eu-stop-letting-corporations-trample-our-laws-for-profit-end-isds-now; Amandine Van Den Berghe, *Investor-State Dispute Settlement Must Go to Protect Our Environment*, Client Earth (17 May 2019), https://www.clientearth.org/investor-state-dispute-settlement-must-go-to-protect-our-environment/; *Unfair Privileges for Investors*, Friends of the Earth Europe, https://www.foeeurope.org/isds.
3. *Rockhopper Exploration Plc, Rockhopper Italia S.p.A. and Rockhopper Mediterranean Ltd v. Italian Republic* (ICSID Case No. ARB/17/14).
4. *See*, for example, section 7 of the statement published by European Federation for Investment Law and Arbitration (EFILA), *A response to the criticism against ISDS*, EFILA (May 2015), https://efila.org/wp-content/uploads/2015/05/EFILA_in_response_to_the-criticism_of_ISDS_final_draft.pdf.

reallocation of investment capital away from carbon-intensive energy and into low-carbon (primarily, renewable) energy.[5] Indeed, investment has been labelled the 'lifeblood' of the global energy system, and low-carbon investments 'the vehicle for the energy system transformation'.[6] Yet political and regulatory frameworks governing renewable energy investment are notoriously prone to change. In this context, it is timely to critically examine the potential for ISDS, as provided under the ECT, to play an active role in the global clean energy transition.

§12.03 REGULATORY AND POLITICAL RISK IN THE RENEWABLE ENERGY SECTOR

[A] The Need for Further Investment in Low-Carbon Energy

Investment in the renewable energy sector, particularly solar and wind power production, has experienced rapid growth in recent years.[7] However, to chart a course towards achieving the targets espoused by the Paris Agreement, a more dramatic, structural change to the global energy investment portfolio is required. A 2018 study, which drew on six energy-economy models to evaluate future energy-related investment needs, concluded that in order to meet the Paris Agreement targets, low-carbon investments would need to account for more than 50% of all energy supply investments by around 2025, and then climb to 80% or greater by around 2035 (in the 1.5°C pathway) or 2050 (in the 2°C pathway).[8] In other words, annual investments in low-carbon energy would need to overtake fossil investments globally around 2025 or before.[9] Using 'the language of dollars', the authors estimated that:

> to achieve the [Nationally Determined Contribution], 2°C or 1.5°C targets globally, there exists a low-carbon energy and energy efficiency investment 'gap' of approximately 130 billion, 320 billion or 480 billion US dollars per year (to 2030; model averages), respectively, representing upwards of one-quarter of total energy investments otherwise foreseen in a baseline scenario; and for some major economies (such as China and India), up to one-half.[10]

In its 2019 report on World Energy Investment, the IEA similarly observed that 'energy investment is misaligned with where the world appears to be heading, and also far out of step with where it needs to go'.[11] Particularly, it was noted that even taking into account decreased costs in certain areas of the renewables sector, a rapid boost in

5. IEA, *World Energy Investment 2019*, 30–31 (IEA, 2019). 'Low-carbon' energy investment, as defined by the IEA, includes energy efficiency, renewable power, renewables for transport and heat, nuclear, battery storage and carbon capture utilization and storage.
6. David L. McCollum, et al., *Energy investment needs for fulfilling the Paris Agreement and achieving the Sustainable Development Goals*, 3 Nature Energy 589, 589 (2018).
7. The IEA reported that in 2018, investment in low-carbon energy represented approximately 35% of all investments in the global energy system. IEA, *supra* n. 5, at 34.
8. McCollum, et al., *supra* n. 6, at 595.
9. *Ibid.*, 589.
10. *Ibid.*, 589–590.
11. IEA, *supra* n. 5, at 30.

total investment across low-carbon energy supply and efficiency will be required if the goals of the Paris Agreement are to remain in sight.[12] The way forward was summarized as follows:

> To meet long-term sustainability goals in the [Sustainable Development Scenario], even with changing costs, low-carbon investment would need to grow two-and-a-half times by 2030, with its share rising to 65%. Although the needs in networks are comparatively less, the regulated nature of grids points to a need for sustained policy commitment for appropriate levels of investments that supports growing shares of variable renewables.[13]

Despite this pressing demand for a structural shift away from investment in fossil fuels and towards investment in low-carbon energy, the IEA reported that there are 'few signs' of the major reallocation of capital required.[14] The IEA observed that current market and policy signals are failing to adequately incentivise this reallocation of capital,[15] and pointed to an 'insufficient policy focus to address persistent risks' as one reason that investment activity in the low-carbon energy sector is stalling.[16] In this regard, the IEA noted:

> Financing our energy future requires policy makers to better understand the risks faced by investors and to design and implement policies that allow for the efficient allocation and management of these risks, which are key determinants of the cost of capital. Where governments – and in some cases, public financial institutions – provide such frameworks, the private sector responds.[17]

The new investment capital (or reallocation of existing capital) required to fill the identified 'gap' in low-carbon and energy efficiency investment will likely come from a variety of sources. As the authors of the aforementioned study noted, 'funding for individual projects could come from ... businesses, governments, households, banks (private, state-owned, development), multi-lateral climate finance institutions, or via other means. And this funding could be sourced domestically or be provided by foreign entities'.[18]

As such, it is not suggested that foreign direct investment (FDI) will be (or should be) solely responsible for driving the structural shift in energy investment required to meet the Paris Agreement targets. However, it will continue to play a significant role. Yet, according to the United Nations Conference on Trade and Development (UNCTAD), overall global FDI has been on the decline for three consecutive years, and in 2018, reached its lowest level since the global financial crisis.[19] UNCTAD cited declining rates of return, increasingly asset-light forms of investment, and a less

12. *Ibid.*, 31.
13. *Ibid.*, 34.
14. *Ibid.*, 6.
15. *Ibid.*, 2.
16. *Ibid.*, 6.
17. *Ibid.*
18. McCollum, et al., *supra* n. 6, at 597.
19. Falling 13% to USD 1.3 trillion. UNCTAD, *World Investment Report 2019: Special Economic Zones*, iii (United Nations, 2019).

favourable investment policy climate as key drivers for the slowdown in FDI,[20] and observed, 'The significant acceleration required to meet the investment needs associated with the Sustainable Development Goals is not yet apparent. We need to raise ambition on climate action, address debt vulnerabilities and reduce trade tensions to foster environments that are conducive to scaling up long-term and sustainable investment.'[21]

[B] The Ongoing Need for Supportive, Stable Political and Regulatory Conditions

Given the capital-intensive nature of renewable energy projects, the sector remains – at least in part – reliant on favourable regulatory frameworks and supportive government policies. This support can take many forms, including improvements in efficiency, the implementation of tradable certificate schemes, and the payment of fixed feed-in tariffs or market premiums to electricity producers from renewable sources.[22] However, support of this nature is something of a double-edged sword. In 2012, Anatole Boute asserted that the level of governmental support was 'the most important element influencing expected profit', and as such, from a renewable investor's perspective, changes to the support system constituted the most important risk factor for investments in renewable energy.[23] Boute posited that the success of government schemes designed to support renewable energy would be dependent on the 'credibility of the public authority's long-term commitment'.[24] As the experience of Spain and other European states has demonstrated, incentive schemes have indeed proven to be prone to reduction and retraction in times of economic crisis.

Some commentators have argued that political risk (as exemplified by the retraction or reduction of incentive schemes) is of declining significance to the renewable energy sector, and consequently, ISDS will no longer have such a significant role to play in protecting renewable energy investments.[25] This assertion is based on technological developments and the reasoning that the cost of renewable energy supply has decreased, will continue to decrease, and has either reached, or will eventually reach, a tipping point, at which time the sector will no longer require government support in the form of subsidies.

Economic determinates will no doubt continue to drive renewable investment decisions, as with all investment decisions. Given the vast improvements in technology, future cost savings plausibly will be derived less from research and development

20. *Ibid.*, xi.
21. *Ibid.*, iii.
22. Anatole Boute, *Combating Climate Change Through Investment Arbitration*, 35(7) Fordham Int. L. J. 614, 622 (2012).
23. *Ibid.*, 624.
24. *Ibid.*
25. Kyla Tienhaara and Christian Downie, *Risky Business? The Energy Charter Treaty, Renewable Energy, and Investor-State Disputes*, 24(3) Global Governance 451, 457 (2018).

and more from expanding manufacturing and delivering greater economies of scale.[26] However, governments still will need to continue to develop attractive policies to further improve the economics of renewable investment. According to a 2018 Massachusetts Institute of Technology study, government policy is one of the key reasons for the price of solar panels having decreased by as much as 99% in the past four decades.[27] Accordingly, political risk and economic determinates cannot readily be extricated from one another. Despite the importance of a stable energy system to economies worldwide, local, national and multinational energy markets are continually evolving. This is driven, at least in part, by the frequent policy and regulatory changes made by governments. Therefore, at such a critical time in the global energy transition, the impact of political and regulatory risk, and measures designed to mitigate those risks, should not be downplayed.

§12.04 THE ECT AND INVESTMENTS IN THE RENEWABLE ENERGY SECTOR

[A] Background to the ECT

The ECT is a multilateral investment treaty, which was signed in Lisbon in December 1994, and came into force in April 1998, with the aim of promoting international cooperation in the energy sector.[28] At that time, former Soviet states were in dire need of foreign investment to harness their vast energy resources. Taking into account the recent withdrawals of Italy in 2015 (effective as of 2016) and Russia (which had signed but not ratified the ECT) in 2009, the ECT currently has fifty-three signatories. Three of those signatories, including Australia, have signed but not ratified the ECT. As of 2019, eighty-three countries have signed the new International Energy Charter (IEC), a non-binding declaration of political intention aiming at strengthening energy cooperation, introduced in 2010.

[B] How Does the ECT Protect Renewable Energy Investments from Adverse Regulatory and Political Changes?

Generally speaking, any reference to the 'protection' of investments under the ECT simply means the ability for the investor to seek a remedy, in the form of payment and/or compensation, for a breach of a treaty obligation by the host state. There is, of course, no guarantee that any given claim will ultimately be successful, and no ability for an investor through ISDS to stop the implementation of a legislative or regulatory measure, no matter how dramatic or destructive its potential impact. Simplifying matters, the only final remedy available to an investor under ISDS, where the measure

---

26. Goksin Kavlak, et al., *Evaluating the Causes of Cost Reduction in Photovoltaic Modules*, 123 Energy Policy 700 (2018).
27. *Ibid.*
28. Energy Charter Treaty, 1994 O.J.L. 380/24 (ECT).

in question has been implemented to the detriment of its investment, is a monetary award.

The ECT's investment protection regime is applicable to any investment associated with an 'economic activity in the energy sector'.[29] Such activity includes the 'construction and operation of power generation facilities, including those powered by wind and other renewable energy sources',[30] while also encompassing investments in battery power and storage and energy efficiency, among others. However, the ECT may not fully cover new investment trends, particularly in respect of renewable energy technology, and the increasing digitalization of the energy sector.[31] This is discussed further in §12.06.

There are numerous examples of how the treaty protections set out in the ECT may be invoked, through ISDS, to protect renewable energy projects from the financial impact of political or regulatory changes. Indeed, available data suggests that of the ISDS claims initiated under the ECT to date, approximately 54% (69 of 128) are claims made by investors in the renewable energy sector. Of the twenty-five claims by renewable energy investors which have been decided at the time of writing (which are listed in Table 12.1), 52% were decided in favour of the investor.[32] This is slightly higher than the overall investor success rate of 46% (including cases where the arbitral tribunal found a breach of the ECT, but no damages were awarded).[33]

Table 12.1 Outcome of Decided ECT Claims by Renewable Energy Investors[34]

No.	*Claimant Investor*	*Respondent State*	*Subject of Claim*	*Outcome*
1.	Charanne BV Constructions Investments S.a.r.l	Spain	Legal reforms affecting the renewable energy sector	Investors' claims dismissed / Award rendered in favour of host state

29. ECT, art. 1(6). 'Economic Activity in the Energy Sector' is defined at Art. 1(5) to mean an economic activity concerning the exploration, extraction, refining, production, storage, land transport, transmission, distribution, trade, marketing, or sale of Energy Materials and Products (with certain specified exclusions) or concerning the distribution of heat to multiple premises.
30. ECT, art. 1(5)(ii).
31. European Commission, *ANNEX to the Recommendation for a Council Decision Authorising the Entering into Negotiations on the Modernisation of the Energy Charter Treaty*, COM(2019) 231 (14 May 2019), https://ec.europa.eu/transparency/regdoc/rep/1/2019/EN/COM-2019-231-F1-EN-MAIN-PART-1.PDF.
32. Any reference to an award decided in favour of the host state is an award in which the investor's claims were dismissed, and an award decided in favour of the investor is an award in which the investor succeeded on the merits, in whole or in part, and was entitled to payment and/or compensation.
33. *Statistics of ECT Cases (as of 23/10/2019)*, Energy Charter Secretariat (2019), https://www.energycharter.org/fileadmin/DocumentsMedia/News/All_statistics_-_23_October_2019.pdf.
34. *Statistics of ECT Cases*, Energy Charter Secretariat (October 23, 2019), https://www.energycharter.org/fileadmin/DocumentsMedia/News/All_statistics_-_23_October_2019.pdf.

No.	*Claimant Investor*	*Respondent State*	*Subject of Claim*	*Outcome*
2.	Antaris Solar GmbH Dr. Michael Göde	Czech Republic	Legal reforms affecting the renewable energy sector	Investors' claims dismissed / Award rendered in favour of host state
3.	Voltaic Network GmbH	Czech Republic	Legal reforms affecting the renewable energy sector	Investors' claims dismissed / Award rendered in favour of host state
4.	ICW Europe Investments Limited	Czech Republic	Legal reforms affecting the renewable energy sector	Investors' claims dismissed / Award rendered in favour of host state
5.	Photovoltaik Knopf Betriebs-GmbH	Czech Republic	Legal reforms affecting the renewable energy sector	Investors' claims dismissed / Award rendered in favour of host state
6.	WA Investments-Europa Nova Limited	Czech Republic	Legal reforms affecting the renewable energy sector	Investors' claims dismissed / Award rendered in favour of host state
7.	EVN AG	Bulgaria	Legal reforms affecting the pricing of electricity and the renewable energy sector	Investors' claims dismissed / Award rendered in favour of host state
8.	Isolux Infrastructure Netherlands B.V.	Spain	Legal reforms affecting the renewable energy sector	Investors' claims dismissed / Award rendered in favour of host state
9.	RREEF Infrastructure (G.P.) Limited RREEF Pan-European Infrastructure Two Lux S.à r.l.	Spain	Legal reforms affecting the renewable energy sector	Breach of Art. 10(1) FET, award rendered in favour of investors
10.	Antin Infrastructure Services Luxembourg S.à.r.l. Antin Energia Termosolar B.V.	Spain	Legal reforms affecting the renewable energy sector	Breach of Art. 10(1) FET, award rendered in favour of investors

No.	*Claimant Investor*	*Respondent State*	*Subject of Claim*	*Outcome*
11.	Eiser Infrastructure Limited Energia Solar Luxembourg S.a r.l	Spain	Legal reforms affecting the renewable energy sector	Breach of Art. 10(1) FET, award rendered in favour of investors
12.	Masdar Solar & Wind Cooperatief U.A.	Spain	Legal reforms affecting the renewable energy sector	Breach of Art. 10(1) FET, award rendered in favour of investors
13.	Blusun S.A. Jean-Pierre Lecorcier Michael Stein	Italy	Legal reforms affecting the renewable energy sector	Investors' claims dismissed / Award rendered in favour of host state
14.	NextEra Energy Global Holdings B.V. NextEra Energy Spain Holdings B.V.	Spain	Legal reforms affecting the renewable energy sector	Breach of Art. 10(1) FET, award rendered in favour of investors
15.	InfraRed Environmental Infrastructure GP Limited	Spain	Legal reforms affecting the renewable energy sector	Award rendered in favour of investors
16.	Stadtwerke München GmbH AS 3 Beteiligungs GmbH Andasol 3 Kraftwerks GmbH Andasol Fonds GmbH & Co. KG Ferranda GmbH Ferrostaal Industrial Projects GmbH RWE Innogy GmbH RheinEnergie AG Marquesado Solar S.L.	Spain	Legal reforms affecting the renewable energy sector	Investors' claims dismissed / Award rendered in favour of host state
17.	9REN Holding S.a.r.l	Spain	Legal reforms affecting the renewable energy sector	Breach of Art. 10(1) FET, award rendered in favour of investors

No.	*Claimant Investor*	*Respondent State*	*Subject of Claim*	*Outcome*
18.	Cube Energy S.C.A. Cube Infrastructure Fund SICAV Cube Infrastructure Managers S.A. Demeter 2 FPCI Demeter Partners S.A.	Spain	Legal reforms affecting the renewable energy sector	Breach of Art. 10(1) FET, award rendered in favour of investors, Partial Dissenting Opinion
19.	Greentech Energy Systems Novenergia	Italy	Legal reforms affecting the renewable energy sector	Breach of Art. 10(1) FET; (10.1) Unreasonable or discriminatory measures; (10.1) Umbrella clause, award rendered in favour of investors,
20.	OperaFund Eco-Invest SICAV PLC Schwab Holding	Spain	Legal reforms affecting the renewable energy sector	Breach of Art. 10(1) FET, award rendered in favour of investors
21.	SolEs Badajoz GmbH	Spain	Legal reforms affecting the renewable energy sector	Breach of Art. 10(1) FET, award rendered in favour of investors
22.	Belenergia S.A	Italy	Legal reforms affecting the renewable energy sector	Investors' claims dismissed / Award rendered in favour of host state
23.	CEF Energia BV	Italy	Legal reforms affecting the renewable energy sector	Breach of Art. 10(1) FET, award rendered in favour of investors
24.	Novenergia II – Energy & Environment (SCA) (Grand Duchy of Luxembourg), SICAR	Spain	Legal reforms affecting the renewable energy sector	Breach of Art. 10(1) FET, award rendered in favour of investors

No.	Claimant Investor	Respondent State	Subject of Claim	Outcome
25.	Greentech Energy Systems A/S Foresight Luxembourg Solar 1 Sarl Foresight Luxembourg Solar 2 Sarl GWM Renewable Energy I SPA GWM Renewable Energy I SPA	Spain	Legal reforms affecting the renewable energy sector	Breach of Art. 10(1) FET, award rendered in favour of investors

Of course, the mere fact that renewable energy investors are accessing ISDS to protect their investments does not mean that the system of ISDS itself is becoming 'greener'. Indeed, one might ask whether there is any difference in the way a claim by a renewable energy investor is likely to be treated, compared to that of an investor in respect of a traditional energy project. The ECT does not, for example, require a tribunal to treat a renewable energy investor more favourably than it would any other energy investor. Moreover, due to their neutral wording, the investment protection provisions in the ECT are often described, in pejorative terms, as being 'vague'. As such, can the ECT truly be credited with 'protecting' investments in the renewable energy sector? The answer may lie not in the wording of the ECT's substantive provisions, or its overall purpose, but rather, in the interpretation of its provisions by ISDS tribunals, and in the principles governing that interpretation.

[C] The Interpretation of Available Protections in Cases Involving Renewable Energy Investments

An analysis of recent ECT cases demonstrates that where renewable energy investors have been successful, it is not because their projects have been given 'special treatment' or deemed so important as to outweigh the operation of the host state's sovereign right to regulate. In fact, there is nothing remotely 'activist' in the reasoning offered by tribunals in such cases. Rather, the outcome is typically arrived at following a fact-intensive, but distinctly apolitical, process. Throughout that process, tribunals are plainly concerned with the need to strike a balance between, on the one hand, the investors' desire for a fair and consistent regulatory framework, and on the other, the host states' mandate to implement legal and regulatory changes.

Taking the example of the fair and equitable treatment (FET) standard, which is expressed in the following way in Article 10(1) of the ECT:

> Each Contracting Party shall, in accordance with the provisions of this Treaty, encourage and create stable, equitable, favourable and transparent conditions for Investors of other Contracting Parties to make Investments in its Area. Such conditions shall include a commitment to accord at all times to Investments of

> Investors of other Contracting Parties fair and equitable treatment. Such Investments shall also enjoy the most constant protection and security and no Contracting Party shall in any way impair by unreasonable or discriminatory measures their management, maintenance, use, enjoyment or disposal. In no case shall such Investments be accorded treatment less favourable than that required by international law, including treaty obligations. Each Contracting Party shall observe any obligations it has entered into with an Investor or an Investment of an Investor of any other Contracting Party.

In assessing whether or not a breach of the FET standard has occurred, tribunals have turned their minds to, among other issues, whether the host state (by its own conduct) fostered an objective expectation in the mind of the investor that its investment would be treated with a certain degree of 'predictability, stability, and non-arbitrariness'.[35] In order to determine the legitimacy and scope of the investor's expectations, the following types of questions are likely to be considered:[36]

- On an objective analysis, did the host state actively encourage or instil this expectation in the investor?
- Was the host state's conduct equivalent to a promise, whether express or implied?
- Did the investor rely on that promise?
- Were the investors' expectations rigid and unrealistic, or did they allow for reasonably foreseeable changes?

These questions essentially ask: Did the investor do its homework? In this way, the 'legitimate expectations' principle puts the onus on the investor to establish why its expectations were reasonable from an objective standpoint, and why the conduct of the host state should be held to have contravened those expectations. It is here that the precise nature of both the investment and the change imposed by the state become relevant. For example, the tribunal will consider whether the investment was procured on the basis of a specific promise or commitment by the host state (e.g., that the host state would not make changes to a favourable regulatory framework, or that if it did, those changes would not impact the investment in question). The tribunal will also consider the nature and intent of the changes imposed by the host state, and the extent to which it is underscored by a clear public interest objective. This does not involve the making of a value judgment about the perceived necessity or quality of the regulatory measure in question. Rather, the measure is assessed through the lens of whether or not the investor, in the precise circumstances of each case, ought to have expected it.[37]

In cases involving sensitive policy areas, the so-called vagueness of treaty obligations (such as the FET standard) enables tribunals to adopt an interpretative

35. Florian Dupuy and Pierre-Marie Dupuy, *What to Expect from Legitimate Expectations? A Critical Appraisal and Look into the Future of the 'Legitimate Expectations' Doctrine in International Investment Law*, in *Festschrift Ahmed Sadek El-Kosheri: From the Arab World to the Globalization of International Law and Arbitration* 273, 279 (M.A. Raouf, et al. eds., Kluwer Law International 2015).
36. Ella Wisniewski, *A Changing Climate: The Future of 'Legitimate Expectations' in Energy Investment Disputes*, 4 ICC Dispute Resolution Bulletin 53, 53–54 (2018).
37. *Ibid.*, 60.

approach which involves sensitivity to, and close scrutiny of, the particular circumstances of the investor and the host state in each case. This 'vagueness' should perhaps be viewed not as a shortcoming but as an inherent safeguard. The fact that tribunals may arrive at very different conclusions in their interpretation of treaty protections (for which ISDS has been criticized as 'unpredictable'[38]) might simply be an indication that the system is working. After all, the FET standard is not a rigid, 'one size fits all' obligation. It requires a nuanced application, with due regard for the relevant political, economic and social factors at play, allowing tribunals the flexibility to determine the appropriate standard of treatment owed to investors in each case. Tribunals must consider, on the one hand, the host state's sovereign mandate to enact regulatory reform, and on the other, the host state's commitment (also an exercise of its sovereign prerogative) to afford investors in its territory a certain standard of protection.[39] To illustrate this, it is helpful to consider the outcome of recent claims by renewable energy investors, involving alleged breaches of the FET standard, which – at first blush – appear to be remarkably similar.

Charanne v. Spain was the first decision of dozens of pending ECT claims by solar energy investors against the Kingdom of Spain.[40] The claims concerned Spain's implementation in 2007, of a generous incentive scheme designed to attract foreign investment in renewable energy projects within Spain (the 'Special Regime'). Some of the benefits of the Special Regime included a feed-in tariff for twenty-five years, followed by a reduced tariff beyond that period. The Special Regime achieved its aim of attracting foreign investors. However, it soon became clear that that the feed-in tariffs paid to the solar energy producers were overly generous or at least unsustainable for Spain's budget, resulting in a widening deficit in the market. The argument was that if Spain took no action to modify the Special Regime, this deficit would steadily worsen, to the detriment of the end consumer and to the energy market as a whole. Therefore, in 2010, Spain enacted the first round of reforms to the Special Regime, establishing a transmission fee, eliminating the feed-in tariff beyond the initial twenty-five-year period, and capping the number of annual operating hours that would be eligible for the feed-in tariff.

In making their claim, the investors in *Charanne* argued that in all of the circumstances, the Special Regime amounted to a specific commitment by Spain, and that the reforms enacted in 2010 amount to a frustration of their legitimate expectations. The fundamental expectation, they asserted, was that Spain would maintain a stable and predictable regulatory framework, based on that which existed at the time of the decision to invest. The tribunal ultimately found that, although enacted with a particular class of investors in mind, the Special Regime was general in nature and, therefore, was not a specific commitment to individual investors (akin to, for example,

38. Tienhaara and Downie, *supra* n. 25, 459.
39. *See El Paso Energy International Company v. Argentina* (Award, ICSID Case No. ARB/03/15, 31 October 2011).
40. *Charanne B.V. & Construction Investments S.A.R.L v. The Kingdom of Spain* (Award, SCC, Case No V 062/2012, 21 January 2016) ('*Charanne v. Spain*').

a stabilization clause). As a result, the possibility of changes such as those implemented in 2010 ought to have fallen within the scope of the investors' expectations. The claim was dismissed.

However, in the past two years, nine cases dealing with the Special Regime have been decided against Spain, in favour of solar energy investors. In these more recent decisions, the tribunals also had to consider further amendments to the Special Regime, which were made from 2012 onwards. Crucially, those amendments were increasingly significant in effect. By 2014, Spain had also issued a decree imposing a tax on electricity production, the feed-in tariff (which was reduced in 2010) was eliminated altogether, and a new regime governing renewable energy was established. The new regime calculated a reasonable rate of return for investors based on the standard of an efficient hypothetical solar energy plant.

In *Eiser v. Spain*, the tribunal decided that the investor was entitled to expect that Spain would not revise the Special Regime to such a degree that all value in its investment was lost.[41] That expectation was also said to have been founded on Spain's actions between 2010 and 2011. For example, Spain had confirmed that the claimant's solar plants would continue to benefit from the original Special Regime, albeit to a lesser extent. However, in contrast to the amendments implemented in 2010, the later amendments were found to have amounted to a 'total and unreasonable change' to the regulatory framework.[42] Similar reasoning was echoed in subsequent cases: *Novenergia,*[43] *Antin Infrastructure,*[44] *Masdar,*[45] and most recently, *NextEra,*[46] *9REN Holding,*[47] *Cube Infrastructure,*[48] *Foresight,* and *SolEs Badajoz,*[49] which have been decided in favour of the investors in the past two years. Indeed, despite agreeing that the investors' due diligence was 'thin',[50] the tribunal in *Cube Infrastructure* affirmed that 'if the [host state] makes a representation that induces investment, it must either deliver on that representation or ensure that any adjustments do not significantly alter the economic basis of the investments made in reliance on that representation'.[51]

41. *Eiser Infrastructure Limited and Energía Solar Luxembourg S.à r.l. v. The Kingdom of Spain* (Award, ICSID, Case No ARB/13/36, 4 May 2017) (*Eiser v. Spain*).
42. *Ibid.*, [368]-[369], [363].
43. The 2013/2014 reforms were described as a 'radical and unexpected' departure from the Special Regime: *Novenergia II – Energy & Environment (SCA) (Grand Duchy of Luxembourg), SICAR v. The Kingdom of Spain* (Award, SCC, Case No 2015/063, 15 February 2018).
44. *Antin Infrastructure Services Luxembourg S.à.r.l. and Antin Energia Termosolar B.V. v. Kingdom of Spain* (Award, ICSID, Case No ARB/13/31, 15 June 2018).
45. *Masdar Solar & Wind Cooperatief U.A. v. Kingdom of Spain* (Award, ICSID, Case No ARB/14/1, 16 May 2018).
46. *NextEra Energy Global Holdings B.V and NextEra Energy Spain Holdings B.V. v. Kingdom of Spain* (Award, ICSID Case No. ARB/14/11, 31 May 2019).
47. *9REN Holding S.a.r.l v. Kingdom of Spain*, (Award, ICSID Case No. ARB/15/1, 31 May 2019).
48. *Cube Infrastructure Fund SICAV and Others v. Kingdom of Spain* (Award, ICSID Case No. ARB/15/20, 26 June 2019), [394] ('*Cube Infrastructure*').
49. *SolEs Badajoz v. Spain* (Award, ICSID Case No. ARB/15/38, 31 July 2019).
50. *Cube Infrastructure, supra* n. 48, [394].
51. Jake Lowther and Ignacio Torterola, *TDM IACL Case Report – Cube Infrastructure Fund SICAV and Others v. Kingdom of Spain (ICSID Case No. ARB/15/20) – Award and Dissenting Opinion – 15 July 2019*, Transnational Dispute Management – International Arbitration Case Law (2019), https://www.transnational-dispute-management.com/legal-and-regulatory-detail.asp?key=23904.

These cases show that investors must be cognisant of the 'predictability of change'.[52] In *Charanne,* Spain was found not to have frustrated the investors' expectations by scaling back the Special Regime while maintaining its essential characteristics. Without an explicit commitment by Spain that the Special Regime would not be modified, such changes should, in the Tribunal's reasoning, have been contemplated by the investors and incorporated into their expectations accordingly. However, in subsequent cases, the more dramatic regulatory changes were found to constitute a breach of the FET standard. Thus, even where tribunals take a deferential approach to the regulatory prerogative of states, investors can remain reasonably confident in their protection against measures which amount to a 'total and unreasonable change'. Those will typically be the type of measures which, even if they had 'done their homework', the investor could not have anticipated.

For investors, the ECT claims raised against Spain and other European states offer at least two important lessons. The first is that the pursuit of stability must be largely driven by the investor's own efforts. Political, economic, and environmental considerations are necessarily dynamic, and consequently, an investor must be able to demonstrate that it exercised due diligence in appraising the landscape of its potential investment. The second is that an investor cannot eliminate the possibility that the host state will exercise its prerogative to implement new measures, or to increase the impact of existing measures, in accordance with a legitimate public interest objective.[53]

Given the targets set in the Paris Agreement, alongside the United Nation's Sustainable Development Goals, it is reasonable to expect that the regulatory landscape in the energy sector will continue to evolve in a manner favourable to the renewable energy sector. Where renewable energy investors 'do their homework' and conduct an adequate risk assessment, the ECT as it stands is well placed to protect their investments.

§12.05 THE ABILITY OF THE ECT TO PROMOTE THE INFLOW OF FOREIGN CAPITAL AND TECHNOLOGY IN THE FIELD OF RENEWABLE ENERGY

As discussed in §12.04, the system of ISDS is already equipped to protect renewable energy investments, and the ECT has a proven track record in this regard. This is not a result of renewable or low-carbon energy friendly provisions, but rather, owing to the inherent flexibility afforded to tribunals in the interpretation of existing substantive protections. However, the capacity of ISDS to *promote* or attract new investment specifically in the renewable energy sector is largely untested.

52. Dupuy and Dupuy, *supra* n. 35, 291.
53. As the tribunal observed in *Philip Morris Brands SÀRL, Philip Morris Products S.A. and Abal Hermanos S.A. v. Oriental Republic of Uruguay* (Award, ICSID, Case No ARB/10/7, 8 July 2016) ('*Philip Morris v Uruguay*') at [422], the requirements of the FET standard did not affect 'the State's right to exercise its sovereign authority to legislate and to adapt its laws to changing circumstances'.

When referring to foreign investment more generally, commentators have pointed out that the availability of ISDS reduces the cost of investing in countries with high sovereign risk, since by citing the existence of treaty protection, an investor may be able to negotiate more favourable terms with its lenders.[54] However, in addition to the fact that project financing data is confidential, the impact of treaty protection on the cost of capital is difficult to quantify.[55] More broadly, the question of whether there is a causal link between the availability of ISDS under any international investment agreement (IIA) and increased FDI has not been answered in any definitive way. As Boute asserts in general terms, a guarantee of protection against sovereign risk 'may reduce the required returns and thus stimulate these investments'.[56] Conversely, where treaty protections are not available, an investor cannot seek to rely on the 'backing' of ISDS to assert that the overall sovereign risk of a project is lower or to negotiate more favourable terms, on that basis.[57]

In 2016, as part of the internal negotiation phase of the Trans-Pacific Partnership (TPP), the Australian Government held a public hearing in relation to ISDS. An Australian mining company, at that time, one of ten Australian investors known to have invoked ISDS provisions against other countries, made the following submission to the Joint Standing Committee on Treaties, in relation to the relevance of access to ISDS provisions in the making of a foreign investment decision:

> It is not the case that foreign investors can never get justice from the courts of a host state, but it is predominantly the case, in developing countries, that foreign investors face a difficult and often hostile environment from the host country's justice system. Where a difficult and hostile environment exists in a particular country, such as Indonesia, potential investors will mark that investment destination down appropriately.
>
> Where a country that is otherwise marked down as an investment destination has a free trade agreement or treaty which provides for independent international dispute resolution for the investor, any such marking down will be qualified or even overlooked, as the investor will draw confidence from being spared exposure to a hostile justice environment and, importantly and vitally for the investor, it will know that if an independent international dispute resolution goes its way then it will have means, under international law, to recover the damages it is awarded. Conversely, where a prospective investor sees an investment proposal which would involve that investor being denied any meaningful way of recovering its lost

54. *See*, e.g., *ISDS as an Instrument for Investment Protection and Facilitation*, Asia-Pacific Economic Cooperation (APEC) (October 2019), https://www.apec.org/Publications/2019/11/ISDS-as-an-Instrument-for-Investment-Promotion-and-Facilitation; Lindsay Oldenski, *What Do the Data Say about the Relationship between Investor-State Dispute Settlement Provisions and FDI?*, Peterson Institute for International Economics (11 March 2015), https://www.piie.com/blogs/trade-investment-policy-watch/what-do-data-say-about-relationship-between-investor-state; Matthias Busse, et al., *FDI Promotion through Bilateral Investment Treaties: More than a Bit?*, 146 Rev. of World Economics 147 (2010); Columbia Center on Sustainable Investment, *Costs and Benefits of Investment Treaties*, Columbia University (March 2018), http://ccsi.columbia.edu/files/2018/04/Cost-and-Benefits-of-Investment-Treaties-Practical-Considerations-for-States-ENG-mr.pdf.
55. Sam Luttrell, *Why ISDS is Good for Australia*, 42(11) Brief 10, 11 (2015).
56. Boute, *supra* n. 22, at 615.
57. Luttrell, *supra* n. 55, 11.

> investment as a result of the host country's government's intervention, then I say, with a measure of certainty, that the investment proposal would not be accepted.[58]

In its report, the Joint Standing Committee on Treaties noted that 'the inclusion of ISDS provisions in an agreement Australia is party to, makes it cheaper and more attractive for Australians to invest in that country'.[59]

Indeed, from the perspective of host states seeking to attract inbound foreign capital, ISDS is an important investment promotion tool. The host state's acceptance of ISDS-backed treaties demonstrates to foreign investors that its legal framework, as applicable to the prospective investment, is aligned with international norms and standards. Conversely, if ISDS is not available through the host state's treaty programme, the investor will need to consider whether it can secure a direct agreement with the state. Depending on the investors' bargaining power, this may not be available.[60] Accordingly, the availability of ISDS will likely continue to be used as a tool to attract and maintain inbound capital flows. This is particularly the case for developing countries and emerging markets, where risk is often higher and where there is considerable need for foreign capital.[61] In such circumstances, where it is in the interest of the host state to encourage long-term foreign investment in innovative and challenging projects within its territory, participation in the system of ISDS is a calculated exercise of state sovereignty. It is therefore uncontroversial to conclude that the ECT is capable of promoting foreign investment. However, this is applicable to all foreign investment, and the relevant question here is whether the ECT can, or should, be capable of promoting 'clean' energy investment.

§12.06 MODERNIZATION OF THE ECT

[A] Common Criticisms of the ECT

The ECT, in its current form, has been labelled a 'major threat to carbon neutrality', on the basis that it allegedly protects fossil fuel-based investments.[62] For example, one commentator has asserted, 'Signatories of the ECT who have already adopted/announced their carbon neutrality target will have to allocate part of their public budget to compensate foreign investors for the "legitimate" expected revenues investors may lose due to adaptation of current regulations to the 1.5°C target.'[63] To date, there do not appear to have been any ISDS claims initiated under the ECT in response to a state's adoption of a carbon neutrality target. On the contrary, and as noted above, the majority of recent ECT cases (i.e., cases determined in the past five

58. Parliament of Australia, Joint Standing Committee on Treaties, *Trans Pacific Partnership*, Report No 165, [6.26] (David Quinlivan, Chairman, Planet Mining Pty Ltd) (November 2016).
59. *Ibid.*, [6.27].
60. Luttrell, *supra* n. 55, 12.
61. *Ibid.*
62. Yamina Saheb, *It's time to Scrap the Energy Charter Treaty*, Euractiv (10 October 2019), https://www.euractiv.com/section/energy/opinion/its-time-to-scrap-the-energy-charter-treaty/.
63. *Ibid.*

years) in which the claimant investor has been successful are those which were initiated by a renewable energy investor, seeking compensation in respect of a measure or measures which have negatively impacted a renewable energy project.

More generally, the fact that ECT protections are applicable to investments in fossil fuel energy by virtue of the investment having being made by a foreign investor in an applicable host state, does not automatically translate to a host state being liable for any payment, to any investor, under the ECT. Such assertions presuppose that claims will be made by specific investors in respect of specific regulatory or legislative measures, and that the arbitral tribunal in each case will decide the claim in favour of the investor. The risk of host states losing ISDS claims generally was addressed in an open letter signed by over forty international law professors, in response to a letter circulated by the 'Alliance for Justice' in March 2015.[64] The response letter highlighted the difference between actual risk and realized risk:

> Simply proclaiming that states might lose a case is not a reason for dismantling a rule of law adjudicative mechanism. Indeed, holding states responsible for violating fundamental norms is part of any regime based on the rule of law, whether the protections in questions are based in a constitution, in national law, or in an international treaty. Likewise, affirming when state conduct is a proper exercise of sovereignty is also a fundamental value of any rule of law regime.[65]

The prevailing approach taken by ISDS tribunals in recent arbitral awards strongly indicates that a change made with a clear public interest objective, in a sensitive policy area, is likely to be upheld. For example, in *Philip Morris v. Uruguay*, the state prevailed over investors who brought claims of expropriation under the Switzerland-Uruguay bilateral investment treaty (BIT) following the introduction of mandatory plain packaging standards for tobacco products (to reduce smoking rates and improve public health).[66] This demonstrates that the critics' concerns in respect of public interest objectives may be exaggerated. Climate change is a political and economic issue of ever-increasing primacy, and global trends suggest that regulatory measures in pursuit of climate goals, such as the Paris Agreement, will continue to increase in significance and urgency. Accordingly, and in the absence of a specific commitment by a host state to the contrary, investors will likely be held to expect the implementation of increasingly disruptive measures intended to mitigate the effects of climate change.

[B] Could Criticisms of the ECT Be Addressed with Improved Drafting?

Notwithstanding the nuanced interpretation and application of existing treaty protections by arbitral tribunals, critics of ISDS have called for 'a new model of trade that

64. Payam Akhavan, et al., *An Open Letter About Investor-State Dispute Settlement*, McGill University (20 April 2015), https://www.mcgill.ca/fortier-chair/isds-open-letter.
65. *Ibid.*
66. In its decision, the tribunal urged investment tribunals to 'pay great deference to governmental judgments of national needs in matters such as the protection of public health'. *Philip Morris v. Uruguay, supra* n. 53, [399].

protects communities and the environment'.[67] This raises the question of whether the drafting of ISDS provisions within IIAs, or updates to existing IIAs, may have a role to play to reinforce the credibility and effectiveness of climate change mitigation policies. As the Secretary General of the Arbitration Institute of the Stockholm Chamber of Commerce said:

> measures to combat climate change need to be enhanced by aligning with economic incentives. Smart drafting of future treaty terms could contribute to this development, and in applying the precedent that has been set by enforcement of treaty undertakings by means of ISDS, states would have to live up to their promise.[68]

This 'smart drafting' could include, among other things, a combination of mandatory clauses and exceptions in respect of sensitive policy areas. For example, all three free trade agreements recently entered into by Australia contain general exceptions pertaining to measures that are necessary to protect human, animal or plant life or health, or related to the conservation of living or non-living exhaustible natural resources, provided that they are not discriminatory and do not constitute a disguised restriction on international trade or investment.[69] The incorporation of express carve outs for sensitive policy areas in IIAs raises the question of whether the ECT could, and should, be amended to support host countries and investors in fostering a low-carbon energy transition. If so, could this be achieved while maintaining its application to energy investments of all kinds, including those which are fossil fuel based? Such questions are likely to be considered in the near future, as negotiations on the modernization of the ECT are presently underway.[70]

Among the list of topics for the proposed modernization of the ECT is the definition of 'economic activity in the energy sector'.[71] Luxembourg has proposed a modification to 'adapt the Treaty to the Energy Transition / Decarbonisation Processes and Contracting Parties Climate Change Commitments and therefore cover new investment trends and new technologies ...'.[72] The EU observed that 'the definition may not cover new trends in investment, in particular with regard to renewable

67. Ben Beachy and Ilana Solomon, *A Dirty Deal*, Sierra Club (2 December 2015), https://www.sierraclub.org/compass/2015/12/dirty-deal.
68. Annette Magnusson, *Future Treaty Making* (Speech), EFILA Inaugural Conference: EU Law and Investment Treaty Law: Convergence, Conflict, or Conversation? (London, 23 January 2015), https://sccinstitute.com/media/49813/scc-annette-magnusson-speech-at-efila-london-23-january-2015.pdf.
69. *See*, e.g., ChAFTA Art. 9.8; JAEPA Art. 14.15; KAFTA Art. 22.1(3).
70. *Energy Charter Conference Gives Green Light for Negotiations on Modernisation of the ECT*, International Energy Charter (7 November 2019), https://www.energycharter.org/media/news/article/energy-charter-conference-gives-green-light-for-negotiations-on-modernisation-of-the-ect/.
71. *Decision of the Energy Conference: Modernisation of the Energy Charter Treaty*, Energy Charter Secretariat (27 November 2018), https://www.energycharter.org/fileadmin/DocumentsMedia/CCDECS/2018/CCDEC201818_-_STR_Modernisation_of_the_Energy_Charter_Treaty.pdf.
72. *Decision of the Energy Conference: Adoption by Correspondence – Policy Options for Modernisation of the ECT*, Energy Charter Secretariat (6 October 2019), https://www.energycharter.org/fileadmin/DocumentsMedia/CCDECS/2019/CCDEC201908.pdf.

energy', and proposed a definition which addresses 'the challenges and opportunities of the transition to a safe and sustainable low-carbon'.[73]

Another topic for the proposed modernization of the ECT is 'Sustainable Development and Corporate Social Responsibility'. Again, Luxembourg is the source of the most ambitious proposal, which would incorporate a new article with reference to 'Climate Change Commitments, Decarbonisation process, Corporate Social Responsibility and Sustainable Development instruments'. Among the instruments Luxembourg proposes to include are the revised OECD Guidelines for Multinational Enterprises (2011), the UN Framework Convention on Climate Change (1992), and the Paris Agreement.[74]

The ECT already contains provisions relating to environmental protection and the development of renewable energy sources. For example, Article 19(d) provides that Contracting Parties are to 'have particular regard to Improving Energy Efficiency, to developing and using renewable energy sources, to promoting the use of cleaner fuels and to employing technologies and technological means that reduce pollution'. However, such provisions are non-binding in nature. That is, there is no remedy available for a failure to act in accordance with their terms. Given the wide range of views among signatories with respect to the modernization of the ECT, it is reasonable to expect that any modifications or additions would also be non-binding in nature.

Since 1994, when the ECT was first signed, there have been transformative developments in the fields of energy production and technology. At least among so-called developed countries, the harnessing and proliferation of energy from fossil fuel sources is – to put it lightly – no longer the order of the day. Further, it has recently been observed that within the low-carbon energy sector, there is a greatly increased need for investment in electricity storage, transmission and delivery, driven by 'greater demands for delivering electricity to the end-use sectors (buildings, industry and transport) and by the intermittency of variable renewable electricity sources'.[75] To reflect these changes, it would appear appropriate to pare back the definitions of the ECT so that its operative provisions encompass as broad a range of energy production and storage activities as possible. In this respect, the preservation of effective neutrality would have a modernizing effect.

Alternatively, and in response to what is arguably the prevailing mood of the day (and assuming consensus between signatories is achievable), a more activist stance could be adopted. This could involve the use of binding provisions to promote 'clean' (i.e., renewable or low-carbon) energy, energy efficiency, and the achievement of global climate goals. However, such an approach would be one of the greater risks. It would limit the flexibility inherent in the ECT, and thus would likely be met with resistance on the international and domestic political stage. It would also demand a consensus on problematic questions such as the definition of 'clean' energy (e.g., would this include nuclear energy?), the types of projects, which would be deemed 'acceptable' (in terms of satisfying a positive obligation to contribute to 'clean' energy

73. *Ibid.*
74. *Ibid.*
75. McCollum, et al., *supra* n. 6, 591.

targets), and how to deal with future technological developments, some of which may be controversial. More critically, and assuming the activist approach were achievable, it would be a dramatic shift away from the current purpose of the ECT and of the ISDS system more generally. Rather than existing to protect investments from breaches of established international norms, the ECT arguably would be tilted towards the regulation of foreign investor activity (currently a matter for states) at the supranational level.

For these reasons, the neutrality approach is preferable. The ECT's investment protection provisions have proven sufficiently effective. While the increased significance of global climate goals arguably requires the adaptation of the ECT, this should not be a 'whole-cloth' reinvention, but rather a modification and supplementation of existing definitions, rules and procedures. Such changes, though having the effect of modernizing the ECT, by reference to the context in which it was originally drafted, would be neutral in nature, and therefore, more likely to be achievable.

§12.07 THE LIKELIHOOD OF FURTHER WITHDRAWAL FROM THE ECT

In view of Italy's withdrawal from the ECT, and the raft of over forty claims pending against Spain, one is prompted to ask: Could the success of renewable energy investors in enforcing ECT protections cause states to abandon the system of ISDS altogether? Given the long-term nature of most foreign investments, the stakes are understandably high for investors and host states alike. As an illustration, in *Eiser v. Spain*, the investors claimed EUR 298 million and were awarded EUR 128 million (plus interest), while in *NextEra v. Spain*, the investor sought EUR 393.6 million and was ultimately awarded EUR 290.6 million (plus interest). Such figures have the capacity to seriously affect the finances of a state, particularly at times of economic difficulty. For many critics, this quandary is central to a perception of ISDS as an increasingly unattractive system for host states.

However, in addition to its role as an investment protection tool, ISDS offers an overarching macroeconomic benefit in terms of its role in minimizing the need for resolution of investment disputes at the inter-state level. That is to say, the process of ISDS allows states to avoid the cost of intervening on behalf of their investors (often referred to as 'gunboat diplomacy'), and the associated risk of damaging the bilateral trade and diplomatic relationship between the host state and the home state of the investor. While difficult to quantify, this benefit should not be overlooked.

During the treaty negotiation period for the TPP, Australia's Joint Standing Committee on Treaties noted, as a 'worst case scenario' of sorts, that in the event of an ISDS tribunal finding against the Australian Government, it would mean one of two things: either the regulation was poor policy or the ISDS provisions are not functioning as intended. In relation to the first possibility, the committee noted, 'If the regulation was poor policy, then the Australian Government has treated a foreign investor badly, and that foreign investor deserves their compensation.'[76] In relation to the second possibility, the committee observed:

> If the ISDS provisions are not functioning as intended, the ISDS tribunal still cannot prevent the Australian Government from progressing with public interest regulation. In addition, because the parties to the TPP are countries that might have similar findings made against them, they would all recognise the need to amend the ISDS provisions so those provisions work as intended.[77]

The framing of the second possibility is a timely reminder that entering into IIAs, negotiating and agreeing to be bound by certain obligations, and participating in ISDS, as the 'teeth' that render those obligations binding, are each activities which constitute a calculated exercise of state sovereignty. Were there no benefits likely to flow from such decisions, in terms of increased opportunity for the home state's investors abroad, or the prospect of increased inbound foreign capital, states would presumably exercise their right to refrain therefrom. As observed in the open letter referred to above, 'Of course, by opening themselves to arbitration, states open themselves to the risk of losing some cases. But creating such a risk is our sovereign right, and it is an incentive to gain international cooperation that benefits not just foreign states but our nation as well.'[78]

Furthermore, in negotiating IIAs, states have an opportunity to include provisions which clarify substantive protections and standards or the procedure by which parties may access ISDS. It is foreseeable that IIAs will continue to include precise exception clauses in respect of sensitive policy areas, such as those negotiated by Australia.[79] While withdrawing from the system of ISDS may appear an effective solution for states seeking to preserve their unfettered regulatory mandate, the longer-term consequence of this withdrawal may be a reduction in foreign capital, including in the areas where investment is critically needed, such as the development of low-carbon energy infrastructure.

§12.08 CONCLUSION

Regulatory and political risk continues to impact the flow of foreign capital and technology into the renewable energy sector. The ECT continues to offer an effective means of protecting existing investments from the impact of adverse regulatory and political change. The protections in the ECT may be invoked by traditional energy investors, including – theoretically – to recover losses suffered as a result of measures implemented to protect the environment. However, when dealing with sensitive policy

76. Joint Standing Committee, *supra* n. 58, [6.47].
77. *Ibid.*, [6.48].
78. Payam Akhavan, et al., *supra* n. 64.
79. *See*, e.g., ChAFTA Art. 9.8; JAEPA Art. 14.15; KAFTA Art. 22.1(3).

areas, arbitral tribunals have, by and large, adopted nuanced and increasingly deferential approaches to state conduct. As such, the ECT's investment protection provisions are working, and their interpretation by arbitral tribunals has proven sufficiently flexible to protect investments in the renewable energy sector.

Of course, the fact that renewable energy investors are enforcing the ECT's operative provisions does not mean that the ECT should be deemed exempt from change. It was drafted in 1994, and borne out of an energy industry that was fixated on fossil fuels. However, it is difficult to foresee the signatories to the ECT agreeing to the implementation of binding provisions to safeguard low-carbon energy infrastructure or to actively impose constraints on traditional energy investments. Such changes, even if they could be agreed, would fundamentally shift the current purpose of the ECT - the protection of investments - and would also jeopardize the flexibility that is the hallmark its operative provisions.

Accordingly, while the increased significance of global climate and environment protection goals arguably requires the adaptation of the ECT, this should not be a 'whole-cloth' reinvention, but rather a modification and supplementation of existing definitions, rules and procedures, in order to ensure effective neutrality. Changes designed to bring the core definitions and terms of the ECT in line with the current state of the energy sector (thereby ensuring effective neutrality) could potentially extend (or clarify) protections to a broader range of investments. It is foreseeable that investment in new areas of energy supply, storage, transmission and efficiency (particularly, those at the forefront of the regulatory and technological landscape) will make a positive contribution to the energy sector. It is precisely this type of contribution which is needed to meet the demands of an energy-hungry globe, while keeping the targets of the Paris Agreement in sight, and which would stand to benefit from the protections enshrined in the ECT.

CHAPTER 13

Addressing Financial Access to Justice in Investment Treaty Arbitration

Victoria Shannon Sahani

Investors and States are stuck in their roles as claimant and respondent, respectively, because the implementation of the Investor-State Dispute Settlement (ISDS) system echoes world economic power dynamics that have historically been more rigid than the text of the ISDS-governing documents. Third-party funding is a lens through which to analyze one consequence of this overarching structural inequality in ISDS: lack of financial access to justice. This chapter explains how third-party funding shines a spotlight on this pervasive lack of financial access to justice in ISDS and presents suggestions for how to address financial access to justice in ISDS without requiring the renegotiation of thousands of investment treaties.

§13.01 THE STRUCTURAL PROBLEM IN ISDS

Pursuant to a contract, such as a concession contract, the investor and host State each have an equal opportunity to bring claims against each other in arbitration.[1] When

1. *See* Harshad Pathak, *Consenting to Counterclaims Under the ICSID Convention*, 19 Pepperdine Disp. Resol. L. J. 101, 112 (2019); Yaraslau Kryvoi, *Counterclaims in Investor-State Arbitration*, 21 Minnesota J. Int'l L. 216, 217, 240, 242, 252 (2012); Andrea K. Bjorklund, *The Role of Counterclaims in Rebalancing Investment Law*, 17 Lewis & Clark L. Rev. 461, 470 (2013); Thomas Kendra, *State Counterclaims in Investment Arbitration – A New Lease of Life?*, 29 Arb. Int'l 575, 578 (2013); Kevin T. Jacobs and Matthew G. Paulson, *The Convergence of Renewed Nationalization, Rising Commodities, and "Americanization" in International Arbitration and the Need for More Rigorous Legal and Procedural Defenses*, 43 Tex. Int'l L. J. 359, 385 (2008); Frederic Gilles Sourgens, *Supernational Law*, 50 Vanderbilt J. Transnat'l L. 155, 196, 197, 199 (2017); Tomoko Ishikawa, *Counterclaims and the Rule of Law in Investment Arbitration*, 113 AJIL Unbound 33, 34 (2019).

there is no pre-dispute arbitration clause or contract between the investor and the host State, however, classic investment treaties provide for rights only for investors and obligations only for the host State.[2] Thus, the State is always the respondent, and it is extremely rare for investment treaties to require that the investor consent to the host States bringing counterclaims.[3] Without this express consent, respondents face an uphill battle to convince a tribunal to assert jurisdiction over their counterclaim in ISDS pursuant to a treaty in the absence of a contract.[4]

In essence, investors and States are stuck in their roles as claimant and respondent, respectively, because the implementation of the ISDS system echoes world economic power dynamics that are more rigid than the text of the ISDS-governing documents.[5] Investment arbitration tribunals hearing cases under the International Centre for Settlement of Investment Disputes (ICSID) Rules are largely hesitant to entertain State counterclaims due to the difficulty in reconciling Article 36 (consent) and Article 46 (jurisdiction) of the ICSID Convention with respect to classic investment treaties.[6] The historical analysis strongly suggests that the ICSID Convention was not intended to bar claims or counterclaims by States.[7] Nevertheless, it has been interpreted to preclude claims and counterclaims by States unless those claims can

2. *See* Barnali Choudhury, *Spinning Straw into Gold: Incorporating the Business and Human Rights Agenda into International Investment Agreements*, 38 U. Penn. J. Int'l L. 425, 472 (2017); Charles N. Brower and Stephen W. Schill, *Is Arbitration a Threat or a Boom to the Legitimacy of International Investment Law?*, 9 Chi. J. Int'l L. 471, 476, 484 (2009); Frederic Gilles Sourgens, *Supernational Law, supra* n. 1, at 172; Tomoko Ishikawa, *Counterclaims and the Rule of Law in Investment Arbitration, supra* n. 1, at 33; Yaraslau Kryvoi, *Counterclaims in Investor-State Arbitration, supra* n. 1, at 244; Jackson Shaw Kern, *Investor Responsibility as Familiar Frontier* 113 AJIL Unbound 28, 31 (2019); Anthea Roberts, *Power and Persuasion in Investment Treaty Interpretation: The Dual Role of States* 104, Am. J. Int'l L. 179, 184 (2010).
3. *See* Andrea K. Bjorklund, *The Role of Counterclaims in Rebalancing Investment Law, supra* n. 1, at 473–475; Harshad Pathak, *Consenting to Counterclaims under the ICSID Convention, supra* n. 1, at 103, 104, 115; Yaraslau Kryvoi, *Counterclaims in Investor-State Arbitration, supra* n. 1, at 225; Bradley Larschan and Guive Mirfendereski, *The Status of Counterclaims in International Law, with Particular Reference to International Arbitration Involving a Private Party and a Foreign State*, 15 Denver J. Int'l L. & Pol'l 11, 31 (1986).
4. *See* Tomoko Ishikawa, *Counterclaims and the Rule of Law in Investment Arbitration, supra* n. 1, at 37; Yaraslau Kryvoi, *Counterclaims in Investor-State Arbitration, supra* n. 1, at 218, 223; Frederic Gilles Sourgens, *Supernational Law, supra* n. 1, at 198; Andrea K. Bjorklund, *The Role of Counterclaims in Rebalancing Investment Law, supra* n. 1, at 480.
5. *See* James Gathii and Sergio Puig, *Introduction to the Symposium on Investor Responsibility: The Next Frontier in International Investment Law*, 113 AJIL Unbound 1, 3 (2019); Bradley Larschan and Guive Mirfendereski, *The Status of Counterclaims in International Law, with Particular Reference to International Arbitration Involving a Private Party and a Foreign State, supra* n. 3, at 33; Harshad Pathak, *Consenting to Counterclaims under the ICSID Convention, supra* n. 1, at 110; Andrea K. Bjorklund, *The Role of Counterclaims in Rebalancing Investment Law, supra* n. 1, at 471, 472.
6. *See* Luis Miguel Velarde Saffer and Amir Ardelan Farhadi, *Lessons from the Deathbed of the Trans-Pacific Partnership (TPP): Are Recent Critiques of the Investor-State Dispute Settlement (ISDS) System Warranted*, 11 Disp. Resol. Int'l 3, 18 n. 61 (2017); Harshad Pathak, *Consenting to Counterclaims under the ICSID Convention, supra* n. 1, at 108, 110, 111, 114; Thomas Kendra, *State Counterclaims in Investment Arbitration – A New Lease of Life?, supra* n. 1, at 577, 593, 595.
7. *See supra* references cited in n. 5.

overcome the investor consent and subject matter jurisdiction hurdles erected by Articles 36 and 46, respectively.[8]

Third-party funding is a lens through which to analyze one consequence of this overarching structural inequality in ISDS: lack of financial access to justice. Because of the rigidity of the parties' roles in classic investment treaties, third-party funders typically fund only investor-claimants in investment arbitrations brought exclusively under a treaty; respondent-side funding in investment treaty-based arbitrations is nearly nonexistent.[9] The funder is always paid from the funds of the respondent in any type of dispute resolution; therefore, the funder is always paid with funds from the respondent State in investment arbitration.[10] In essence, States are the sole payers for third-party funding for investment treaty arbitration, but they are unable to enjoy a benefit equivalent to investors' benefits. This is a microcosm of the larger problem of lack of financial access to justice for respondent States of which third-party funding is just one aspect, but a thorough discussion of financial access to justice in ISDS is beyond the scope of this chapter.[11] This chapter focuses on how third-party funding in particular shines a spotlight on this pervasive lack of financial access to justice in ISDS and presents suggestions for how to address financial access to justice in ISDS through third-party funding without requiring the renegotiation of thousands of investment treaties.

§13.02 CLASSIC THIRD-PARTY FUNDING IN ISDS

It is presently uncontroversial that ISDS is controversial.[12] The explosion of third-party funding in investor-State arbitration and the frequent publicity of such funding have

8. *See supra* references cited in n. 6.
9. *See* Victoria Anne Shannon, *Harmonizing Third-Party Litigation Funding Regulation*, 36 Cardozo L. Rev. 861, 867 (2015) (addressing the lack of defense-side funding); *The ICCA Reports No. 4: ICCA Queen Mary Task Force Report on Third-Party Funding in International Arbitration*, 244, 246–247 (Int'l Council for Commercial Arb. 2018).
10. *See* Lisa Bench Nieuwveld and Victoria Shannon Sahani, *Third-Party Funding in International Arbitration* 34–35, 37 (Wolters Kluwer 2d ed. 2017).
11. For discussions of access to justice more generally in ISDS, *see*, e.g., Nan Aron, *ISDS denies equal access to justice*, The Hill (June 9, 2015); Investment Division, Directorate for Financial and Enterprise Affairs, *Government perspectives on investor-state dispute settlement: a progress report*, Organisation for Economic Co-operation and Development (OECD) (December 14, 2012), https://www.oecd.org/daf/inv/investment-policy/ISDSprogressreport.pdf.
12. *See*, e.g., Frank J. Garcia, *The Case Against Third-Party Funding in Investment Arbitration*, Investment Treaty News, Int'l Institute for Sustainable Development (July 30, 2018), https://www.iisd.org/itn/2018/07/30/the-case-against-third-party-funding-in-investment-arbitration-frank-garcia/; Chris Hamby, *Secrets of a Global Super court: A BuzzFeed News Investigation* BuzzFeed.com (August 28–October 12, 2016), https://www.buzzfeed.com/badge/global supercourt (a six-article series); Rebecca Lowe, *Speculate and Arbitrate to Accumulate*, IBA Global Insight (April/May 2013), https://www.ibanet.org/Article/NewDetail.aspx?ArticleUid=804E46E3-DFC0-4966-B16E-31627803970C; Pia Eberhardt, *A Response to the Critics of "Profiting from Injustice,"* Kluwer Arb. Blog (January 2, 2013), http://arbitrationblog.kluwerarbitration.com/2013/01/02/a-response-to-the-critics-of-profiting-from-injustice/; Transnational Institute and Corporate Europe Observatory, *Profiting from Injustice* (Brussels/Amsterdam, November 2012), https://corporateeurope.org/sites/default/files/publications/profiting-from-injustice.pdf.

arguably made ISDS even more controversial.[13] Many pages have been printed arguing against allowing third-party funding in investment arbitration for a variety of reasons.[14] In contrast, third-party funding has been relatively well received by the international commercial arbitration system, with the caveat that there are justifiable concerns about disclosure requirements, evidentiary privileges, and conflicts of interest that must be addressed through international rules, guidelines, and norms.[15] Many discussions about third-party funding address international commercial and investment arbitration together.[16] However, third-party funding affects investment arbitration differently than commercial arbitration due to structural differences in the investment arbitration system.

Upon a cursory glance, one may draw the conclusion that the participation of an unobtrusive third-party funder should not have any effect on an ISDS case. In fact, the traditional view of investment arbitration tribunals is that the mere presence of a third-party funder has no effect on the arbitration proceedings. For example, the tribunal in *Oxus Gold v. Uzbekistan* articulated the traditional view that third-party funding has no impact on the merits portion of the arbitration process: "It is undisputed that Claimant is being assisted by a third-party funder in this arbitration proceeding. The Arbitral Tribunal has mentioned this fact in its Procedural Order Nos. 6 and 7. However, this fact has no impact on this arbitration proceeding."[17] The treatment of third-party funding may vary from tribunal to tribunal however, since there are no mandatory substantive precedents in investment arbitration regarding third-party funding yet.[18] Nevertheless, most tribunals that have addressed third-party funding in their awards – if at all – have simply acknowledged the presence of the funder and moved on to addressing other aspects of the case.

However, there is more to third-party funding's effect on ISDS than meets the eye. Most funding happens on the claim side in any system of dispute resolution – litigation, commercial arbitration, or investment arbitration – because claim-side funding is more financially attractive to most funders than respondent-side funding.[19] This is because the bulk (if not all) of any third-party funder's eventual payout will come from the respondent in the case. For example, if a funded claimant wins, then the funder is paid

13. *See supra* references cited in n. 12.
14. *See ibid.*
15. *See generally The ICCA Reports No. 4: ICCA Queen Mary Task Force Report on Third-Party Funding in International Arbitration* (Int'l Council for Commercial Arb. 2018).
16. *See generally The ICCA Reports No. 4: ICCA Queen Mary Task Force Report on Third-Party Funding in International Arbitration* (Int'l Council for Commercial Arb. 2018); Victoria Shannon Sahani, *Third-Party Funders as Stakeholders in International Arbitration* in *Cambridge Compendium of International Commercial and Investment Arbitration* (Andrea Bjorklund, Franco Ferrari and Stefan Kröll eds, Cambridge University Press (forthcoming)).
17. *Oxus Gold PLC v. Republic of Uzbekistan*, UNCITRAL Arb., Final Award (December 17, 2015), para. 127.
18. However, this will change after ICSID adopts its proposed rule changes, which include adding provisions regarding third-party funding. *See* ICSID, *Working Paper #4: Proposals for Amendment of the ICSID Rules*, World Bank Group (February 2020), https://icsid.worldbank.org/en/Documents/WP_4_Vol_1_En.pdf (proposing adding rules or modifying rules to address third-party funding, including Arbitration Rule 14 and Additional Facility Rule 23 on disclosure and Arbitration Rule 53 and Additional Facility Rule 63 on security for costs).
19. *See supra* references cited in n. 9.

from the awarded amount collected from the respondent. In addition, a winning funded claimant may also obtain an adverse costs order against the respondent, which also helps the claimant repay its third-party funder.[20] In contrast, respondent-side funding is only financially attractive if the funding arrangement is structured in a certain way, such as legal expenses insurance or after-the-event insurance.[21] If a funded respondent wins (or, depending on the financing structure, even if the respondent loses), the respondent must pay the funder a fee according to the terms of its funding contract; this fee is often structured like an "insurance" premium or a success fee.[22] Only if a funded respondent brings a successful monetary counterclaim or a successful costs application against the claimant can the funded respondent obtain money from the claimant that it can use to pay its third-party funder.[23] In commercial arbitration, having the respondent always serve as the source of funds for the funder is tolerable, because corporations could just as easily be respondents as claimants in commercial cases. Furthermore, respondents in international commercial arbitration under a contract have the ability to bring counterclaims that funders may choose to fund. Similarly, when the investor and host State sign a separate contract, such as a concession agreement, they each have an equal opportunity to bring claims against each other according to their contractual dispute resolution method, which may be arbitration.[24]

States and State-owned entities that are parties to a contract-based international arbitration proceeding, however, are in a fundamentally different position than respondent States sued in investment treaty-based arbitration. Unlike in commercial arbitration, the rigidity of the parties' roles in investment treaty-based arbitration may create lopsided funding incentives. The funder is always paid from the funds of the respondent any type of dispute resolution; therefore, the funder is always paid with funds from the respondent State in investment arbitration. In essence, States are the sole payers in a system of third-party funding for investment treaty arbitration in which they are unable to enjoy a benefit equivalent to investors' benefits. While there have been a few notable examples of third-party funding of respondent States, it is generally

20. *See generally The ICCA Reports No. 4: ICCA Queen Mary Task Force Report on Third-Party Funding in International Arbitration* 145–184 (Int'l Council for Commercial Arb. 2018) (addressing costs and security for costs).
21. For example, Narghis Torres, Co-Founder and CEO of LexFinance, www.lex-finance.com, publicly stated that his firm regularly finances respondent States in investment arbitration at an event titled "Third-Party Funding in Investor-State Dispute Settlement" hosted by Columbia Law School on October 17, 2017 at which the Author was present.
22. *See* Jonathan T. Molot, *A Market in Litigation Risk*, 76 U. Chi. L. Rev. 367, 377–380 (2009) (proposing defense-side funding in the United States that would be similar to after-the-event insurance in Europe); Bernardo M. Cremades Jr, *Third Party Litigation Funding: Investing in Arbitration*, Transnat'l Disp. Mgmt (October 2011), 16–25 (discussing several arrangements for defense-side funding in which the funder is only paid if the defendant/respondent wins the case).
23. *See generally The ICCA Reports No. 4: ICCA Queen Mary Task Force Report on Third-Party Funding in International Arbitration* 145–184 (Int'l Council for Commercial Arb. 2018) (addressing costs and security for costs).
24. The other common alternative is the local courts of the host State.

not common.[25] Even if a funder funds a respondent State's defense, the winning respondent State still must pay the funder from its own coffers, because even if the winning funded respondent obtains an adverse costs order against the claimant, the amount awarded is unlikely to cover the full cost of third-party funding absent a unicorn-like ruling such as the United Kingdom Commercial Court's decision in *Essar v. Norscot*.[26]

Besides defense-side funding, the other vehicle for third-party funding of States is through a counterclaim. As mentioned previously, investment arbitration tribunals hearing cases under the ICSID Rules are largely hesitant to uphold State counterclaims due to the difficulty in reconciling two provisions of the ICSID Convention.[27] Article 36 of the ICSID Convention states that the request for arbitration shall contain "information concerning ... [the parties'] consent to arbitration."[28] When there is no pre-dispute arbitration clause or contract between the investor and the host State, the consent to arbitrate must be found in the bilateral investment treaty (BIT) between the host State and the investor's home State. The investor is not a party to the treaty, so the investor's "written" consent is evidenced by the investor filing a claim under Articles 25 and 28 of the ICSID Convention or under provisions of the BIT.[29] In addition, Article 46 of the ICSID Convention requires a tribunal to determine "if requested by a party ... any incidental or additional claims or counterclaims arising directly out of the subject-matter of the dispute provided that they are within the scope of the consent of the parties and are otherwise within the jurisdiction of the Centre."[30] Since nearly all BITs expressly protect investor rights, but not necessarily host State rights, it is unclear whether claims involving the host State's rights "are within the scope of the consent of the parties" or whether counterclaims brought by the State are "within the jurisdiction of the Centre." Given these uncertainties, several cases have dealt with counterclaims on a case-by-case basis with varying results, and there is no clear norm regarding what

25. For example, it is widely known that the Bloomberg Foundation, through its "Campaign for Tobacco-Free Kids" in the United States, funded pro bono Uruguay's winning defense of its tobacco plain packaging laws in an investment arbitration brought by Philip Morris, a multinational tobacco corporation. This example is unusual, however, because it involved not-for-profit or ideological funding rather than for-profit funding. *See* Kelly Henning, *Supporting Uruguay in their Fight Against Big Tobacco*, Bloomberg Philanthropies Public Health Team (July 18, 2013), https://www.bloomberg.org/blog/supporting-uruguay-in-their-fight-against-big-tobacco/. Not-for-profit funding is being offered to other respondent States defending against claims by tobacco companies. *See Bloomberg Philanthropies & The Bill & Melinda Gates Foundation Launch Anti-Tobacco Trade Litigation Fund*, Bloomberg Philanthropies Press & Media (March 18, 2015), www.bloomberg.org/press/releases/bloomberg-philanthropies-bill-melinda-gates-foundation-launch-anti-tobacco-trade-litigation-fund/.
26. *See Essar Oilfields Services Ltd v. Norscot Rig Management Pvt Ltd* [2016] EWHC 2361 (Comm) (September 15, 2016), http://www.bailii.org/ew/cases/EWHC/Comm/2016/2361.html (upholding the decision of the ICC arbitral tribunal that had ruled that Essar had to pay the full cost of Norscot's third-party funding, because Essar had engaged in overly egregious conduct that had forced Norscot to obtain third-party funding to vindicate its rights in arbitration).
27. *See supra* n. 6 and accompanying text.
28. Convention on the Settlement of Investment Disputes between States and Nationals of Other States (1965), Art. 36.
29. *Ibid.*, Arts 25, 28.
30. *Ibid.*, Art. 46.

the rule should be.[31] Thus, third-party funders typically fund only investor-claimants in investment arbitrations brought exclusively under a treaty; respondent-side funding in investment treaty-based arbitrations is nearly nonexistent.

§13.03 NOT-FOR-PROFIT THIRD-PARTY FUNDING IN ISDS

Another phenomenon that affects financial access to justice in ISDS is that some third-party funders are participating in ISDS without a profit-making motive or with profit not being the primary goal. Such funders might be termed "not-for-profit funders" or "ideological funders."[32] Not-for-profit funders are primarily motivated by goals other than reaping a profit, such as creating a favorable precedent for future claims, gathering information about parties, or supporting or fighting against an industry. A not-for-profit funder may still receive reimbursement or profit from the case, but that is not the driving force behind the funder supporting the case.

A famous example of a defense-side, industry-specific, not-for-profit third-party funder is the Anti-Tobacco Trade Litigation Fund created by Bloomberg Philanthropies and the Bill and Melinda Gates Foundation to help low- and middle-income countries finance their defenses against tobacco companies' claims under investment treaties.[33] In one case, the Bloomberg Foundation and its Campaign for Tobacco-Free Kids famously provided financial support and technical assistance to the government of Uruguay for its defense against the tobacco company Philip Morris in the ICSID case *Philip Morris v. Uruguay*, in which Philip Morris challenged State regulations requiring plain packaging of tobacco products.[34]

---

31. *Ibid.*
32. *See*, e.g., Eric de Brabandere and Julia Lepeltak, *Third-Party Funding in International Investment Arbitration*, 27(2) ICSID Rev. 379 (2012); Eugene Kontorovich, *Opinion: Peter Thiel's funding of Hulk Hogan-Gawker litigation should not raise concerns*, The Washington Post (May 26, 2016), www.washingtonpost.com/news/volokh-conspiracy/wp/2016/05/26/peter-thiels-funding-of-hulk-hogan-gawker-litigation-should-not-raise-concerns ("Anyone who donates to the ACLU or a Legal Aid fund is basically underwriting third-party litigation. Most recently, private profit-motivated litigation finance has emerged as an industry in its own right, unburdened by any concern over the old common law rules. ... By current standards, Thiel's funding should raise no eyebrows – unless one also wants to revisit public interest litigation, class actions and contingent fees. Critics of Thiel's role in the Gawker case argue that it is particularly inappropriate because they think he is motivated by 'revenge' over the gossip site's earlier publication of stories about his private life. But if the lawsuit is not frivolous, it is hard to see how the motivations of funders are relevant (or discernible). One would not say a civil rights organization could not accept donations from philanthropists angered by a personal experience with discrimination. All Thiel has done is cut out the middleman. Indeed, Thiel's conduct fits into the 'public interest' or 'ideological' litigation paradigm"); Victoria Shannon Sahani, *Third-Party Funders as Stakeholders in International Arbitration* in *Cambridge Compendium of International Commercial and Investment Arbitration* (Andrea Bjorklund, Franco Ferrari and Stefan Kröll eds., Cambridge University Press (forthcoming)).
33. In addition, the Author was present when former New York City Mayor Michael Bloomberg appeared in person at the January 2016 Annual Meeting of the Association of American Law Schools and pledged in his remarks that his foundation would support countries that did not have the financial means to defend against arbitrations brought by tobacco companies like Philip Morris.
34. *See supra* references cited in n. 25.

Similarly, an example of a precedent-seeking funder appears in *Quasar de Valores v. Russia* in which the funder, Group Menatep Limited, was a former majority shareholder in the Russian oil company Yukos.[35] There was no contract in place requiring the claimant to reimburse Menatep; instead, Menatep was seeking to create a favorable interpretive "precedent" in hopes that such a precedent would be applied in its future, much larger, shareholder dispute against Russia under the Energy Charter Treaty, in which it expected to win a massive monetary award. Moreover, in *Quasar de Valores v. Russia*, the tribunal denied the funded party's request to recover costs, because the third-party funder was merely trying to create a favorable precedent and was not entitled to receive repayment from the funded party, even if the funded party won the case. While the term "not-for-profit funder" may not be entirely accurate with respect to Menatep's ultimate motives in this case, Menatep is certainly a different type of funder than the traditional third-party funders that fund multiple unrelated cases purely for profit.

The foregoing scattered references to not-for-profit funders in ISDS may not yet seem very noteworthy. Nevertheless, ISDS is likely to see a rise in the participation of not-for-profit funders in the future, on both the claim side and the defense side, as potential financiers worldwide take a greater interest in international arbitration as a vehicle for bringing about the changes they seek in global political and economic dynamics.

Regardless of whether the third-party funding is for profit or for other reasons, there is a widespread perception that third-party funding is unbalancing our notions of party-driven dispute resolution processes and evenhanded tribunals.[36] Third-party funding indisputably puts a gold-weighted thumb on the scale in favor of funded investors, but respondent States have almost no access to such funding, even though respondent States win most ISDS cases.[37] Respondent States without counterclaims need hefty funds at their disposal through which to pay the funder either a periodic premium or need to be able to pay the funder from their own pockets (rather than from the proceeds of an award) upon winning the case.[38] In addition, even if the respondent State is able to submit a counterclaim seeking a nonfinancial remedy, such as an injunction against an investor polluting the environment, a funder will not view that as an attractive investment opportunity, since there will be no monetary judgment upon winning the injunction. As mentioned previously, not-for-profit dispute financiers may be willing to step into the breach for some respondents, but they will not do so

35. *See Quasar de Valores SICAV S.A. et al. v. The Russian Federation*, SCC Arb. No. 24/2007, Award of July 20, 2012, para. 223.
36. *See supra* references cited in n. 12.
37. *Compare* Susan D. Franck, *Development and Outcomes of Investment Treaty Arbitration*, 50 Harvard Int'l L. J. 435, 447 (2009) ("First, governments can and did win investment disputes. In fact, governments (57.7%) were more likely than investors (38.5%) to win cases and have no damages awarded for alleged treaty breaches. Second, the average amount awarded (approximately USD 10 million) was a fraction of what investors typically requested (approximately USD 343 million)") (parentheses in original) *with* Andrea K. Bjorklund, *The Role of Counterclaims in Rebalancing Investment Law, supra* n. 1, at 464 ("It might be said that, absent the ability to submit a counterclaim, a state cannot win; the most it can hope to do is not to lose").
38. *See supra* references cited in n. 21.

systematically, regularly or predictably and, therefore, do not present a viable solution to this problem.[39] Similarly, classic attorney contingent, conditional, or damages-based fee agreements are not an appropriate vehicle for reforming financial access to justice in ISDS either, due to the rigidity of the classic roles of investor-claimants and State-respondents. Therefore, something must change in the structure of the ISDS system in order to create alternative sources of funding for arbitration costs to increase financial access to justice for respondent States, which would hopefully also bolster States' confidence in the ISDS system.

This highlights a crucial point about access to justice. Any proper assessment of "access to justice" must examine the situation of parties that have no choice in the matter: respondents. Respondents in all types of arbitration have no choice regarding whether the arbitration will bind them, regardless of whether they are financially able to participate in the arbitration or not. Thus, respondents *must* have access to financial resources for arbitration costs in order for the ISDS system to be considered "just" at all.

§13.04 PROPOSALS FOR FINANCIAL ACCESS TO JUSTICE IN ISDS

There are respondents in both international commercial arbitration and investment treaty arbitration that have enough financial means to fund their own costs; for them, the availability of alternative sources of funding for arbitration costs is irrelevant. If a respondent State does not have sufficient financial resources to self-finance, however, the respondent State may choose not to participate in the arbitration. The logic here is that the respondent State will attempt to make itself "judgment-proof," meaning that, even if the investor wins, the investor will not be able to collect the money.[40] Similarly, some States participate in the arbitration and then attempt to thwart enforcement of the award after they lose.[41] Both of these responses by States delegitimize and undermine the ISDS system. Therefore, solutions should be implemented to encourage States to vigorously participate in the system and abide by its results. This section describes and analyzes several possible solutions to the financial access to justice problem in ISDS.

As described above, respondents in international commercial arbitration and ISDS generally are not attractive targets for investment by classic for-profit dispute financiers, like third-party funders and law firms.[42] One potential solution is to make respondents more attractive to for-profit dispute financiers. For example, funders are

39. *See* Victoria Shannon Sahani, Mick Smith and Christiane Deniger, *Third-Party Financing in Investment Arbitration* in *Contemporary and Emerging Issues on the Law of Damages and Valuation in International Investment Arbitration* 49 (Christina Beharry ed., Brill Nijhoff 2018) ("In addition, not-for-profit funding may be a viable option for respondents in international arbitration – particularly respondent States in investment arbitration – since a financial return on investment would not normally be required"). For examples of not-for-profit funding, *see supra* references cited in n. 25 and s. 3.03.
40. *See* Lisa Bench Nieuwveld and Victoria Shannon Sahani, *Third-Party Funding in International Arbitration* 34–35, 37 (Wolters Kluwer 2d ed. 2017).
41. *See ibid.*
42. There is one potential dispute financier called LexFinance that would finance a respondent State's defense, but one dispute financier is not enough to solve a systemic, structural problem. *See supra* references cited in n. 21.

still fighting the public relations battle, and there are still many groups and organizations that oppose third-party funding, especially in ISDS.[43] There are reputational benefits if third-party funders, after-the-event insurers, and law firms engage in pro bono funding or reduced-fee funding for a subset of worthy claims or defenses by respondents. Firms that are seen as supporting impecunious respondents or worthy defenses may be viewed more positively within the larger funding market. This is one reason that law firms engage in domestic pro bono work and reduced-fee work already in their local communities. If a concrete reputational benefit were promised to firms that engage in pro bono or reduced-fee financial access to justice for respondents, then perhaps these for-profit entities would be incentivized to engage in offering such services. That concrete reputational benefit could be inclusion on a list of commendable law firms that are increasing financial access to justice in ISDS, and this list that could be compiled, maintained and published by an international organization like the ICSID at the World Bank, United Nations Commission on International Trade Law (UNCITRAL), United Nations Conference on Trade and Development (UNCTAD), or the Permanent Court of Arbitration (PCA). The drawback to this is that reputational benefits are nearly impossible to quantify and the time horizon for realizing financial benefits from reputational benefits may be too long for for-profit entities. That said, the recent widespread adoption of the Equal Representation in Arbitration pledge, aimed at increasing the number of women arbitrators, despite any quantifiable, immediate effect on the profits of the signatory firms, is admirable and may provide a useful model.[44]

Another potential solution is public funding of States, perhaps through a non-governmental organization (NGO) fund into which all ISDS Member States pay and then impecunious States can apply for assistance for their defenses. A mechanism like this exists at the World Trade Organization (WTO) for its dispute settlement process, and third-party funders seem to be trying to create a WTO dispute settlement funding market as well.[45] Tangentially, this could also include not only funding from not-for-profit organizations but also crowdfunding.[46] A drawback of this approach is that it would be highly political. There will be politics involved in which States pay into the fund, which States receive assistance from the fund, whether or how States must repay the aid, and which not-for-profit entities or crowdfunding platforms are supporting which issues and causes. In sum, a public funding solution would likely bring more

43. *See supra* references cited in n. 12.
44. An alphabetized list of more than 750 organizations and individuals that have signed the Equal Representation in Arbitration pledge to increase the number of women in arbitration is available at http://www.arbitrationpledge.com/organisations.
45. For a proposal for funding developing States in WTO dispute settlement, *see*, e.g., Mauritius Nagelmueller, *Access to Justice for Developing Countries: Third Party Funding for Sovereigns in WTO Disputes*, Litigation Finance J. (October 4, 2017) (guest post), https://litigationfinancejournal.com/access-justice-developing-countries-third-party-funding-sovereigns-wto-disputes/ (proposing that for-profit dispute financiers should provide financing to developing States in WTO dispute settlement proceedings).
46. *See generally* Manuel A. Gomez, *Crowdfunded Justice: On the Potential Benefits and Challenges of Crowdfunding as a Litigation Financing Tool*, 49 U.S.F. L. Rev. 307 (2015); Ronen Perry, *Crowdfunding Civil Justice*, 59 B.C. L. Rev. 1357 (2018).

politics into an ISDS system that, in theory, was designed to be apolitical, or at least less political, than other international fora.

A third potential solution involves financiers modifying their criteria when deciding which cases to fund. For example, a third-party funder might modify its algorithms and decision-making processes to include other ideals as factors to weigh in determining whether to fund a case in order to increase access to justice in international arbitration. One of those ideals could be ensuring that respondent States have access to justice by having access to third-party funding. Respondent States may also have merit-based winning claims or counterclaims that are too expensive to pursue relative to their claim value when offset by the cost to defend against the investor's original claim. As mentioned previously, third-party funders have a much more dubious reputation in investment arbitration, when compared to commercial arbitration. If third-party funders financed some respondent States in investment arbitration, then perhaps the participation of third-party funders in investment treaty cases would be viewed as more balanced, perhaps even viewed positively. In addition, investment arbitration, as a whole, may be viewed as more legitimate if respondent States have more regular access to third-party funding.

This third solution departs from the poverty paradigm that is often used to argue that dispute financiers should modify their choices regarding which cases to fund to promote access to justice.[47] For example, since so few respondent States are currently being funded, both poor and wealthy respondent States alike are equally denied third-party funding from most for-profit funders. Other worthy aspects of the case itself may be the true foundation of "access to justice" that funders should espouse and support financially, such as upholding the health and safety laws of a country,[48] defending against abusive investment practices, ensuring the stability of a country's legal system, stopping damaging environmental practices of investors, clarifying the meaning of ambiguous treaty language, and so on. Those are worthy ideals worth pursuing and financing regardless of the wealth or poverty of the respondent nation or the potential for profit (or lack thereof).

A fourth potential solution is the renegotiation of investment treaties to allow for claims by host States against investors as well as counterclaims by respondent States.[49]

---

47. *See*, e.g., United Nations Office of the High Representative for the Least Developed Countries, Landlocked Developing Countries and Small Island Developing States (UNOHRLLS) and the International Development Law Organization (IDLO), *Investment Support Programme for the Least Developed Countries (ISP/LDCs): Programme Document*, para. 5 and n. 11 (September 6, 2017), https://res.cloudinary.com/lbresearch/image/upload/v1506335575/isp_ldcs_programme_document_6_september_258117_1133.pdf (proposing a system for providing support to poor States for, among other endeavors, "[f]oreign investment-related dispute settlement between the Client and a foreign entity, including arbitration or any other alternative dispute resolution proceeding" and "if the applicable rules to the dispute allow, the ISP/LDCS may also seek to identify and field the Client's party-appointed arbitrator").
48. *See supra* references cited in n. 25 for an example of a nonprofit funder supporting a State's laws regarding packaging of tobacco products for public health and safety reasons.
49. *See* Meredith A. Strike, *Investor-State Dispute Settlement in Sub-Saharan Africa: Suggestions for Reform*, 27 African J. Int'l & Comp. L. 150, 160 (2019); Yaraslau Kryvoi, *Counterclaims in Investor-State Arbitration*, *supra* n. 1, at 226.

If the treaties change to allow host States to become claimants against investor-respondents, or if arbitral tribunals coalesce around a "common law" rule regarding when they will exercise jurisdiction over host State counterclaims, then this would help even the playing field for States with respect to access not just to third-party funding, but also to contingency and conditional fee arrangements with attorneys. Under this new regime, if the funded State-claimant or State-counterclaimant wins, then the funder would be paid from the private investor-respondent's funds. Similarly, a funded investor-respondent would pay for its defense-side third-party funding from its own funds, the cost of which could be offset by additional claims or counterclaims against the State. In sum, if treaties allowed host States to be claimants and counterclaimants, then third-party funding of investment arbitration would look a lot more like third-party funding of commercial arbitration.

An advantage of this approach is that States can create bespoke agreements between them. Perhaps ISDS does not have to look the same for all States. While the ICSID Arbitration Rules are the same for all States, each pair or group of States entering into an investment treaty can develop their own nuanced arbitration procedures. Arbitration is fundamentally a creature of agreement, so States should be able to agree to whatever process they want. The major drawback to bespoke arbitration procedures in treaties, of course, is logistics. If every treaty "reinvented the wheel" so to speak regarding arbitration procedure, then this would impose huge costs on the global dispute resolution system because arbitrators would have to learn a new system with each new dispute and institutions would be able to administer proceedings as efficiently and effectively, and they may even be unable to ensure the integrity of the result. Some degree of customization is useful, but too much customization actually makes arbitration too difficult to administer, which frustrates the basic purpose of a dispute resolution system that is meant to freely encourage foreign direct investment.

Another drawback of this approach is the theoretical expectation that widespread treaty revision will be nearly impossible to implement, since many countries no longer have the political will to ratify a renegotiated treaty, no matter how problematic the existing treaty may be. The surprising reality, however, is that more countries have expressed openness to reexamining and revising treaty provisions than the academic literature would suggest. In addition, some countries whose investment treaties have expired, who are engaged in renegotiating their treaties for other reasons or who are entering into new treaties, could consider including provisions to allow for host State claims. For example, several new BITs and ICSID's forthcoming arbitration and conciliation rule revisions contain provisions requiring disclosure of third-party funding in recognition that third-party funding is here to say.[50] Such an explicit reference to

50. *See*, e.g., Comprehensive Economic and Trade Agreement (CETA), Art. 8.1, http://data.consilium.europa.eu/doc/document/ST-10973-2016-INIT/en/pdf ("any funding provided by a natural or legal person who is not a disputing party but who enters into an agreement with a disputing party in order to finance part or all of the cost of the proceedings either through a donation or grant, or in return for remuneration dependent on the outcome of the dispute"); Comprehensive Economic and Trade Agreement (CETA), Art. 8.26, http://data.consilium.europa.eu/doc/document/ST-10973-2016-INIT/en/pdf (requires disclosure of only the name and address of the third-party funder "at the time of the submission of a claim, or, if the

third-party funding in something as permanent as a treaty or an arbitration rule arguably is tantamount to rolling out the proverbial "red carpet" to welcome third-party funders. Moreover, the Morocco-Nigeria BIT concluded in 2018 innovatively includes investor obligations that the host State may redress in its domestic State courts as well as a "disputes prevention" mechanism.[51] Furthermore, the biggest recent development in this space is the European Union (EU) Member States signing a new treaty in May 2020 to terminate and replace all preexisting intra-EU BITs.[52] The termination treaty eliminated investment arbitration for all intra-EU disputes, but it is unclear whether intra-EU commercial arbitration will be eliminated as well by forthcoming case law.

A fifth solution is to leave the multitude of treaties as they are and instead change the jurisdictional language in the major arbitration rules used in ISDS to expressly allow counterclaims in investment arbitration.[53] An advantage of the fifth approach of

---

financing agreement is concluded or the donation or grant is made after the submission of a claim, without delay as soon as the agreement is concluded or the donation or grant is made"); Transatlantic Trade and Investment Partnership (TTIP) (European Union draft), Ch. II, s. 3, subs. (1), Art. 1, http://trade.ec.europa.eu/doclib/docs/2015/september/tradoc_153807.pdf (nearly identical to CETA Art. 8.1); Transatlantic Trade and Investment Partnership (TTIP) (European Union draft), Ch. II, s. 3, subs. (3), Art. 8, http://trade.ec.europa.eu/doclib/docs/2015/september/tradoc_153807.pdf (nearly identical to CETA Art. 8.26); EU-Vietnam Investment Protection Agreement, Ch. 3, s. B, subs. (1), Art. 3.28(i), https://trade.ec.europa.eu/doclib/docs/2018/september/tradoc_157394.pdf (defines third-party funding as "any funding provided by a natural or juridical person who is not a party to the dispute but who enters into an agreement with a disputing party in order to finance part or all of the cost of the proceedings in return for a remuneration dependent on the outcome of the dispute or in the form of a donation or grant"); EU-Vietnam Investment Protection Agreement, Ch. 3, s. B, subs. (3), Art. 3.37, https://trade.ec.europa.eu/doclib/docs/2018/september/tradoc_157394.pdf (provides for a similar disclosure requirement as CETA, except it also adds a required disclosure regarding the "nature of the funding arrangement" and requires that the arbitral tribunal considers the presence of third-party funding when making decisions regarding costs and security for costs); EU-Vietnam Investment Protection Agreement, Ch. 3, s. B, subs. (5), Art. 3.54(7), https://trade.ec.europa.eu/doclib/docs/2018/september/tradoc_157394.pdf (stating that Art. 3.37 regarding third-party funding applies in the appeal procedure); *supra* reference cited in n. 18 (describing forthcoming ICSID Rule revisions to address third-party funding).

51. *See* Thomas Kendra, Robert Bradshaw and Ilham Kabbouri, *The Morocco-Nigeria BIT: A New Breed of Investment Treaty?*, Thomas Reuters Practical L. Arb. Blog (November 16, 2017), http://arbitrationblog.practicallaw.com/the-morocco-nigeria-bit-a-new-breed-of-investment-treaty/ (describing the key features of the treaty and explaining that "while the BIT specifies that breach of investor obligations may lead to liability before domestic courts, it does not expressly address whether such claims may also be raised by a respondent State in arbitration. International tribunals do appear increasingly to admit counterclaims by States, so this may nevertheless remain a possibility").
52. *See* Tom Jones, *UK and Finland Face Legal Action over Intra-EU BITs*, Global Arb. Rev. (May 14, 2020), https://globalarbitrationreview.com/article/1226878/uk-and-finland-face-legal-action-over-intra-eu-bits; *A defining moment for arbitration within Europe*, Global Arb. Rev. (May 13, 2020), https://globalarbitrationreview.com/article/1226781/a-defining-moment-for-arbitration-within-europe. It is also unclear how the EU BIT termination treaty and the convoluted Brexit political situation will interact with respect to BITs between the United Kingdom and other EU Member States, and it is unclear whether the United Kingdom will still be part of the EU at the time this book is published.
53. The major arbitration rules used in ISDS include the ICSID Arbitration Rules, the UNCITRAL Arbitration Rules, the International Court of Arbitration of the International Chamber of Commerce (ICC) Arbitration Rules, the PCA Rules, and others.

changing the arbitration rules is that, with the stroke of a pen, the arbitration rules can harmonize the implementation of the jurisdiction requirements of the treaties in the ISDS system. Many of the existing investment treaties are decades old, yet the arbitration rules that they referenced have undergone several revisions and overhauls in the ensuing decades. The newly revised rules still apply to the preexisting BITs, even if the new rules look very little like the ones that existed at the time the treaty was originally ratified. There have not been many objections from States or investors regarding the use of the current version of the investment arbitration rules at the time the claim is filed, with the exception of some objections to the emergency arbitrator procedures incorporated within some rules of arbitration. Given this norm, changing the arbitration rules, in effect, could function as a shortcut to changing the system. In addition, changing the arbitration rules is far easier than revising a treaty, because there is no State ratification required, and the arbitration rule revision process may be viewed as more egalitarian and pluralistic in terms of making sure that all voices and viewpoints are considered during the redrafting process. This contributes greatly to legitimacy, harmonization, and trust in the ISDS system.

Another advantage of this fifth solution is that, since the present treaties are all different, the multinational corporations can shop around and choose the treaty that is best for them, thereby circumventing the protections that are put in place by their home jurisdiction or the host jurisdiction vis-à-vis investors from certain countries. The problem with this is that many treaties do not take into account that multinational corporations often have multiple nationalities, which has made "treaty shopping" by investor-claimants even more of a problem in recent years. Multinational corporations can "treaty shop" by using shell companies and single-purpose vehicles.[54] The system is lopsided because a host State cannot change its nationality to "treaty shop." Therefore, each individual treaty that is revised, renegotiation, or newly ratified creates a new opportunity for treaty shopping among multinational corporations, especially if the multinational corporations agree or disagree with certain treaty revisions. This exacerbated by the fact that host States cannot bring claims under most existing treaties, and the investor gets to choose the treaty in the first place by filing the original claim before the host State, can bring a counterclaim under a treaty that allows counterclaims. States are only fully empowered by revised treaties if they can choose the treaty and file the original claim, rather than merely being a counterclaimant. This is also a drawback to the fourth solution, described above, of allowing States to modify the ISDS system purely by treaty; the fifth solution appears to solve this problem.

Nevertheless, the fifth solution also has two major drawbacks. First, arbitral institutions themselves have no direct power over the States.[55] If the institutions make

54. *See* Jackson Shaw Kern, *Investor Responsibility as Familiar Frontier, supra* n. 2, at 29; Gus van Harten and Martin Loughlin, *Investment Treaty Arbitration as a Species of Global Administrative Law,* 17 European J. Int'l L. 121–150, 137–138 (2006).

55. Nevertheless, several articles have called for or examined the increasing institutionalization of investment arbitration, including perhaps the creation of either an appellate body or a permanent multilateral investment court of some type. *See, e.g.*, Andrea K. Bjorklund, *The Role of Counterclaims in Rebalancing Investment Law, supra* n. 1, at 480; Nicolis M. Perrone, *The "Invisible" Local Communities: Foreign Investor Obligations, Inclusiveness, and the International*

rule changes that the States strongly oppose, then they can vote with their feet in revised or newly ratified treaties by deleting those arbitration rules from the approved list in the treaties. Second, arbitration rules are supposed to be treaty neutral, also known as trans-substantive.[56] If one treaty allows counterclaims and another treaty does not, the same set of UNCITRAL Arbitration Rules, for example, need to be able to apply to both treaties. Furthermore, the arbitral institutions would not want to make any rule changes that would make them lose market share. Therefore, arbitration rulemaking bodies are very unlikely to take on the counterclaim issue directly, although this thought experiment shows how interesting it would be if they could.

Finally, a sixth solution is to create an investment court, with judges instead of arbitrators, to replace investment treaty arbitration. So far, proposals for such investment courts have not garnered enough support yet to be translated into a definitive implementation plan. Therefore, delving into the nuances, benefits, and drawbacks of that potential solution is beyond the scope of this chapter, although the topic has been explored extensively by other scholars.[57] Therefore, it is important to at least acknowledge that this solution is percolating and may gain more support, particularly in the aftermath of the EU's recent termination treaty.

§13.05 CONCLUSION

This chapter has highlighted the challenges and imbalances in the current structure of the ISDS system by viewing the system through the lens of third-party funding. This

Investment Regime, 113 AJIL Unbound 16, 21 (2019); Stephan W. Schill, *Reforming Investor–State Dispute Settlement: A (Comparative and International) Constitutional Law Framework*, 20 J. Int'l Econ. L. 649–672, 662, 665, 668 (2017); Jeswald W. Salacuse, *The Emerging Global Regime for Investment*, 51 Harvard Int'l L. J. 427, 451 (2010).

56. *See* Andrea K. Bjorklund, *The Role of Counterclaims in Rebalancing Investment Law, supra* n. 1, at 480. To explore the debate regarding the efficacy of trans-substantive procedural rules, *compare* Robert M. Cover, *For James Wm. Moore: Some Reflections on a Reading of the Rules*, 84 Yale L. J. 718, 718 (1975) ("We have become so transfixed by the achievement of James Wm. Moore and his colleagues in creating, nurturing, expounding and annotating a great trans-substantive code of procedure that we often miss the persistent and inevitable tension between procedure generalized across substantive lines and procedure applied to implement a particular substantive end. There are, indeed, trans-substantive values which may be expressed, and to some extent served, by a code of procedure. But there are also demands of particular substantive objectives which cannot be served except through the purposeful shaping, indeed, the manipulation, of process to a case or to an area of law. What follows is by no means an attempt to denigrate or undermine the ongoing trans-substantive achievement of the [US] Federal Rules of Civil Procedure. Rather it is an exploration to rediscover the feel of a tension") *with* Geoffrey C. Hazard, Jr., *Discovery Vices and Trans-Substantive Virtues in the Federal Rules of Civil Procedure*, 137 U. Pa. L. Rev. 2237, 2244 (1989) ("The second principal criticism of the [US] Federal Rules is that they indiscriminately govern all kinds and types of litigation, whereas civil procedure rules properly constructed would be shaped to the needs of specific categories of litigation. This critique contemplates separate sets of rules for civil rights cases, antitrust cases, routine automobile cases, and so on. The criticism has been expressed perhaps most incisively by Professor Robert Cover, esteemed colleague prematurely gone from us. Yet despite the great respectability of its source, the 'trans-substantive' critique seems misguided to me. It overstates the reach of the [US] Federal Rules and underestimates the technical and political difficulties of trying to tailor procedures to specific types of controversies").
57. *See supra* references cited in n. 55.

examination has highlighted the lack of access to financial justice among respondent States in ISDS. There is no easy solution to this problem, but a solution must be devised because States are calling for either reforming or replacing the system. This chapter has suggested several solutions to this problem, including making respondents more attractive to for-profit dispute financier, public funding of respondent States, enticing financiers to expand their case selection criteria, renegotiating investment treaties, changing jurisdictional language in the major arbitration rules, and creating a permanent investment court. These are just a few of the solutions that are being considered globally regarding the future of ISDS. UNCITRAL Working Group III remains hard at work on proposed changes.[58] It remains to be seen which suggested routes to change will gain traction. One way or another, it is clear that ISDS is headed toward change, at least with respect to the forthcoming sweeping revisions to the ICSID Arbitration Rules and more changes are likely to follow soon afterward. This chapter adds to the conversation about ways in which to improve the ISDS system without requiring a massive multilateral treaty. Yet, perhaps the galvanizing, collaborative effort of a massive multilateral treaty is exactly what the world needs to come together right now.[59]

58. *See generally* United Nations Commission on International Trade Law (UNCITRAL) Working Group III: Investor-State Dispute Settlement Reform, *Status of preparatory work on reform options and schedule of events* (May 14, 2020), https://uncitral.un.org/en/working_groups/3/investor-state.

59. *See*, e.g., United Nations Commission on International Trade Law (UNCITRAL) Working Group III: Investor-State Dispute Settlement Reform, *Multilateral Instrument on ISDS Reform Webinar* (April 23, 2020), https://uncitral.un.org/en/multilateralinstrumentwebinar ("The UNCITRAL Secretariat and the ISDS Academic Forum organized a webinar on the topic of a multilateral instrument on ISDS reform on 23 April 2020. Topics for discussion included the possible architecture of a multilateral instrument that would aim at providing the framework for the implementation of various reform options: the instrument could include specific provisions and annexes, addressing various reform options; it can also foresee the preparation of protocols for addressing possible developments; a further possibility would be for the instrument to also set-up a multilateral institution for investment dispute settlement that would allow States to choose among different modes of dispute settlement administered by the institution (reformed investor-State arbitration, inter-State arbitration, use of a multilateral standing mechanism, domestic remedies)").

CHAPTER 14

Regulating Third-Party Funding in Investor-State Arbitration Through Reform of ICSID and UNCITRAL Arbitration Rules: Holding Global Institutions to Their Development Mandates

Brooke S. Güven, Frank J. Garcia, Karl M.F. Lockhart & Michael R. Garcia[*]

The role of third-party funding (TPF) in international investment arbitration is a recent and growing phenomenon. However, given a lack of disclosure and transparency, it is exceedingly difficult to know its prevalence or the terms by which it is provided to claimants. While TPF in investor-State dispute settlement (ISDS) is often justified on the basis of access to justice or its ability to level the playing field between parties, claims which are themselves open to question, the realities of TPF in ISDS, even given the early and imperfect nature of the empirical record to date, suggest reasons for concern about its impacts. This chapter focuses on the key role that arbitration rules can play in restricting or regulating TPF in ISDS. In particular, reforming the International Center for the Settlement of Investment Disputes (ICSID) Arbitration Rules, the ICSID Additional Facility Rules, and the United Nations Commission on International Trade Law (UNCITRAL) Arbitration Rules will be a critical component in any successful TPF regulatory response, given their prominence in ISDS disputes. Given the reform processes in which both institutions are currently engaged, the time is ripe to use these processes to effect TPF reform through reform of these key arbitration rules.

* The authors wish to thank Lise Johnson and Nehal Khorraminejad for their very helpful comments on earlier drafts, and Keith Kaminski and Gina Makarem for their able and timely research assistance.

§14.01 INTRODUCTION

The role of TPF in international investment arbitration is a recent and growing phenomenon of some concern. As used herein, TPF refers to a financial investment in an ISDS claim in exchange for the investor being granted an interest in an eventual award on a non-recourse basis. TPF in ISDS is often justified on the basis of access to justice or its ability to level the playing field between parties, claims which are themselves open to question. Moreover, the realities of TPF in ISDS, even given the early and imperfect nature of the empirical record to date,[1] suggest reasons for concern about its impacts—especially with respect to the nature and number of claims filed, the management of cases, and its role in exacerbating the regulatory and financial pressures already facing respondent States, many of which are developing countries.

Whether one favors fully or partially restricting TPF investments[2] or other kinds of regulation (e.g., transparency), one of the most important sites for addressing the potential risks and harms caused by TPF in the ISDS context is through reform of arbitration rules used in ISDS disputes. Arbitration rules are a natural focal point and

1. It is difficult to determine with any precision the exact extent of TPF activity in investment arbitration, principally because it is almost entirely unregulated, and absent even the most basic transparency requirements (or case-specific orders), TPF funders and funded litigants do not typically disclose the presence of TPF, the identity of the funder, or the terms on which TPF is being provided. There is, however, general consensus even within the arbitral community that the TPF presence is significant and increasing. *See* William Park and Catherine A. Rogers, *Third-Party Funding in International Arbitration: The ICCA Queen-Mary Task Force, in Austrian Yearbook on International Arbitration* 113, 115 (Christian Klausegger et al. eds., 2015) (according to an estimate from a major funder on the Queen Mary Task Force, "at least two-thirds of ICSID cases filed in 2013 implicated claimants which had sought resources from a major funder."); *see also* David Gaukrodger and Kathryn Gordon, *Investor-State Dispute Settlement: A Scoping Paper for the Investment Policy Community* 37 (OECD Working Papers on Int'l Inv., No. 2012/03, 2012), https://papers.ssrn.com/sol3/papers.cfm?abstract_id=2207366 ("Commercial third party funders generally prefer not to disclose their role to the other parties or to the adjudicators, and funders and parties appear to consider that no clear disclosure requirements currently exist. Accordingly, it is not possible to determine the scope of third-party funding in ISDS. However, available evidence suggests an already significant role."); Zoe Williams and Florence Dafe, *Banking on courts; financialization and the rise of third-party funding in investment arbitration,* Review of International Political Economy, 1, 5 (May 2020) ("Our interviewees supported the view that the lack of disclosure requirements renders it difficult to establish the proportion of funded arbitral claims.").
2. A full restriction would completely prohibit the third-party funding of ISDS claims. A partial restriction may permit third-party funding of claims under specific circumstances. United Nations Commission on International Trade Law's (UNCITRAL's) Working Group III (WG III) has, for example, suggested that TPF may be usefully be permitted when a claimant is impecunious, a small- or medium-sized enterprise, has a claim of a certain nature, or another category. "Report of Working Group III (Investor-State Dispute Settlement Reform) on the work of its thirty-eighth session" U.N. Doc. A/CN.9/1004 (October 23, 2019), pp. 16, para. 83. UNCITRAL's WG III has also suggested that TPF could, for example, be prohibited "for certain types of claims, such as frivolous claims, claims made in bad faith or without legitimate reasons and claims with political purposes." *Ibid.* It has also suggested that there "could be a prohibition on speculative funding, funding provided on a non-recourse basis in exchange for a success fee, and other forms of monetary remuneration or reimbursement wholly or partially dependent on the outcome of a proceeding or portfolio of proceedings," and it "was noted that the prohibition of third-party funding along with exceptions could provide an appropriate approach for regulating the practice." *Ibid.*

opportunity for TPF reform given their critical role in balancing the procedural rights of investor-claimants and respondent-States. They are also of central importance due to their relative susceptibility to change. While treaties are difficult to amend, the sets of arbitration rules used most frequently in ISDS are currently at key inflection points, making them ripe for reform.

In particular, reforming the ICSID Arbitration Rules, the ICSID Additional Facility Rules, and the UNCITRAL Arbitration Rules will be a critical component in any successful TPF regulatory response, given their prominence in ISDS disputes. In the vast majority of existing international investment agreements (IIAs), States provide advance consent to arbitrate under one or more of these three specific sets of rules (with the ability to agree at the time of a dispute to arbitrate under other rules). Unsurprisingly, the vast majority of investor-State disputes to date—over 90%—have taken place under one of these sets of rules.[3]

ICSID is currently engaged in its fourth Arbitration Rule reform process, with TPF an agreed agenda item. Moreover, States are working within UNCITRAL's Working Group III (WG III) to address ISDS reform, and TPF reform has been flagged as a concern that warrants multilateral action. This could potentially result in a recommendation to the UNCITRAL Commission to amend its arbitration rules. The time is ripe to use these processes to effect TPF reform through changes to these key arbitration rules.

This chapter focuses on the role of amendments to the ICSID and UNCITRAL arbitration rules as part of a comprehensive approach to TPF regulatory reform. After a brief introduction to TPF and its role in ISDS—which concludes that the risks posed by TPF are sufficient to warrant an immediate regulatory response under the precautionary principle—the chapter presents an overview of current TPF regulatory efforts. It then focuses on the role of arbitral rule reform in general, and ICSID and UNCITRAL rules reform in particular, in addressing TPF. We argue that ICSID arbitration rules reform and UNCITRAL ISDS reform efforts currently underway are a necessary and critical opportunity to address the systemic risks and costs TPF introduces into ISDS, and by extension the international investment regime in general. Not only are the ICSID and UNCITRAL arbitration rules central to the investment arbitration system, but both institutions also hold mandates to pursue broader sustainable development objectives, objectives which TPF in ISDS appears to undermine. We conclude that current WG III reform efforts are still at a phase in which they can be formulated to address many of the major systemic concerns surrounding the use of TPF in ISDS, in particular through UNCITRAL Arbitration Rules reform. In contrast, the current ICSID rule reform process, which is in its final stages, may fail to regulate TPF in a manner that supports

3. Of the 1023 known treaty-based ISDS cases as of December 31, 2019, 32% of them were administered under the UNCITRAL rules, and 59% under ICSID or ICSID Additional Facility rules. This means that together UNCITRAL and ICSID rules comprise 91% of all treaty-based ISDS cases filed since 1987. The remaining 9% of cases either use the rules of the International Chamber of Commerce, the Cairo Regional Center for International Commercial Arbitration, the London Court of International Arbitration, the Moscow Chamber of Commerce and Industry, or the Stockholm Chamber of Commerce; were ad hoc; or it is not known what rules were used. *Investment Dispute Settlement Navigator*, UNCTAD Investment Policy Hub (last updated December 31, 2019) https://investmentpolicy.unctad.org/investment-dispute-settlement.

sustainable development objectives; it should be fundamentally reconsidered so that this important opportunity is not lost.

§14.02 THE NATURE OF TPF IN ISDS AND THE OBJECTIVES OF TPF REGULATION

[A] What Is TPF?

In its broadest sense, TPF is the generic term used to describe situations in which an otherwise disinterested third party provides financial or other support of value to a party in a legal dispute in order to pay or offset expenses incurred in advancing a claim.[4] The relationship between the funder and the claimant is governed by contractual arrangements, generically referred to as the "funding agreement." While definitions of third-party funder and TPF can be broad or narrow,[5] as used in this chapter, third-party funders are investment funds that invest in an investor-State claim on a non-recourse basis in exchange for an interest in any eventual award.[6] In addition to investments in specific claims, third-party funders may also arrange portfolio investments by bundling and cross-collateralizing claims around a law firm or a claimant, which reduces funder risk and thus the cost of capital provided.[7]

Successful third-party funders bring deep expertise in analyzing the legal basis for a claim and how a tribunal is likely to apply applicable law to the underlying facts. As repeat players in the arbitration system, they also provide great depth in specific resources, such as know-how, case management experience, networks, and familiarity with arbitrators, experts, and counsel. Some funders take a fairly hands-off approach to how a claimant and its counsel decide to manage a claim, while others monitor and provide input on a much greater level.[8] In addition, some funders have contractual

4. *Report of the ICCA–Queen Mary task force on third-party funding in international arbitration*, The ICCA Reports No. 4 (April 2018), 44–80 (ICCA-QM Report). This broad definition captures philanthropic grants (e.g., Bloomberg Philanthropies' support of Uruguay in *Philip Morris v. Uruguay*, ICSID Case No. ARB/10/7, Award (July 8, 2016)) pro-bono legal representation, contingent fee representation, and other recourse- or non-recourse-based financing models in addition to more "traditional" forms of third-party funding described in this paragraph.
5. ICCA-QM Report, *supra* n. 4.
6. The narrow definition of third-party funding used in this paper excludes various forms of arbitration financing, such as, for example, contingency fee arrangements, litigation insurance, after-the-event insurance, philanthropic funding, or pro-bono services. Equity arrangements are increasingly common investments made by litigation funders and complicate definitional matters. But they are also excluded from the definition used in this chapter because equity investments can result in a different and greater alignment of interest between shareholders and the claim being advanced. Equity investments also implicate fundamental tenants of corporate law, thus raising different issues as to how and under what circumstances the interests of a shareholder in the claim, and shareholder claims more generally, should or could be regulated in the investor-State context, and the most appropriate way in which to achieve that objective. *See* David Gaukrodger, *Investment Treaties and Shareholder Claims for Reflective Loss: Insights from Advanced Systems of Corporate Law* (OECD, Working Papers on International Investment, 2014).
7. *See* ICCA-QM Report, *supra* n. 4, at 38–39.
8. *Ibid.*, at 28.

rights to approve or not approve certain decisions, such as the amount and terms of settlement with a respondent State.[9]

[B] How Is TPF Used in ISDS?

Outside of a small handful of newer treaties (and some new model treaties),[10] the vast majority of treaties and arbitration rules are silent on TPF and do not contain any rules requiring its use to be disclosed. As such, it is exceedingly difficult to know TPF's prevalence with certainty[11] or the terms by which it is provided to claimants.[12] Due to the specific circumstances of particular cases, the existence of funding (and in some cases, the funder or the terms on which funding has been provided) becomes known to the parties or made public more generally. Currently, there are approximately forty publicly known funded claims, although the actual number is likely much, if not multiples, higher.[13]

9. *See ibid.*
10. *For example,* Investment Protection Agreement Between the European Union and the Socialist Republic of Viet Nam, E.U.-Viet., June 30, 2019, 2019 O.J. (L 177) (not in force) (hereinafter E.U.-Vietnam Investment Protection Agreement); Indonesia - Australia Comprehensive Economic Partnership Agreement, Indon.-Austl., March 4, 2019, https://www.dfat.gov.au/trade/agreements/in-force/iacepa/iacepa-text/Pages/default (shall enter into force July 5, 2020); Investment Protection Agreement Between the European Union and the Republic of Singapore, E.U.-Sing., October 15, 2018, 2018 O.J. (L267) 1 (not in force) (hereinafter E.U.-Singapore Investment Protection Agreement); Agreement for the Reciprocal Promotion and Protection of Investments between the Argentine Republic and the United Arab Emirates, Arg.-U.A.E. April 16, 2018, (not in force) (hereinafter Argentina-U.A.E. BIT) (banning third-party funding); Comprehensive Economic and Trade Agreement between Canada and the European Union, Can.-E.U., October 30, 2016, https://www.international.gc.ca/trade-commerce/trade-agreements-accords-commerciaux/agr-acc/ceta-aecg/text-texte/toc-tdm.aspx?lang=eng (not in force) (hereinafter Canada-E.U. Comprehensive Economic and Trade Agreement). In addition, at least two recently-published model bilateral investment treaties address third-party funding. *See* Netherlands Model Investment Agreement, March 22, 2019, https://investmentpolicy.unctad.org/international-investment-agreements/treaty-files/5832/download (hereinafter Netherlands Model BIT); Agreement between the Slovak Republic and ... for the Promotion and Reciprocal Protection of Investments, 2019, https://investmentpolicy.unctad.org/international-investment-agreements/treaty-files/5917/download (hereinafter Slovakia Model BIT).
11. Results of a 2018 survey of international arbitration practitioners show that nearly half (42%) of survey respondents have encountered TPF in practice either by using it themselves (16%) or by seeing it used (26%); 56% were aware of it but had not seen it in practice; 3% were not aware of TPF. School of International Arbitration at Queen Mary University of London, *2018 International Arbitration Survey: The Evolution of International Arbitration* (White & Case LLP, 2018), 24, https://www.whitecase.com/sites/whitecase/files/files/download/publications/2018-international-arbitration-survey.pdf. *See also* Williams and Dafe, *supra* n. 1, at 12–17.
12. In the investor-State context, respondent funding is a very different type of investment because of the one-way nature of obligations in investment treaties. Under most existing treaties, States can advance claims for damages against States, but States cannot claim (or in most cases, counterclaim) against investors for damages. Thus, the financial "up-side" for a funder is not the same in these two contexts. This paper considers only claimant funding. For a discussion of and comparisons with respondent funding *see* Brooke Guven and Lise Johnson, *The Policy Implications of Third-Party Funding in Investor-State Dispute Settlement* 5–11 (CCSI, Working Paper, 2019).
13. Sherry Xin Chen and Kirrin Hough, *Researching Third-Party Funding in Investor-State Dispute Settlement*, GlobaLex (May 2019), s. 5.2, https://www.nyulawglobal.org/globalex/Third-Party

Since the late 2000s, and in particular since the 2008 global financial crisis, TPF has increasingly been viewed as an attractive asset class for its ability to produce significant returns.[14] As a result, the amount of capital available for funders has increased significantly over the past few years to its current estimate in the tens of billions of dollars, with more money in the market than cases meriting investment.[15] Funders face pressure by their own investors to deploy these funds.[16]

While it may be too early to predict the impact of COVID-19 on TPF, it would be reasonable to assume that TPF's role in ISDS will increase as it did following the 2008 financial crisis. This may particularly be the case as global liquidity dries up and institutional investors seek to allocate capital to investments that are able to produce returns. Indeed, law firms are already sending out client alerts relating to the myriad of potential investment treaty breaches arising out of government responses to manage the effects of COVID-19.[17] It is certain that some of these claims will be attractive to, if not partially driven by, third-party funders. Given the current climate, it is not difficult to envision another substantial increase in TPF and the number of funded claims in the years to come.

Empirical evidence regarding the circumstances in which TPF is used is crucial for fully analyzing the role and impact of TPF in the investor-State context. Understanding the case-specific and systemic costs and benefits of funding will better permit policy-makers to determine whether and under what, if any, conditions TPF should be permissible. This information will also allow government officials to consider what tools are available, or should be available, to ensure that TPF serves the objectives States intended when entering into investment treaties, rather than producing unintended or undesirable effects. But such data is lacking. It is therefore important to consider how, and based on what principles, to regulate or otherwise advance policy objectives in the face of uncertainty, and what inferences should be drawn given that the potentially regulated actors in the practice are the key holders of the relevant data. It is also crucial to consider what steps must be taken to advance policy objectives and close knowledge gaps in order to improve policy responses in the future.

[C] What Are the Objectives of TPF Regulation?

ISDS is integrated into investment treaties to advance, not undermine, their object and purpose. The object and purpose of investment treaties are to promote investment that fosters the sustainable economic development and prosperity of the State parties to the

_Funding_Investor-State_Dispute_Settlement.html (this list has been updated by and is on file with the authors); Williams and Dafe, *supra* n. 1, at 5–6.

14. Williams and Dafe, *supra* n. 1, at 12.
15. *Ibid.* at 13–14. ("Burford Capital's claim to have access to about £2.3bn of financing, and Steven Friel, chief executive of Woodsford Litigation Funding's view that worldwide a figure of £70bn was a reasonable estimate of the amount of money available to both funders and law firms ....")
16. *Ibid.* at 14.
17. *See* Pia Eberhardt, *Cashing in on the pandemic: How lawyers are preparing to sue states over COVID-19 response measures*, Longreads (May 19, 2020), https://longreads.tni.org/cashing-in-on-the-pandemic/.

treaty and, by extension, the stakeholders within them.[18] Investment treaties are thus instrumentalist agreements that protect foreign investors and investments as a means to a greater end, not simply as an ends in themselves.[19] Therefore, when assessing the costs and benefits of TPF in this context, it is important to understand how its operation, and the incentives created by its financial structure, affect ISDS in its capacity to advance a holistic notion of prosperity consistent with and supportive of the treaties' sustainable development objectives.[20]

The ISDS mechanism itself is already highly controversial and facing a "legitimacy crisis."[21] While the causes of its dethroning are multifaceted, the one-way nature of a system that grants only foreign investors – even those with "unclean hands" who may have violated applicable domestic laws or other norms – a privileged avenue to sue States for good-faith conduct based on vague treaty standards is now widely

18. *For example,* Treaty between the United States of America and the Argentine Republic Concerning the Reciprocal Encouragement and Protection of Investment, U.S.-Arg., November 14, 1991, 31 I.L.M. 124 (entered into force October 20, 1994) Preamble ("Recognizing that agreement upon the treatment to be accorded such investment will stimulate the flow of private capital and the economic development of the parties"); Agreement for the Promotion and Protection of Investments, S. Kor.-Para., December 22, 1992, 1766 U.N.T.S. 344 (entered into force August 6, 1993) Preamble ("Recognizing the important complementary role of foreign investment in the economic development process ... ."); Agreement on Encouragement and Reciprocal Protection of Investments, Neth.-Bangl., November 1, 1994, 1942 U.N.T.S. 112 (entered into force June 1, 1996) Preamble ("Recognizing that agreement upon the treatment to be accorded to such investments will stimulate the flow of capital and technology and the economic development of the Contracting Parties ... ."); Agreement between The Swiss Confederation and The Arab Republic of Egypt on the Promotion and Reciprocal Protection of Investments, Switz.-Egypt, June 7, 2010, (entered into force May 15, 2012) Preamble ("Recognizing the need to promote and protect foreign investments with the aim to foster the economic prosperity and sustainable development of both States"); Agreement between Canada and Mongolia for the Promotion and Protection of Investments, Can.-Mong., September 8, 2016, https://investmentpolicy.unctad.org/international-investment-agreements/treaty-files/5373/download (entered into force February 24, 2017) Preamble ("Recognizing that the promotion and the protection of investments of investors of one Party in the territory of the other Party will be conducive to the stimulation of mutually beneficial business activity, to the development of economic cooperation between them and to the promotion of sustainable development ... ."). *See also* Lise Johnson, *Aligning Swiss Investment Treaties with Sustainable Development: An Assessment of Current Policy Coherence and Options for Future Action* (October 2015) (a report commissioned by the Swiss Agency for Development and Cooperation that focuses on the extent to which Swiss treaties are aligned with sustainable development); Lise Johnson, Lisa Sachs and Nathan Lobel, *Aligning International Investment Agreements with Sustainable Development Goals*, 58 Columbia Journal of Transnational Law 58 (2020).
19. *See* Gus Van Harten, *Investment Treaty Arbitration and Public Law*, 140 (Oxford University Press 2008).
20. While all States have nuanced definitions and priorities relating to sustainable development and sustainability objectives, all States have agreed to a universal definition embodied in the United Nations 2030 Agenda for Sustainable Development, including 17 Sustainable Development Goals, which is used as a general framing for the term as used in this chapter, notwithstanding the more State-specific intentions that may be embodied within any one treaty or advanced by any specific State. G.A. Res. 70/1, Transforming Our World: The 2030 Agenda for Sustainable Development (October 21, 2015).
21. *For example,* UNCITRAL, "Possible future work in the field of dispute settlement: Reforms of investor-State dispute settlement (ISDS) – Note by the Secretariat" A/CN.9.917 (April 20, 2017), para. 12.

questioned and criticized.[22] When the unclear substantive and procedural standards contained in most of the existing investment treaties are interpreted and applied by ad hoc arbitrators in a system that does not apply precedent, appellate review, or other control mechanisms for constraining arbitrator discretion, uncertain and unpredictable outcomes result.[23] Respondent States have exceptionally narrow bases to advance counterclaims. Most treaties contain little to no guidance on damages calculations, and there can be rather large gaps between amounts claimed and those awarded.[24] Awards, which are frequently in the millions or billions of dollars,[25] fall disproportionately on developing States[26] and can represent sizeable proportions of a State's GDP.[27] What is more, these awards are highly enforceable in most countries around the world.[28] Even a cash-strapped respondent State has little choice but to pay, given the importance of its credit rating in global financial markets,[29] and the high costs of compliance are borne by its citizens.[30] Importantly, international human rights experts have concluded that IIAs and their ISDS mechanism have often proved to be incompatible with the human rights obligations of the States party to these treaties and with the rule of law more generally.[31]

---

22. *See*, e.g., *Selected Statements and Actions Against Investor-State Dispute Settlement (ISDS)*, Public Citizen, (last updated April 20, 2018), https://www.citizen.org/wp-content/uploads/selected_statements_and_actions_against_isds_1.pdf.
23. UNCITRAL, "Possible Reform of Investor-State Dispute Settlement (ISDS): Consistency and Related Matters – Note by the Secretariat" A/CN.9/WG.III/WP.150 (August 28, 2018); Lise Johnson and Lisa Sachs, *Inconsistency's Many Forms in Investor-State Dispute Settlement and Implications for Reform*, CCSI Briefing Note (November 2018), http://ccsi.columbia.edu/files/2018/11/Inconsistencies_ISDS_Briefing-Note_11.28.18.pdf.
24. Daniel Behn and Ana Maria Daza, *The Defense Burden in International Investment Arbitration*, PluriCourts Working Paper (forthcoming, 2020).
25. *Ibid.*
26. Kevin P. Gallagher and Elen Shrestha, *Investment Treaty Arbitration and Developing Countries: A Re-Appraisal* (Global Development and Environment Institute, Working Paper No. 11-01, 2014).
27. For example, the nearly USD 6 billion award (pre-interest) issued against Pakistan in *Tethyan v. Pakistan* represented nearly 2% of its GDP. ICSID Case No. ARB/12/1, Award (July 12, 2019).
28. ISDS Awards are enforceable in most countries in the world through the New York and ICSID Conventions. Convention on the Recognition and Enforcement of Foreign Arbitral Awards, June 10, 1958, 330 U.N.T.S. 3 [hereinafter New York Convention]; Convention on the Settlement of Investment Disputes, March 18, 1965, 575 U.N.T.S. 159 [hereinafter Washington Convention].
29. Ignoring an investment arbitral award is a risky course of conduct for any State concerned with its investment rating. *See generally, Argentina's Post-Crisis Economic Reform: Challenges for U.S. Policy*, CRS (April 15, 2013), https://fas.org/sgp/crs/row/R43022.pdf (detailing effects of Argentina's public and private debt defaults on access to international markets); *Sovereign Rating Methodology*, S&P Global Ratings (December 18, 2017), https://www.spratings.com/documents/20184/4432051/Sovereign + Rating + Methodology/5f8c852c-108d-46d2-add1-4c20c3304725 (explaining rating agency's methodology for factoring defaults into sovereign credit ratings).
30. The public pays in the form of both fiscal and welfare burdens because losses and settlements must (1) be paid out of the public treasury, with (2) money that is therefore no longer available for social welfare or other government spending priorities. Frank J. Garcia, *Third-Party Funding as Exploitation of the Investment Treaty System* 59 B.C.L. Rev. 2911, 2922 (2018).
31. "Letter from the Mandates of the Working Group on the issue of human rights and transnational corporations and other business enterprises; the Special Rapporteur on the right to development; the Special Rapporteur on the issue of human rights obligations relating to the enjoyment of a safe, clean, healthy and sustainable environment; the Independent Expert on the effects of

At the same time, no clear evidence exists that these significant costs of ISDS are offset by its hoped-for benefits. In particular, there is a lack of evidence as to treaties' role in increasing investment flows that support treaty parties' economic development or improving the quality of institutions governing investment.[32] This glaring disparity between costs and benefits will inevitably become more extreme during the global recession in the wake of COVID-19 and the ISDS claims that will almost certainly result.[33]

From this perspective, there are concerns that the introduction of TPF into ISDS further skews the outcomes of the system and the incentives and priorities of its key actors, away from the treaties' development objectives and toward decision-making frameworks that benefit financiers seeking speculative profits.[34] TPF in ISDS may negatively influence: (1) investor decisions and conduct (including with respect to the number of claims, the nature and motives to bring claims, and decisions to remain invested in the host country or to divest); (2) the development of the law and outcomes of specific claims (including the quality of claims, the substantive development of the law, and decisions to settle claims); and (3) respondent States and their governance of investment (including regulatory chill and overdeterrence, and concentrated impacts on certain types of investment and respondent States).[35]

Given the asymmetric nature of ISDS, the costs of TPF will be disproportionately borne by the citizens of developing countries.[36] This will particularly be the case where

---

foreign debt and other related international financial obligations of States on the full enjoyment of all human rights, particularly economic, social and cultural rights; the Special Rapporteur on the rights of indigenous peoples; the Independent Expert on the promotion of a democratic and equitable international order; and the Special Rapporteur on the human rights to safe drinking water and sanitation, to the UNCITRAL Secretariat and Member States", U.N. Doc. OL ARM 1/2019 (March 7, 2019), https://uncitral.un.org/sites/uncitral.un.org/files/public_-_ol_arm_07.03.19_1.2019_0.pdf.

32. Other objectives cited by treaty parties include depoliticization of disputes and advancement of the rule of law. For an overview of these objectives, and the lack of evidence showing that ISDS supports their achievement, *see*, e.g., Joachim Pohl, *Societal Benefits and Costs of International Investment Agreements: A Critical Review of Aspects and Available Empirical Evidence* (OECD, Working Paper No. 2018/01, 2018), https://doi.org/10.1787/e5f85c3d-en; Lise Johnson, Brooke Güven and Jesse Coleman, *Investor-State Dispute Settlement: What Are We Trying to Achieve? Does ISDS Get Us There?*, CCSI Blog Series (2017), http://ccsi.columbia.edu/2017/12/11/investor-State-dispute-settlement-what-are-we-trying-to-achieve-does-isds-get-us-there/.
33. Nathalie Bernasconi-Osterwalder, Sarah Brewin and Nyaguthii Maina, *Protecting Against Investor-State Claims Amidst COVID-19: A call to action for governments*, IISD Commentary (April 2020); CCSI is leading a call for an immediate moratorium on all ISDS claims and a permanent restriction on all arbitration claims related to government measures targeting health, economic, and social dimensions of the pandemic and its effects. *See Call for ISDS Moratorium During Covid-19 Crisis and Response*, Columbia Center on Sustainable Investment (May 6, 2020), http://ccsi.columbia.edu/2020/05/05/isds-moratorium-during-covid-19/.
34. These incentives and outcomes may be, but are not necessarily, aligned with the interests of claimants. For example, claimants may have interests in settling or not settling a claim, in settling at an amount above a specific amount, or settling for a specific regulatory concession—all or some of which outcomes may not align with the interests of a funder investing in the relevant claim.
35. Guven and Johnson, *supra* n. 12, at 11–45.
36. The equities of TPF in ISDS are thus markedly different from the equities of domestic TPF litigation between commercial parties, where the costs of losing the case are borne by a commercial entity and its shareholders. Garcia, *supra* n. 30, at 2922–2923.

the development status of the respondent may be a factor in how TPF funders evaluate claims in which to invest.[37] TPF thus both exacerbates existing concerns about the balance of costs and benefits in ISDS and introduces new ones.

At the same time as these serious concerns about the impact of TPF arise, its systemic benefits have not been demonstrated. While TPF is often portrayed as a means of providing access to justice for claimants who would not otherwise have the funds to seek remedies, this justification is difficult to fully assess, absent more information about which claimants are accessing TPF and under what circumstances. However, in a growing number of known funded cases, claimants are seeking funding not because they are impecunious, but because they wish to pursue claims with as little impact as possible on cash flows or other financing.[38] Existing arguments about the "need" for TPF in ISDS to ensure "access to justice" overstate both the "need" for this particular form of support, and the role of ISDS in ensuring "access to justice."[39]

TPF is also often justified in its ability to create market efficiencies by facilitating a greater alignment of risk-tolerance between disputing parties.[40] These arguments claim that when a risk-averse party aligns with a funder, bargaining dynamics between the disputing parties may become more even such that settlement outcomes align with the objective merits of the claim.[41] However, this reasoning does not characterize most ISDS claims with States, which have unique characteristics that may result in risk-aversion, particularly given the one-way nature of claims in the investment law system. Most States face few claims,[42] and the vast majority of States that do face claims are revenue-constrained low- or middle-income countries[43] that may be concerned about the reputational impacts of an ISDS claim being lodged against them.[44] Critically,

37. TPF funders have reported considering the level of development, expertise, and legal capacity of the respondent State, with preference given to claims against developing or newly industrialized States with both a capacity to pay the award and a respectable investment rating they are eager to protect, while having only modest legal capacity and legal defense budgets. *Third Party Funding in Investor-State Dispute Settlement: Round Table Discussion on Third Party Funding in Investor-State Dispute Settlement with ICCA-Queen Mary Task Force on Third-Party Funding in International Arbitration Draft Report for Public Discussion*, Columbia. Center on Sustainable Investment (October 17, 2017), http://ccsi.columbia.edu/files/2017/11/Third-Party-Funding-in-ISDS-Roundtable-Outcome-Document-FINAL-2.pdf [hereinafter Round Table].
38. ICCA-QM Report, *supra* n. 4, at 20.
39. Williams and Dafe, *supra* n. 1, at 10–11.
40. *See*, e.g., Jonathan Molot, *Litigation Finance: A Market Solution to a Procedural Problem*, 99 Geo. L. J. 65, 84 (2010).
41. *Ibid.*
42. Of 135 States studied, twenty-seven had faced one claim; fifty-four had faced between two and five claims; twenty-five had faced six to nine claims; and twenty-nine had faced ten or more claims. Behn and Daza, *supra* n. 24.
43. Out of 135 respondents analyzed, thirty-five are World Bank Group classified low income, forty-two classified as lower-middle income, forty classified as upper-middle income, and thirty-five classified as upper-income. Upper-income countries are also primarily sued by investors from other upper-income countries, whereas the claims against lower-income countries are primarily by upper-income country investors, but also include some low- or middle-income investors. *Ibid.*
44. Todd Allee and Clint Peinhart, *Contingent Credibility: The Impact of Investment Treaty Violations on Foreign Direct Investment*, 65 Int'l Organization 401 (2011) (calculating drops in FDI associated with even ultimately unsuccessful claims).

developing countries are more likely to settle even unmeritorious claims than developed countries.[45] All these factors are likely to become exponentially more pronounced in the post-COVID-19 recession, when States will be increasingly revenue constrained and sensitive to their reputations as investment destinations in an effort to attract diminished investment.

From this perspective, tilting the already-unbalanced system of ISDS by adding a new and well-resourced player that also has a stake in the system remaining unbalanced—as measured by third-party funders' interest in extracting financial payments from governments, expanding interpretations of vague treaty standards, liberalizing standing, and increasing the number of claims—is of profound concern. Rather than leveling the playing field or facilitating access to justice, it seems that third-party funders are profiting from a malfunctioning system of justice, distorting it into a speculative investment vehicle for the benefit of investment funds and their shareholders.[46] TPF in ISDS appears unlikely to be justifiable as a matter of balancing the benefits, costs, and risks when assessed on the basis of advancing treaty objectives.

In the absence of information to dispel these concerns—and in light of the fact that funders and claimants hold much of the information relevant for a deeper analysis of these issues—the precautionary principle should govern policy approaches.[47] The precautionary principle requires regulators to protect the public from exposure to harm when a serious substantive investigation has found a plausible risk based on information known at the time and requires them to act to prevent such harms even while the full factual record is under development.[48] Creating a full factual record as to the impacts of TPF on State treaty parties and treaty objectives is impossible absent greater transparency surrounding these kinds of investments. At the same time, based on what is known about TPF, its role in ISDS, and its place in the investment treaty system more broadly, it is clear that TPF poses systemic risks. These risks may be undermining the very purposes for which States entered into these treaties in the first place. It is inconsistent with investment treaty objectives—the sustainable development of States and their citizens—to risk ceding such an important engine for economic development and prosperity as foreign investment to the private, profit-maximizing objectives that have now been introduced into the bilateral investment treaty (BIT) regime by investment funds.

Similarly, for the reasons set forth above, regulatory activity should aim at restricting TPF in ISDS rather than simply regulating it through a disclosure-based

45. Anton Strezhnev, "Why Rich Countries Win Investment Disputes: Taking Selection Seriously" (September 22, 2017) (unpublished draft) (on file with authors).
46. Garcia, *supra* n. 30, at 2919–2923.
47. *Ibid.* at 2930 (advocating precautionary approach to third-party funding regulation in view of potential risks and magnitude of funding already involved).
48. *See ibid.* The precautionary principal is defined by the United Nations in the Rio Declaration on Environment and Development: "In order to protect the environment, the precautionary approach shall be widely applied by States according to their capabilities. Where there are threats of serious or irreversible damage, lack of full scientific certainty shall not be used as a reason for postponing cost-effective measures to prevent environmental degradation." Rio Declaration on Environment and Development, Report of the United Nations Conference on Environment and Development (Vol. 1), at princ. 15, U.N. Doc. A/CONF.151/26/REV.1 (1992).

regime. Simple disclosure is not an adequate solution when the structural risks to the system introduced by TPF are already present and profound and the ISDS regime so prone to exploitation. ISDS already creates inter- and intra-national inequalities,[49] and allowing TPF to operate within ISDS—even under an enhanced disclosure regime—exacerbates the fundamental problems with ISDS that reform efforts are now attempting to address. Furthermore, TPF introduces new problems of its own. What was intended as a system of justice becomes a speculative investment opportunity with widespread externalities. This is the kind of economic distortion of dispute resolution that traditional prohibitions on maintenance and champerty were designed to prevent.

Many of these concerns have been increasingly articulated by States as reasons for which a full or partial restriction or other regulation of TPF should be advanced.[50] For example, within the context of WG III, multilateral approaches to regulating TPF in ISDS are being developed.[51] ICSID's draft reformed rules appear poised to enact some

49. Lisa Sachs and Lise Johnson, *Investment Treaties, Investor-State Dispute Settlement and Inequality: How International Rules and Institutions Can Exacerbate Domestic Disparities*, Columbia Center on Sustainable Development (September 11, 2019), http://ccsi.columbia.edu/files/2017/11/ISDS-and-Intra-national-inequality.pdf.

50. *See*, for example, certain written submissions made by States to UNCITRAL's WG III: "Possible reform of investor-State dispute settlement (ISDS): Submission from the Government of Morocco," A/CN.9/WG.III/WP.161 (March 4, 2019), pp. 5, paras 26–30; "Possible reform of investor-State dispute settlement (ISDS): Submission from the Government of South Africa," A.CN.9/WG.III/WP.176 (July 17, 2019), pp. 11, paras 67–69; "Possible reform of investor-State dispute settlement (ISDS): Submission from the Republic of Korea," A/CN.9/WG.III/WP.179 (July 31, 2019) pp. 4–6. *See also* statements made by States in UNCITRAL's WG III: *Audio Recordings 35th Session, Working Group III (Investor-State Dispute Settlement Reform)*, UNCITRAL (April 25, 2018) https://uncitral.un.org/en/audio (last visited April 29, 2019). Nigeria stated that third-party funding "[r]aises a moral, ethical and public policy issues why a total stranger who has suffered no injury should be allowed to benefit from the injury caused to others ..." and after noting systemic concerns surrounding third-party funding, including an increase in frivolous or unmeritorious claims and impacts on settlements, suggested that increased transparency or an outright ban may be considered to deal with these concerns. [10:49:26]. Burkina Faso noted the ethical and other concerns regarding third-party funding in ISDS said that potential regulations, or a ban may be an appropriate result. [16:25:59]. Kenya raised the question of whether third-party funding should be banned in ISDS. [16:28:31]. South Africa, noting the increase in funding of non-pecunious investors, the financial value of claims being funded, and the targeting of certain profiles of countries, along with the significant impact that funders can have on case management and settlement, called for third-party funding to be seriously addressed, and noted Kenya's call for a detailed analysis as to what can be done, including a ban, or a very comprehensive transparency requirement including the terms of the funding agreement and ethical requirements [16:46:23]. India stated "third-party funding ... has the potential to derail the system from its very objective of providing justice." [10:24:31]. *Audio Recordings 37th Session, Working Group III (Investor-State Dispute Settlement Reform)*, UNCITRAL (April 1, 2019), https://icms.unov.org/CarbonWeb/public/uncitral/speakerslog/9e4160d4-6cef-4de6-83c0-d9c4645bf253 (last visited April 30, 2019). Uruguay noted that given the option between regulation and a ban it supports regulation, and if banning third-party funding were not difficult, this is the option that it would choose. [12:06:31]. Morocco raised concerns about the possibility of speculative and abusive use of third-party funding by investors and while awaiting the adoption of rules that could effectively regulate third-party funding, propose a ban on third-party funding in context of UNCITRAL reform. [12:10:15]. Argentina intervened to remind delegations that a ban remains on the table. [12:28:20].

51. At its 37th Session Working Group III concluded that it would be desirable that reforms be developed by UNCITRAL in order to address concerns related to the definition, and to the use or regulation of third-party funding in ISDS "Report of Working Group III (Investor-State Dispute

level of regulation of TPF.[52] Some States, such as Argentina and the United Arab Emirates, have already banned the practice in treaties.[53]

However, restricting or regulating TPF in ISDS is not an easy task. Moreover, perhaps in large part due to the paucity of empirical data on the role of TPF in ISDS, States have differing perspectives of the scope of the problem and, as a result, the most appropriate policy response to solve it. In this context, agreement on how to regulate these kinds of investments may present considerable hurdles. Moreover, the very ad hoc nature of investment law and dispute settlement, with overlapping and customizable rules and legal frameworks, makes coherent regulation a significant challenge. The following section will turn to address the practicalities of these issues.

§14.03 WHAT IS REQUIRED TO EFFECTIVELY RESTRICT OR REGULATE TPF IN ISDS?

An effective response to the costs and risks of TPF in ISDS requires that reform efforts proceed on a number of fronts: in treaties (unilaterally, bilaterally, and multilaterally); through arbitral association rules reform; and in domestic law. We will first address the role of treaties, before briefly introducing the role of arbitral association rule reform (which will be the subject of its own section to follow). We conclude this section with the role of domestic regulation.

[A] Treaty-Based TPF Reform

Investment treaty reform is a logical starting point for assessing TPF reform options and strategies. To the extent a treaty restricts or regulates TPF, such restriction or regulation will apply to any ISDS dispute brought under such treaty, regardless of what rules or seat are chosen.[54] However, while newer treaties are starting to include TPF regulatory provisions in their text, the vast majority of disputes are brought under treaties entered into prior to 2010. The process of reforming over 3,000 existing treaties, nearly all of which are silent on TPF, is an uncertain one and would take a considerable amount of time to achieve.

[1] New and Future Treaties

Some recent IIAs, and a growing number of model investment treaties, incorporate provisions restricting or otherwise regulating TPF. For example, the 2018 BIT between

Settlement Reform) on the Work of its Thirty-Seventh Session" A/CN.9/970 (April 9, 2019), p. 6, para. 25; "Third-party funding – Possible solutions" A/CN.9/WG.III/WP.172 (August 2, 2019).

52. *See infra* §14.04[B] (discussing the current ICSID rule reform process).
53. Argentina-U.A.E. BIT, *supra* n. 10, at Art. 24.
54. *For example, ibid.*, Art. 24 ("Third party funding is not permitted.").

Argentina and the United Arab Emirates fully restricts TPF of claims.[55] Other recent treaties have opted to regulate but not restrict TPF. For example, the European Union's (EU) recent agreements, including the 2019 EU–Vietnam Investment Protection Agreement and the 2016 Comprehensive and Economic Trade Agreement between the EU and Canada, provide for disclosure of the existence of TPF, as well as the name and address of the funder.[56] Australia and Indonesia recently signed a BIT requiring the same disclosures.[57] Similarly, the model bilateral investment treaties of the Netherlands and Slovakia require parties benefiting from TPF to disclose the name and address of the funder.[58]

In all these cases, States have left (or in the case of models, suggest leaving) the tribunal fairly broad (if not absolute) discretion in defining TPF,[59] determining whether the parties use of TPF complies with the treaty requirements, and constructing and applying penalties for violations of treaty terms.[60] To the extent States wish to have more control over the way in which TPF is regulated and used in disputes under their treaties, they may wish to consider including specific terminology, defined terms, and specific penalties and enforcement procedures for a party's breach of treaty terms.[61] Such provisions could be included directly in new agreements, or, as discussed in the following section, via a bi- or multilateral amendment to existing treaties.

55. Argentina-U.A.E. BIT *supra* n. 10. Art. 24 of the Argentina-UAE bilateral investment treaty states simply that "[t]hird party funding is not permitted" (third-party funding is not otherwise defined).
56. E.U.-Vietnam Investment Protection Agreement, *supra* n. 10, at Art. 3.37(1); Canada-E.U. Comprehensive Economic and Trade Agreement, *supra* n. 10, at Art. 8.26; *see also* E.U.-Singapore Investment Protection Agreement, *supra* n. 10, Art. 3.8(1).
57. Indonesia-Australia Comprehensive Economic Partnership Agreement, *supra* n. 10, Art. 14.32 (1).
58. Netherlands Model BIT, *supra* n. 10, Art. 19.8; Slovakia Model BIT, *supra* n. 10, Art. 21(1).
59. For example, the Canada-E.U. Comprehensive Economic and Trade Agreement defines TPF broadly as "any funding provided by a natural or legal person who is not a party to the dispute but who enters into an agreement with a disputing party in order to finance part or all of the cost of the proceedings either through a donation or grant, or in return for remuneration dependent on the outcome of the dispute." *Supra* n. 10, at Art. 8.1. This definition is fairly typical. In contrast, the Indonesia – Australia Comprehensive Economic Partnership Agreement contains no definition of TPF, giving the tribunal absolute discretion to define the term. *Id. See also* Netherlands Model BIT. *Ibid.*
60. *See*, e.g., EU – Vietnam Investment Protection Agreement, *supra* n. 10, at Art. 3.37 (allowing tribunal discretion to interpret and enforce provision requiring parties to disclose TPF "without delay"); Netherlands Model BIT, *supra* n. 10, Art. 19.8 (requiring disclosure of TPF but providing no definition of TPF or guidance for the tribunal in terms of oversight or penalties for violation). In contrast, the Indonesia – Australia Comprehensive Economic Partnership Agreement has more teeth. *Ibid.*, Art. 14.32, para. 3. ("If a disputing investor fails to disclose third party funding under this Article, the tribunal may order the suspension or termination of the proceedings.")
61. An example of language that could be incorporated into treaties to define, restrict and regulate TPF in ISDS can be found in Draft Text Providing for Transparency and Prohibiting Certain Forms of Third-Party Funding in Investor-State Dispute Settlement (CCSI, IIED, IISD, July 15, 2019) (submitted to UNCITRAL's WG III) https://uncitral.un.org/sites/uncitral.un.org/files/media-documents/uncitral/en/wgiii_transparency_0.pdf.

[2] Existing Treaties

Given that the dramatic rise of TPF in ISDS is a relatively recent phenomenon, the vast majority of treaties are silent on the topic. Virtually all known investment disputes have been brought under "old-generation" treaties concluded before 2010.[62] These treaties typically feature broad and vague formulations of terms, include few exceptions or safeguards, and do not address the more recent ascent of TPF in ISDS. As such, including TPF restrictions in new treaties, important as this is, will therefore be largely ineffective in restricting TPF in the majority of claims likely to be brought now and in the near (or even not-so-near) future. Therefore, reform of existing treaties will be an essential adjunct to arbitral rules reform for effective and systemic TPF regulation.

The amendment of existing treaties to include TPF provisions can be done on a treaty-by-treaty basis, or via a multilateral instrument that could apply amendments to a broader number of existing treaties. To begin with, States could amend specific treaties pursuant to their terms. In practice, however, amendments or joint interpretations of bilateral treaties can be challenging due to time constraints on the part of government officials, as well as the asymmetric power relations that often exist in BITs between historically capital-exporting and capital-importing States.[63] Generally speaking, proposals for amendments or interpretations that benefit the State proposing the amendment are likely to be only acknowledged or accepted to the extent they are also beneficial (and not merely neutral) to the other treaty-party.[64] When treaties are highly asymmetrical, it becomes unlikely that a State seeking to restrict TPF (i.e., a capital-importing State) will achieve much success through joint statements or amendments to BITs or regional trade agreements' investment chapters unless the dominant partner (i.e., the capital-exporting State) also favors TPF reform.

From a purely practical perspective, given the many competing substantive and time-management priorities of treaty negotiators and decision-makers, most bilateral amendments or joint interpretations may only be possible in theory. In any event, amendments or interpretations of all existing treaties on a treaty-by-treaty basis are likely to be a slow and incremental process.

States could also approach reform of existing treaties via a multilateral instrument that could apply to existing and/or future agreements, following the example of the Mauritius Convention in the ISDS transparency context, or the Multilateral

62. UNCTAD, *Phase 2 of IIA Reform: Modernizing the Existing Stock of Old-Generation Treaties*, IIA Issues Note 2, June 2017, at 4, https://unctad.org/en/PublicationsLibrary/diaepcb2017d3_en.pdf.
63. On the dynamics between unequal States and how they affect treaty negotiations in international economic law, *see* Frank J. Garcia, *Consent and Trade: Trading Freely in a Global Market* (2018). For a penetrating analysis of the effects of such dynamics specifically in investment treaties, *see* Alessandra Arcuri, *The Great Asymmetry and the Rule of Law in International Investment Arbitration in Yearbook on International Investment Law and Policy 2018* (Lisa Sachs, Lise Johnson and Jesse Coleman eds., 2020).
64. *See* Garcia, *supra* n. 63, at 70–80 (effects of asymmetry bilaterally and regionally in market access negotiations), 104–105 (effects multilaterally in WTO TRIPS negotiations).

Instrument in the base erosion and profit shifting (BEPS) context.[65] Indeed, one outcome of the WG III process may be such a treaty.[66] However, the negotiation of such an instrument may take years, and to the extent many States (and, importantly, capital-exporting States) do not ratify it, or investors retain the ability to "treaty-shop" around such an instrument, its effectiveness may ultimately be questionable or limited.

Despite these challenges, treaties will continue to be an important piece of the TPF regulatory puzzle. They can complement arbitration rule reform efforts by providing for stronger, more nuanced, or more certain outcomes when States desire to do so.[67] But since the investment treaty regime remains so fragmented, and the political economy of treaty reform so daunting, an effective and efficient response to TPF's costs and risks in ISDS will likely depend on arbitration rules reform.

[B] Restricting or Regulating TPF Through Reform of Arbitration Rules

Arbitration associations and their rules are a natural focal point and opportunity for TPF reform given their position and role within the ISDS regime and the resulting efficiencies to be gained. Arbitration is built on the premise of agreed-to terms and customization; parties can choose to specify and tailor a multiplicity of details

65. The Mauritius Convention on Transparency establishes a mechanism pursuant to which parties can efficiently and effectively apply the UNCITRAL Rules on Transparency in Treaty-Based Investor-State Arbitration (the "Transparency Rules") to existing treaties to which the Transparency Rules do not apply, and also to disputes under treaties conducted under rules other than the UNCITRAL arbitration rules. United Nations Convention on Transparency in Treaty-Based Investor State Arbitration, G.A. Res. 69/116, U.N. Doc. A/RES/69/116 (December 10, 2014). *See generally Multilateral Convention to Implement Tax Treaty Related Measures to Prevent Base Erosion and Profit Shifting: Information Brochure*, OECD (2018), http://www.oecd.org/tax/treaties/multilateral-instrument-BEPS-tax-treaty-information-brochure.pdf. The MLI is an innovative multilateral legal instrument to amend bilateral income tax treaties in order to implement Base Erosion and Profit Sharing ("BEPS") standards through a single-instrument unifying framework that offers flexibility to signing countries to: (i) identify the treaties they are willing to amend and (ii) identify optional amendments they agree to adopt in those treaties they propose to amend, in addition to the minimum standards required by the treaty. *Ibid.* Over 80 countries have agreed to amend income tax treaties under this instrument (subject to individual country ratification procedures), which entered into force on July 1, 2018. *Signatories and Parties to the Multilateral Convention to Implement Tax Treaty Related Measures to Prevent Base Erosion and Profit Sharing*, OECD (July 23, 2018), http://www.oecd.org/tax/treaties/beps-mli-signatories-and-parties.pdf.
66. *See* "Possible reform of investor-State dispute settlement – Multilateral instrument on ISDS reform" U.N. Doc. A/CN.9/WG.III/WP.194 (January 16, 2020); Colombia, for example, in a written submission to UNCITRAL on this topic, includes TPF regulation as an element of ISDS reform that could be addressed by a multilateral instrument. "Possible reform of investor-State dispute settlement (ISDS): Submission from the Government of Columbia" A/CN.9/WG.III/WP.173 (June 14, 2019).
67. Even if and to the extent States were to successfully pursue restriction of TPF through ICSID and UNCITRAL arbitration rules reform, some States may wish to more specifically tailor the ways in which TPF should be regulated or restricted in claims against them under their treaties, or prevent future arbitration rules amendments with which they may not agree. States can achieve this more nuanced control by incorporating TPF provisions into their treaties.

regarding the governance of any dispute.[68] Among these options is the choice of arbitral rules and, in many cases (unless the arbitration is ad hoc), the choice of administering institution.[69] Many arbitration institutions have established their own arbitration rules. However, most of these institutions also administer arbitrations under rules other than the proprietary rules of the institution. In particular, some rules, such as the UNCITRAL Arbitration Rules, were developed to be used by disputing parties in ad hoc or administered arbitrations but are not tethered to a specific arbitration institution.[70]

In the context of investment arbitration, this customization (at least as far as the investor-claimant is concerned) is limited to some extent by the terms that home and host States have established in the underlying investment treaty itself. In their BITs, State parties may consent in advance to arbitration with respect to claims for alleged treaty breaches brought by covered investors relating to covered investments, pursuant to the treaty's terms. While a treaty may not specify all elements of how and on what terms disputes under the treaty will proceed, it will broadly specify the contours and general conditions of State consent, such as governing law.[71] States also designate in their treaties a menu of arbitration rules from which investors may choose from to govern the dispute. Treaties also typically provide that, in addition to the specified arbitration rules, States and investors may agree to arbitrate under rules other than those designated.[72]

For these reasons, addressing TPF through arbitral rules reform is a critical element in any TPF regulatory strategy. While TPF reform of one BIT or FTA at a time can be important and meaningful, arbitral rules reform solves the collective action issues attendant to BIT reform and offers important efficiency gains and multiplier effects due to the centrality of these rules. All investment arbitrations proceed under some set of rules, with the vast majority (over 90%, as will be discussed below) held under either ICSID or UNCITRAL rules.[73] Regulating TPF through arbitration rules

---

68. Latham & Watkins LLP, *Client Alert Commentary Number 1563: Investment Treaty Arbitration: A Primer 4* (July 29, 2013) https://www.lw.com/thoughtLeadership/LW-investment-treaty-arbitration-primer. ("Investment treaties often provide investors a choice between various forms of arbitration for the purpose of settling disputes with host States.").
69. Arbitration rules set forth and govern the procedure by which an arbitration will proceed, such as the composition of the tribunal and how it is constituted, requirements for statements and filings, requests for interim measures, and evidentiary burdens, among other issues.
70. *Frequently Asked Questions - Arbitration*, UNCITRAL, https://uncitral.un.org/en/texts/arbitration/faq#arbitration (last visited May 22, 2020) ("Does UNCITRAL ... administer arbitrations ....? No ... ."). *See also* discussion of UNCITRAL rule reform efforts at *infra* §14.04[C].
71. For example, most investment treaties designate that the tribunal shall apply the provisions of the treaty and applicable rules of international law to any dispute. For example, U.S. Model Bilateral Investment Treaty, 2012, https://ustr.gov/sites/default/files/BIT%20text%20for%20ACIEP%20Meeting.pdf, Art. 30(1) ("the tribunal shall decide the issues in dispute in accordance with this Treaty and applicable rules of international law."); ("the tribunal shall decide the issues in dispute in accordance with this Treaty and applicable rules of international law.").
72. *For example*, Comprehensive Economic and Trade Agreement, Can.-E.U., October 30, 2016, (entered into force September 21, 2017), Art. 8.23(2) [hereinafter CETA]; United States Mexico Canada Agreement, November 30, 2018, Art. 14.D.3(3) [hereinafter known as USMCA]; Comprehensive and Progressive Agreement for Trans-Pacific Partnership, March 8, 2018 (entered into force December 30, 2018), Art. 9.19(4) (hereinafter CPTPP).
73. *See infra* n. 88 and §14.04[B].

reform may offer significant benefits in terms of standardization of rules, which may also help to establish shared norms and standards around the appropriate role, if any, for TPF in ISDS.[74]

[C] Additional Considerations Related to Domestic Law

Despite the international nature of treaty-based arbitration, domestic laws are still relevant to the legal, policy, and practical considerations that can impact the regulation or use of TPF in ISDS disputes. As a general matter, domestic regulation of TPF can be distinguished as between civil law and common law approaches, with civil law countries being more permissive of litigation funding as a general matter.[75] A separate distinction can be drawn between how a civil or common law jurisdiction treats the TPF of claims in commercial disputes between private parties, and how the same jurisdiction may treat differently the TPF of claims in disputes against a sovereign.[76] This latter question is more closely aligned with how such jurisdictions may assess TPF in ISDS, as it similarly involves claims of private parties against a government. Whatever the system, domestic laws can impact the role of TPF and the attractiveness of a claim as an investment in several ways, including (but not limited to) when TPF is unlawful in the jurisdiction of the seat of the arbitration, the jurisdiction in which enforcement is sought, the claimant's jurisdiction, or the jurisdiction in which the funder is located.[77]

With respect to the law of the seat, the law of the designated "seat" of the arbitration will fill in any gaps that are not addressed by arbitral rules or the relevant

74. Zacchaeus Andangor and Success Gilbert, *Future of International Arbitration: What Changes Are on the Horizon*, 9 J. Prop. L. & Contemp. Issues, 195, 196 (2019).
75. In many civil law countries, third-party funding may be relatively new and/or unregulated, or may even be expressly authorized. *Handbook on Third Party Funding in Investment Arbitration* part II (Nikolaus Pitkowitz ed., Juris 2018): Country Reports (e.g., Brazil has no rules on third-party funding, but it is regulated within the broader context of financial services regulation; third-party funding is recognized as validly practiced in France; third-party funding in Germany is largely unregulated; the Netherlands does not have specific rules on third-party funding but the parliament is discussing what rules should apply within the broader context of allowing the practice). In contrast, common law jurisdictions have historically prohibited maintenance, or the support of litigation by another party who lacks a legitimate interest in the lawsuit, and champerty, akin to maintenance but with the specific feature of supporting the litigation in exchange for a return of a share of the proceeds. These legal regulations grew out of a desire to prevent the wealthy or powerful from using the medieval English legal system to gain material wealth by putting power behind unmeritorious or socially undesirable claims. Michael K. Velchik and Jeffrey Y. Zhang, *Islands of Litigation Finance*, Discussion Paper No. 71, 10–12, John M. Olin Center for Law, Economics, and Business, Fellows' Discussion Paper Series (April 25, 2017).
76. In the United States, for example, the third-party funding of claims against the government is regulated separately and much more rigorously than the use of third-party funding in the context of two private parties. The U.S. Anti-Assignment of Claims Act largely prohibits third-party funding of claims against the government. 31 USC § 3727. For a discussion of this act in the context of third-party funding of ISDS claims *see* Guven and Johnson, *supra* n. 12.
77. Williams and Dafe, *supra* n. 1, at 9 (One funder has explained that he would only invest in a claim if the various relevant jurisdictions permitted TPF: his own, that in which the claimant's assets were located, that in which the claimant had its legal seat, and the seat of the arbitration.).

investment treaty.[78] For TPF, this means that the domestic legal framework can thus restrict the ways in which TPF can be used in any international arbitration seated in that jurisdiction.[79] Moreover, to the extent TPF were to be made illegal in the seat, any resulting award could be set aside.[80]

TPF does remain regulated, or even illegal, in certain domestic jurisdictions. But an increasing number of common law jurisdictions such as Australia, Canada and the US have liberalized TPF in recent years. Others such as Singapore and Hong Kong, key players in international arbitration, have acted at the domestic law level to specifically permit TPF in arbitration, even while otherwise restricting TPF. This is, at least in part, to build up their profile as globally competitive hosts of arbitrations. Third-party funders heralded these changes,[81] and at least one major funder had actually lobbied in favor of them.[82] These situations demonstrate the competition that jurisdictions hosting major arbitration centers face and the competitive nature of the arbitration landscape in attracting business.[83] This sort of regulatory race to the bottom driven by

78. *Guide to Leading Arbitral Seats and Institutions*, K&L Gates (2012), at 1, http://www.klgates.com/files/upload/guidetoleadingarbitralseatsandinstitutions.pdf; *Frequently Asked Questions* LCIA, https://www.lcia.org/Frequently_Asked_Questions.aspx (last updated 2020), at No. 17; *Guide to International Arbitration*, Latham and Watkins (2017), at 2, https://www.lw.com/thoughtleadership/guide-to-international-arbitration-2017.
79. With respect to policy considerations, it is often noted that the trend in domestic regulation of third-party funding is one of liberalizing, and not tightening, restrictions on third-party funding. However, these trends are not necessarily instructive for considering the specific policy objectives of third-party funding in ISDS. Rather, what would be a more instructive guide and basis for comparison would be to what extent, why, and under what circumstances, governments permit the funding of domestic legal claims *against themselves*. In the United States, for example, this practice is regulated separately and much more rigorously than the use of third-party funding in the context of two private parties. The U.S. Anti-Assignment of Claims Act largely prohibits third-party funding of claims against the government. 31 USC § 3727. For a discussion of this act in the context of third-party funding of ISDS claims *see* Brooke Guven and Lise Johnson, *The Policy Implications of Third-Party Funding in Investor-State Dispute Settlement* (2019) 16–18 CCSI Working Paper 2019.
80. New York Convention, *supra* n. 28, at Art. V(1)(a).
81. Charlie Morris, *Law Takes Its Course: The Impact of Third Party Funding on Hong Kong as Centre for International Arbitration*, 146 Intercontinental Finance & Law 16, 17 (2017), https://woodsfordlitigationfunding.com/us/wp-content/uploads/sites/3/2017/08/ICFL-HK-article.pdf (Woodsford); Quentin Pak, "Hong Kong Allows Third Party Funding of Arbitration," Buford Finance Blog (December 12, 2018), https://burfordcapital.com/insights/insights-container/hong-kong-allows-third-party-funding-of-arbitration/ (Burford); Marla Decker, International Arbitration and Third-Party Funding in Hong Kong: Q&A With the Secretary-General of the Hong Kong International Arbitration Centre, Above the Law (February 27, 2019) https://abovethelaw.com/2019/02/international-arbitration-and-third-party-funding-in-hong-kong-qa-with-the-secretary-general-of-the-hong-kong-international-arbitration-centre/?rf=1 (Lake Whillans).
82. Burford Capital, 2017 Annual Report 11 (2017). ("[B]oth Hong Kong and Singapore had prohibited litigation finance (except in insolvency), and indeed any form of risk-based litigation activity, including lawyers taking risk on their own fees. However, following significant education and lobbying by Burford, both jurisdictions passed legislation in 2017 that enabled litigation finance for arbitration.")
83. Decker, *supra* n. 81 ("As jurisdictions compete for status as premier international arbitration hubs, a differentiating factor (or, increasingly, a must-have factor) is whether the jurisdiction's legal framework allows for third-party funding in arbitrations seated there."); Morris, *supra* n. 81, at 17 ("Until now, an Asian-based corporate may have opted to have its arbitration heard in a venue where funding has long been permitted, such as London or Paris. Now, thanks to the reforms in Asia, that same corporate may prefer to select Hong Kong or Singapore as its venue

financial incentives demonstrates the benefits of restricting or regulating TPF through key arbitration rules as a solution to collective action problems.[84]

With respect to the domestic law of the jurisdiction in which enforcement is sought—specifically, when enforcement proceedings occur pursuant to the New York Convention—domestic courts may refuse to recognize or enforce an award under circumstances in which recognition or enforcement of the award would be "contrary to the public policy" of the enforcing State.[85] To the extent there is a strong public policy against TPF in the enforcing jurisdiction, there is a risk for the funder and claimant that a domestic court could rely on this exception to refuse enforcement of awards in which TPF was involved.[86] However, domestic jurisdictions have increasingly relaxed prohibitions on TPF, particularly in common law countries that have begun to roll back long-maintained bans against champerty and maintenance. These changes may make such public policy arguments difficult to sustain in such jurisdictions where trends are toward liberalizing these practices, even if not yet fully liberalized.[87] Nevertheless, although this argument has never been litigated, existing case law suggests that such an argument could prevail in jurisdictions where enforcing such an award would violate the clear policy of the forum State as expressed in its domestic TPF statutes.[88]

---

of choice."); ("[T]he change swiftly follows a similar liberalisation of regional rival Singapore's funding regime earlier in the year. ... Hong Kong possibly found itself at a significant competitive disadvantage when measured against rival arbitral seats—not just Singapore but London, Paris, New York and Geneva too.").

84. *See*, e.g., David Gaukrodger, "Appointing Authorities and the Selection of Arbitrators in Investor-State Dispute Settlement: An Overview," OECD Consultation Paper (March 2018), para. 259 (discussing how a competitive market may lead to appointing authorities more frequently selecting arbitrators with a commercial arbitration background that lean toward higher degrees of investor protection).
85. New York Convention, *supra* n. 28, at Art. V(2)(b). The ICSID Convention does not contain a public policy exception. Outside of the New York Convention, a national court hearing an action to recognize and enforce a foreign arbitral award has broad discretion to refuse either to recognize it or enforce it, subject to that State's laws and to principles of comity. Leonard V. Quigley, *Accession by the United States to the United Nations Convention on the Recognition and Enforcement of Foreign Arbitral Awards*, 70 Yale L.J. 1049, 1058–1059 (1961) ("With regard to enforcing foreign arbitral awards abroad [prior to the Convention], the answer [varied] with the national law of the countries involved and their status as parties or non-parties to the Geneva Convention of 1927. The Geneva Convention require[d] enforcement of awards rendered between nationals of the signers according to local procedural rules. The actual effectiveness of the obligation incurred under the Geneva Convention thus depend[ed] on the supplementary national legislation. Between non-parties to the Geneva Convention, there [was] little uniformity. [For example], [e]nforcement of an award rendered and reduced to judgment in New York was denied by the Supreme Court of Portugal. On the other hand, the Supreme Court of Colombia granted execution upon a New York judgment based upon a New York award.") (internal citations omitted).
86. A public policy against TPF may result from the jurisdiction not liberalizing existing rules against it; or because the jurisdiction has allowed TPF in domestic litigation but has not legalized it with respect to actions against the sovereign, such as is the case in the U.S., or more narrowly, not allowed it in investment arbitrations to which the sovereign is the Respondent.
87. Williams and Dafe, *supra* n. 1, at 7–8.
88. Under the most commonly applied U.S. standard, for example, courts may refuse to enforce an award where "enforcement would violate the forum State's most basic notions of morality and justice" (*Parsons & Whittemore Overseas Co. v. Societe Generale De L'Industrie Du Papier (RAKTA)*, 508 F.2d 969, 974 (2d Cir. 1974)) or would be "repugnant to fundamental notions of what is decent and just." (*Argentina v. GB Group PLC*, 764 F. Supp.2d 21, 39 (D.C. 2011)

A key consideration in this respect would be whether the State has a distinct public policy regarding the TPF of awards against sovereigns, in addition to its policies regarding TPF more generally.

Finally, with respect to the law of the claimant's jurisdiction, a key consideration is the way in which a domestic court may choose whether or not to recognize the contractual rights of a third-party funder. Funders wish to ensure that they will be able to enforce their rights to collect their share of the proceeds of an award from a claimant, and this is a topic on which domestic law may have some bearing.

The role of domestic law can thus be key in TPF regulation, in particular as it more practically relates to the enforcement of any award or a funder's rights to a portion of an award. However, while certain domestic approaches may discourage funders from certain claims, regulation through domestic law is not a viable approach to systemic and coherent regulation of TPF for both practical and normative reasons.

§14.04 ICSID AND UNCITRAL RULE REFORM AS A PRIORITY

[A] Why ICSID and UNCITRAL and Why Now?

In nearly all existing investment treaties, State parties provide advance consent to investor-State arbitration under the ICSID Arbitration Rules, the ICSID Additional Facility Rules, or the UNCITRAL Arbitration Rules.[89] Perhaps unsurprisingly, these arbitration rules govern the vast majority of ISDS disputes. Of the 1,023 known treaty-based ISDS cases as of 31 December 2019, 32% of them were administered

(quoting *Ackerman v. Levine*, 788 F.2d 830, 841 (2d Cir. 1986) and *Tahan v. Hodgson*, 662 F.2d 862, 864 (D.C.Cir.1981)). The prevailing standard in the United Kingdom is similarly strict. *See Deutsche Schachtbau-und Tiefbohrgesellschaft M.B.H. (D.S.T.) v. Ras Al Khaimah Nat'l Oil Co. (Rakoil)*, (1987) 2 Lloyd's Rep. 246, 254 (C.A.) (holding that in order for an English court to vacate an arbitral award on the basis of the public-policy defense, the advocating party must show that there is "some element of illegality or that the enforcement of the award would be clearly injurious to the public good or, possibly, that enforcement would be wholly offensive to the ordinary reasonable and fully informed member of the public on whose behalf the powers of the State are exercised." Although difficult to meet, these standards are not insurmountable, particularly in view of the nature of the risks posed by TPF. If the enforcement action is in the US, for example, it would be significant that the US itself does not permit TPF in cases bringing claims against the sovereign. Moreover, in or out of the US, where the jurisdiction has specifically legislated to ban TPF from all cases or at least from investment disputes, it is not difficult to see how a reviewing court would find enforcement against an express legislative determination to violate the forum's public policy. Finally, given the risk that TPF may in fact operate as an exploitation the ISDS regime for the benefit of third parties, a court could deem such a practice as contravening the forum's basic notions of justice. *See* Garcia, *supra* n. 30, at 2919–2923.

89. *See International Investment Agreements Navigator*, UNCTAD Investment Policy Hub, https://investmentpolicy.unctad.org/international-investment-agreements (last visited May 3, 2020) (showing approximately 2,363 of 2,577 treaties mapped provide for either ICSID or UNCITRAL rules, or both). Joachim Pohl, Keke Mashigo and Alexis Nohen, *Dispute settlement provisions in international investment agreements: A large sample survey*, 20–21 (OECD Working Papers on Int'l Inv., No. 2012/2, 2012). ("ICSID as well as ad hoc tribunals established according to UNCITRAL rules are by far the most often mentioned as possible fora for ISDS, while the ICC comes a distant third. Other fora, including treaty designed ad hoc tribunals and regional tribunals in Stockholm, Cairo, Bogota, etc. are mentioned infrequently.")

under the UNCITRAL Rules and 59% under ICSID or ICSID Additional Facility Rules.[90] This means that together, UNCITRAL and ICSID rules have governed or are governing 91% of all known treaty-based ISDS cases filed since 1987.[91] Moreover, treaties typically provide advance consent to arbitrate only under one or more of these rules. So to the extent respondent States do not wish to use ad hoc or institutional rules that do not provide for TPF regulation, they could always refuse consent to arbitrate under such other rules at the time of the dispute.[92] Alternatively, as a condition of their consent, States could stipulate and agree with the claimant how TPF would be treated in any specific arbitration. Thus, efficient and effective regulation of TPF in ISDS can occur, at least in theory, through the amendment of the ICSID and UNCITRAL arbitration rules.

It is therefore extremely important for the success of TPF reform that States act now, because ICSID Member States are currently engaged in reform of the ICSID rules on a number of fronts, and WG III is currently engaged in developing solutions to address identified concerns surrounding TPF in ISDS. WG III's solutions could include a recommendation to the UNCITRAL Commission to amend its Arbitration Rules. As such, this is a critical moment for governments engaged in TPF reform under each of these processes to effect reforms; reforms that will advance the development objectives of their investment treaties and align with the broader development mandates of ICSID, a World Bank Group institution, and UNCITRAL, a United Nations institution.

[B] ICSID Rule Reform

ICSID is the most popular forum for resolving ISDS disputes, having administered at least 630 arbitrations between States and investors.[93] Its sets of rules have been used in

90. *See* UNCTAD Investment Policy Hub, *supra* n. 3 (showing 540 cases under ICSID rules and 326 cases under UNCITRAL rules out of a total of 1,023 known cases in the database). The remaining 9% of cases either use the rules of the International Chamber of Commerce, the Cairo Regional Center for International Commercial Arbitration, the London Court of International Arbitration, the Moscow Chamber of Commerce and Industry, or the Stockholm Chamber of Commerce; or were ad hoc; or it is not known what rules were used.
91. Of course, unknown or non-transparent claims are not included in this calculation. *See Mapping of IIA Content*, UNCTAD Investment Policy Hub, https://investmentpolicy.unctad.org/international-investment-agreements/iia-mapping (last visited May 3, 2020) (showing approximately 2,363 of 2,577 treaties mapped provide for either ICSID or UNCITRAL rules, or both) (data shows that 870 out of 2577 mapped investment treaties allow for arbitration under neither ICSID nor UNCITRAL rules, and that of these 870, only thirty-three of them require documents to be made publicly available and hearings to be open to the public, leaving 836 treaties which allow for non-ICSID, non-UNCITRAL arbitrations with no transparency provisions – meaning that potentially 32% of the mapped treaties allow for undisclosed investment disputes).
92. The Energy Charter Treaty, which accounts for 9% of disputes administered by ICSID (ICSID Caseload Statistics, 2020-1) provides for arbitration under these three rules as well as the Arbitration Rules of the Stockholm Chamber of Commerce. As dispute settlement under this treaty represents an outsized proportion of overall claims, a case can be made that TPF under the SCC Rules would also need to be addressed.
93. *Case Administration*, ICSID, https://icsid.worldbank.org/en/Pages/Services/Case-Administration.aspx (last updated 2019); *How to File a Non-ICSID Arbitration*, ICSID, https://icsid.worldbank.org/en/Pages/process/How-to-file-a-Non-ICSID-Arbitration.aspx (last updated 2019).

at least 540 disputes.[94] ICSID is unique among arbitration institutions in that it is one of the five divisions of the World Bank Group, meaning that it shares the World Bank Group's sustainable development objectives. Of particular importance to TPF reform, the World Bank Group's goals include ending extreme poverty and boosting shared prosperity based on justice and the rule of law, with international investment seen as a mechanism to advance these objectives.[95] Through its membership in the World Bank Group, ICSID is committed to cooperation with United Nations (UN) efforts to implement these and other Sustainable Development Goals.[96]

In particular, the ICSID Convention itself references its development objective and the role of investment in the very first sentence of its Preamble, which cites "the need for international cooperation for economic development, and the role of private international investment therein[.]"[97] ICSID is also unique among arbitration institutions in that it is an intergovernmental institution, created by a multilateral treaty—the ICISD Convention—with 154 Member States.[98] Article 6 of the ICSID Convention clarifies that ICSID has full legal personality under international law and is therefore also subject to the human rights and development obligations applied to any international organization.[99]

In furtherance of these development objectives, ICSID has developed two different sets of arbitration rules: the ICSID Arbitration Rules, for use by parties to the ICSID

---

94. UNCTAD Investment Policy Hub, *supra* n. 3.
95. *About ICSID*, ICSID, https://icsid.worldbank.org/en/Pages/about/default.aspx (last updated 2019); *ICSID and the World Bank Group*, ICSID, https://icsid.worldbank.org/en/Pages/about/ICSID%20And%20The%20World%20Bank%20Group.aspx (last updated 2019). *See also*, *History*, World Bank Group, https://www.worldbank.org/en/about/history (last updated 2020). ("The subsequent launch of the International Centre for Settlement of Investment Disputes ... further rounded out the Bank Group's ability to connect global financial resources to the needs of developing countries.")
96. *World Bank Group and the 2030 Agenda*, World Bank, https://www.worldbank.org/en/programs/sdgs-2030-agenda (last visited June 2, 2020). ("The World Bank Group has a treaty-based relationship with the United Nations (UN) that dates back to its founding, and through that relationship, works to build a partnership that supports Member States and contributes to effective development outcomes while preserving the distinct mandates of each institution. Over the years, the WBG has collaborated with the UN in nearly every region and sector, and its engagement has deepened since the adoption of the Millennium Development Goals (MDGs), and now with the Sustainable Development Goals (SDGs).")
97. ICSID Convention, Convention on the Settlement of Investment Disputes Between States and Nationals of Other States, March 18, 1965, 575 U.N.T.S. 159 (entered into force October 14, 1966), at 11 (hereinafter ICSID Convention).

    The role of the private sector in advancing sustainable economic development consistent with human rights is also now the subject of certain binding and non-binding governance frameworks, which thus provide normative guidelines as to how and under what circumstances such private international investment should contribute to the development objectives of the ICSID Convention. *See*, e.g., *OECD Guidelines for Multinational Enterprises*, OECD (2011), http://mneguidelines.oecd.org/guidelines/; UN Guiding Principles on Business and Human Rights, United Nations Human Rights Office of the High Commissioner (2012), https://www.ohchr.org/documents/publications/guidingprinciplesbusinesshr_en.pdf.
98. *Ibid.*
99. *Ibid.*, Art. 6. *See*, e.g., Carla Ferstman, *International Organizations and the Fight for Accountability: The Remedies and Reparations Gap* (Oxford 2017) (international organizations are subject to core human rights duties as a function of their international legal personality and, in appropriate cases, their specialized functions).

Convention; and the ICSID Additional Facility Rules, for use when either the claimant or respondent is not an ICSID party or a national of an ICSID party. The ICSID Arbitration Rules were adopted in 1967 and effective as of 1 January 1968. The Additional Facility Rules were enacted in 1978.[100] Both sets of rules have been amended three times, effective as of 1984, 2003, and 2006.[101] Amendments to the ICSID Arbitration Rules require a vote in favor by two-thirds of ICSID Member States,[102] whereas amendments to the Additional Facility Rules only require a simple majority vote.[103] Since 2016, ICSID has been engaged in its fourth rule amendment process, which will amend in largely the same ways both the ICSID Arbitration Rules and the ICSID Additional Facility Rules (Proposed ICSID Rules).[104]

Among other topics, the current round of ICSID rules amendments is seeking to craft rules that regulate TPF in proceedings under the ICSID rules.[105] The most recent ICSID Rule Amendment Working Paper (no. 4), proposes a minimum amount of TPF regulation, limited to disclosure of the existence of TPF as well as the name and the

100. The ICSID Convention enabled ICSID to administer arbitrations under the ICSID Rules between investors and States where both the investor's home State and the disputing State were parties to the ICSID convention. For disputes in which one party fell outside the scope of the Convention, ICSID enacted the Additional Facility Rules in 1978. *Additional Facility Rules*, ICSID, https://icsid.worldbank.org/en/Pages/icsiddocs/ICSID-Additional-Facility-Rules.aspx (last updated 2019).
101. *A Brief History of Amendment to the ICSID Rules and Regulations*, ICSID https://icsid.worldbank.org/en/amendments/Pages/Background%20Material/History-Amendment-ICSID-Rules.aspx (last updated 2019).
102. ICSID Convention, *supra* n. 97, at Ch. I, s. 2, Art. 6(1). Each Member State has one representative on the Administrative Council. Administrative Council, *ICSID* (2019) https://icsid.worldbank.org/en/Pages/about/Administrative-Council.aspx.
103. Since proceedings under the Additional Facility Rules are not specifically provided for in the ICSID Convention. Administrative and Financial Regulation Ch. 1, Reg. 7(1) applies to the amendment of the Additional Facility Rules—which only requires a majority vote of the Administrative Council. *See Additional Facility Rules*, ICSID, https://icsid.worldbank.org/en/Pages/icsiddocs/ICSID-Additional-Facility-Rules.aspx (last updated 2019), at Art. 3; ICSID Administrative and Financial Regulation Ch. 1, Reg. 7(1) https://icsid.worldbank.org/en/Documents/resources/2006%20CRR_English-final.pdf; *see also* Aurélia Antonietti, *The 2006 Amendments to the ICSID Rules and Regulations and the Additional Facility Rules*, 21 ICSID Rev. 427, 427 (2006); Antonio R. Parra, *The Development of the Regulations and Rules of the International Centre for Settlement of Investment Disputes*, 22 ICSID Rev. 55, 57 (2007).
104. As the amendments to the ICSID Additional Facility Arbitration Rules that relate to TPF are identical to those in the ICSID Arbitration Rules, they will be discussed together, and the term "ICSID Rules" will be used to refer to both. *See Proposals for Amendment of the ICSID Rules*, (ICSID, Working Paper No. 4, February 2020) at 403–404, https://icsid.worldbank.org/en/Documents/WP_4_Vol_1_En.pdf [hereinafter Working Paper #4] (ICSID Additional Facility Proposed Rule 23 "Notice of Third-Party Funding," mirroring ICSID Proposed Rule 14); Working Paper #4 at 426 (ICSID Additional Facility Proposed Rule 63(4), mirroring ICSID Proposed Rule 53(4)). Subsequent references will be made to the Proposed ICSID Arbitration Rules, which can be found in the Proposed ICSID Additional Facility Rules at the corresponding Rules given the linkage just mentioned.
105. In late 2016, ICSID invited States to propose topics to be considered for future rule change, and one of the ideas that was suggested was to "Explore Possible Provisions on Third Party Funding." *List of Topics for Potential ICSID Rule Amendment*, ICSID, https://icsid.worldbank.org/en/Documents/about/List%20of%20Topics%20for%20Potential%20ICSID%20Rule%20Amendment-ENG.pdf.

address of the funder.[106] Disclosure would not (necessarily) be public but would be provided to the ICSID Secretariat, who would then transmit it to the parties and the arbitrators.[107]

While public comments submitted on earlier ICSID Working Papers have advocated for more regulation,[108] and even restriction, of TPF under the ICSID Rules,[109] ICSID has rejected such reforms, deeming them beyond the scope of TPF problems that the ICSID rule reform process is attempting to address. Instead, ICSID appears solely concerned with possible conflicts of interest that may arise between arbitrators and third-party funders.[110] As such, a minimum amount of transparency around the existence of funding and the identity of the funder has been deemed a sufficient fix.

However, it is precisely because of this narrow and circumscribed definition of the problem that ICSID is now missing the mark.[111] States and others have identified vastly more wide-ranging concerns about the role that TPF is playing in ISDS. These concerns include an increase in the number of claims fueled by these new financial

---

106. *Proposals for Amendment of the ICSID Rules* (ICSID, Working Paper No. 1, August 2018), https://icsid.worldbank.org/en/amendments/Pages/Proposals/Working-Paper.aspx; *Proposals for Amendment of the ICSID Rules* (ICSID, Working Paper No. 2, March 2019) https://icsid.worldbank.org/en/Documents/Vol_1.pdf; *Proposals for Amendment of the ICSID Rules* (ICSID, Working Paper No.3, August 2019) https://icsid.worldbank.org/en/Documents/WP_3_VOLUME_1_ENGLISH.pdf [hereinafter Working Paper #3]; Working Paper #4, *supra* n. 104.
107. Proposed Rule 14, Working Paper #4, *supra* n. 104, at 294–296.
108. The ICSID amendment proposal addresses third-party funding in Rule 13. *Proposals for Amendment of the ICSID Rules*, (ICSID, Working Paper No. 2, Vol. 1, March 2019). Paragraph 139 explains: "Some commentators suggested that AR 13 should require disclosure of the entire funding agreement. AR 13 requires disclosure of the fact of funding and the name of the funder only, as nothing further is required to achieve the purpose of the rule, avoidance of conflicts of interest. This approach is in line with current treaty practice and most other arbitration rules that address this topic. If the disclosure of further information about the third-party funding arrangement becomes relevant to another aspect of the proceeding, Tribunals have discretion under the general rules on evidence to order disclosure of relevant materials." Working Paper #3, *supra* n. 106, at 130–131, 135 ("There is potential for a conflict of interest when an undisclosed entity provides TPF to a party in arbitration. ... Absent disclosure, parties and arbitrators may be unaware of such conflicts, which could affect the integrity of ISDS and could give rise to challenges that delay the proceedings."); *see also Backgrounder on Proposals for Amendment of the ICSID Rules 2–3*, ICSID (2018), https://icsid.worldbank.org/en/Documents/Amendment_Backgrounder.pdf.
109. *See*, e.g., Frank J. Garcia and Kirrin Hough, *Third Party Funding in International Investor-State Arbitration* (Submission to ICSID Secretariat, November 27, 2018) ("effective regulation of third-party funding requires a closer examination of the role of third-party funding in investment arbitration and more comprehensive reform to the ICSID arbitration rules"); Columbia Center on Sustainable Investment, *Illustrative Suggestions for Amendments to the ICSID Arbitration Rules* (Submission to ICSID Secretariat, March 31, 2017). ("It is crucial to launch a multi-stakeholder dialogue on the role of third-party funders in ICSID investor-State arbitration, and to consider rules for governing whether, in what circumstances, and under what conditions different funding arrangements may be permitted.")
110. *Ibid.*
111. The definition of TPF used by ICSID is also broad and captures pro-bono, philanthropic and other kinds of financial arrangements that do not result in the same profit-motivated incentives, and thus systemic and problematic outcomes, that a narrower definition would. The current draft defines TPF as "any non-party from which the party, directly or indirectly, its affiliate or its representative has received funds for the pursuit or defense of the proceeding through a donation or grant, or in return for remuneration dependent on the outcome of the proceeding." Proposed Rule 14(1), Working Paper #4, *supra* n. 104, at 294–296.

resources available to investors but not States; the deliberate targeting of developing countries for funded claims; skewed incentives in the decision to threaten or actually bring claims; shifting priorities in the management of cases, including on which terms and when settlement can and should occur; and structural distortion of the BIT/ISDS regime itself, away from serving economic development and into a vehicle for speculative profits for unrelated third parties.[112] The vast majority of those concerns cannot and will not be addressed through transparency, particularly non-public transparency, which is the extent of ICSID's contemplated action on TPF.[113]

Such questions about the role of TPF in ISDS, identified in WG III (discussed in the following section) and elsewhere, highlight systemic concerns that, if accurate, threaten to undermine the development objectives of the ICSID Convention itself and the World Bank Group as an institution. Moreover, the WG III process itself constitutes a growing international dialog on the role of TPF in ISDS, facilitated by a UN body, that has already moved beyond ICSID's own limited consideration of these issues. As States' positions on TPF in ISDS coalesce through the WG III process, they will represent a new consensus on TPF that already seems likely to eclipse ICSID's own reforms. Such an outcome would hardly be in line with ICSID's mandate to support "international cooperation for economic development" through its rules and policies on foreign investment.

In keeping with its own development-oriented mandate, ICSID has a duty to consider the broader impacts of its rules and how its rules align with, or undermine, its own mission. Where not aligned, as is currently the case with its approach to TPF in ISDS, ICSID and its members have a duty to incorporate changes to its rules through the rule amendment process that would put its approach to TPF on track to achieve the objectives of the Convention and the World Bank Group.[114]

[C] UNCITRAL Arbitration Rules Reform

UNCITRAL was established by the UN General Assembly in 1966.[115] Its main objective is to promote the progressive harmonization and unification of international trade law in furtherance of Article 1, paragraph 3 of the UN Charter.[116] This article sets out one of the purposes of the UN, which is "[t]o achieve international co-operation in solving

112. *See ibid.*, s. 2.2.
113. *See generally.*, Williams and Dafe, *supra* n. 1 (arguing that the financialization of third-party funding in ISDS has resulted into transformational, fundamental and systemic impacts on the workings for the international investment law regime and legal system); Guven and Johnson, *supra* n. 12, at 5-11; Frank J. Garcia, *supra* n. 30, at 2928-2931; Maya Steinitz, *Whose Claim Is This Anyway? Third Party Litigation Funding*, 95 Minn. L. Rev. 1268 (2011) (describing TPF and the various legal fields in which it is used).
114. It remains uncertain whether this fourth draft will be the final draft or whether another round of proposed revisions and opportunity for State and public comment will occur. Working Paper #4 expresses an intent that final rules be voted on "in the latter half of 2020" with a goal of having them enacted by early 2021. Working Paper #4, *supra* n. 104, at 1.
115. G.A. Res. 2205, U.N. GAOR, 21st Sess., Supp. No. 16, vol. 1, at 99, U.N. Doc. A/RES.2205(XXI) (1966).
116. *Ibid.*

international problems of an economic, social, cultural, or humanitarian character, and in promoting and encouraging respect for human rights and for fundamental freedoms for all without distinction."[117] Thus, UNCITRAL's mandate lies in contributing to the development of international trade law in pursuit of greater international co-operation in economic and social fields and with respect for human rights.[118]

UNCITRAL is a technical body that prepares and promotes the use and adoption of legislative and non-legislative instruments in key areas of commercial law.[119] Structurally, it is led by a Commission, composed of sixty UNCITRAL Member States, which carries out its work at annual sessions.[120] The Commission has established six working groups to advance its work based on mandates granted to them.[121]

While UNCITRAL itself does not administer arbitrations, the Commission has adopted a set of arbitration rules that may be used in investor-State proceedings. The UNCITRAL Arbitration Rules were adopted in 1976, and amended in 2010 and again in 2013.[122] The 2010 UNCITRAL Rules revisions incorporated new developments in arbitration practice and enhanced procedural efficiency. In 2013, the UNCITRAL Rules were once again updated to include a paragraph incorporating the newly adopted UNCITRAL Rules on Transparency in Treaty-Based Investor-State Arbitration.

In 2015, the UNCITRAL Commission granted WG III a "broad mandate to work on the possible reform of investor-State dispute settlement."[123] WG III has identified TPF in ISDS as a concern meriting multilateral reform.[124] Notably, the concerns about TPF identified by WG III, especially when compared to concerns about TPF identified in the context of the ICSID amendment process, are wide-ranging, systemic, and multifaceted.

117. U.N. CHARTER, Art. 1, para. 3.
118. *See* Letter to UNCITRAL Member States from UN Special Procedures Mandate Holders, OL ARM 1/2019 (March 7, 2019) https://uncitral.un.org/sites/uncitral.un.org/files/public_-_ol_arm_07.03.19_1.2019_0.pdf (Submitted to UNCITRAL Secretariat in the context of Working Group III's ISDS Reform mandate).
119. *A Guide to UNCITRAL: Basic facts about the United Nations Commission on International Trade Law,* UNCITRAL (2013) at 1, https://uncitral.un.org/sites/uncitral.un.org/files/media-documents/uncitral/en/12-57491-guide-to-uncitral-e.pdf.
120. *Ibid.,* at 2.
121. *Ibid.,* at 7.
122. *UNCITRAL Arbitration Rules,* UNCITRAL (2013), https://uncitral.un.org/en/texts/arbitration/contractualtexts/arbitration.
123. Official Records of the General Assembly, GAOR, 71st Session Supplement No. 17, at para. 264, U.N. Doc A/71/17 (2016). The work being done by UNCITRAL's WG III is proceeding on a three-phase mandate: (1) to identify and consider concerns regarding ISDS; (2) to consider whether reform was desirable in light of any identified concerns; and (3) if the Working Group were to conclude that reform was desirable, develop any relevant solutions to be recommended to the UNCITRAL Commission. *Ibid.* As the WG III has recently moved into phase III of its mandate, it will soon begin to develop solutions to address this concern. The mandate of WG III has been interpreted to be limited to procedural, and not substantive, concerns and corresponding solutions. "Report of the Working Group III (Investor-State Dispute Settlement Reform) on the work of its thirty-fourth session," A/CN.9.930 (December 19, 2017), p. 5, para. 20.
124. "Report of Working Group III (Investor-State Dispute Settlement Reform) on the Work of its Thirty-Seventh Session," *supra* n. 51, at pp. 6, para. 25.

Concerns about TPF articulated by States in WG III include an increase in frivolous or unmeritorious claims; impacts on case management and decisions to settle claims; the targeting of certain profiles of respondent States; the moral, ethical, and political issues involved in permitting a funder to benefit from injury caused to others; and the potential of TPF "to derail the system from the very objective of providing justice."[125] The UNCITRAL Secretary-General, in addressing delegates during WG III's 38th Session, explained why the Secretariat had prepared a background paper on TPF without working together with ICSID (or other institutions), stating that:

> [W]e are looking at a much broader issue when tackling third-party funding. We [are] not only looking at potential conflict of interest, for instance, or the possible disruption of an arbitral procedure. So it is really with this broader perspective of the interaction of third-party funding with the entire ISDS system that we are looking into reforming that we have prepared this paper.[126]

The procedural solutions that may be developed to address these concerns articulated within WG III have yet to be specifically discussed or assessed.[127] But one potential solution could be for WG III to recommend to the Commission that the UNCITRAL Arbitration Rules be amended to incorporate restrictions on TPF in disputes governed by the UNCITRAL rules.[128] Such reforms to the UNCITRAL Arbitration Rules will require not only a recommendation by WG III to the UNCITRAL Commission but also that the Commission recommend such amendments to the UN General Assembly for adoption.

As noted above, the ICSID rule reform process has very narrowly defined the problem of TPF to be one of conflicts of interest and, as such, is proceeding to address this problem by applying transparency as a solution. To the contrary, in the context of UNCITRAL's ISDS reform process, States have articulated a much broader spectrum of concerns, many of which are more profoundly intertwined with the role of ISDS in advancing the object and purpose of investment treaties themselves. Transparency will do little, if anything, to address these more fundamental concerns and impacts. It is for this reason that States in UNCITRAL have been focused to a much greater extent on more robust solutions, including complete restrictions on TPF. In light of the systemic

125. "Possible reform of investor-State dispute settlement (ISDS): Submission from the Government of Morocco" *supra* n. 50; "Possible reform of investor-State dispute settlement (ISDS): Submission from the Government of South Africa." *Ibid.*; "Possible reform of investor-State dispute settlement (ISDS): Submission from the Republic of Korea." *Ibid.*; *Audio Recordings 35th Session, Working Group III (Investor-State Dispute Settlement Reform). Ibid.*; *Audio Recordings 37th Session, Working Group III (Investor-State Dispute Settlement Reform). Ibid.*

126. Working Group III 38th Session, Audio recordings (October 17, 2019, Morning Session), at 10:15:50 – 10:17:17, https://conferences.unite.un.org/carbonweb/public/uncitral/speakerslog/c6721e1b-0259-4e89-a0ec-0597fceb948c. The background paper in question is A/CN.9/WG.III/WP.172.

127. The UNCITRAL Secretariat has elaborated certain possible solutions in A/CN.9/WG.III/WP.172.

128. Another potential, and complementary, recommendation could be a multilateral instrument that could be used to amend existing treaties to incorporate TPF regulations. *See* "Possible reform of investor-State dispute settlement (ISDS) – Multilateral instrument on ISDS reform", *supra* n. 66.

risks contemplated by WG III, restricting TPF appears as a more appropriate policy response.

[D] Reform of Other Arbitration Rules

Under the majority of existing investment treaties, States consent in advance to arbitration only under one or more of the ICSID, ICSID Additional Facility, and/or UNCITRAL Rules.[129] However, in order to effect systemic reform of TPF in ISDS, it may ultimately be necessary—and would, in any event, be desirable—for all significant arbitration rules to be amended. Coordinated and consistent TPF regulation in all investment arbitration rules would help establish a norm as to the appropriate and acceptable role for speculative finance to play in ISDS, and could help prevent any regulatory arbitrage or temptations toward a "race to the bottom" by arbitration institutions to attract business.[130]

While mechanisms for collective action by all arbitration institutions do exist,[131] reforming TPF through changes to other arbitration rules faces significant hurdles. Unlike ICSID and UNCITRAL, other institutions do not have specific mandates to advance sustainable development. In fact, they would appear to have a financial interest in allowing TPF in international arbitration insofar as TPF, to the extent it facilitates cases that otherwise would or could not be brought, increases the number of ISDS cases, which translates to increased revenue for administering institutions.

129. UNCTAD Investment Policy Hub, *supra* n. 91 (showing that only 870 of 2577 (33%) of mapped treaties provide in advance for arbitration under another set of rules, in addition to or exclusive of ICSID and/or UNCITRAL). The Energy Charter Treaty, which accounts for 9% of disputes administered by ICSID (ICSID Caseload Statistics, 2020-1) provides for arbitration under these three rules as well as the Arbitration Rules of the Stockholm Chamber of Commerce. As dispute settlement under this treaty represents an outsized proportion of overall claims, a case can be made that TPF under the SCC Rules would also need to be addressed.

130. Williams and Dafe, *supra* n. 1, at 8. Besides ICSID, the top institutions are the International Chamber of Commerce (ICC), the London Court of International Arbitration (LCIA), the Singapore International Arbitration Centre (SIAC), the Hong Kong International Arbitration Centre (HKIAC), the Arbitration Institute of the Stockholm Chamber of Commerce (SCC), and the International Centre for Dispute Resolution (ICDR). Queen Mary University of London, *supra* n. 11. Notably absent from this list is the Permanent Court of Arbitration, which also has its own rules. However, according to UNCTAD's Investment Dispute Settlement Navigator, of the 166 arbitrations administered by the PCA, the vast majority have been conducted under UNCITRAL rules. UNCTAD Investment Policy Hub, *supra* n. 3. *See also 119th Annual Report*, Permanent Court of Arbitration (2019), 24-32, https://docs.pca-cpa.org/2020/03/7726c41e-online-pca-annual-report-2019-final.pdf.

131. Such work could proceed, for example, through the International Federation of Commercial Arbitration Institutions or another similar other setting. IFCAI is a trade group consisting of fifty-two arbitration institutions across the globe. One of the goals of IFCAI is "To canvass and coordinate the views of Members on developments of mutual interest, such as the amendment, or enactment, of legislation; the introduction and/or imposition of regulations; and the promulgation of codes of ethics or practice guidelines affecting arbitration." *About IFCAI*, IFCAI, http://www.ifcai-arbitration.org/about-ifcai/ (last updated 2020). A number of arbitration institutions, for example, have recently "spoken with one voice" regarding their ability to cooperate and collaborate in response to certain collective challenges. *Arbitration and COVID -19*, Arbitration Institute of the Stockholm Chamber of Commerce, https://sccinstitute.com/media/1658123/covid-19-joint-statement.pdf (last visited May 23, 2020).

Because ISDS, when compared to commercial arbitration cases, often have some of the largest claims,[132] and because many institutions price dispute services based on the size of claims,[133] TPF may be attractive to institutions if it increases the overall number of ISDS claims.[134] However, these institutions may ultimately risk marginalizing themselves in the growing dialogue on TPF regulation if they do nothing.

§14.05 CONCLUSION

In the late nineteenth century, a court in the City of London began to plan for a new tribunal, a predecessor to what would later become the London Court of International Arbitration. Upon its inauguration, a leading law journal of the time remarked on the goals of the new institution, "This Chamber is to have all the virtues which the law lacks. It is to be expeditious where the law is slow, cheap where the law is costly, simple where the law is technical, a peacemaker instead of a stirrer-up of strife."[135]

TPF in ISDS risks converting an already imperfect system of justice into a "stirrer-up of strife" by distorting incentives in the advancement and management of claims, the development of the law, and the outcomes of claims. In short, it negatively impacts the ways in which States govern investment. This undermines the role of foreign investment in the sustainable development of State treaty-parties and risks turning the ISDS regime into a vehicle for unrelated financial investors' speculative gains. As such, it is critical to address the role of TPF in ISDS while there is still time and space for regulatory action. The scale and increasing rate of current TPF investment – even if imperfectly estimated – and the magnitude of the systemic risks to States, their development, and their citizens, mandates a precautionary approach, one which must restrict, not simply regulate, TPF.

132. *Compare* Diana Rosert, *The Stakes Are High: A Review of the Financial Costs of Investment Treaty Arbitration,* International Institute for Sustainable Development Research Report, 2 (2014) (noting 52 ISDS claims over USD1 billion in 2013 and that the average claim was USD 492 million) *with,* e.g., *ICC Arbitration figures reveal new record for awards in 2018,* ICC (November 6, 2019) https://iccwbo.org/media-wall/news-speeches/icc-arbitration-figures-reveal-new-record-cases-awards-2018/ (claiming the average value of all pending disputes before the ICC at the end of the 2018 was USD 131 million); SIAC, 2019 Annual Report 15 (2020) (stating the average value of new cases filed in 2019 was USD 31 million); *2019 Annual Report,* LCIA (2020), https://www.lcia.org/News/annual-casework-report-2019-the-lcia-records-its-highest-numbe.aspx, at 12 (2020) (relating that only 9% of new cases filed in 2019 claimed over USD 50 million); *2019 Statistics,* HKIAC (2019), https://www.hkiac.org/about-us/statistics (average amount in dispute in 2019 was USD 19.9 million). *See* Williams and Dafe, *supra* n. 1, at 12 (comparing the attractiveness of funding of investment versus domestic legal claims because of the larger size of the former).
133. *See,* e.g., *Costs and Payments,* ICC https://iccwbo.org/dispute-resolution-services/arbitration/costs-and-payments/ (last visited May 28, 2020), ("ICC's administrative costs and the arbitrators' fees are fixed according to a scale of costs based on the monetary value of the claims."); *SIAC Schedule of Fees,* SIAC (August 1, 2016), https://www.siac.org.sg/estimate-your-fees/siac-schedule-of-fees (showing a scale of costs increasing based on the sum in dispute).
134. *Supra* n. 83.
135. IX Law Quarterly Review 86 (1893); *see also* History, LCIA, https://www.lcia.org/LCIA/history.aspx.

Reform of ICSID and UNCITRAL arbitration rules should and will play a key role in any TPF regulatory scenario. Given their mandates, ICSID and UNCITRAL, a World Bank Group organization and a United Nations commission, must advance their stated objectives of promoting the sustainable development of States and the citizens within them. The arbitration rules created by each of these institutions should both align with the mandates of these institutions and with the development objectives articulated in investment treaties.

The UNCITRAL process has identified wide-ranging concerns about TPF in ISDS that go to the very heart of sustainable development and the object and purpose of investment treaties. WG III is poised to seize this opportunity to enact meaningful reforms that further States' broader development objectives. The ICSID rule reform process, on the other hand, has honed in on an exceedingly narrow range of concerns about TPF in ISDS. ICSID is set to drastically miss the mark on the extent of reforms necessary to advance, or even remain consistent with, ICSID's own mandate. ICSID and ICSID Member States should take this opportunity to reconsider the scope of the concerns surrounding TPF and, in light of these concerns, broaden proposed TPF restrictions before the rule reform process has finished.[136] It is critically important that this opportunity to improve the strength and integrity of the international investment regime – and its ability to work for sustainable development goals – not be missed.

136. During UNCITRAL's Resumed 38th Session, "it was suggested that the definition of third-party funding in investment treaties and domestic legislation as well as that proposed in the ICSID Regulations and Rules amendment process could provide useful guidance." "Report of Working Group III (Investor-State Dispute Settlement Reform) on the work of its thirty-eighth session" *supra* n. 2, at para. 88. While tempting for normative, strategic, and political reasons, to have a common or similar set of rules, this is only true to the extent collaborative efforts result in outcomes that both consider and address the systemic risks that the use of TPF in ISDS poses to States and to the object and purpose of their investment treaties.

CHAPTER 15

Alternatives to Arbitration in Reforming Investor-State Dispute Settlement

Kinda Mohamadieh

In the ongoing debate about reforming Investor-State Dispute Settlement (ISDS), one question underlying the deliberations at United Nations Commission on International Trade Law (UNCITRAL) Working Group III (WG III) is whether the reform focuses on making arbitration work better or whether it also encompasses considerations of alternatives to arbitration as means to resolve investment disputes. This chapter discusses mediation, the role of domestic courts, and the role of State-to-State led mechanisms as potential alternatives to arbitration in redesigning the investment dispute settlement regime. Effectively addressing and integrating such alternatives in the envisioning of a reformed investment dispute settlement system could contribute towards enhancing the relevance and legitimacy of the outcome from WG-III deliberations.

§15.01 INTRODUCTION

In the ongoing debate about reforming ISDS, one question underlying the deliberations at UNCITRAL WG III is whether the reform merely focuses on making arbitration work better, or whether it also encompasses designing and utilizing alternatives to arbitration as means to resolve investment disputes. During the fiftieth session of UNCITRAL that adopted the mandate of WG III, country representatives approached the mandate in a broad manner that extended beyond thinking solely of correcting arbitration. For example, the report of the fiftieth session notes that '[t]he suggestion was made that it would be useful to consider the role of domestic courts, State-to-State dispute settlement mechanisms and any other means of investment dispute resolution'.[1] The deliberations at WGIII have touched on suggestions for alternatives and proposals that could change the status of arbitration as the norm for investment dispute resolution. Means of alternative dispute settlement is one of the issues placed for discussion on the agenda of the 39th session of WG III.[2]

This chapter examines and discusses the viability of alternatives to arbitration as potential options in a reform package that could emerge from WG III deliberations. It broadly considers the concept of an 'alternative to arbitration'. It envisions hybrid approaches that could mix arbitration with other tools for dispute settlement as well as approaches that would introduce systemic changes and alter the dynamics and incentives underlying the current arbitration model. For those purposes, the chapter discusses the added value and potential challenges associated with three main alternatives to investor-State arbitration, including mediation and conciliation, use of domestic courts, and reliance on State-to-State mechanisms. It investigates the extent to which such alternatives have been part of the deliberations at WGIII and the nature of the proposals presented in that regard. It highlights that alternatives to arbitration, such as reliance on domestic courts and State-to-State dispute settlement mechanisms, are evident in State practice. Consequently, the chapter proposes that effectively addressing and integrating such alternatives in the envisioning of a reformed investment dispute settlement system would contribute towards enhancing the relevance and legitimacy of the outcome from WGIII deliberations.

§15.02 ALTERNATIVES TO ARBITRATION IN STATE PRACTICES PERTAINING TO SETTLING INVESTMENT DISPUTES

While ISDS has developed rapidly over the last twenty years, the history of international investment agreements (IIAs) has not always incorporated ISDS. For example, the first bilateral investment agreement between Germany and Pakistan, concluded in 1959, did not include a direct ISDS clause.[3] The International Centre for Settlement of Investment Disputes (ICSID) was established in 1966 and its first case, *Holiday Inns et al v. Morocco*,[4] was only registered in 1972. The preamble of the ICSID Convention of 1966 provides that 'while such disputes would usually be subject to national legal processes, international methods of settlement may be appropriate in certain cases'.[5] This reflects a recognition that international arbitration should come to complement

1. UNCITRAL, Report of fiftieth session that adopted WGIII mandate (A/72/17), para. 256, http://www.uncitral.org/uncitral/en/commission/sessions/50th.html.
2. UNCITRAL, Secretariat paper, A/CN.9/WG.III/WP.190 (15 January 2020), https://undocs.org/en/A/CN.9/WG.III/WP.190 & UNCITRAL, Secretariat note A/CN.9/WG.III/WP.166 (July 2019), https://undocs.org/en/A/CN.9/WG.III/WP.166. For more information on the 39th session of WGIII, visit: https://uncitral.un.org/en/working_groups/3/investor-state.
3. Germany-Pakistan IIA (1959), https://investmentpolicy.unctad.org/international-investment-agreements/treaties/bilateral-investment-treaties/1732/germany---pakistan-bit-1959-.
4. *Holiday Inns S.A. and others v. Morocco*, ICSID Case No. ARB/72/1.
5. ICSID Convention, Regulations and Rules, https://icsid.worldbank.org/en/Documents/resources/2006%20CRR_English-final.pdf.

other means of dispute settlement, particularly domestic legal processes, and that investment arbitration was not been initially designed as a total replacement of the latter. It was only in 2001 that the benchmark of ten new ICSID cases was registered in one year.[6] According to ICSID, while only eighteen arbitration cases were registered in its first twenty years (1965–1984), the next twenty years saw 150 new cases (1985–2004), and a further 242 cases were registered in the following eight years alone (2005–2012).[7] The latest aggregate number of known treaty-based ICSID and non-ICSID cases has exceeded 1,000.[8] Thus, while it is difficult to imagine IIAs today without investment arbitration, the two were not necessarily so closely wedded throughout the history of IIAs. Moreover, the relevance of IIAs is not contingent upon arbitration as the means for settling disputes between foreign investors and States.

In 2015, the United Nations Conference on Trade and Development (UNCTAD) published a set of options for reforming investment dispute settlement, including the two options of replacing the existing investor-State arbitration or reforming it.[9] In 2019, UNCTAD published a list of ISDS reforms highlighting States' approaches to dispute settlement in new IIAs signed during 2018.[10] The list showed that several States have chosen to move away from arbitration or limit reliance on arbitration in their new treaty practice. For example, some agreements do not include ISDS or they subject ISDS to the State's consent on a case-by-case basis.[11] Some States limit ISDS by including a requirement to exhaust local judicial remedies or to litigate in local courts for a prolonged time period before turning to arbitration. Others narrow the ISDS subject-matter scope and/or set a time limit for submitting ISDS claims.[12]

The idea that arbitration would be less costly, faster, and seal-off conflicts of interest in comparison to other means of settling investment disputes did not hold true in the realm of practice. Furthermore, arbitration as means to depoliticize the dispute settlement process has been challenged both factually and as a policy matter, whereby government decisions to provide special treatment to investors over other constituencies have been seen as political and decried.[13] There is also evidence that diplomatic pressures continue to be applied in the context of investment disputes notwithstanding

6. Richard Happ and Sebastian Wuschka, *From the Jay Treaty Commissions Towards a Multilateral Investment Court: Addressing the Enforcement Dilemma*, Indian Journal of Arbitration Law, https://www.luther-lawfirm.com/uploads/tx_fwluther/IJAL_Volume_6_Issue_1_Richard_Happ___Sebastian_Wuschka_01.pdf.
7. ICSID, *The ICSID Caseload Statistics* (Issue 2019-1), https://icsid.worldbank.org/en/Documents/resources/ICSID%20Web%20Stats%202019-1(English).pdf.
8. UNCTAD, Investment Dispute Settlement Navigator, https://investmentpolicy.unctad.org/investment-dispute-settlement.
9. UNCTAD, World Investment Report (2015), https://unctad.org/en/PublicationsLibrary/wir2015_en.pdf.
10. UNCTAD IIA Issues Note, *Reforming Investment Dispute Settlement: A Stocktaking* (March 2019), https://unctad.org/en/PublicationsLibrary/diaepcbinf2019d3_en.pdf.
11. *Ibid.*, p. 6. Examples of treaties that do not include ISDS: Brazil–Ethiopia bilateral investment agreement (BIT), Brazil–Guyana BIT, Brazil–Suriname BIT, USMCA (Canada–Mexico, Canada–United States), Regional Comprehensive Economic Partnership Agreement (RCEP).
12. UNCTAD, *supra* n. 9.
13. Organization of Economic Cooperation and Development (OECD), *FDI Qualities Indicators: Measuring the Sustainable Development Impacts of Investment* (2019).

the availability of ISDS.[14] This encourages States to look towards alternatives to arbitration in their reformed dispute settlement practice.

§15.03 DISCUSSIONS AT UNCITRAL: THE CONTEXT

Discussions on reforming ISDS held at WG III are taking place during a period when there is close to an international consensus on the need to focus on linking foreign direct investment (FDI) with development objectives for the purposes of achieving the Sustainable Development Goals (SDGs).[15] Work has been undertaken on clarifying the sustainability characteristics of FDI and addressing obligations of investors under IIAs, both of which are subjects that are garnering increasing attention. In this context, the responsibilities of businesses and related accountability frameworks are increasingly becoming a mainstream issue in multiple fora.

For example, a recent publication entitled *Towards an Indicative List of FDI Sustainability Characteristics*[16] focuses on 'assessing the contribution of foreign investment to sustainable development and identifying policies to maximise positive impacts and minimise potential negative impacts'.[17] Additionally, the Guiding Principles on Business and Human Rights, which is a consensual document accepted by the international community under the auspices of the United Nations Human Rights Council (HRC), provides that 'business enterprises should respect human rights. This means that they should avoid infringing on the human rights of others and should address adverse human rights impacts with which they are involved'.[18] A legally binding instrument on business and human rights is being discussed in an intergovernmental working group under the auspices of the HRC.[19]

UNCTAD points out that one of the salient features of new IIAs is the balance between investor protections and investor obligations through the investor's duty to comply with host State domestic laws and regulations, abstain from corruption, uphold labour rights, undertake impact assessments and meet corporate social responsibility

---

14. *Ibid.*
15. The SDGs by UN Member States under the 2030 Agenda for Sustainable Development, https://sustainabledevelopment.un.org/?menu=1300.
16. Karl P. Sauvant and Howard Mann, *Towards an Indicative List of FDI Sustainability Characteristics*, ICTSD and WEF (1 October 2017), https://ssrn.com/abstract=3055961. One definition of 'sustainable investment' is 'commercially viable investment that makes a maximum contribution to the economic, social and environmental development of host countries and takes place in the framework of fair governance mechanisms'. *Ibid.*, at 2. This work focuses on FDI, particularly on five clusters of FDI qualities including productivity and innovation, employment and job quality, human capital and skills, gender equality, and carbon footprint.
17. OECD, 'FDI Qualities Indicators: Measuring the Sustainable Development Impacts of Investment', Paris (2019), 30.
18. United Nations Guiding Principles on Business and Human Rights, https://www.ohchr.org/Documents/Publications/GuidingPrinciplesBusinessHR_EN.pdf.
19. Information available at: https://www.ohchr.org/en/hrbodies/hrc/wgtranscorp/pages/igwgontnc.aspx.

(CSR) standards.[20] The 2020 Organisation for Economic Co-operation and Development (OECD) Investment Treaty Conference addresses how governments approach issues of business responsibilities in their trade and investment treaties. It also explores related issues such as policy space for governments, provisions that buttress domestic law and its enforcements in areas such as labour, environment, anti-corruption and human rights, and provisions that speak directly to investors, such as establishing conditions for access to investment treaty benefits.[21] According to an OECD consultation paper, responsible business conduct is 'a broad concept that focuses on two aspects of the business-society relationship: (i) the positive contribution businesses can make to sustainable development and inclusive growth; and (ii) avoiding adverse impacts on others and addressing them when they do occur'.[22]

At WG III, multiple submissions by participating Member States have pointed towards the need to more actively situate ISDS reform in this broader context, which considers the needed reforms as part of a process of aligning investment policies, including the role of ISDS, with broader developmental objectives. For example, Morocco noted a belief 'that ISDS reform is likely to lead to responsible international investment that will promote achievement of the Sustainable Development Goals'.[23] South Africa elaborated on this interface by noting that 'ISDS reform must be consistent with broader sustainable development objectives' and that '[p]romoting and attracting investment should not be an end in itself, but a step towards realising the broader objectives of the SDGs and the human rights obligations'.[24] South Africa stressed on 'policy space to regulate' as one of the principles to guide ISDS reforms.[25] Mali's submission reflected support for a 'comprehensive investor-State dispute settlement reform that fosters sustainable development by, inter alia, safeguarding the right of States that receive investments to establish regulations aimed at promoting the development goals'.[26] Mali stressed its support for 'a system whereby responsible, sustainable investment that creates stable and decent jobs is promoted and facilitated'.[27] Korea's submission to WG III 'reflects diverse opinions from academia and civil society', part of which are positions of several Korean civil society groups that proposed work towards 'a more democratic and human rights-friendly investment

20. UNCTAD, *Taking Stock of IIA Reform: Recent Developments* (June 2019), available at: https://unctad.org/en/PublicationsLibrary/diaepcbinf2019d5_en.pdf.
21. http://www.oecd.org/investment/conference-investment-treaties.htm. David Gaukrodger, *Business Responsibilities and Investment Treaties*, OECD (January 2020), http://www.oecd.org/daf/inv/investment-policy/Consultation-Paper-on-business-responsibilities-and-investment-treaties.pdf.
22. *Ibid.*, OECD consultation paper.
23. *Possible reform of investor-State dispute settlement*, Submission from the Government of Morocco, A/CN.9/WG.III/WP.161, para. 4 (4 March 2019), https://undocs.org/en/A/CN.9/WG.III/WP.161.
24. *Possible reform of Investor-State dispute settlement*, Submission from the Government of South Africa, A/CN.9/WG.III/WP.176 (July 2019), https://undocs.org/en/A/CN.9/WG.III/WP.176.
25. *Ibid*, South Africa, para. 30.
26. *Possible reform of investor-State dispute settlement*, Submission from the Government of Mali, A/CN.9/WG.III/WP.181, para. 1, September 2019, available at: https://undocs.org/en/A/CN.9/WG.III/WP.181.
27. *Ibid.*, Mali.

policy, based on the United Nations' Sustainable Development Goals and Millennium Development Goals'.[28] Indonesia's submission stressed that 'ISDS reform process should reflect an effort to strike a balance between the rights and obligations of all relevant stakeholders, protecting investors and their rights while preserving a State's policy space and right to regulate foreign investments in its territories.'[29] The Group of seventy-sevn, which is the largest intergovernmental grouping of developing countries in the United Nations, presented WG III with a collective statement on behalf of its group that pointed out 'the impact of ISDS on the development process'.[30] The Group stressed the importance of sustainable development, fairness, transparency, the respect of the right to regulate and the flexibility of States to protect legitimate public welfare objectives, as well as the need to appropriately address the rights and responsibilities of foreign investors.[31]

Aligning ISDS reform with developmental objectives requires a recognition that cases and measures that ISDS touches on have different implications from a sustainable development and public policy perspective. Consequently, investor-State arbitration does not necessarily provide the most effective avenue for dealing with all of the cases that might arise, even if some procedural changes to arbitration are to be adopted. In light of this, reforming ISDS ought to extend beyond just seeking to regain legitimacy of the arbitration system. Rather, there is a need for a broader re-envisioning of the dispute settlement system. For example, South Africa's submission raises a point pertaining to the 'necessity of investor-State Dispute Settlement' pointing out that '[c]ountries must consider whether there is a real need for ISDS mechanisms'.[32] South Africa posits that the starting point or question is whether ISDS mechanisms are desirable or necessary in the first place. Countries must not rush into assuming that ISDS policies must be a part of their investment agreements and must be mindful of the origins of the ISDS. It was never seen as a substitute for domestic legal dispute settlement, but as a stopgap in cases of extreme maladministration carried out by governments.[33]

§15.04 DISCUSSIONS AT UNCITRAL: THE PROPOSED REFORMS

The deliberations at WG III had identified four general categories of concerns with ISDS: cost and duration of proceedings; inconsistency, incoherence, unpredictability and incorrectness of decisions; arbitrators' and decision-makers' appointment methods

28. *Possible reform of investor-State dispute settlement*, A/CN.9/WG.III/WP.179, Submission from the Republic of Korea (July 2019), https://uncitral.un.org/sites/uncitral.un.org/files/wp179_new.pdf.
29. *Possible reform of Investor-State dispute settlement*, submission by the Government of Indonesia, A/CN.9/WG.III/WP.156, para 6 (November 2018), https://undocs.org/en/A/CN.9/WG.III/WP.156.
30. Available at: https://www.g77.org/doc/.
31. Statement on behalf of the Group of 77 and China, at UNCITRAL Working Group III Meeting on Investor-State Dispute Settlement Reform, https://uncitral.un.org/sites/uncitral.un.org/files/media-documents/uncitral/en/uncitral_wgiii_-_35th_session_-_g77_statement.pdf.
32. Submission by South Africa, *supra* n. 24, para. 37.
33. *Ibid.*

and ethics; and third-party funding.[34] WG III has also identified a number of 'cross-cutting issues' that were mainly raised by developing countries. These include means other than arbitration to resolve investment disputes as well as dispute prevention methods, exhaustion of local remedies, third-party participation, counterclaims and investor obligations, regulatory chill, and calculation of damages.[35] There was an agreement in WG III that these issues will be taken into account as the working group develops tools to address various concerns.[36] Yet, whether these issues would be addressed in an integrated manner as discussions on reform options evolve remains to be seen.

Working papers of WG III, in the form of notes prepared by the UNCITRAL Secretariat, approach and conceptualize alternative means to dispute settlement as synonymous to the notion of alternative dispute resolution (ADR) that particularly focuses on mediation and conciliation.[37] For example, the UNCITRAL Secretariat's paper, 'Dispute prevention and mitigation - Means of alternative dispute resolution', focuses on mediation and conciliation presenting them as 'an alternative to both investment treaty arbitration and resort to national courts'.[38] The role of options like resorting to domestic courts or State-to-State dispute settlement as an alternative to investor-State arbitration is not comprehensively weaved into the notion of alternative means for investment dispute resolution as currently being handled at WG III. These options, however, are integrated into the submissions of several participating Members States.[39]

Civil society groups participating in WG III have conceptualized the notion of 'means other than arbitration to resolve investment disputes' as encompassing alternatives to ISDS, such as domestic courts, ombudsmen, ADR and State-to-State dispute settlement.[40] They also pointed out that this discussion requires consideration of limits on the causes of action that can be pursued through ISDS (e.g., to denial of justice) and rules on referral to other courts and/or expert bodies and on staying ISDS disputes while related proceedings are pending.[41]

The role of domestic courts and exhaustion of local remedies were captured in a preliminary note produced by the UNCITRAL Secretariat on possible options for

34. Report of WG III on the work of its thirty-sixth session, A/CN.9/964 (Vienna, 29 October–2 November 2018), https://uncitral.un.org/en/working_groups/3/investor-state. Third-party funding was added subsequently as an additional area for the development of reforms.
35. Report of WG III on the work of its thirty-seventh session (New York, 1-5 April 2019), paras 26–40, A/CN.9/970 (April 2019), available at https://undocs.org/en/A/CN.9/970.
36. *Ibid.*, UNCITRAL, para. 37, p. 8.
37. UNCITRAL, A/CN.9/WG.III/WP.190, *supra* n. 2.
38. *Ibid.*, UNCITRAL, referencing and restating a point made in the submission from the Government of South Africa, A/CN.9/WG.III/WP.176, para. 40.
39. *Ibid.*, Submission by South Africa, *supra* n. 24.
40. International Institute for Environment and Development (IIED), Columbia Center on Sustainable Investment (CCSI) & International Institute for Sustainable Development (IISD), *Shaping the Reform Agenda: Concerns Identified and Cross-Cutting Issues*, Submission to UNCITRAL WG III on ISDS Reform, https://uncitral.un.org/sites/uncitral.un.org/files/media-documents/uncitral/en/wgiii_crosscuttingissues__0.pdf.
41. *Ibid.*

reform.[42] This preliminary note presents an overview of all possible reforms proposed by Member States during the deliberations of WG III and in their submissions. State-to-State mechanisms were discussed in reference to preliminary consideration of issues in a dispute, including through technical consultations, decisions taken by the respective State authorities, setting up a joint review committee by the treaty parties, setting a review or appellate mechanism or a State-to-State body to which application could be made if the claim cannot be settled at the technical level in a given time period.[43]

Keeping the role of domestic courts and State-to-State dispute settlement outside the notion of means of dispute resolution alternative to arbitration would practically focus the discussion of ISDS reform on changes that allow a re-legitimation of the existing system of investment dispute settlement. It will move the discussion away from a more fundamental rethink of the system. The next sections discuss three reform possibilities that would provide means for investment dispute settlement alternative to arbitration, including mediation and conciliation, domestic courts and State-to-State led mechanisms.

[A] Mediation and Conciliation: The Current Practice, Prospects and Potential Challenges[44]

Mediation and conciliation are not frequently used.[45] This is despite the availability of multiple rules and institutions administering mediation and conciliation. Moreover, there is an increasing number of references to these methods in recent investment treaties. These refer to mediation either as a precondition to arbitration or as a stand-alone mechanism for resolving disputes.[46] However, the complete picture is not

42. UNCITRAL Note by the Secretariat, *Possible reform of investor-State dispute settlement* (July 2019), https://undocs.org/en/A/CN.9/WG.III/WP.166.
43. *Ibid.*, UNICTRAL, para. 34. *See also* UNCITRAL, *Tabular Form on Possible Reforms*, https://undocs.org/en/A/CN.9/WG.III/WP.166/Add.1.
44. The terms 'mediation' and 'conciliation' are often used as if they were interchangeable. A mediator is an independent third person that will listen to the parties and try to persuade them to focus on their real interests rather than what they see as their legal rights. The conciliator usually focuses on making proposals for settlement, which in the words of the UNCITRAL Conciliation Rules, Art. 7(1), to 'assist the parties in an independent and impartial manner in their attempt to reach an amicable settlement of their dispute'. Nigel Blackaby, Constantine Partasides, Alan Redfern, Martin Hunter, *An Overview of International Arbitration* (2015), Investment Claims, Oxford University Press, http://oxia.ouplaw.com.
45. UNCITRAL, A/CN.9/WG.III/WP.190, *supra* n. 2.
46. Six hundred and twenty-seven out of the 2,577 IIAs mapped by UNCTAD include either voluntary or compulsory conciliation and mediation. *See* UNCTAD IIA Navigator, available at: https://investmentpolicy.unctad.org/international-investment-agreements/iia-mapping. *See also* Frauke Nitschke, *A Preview of ICSID's New Investor-State Mediation Rules* (10 January 2020), http://mediationblog.kluwerarbitration.com/author/fraukenitschke/?doing_wp_cron=1590665138.3794920444488525390625.

obtainable because these processes usually remain confidential with no publicly available data pertaining to them.[47]

ICSID's overall numbers released in 2019 point to twelve registered conciliation cases, including two additional facility conciliation cases, and no cases under the ICSID Fact-Finding Additional Facility Rules.[48] ICSID has increased its focus on mediated outcomes and proposed a new set of investor-State mediation rules, which, if agreed, would be the first set of institutional mediation rules designed specifically for investment disputes.[49] Other institutions, including the Permanent Court of Arbitration (PCA), International Chamber of Commerce (ICC), the Stockholm Chamber of Commerce (SCC), and the International Centre for Dispute Resolution, offer mediation rules and mediation support services. The PCA has so far not administered mediation proceedings based on a treaty.[50] Similarly, neither the Energy Charter Secretariat nor the SCC has administered any investor-State mediations, while the ICC has so far administered only one treaty-based mediation.[51]

The relevance of mediation as a choice for dispute settlement, particularly from the point of view of investors, could be bolstered by the addition of the United Nations Convention on International Settlement Agreements Resulting from Mediation (i.e., the Singapore Convention) that focuses on the enforcement of international settlements that result from mediation.[52] The Singapore Convention is the result of negotiations undertaken in UNCITRAL Working Group II.[53] It provides a framework and a set of multilateral standards to facilitate cross-border enforcement of settlements emerging from mediation, including between an investor and a host government, in a similar way in which the New York Convention on the Recognition and Enforcement of Foreign Arbitral Awards does in the case of international arbitration. If a country joins the Singapore Convention, it makes it easier for investors to enforce settlements, to which the country is party to, in other jurisdictions party to the Convention.[54]

47. ICSID statistics indicate that about 34% of ICSID cases were settled or otherwise discontinued, which might indicate the use of ADR by the parties to some extent. Reference: UNCITRAL *supra* n. 2 footnote 52.
48. *See* ICSID caseload – statistics, issue 2019-2 statistics, available at: https://icsid.worldbank.org/en/Documents/ICSID_Web_Stats_2019-2_(English).pdf, referenced in UNCITRAL paper A/CN.9/WG.III/WP.190.
49. ICSID Investor-State Mediation webpage, available at: https://icsid.worldbank.org/en/Pages/process/adr-mechanisms--mediation.aspx.
50. UNCITRAL paper A/CN.9/WG.III/WP.190, partially referencing C. Titi, K., Fach Gómez, K., *Mediation in International Commercial and Investment Disputes*.
51. *Ibid.*
52. Available at: https://www.singaporeconvention.org/.
53. Official Records of the General Assembly, Seventy-second Session, Supplement No. 17 (A/72/17), paras 238–239. *See also* Resolution adopted by the General Assembly 73/198 (20 December 2018).
54. *See* Art. 3 (General Principles) of the Singapore Convention, which provides, 'Each Party to the Convention shall enforce a settlement agreement in accordance with its rules of procedure and under the conditions laid down in this Convention.' Accordingly, each party to the Convention undertakes the commitment to enforce a settlement agreement covered under the Convention. Reservations provided under Art. 8.1 of the Convention are narrow, allowing a State Party to reserve its right to not have to enforce a settlement between its government and an investor and to take a reservation based on reciprocity. *See* Iris Ng, *The Singapore Mediation Convention: What Does It Mean for Arbitration and the Future of Dispute Resolution?*, http://arbitrationblog

The confidentiality of mediation is sometimes considered an advantage given the reputational costs associated with publicly known ISDS cases and is argued to be essential to the mediation process.[55] Yet, increasing reliance on confidentiality-centred processes within the context of a dispute settlement system that has already acknowledged the shortcomings of secrecy and accepted the need to move towards transparency could lead to serious setbacks from the advances on transparency achieved so far. To deal with transparency challenges in ISDS, the UNCITRAL Rules on Transparency in Treaty-Based Investor-State Arbitration and the United Nations Convention on Transparency in Treaty-Based Investor-State Arbitration were adopted and additional reforms are being discussed by WGIII.[56]

The role of mediation as an alternative to arbitration could have different implications depending on the nature of the disputed issues. Indeed, there is ample difference between a dispute concerning the valuation of a direct uncompensated expropriation in comparison to a dispute arising out of action taken by a government for environmental, human rights, or other public interest objectives.[57] The latter raises important issues pertaining to third-party rights, developmental and public policy considerations, and the role of domestic legal processes. Part of the problem of the current ISDS regime has been its failure to attend to these specificities.

The use of mediation has been questioned in sensitive cases pertaining to public interest measures or other issues of grave concern to the involved State. In such cases, it might be hard for public officials to take a decision to enter mediation or justify a voluntary compensation to investors for a decision or a regulation it sets in place for the public interest.[58] This is especially so in the context of an investor-State dispute where domestic opposition in the concerned country is ready to use the process to smear incumbents.[59] On a more technical level, officials, including those responsible for the measure that is the subject of the claim, arguably may take time to convey all the needed information and other endogenous elements related to the issues at hand. This makes it harder to undertake an assessment that enables a decision on whether to go

.kluwerarbitration.com/2019/08/31/the-singapore-mediation-convention-what-does-it-mean-for-arbitration-and-the-future-of-dispute-resolution/?doing_wp_cron=1590567273.618558883 6669921875000. *See also* Nandakumar Ponniya, Celeste Ang and Wong Tjen Wee, *Singapore Mediation Convention Strengthens Enforcement of Mediation Settlements*, Baker McKenzie (August 2019), https://www.lexology.com/library/detail.aspx?g=6cc668a2-1220-44a7-9488-a4811c31f150.

55. *Mediation in International Commercial and Investment Disputes* (Catharine Titi and Katia Fach Gómez, eds), pp. 35, 36.
56. Rules on Transparency in Treaty-Based Investor-State Arbitration, https://uncitral.un.org/sites/uncitral.un.org/files/media-documents/uncitral/en/rules-on-transparency-e.pdf. The Convention on Transparency in Treaty-Based Investor-State Arbitration, https://uncitral.un.org/sites/uncitral.un.org/files/media-documents/uncitral/en/transparency-convention-e.pdf.
57. Brooke Skartvedt Güven, *Investor-State Mediation: An Opportunity to Advance Sustainable Outcomes* (3 January 2020), http://ccsi.columbia.edu/2020/01/03/investor-state-mediation-an-opportunity-to-advance-sustainable-outcomes/.
58. Catharine Titi and Katia Fach Gómez, *supra* n. 55 (referencing Welsh and Schneider, *The Thoughtful Integration of Mediation in Bilateral Investment Treaty Arbitration*, Harvard Negotiation L. Rev. 71,77 (2013)).
59. *Ibid.*, p. 36.

forward with mediation seeking a settlement or to continue to arbitrate.[60] In other cases, officials may not be at liberty to settle with foreign investors,[61] or might not want to do that and undertake the potential risk of a backlash from their domestic constituency.[62]

A note by the UNCITRAL Secretariat on treaty interpretation points out that divergent treaty interpretations adopted by ISDS tribunals make it difficult to assess the strengths and weaknesses of a State's position and to thus decide whether settling is the right path to follow in a specific case.[63] While mediation is often characterized as a 'win-win' situation, whether a party effectively 'wins' as a result of mediation depends on what it could potentially have achieved through other means of dealing with the dispute. The encouragement of early settlements, through mediation or other confidential means, risks increasing the number of 'wins' that investors accrue without having to make their case, especially if there is a significant imbalance between the economic power of the investor and that of the host State. This could in turn exacerbate the current challenges resulting from the existing model of ISDS, and potentially intensify the chilling effect on the regulatory process. Resorting to mediation and conciliation as an option for reforming ISDS would require effective address of the potential implications arising from lack of transparency, imbalance between the parties, selection of mediators and conciliators and its potential implications on the regulatory and public policy processes. Otherwise, mediation could repeat the same pitfalls of ISDS based on arbitration.

[B] Domestic Courts, Their Interface with Arbitration and Their Role as an Alternative

Considering the interface between domestic courts and arbitration is necessary for the redesign of the investment dispute settlement regime. Otherwise, arbitration would continue to evolve into a completely parallel justice system that marginalizes the role and contribution of domestic courts in the realm of investment law.[64] As recalled earlier in §15.02, the ICSID Convention preamble[65] recognizes that while subjecting investment disputes to international methods of dispute settlement may be appropriate in certain cases, national legal processes would be the usual recourse for such disputes. This reflects an understanding that '[i]t is not inherently unreasonable to require that the investor make some efforts domestically to obtain redress before seizing an

60. *Ibid.*, p. 37.
61. Silvia Constain, *Mediation in Investor-State Dispute Settlement: Government Policy and the Changing Landscape*, ICSID Review-Foreign Investment Law Journal (2014).
62. In *Southern Pacific Properties v. Egypt*, ICSID Case No. ARB/84/3, a tentative settlement was possible but was rejected in favour of arbitration by the prime minister, who expected that settling would open him to attacks by opponents and the media. Later a settlement was reached after arbitration commenced and for a higher amount. Reference made in *supra* n. 55, p. 37.
63. UNCITRAL, *Possible reform of investor-State dispute settlement (ISDS) Interpretation of investment treaties by treaty Parties*, A/CN.9/WG.III/WP.191 (January 2020), https://undocs.org/en/A/CN.9/WG.III/WP.191.
64. Submission by South Africa, *supra* n. 24, para. 44.
65. *Supra* n. 5.

international tribunal'.[66] A usual objection to such a proposition is the claim that domestic courts are usually overburdened and often not efficient in addressing investment cases where the investor is looking for a fast decision.[67] Consequently, the requirement to exhaust local remedies is often opposed under the argument that it would lead to delays in the resolution of the disputes and consequently could increase costs. While these critiques may apply to many domestic courts, they also apply to international investment arbitration, which is evident by the fact that issues of duration and cost are some of the concerns under discussion at WG III. Thus, the fact that domestic systems might need improvement should not be a barrier for discussing their role in settling disputes between the investor and the host State. For those purposes, reform of ISDS could include a process targeting the strengthening of domestic systems. UNCTAD pointed out that increased reliance on domestic courts, coupled with support for States whose legal systems are less developed, can strengthen the rule of law and consistency in the jurisprudence, and remedy some deficiencies that are used to justify ISDS.[68] Domestic reforms could include considering the utility of conferring certain courts, such as those dealing with administrative issues, exclusive competence to deal with investment disputes, or establishing specialized courts to deal with such disputes.

WG III had agreed that requiring investors to exhaust local remedies before bringing their claims to investment arbitration is a tool to be considered in reforming ISDS.[69] Besides this option, domestic courts could also be considered as a full alternative to arbitration, to deal with all claims or certain subject-matter disputes. Furthermore, domestic courts could contribute towards addressing challenges faced in the interpretation of domestic law by arbitral tribunals by serving as a reference point for arbitral tribunals on domestic law interpretation. Indeed, arbitral tribunals could be over-influenced by commercial rather than public policy considerations, resulting in a balance tipped in favour of private rather than public interests.[70] These different approaches to the role of domestic courts have not been comprehensively addressed in

66. H. Wehland, *Domestic Courts and Investment Treaty Tribunals: The Effect of Local Recourse Against Administrative Measures on the Breach of Investment Protection Standards* (2019), 36 J. Int'l Arb. 207–229 (March 2019) (referencing C. Schreuer, *Calvo's Grandchildren: The Return of Local Remedies in Investment Arbitration*, 4 The L. & Practice of Int'l Courts and Tribunals, 1–17 (2005)).
67. According to UNCTAD, among the main arguments made against local litigation requirements are '[c]oncerns that some host States cannot guarantee an efficient and well-functioning domestic court system'. UNCTAD, *Improving Investment Dispute Settlement*, IIA Issues Note (November 2017), p. 11, https://unctad.org/en/PublicationsLibrary/diaepcb2017d8_en.pdf.
68. UNCTAD, *World Investment Report* (2015), p. 149, https://unctad.org/en/PublicationsLibrary/wir2015_en.pdf.
69. UNCITRAL, Report of Working Group III, *Investor-State Dispute Settlement Reform*, A/CN.9/970, p. 7, https://undocs.org/en/A/CN.9/970.
70. South Africa submission, *supra* n. 24, para. 45. For example, the unrestricted mandate of arbitrators has led to cases where arbitral tribunals have also questioned decisions by the higher courts of several countries, such as in ISDS cases against India and Ecuador. *See White Industries Australia Limited v. The Republic of India*, UNCITRAL (2011); *Chevron Corporation and Texaco Petroleum Corporation v. The Republic of Ecuador*, UNCITRAL, PCA Case No. 2009-23.

WG III. Yet, several country submissions to WG III have referred to the role of domestic courts, including, but not limited to, the requirement of exhaustion of local remedies.[71]

Country practices show multiple experiences where domestic courts are taken as the only resort of choice. For example, the Australia-United States Free Trade Agreement (FTA) and the Australia-Japan Economic Partnership Agreement do not include arbitration as a choice for resolving disputes. Under these treaties, in case of a dispute, foreign investors must resort to domestic courts. Investors going abroad can insure their investment against political risks by purchasing private insurance, rather than relying on ISDS. In the renegotiations of North American Free Trade Agreement (NAFTA) (renamed the United States-Mexico-Canada Agreement (USMCA)), ISDS was eliminated between the United States and Canada. After a transition period of three years for investors already established in the foreign jurisdiction, the investors will have to revert to domestic courts. Canada had been subject to more investor-State claims under NAFTA Chapter 11 than either the United States or Mexico and has lost eight.[72] The United States has never lost a NAFTA Chapter 11 case.[73] Between the United States and Mexico, new dispute settlement rules require exhaustion of local remedies through initiating domestic remedies and seeing them through until a final decision or until thirty months have passed with no decision.[74] South Africa is another country that chose to move investment disputes away from international arbitration and towards domestic courts. Under its Protection of Investment Act (2015), which was set in place after it terminated its IIAs, investors have recourse to domestic courts, as well as to the option of referring any investment dispute with the government to a mediation process facilitated by the South African Department of Trade and Industry.[75]

Another approach could be where countries choose to reserve certain disputes for the domestic courts, such as those involving taxation, natural resources, obligations in treaties with Indigenous Peoples, or other issues pertaining to crucial public interest considerations and non-discriminatory regulatory interventions.[76] This could require a

71. Submission by Morocco, A/CN.9/WG.III/WP.161, para. 14; Submission by Indonesia, A/CN.9/WG.III/WP.156, para. 12; Submission by South Africa, *supra* n. 24, para. 12, https://uncitral.un.org/en/working_groups/3/investor-state.
72. Daniel Garcia-Barragan, Alexandra Mitretodis and Andrew Tuck, *The New NAFTA: Scaled-Back Arbitration in the USMCA*, 36 J. Int'l Arb. 739–754 (2019), https://www.alston.com/-/media/files/insights/publications/2019/12/the-new-nafta.pdf. For more information, *see* UNCTAD ISDS Navigator, https://investmentpolicy.unctad.org/investment-dispute-settlement/country/35/canada.
73. *Ibid.*
74. Annex 14-D of revised NAFTA entitled *Mexico-United States Investment Disputes. See also* Public Citizen, *Analysis of the NAFTA 2.0 Text Relative to the Essential Changes We Have Demanded to Stop NAFTA's Ongoing Damage*, https://www.citizen.org/sites/default/files/nafta_2.0_text_ana lysis.pdf; Nathalie Bernasconi, *USMCA Curbs How Much Investors Can Sue Countries – Sort of*, https://www.iisd.org/library/usmca-investors.
75. Protection of Investment Act South Africa, s. 13, available at: https://www.thedti.gov.za/gazzettes/39514.pdf. *See also* Peter Leon and Ernst Muller, *New Dispute Resolution Rules for Foreign Investors in South Africa* (February 2017), https://hsfnotes.com/arbitration/2017/02/16/new-dispute- resolution-rules-for-foreign-investors-in-south-africa/.
76. Jane Kelsey, *UNCITRAL Working Group III: Promoting Alternatives to investor-State arbitration as ISDS Reform*, International Institute for Sustainable Development, Investment Treaty News, vol. 10, no. 4 (October 2019).

filter for such cases away from international dispute settlement and towards domestic courts or other means such as State-to-State dispute settlement. A filter could be created as a State-to-State mechanism involving the States Parties to the investment treaty, or another type of autonomous mechanism set up by the States Parties to the treaty, and may serve to filter cases before they proceed to arbitration.[77] For example, the Australia-China FTA provides for a State-to-State filter, whereby both States could agree that a potential ISDS claim is about a non-discriminatory regulatory issue and should not proceed to arbitration.[78]

Exhaustion of local remedies is another potential approach to integrating the role of domestic courts in the redesign of the investment dispute settlement regime. The current lack of a rule on exhaustion of local remedies in relation to disputes under investment treaty law stands out in comparison to the usual practice under international law. Exhaustion of local remedies is of fundamental importance to the law of State's international responsibility and the international procedural law of diplomatic protection.[79] Under these principles of diplomatic protection, a State can bring international proceedings based on the violation of the rights of one of its nationals only once the latter has exhausted any remedies available to it in the local courts of the opposing State.[80] Even in human rights law, the person who has allegedly suffered a violation must first turn to domestic authorities with his or her grievance, thus allowing them to correct any injustice that may have occurred before proceeding to regional or international mechanisms.[81]

UNCTAD's mapping of IIAs reveals that 1,616 out of 2,577 mapped treaties include reference to the domestic courts of the State among the ISDS forum options.[82] Most of these (781 treaties) do not attempt to organize the relationship between domestic proceedings and international arbitration.[83] According to the same mapping, 82 of the 1,616 agreements require exhaustion or pursuit of local remedies before proceeding to international arbitration.[84] Some countries are adopting more details to clarify the interface between domestic and international remedies. For example, India adopts the rule of exhaustion of local remedies in its revised approach to IIAs. Under the 2018 India-Belarus BIT, the investor is required to pursue domestic judicial or administrative remedies related to the measure for at least five years from when it

77. Trishna Menon and Gladwin Issac, *Developing Country Opposition to an Investment Court: Could State-State Dispute Settlement be an Alternative?* (February 2018), http://arbitrationblog.kluwerarbitration.com/2018/02/17/d eveloping-country-opposition-investment-court-state-state- dispute-settlement-alternative.
78. *See* Rodrigo Polanco, *The Return of the Home State to Investor-State Disputes: Bringing Back Diplomatic Protection* (Cambridge, 2019), 89.
79. Z. Douglas, *The Hybrid Foundations of Investment Treaty Arbitration*, 74 *British Yearbook of International Law*, 240 (2003).
80. *See Interhandel (Switzerland v. United States)*, Judgment of 21 March 1959, [1959] ICJ Reports 27.
81. South Africa submission, *supra* n. 19, para. 46, A/CN.9/WG.III/WP.176.
82. UNCTAD IIA Mapping, https://investmentpolicy.unctad.org/international-investment-agreements/iia-mapping.
83. *Ibid.*
84. *Ibid.*

became aware of the measure, after which an investor may pursue ISDS.[85] A fork-in-the-road clause requires the investor who initiates arbitration to abandon any ongoing domestic proceedings with respect to the same measure. The agreement also prohibits an arbitral tribunal from reviewing the merits of a decision given by a domestic judicial authority.[86]

There are multiple issues to consider in designing the interface between the role of domestic courts and international arbitration in investment dispute settlement, particularly if designing a hybrid dispute settlement system that integrates a role for both. For example, it is not enough to provide the investor with the option of recourse to domestic courts through a 'fork-in-the-road' clause. Such clauses make it unlikely for investors to direct disputes to domestic courts,[87] and thus would have very limited implications in the process of redesigning the ISDS regime. A more express and unequivocal provision of exhaustion of local remedies would require that the investor 'shall' exhaust local remedies before initiating international arbitration and would determine the legal nature of the remedies to be exhausted, whether administrative or judicial.[88]

Another of these issues, which represents a concern particularly for governments, is that treaty tribunals might set themselves up as courts of appeal vis-à-vis a host State's domestic courts.[89] Different tribunals have exhibited different approaches to judgments of local courts. Tribunals usually accept that the judgment of a local court can have certain binding effects in a later treaty arbitration but have exhibited different views regarding the extent of such a binding effect.[90] For example, in *Robert Azinian & others v. United Mexican States*,[91] the tribunal decided that it would not review any administrative measure that had already been conclusively examined in the local courts. According to the decision in this case, '[a] governmental authority ... cannot be faulted for acting in a manner validated by its courts, unless the courts themselves are disavowed at the international level'.[92] In *Helnan Int'l Hotels A/S v. Arab Republic of*

85. Treaty between the Republic of Belarus and the Republic of India on investments, 24 September 2018 (not in force), Arts 15.1 and 15.2, https://investmentpolicy.unctad.org/international-investment-agreements/treaties/bilateral-investment-treaties/3839/belarus---india-bit-2018.
86. *Ibid.*, Art. 13.4(i).
87. Bahakal Yimer, Nicolas Cisneros, Laura Bisiani and Rahul Donde, *Application of International Investment Agreements by Domestic Courts*, p. 61, Trade Law Clinic (June 2011), https://www.tradelab.org/single-post/2018/03/02/Application-of-International-Investment-Agreements-by-Domestic-Courts.
88. Martin Dietrich Brauch, *Exhaustion of Local Remedies in International Investment Law*, International Institute for Sustainable Development (January 2017), https://www.iisd.org/sites/default/files/publications/best-practices-exhaustion-local-remedies-law-investment-en.pdf. For an example of a similar wording, *see* the SADC Model BIT (SADC, 2012, art. 28, para. 4(a)), available at: https://www.iisd.org/itn/wp-content/uploads/2012/10/sadc-model-bit-template-final.pdf.
89. Schreuer, *supra* n. 66.
90. Wehland, *supra* n. 66.
91. *Robert Azinian & others v. United Mexican States*, ICSID Case No. ARB (AF)/97/2, Award (1 November 1999). *See also Fouad Alghanim & Sons Co. for General Trading & Contracting & others v. Hashemite Kingdom of Jordan*, ICSID Case No. ARB/13/38, Award (14 December 2017).
92. *Robert Azinian & others v. United Mexican States*, para. 97.

Egypt,[93] the tribunal considered that it would have to accept the decision of a local forum pertaining to a certain domestic measure as binding merely as a matter of domestic law.[94] This does not prevent the tribunal from reviewing the measure and determining whether there exists a treaty breach as a result of it.[95] If such an approach is taken, international tribunals do not need to be restricted by determinations of national courts and would treat them as merely 'convincing authority for the purposes of their own decision-making'.[96]

For all those reasons, a redesign of the investment dispute settlement system into one that integrates roles for domestic courts and international arbitration ought to include clarification of how international tribunals should approach determinations by domestic courts. This is particularly important for the purpose of advancing consistency and coherence. Building on the experience with the application of the principle of subsidiarity in the European Union (EU) legal context, a standard of review built on the principles of deference could play a useful role in organizing this interface. If adopted, then international adjudicators would only review whether domestic courts' interpretation and application of international standards was outside the boundaries of reasonable construction and factual appreciation.[97] For example, Article 5 of the Treaty on European Union defines the principle of subsidiarity as follows:

> Under the principle of subsidiarity, in areas which do not fall within its exclusive competence, the Union shall act only if and in so far as the objectives of the proposed action cannot be sufficiently achieved by the Member States, either at central level or at regional and local level, but can rather, by reason of the scale or effects of the proposed action, be better achieved at Union level.

Procedural issues such as duration and costs that could arise as a result of a requirement to exhaust local remedies could be addressed with procedural rules that set time limitations or the establishment of particular domestic procedures, such as single-instance court proceedings.[98] However, these time limits should not be too short. Otherwise, the requirement to exhaust local remedies or attempt a settlement in the host State's domestic courts would yield no meaningful outcomes.

When considering the expansion of the role of domestic courts in dealing with investment claims, countries would need to consider how IIAs would apply in their domestic courts, which will potentially vary in different countries. This would depend on nuances of each jurisdiction such as its legal system, whether it is a dualist or monist system and its constitutional order, as well as the content of the dispute settlement

93. *Helnan Int'l Hotels A/S v. Arab Republic of Egypt*, ICSID Case No. ARB/05/19, Decision on Annulment (14 June 2010), paras 125, 131.
94. *Ibid.*, para. 131.
95. Wehland, *supra* n. 66.
96. *Ibid.*, p. 229.
97. Nico Krisch, *Institutionalizing Subsidiarity in the Reform of Investment Adjudication*, discussion paper for the Preparatory Session for UNCITRAL Working Group III (January 2020). *See also* Markus Jachtenfuchs and Nico Krisch, *Subsidiarity in Global Governance*, 79 Law & Contemporary Problems (2016).
98. *Ibid.*, Krisch.

clause itself.[99] For example, in some countries IIAs do not have direct effect. Consequently, investors cannot invoke IIAs in domestic courts.[100] In others, like Argentina, IIAs do have such a direct effect and may be invoked before domestic courts.[101] However, studies have found that classical distinctions between monist and dualist systems do not provide a rule of thumb whether domestic courts apply IIAs and thus cannot be determinative to the outcome of an IIA application by domestic courts.[102] Furthermore, it is important that countries consider and address the implications of the most-favoured-nation (MFN) clause integrated into many of their agreements on the effectiveness of the reform they will adopt. For example, in *Maffezini v. Spain*[103] and *Siemens v. Argentina*,[104] the claimants were able to rely on MFN clauses to avoid a requirement of exhaustion of local remedies. The tribunals in these two cases differentiated between the condition of exhaustion of local remedies and a resort to domestic courts over the course of a certain period,[105] consequently finding that the latter could be overcome by way of the MFN clause.

[C] State-to-State Mechanisms for Investment Dispute Settlement

Strengthening the involvement of State authorities has been integrated as one of the reform options considered by WG III. But WG III has not effectively addressed State-to-State dispute settlement as an alternative to investor-State arbitration. An UNCITRAL working paper on ISDS reform possibilities discussed strengthening State-to-State preliminary consideration of issues in a dispute.[106] This, according to UNCITRAL, could possibly include technical consultations among States, setting up a joint review committee by the treaty parties or State-to-State body to which application could be made if the claim cannot be settled at the technical level.[107] The conceptualization of alternative dispute settlement under the UNCITRAL Secretariat's papers does not include State-to-State dispute settlement as an alternative to ISDS but seem to focus on State-to-State cooperation in dispute prevention.[108]

Reliance on State-to-State prevention and dispute settlement mechanisms has been expanding in State treaty practice. A system for dispute prevention has been adopted by Brazil under its investment facilitation and cooperation model (CFIA). The

99. Bahakal Yimer, Nicolas Cisneros, Laura Bisiani, Rahul Donde, *supra* n. 87, p. 61.
100. The exercise by the European Union of its competence over FDI acquired through the Lisbon Treaty excludes the possibility for domestic courts to directly apply IIA provisions. *See*, for example, the European Union-Canada Comprehensive Trade and Economic Agreement (CETA).
101. *Supra* n. 87, p. 61.
102. *Ibid.*
103. *Emilio Agustín Maffezini v. Kingdom of Spain*, ICSID Case No. ARB/97/7.
104. *Siemens A.G. v. The Argentine Republic*, ICSID Case No. ARB/02/8.
105. Schreuer, *supra* n. 66, pp. 4, 5.
106. UNCITRAL, *Possible reform of investor-State dispute settlement*, Addendum (July 2019), A/CN.9/WG.III/WP.166/Add.1, https://uncitral.un.org/en/working_groups/3/investor-state.
107. *Ibid.*
108. UNCITRAL, A/CN.9/WG.III/WP.190, paras 24, 25, https://uncitral.un.org/en/working_groups/3/investor-state.

institutional core of the CFIA prevention pillar is the joint committee and the ombudsman. The 'joint committee for administration of the Agreement' is composed of government representatives of both parties designated by their respective governments. The agreement also establishes 'focal points or ombudsmen', which have as their main responsibility the provision of support to investors from the other party.[109] The Brazilian approach was influenced by the experience of the Korean Office of the Foreign Investment Ombudsman (OFIO), which includes providing investment aftercare to support investors who face grievances in their day-to-day business in order to make sure that the investment environment is appropriate. The Brazilian Direct Investment Ombudsman (DIO) was established within the Foreign Trade Board. It coordinates a focal point network comprised of main agencies and entities of the public administration at the national and subnational levels, including the investment promotion agencies. It handles complaints related to the federal government and to Brazil's different States.[110] In a submission to UNCITRAL WG III, Brazil notes that '[i]n extensive consultations with Brazilian multinational companies, the government realized that investors were more interested in the improvement of the institutional framework for investment with foreign governments than in after-the-fact remedies that would provoke long and expensive litigation'.[111] In addition, Brazil provides for State-to-State dispute settlement as one element of the model it adopts under the CFIA. The CFIA does not include ISDS. For example, the Brazil-India bilateral investment treaty (2020) provides that '[a]ny dispute between the Parties which has not been resolved after being subject to the Dispute Prevention Procedure may be submitted by either Party to an ad hoc Arbitral Tribunal, ... [or] ... to a permanent arbitration institution for settlement of investment disputes'.[112] Yet, in the Brazil-India treaty, the purpose of the arbitration is to decide on the interpretation of the treaty or the observance by a party of the terms of the treaty. However, the arbitral tribunals cannot award compensation.[113]

Other examples include the South Africa's Protection of Investment Act of 2015, which provides for the possibility of State-to-State arbitration after exhaustion of domestic legal remedies, with the States' consent required on a case-by-case basis.[114] The Southern African Development Community (SADC) have also decided to amend its Finance and Investment Protocol in 2016 to exclude the ISDS clause, leaving State-to-State dispute settlement as the only option.[115] Furthermore, the process of reforming

109. Felipe Hees, Pedro Mendonça Cavalcante and Pedro Paranhos, *The Cooperation and Facilitation Investment Agreement (CFIA) in the context of the discussions on the reform of the ISDS system*, South Centre (May 2018), https://www.southcentre.int/investment-policy-brief-11-may-2018/#more-11005.
110. Ricardo Figueiredo de Oliveira, *The Useful Institution of an Investment Ombudsperson*, Columbia FDI Perspectives, No. 273 (9 March 2020).
111. Submission by Brazil to WG III, https://undocs.org/en/A/CN.9/WG.III/WP.171.
112. Brazil-India BIT (2020), Art. 19.1, https://investmentpolicy.unctad.org/international-investment-agreements/treaty-files/5912/download.
113. *Ibid.*, Art. 19.2.
114. South African Government, *Protection of investment act 22 of 2015* (2015), https://www.gov.za/documents/protection-investment-act-22-2015-15-dec-2015-0000.
115. Protocol, available at: http://www.sadc.int/documents- publications/protocols/. SADC is constituted of 16 African States, https://www.sadc.int/index.php?cID=142.

the dispute settlement mechanisms under the Organization of Islamic Conference (OIC) investment agreement includes a proposal to adopt a State-to-State mechanism. As proposed, this mechanism would be operational after the exhaustion of local remedies, in case the investor is not satisfied and claims there is a denial of justice. At that stage, a State-to-State mechanism could be resorted to in order to arrive at an amicable settlement and avoid the movement towards arbitration.[116] The proposition by the EU for a multilateral investment court, which is being discussed at WG III, integrates the possibility of using the proposed court for State-to-State dispute settlement.[117] This reflects a recognition by the EU that States are increasingly choosing to rely on State-to-State dispute settlement as a substitute for ISDS.

State practices and multilateral intergovernmental experiences point that State-to-State led mechanisms, including State-to-State dispute settlement, could be viable options and do not necessarily have to be tainted with politicization. In the multilateral context, the World Trade Organization (WTO) dispute settlement system that is State-led in terms of its design, assignment of adjudicators, bringing cases and overseeing decisions have proved successful in attending to trade-related claims. The WTO State-to-State dispute settlement covers cases on investment-related measures falling under the scope of the WTO Agreement on Trade-Related Investment Measures (TRIMS), which are of a similar type to those covered under IIAs.[118] States do not need to establish a standing body, as the WTO Dispute Settlement Body, in order to advance State-to-State dispute settlement in investment cases. If States want to move away from the ad hoc case-by-case appointments, one option could be establishing treaty-specific dispute settlement commissions appointed by State parties to that treaty. These could be envisioned based on the experience of the Jay Treaty of November 1794 that was concluded to settle disputes between the United States and Great Britain resulting from the American War of Independence.[119] The arbitrations under the Jay Treaty have been considered the root or starting point for the development of modern international arbitration.[120] In the context of existing IIAs, each party to the treaty could nominate a commissioner (or more) who would be preselected from among national judges or retired judges[121] and pre-delegated by their respective State to serve on a commission

116. Mouhamadou Kane, Presentation, *Structural Reforms of the Dispute Settlement System under the OIC Investment Treaty*, CCSI preparatory session for the UNCITRAL WGIII resumed 38th session (January 2020).
117. Submission from the European Union and its Member States to WG III, *Possible reform of investor-State dispute settlement* (24 January 2019), A/CN.9/WG.III/WP.159/Add.1, p. 6, https://undocs.org/en/A/CN.9/WG.III/WP.159/Add.1.
118. Jane Kelsey, *Learnings for UNCITRAL WGIII from the WTO's Dispute Settlement Regime*, Third World Network, https://twn.my/title2/briefing_papers/nontwn/BriefingPaperJaneKelsey.pdf. *See* TRIMS related cases at https://www.wto.org/english/tratop_e/dispu_e/dispu_agreements_index_e.htm.
119. Treaty of Amity, Commerce, and Navigation, between His Britannic Majesty and the United States of America, 19 November 1794, 52 C.T.S. 243.
120. Richard Happ and Sebastian Wuschka, *supra* n. 6. *See also* Georg Schwarzenberger, *Present-Day Relevance of the Jay Treaty Arbitrations*, 53 Notre Dame L. Rev. 715 (1978), http://scholarship.law.nd.edu/ndlr/vol53/iss4/3.
121. *See* Royal Commissions appointment by the Australian Government, https://www.royalcommission.gov.au/; Judicial Conference of Australia, *Retired Judicial Officers Available for Public Service*, https://www.jca.asn.au/retired-judges/.

in case an investment dispute arises. A third adjudicator could be selected by the other two to preside over the commission on a case-by-case basis, which could also help fill a need for a specific expertise depending on the case at hand. This model could help avoid the costs associated with financing a standing international investment court. Case management and procedural rules could deal with any potential backlogs at the national level for the judge 'seconded' to serve on such international commission. The commissions could be served by the secretariats of existing international institutions specialized in investment dispute settlement or opt for ad hoc rules.[122]

Generally, it is important to effectively consider the potential role of State-to-State led mechanisms in the redesign of the investment dispute settlement system. In cases where both State-to-State dispute settlement and ISDS would live side by side, it will be important to clarify the role of each and the relationship between the two. This includes, for example, how one decision in a State-to-State dispute settlement might influence an ISDS case that deals with the same issues, including situations where the former should be binding in subsequent State-to-State or investor-State cases. States could also clarify how parallel State-to-State and ISDS cases might be coordinated, for example, if one has to be suspended in certain circumstances.

§15.05 CONCLUSION

The conceptualization of means of dispute settlement alternative to investor-State arbitration in WG III, particularly as presented in the UNCITRAL Secretariat notes, does not comprehensively cover the role of domestic courts and State-to-State dispute settlement mechanisms. The current conceptualization is focused on mediation and conciliation as steps preceding investor-State arbitration. The discussion of a role for domestic courts in WG III primarily focuses on exhaustion of local remedies. It neither considers domestic courts as an alternative to arbitration nor addresses the role of domestic courts as a reference point for arbitral tribunals regarding the interpretation of national law. The discussion of State-to-State led mechanisms in WG III focuses on State-to-State cooperation in dispute prevention and not on State-to-State dispute settlement as an alternative to ISDS. Yet, as shown in this chapter, recent practice of several States shows openness to the reliance on domestic courts and State-to-State led mechanisms in designing models for investment dispute settlement. Several submissions by States participating in WG III have also reflected upon this. Moreover, the historical record shows that IIAs were initially designed with no ISDS in place and that IIAs survived long before ISDS became an active ingredient within the international investment regime. Furthermore, international arbitration was not meant as a complete substitute to national procedures and other means of dispute settlement, which is

122. For example, in the Cuba-Italy bilateral investment treaty, arbitration provisions provide an overlap between the procedures for ISDS and SSDS, whereby tribunals for both types of cases are composed using the State-to-State procedures. The tribunal, whether for ISDS or SSDS, is constituted primarily by the treaty parties. Investors thus have no formal role in constituting an ISDS tribunal under this treaty. Treaty text available at: https://investmentpolicy.unctad.org/international-investment-agreements/countries/52/cuba.

particularly evident given the recognition of this complementarity in the ICSID Convention preamble.

The assumptions that arbitration would be advantageous to other means of dispute settlement have been already discredited. The mandate of WG III allows for deliberations over such alternatives as the role of domestic courts and State-to-State dispute settlement. Thus, it is of ample importance that all reform options, including alternatives to investor-State arbitration, get properly and effectively discussed in WG III. This will contribute towards ensuring the relevance and legitimacy of the outcome that could result from these deliberations. It will allow the discussion to move beyond a mere focus on making arbitration work better and regain legitimacy. Consequently, the outcome might better serve the objective of aligning the international investment regime with countries' development processes and objectives.

CHAPTER 16

Mediation as a Method to Settle International Trade and Investment Disputes

Herman Verbist[*]

Mediation is often provided in commercial contracts and also increasingly in investment treaties as a possible method for the settling of disputes, often as a first step before an arbitration can be commenced. However, little data are available on disputes submitted to mediation. This chapter examines the available data on mediation and also the existing framework for commercial mediation and for investor-state mediation. A special focus is given to the work of the United Nations Commission on International Trade Law (UNCITRAL) and also of Working Group III (WG III) on possible (investor-State dispute settlement) ISDS Reform.

§16.01 INTRODUCTION

Even though arbitration continues to be the go-to dispute solution mechanism for resolving cross-border disputes, parties are increasingly resorting to various forms of alternative dispute resolution (ADR) in the hope that a swifter and more cost-efficient resolution to disputes can be found, as was indicated in the International Arbitration Survey organized by Queen Mary University London in 2018.[1] The 'UNCITRAL' Model Law defines mediation as 'a process where parties request a third person or persons to

* The author thanks Ms Maureen Martins, attorney at the Brussels Bar and an associate with the law firm Everest Attorneys, for her assistance in the preparation of this chapter.

1. *2018 International Arbitration Survey: The Evolution of International Arbitration*, Queen Mary University of London/White & Case, 6, available at: http://www.arbitration.qmul.ac.uk/research/2018/ (accessed 4 June 2020).

assist them in their attempt to reach an amicable settlement of their dispute arising out of, or relating to, a contractual or other legal relationship'.[2] Mediation, as a method to settle international trade and investment disputes, has various benefits. These include reducing the instances where a dispute leads to the termination of a commercial relationship, facilitating the administration of international transactions by commercial parties, and producing savings in the administration of justice by States. Because of these benefits, the number of mediations has increased over the past decade, and answers should be found to fulfil the need for mediation.

This chapter first presents current answers to the growing need for mediation in the field of international trade. Second, it discusses the present mediation methods available in investment disputes. It concludes that there are only a few investor-State disputes submitted so far to mediation but notes that UNCITRAL adopted already some instruments in order to answer the growing need for mediation as a method to settle international trade and investment disputes, including the Singapore Convention on Mediation and a revised Model Law on Mediation.

§16.02 MEDIATION IN INTERNATIONAL TRADE DISPUTES

[A] Statistics on ICC Mediations

There is an increased use of mediation in international commercial disputes. Mediation offers numerous advantages, such as speed, lower costs and confidentiality. In 2014, the International Chamber of Commerce (ICC) Mediation Rules, which replaced the ICC ADR Rules of 2001 entered into force.[3] The term 'mediation' as used in the ICC Mediation Rules includes not only mediation but any other amicable settlement technique or combination of techniques the parties may prefer. The Mediation Rules provide that disputes filed under these Rules will be settled by mediation unless the parties choose otherwise. Cases brought under the Mediation Rules, as under the ADR Rules, are initiated either on the basis of a prior agreement between the parties to use the Rules, or by a unilateral request by one or more parties accepted by the other(s). Mediators and neutrals are either nominated by the parties and confirmed by the ICC International Centre for ADR (Centre) or, if the parties fail to agree, appointed by the Centre. As a neutral and flexible procedure, ICC mediation lends itself to disputes

2. A/CN.9/WG.II/WP.205, para. 5 (23 November 2017) (Working Group II (WG II) 68th session, 5-9 February 2018); note 3 in document A/CN.9/WG.II/WP.205/Add.1 (23 November 2017) (WG II 68th session, 5-9 February 2018); Report of Working Group II (Dispute Settlement) on the work of its 67th session (Vienna, 2-6 October 2017), A/CN.9/929, para. 104. It has been proposed that this change of terminology should also apply to the UNCITRAL Conciliation Rules (1980), A/CN.9/WG.II/WP.205, para. 4 (23 November 2017) (WGII 68th session, 5-9 February 2018).
3. Available at: https://iccwbo.org/dispute-resolution-services/mediation/mediation-rules (accessed 2 June 2020). Before the ADR Rules, the ICC had Conciliation Rules. The first Rules of Conciliation were established in 1922. *See The New ICC Mediation Rules*, 24 ICC ICArb. Bull. 2, 5-24 (2013); A. Mukhopadhyay and K.-U. Karl, *Does Business Need Mediation?*, 24 ICC ICArb. Bull. 2, 25-31 (2013); H. Verbist, *The 2014 ICC Mediation Rules*, in *Festschrift für Siegfried Elsing zum 65. Geburtstag*, 591-608 (W. Ebke, D. Olzen and O. Sandrock eds, Frankfurt-am-Main: Verlag Recht und Wirtschaft, 2015).

between parties from distant countries and contrasting cultures. The ICC established in 2018 a Mediation Request Form.

In 2014, the Centre received twenty-five filings for amicable dispute resolution, all but one of which were administered under the new Rules.[4] The exception was a case in which the parties maintained their choice of the ICC ADR Rules, predecessor to the Mediation Rules. Mediation was the settlement technique chosen in fifteen of the twenty-five cases filed; conciliation was chosen in one case; and in the remaining nine cases the disputes were withdrawn before a choice was made. Of the cases filed in 2014, 72% were filed on the basis of a prior dispute resolution agreement providing for ICC mediation or ADR, followed in most cases by ICC arbitration. Such agreements provide parties with the security of knowing how disputes will be approached ahead of their occurrence, and their widespread use reflects their usefulness in practice. All but four of the mediation and ADR filings in 2014 were international cases involving parties from two or more countries. Eleven of the nineteen mediators and neutrals selected in the cases filed in 2014 were chosen by the parties and the remaining eight were appointed by the Centre. In six cases the nomination or appointment was made on the basis of an initial list of potential candidates drawn up by the Centre, sometimes with the aid of proposals from ICC National Committees and Groups. Mediators and neutrals of nine different nationalities were selected in 2014. Ten of the cases filed in 2014 were settled within the year. The average duration of cases from start to finish was around three months, and the average time taken to reach a settlement after the first meeting between the parties and the mediator/neutral is one month. ICC mediations would appear to be fulfilling the expectations of greater efficiency and rapidity raised by the new Rules.

In 2015, the Centre registered sixteen new filings under the ICC Mediation Rules.[5] In twelve cases, the request was made on the basis of a prior agreement between the parties to submit disputes to the ICC Mediation Rules. Of the four remaining, unilateral requests for mediation, three were refused by the other party or parties, so the cases could not proceed. No requests were received in which the parties opted for settlement procedures other than mediation (as is possible under the ICC Mediation Rules), which demonstrates a clear preference for mediation over other amicable dispute resolution procedures. The mediation requests filed in 2015 involved parties from a total of twenty countries throughout the world. Nine of the cases registered in 2015 were between parties from different regions of the world and all but four between parties from different countries. The parties included two States: one in North Africa and the other in South East Asia. In thirteen cases, the mediation proceeded beyond the initial request. The mediators in these thirteen cases included four women and nine men. Roughly half of the mediators were nominated by the parties (in one case, the parties' nominee was chosen from a list of suitable candidates provided by the Centre). The other mediators were appointed by the Centre in the absence of agreement between the parties on a joint nominee. Of the thirteen mediations that were set in motion during

4. ICC DR Bull. 2015/1, 17–20.
5. ICC DR Bull. 2016/1, 19.

the year, four reached a settlement before the year end. The average time taken to reach the settlement in these cases was five months from the filing of the request.

In 2016, the ICC Centre registered thirty-two new filings under the ICC Mediation Rules.[6] Also in 2016, parties overwhelmingly opted for mediation. The eighty-one parties in the 2016 filings came from thirty-two countries and independent territories across the world. A total of twenty-three neutrals of ten different nationalities were nominated or appointed in those cases in which settlement proceedings took place. Six of the neutrals were women and seventeen were men. In those cases settled with the assistance of neutrals during the year, the settlement was achieved within an average of sixty days of the file being transmitted to the neutral. In several cases, no neutral was required as the parties settled their disputes themselves.

In 2017, the ICC Centre registered thirty new filings under the ICC Mediation Rules.[7] In the 2017 filings, apart from two requests for conciliation, parties overwhelmingly opted for mediation. The eighty-six parties in the 2017 filings came from thirty-one countries and independent territories across the world. Parties from the Americas were predominant (representing 41% of all parties), and the US and Brazil accounted for the highest number of parties (ten each). A total of seventeen neutrals of seven different nationalities were nominated by the parties or appointed by the Centre. Four neutrals were women and twelve were men. In those cases settled with the assistance of neutrals during the year, the settlement was achieved within an average of six weeks of the file being transmitted to the neutral.

In 2018, the Centre registered thirty-seven new filings under the ICC Mediation Rules.[8] In the 2018 filings, apart from one request for conciliation, parties overwhelmingly opted for mediation. The ICC mediation cases in 2018 involved a hundred parties from thirty-six countries and independent territories. While parties from the Americas took the lead in 2017, European parties were predominant (representing 54% of all parties) in 2018. Countries accounting for the highest number of parties were the United Kingdom, Italy, US and the United Arab Emirates. Eight parties were States or State entities (originating from the MENA region and Asia). A total of eighteen neutrals were nominated by the parties or appointed by the Centre. The neutrals came from eleven different jurisdictions, including the Czech Republic, France, India, Italy, Mexico, the Netherlands, Panama, Spain, Switzerland, the United Kingdom, and the US. Four women acted as neutrals in 2018 (from the United Kingdom, Italy, France and Panama). The disputes covered a wide range of business sectors. Construction and engineering disputes were the most frequent, accounting for almost 35% of cases, followed by disputes relating to energy and telecommunication. In 2018, the value of disputes ranged from USD 250,000 to USD 860 million. The cost of proceedings in which mediators were appointed (covering ICC administrative expenses and the fees and expenses of the neutral) was USD 18,500.00 on average.

6. ICC DR Bull. 2017/2, 114–115.
7. ICC DR Bull. 2018/2, 64–65.
8. ICC DR Bull. 2019/1, 26.

[B] From Arbitration to Mediation Proceedings

Approximately 47% of ICC arbitrations are withdrawn before a final award is rendered.[9] The ICC Court Secretariat is not always informed of the reasons for such withdrawal, but they occur mostly when there is a settlement of the dispute. The parties can ask an arbitral tribunal to record the terms of the settlement agreement in an award by consent pursuant to Article 32 of the ICC Rules of Arbitration, but this does not frequently happen. The parties are free to resort to ADR or mediation at any stage during the arbitration, and the ICC encourages them to do so.[10] Settlement is usually a better option than proceeding with an arbitration as it can reduce time and cost and preserve commercial relationships. The escalating use of international arbitration in conjunction with ADR is generally only resorted to in cases where there is a contractual mandate to do so, i.e., through multi-tiered escalation clauses, as was indicated in the International Arbitration Survey organized by Queen Mary University London in 2018.[11]

The involvement of the arbitral tribunal in settlement discussions and the use of hybrid procedures such as so-called arb-med are somewhat controversial. Nonetheless, such procedures are not incompatible with the ICC Rules of Arbitration. Where agreed between the parties and the arbitral tribunal, the arbitral tribunal may take steps to facilitate settlement. However, there is an important caveat: every effort should be made to ensure that any subsequent award is enforceable. Therefore, before adopting a settlement procedure that requires its participation, the arbitral tribunal should verify whether such an approach may give rise to difficulties either at the place of arbitration or at likely places of enforcement. In particular any form of separate party caucusing (private discussions between an arbitrator and a party) is likely to give rise to such concerns.[12]

In the Anglo-Saxon system, the initiative to settle is traditionally taken by the parties' legal counsel or the parties themselves, although arbitral tribunals may strongly encourage the parties to settle. In certain civil law traditions, notably in Germany, Austria and parts of Switzerland, arbitral tribunals may be very proactive in encouraging the parties to settle the case and even go as far as proposing terms or offering preliminary views on the outcome of the case.[13] The ICC Rules of Arbitration are amenable to both approaches. Article 51 of the Arbitration Law of the People's Republic of China of 1994 authorizes the arbitrator to act as conciliator and, if a settlement is reached, to prepare a conciliation statement, which is to have the same legal force as an arbitral award, or shall prepare an award based on the settlement. Article 33 of the Hong Kong's Arbitration Ordinance (2015) authorizes the arbitrator to

9. J. Fry, S. Greenberg and F. Mazza, *The Secretariat's Guide to ICC Arbitration* (Paris: ICC Publication No. 729 E, 2012) 323, para. 3-1163.
10. *Ibid.*, 436, para. 4-51.
11. *2018 International Arbitration Survey: The Evolution of International Arbitration*, Queen Mary University of London/White & Case, 6; available at: http://www.arbitration.qmul.ac.uk/research/2018/ (accessed 4 June 2020).
12. Fry, Greenberg and Mazza, *supra* n. 9, 264–265, para. 3-922.
13. *2018 International Arbitration Survey: The Evolution of International Arbitration*, *supra* n. 11.

act as mediator, if all parties consent. If no settlement is reached, any confidential information obtained by an arbitrator from a party during the mediation proceedings conducted by the arbitrator as a mediator must be disclosed by the arbitrator before resuming the arbitral proceedings to all other parties. However, the arbitrator must disclose only as much of that information as the arbitrator considers is material to the arbitral proceedings.

§16.03 UNCITRAL MEDIATION INSTRUMENTS

After four years of preparation, UNCITRAL adopted two instruments that provide for common legislative standards for the enforcement of international commercial settlement agreements resulting from mediation and make such type of dispute settlement more efficient: a Convention on International Settlement Agreements Resulting from Mediation (Singapore Convention) and the UNCITRAL Model Law on International Commercial Mediation and International Settlement Agreements Resulting from Mediation, 2018. UNCITRAL adopted both instruments without creating any expectation that interested States may adopt either instrument.[14] Both instruments provide common legislative standards for the enforcement of international commercial settlement agreements resulting from mediation and make such type of dispute settlement more efficient. The General Assembly of the United Nations adopted the Singapore Convention on 20 December 2018. It called upon the Members States and regional economic integration organizations (REIOs) that wish to strengthen the legal framework on international dispute resolution to consider becoming a party to the Convention.[15] The Singapore Convention was opened for signature on 7 August 2019. At this same session, the General Assembly also recommended that all States give favourable consideration to the Model Law on International Commercial Mediation and International Settlement Agreements resulting from Mediation 2018, amending the UNCITRAL Model Law on International Commercial Conciliation 2002, when the States revise or adopt legislation relevant to mediation, bearing in mind the desirability of uniformity of the law of mediation procedures and the specific needs of international commercial mediation practice.[16]

Both instruments were prepared by Working Group II (Dispute Resolution) of UNCITRAL. The amended Model Law was adopted by the Commission of UNCITRAL on 25 June 2018. According to the practice at the United Nations, the Singapore

14. Report of Working Group II (Dispute Settlement) on the work of its 68th session (New York, 5–9 February 2018), A/CN.9/934, paras 140–142.
15. UN General Assembly Document, 73rd session (2018–2019), A/RES/73/198, adopting document A/73/496, 10–17, available at: http://research.un.org/en/docs/ga/quick/regular/73; Singapore Convention on mediation available at: http://undocs.org/en/A/RES/73/198 (accessed 17 March 2019). *See also* H. Verbist, *UNCITRAL Instruments on Enforcement of International Commercial Settlement Agreements Resulting from Mediation*, TMD 2018-4, 6–22; H. Verbist, *UNCITRAL Working Group II Instruments on Enforcement of International Commercial Settlement Agreements Resulting from Mediation*, January 2019, available at: https://static1.squarespace.com/static/5a4599e6bce17688a9e7bde2/t/5c3a6bb5562fa75d70fc4da3/1547332534675/H+Verbist+WG+II+Paper+and+Appendices+-+JAN2019.pdf (19 March 2019).
16. UN General Assembly Document, 73rd session (2018–2019), A/RES/73/198, *supra* n. 15.

Convention needed the approval of the General Assembly. In October 2017, in Vienna, there was a consensus that the instruments should refer to 'mediation' instead of 'conciliation', as 'mediation' is a more widely used term.[17] The then-proposed amended Model Law added a footnote to define mediation as 'a process where parties request a third person or persons to assist them in their attempt to reach an amicable settlement of their dispute arising out of, or relating to, a contractual or other legal relationship'.[18] This change in terminology does not have any substantive or conceptual implications.[19]

[A] The Model Law on International Commercial Mediation and International Settlement Agreements Resulting from Mediation 2018

The Model Law was initially adopted in 2002. It was amended in 2018 with the addition of a new section on international settlement agreements and their enforcement. The Model Law aims to assist States in reforming and modernizing their laws on mediation procedure.[20] The Model Law 2018 consists of three sections, structured as follows: Section 1 - General Provisions (Articles 1 and 2); section 2 - International Commercial Mediation (Articles 3–15); section 3 - International Settlement Agreements (Articles 16–20). The Model Law applies to international commercial mediation and to international settlement agreements. If the parties conclude an agreement settling the dispute, that settlement is binding and enforceable (Article 15). Article 19 provides an exhaustive list of grounds for the competent authority of a State to refuse to grant relief. Such an authority may refuse to grant relief if (a) a party to the settlement agreement was under some incapacity; or (b) the settlement agreement is null and void, inoperative or incapable of being performed under the law to which the parties have validly subjected it or, failing any indication thereon, under the law deemed applicable by the competent authority. Legislation based on or influenced by the UNCITRAL Model Law on

17. Report of Working Group II (Dispute Settlement) on the work of its 67th session (Vienna, 2–6 October 2017), A/CN.9/929, para. 104. It has been proposed that this change of terminology should also apply to the UNCITRAL Conciliation Rules (1980), A/CN.9/WG.II/WP.205, para. 4 (23 November 2017) (WGII 68th session, 5–9 February 2018).
18. A/CN.9/WG.II/WP.205, para. 5 (23 November 2017) (WGII 68th session, 5–9 February 2018); note 3 in document A/CN.9/WG.II/WP.205/Add.1 (23 November 2017) (WG II 68th session, 5–9 February 2018); Report of Working Group II (Dispute Settlement) on the work of its 67th session (Vienna, 2–6 October 2017), A/CN.9/929, para. 104. It has been proposed that this change of terminology should also apply to the UNCITRAL Conciliation Rules (1980), A/CN.9/WG.II/WP.205, para. 4 (23 November 2017) (WGII 68th session, 5–9 February 2018).
19. UNCITRAL Commission Report, 51st session, 25 June–13 July 2018, New York, A/73/17, Annex II, p. 56, note 2; J. Knieper and C. Montineri, *UNCITRAL and a New International Legislative Framework on Mediation*, TMD 2018-4, 23, 24.
20. UN General Assembly Document, 73rd session (2018–2019), A/RES/73/199, available at: http://research.un.org/en/docs/ga/quick/regular/73; Report of the United Nations Commission on International Trade Law, Fifty-first session, 25 June–13 July 2018, A/73/17, 56–62, available at: https://undocs.org/en/A/73/17%20. *See also* H. Verbist, '*The amended UNCITRAL Model Law on International Commercial Mediation 2018*', in *Liber Amicorum 50 years of solutions – 50 ans de solutions – 50 jaar oplossingen Cepani 1969–2019* (D. De Meulemeester, M. Berlingin and B. Kohl, eds (Mechelen: Wolters Kluwer, 2019), 457–482.

International Commercial Conciliation (2002) has been adopted in thirty-three States in a total of forty-five jurisdictions.[21] The UNCITRAL website does not yet mention legislation based on or influenced by the UNCITRAL Model Law on International Commercial Mediation and on International Settlement Agreements resulting from Mediation (2018).

[B] The Singapore Convention

The Singapore Convention complements the existing legal framework on international mediation and contributes to the development of harmonious international economic relations. It provides States with consistent standards on the cross-border enforcement of international settlement agreements resulting from mediation.[22] The Singapore Convention contains a preamble and sixteen articles. It does not require the disputing parties to have had an agreement to mediate. It applies regardless of whether the parties had a prior agreement or not. As a consequence, an eventual settlement agreement may address issues outside of the scope of an agreement to mediate, unlike the New York Convention's requirement that an arbitral award may only address issues within the scope of an agreement to arbitrate.[23] The Singapore Convention does not apply to settlement agreements concluded to resolve a dispute arising from transactions engaged in by one party as a consumer for personal, family or household purposes and does not apply to settlement agreements relating to family, inheritance or employment law. Also, the Singapore Convention does not apply to settlement agreements that have been approved by a court or concluded in the course of proceedings before a court. It also does not apply to settlement agreements that are enforceable as a judgment in the State of that court. Furthermore, it does not apply to settlement agreements that have been recorded and are enforceable as an arbitral award. This exclusion was highly debated, as the Working Group had confirmed at a certain stage of the discussion that the mere involvement of a judge or arbitrator in the conciliation or mediation process should not result in the settlement agreement being excluded from the scope of the instrument.[24] Article 1(3) of the Singapore Convention provides that it will be for the competent authority where enforcement is sought to

---

21. Available at: https://uncitral.un.org/en/texts/arbitration/modellaw/commercial_conciliation/status (accessed 21 May 2020).
22. UN General Assembly Document, 73rd session (2018–2019), A/RES/73/198, *supra* n. 15. *See also* A. Anderson, B. Beaumont and H. Verbist, *The United Nations Convention on International Settlement Agreements Resulting from Mediation: Its Genesis, Negotiation and Future*, in *International Mediation, The Comparative Law Yearbook of International Business* Vol. 41a (C. Campbell ed., Alphen aan den Rijn: Wolters Kluwer, 2020), 35–62.
23. T. Schnabel, *The Singapore Convention on Mediation: A Framework for the Cross-Border Recognition and Enforcement of Mediated Settlements*19 Pepperdine Disp. Resol. L.J. 1 (2019), available at: https://papers.ssrn.com/sol3/papers.cfm?abstract_id = 3239527. Mr Schnabel negotiated the Singapore Convention on behalf of the United States in UNCITRAL Working Group II.
24. Report of Working Group II (Dispute Settlement) on the work of its 65th session (Vienna, 12–23 September 2016), 30 September 2016, A/CN.9/896, 4, paras 53–54.

determine under its law whether a settlement agreement reached out-of-court can be laid down in a judgment or not.

Each party to the Singapore Convention shall enforce a settlement agreement in accordance with its rules of procedure and under the conditions laid down in it. The rules of procedure may thus differ in the States adhering to the Singapore Convention. It does not contain in its title the term 'enforcement', but provides for a 'direct' enforcement of settlement agreements resulting from mediation, in accordance with the rules of procedure of the State for enforcement and the conditions laid down in it. If a dispute arises concerning a matter that a party claims was already resolved by a settlement agreement, a party to the Singapore Convention allows the party to invoke the settlement agreement in accordance with its rules of procedure and under the conditions laid down it, in order to prove that the matter has already been resolved.[25]

Article 4 sets out the requirements of form for a party in a dispute to rely on a settlement agreement. The requirements laid down in Article 4.1 are: (a) there must be a written settlement agreement signed by the parties, and (b) evidence that the settlement agreement resulted from mediation. Article 4(1)(b) of the Singapore Convention provides a list of means to evidence that the settlement agreement resulted from mediation.[26] The evidence that the settlement agreement resulted from mediation can be given by: the mediator's signature on the settlement agreement; a document signed by the mediator indicating that he or she carried out the mediation; or an attestation by the institution that administered the mediation; or by any other evidence acceptable to the competent authority in the country where enforcement is sought. The understanding is that only if that other evidence mentioned could not be produced, then would the requesting party be allowed to submit any other evidence.[27] Article 4 reflects a balance between the formalities that are required to ascertain that a settlement agreement resulted from mediation and the need for the Singapore Convention to preserve the flexible nature of the mediation process.[28] Article 5 lays down the grounds for which a court can refuse to enforce a settlement agreement resulting from mediation. Following the model of Article V of the New York Convention on the enforcement of foreign arbitral awards, Article 5(1) lists the grounds which a party against whom enforcement of a settlement agreement is sought must prove, while Article 5(2) lists the grounds which a court may raise at its own initiative in order to refuse enforcement of the settlement agreement.[29] The grounds listed in Article 5 are exhaustive. However, they are stated in general terms, giving flexibility to the enforcing authority with regard to their interpretation.[30] All of Article 5 grounds for refusal are

---

25. Report of Working Group II (Dispute Settlement) on the work of its 67th session (Vienna, 2-6 October 2017), 11 October 2017, A/CN.9/929, pp. 8-9, paras 43-48.
26. *Ibid.*, paras 52-59.
27. Report of Working Group II (Dispute Settlement) on the work of its 68th session (New York, 5-9 February 2018), A/CN.9/934, para. 38.
28. Report of the United Nations Commission on International Trade Law, (UNCITRAL Commission 51st session, New York, 25 June-13 July 2018), A/73/17, para. 28.
29. T. Schnabel, *supra* n. 23; N. Alexander and S. Chong, *An Introduction to the Singapore Convention on Mediation – Perspectives from Singapore*, TMD, 2018-4, 37, 44-50.
30. Report of Working Group II (Arbitration and Conciliation) on the work of its 63rd session (Vienna, 7-11 September 2015), 17 September 2015, A/CN.9/861, para. 93.

permissive rather than mandatory; a court can choose to provide relief even if a particular exception might apply, and if a state implements the Singapore Convention through legislation, it has no obligation to permit courts to use all the grounds for refusal.[31] Moreover, Article 8 provides the possibility for States to make two reservations when signing it. This allows States to declare that the Singapore Convention shall not apply to settlement agreements to which they are themselves or to which State agencies are a party (Article 8(1)(a)). States may also make the reservation that the Singapore Convention shall only operate on an opt-in basis, if the parties to a settlement agreement have agreed to the application of it (Article 8(1)(b)).[32] Moreover, even without an explicit provision in the Singapore Convention, parties to a settlement agreement will be able to exclude its application.[33] The Singapore Convention also provides flexibility for the timing at which States may declare a reservation (Article 8(3)) or withdraw it (Article 8(5)). Pursuant to Article 8, the Singapore Convention will apply to settlements reached in the context of investment disputes,[34] unless the States would formulate a reservation or a declaration excluding such settlements.[35]

Forty-six countries signed the Convention on 7 August 2019, the day it opened for signatures. This is the highest number of first-day signatories of a UNCITRAL convention to date.[36] Singapore was the first country to sign.[37] Meanwhile, six countries have ratified the Convention.[38] Pursuant to Article 14, the Singapore Convention shall enter

31. T. Schnabel, *supra* n. 23.
32. Report of Working Group II (Dispute Settlement) on the work of its 68th session (New York, 5-9 February 2018), 19 February 2018, A/CN.9/934, paras 38-39.
33. *Ibid.*, para. 38.
34. F. Nitschke, *A Preview of ICSID's New Investor-State Mediation Rules*, available at: http://mediationblog.kluwerarbitration.com/2020/01/10/a-preview-of-icsids-new-investor-state-mediation-rules/?doing_wp_cron=1591366099.2868781089782714843750 (accessed 5 June 2020).
35. Report of Working Group II (Arbitration and Conciliation) on the work of its 63rd session (Vienna, 7-11 September 2015), A/CN.9/861, paras 44-46 on pp. 9-10; A/CN.9/WG.II/WP.198, para. 24 (30 June 2016) (WGII 65th session, Vienna, 12-23 September 2016); Report of Working Group II (Dispute Settlement) on the work of its 65th session (Vienna, 12-23 September 2016), A/CN.9/896, paras 61-62 on pp. 11-12; A/CN.9/WG.II/WP.205, para. 28, pp. 6-7 (23 November 2017) (WGII 68th session, 5-9 February 2018). For the discussion at UNCITRAL Working Group II on Art. 8 of the Singapore Convention on Mediation, *see* Report of UNCITRAL Working Group II (Dispute Settlement) on the work of its 68th session (New York, 5-9 February 2018), A/CN.9/934, paras 72-93, pp. 12-14.
36. Herbert Smith Freehills, *46 Countries Sign the Singapore Convention on Mediated Settlements Today*, 7 August 2019; A. Komindr, *UNCITRAL and Legal Innovations in International Commercial Mediation*, 11 Korean Arb. Rev., 2020, 26, at 31.
37. The forty-six signatories of the Singapore Convention as of 7 August 2019 are: Afghanistan, Belarus, Belize, Brunei, Chile, China, Colombia, Republic of the Congo, Democratic Republic of the Congo, Kingdom of Eswatini, Fiji, Georgia, Grenada, Haiti, Honduras, India, Iran, Israel, Jamaica, Jordan, Kazakhstan, Laos, Malaysia, Maldives, Mauritius, Montenegro, Nigeria, North Macedonia, Palau, Paraguay, Philippines, Qatar, South Korea, Samoa, Saudi Arabia, Serbia, Sierra Leone, Singapore, Sri Lanka, Timor Leste, Turkey, Uganda, Ukraine, the US, Uruguay and Venezuela. Subsequently, 6 other countries signed the Singapore Convention: Armenia (26 September 2019), Chad (26 September 2020), Ecuador (25 September 2020), Gabon (25 September 2020), Guinea-Bissau (25 September 2020) and Rwanda (28 January 2020); *see* UNCITRAL website: https://uncitral.un.org/en/texts/mediation/conventions/international_settlement_agreements/status (accessed 21 May 2020).
38. The six countries having ratified the Singapore Convention are: Belarus (15 July 2020), Ecuador (9 September 2020), Fiji (25 February 2020), Qatar (13 March 2020), Saudi Arabia (5 May 2020)

into force six months after the deposit of the third instrument of ratification, acceptance, approval, or accession. With the deposit of the instrument of ratification by Qatar on 12 March 2020, the Singapore Convention entered into force on 12 September 2020.[39]

[C] UNCITRAL Mediation Rules

In addition to the two instruments which provide for common legislative standards for the enforcement of international commercial settlement agreements resulting from mediation, UNCITRAL has also prepared Rules on Mediation which can be used ad hoc by the parties in conducting mediations. The draft UNCITRAL Mediation Rules (2020) contain thirteen articles and update the UNCITRAL Conciliation Rules (1980). The draft Mediation Rules (2020) are submitted for adoption to the Commission of UNCITRAL at its 53rd session, 14–18 September 2020.[40]

These rules should apply when the parties agree to them (Article 1.1). The parties may agree to exclude or vary any provision of the Rules (Article 1.4). Some provisions of the Rules are consistent with the UNCITRAL Model Law on Mediation, such as the Articles of the Conduct of Mediation and Confidentiality. As in the Model Law, the Rules provide that the parties may agree on the manner in which the mediation is to be conducted. Otherwise, the mediator may determine the conduct of the mediation in consultation with the parties, taking into account the circumstances of the case, any wishes that the parties may express and the need for a speedy settlement of the dispute (Article 4.1). Also, unless otherwise agreed by the parties, all information relating to the mediation, including, if relevant, the settlement agreement, shall be kept confidential by those involved in the mediation, except where disclosure is required by the law or where a signed settlement agreement can be used as evidence that it resulted from mediation (Article 6). Pursuant to the Rules, mediation may take place at any time regardless of whether arbitral, judicial or other dispute resolution proceedings have been already initiated (Article 10.1). Unless otherwise agreed by the parties, the parties and the mediator agree that the mediator shall not act as an arbitrator or as a representative or counsel of a party in any arbitral, judicial or other dispute resolution proceedings in respect of the dispute that is related to the mediation. The parties also agree that they shall not present the mediator as a witness in any such proceedings (Article 12).

---

and Singapore (25 February 2020); *see* UNCITRAL website: https://uncitral.un.org/en/texts/mediation/conventions/international_settlement_agreements/status (accessed 20 September 2020).

39. Available at: http://www.unis.unvienna.org/unis/en/pressrels/2020/unisl293.html (accessed 21 May 2020).
40. A/CN.9/1026, 3 January 2020; available at: https://undocs.org/en/A/CN.9/1026.

[D] UNCITRAL Notes on Mediation

UNCITRAL also drafted Notes on Mediation (Notes) taking account of the newly adopted instruments on international commercial mediation.[41] The Notes list and briefly describe matters relevant to mediation, with a focus on international mediation. Because of the flexibility that characterizes mediation, the Notes stress that procedural styles, practices and methods to foster a settlement between parties vary. The Notes do not seek to promote any particular practice as best practice. They seek to assist parties in better understanding mediation including the wide and flexible range of possible outcomes. The new Notes have been submitted for approval to the Commission in September 2020.

The Notes first state the main features of mediation: it is a non-adjudicatory, flexible and voluntary process based on party autonomy and the legal framework: the Singapore Convention, Mediation Laws and the Mediation Rules. The Notes further list and briefly describe matters relevant to mediation pursuant to the different phases of mediation, which are commencement of the mediation; selection and appointment of a mediator; preparatory steps; conduct of the mediation; settlement agreement; termination of the mediation; mediation in the ISDS context. Regarding the preparatory steps, the Notes state that it is common for the parties and the mediator to sign terms of reference which will cover various elements of the mediation and mediators' involvement in the process. The terms of reference may contain an outline of the dispute, relevant rules determining the conduct of the mediation, such as the ethical standards applicable to the mediator and relevant disclosure obligations as well as the parties' agreement regarding confidentiality (Point 3(a)).

The Notes add that it is advisable for the parties to consider at the outset of the mediation the extent to which they wish the mediation to remain confidential, and to check applicable law and rules to ensure that the confidentiality obligations are clearly spelled out and sufficiently safeguarded (Point 3(d)). The Notes describe the role of mediators to build trust between the parties and in the process so as to reach a settlement of the dispute. Mediators apply varying degrees of influence in accordance with the parties' expectations, the circumstances of the case and different practices (Point 4(a)). As to the enforceability of the settlement agreement, the Notes observe that generally the parties comply voluntarily with the obligations set forth in the agreement. If necessary, the settlement agreement may be enforced in accordance with the procedure of the State in which enforcement is sought. States that are party to the Singapore Convention and States that have enacted legislation based on the Model Law follow the enforcement procedure defined therein. It is advisable that the parties state their understanding that the settlement agreement can be used as evidence that resulted from mediation and that it can be relied upon for seeking relief under the applicable legal framework (Point 5(c)).

The Notes also refer to mediation in the ISDS context and address the issue of third parties. Mediation can be efficiently used during the 'cooling-off period', as well

41. A/CN.9/1027, 3 January 2020, available at: https://undocs.org/en/A/CN.9/1027.

as in parallel track during or even after arbitral, judicial or other dispute resolution proceedings have been commenced or concluded. A number of specific issues are highlighted which may arise in the ISDS context and which should be envisioned at the start of the mediation: (a) selection and appointment of a mediator; (b) confidentiality and transparency; (c) third parties; (d) authority to settle. A dispute may affect and concern the civil society and/or other interested stakeholders. These third parties may be allowed by the parties to participate in the mediation and make submissions, if they meet certain criteria as agreed by the parties. If the parties have agreed that third parties may attend mediation sessions, the mediator and the parties should be mindful of the interests that are represented and the authority of each representative (Point 7(c)).

[E] UNCITRAL WG III on Possible ISDS Reform

Over the past decade, the concept of resolving investment disputes through mediation has been widely discussed in the ISDS community, among States, practitioners and academics.[42] Since 2017, UNCITRAL WG III started discussing a possible reform of ISDS.[43] WG III noted that resort to arbitration is the predominant means used in resolving investor-State disputes and it observed that alternative dispute resolution methods are available, but they seem to be rarely used, despite the existing legal framework.[44] The UNCITRAL Commission entrusted WG III with a broad mandate to work on the possible reform of ISDS. In line with the UNCITRAL process, WG III would, in discharging that mandate, ensure that the deliberations, while benefitting from the widest possible breadth of available expertise from all stakeholders, would be Government-led, with high-level input from all Governments, consensus-based and fully transparent. The Working Group would proceed to: (a) first, identify and consider concerns regarding ISDS; (b) second, consider whether reform was desirable in the light of any identified concerns; and (c) third, if WG III were to conclude that reform was desirable, develop any relevant solutions to be recommended to the Commission.[45]

WG III started its discussions on possible ISDS Reform at its thirty-fourth session in Vienna, with a discussion on concerns regarding costs and duration and procedural issues of ISDS arbitrations, and coherence and consistency in ISDS outcomes.[46] From the start of its discussions the Working Group considered whether work should be

42. United Nations Conference on Trade and Development, '*Investor-State Disputes: Prevention and Alternatives to Arbitration*', United Nations, New York and Geneva, 2010, available at: https://unctad.org/en/Docs/diaeia200911_en.pdf (accessed 5 June 2020).
43. Working papers and submissions of governments for UNCITRAL Working Group III on Investor-State Dispute Settlement Reform are available at: https://uncitral.un.org/en/working_groups/3/investor-state (accessed 5 June 2020).
44. A/CN.9/WG.III/WP.190, para. 37 (15 January 2020) (WGIII 39th session, 30 March–3 April 2020).
45. UNCITRAL Commission Report, 50th session, 3–21 July 2017, Vienna, A/72/17, para. 264, available at: https://uncitral.un.org/en/commission.
46. Report of Working Group III (Investor-State Dispute Settlement Reform) on the work of its 34th session (Part I – 19 December 2017) (Vienna, 27 November–1 December 2017), A/CN.9/930/Rev.1; Report of Working Group III (Investor-State Dispute Settlement Reform) on

limited to arbitration or should include other types of existing ISDS mechanisms. There was a generally shared view that ADR methods, including mediation, ombudsman, consultation, conciliation and any other amicable settlement mechanisms, could operate to prevent the escalation of disputes to arbitration and could alleviate concerns about the costs and duration of arbitration. WG III decided to concentrate its work first on identifying concerns regarding arbitration and to consider other types of ISDS mechanisms subsequently as part of a holistic approach to addressing those concerns.[47] At its thirty-fifth session, WG III continued its discussion on concerns with respect to coherence and consistency of the ISDS outcomes and lack of sufficient guarantees of independence and impartiality on the part of arbitrators.[48] At its thirty-sixth session, WG III continued its discussion on concerns with respect to coherence and consistency of the ISDS outcomes and on concerns pertaining to arbitrators and decision makers as well as on costs and duration of ISDS proceedings.[49] At its thirty-seventh session, WG III discussed on concerns pertaining to third-party funding in ISDS proceedings as well as on proposals for a work plan during the third phase of its mandate.[50] At its thirty-eighth session, WG III agreed on a project schedule on reform options and requested the Secretariat to undertake preparatory work on dispute prevention and mitigation as well as on means of ADR. Also, WG III started its work of the third phase with a discussion on the establishment of an advisory centre and a code of conduct for ISDS tribunal members and on third party funding. The WG III thereby asked the Secretariat to work closely with the International Centre for the Settlement of Investment Disputes (ICSID) and other institutions to prepare a draft code of conduct for its consideration and also in regard to further preparatory work on third-party funding.[51] Due to the coronavirus (COVID-19) situation, the thirty-ninth session of UNCITRAL WG III had to be postponed until further notice.[52] However, in order to allow making progress on the working papers prepared for consideration at

the work of its 34th session (Part II - 26 February 2018)(Vienna, 27 November–1 December 2017), A/CN.9/930/Add.1/Rev.1 (21 June 2020), available at: https://undocs.org/en/A/CN.9/930/Rev.1.

47. Report of Working Group III (Investor-State Dispute Settlement Reform) on the work of its 34th session (19 December 2017) (Part I - 19 December 2017) (Vienna, 27 November–1 December 2017), A/CN.9/930/Rev.1, 6, paras 31–33 and 11, para. 74.
48. Report of Working Group III (Investor-State Dispute Settlement Reform) on the work of its 35th session (14 May 2018) (New York, 23–27 April 2018), A/CN.9/935, available at: https://undocs.org/en/A/CN.9/935.
49. Report of Working Group III (Investor-State Dispute Settlement Reform) on the work of its 36th session (6 November 2018) (Vienna, 29 October–2 November 2018), A/CN.9/964, available at: https://undocs.org/en/A/CN.9/964.
50. Report of Working Group III (Investor-State Dispute Settlement Reform) on the work of its 37th session (9 April 2019) (New York, 1–5 April 2019), A/CN.9/970, available at: https://undocs.org/en/A/CN.9/970.
51. Report of Working Group III (Investor-State Dispute Settlement Reform) on the work of its 38th session (23 October 2019) (Vienna, 14–18 October 2019), A/CN.9/1004, paras 25, 78 and 98, available at: https://undocs.org/en/A/CN.9/1004.
52. The 39th session of Working Group III (Investor-State Dispute Settlement Reform) was scheduled to take place on 30 March–3 April 2020 in New York: for the provisional agenda of the 39th session (16 January 2020), available at: https://undocs.org/en/A/CN.9/WG.III/WP.189.

this session, a number of online webinars were organized by the UNCITRAL Secretariat in cooperation with the Academic Forum.[53]

One of the topics that was scheduled for discussion at the thirty-ninth session of WG III was the topic of dispute prevention, mitigation and mediation. The UNCITRAL Secretariat prepared for this discussion a note in which it makes proposals focusing on the 'prevention' of disputes, rather than 'post-dispute' regulation as cost-effective approach to the reform of ISDS.[54] The Secretariat sets out in its note that a number of initiatives have been developed already at the national level by some States, such as: (a) identifying a lead agency, which usually aims at establishing a unique channel of communication between the investor and the State; (b) mapping of information and making it available; (c) monitoring communication with investors; (d) raising awareness on investment obligations among government officials and training; (e) early settlement discussions and handling disputes. As regards initiatives developed by some States at a bilateral or multilateral level, the Secretariat in its note refers to: (a) State-to-State cooperation in dispute prevention; and (b) capacity-building.

With respect to ADR methods, the Secretariat's note points out that investment treaties foresee a time frame, more commonly known as the 'cooling-off' period, ranging from three to eighteen months during which the disputing parties may attempt amicable settlement, before arbitration. Often, investment treaties include a two-tiered dispute settlement clause, providing first for some form of ADR before culminating, at the second tier, with a resolution of the investor-State dispute by an arbitral-tribunal.[55] The Secretariat's note points out that it is difficult to collect accurate data on the use of ADR methods, as these methods are usually confidential. The Secretariat also refers to studies and publications made on the subject of obstacles to settlement in ISDS that identify many reasons for the difficulties encountered, such as fear of public criticism, fear of allegations of corruption, fear of setting a precedent, difficulties regarding access to public funds to organize the defence, as well as difficulties regarding intergovernmental coordination in short time frames.[56] On 18 June 2020, WG III organized a webinar on the role of mediation in ISDS.[57]

53. The purpose of the Academic Forum is for academics active in the field of ISDS to exchange views, explore issues and options, test ideas and solutions, and make a constructive contribution to the ongoing discussions on possible reform of ISDS, in particular the discussions in the context of WG III; available at: https://www.jus.uio.no/pluricourts/english/projects/leginvest/academic-forum/.
54. A/CN.9/WG.III/WP.190, *supra* n. 44, at para. 5.
55. A/CN.9/WG.III/WP.190, *supra* n. 44, at paras 11–44.
56. A/CN.9/WG.III/WP.190, *supra* n. 44, at para. 44; S. Chew, L. Reed and J.C. Thomas, *Survey on Obstacles to Settlement of Investor-State Disputes*, National University of Singapore, Centre for International Law, November 2016, available at: https://cil.nus.edu.sg/wp-content/uploads/2018/09/NUS-CIL-Working-Paper-1801-Report-Survey-on-Obstacles-to-Settlement-of-Investor-State-Disputes.pdf (accessed 21 June 2020). *See also* C. Titi and K. Fach Gomez, *Mediation in International Commercial and Investment Disputes* (Oxford University Press, 2019), available at: https://global.oup.com/academic/product/mediation-in-international-commercial-and-investment-disputes-9780198827955?cc=be&lang=en& (accessed 21 June 2020).
57. The papers presented at the webinar are available on the website of UNCITRAL: https://uncitral.un.org/en/mediationwebinar (accessed 21 June 2020): C. Kessedjian, A. van Aaken, R. Lie and L. Mistelis, *Mediation in Future Investor-State Dispute Settlement*, Academic Forum; A. Bell, *From Two-Party to Multi-Party Dispute Resolution: A Negotiation Analysis Perspective*, Harvard

§16.04 MEDIATION AND CONCILIATION IN INVESTMENT DISPUTES

[A] ICSID Rules

As the world's leading institution devoted to international investment dispute settlement, ICSID has significant process expertise in investment arbitration and conciliation. The Convention on the Settlement of Investment Disputes between States and Nationals of Other States ('ICSID Convention')[58] established ICSID and provides procedures for the settlement by conciliation or arbitration of investment disputes between States and foreign investors.[59] The purpose was to set up a body to which foreign investors might have access for resolving disputes with their host governments, without having to enlist the support of their home governments to present claims on their behalf.[60] While there already existed international commercial arbitration institutions in the 1950s and while the New York Convention on the Recognition and Enforcement of Foreign Arbitral Awards had been opened for signature in 1958, it was judged that a separate arbitral body not identified with a commercial approach might be more readily acceptable to the governments of some capital-receiving countries in matters involving the rights and assets of foreign investors.[61] At the outset, conciliation was the preferred method for investment dispute settlement because (a) the World Bank had successful experience with conciliation, and (b) conciliation did not in any way infringe or appear to infringe upon a country's sovereignty. Conciliation being more acceptable than arbitration, it was likely to be more effective.[62] The drafters of the Convention envisioned conciliation and arbitration to be on an equal footing.[63] In actual practice, resort to conciliation has been minimal.[64] The main procedural provisions are contained in Chapters III and V to VII of the Convention. These provisions cross-reference other provisions, such as Article 14(1) of the Convention concerning the required qualities of a conciliator. The conditions for jurisdiction are contained in Chapter II. All provisions of the Convention are mandatory except when the Convention allows parties to agree otherwise. Article 33 of the ICSID Convention

University; D. Masucci, *Mediating Collective Interests*; B. Legum, *Investor-State Mediation and State Authority*; F. Nitschke, *Expanding the Pie in Investment Dispute Settlement: ICSID's Proposed Mediation Rules*.

58. The Convention was adopted on 16 March 1965 by the World Bank in Washington and has thus far 154 Contracting States and nine Signatory States. Available at: https://icsid.worldbank.org/en/Pages/about/Database-of-Member-States.aspx (accessed 21 June 2020).
59. A. Parra, *The History of ICSID* (Oxford University Press, 2012), 1.
60. *Ibid.*, 16.
61. *Ibid.*, 17(referencing 'The Promotion of the International Flow of Private Capital: Progress Report by the Secretary General', United Nations Economic and Social Council, E/3325 (26 February 1960), 80–81).
62. *See History of the ICSID Convention*, Vol. II-1, 14, para. 9, available at: https://icsid.worldbank.org/en/Documents/resources/History%20of%20ICSID%20Convention%20-%20VOLUME%20II-1.pdf (accessed 21 June 2020); F. Nitschke, *The ICSID Conciliation Rules in Practice*, in *Mediation in International Commercial and Investment Disputes* (C. Titi and K. Fach Gomez eds) (Oxford University Press, 2019), 123.
63. *See* F. Nitschke, *supra* n. 62, at para. 123.
64. C. Schreuer, *The ICSID Convention: A Commentary* (Cambridge University Press, 2001), 8, para. 22.

provides that conciliations will be conducted in accordance with the Conciliation Rules in effect on the date on which the parties consented to conciliation, except as the parties otherwise agree. If a question of procedure arises which is not covered by the Convention or by the applicable Conciliation Rules, the Commission has discretion to decide the question.

The Conciliation Rules containing thirty-four Rules govern the conciliation proceeding once a request for conciliation has been registered. They complement the ICSID Convention procedural provisions. The original Conciliation Rules were adopted on 25 September 1967 and were effective as of 1 January 1968. These were published with non-binding explanatory notes. The ICSID Conciliation Rules have subsequently been amended three times. The first amendment was approved and took immediate effect on 26 September 1984. The second amendment was approved on 29 September 2002 and was effective on 1 January 2003. The current Conciliation Rules were approved by written vote of the Administrative Council in 2006 and were effective from 10 April 2006.[65]

[B] Statistics on ICSID Conciliations

The latest ICSID caseload statistics indicate that 65% of all arbitration proceedings under the ICSID Convention and Additional Facility Rules are decided by a Tribunal. However, 35% of the disputes are settled or the proceeding is otherwise discontinued, including 5% of cases where a settlement agreement is embodied in an award at the parties' request.[66]

So far, there have been twelve ICSID registered conciliation cases, of which nine are concluded and three are still pending.[67] The first ICSID conciliation case was registered in 1982 and the last – which is still pending – in May 2019.[68] Considering the dates of registration of the cases and of the outcome of the cases, concluded conciliations lasted from five months to three years. Conciliations thus may take several months to several years. These conciliation cases relate to six sectors: oil, gas and mining (five cases); electric power and other energy (two cases); textile (two cases between the same parties); agriculture, fishing and forestry (one case); construction (one case) and water, sanitation and flood protection (one case). Main sectors are thus the oil, gas and mining sector and the electric power and other energy sectors. Most cases (ten cases out of the twelve) involved African parties, mainly as respondents (Cameroon, Central Africa, Equatorial Guinea, Gabon, Madagascar, Niger, Togo). Parties were also Albanian, British, French, German, Greek and from the US. Of the twelve conciliation proceedings registered, conciliation commissions were constituted

65. Available at: https://icsid.worldbank.org/en/Pages/icsiddocs/ICSID-Convention-Conciliation-Rules.aspx.
66. ICSID Caseload Statistics, Issue 2020-1, para. 7, Chart 9.A; available at: https://icsid.worldbank.org/en/Documents/resources/The%20ICSID%20Caseload%20Statistics%202020-1%20Edition-ENG.pdf (accessed 21 June 2020).
67. A/CN.9/1027, available at: https://undocs.org/en/A/CN.9/1027.
68. Available at: https://icsid.worldbank.org/en/Pages/ICSIDSearch.aspx?k=conciliation#k=conciliation. (accessed 21 May 2020).

in eight cases. Most members of the 'Conciliation Commission' are French (six persons). Other nationalities of the members include Belgian, British, German or Swiss. Conciliation cases were conducted in French (four cases), English (four cases) or both languages (two cases). The language of the conciliation proceedings is not always indicated.

The ICSID Statistics on these twelve conciliations indicate that in 78% of the cases, the Conciliation Commission issued a report, while in the remaining 22% the proceeding was discontinued. In the conciliations where the Conciliation Commission issued a report, the report recorded in 86% of the cases a failure of the parties to reach agreement, while in the remaining 14% of the cases, the Conciliation commission recorded an agreement of the parties.[69] The information available at the ICSID website on the twelve conciliations conducted so far under the ICSID Convention and Additional Facility Rules is summarized in Table 16.1 at the end of the chapter.

[C] Conduct of an ICSID Convention Conciliation

The function and role of the Conciliation Commission are described in Article 34 of the ICSID Convention. It is the duty of the Conciliation Commission to clarify the issues in dispute between the parties and to endeavour to bring about agreement between them upon mutually acceptable terms.[70] Conciliation Rule 13(1) provides that the Commission shall hold its first session within sixty days after its constitution or such other period as the parties may agree. Conciliation Rule 20 lists a number of questions of procedure on which the Commission shall preliminarily seek the views of the parties and for which it may invite the parties to a meeting. Conciliation Rule 22 specifies that the Commission shall hear the parties and shall endeavour to obtain any information that might serve to clarify the issues in dispute between the parties. In this respect, it may (a) request from either party oral explanations, documents and other information; (b) request evidence from other persons; and (c) with the consent of the party concerned, visit any place connected with the dispute or conduct inquiries there, provided that the parties may participate in any such visits and inquiries. In order to bring about agreement between the parties, the Commission may, from time to time, at any stage of the proceedings, make - orally or in writing - recommendations to the parties. Pursuant to Conciliation Rules 25(1), the President of the Commission shall within thirty days from its constitution invite each party to file a written statement of its position. Every written statement or other instrument filed by a party may be accompanied by supporting documentation, as set out in Conciliation Rule 26. In accordance with Rule 27, the Conciliation Commission may organize one or more hearings with the parties, whereby it is free to invite the parties separately (also called 'caucus').[71] Each party may, at any stage of the proceeding, request that the Commission hear witnesses and experts whose evidence the party considers relevant (Rule 28)

69. ICSID Caseload Statistics, *supra* n. 66, at para. 8, Charts 10 and 11.
70. Available at: https://icsid.worldbank.org/en/Documents/icsiddocs/ICSID%20Convention%20English.pdf.
71. *See* F. Nitschke, *supra* n. 62, at para. 135.

and in accordance with Rule 22(3) the Commission may also organize a visit to the place connected with the dispute. Pursuant to Conciliation Rule 29, the Conciliation Commission shall decide upon the validity of objections raised against the jurisdiction of the Centre or as to whether the dispute is within the competence of the Commission. The Conciliation Rules specify that decisions of the Commission shall be taken by a majority of votes (Rule 16(1) of the ICSID Conciliation Rules) and may take the form of procedural orders (Rule 19 of the ICSID Conciliation Rules). Article 35 of the Convention states that no party shall be entitled to invoke in any other proceeding, whether before arbitrators or in a court of law or otherwise, any views expressed or offers of settlement made by the other party in the conciliation proceedings, or the report or any recommendations made by the Commission, unless agreed otherwise by the parties.

[D] Proposal for New ICSID Mediation Rules

In 2016, ICSID commenced a Rules amendment project and sought public and state input on potential changes. In the framework of the Rules revision process, the ICSID Secretariat published meanwhile four working papers: a first working paper on 2 August 2018,[72] a second working paper on 15 March 2019,[73] a third working paper on 26 August 2019[74] and a fourth working paper on 28 February 2020.[75] ICSID proposes amendments to the Conciliation Rules, which aim to make the rules more user-friendly and the conciliation process even more flexible, and also in order to allow the parties to benefit from the enforcement mechanism of the Singapore Convention on Mediation.[76] With the revision process, ICSID also proposes a set of stand-alone Mediation Rules. ICSID started working on Mediation Rules in 2018. It does so, while taking into account that about 40% of ICSID arbitrations are either settled amicably or otherwise discontinued.[77] As part of the revision process, ICSID also published a draft Code for Adjudicators in ISDS.[78]

The proposed Mediation Rules complement the existing ICSID Arbitration and Conciliation Rules. They may be used either independently of or in conjunction with arbitration or conciliation proceedings. The proposed Mediation Rules are stand-alone rules, in other words separate from the ICSID Convention and Additional Facility Rules.[79] The proposed Mediation Rules respond to the increased demand for mediation of investment disputes generally, ICSID's activities in this sphere, and requests by

72. Available at: https://icsid.worldbank.org/en/Documents/X.Amendments_Vol_3_AFMR.pdf (accessed 2 June 2020).
73. Available at: https://icsid.worldbank.org/en/Documents/Vol_1.pdf (accessed 2 June 2020).
74. Available at: https://icsid.worldbank.org/en/Documents/WP_3_VOLUME_1_ENGLISH.pdf (accessed 2 June 2020).
75. Available at: https://icsid.worldbank.org/en/Documents/WP_4_Vol_1_En.pdf (accessed 2 June 2020).
76. *See* F. Nitschke, *supra* n. 62, at paras 141, 143.
77. *See ibid.*, at para. 143.
78. Available at: https://icsid.worldbank.org/en/Documents/Draft_Code_Conduct_Adjudicators_ISDS.pdf (accessed 2 June 2020).
79. M. Kinnear, *Modernizing ICSID's Rules for Investment Dispute Resolution*, ICC DR Bull. 2019/1, 55; F. Nitschke, *supra* n. 34.

users and Member States for ICSID mediation. The ICSID Mediation Rules will be the first set of institutional mediation rules designed specifically for investment disputes. The introduction of the Mediation Rules will add to the array of dispute resolution services currently offered by ICSID. The new Mediation Rules will assist Member States to implement their International Investment Agreement provisions offering investment mediation. They provide an investment dispute-specific mediation framework, apt for use either independently of, or in conjunction with, arbitration or conciliation proceedings.

The Working Papers of ICSID for the revision of the Rules provide an explanation of how the mediation framework fits into the ICSID system, as well as an overview of the process contemplated under the proposed Mediation Rules, before explaining the specific proposed provisions. While there are some similarities between the ICSID conciliation framework and the proposed Mediation Rules, the Mediation Rules differ in terms of: (i) the institution of the proceeding; (ii) the appointment of the mediator; (iii) the role of the mediator; (iv) the conduct of the proceeding; and (v) the fact that mediation under the proposed Mediation Rules is an entirely voluntary process, allowing a party to withdraw at any time.[80]

The proposed Mediation Rules contain twenty-two rules. They will have fewer sections than the Arbitration Rules and the Conciliation Rules.[81] The mediator's role is to assist the parties in reaching a mutually acceptable resolution of all or part of the dispute (Rule 17(1) of the draft ICSID Mediation Rules). The Rules provide that the Secretariat is authorized to administer mediation proceedings in relation to an investment involving a State or a REIO, which the parties agree in writing to submit to the Centre (Rule 2(1)). There shall be one mediator or two co-mediators (Rule 13(1)). Each mediator shall be appointed by agreement of the parties. The parties may, at any time, jointly request the Secretary-General to assist them in the appointment of a mediator (Rule 13(3) and (4)). The Rules do not refer to a list of mediators. All information relating to the mediation and all documents generated or obtained during the conciliation are in principle confidential. They will not be confidential if: (a) the parties agree otherwise; (b) the information or documents are independently available; or (c) disclosure is required by law (Rule 10(1)). The fact that the parties have or have had recourse to mediation is not confidential, unless the parties agree otherwise (Rule 10(2)). Any position taken, admissions or offers of settlement made, or views expressed by a party during the mediation is without prejudice to the legal positions it may take in any other proceeding (Rule 11). A party may withdraw from a mediation at any moment (Rule 22(1)). The formal notice of termination (Rule 22(2)) is intended to facilitate the enforcement of any settlement agreement reached as a result of the

80. Available at: https://icsid.worldbank.org/en/Documents/X.Amendments_Vol_3_AFMR.pdf, para. 1328 (accessed 2 June 2020).

81. As set out in the fourth working paper of ICSID of 28 February 2020; available at: https://icsid.worldbank.org/en/Documents/WP_4_Vol_1_En.pdf (accessed 2 June 2020).

mediation, allowing for such settlement to benefit from the framework of the UNCITRAL Convention in International Settlement Agreements Resulting from mediation.[82] In addition, ICSID makes its facilities available for the purpose of supporting efforts by parties to resolve investment disputes through mediation. ICSID has also organized numerous events on investment mediation, including a series of trainings for investor-State mediators, aimed at developing the skills necessary to mediate investment disputes. It also provides an array of information on investment mediation on its website.

[E] Mediation Provisions in Investment Treaties

States have acknowledged the suitability of mediation for the resolution of investment disputes and have included mediation provisions in bilateral and multilateral treaties.[83] In some new treaties, mediation has been introduced as a pre-condition to the commencement of investor-State arbitration.[84] In other treaties, mediation has been introduced as a stand-alone mechanism for dispute resolution, providing an alternative to arbitration or conciliation.[85]

For example, the Energy Charter Treaty (ECT) was signed in December 1994 and entered into force in April 1998.[86] The ECT provides the possibility to settle investment disputes through mediation. Article 26 of the ECT allows parties to a dispute to agree to use good offices, structured negotiation, mediation or conciliation using existing mechanisms or even agreeing on a tailor-made mechanism.[87] Article 7.7 of the ECT provides a specialized conciliation mechanism for transit disputes related to the transit and supply of electricity, natural gas, oil and oil products through cross-border grids

82. Proposals for Amendments of the ICSID Rules, Working Paper 1, 2 August 2018, Vol. 3, para. 1398, available at: https://icsid.worldbank.org/en/Documents/X.Amendments_Vol_3_AFMR.pdf (accessed 2 June 2020).
83. *See*, e.g., Art. 10.15 of the Dominican Republic-Central America FTA (CAFTADR) (2006-7), available at: https://ustr.gov/trade-agreements/free-trade-agreements/cafta-dr-dominican-republic-central-america-fta/final-text (accessed 2 June 2020).
84. For example, Art. 26 of the Investment Agreement for the COMESA Common Investment Area (not yet in force) requires a six-month amicable settlement period, during which the parties '*shall seek the assistance of a mediator*', unless an alternative method of dispute settlement is agreed upon (emphasis added), available at: https://www.iisd.org/toolkits/sustainability-toolkit-for-trade-negotiators/wp-content/uploads/2016/06/rei120.06tt1.pdf; *see also* Ch. 10, and Art. 9.18 of the Comprehensive and Progressive Agreement for Trans-Pacific Partnership (CPTPP), available at: https://international.gc.ca/trade-commerce/trade-agreements-accords-commerciaux/agr-acc/cptpp-ptpgp/index.aspx?lang=eng) (accessed 21 May 2020).
85. For example, Annex 29-C on Mediation in the CETA (not yet in force), https://www.international.gc.ca/trade-commerce/trade-agreements-accords-commerciaux/agr-acc/tpp-ptp/text-texte/09.aspx?lang=eng. *See also* Ch. 8(II)(3)(2), Art. 5 of the EU-Vietnam FTA (not yet in force), http://trade.ec.europa.eu/doclib/press/index.cfm?id=1437; Ch. 3, Art. 3.4, and Annex 6 of the EU-Singapore FTA (not yet in force), https://trade.ec.europa.eu/doclib/press/index.cfm?id=961 (accessed 21 May 2020).
86. Currently there are fifty-three Signatories and Contracting Parties to the Treaty. This includes both the European Union and Euratom. Treaty, available at: https://www.energycharter.org/process/energy-charter-treaty-1994/energy-charter-treaty/ (accessed 21 June 2020).
87. Available at: https://www.energycharter.org/what-we-do/dispute-settlement/amicable-resolution-of-disputes/ (accessed 21 June 2020).

and pipelines. The conciliation rules were last amended in 2015 and a commentary was endorsed by the Conference in 2016.[88]

In 2016, the Energy Charter Conference adopted a Guide on Investment Mediation, recognizing mediation as a helpful instrument to facilitate the amicable resolution of investment disputes and encouraged its Contracting Parties to consider to use mediation on a voluntary basis as one of the options at any stage of the dispute to facilitate its amicable solution and to consider the good offices of the Energy Charter Secretariat. The Guide was prepared with the support of the International Mediation Institute, ICSID, the Arbitration Institute of the Stockholm Chamber of Commerce (SCC), the International Court of Arbitration of the ICC, UNCITRAL and the Permanent Court of Arbitration (PCA).[89] The latest ECT caseload statistics indicate that of the 131 arbitration cases handled thus far under the ECT, nine cases have been settled of which four were embodied in an award.[90]

[F] Permanent Court of Arbitration

The PCA administers many investor-State arbitrations.[91] In 1962, the PCA elaborated a set of 'Rules of Arbitration and Conciliation for settlement of investment disputes between two parties of which only one is a State', which inspired the subsequent adoption of the ICSID Convention by the World Bank.[92] The PCA released in 1996 Optional Conciliation Rules, based on the UNCITRAL Conciliation Rules.[93] The PCA has so far not administered any investor-State mediation.[94]

[G] Stockholm Chamber of Commerce

The SCC administers many investor-State arbitrations.[95] The SCC adopted Mediation Rules in 2014 which may apply to investor-State disputes.[96] The SCC has so far not administered any investor-State mediation.[97]

---

88. Available at: https://www.energycharter.org/fileadmin/DocumentsMedia/CCDECS/2015/CCDEC201511.pdf (accessed 21 June 2020).
89. Available at: https://trade.ec.europa.eu/doclib/press/index.cfm?id=961 (accessed 2 June 2020).
90. Available at: https://www.energychartertreaty.org/fileadmin/DocumentsMedia/Statistics/All_statistics_-_15_June_2020.pdf (accessed 21 June 2020).
91. Statistical information on the PCA available at: https://pca-cpa.org/en/documents/publications/ (accessed 21 June 2020).
92. *Dispute Settlement, General Topics, 1.3. Permanent Court of Arbitration* (New York and Geneva: United Nations, 2003) 6, para. 1.2, available at: https://unctad.org/en/Docs/edmmisc232add26_en.pdf (accessed 21 June 2020).
93. *Ibid.*, 11, para. 5.
94. *See* UNCITRAL Secretariat Note A/CN.9/WG.III/WP.190, *supra* n. 44, at paras 41, 44.
95. Statistical information on the SCC case load available at: https://sccinstitute.com/statistics/ (accessed 21 June 2020).
96. Available at: https://sccinstitute.com/media/49819/medlingsregler_eng_web.pdf (accessed 21 June 2020).
97. *See* UNCITRAL Secretariat Note A/CN.9/WG.III/WP.190, *supra* n. 44, at paras 41, 44.

[H] International Chamber of Commerce

The ICC adopted in 2014 Mediation Rules,[98] which may apply to investor-State disputes. The ICC has so far administered only one-treaty based mediation, which ended unsuccessfully, due to the partial participation of a party.[99]

[I] IBA Rules for Investor-State Mediation

On 4 October 2012 the International Bar Association adopted the IBA Rules for Investor-State Mediation.[100] The IBA Rules are stand-alone rules for the settlement of Investor-State disputes containing eleven articles. They were used in an ICSID Conciliation (Case No CONC/(AF)/12/2).[101] As regards confidentiality, Article 10(3)(a) of the IBA Rules provides that the existence of a mediation process itself is not submitted to confidentiality requirements, but that the documents exchanged and given to the mediator and the mediation process are confidential.[102] Pursuant to Article 4(1), there shall be a sole mediator, unless the parties designate two co-mediators. If the parties have not jointly designated a mediator within twenty-one days, the parties shall within fourteen days agree on an institution or person that shall assist them in choosing a mediator ('Designating Authority') in accordance with the procedure set out in Appendix C ('Choice of Mediator Through Designating Authority') (Article 4(6)). If the parties do not agree on a Designating Authority within fourteen days, then the Secretary-General of the PCA at The Hague shall select a Designating Authority upon the request of either party (Article 4(7)). Article 8(1) provides that the mediation shall be conducted in accordance with the parties' wishes and with the assistance of the mediator. Pursuant to Article 9, as soon as practicable following the mediator's designation, the mediator shall convene a mediation management conference with the parties, whether in person, by telephone or by any other means of telecommunication, to discuss: (a) the conduct of the mediation, in particular any outstanding procedural issues such as the languages and location of the mediation sessions; (b) a provisional timetable for the conduct of the mediation; (c) confidentiality and privacy arrangements, including any legal disclosure obligation that may affect such arrangements; (d) the applicability of any relevant prescription or limitation periods and whether the parties wish to address such periods by agreement; (e) whether the parties wish to agree in writing not to commence or not to continue any arbitral or judicial proceedings relating to the differences or disputes that are the subject of the mediation while the

98. Available at: https://iccwbo.org/dispute-resolution-services/mediation/mediation-rules (accessed 21 June 2020).
99. *See* UNCITRAL Secretariat Note A/CN.9/WG.III/WP.190, *supra* n. 44, at paras 41, 44.
100. *See* https://icsid.worldbank.org/en/Documents/process/IBA%20Rules%20for%20Investor-State%20Mediation%20(Approved%20by%20IBA%20Council%204%20Oct%202012).pdf (2 June 2020).
101. A. Joubin-Bret, *Chapter 10: Investor-State Mediation (ISM): A Comparison of Recent Treaties and Rules*, in *Contemporary Issues in International Arbitration and Mediation: The Fordham Papers* (A. Rovine ed., 2014), 166.
102. *Ibid.*, 162.

mediation is pending; (f) whether special arrangements for the approval of a settlement agreement need to be made; and (g) the financial arrangements, such as the calculation and payment of the mediator's fees and expenses.

§16.05 CONCLUSION

The few statistics available on mediation and conciliation as methods to settle international trade and investment disputes, in particular those provided by the ICC for commercial mediation and by ICSID for investor-State disputes, indicate that there are not yet a large number of disputes submitted to mediation. Investment treaties generally foresee a time frame, more commonly known as the 'cooling-off' period, during which the disputing parties may attempt amicable settlement before arbitration. Moreover, investment treaties include a two-tiered dispute settlement clause, providing first for some form of ADR before culminating, at the second tier, with a resolution of the investor-State dispute by an arbitral-tribunal. However, there still seem to be a number of obstacles to overcome in order to convince parties, and in particular, States, to submit their dispute to mediation. The work undertaken by UNCITRAL WG III on possible ISDS Reform will also focus on these obstacles and this work may give guidance that may lead parties to submit investor-State disputes to mediation. Meanwhile, UNCITRAL has already adopted some instruments in order to answer the growing need for mediation as a method to settle international trade and investment disputes, including the Singapore Convention on Mediation and a revised Model Law on Mediation. The Singapore Convention of 2019, which entered into force on 12 September 2020, facilitates the enforcement of international settlement resulting from mediation both in commercial mediation and in investor-State mediation. Pursuant to Article 8 of the Singapore Convention, it will apply to settlements reached in the context of investment disputes, unless States formulate a reservation or a declaration excluding such settlements. The significance of this Convention in the future will, however, depend on the number of States that will ratify it.

Table 16.1 ICSID Conciliation Cases

ICSID Case Reference	*Dates Registration – Outcome*	*Sector*	*Parties' Nationalities*	*Languages*	*Composition of the Commission*	*Status*
1. 82/1	05/10/1982 – 20/06/1983	Textile	German (C) Malagasy (R)	French	–	**Concluded** *Settlement before constitution Commission*
2. 83/1	26/08/1983 – 27/11/1985	Oil, gas and mining	U.S (C) Trinidad and Tobago (R)	English	British, President	**Concluded** *Settlement agreed by the parties*
3. 94/1	13/06/1994 – 19/07/1996	Textile	German (C) Malagasy (R)	French	Belgian, President French Malagasy	**Concluded** *No information available*
4. 03/1	08/12/2003 – 08/04/2005	Oil, gas and mining	Bahamian (C) Nigerien (R)	English, French	–	**Concluded** *Settlement before constitution Commission*
5. 05/1	20/05/2005 – 06/04/2006	Electric power and other energy	- (C) Togolese (R)	–	Portuguese, President Belgian Canadian	**Concluded** *Non-successful; Subsequent arbitration*

ICSID Case Reference	*Dates Registration – Outcome*	*Sector*	*Parties' Nationalities*	*Languages*	*Composition of the Commission*	*Status*
6. 07/1	13/08/2007 – 13/08/2008	Agriculture, fishing and forestry	French, British (C) Central African (R)	French	French, President French Central African	**Concluded** *Non successful; Commission declared proceeding closed*
7. 11/1	19/09/2011 – 11/06/2013	Oil, gas and mining	- (C) Cameroonian (R)	English, French	Swiss, President U.S. French	**Concluded**
8. 12/1	15/05/2012 –	Oil, gas and mining	- (C) Equatorial Guinean (R)	English	–	**Pending** *Suspension of the constitution of the Commission until 31 January 2018*
9. 12/2	29/06/2012 – 12/05/2015	Oil, gas and mining	Equatorial Guinean (C) U.S (R)	English	Mexican, President	**Concluded** *No information available*
10. 16/1	16/05/2016 –	Construction	Greek (C) Albanian (R)	English	–	**Pending**

11. 18/1	30/03/2018 – 19/09/2018	Electric power and other energy	Gabonese (C) Gabonese (R)	French	Egyptian, President French German	**Concluded** *Subsequent arbitration which resulted in a settlement agreement*
12. 19/1	24/05/2019 –	Water, sanitation and flood protection	Cameroonian (C) Cameroonian, Cameroonian (R)	–	U.S., President Moroccan Cameroonian *Reconstituted:* U.S., President; Moroccan;French/Lebanese	**Pending**

CHAPTER 17

The Duty to Mitigate: A Billion Dollar Mystery of General Principles of Law

Kai-chieh Chan & Chuanyu Fan

Part of the backlash against the investor-State dispute settlement (ISDS) system comes from the anger toward awards with large amounts of damages that are perhaps poorly reasoned. This chapter discusses the principle of mitigation, which is one of the most important, yet controversial, legal aspects of quantum in ISDS. Through a comparative analysis, this chapter argues that while the duty to mitigate is not unanimously found in all major domestic legal systems, it is widely recognized in the field of transnational commercial law. Even if legal notions similar to mitigation can be found in every legal regime, the chapter points out that potential confusions exist between different types of the obligation to mitigate. In the absence of clear principles guiding their reasoning on mitigation, tribunals in ISDS tend to minimize its application, thereby creating more backlash against the system. To avoid further confusion on the principle of mitigation, this chapter submits that future reform or joint interpretation mechanisms can be used to clarify the scope of the obligation to mitigate.

§17.01 INTRODUCTION

On January 28, 2020, *Jeune Afrique* published its criticism of the current system of investment arbitration and the backlash of the African States against that system. Instead of offering a general overview of investment case law concerning the African States, the report centers around critics of a single case: *Process & Industrial Developments (P&ID) v. Nigerian Ministry of Petroleum*, in which the claimant was awarded

USD 6.6 billion despite its initial investment of only USD 40 million.[1] According to the Nigerian government, the award in *P&ID v. Nigerian Ministry of Petroleum* is "an assault on every Nigerian and unfair."[2]

While not an investment treaty arbitration, *P&ID* warrants attention due to its magnitude. With its interest increasing at a rate of USD 1.25 million per day, the award creditor is due to pay more than USD 9.6 billion as of September 2019,[3] three times more than the State's annual budget on health and education combined. The solution suggested by the *Jeune Afrique* critique is to call for more African lawyers to join the system as arbitrators.[4]

The fairness of the majority (comprised of Sir Anthony Evans and Lord Hoffmann)'s decision in *P&ID* is beyond the scope of this chapter. The arbitration was exclusively governed by English/Nigerian laws and the claim was not brought under a treaty. However, one of the major legal disputes in the case concerned that of the duty to mitigate. In *P&ID*, the respondent argued that damages arising out of loss of profits should be limited to three years (and not twenty years, the entire duration of the contract) because the claimant "should have found some other profitable investment" by this time. This argument was swiftly rejected by the tribunal majority, because the government, who had the burden of proof, failed to show both (1) "what this other investment would have been" and (2) any other investment opportunity that is reasonably less risky.[5] These requirements, as will be shown below, are not different from the ones contained in transnational or international law. For the dissenting arbitrator in *P&ID*, who agreed with the respondent on the three years limit on loss of profits, the duty to mitigate implies that the claimant "has the onus to mitigate damages of his cause of action rather than rush to file an action in court."[6] The dissenting arbitrator therefore stated that he would have set the damages at USD 250 million and not USD 6.6 billion.[7]

---

1. Olivier Holmey, *Droit des affaires: l'arbitrage international dans le box des accusés*, Jeune Afrique (January 22, 2020, 12:04), https://www.jeuneafrique.com/mag/885737/economie/droit-des-affaires-larbitrage-internationaldans-le-box-des-accuses/.
2. Camillus Eboh and Libby George, *Nigerian Court Orders Firm That Won $9 Billion Case Against Government to Forfeit Assets*, Reuters (September 19, 2019, 19:08), https://www.reuters.com/article/us-nigeria-arbitration/nigerian-court-orders-firm-that-won-9-billion-case-against-government-to-forfeit-assets-idUSKBN1W42IG.
3. Tom Jones, *Mega-award leads to blowback in Nigeria*, Global Arbitration Review (September 3, 2019), https://globalarbitrationreview.com/article/1197870/mega-award-leads-to-blowback-in-nigeriab.
4. Olivier Holmey, *Droit des affaires: l'arbitrage international dans le box des accusés*, Jeune Afrique (January 20, 2020, 12:04), https://www.jeuneafrique.com/mag/885737/economie/droit-des-affaires-larbitrage-international-dans-le-box-des-accuses/.
5. *Process and Industrial Developments Ltd (P&ID) v. Nigerian Ministry of Petroleum*, Final Award (January 31, 2017) para. 109.
6. *Process and Industrial Developments Ltd (P&ID) v. Nigerian Ministry of Petroleum*, Dissenting Opinion of Bayo Ojo, SAN (January 31, 2017) para. 10. The reason behind his dissent may be that: "[claimant is a new company that was incorporated in 2006. While not denying the fact that the claimant is entitled to be compensated, to demand for general damages of $8.6 billion dollars is like asking for a reward for services not rendered." (at para. 5).
7. *Ibid.*, para. 46.

The duty to mitigate thus plays an important role in arbitration. In investment arbitration, where tribunals often award a significant amount of damages, the duty to mitigate can serve as a mechanism balancing between the rights and duties of States and foreign investors. We will examine the origin of the principle and locate different approaches of its application, before delving into their use in investor-State arbitration and the potential future reforms. This chapter aspires to provide a more comprehensive and daring treatment of the duty of mitigation in investment law.

§17.02 THE DUTY TO MITIGATE IN DOMESTIC AND TRANSNATIONAL LAWS

Lawyers and academics have long regarded quantum of damages "as the 'poor cousin' of more important legal battles about jurisdiction over claims and their merits, and hence [issues of damages and compensation] have received less systematic attention."[8] Likewise, despite its prominence in domestic law, the duty to mitigate has received limited attention and appraisal in discussions pertaining to quantum in investment law. In the classic work by Borzu Sabahi, for instance, it was dealt with in a little more than one page with the opening warning that "[t]here seems to be no mechanical rule regarding what constitutes reasonable mitigation. Everything depends on the facts of a case. The following examples, thus, are only illustrative."[9] Indeed, perhaps owing to the fact-sensitive character of the duty to mitigate, authorities in investment law generally seem prudent in their analysis of it.[10]

It starts with an inquiry into various forms of this duty in domestic and transnational legal systems. This task is necessary because the duty to mitigate is often regarded as a "general principle of law" in the sense of Article 38(1)(c) of the Statute of the International Court of Justice (ICJ), according to which international courts and tribunals have recourse to principles deduced from domestic legal systems with the methodology borrowed from comparative law.[11] While the sufficient number of national legal systems in which a principle must exist has not been indicated by the *travaux* of the Statute, authorities have employed such terms as "great majority of the municipal legal systems of the world," "majority of national legal systems," and "principal legal systems of the world."[12] The next section examines whether the duty to mitigate constitutes a general principle of law.

8. Charles N. Brower and Michael Ottolenghi, "Damages in Investor-State Arbitration," 4 Transnational Dispute Management (2007), 2.
9. Borzu Sabahi, *Compensation and Restitution in Investor-State Arbitration: Principles and Practice* 177 (Oxford University Press, 2011).
10. For another example, *see* Irmgard Marboe, *Calculation of Compensation and Damages in International Investment Law* 128–129 (Oxford University Press, 2015), who only devoted three paragraphs to her analysis of the duty in investment law.
11. Bin Cheng, *General Principles Of Law as Applied by International Courts and Tribunals* 376 (London: Stevens & Sons Ltd., 1953) (stating that "the comparative method of studying the legal systems of different nations is no doubt a valuable and even conclusive test whether a given principle represents a genera judicial truth").
12. *See* Marcelo Vázquez-Bermúdez, *First Report on General Principles of Law* 64–65 (International Law Commission, A/CN.4/732, 2019).

[A] General Principles of Law: A Methodological Note

Some controversies exist surrounding the appropriate methodology to extract general principles of law. For functionalists like Zweigert and Kötz, "[Comparative lawyers] know that they must cut themselves loose from their own doctrinal and juridical preconceptions and liberate themselves from their own cultural context in order to discover 'neutral' concepts."[13] According to this approach, what matters is the underlying legal basis (*ratio legis*) behind different domestic laws and not the substantial similarities between them.[14] Accordingly, Michael Akehurst has noted that "[d]ifferences of detail between different systems of municipal law do not prevent the application of general principles of law where there is an underlying common principle."[15] In the same vein, George Abi-Saab has recently commented in his study on international economic law that "[w]hat counts here is not the denomination of the principle in the different national jurisdictions, which vary widely, but the general legal policy."[16] Accordingly, these principles are applicable not because they are in fact recognized in many States, but because "they are inherent in the logic of legal reasoning" and "that they are the distillation of human wisdom and accumulated experience in the legal field."[17]

To a certain extent, this approach is in conflict with the traditional approach according to which "[t]he existence of general principles of law *must* be established through a comparative study of national legal systems representative of the whole international community."[18] The problem with it is that the more national laws one verifies, the less similarities one may find. As Prosper Weil once stated, *"[d]'une certaine manière, le processus d'abstraction-généralisation est autodestructeur."*[19]

13. Konrad Zweigert and Hein Kötz (Trans. Tony Weir.), *Introduction to Comparative Law*, 10, 35 (Oxford University Press, 1998) (also stating that "the comparatist must eradicate the preconceptions of his native legal system.").
14. *See* Cheng, *supra* n. 11, 377 (stating that "[i]t is necessary to go further and fathom their underlying theoretical basis.").
15. Michael Akehurst, "Equity and General Principles of Law," 25 International and Comparative Law Quarterly 814 (1976).
16. George Abi-Saab, *General Principles of Law in International Economic Law, in Elgar Encyclopedia of International Economic Law* 42 (Edward Elgar, 2017).
17. *Ibid.*
18. For the advocates of this approach in investment law, *see* Tarcisio Gazzini, "General Principles of Law in the Field of Foreign Investment," 10 Journal of World Investment and Trade 107 (2009); *see also* Arnaud de Nanteuil, *Droit international de l'investissement* 123 (Pedone, 2017) (stating that "*en théorie, un tel principe ne peut être formulé que s'il est partagé non seulement par un grand nombre d'État mais encore par des systèmes de différentes nature. Il faudrait donc être capable de vérifier ce qu'il existe non seulement dans les droits européens mais également dans les systèmes de droit asiatique, dans ceux qui sont appuyés sur une tradition islamique, sans oublier les systèmes plus ou moins inspirés de tradition tribales*").
19. "In a sense the process of abstraction-generalization is self-destructive" (translation by the authors). *See generally* Prosper Weil, *Cours général de droit international public*, in 237 *Recueil des Cours de l'Académie de Droit International de La Haye*, 146–148 (1992) (stating that "*[o]n retrouve ici les douces illusions de l'oecuménisme juridique et les dures réalités du multiculturalisme juridique: à moins de s'en tenir à un niveau très élevé d'abstraction et de généralisation ... il y a plus de différences que de ressemblances entre les grands systèmes juridiques du monde*").

If a look into "general legal policy" suffices to identify general principle laws, one can confidently say that the duty to mitigate is a general principle. According to the economic analysis of law, the law of remedies seems to have been influenced by the need to keep the economic machine running with the "least possible disturbance."[20] In this sense, not only the wrongdoers but also the victims must contribute to this objective. Following this logic, one can discern at least two legal policies behind the duty to mitigate. First, it has a *private* function of allocating risks between wrongdoers and victims. It can thus deal with the problem of "moral hazard" potentially arising out of bad faith behavior by the victim. Even though in some cases, such as the "plaintiff's failure to buy in a rising market, involve no waste of community resources yet the defendant is held not to be liable for a loss that could have been avoided," the duty can be said to protect the legitimate expectations of the wrongdoers.[21] Second, the duty fulfills a *public* function by maximizing social value and prohibiting unreasonable waste potentially carried out by the victim.[22]

[B] The Duty to Mitigate: A General Principle of Law?

While the legal policies behind the duty to mitigate sound desirable, the legislature and judges of a State must decide whether to adopt it. In any event, it is widely found in various transnational principles. For example, Article 7.4.8(1) of the Principles of International Commercial Contracts (UNIDROIT Principles) provides that a "non-performing party is not liable for harm suffered by the aggrieved party to the extent that the harm could have been reduced by the latter party's taking reasonable steps." Similarly, under Article 9.504 of the Principles of European Contract Law, the non-performing party "is not liable for loss suffered by the aggrieved party to the extent that the aggrieved party contributed to the non-performance or its effects."[23] Authors discussing *lex mercatoria* have unanimously supported the existence of the duty to mitigate in international contracts.[24] Therefore, in accordance with the spirit of

20. Anne Michaud, "Mitigation of Damage in the Context of Remedies for Breach of Contract", 15 Revue Générale de Droit 301 (1984).
21. Djakhongir Saidov, *The Law of Damages in International Sales* 125–126 (Hart Publishing, 2008); Kurt J. Venzmer, *Mitverursachung und Mitverschulden im Schadensersatzrecht* 101 et seq. (Beck, 1960).
22. Reinhard Greger, "Mitverschulden und Schadensminderungspflicht – Treu und Glauben im Haftungsrecht?", Neue Juristische Wochenschrift 1133 (1985) (describing the duty to mitigate as an obligation one owes toward the society). As stated by the official commentary to Art. 7.4.8 of the UNIDROIT Principles (2010), "it would be unreasonable *from the economic standpoint* to permit an increase in harm which could have been reduced by the taking of reasonable steps" (emphasis added). *See* https://www.unidroit.org/instruments/commercial-contracts/unidroit-principles-2010/406-chapter-7-non-performance-section-4-damages/1030-article-7-4-8-mitigation-of-harm.
23. *See also* the *Acte Uniforme OHADA sur le droit commercial* (OHADA Uniform Act relating to general commercial law), Art. 293; the Convention relating to a Uniform Law on the International Sale of Goods (ULIS) 1964, Art. 88; the Common European Sales Law (CESL), COM (2011) 635 final, Art. 162.
24. Yasuhei Taniguchi, "The Obligation to Mitigate Damages," *in Evaluation of Damages in International Arbitration* 92–95 (Yves Derains and Richard Kreindler eds., ICC Institute of World Business Law, 2006) (citing ICC Cases 8817, 8782, 5037, 4716, 5418, 3880 and 2478).

co-operation between sophisticated businessmen of *lex mercatoria*, parties have the duty to mitigate damages even before contractual non-performance.[25]

If codification efforts in transnational law are unanimous for their endorsement of the duty to mitigate, domestic laws are less so. Arguably, only common law legal systems impose a real obligation to mitigate on victims.[26] The English Sale of Goods Act, for example, provides that damages for non-acceptance should be calculated based on "the difference between the contract price and the market or current price at the time or times when the goods ought to have been accepted or at the time of the refusal to accept."[27] The duty to mitigate is also applicable to torts under English law.[28] In the United States, the Uniform Commercial Code (UCC) allows the seller to resell the goods in case of the buyer's non-acceptance, and similarly permits the buyer to purchase substitute goods from elsewhere in case of the seller's breach. If such a move was carried out "in good faith and in a commercially reasonable manner," the differences between the two prices and incidental costs can be recovered by the aggrieved party.[29]

Some other domestic laws, while explicitly mentioning the duty to mitigate, are less explicit about how it can be carried out and simply provide it as a factor to be taken into account when damages are calculated. For example, the Contract Law of the People's Republic of China requires only a contractual party to take proper measures to "prevent *the enlargement of losses.*" It also provides that "reasonable expenses incurred by the other party in preventing the aggravation of the loss shall be borne by the breaching party."[30] Similarly, while containing no explicit mention of the duty, the Dutch civil code allows for a victim to recover "reasonable costs to prevent or mitigate damage which could be expected as result of the event giving rise to liability."[31] The Russian civil code also allows the court "to reduce the amount of responsibility of the debtor if the creditor has intentionally or through negligence *facilitated the increase* of the amount of losses ... *or has not taken reasonable measures to reduce them.*"[32]

For other domestic laws that do not contain any reference to the duty to mitigate at all, it is often suggested that similar results can be achieved through more general legal principles. However, this solution is not without detriment to legal certainty. In

25. Filali Osman, *Les Principes Généraux de la* Lex Mercatoria 185–186 (L.G.D.J., 1992) (stating, "*l'obligation s'impose bien en amont de la phase de réparation du préjudice. [...] C'est d'elle que dérive l'obligation faite au créancier de la prestation de renégocier de bonne foi le contrat, ou de se renseigner*").
26. Bernard Hanotiau, *Régime juridictionnel et portée de l'obligation de modérer le dommage dans la responsabilité contractuelle et extra-contractuelle*, Revue de droit des affaires internationales 404 (1987) (characterizing the US and UK approaches as "*véritable obligation de modérer le préjudice*").
27. English Sale of Goods Act 1979, s. 50(3); similarly *see* s. 51(3) (mitigation in case of non-delivery).
28. Andrew Burrows, *English Private Law* 1277 (Oxford University Press, 2013).
29. UCC ss. 2-706 (on seller's resale) and 2-712 (on buyer's procurement of substitute goods).
30. Article 119 of the Contract Law of the People's Republic of China (1999). The same article is preserved in full in the draft civil code published in December 2019 (Art. 591).
31. Article 96 (2) (a) of the New Netherlands Civil Code.
32. Article 404(1) of the Civil Code of the Russian Federation, available at: http://www.russian-civil-code.com/PartI/SectionIII/Subsection1/Chapter25.html.(emphases added).

Chile, for instance, the *Código Civil de Bello* is silent on mitigation. While some authors have advocated in favor of the duty to mitigate by referring to the duty of good faith (Article 1546), others (e.g., eminent jurist Jorge López Santa María) considered the approach unfounded because Chilean courts have generally been cautious with the extraction of creative conclusions from the article.[33] One can contrast the case of Chile with that of Colombia, where the latter's Supreme Court had no difficulty extracting a duty to mitigate from the general principle of good faith provided in Article 83 of the *Constitución Política de Colombia* (Constitution), Article 1603 of the Civil Code and Article 871 of the Commercial Code.[34]

In some States, the notion of mitigation is said to be assimilated with that of contributory fault. Section 254 of the German Civil Code, entitled "Contributory negligence," provides that "[w]here fault on the part of the injured person *contributes to the occurrence of the damage*, liability in damages as well as the extent of compensation to be paid depend on the circumstances, in particular to what extent the damage is caused mainly by one or the other party."[35] Similarly, Article 418 of the Japanese Civil Code stipulates that "if the obligee is *negligent regarding the failure of performance* of the obligation, the court shall determine the liability for damages and the amount thereof by taking such elements into consideration."[36] The distinction between contributory fault and duty to mitigate is arguably temporal. While the former relates to actions contributing to the breach before it occurs, the latter arises only after the breach.[37]

On the other side of the spectrum is the rejection of the duty to mitigate as a principle. Most notably, the duty to mitigate is explicitly excluded under French tort law. In a decision dated June 19, 2003, the second chamber of the French Supreme Court (*Cour de cassation*) held that victims of traffic accident are under no obligation to mitigate (in this case by reopening their bakery).[38] Recent authorities generally acknowledge that the rule under French law is that "the perpetrator of an accident must

33. Jorge López Santa María, "Sobre la obligación de minimizar los daños en el derecho chileno y comparado", *in Los Contratos en el Derecho Privado* 331 (Fabricio Mantilla Espinosa and Francisco Ternera Berrios eds., Legis, 2007). Other scholars have proposed to base the duty on Art. 2330 of the Code, which concerns the reduction of damages regarding contractual liabilities. Such a suggestion, however, is rejected by most authors because the article does not apply to torts. *See* Adrián Oscar Morea Fogliato, *El deber de mitigar el daño evitable por parte de la víctima en el ordenamiento jurídico argentino* 335 (Unpublished doctoral thesis at the Pontifical Catholic University of Argentina, 2016).
34. Corte Suprema de Justicia, Sala de Casación Civil y Agraria, Sentencia del 16 de diciembre de 2010. On Colombian law regarding mitigation, *see* Felipe Suescún de Roa, *Mitigación de daños en materia contractual*, 136 Vniversitas (2018), available at: https://revistas.javeriana.edu.co/index.php/vnijuri/article/view/19815 (emphasis added).
35. Translation available at: https://www.gesetze-im-internet.de/englisch_bgb/englisch_bgb.html#p0764 (emphasis added).
36. Translation available at: http://www.japaneselawtranslation.go.jp/law/detail/?id = 2057&vm = 2&re = 02; the corresponding provision for torts is Art. 722(2), which states that "[i]f a victim is negligent, the court may determine the amount of compensation by taking that factor into consideration."
37. For discussion on the distinction under Japanese law, *see* Yoshihito Hasegawa, *Songai baisho chosei no hoteki kozo* ("Legal structure of damages adjustment"), 74 Journal of Private Law (*Shiho*) 165 (2012).
38. Civ. 2e, June 19, 2003, n° 00-22302.

compensate for all the damages caused by it; that the victim is not obliged to limit his or her damage in the interest of the responsible party."[39] The duty to mitigate is also not recognized under French contract law.[40] According to one authoritative source, while a similar result may be achieved with recourse to general notions such as good faith, causal link, and contributory fault, it only allows the adjudicators to consider the *omissions* of the victims, who aggravated its loss. Thus, the victims are not required by law to perform specific *actions* to mitigate their losses.[41]

[C] The Standard of Due Diligence Required in Mitigation

Scholars very often dispute the definition of the duty to mitigate. One authority simply states that the "generally accepted principle of mitigation *allows (and in some cases requires)* a non-breaching party to take acts not contemplated by the contract so as to lower the damages."[42] It is unclear when and which types of mitigating efforts would be a *must*.

For some, the duty to mitigate has never been a real "duty." In the words of Alexander Komarov, the duty "is not matched by any corresponding right. ... As a consequence, there is no sanction for 'breach' of this 'duty'; the only possible result of the plaintiff's failure to mitigate is to reduce the amount of his recovery."[43] This view seemed to be echoed by the International Law Commission (ILC), whose commentary of the *Draft Articles on Responsibility of States for Internationally Wrongful Act* provides that "[a]lthough often expressed in terms of a 'duty to mitigate', *this is not a legal obligation which itself gives rise to responsibility*. It is rather that a failure to mitigate by the injured party *may* preclude recovery to that extent."[44] The practical result of this is that arbitrators or judges should not apply the notion of mitigation ex officio in case of defaults award or judgments (i.e., award/judgment rendered in absentia of the respondent).[45]

Others, however, have little trouble treating the duty to mitigate as a real "duty." In common law, for example, the principle is that "as a matter of law, the plaintiff *must*

---

39. Yvaine Buffelan-Lanore and Virginie Larribau-Terneyre, *Droit civil* 860, para. 2520 (Sirey, 2018); Alain Bénabent, *Droit des obligations* 336, para. 426 (L.G.D.J., 2018). *See* Civ. 2e, October 25, 2012, n° 11-25511: *"l'auteur d'un accident doit en réparer toutes les conséquences dommageables; que la victime n'est pas tenue de limiter son préjudice dans l'intérêt du responsible."*
40. *See*, e.g., Civ. 3e, July 19, 2013, n° 12-13.851.
41. Philippe Malaurie, Laurent Aynès, and Philippe Stoffel-Munck, *Droit des obligations* 564 (L.G.D.J., 2017).
42. Charles T. Kotuby Jr. and Luke A. Sobota, *General Principles of Law and International Due Process: Principles and Norms Applicable in Transnational Disputes* 150 (Oxford University Press, 2017) (emphasis added).
43. Alexander Sergeevich Komarov, "Mitigation of Damages," *in Evaluation of Damages in International Arbitration* 37 (Yves Derains and Richard Kreindler eds., ICC Institute of World Business Law, 2006).
44. *Draft Articles on Responsibility of States for Internationally Wrongful Acts, with commentaries*, 2 Yearbook of the International Law Commission 93 (2001) (emphasis added).
45. Anthony Daimsis, "How Heuristics Misshape Reasoning and Lead to Increased Costs in Arbitration," in *Finances in International Arbitration: Liber Amicorum Patricia Shaughnessy* 100–101 (Sherlin Tung, Fabricio Fortese, Crina Baltag eds., Kluwer Law International, 2019).

mitigate his loss, the jury *must* only award damages representing the loss which the plaintiff would have suffered if he had done so."[46] In arbitration, "the harmed party *must take reasonable steps* to reduce its losses, or else it may find its recovery limited to only those losses it could not have prevented through timely action."[47] This view is supported by Articles 77 and 88 of the UN Convention on Contracts for the International Sale of Goods (CISG). Article 77 provides that "[a] party who relies on a breach of contract must take such measures as are reasonable in the circumstances to mitigate the loss, including loss of profit resulting from the breach." Article 88, in turn, provides that "(1) A party ... *may* sell [the goods] by any appropriate means if there has been an unreasonable delay by the other party in taking possession of the goods or in taking them back ... (2) If the goods are subject to rapid deterioration or their preservation would involve unreasonable expense, a party ... *must* take reasonable measures to sell them." Article 88 of the CISG demonstrates that, under certain conditions, the duty to mitigate might become a legal obligation.[48] According to the UN Compensation Commission, "under the general principles of international law relating to mitigation of damages ... the claimant *was not only permitted but indeed obligated to take reasonable steps* to fight the oil-well fires in order to mitigate the loss, damage or injury being caused."[49]

The controversy above may not be merely rhetorical. True, the duty to mitigate may always be a "weak" duty as long as, on the one hand, the failure to carry it out cannot itself give rise to contractual and tortious liability and, on the other hand, such a failure will not bar the victim from claiming for damages.[50] But from the brief comparative analysis above, one can identify as least three approaches:

- The first approach does not defer to any party and analyze the party's behavior from a reasonable business man's perspective to know what should have and should not have been done. This does not necessarily imply that the victim bears the burden of proof. As one commentator has stated, "even where judges

46. Patrick S. Atiyah, *The Rise and Fall of Freedom of Contract* 425 (Oxford University Press, 1985) (emphasis in the original).
47. Borzu Sabahi, Kabir Duggal and Nicholas Birch, "Principles Limiting the Amount of Compensation," *in Contemporary and Emerging Issues on the Law of Damages and Valuation in International Investment Arbitration* 332 (Christina L. Beharry ed., Brill | Nijhoff, 2018) (emphasis added). *See also* Christian Tietje and Emily Sipiorski, *Offset of Benefits in Damages Calculation in International Investment Arbitration*, 29 Journal of International Arbitration 559–560 (2012) (describing the duty to mitigate as an "obligation for the harmed party" and "duty placed on the claimants").
48. Similarly, in a commentary on Art. 2-172 of the UCC, which provides that the buyer *must* mitigate, Shael Herman recognized that: "[t]rue, the buyer may not be compelled to mitigate, but failure to do so risks having a claim reduced by the amount that mitigation efforts would have cut its loss and thus saved the other party." *See* Shael Herman, "Specific Performance," 7 Edinburgh Law Review 196 (2003). A similar distinction exists in German law between the duty owe to others (*Pflicht*) and the duty towards oneself (*Obliegenheit*).
49. *Well-Blowout Control Claim* (UN Doc. No. S/AC.26/1996/5/Annex), Report and Recommendations Made by the Panel (December 18, 1996), para. 54.
50. For the contrary view (criticized by other scholars) in Japanese law, *see* Uchida Takashi, *Kyosei riko to songai baisho – "songai keigen gimu" no kanten kara* ("Compulsory execution and damages-from the viewpoint of 'Damage reduction obligation'"), 42 Hoso jiho 2643–2644 (1990) (arguing that the failure to mitigate may bar the victim from claiming for damages).

recognise that it is the breaching party who bears the burden of proof (and where it fails to do so), the injured party may still be required to provide evidence of taking measures to mitigate its loss. ... in some other cases, judges and arbitrators themselves appear to have taken the initiative in establishing whether the injured party had mitigated its loss."[51] This approach can be based on the *lex mercatoria* obligation for the parties to cooperate in a breach of contract.[52]

- The second approach defers to the decision of the victim and requires the wrongdoer to establish that the victim had *aggravated* its loss by its action or omission.[53] Under influence of the principle of full compensation, the standard does not require the victim to *actively reduce* the amount that may already be counted as loss.
- The third approach also defers to the decision of the victim but requires the wrongdoer to establish both the aggravation of loss and the failure to reduce the loss.[54] The standard of proof here requires the wrongdoer to construct a hypothetical way that the victim should have reasonably followed.[55] The standard here is that of "reasonableness"[56] or "reasonable family father."[57]

While there may not always be a clear demarcation between these approaches, an illustration can be drawn from *P&ID*. For the majority the inquiry stopped once the respondent failed to demonstrate how the claimant could "have found some other profitable investment and thereby mitigated its loss" (the second or third approach).[58] The dissenting arbitrator decided otherwise and found that it was for the claimant to show how it "will not be able to find an alternative work or project for twenty years" (the first approach).[59]

51. Saidov, *supra* n. 21, 148.
52. In ICC Case No. 2478, for example, the tribunal held that the claimant should have accepted the unreasonably low price proposed by the respondent before initiating the arbitration to seek for adjustment of the price. *See French Buyer v. Rumanian Seller* (ICC Case No. 2478), Award (1974), 3 Yearbook of Commercial Arbitration (1978) 223.
53. For French tort law, *see Projet de réforme du droit de la responsabilité civile* (draft of March 2017) Art. 1263, available at: http://www.justice.gouv.fr/publication/Projet_de_reforme_de_la_responsabilite_civile_13032017.pdf.
54. Here the enlarged loss is excluded, either by the notions of contributory fault and/or causation.
55. Herfried Wöss, Adriana San Román Rivera, Pablo Spiller and Santiago Dellepiane, *Damages in International Arbitration under Complex Long-term Contracts* 216, para. 5.108 (Oxford University Press, 2014) (noting that "the respondent will need to build a new hypothetical situation in which the claimant takes a reasonable mitigation opportunity that it did not take in the actual world. The recoverable damages would be the difference between the claimant's hypothetical situation but for the breach, and the claimant's hypothetical situation if it had mitigated.").
56. *See*, e.g., Sabahi, *supra* n. 9, 177; Komarov, *supra* n. 43, 42 ("reasonable and prudent action").
57. Marboe, *supra* n. 10, 126, para. 3.257 (citing ICC Award No. 5514 which provides the standard "bon père de famille"). *See also* commentary to Trans-Lex Principle, available at: https://www.trans-lex.org/949000/_/duty-to-mitigate/ (stating that "Which measures a party relying on a breach by the other party is required to take in order to mitigate its damages, ... must be determined by application of the standard of reasonableness"). The standard is explicitly mentioned in the Civil Code of the Philippines, Art. 2203 (providing that "[t]he party suffering loss or injury must exercise the diligence of a good father of a family to minimize the damages").
58. *P&ID*, Final Award, *supra* n. 5, para. 109.
59. *P&ID*, Dissenting Opinion of Bayo Ojo, SAN, *supra* n. 6, para. 12.

§17.03 THE DUTY TO MITIGATE IN INTERNATIONAL INVESTMENT ARBITRATION

As shown in section §17.02, there may be doubts with regard to the existence of the duty to avoid loss as a generally accepted principle of law.[60] However, at least the duty not to aggravate loss may be reasonably deduced from the neighboring concepts of proximity, causation or good faith.

Even if a principle is generally well established in various domestic or transnational laws, it does not automatically qualify as a general principle of law. After all, once a principle is found in domestic laws, it must be "transposed" to fit the reality of international relations. As Lord McNair famously put it, "The way in which international law borrows from this source is not by means of importing private law institutions 'lock, stock and barrel', ready-made and fully equipped with a set of rules."[61] More difficult is the problem of whether the same principles applicable in international relations can be applied in the context of investor-State arbitration (or vice versa), where investor and State do not stand as sovereign equals.

Despite these doubts, investment tribunals have so far admitted the existence of the duty to mitigate as a general principle of law. While some just accept the principle without any discussion, the most elaborate justifications have been given by the tribunals in *AIG v. Kazakhstan* and *Clayton/Bilcon v. Canada*. In *AIG*, the tribunal held that:

> Mitigation of damages, as a principle, is applicable in a wide range of situations. It has been adopted in common law and in civil law countries, as well as in International Conventions and other international instruments – as for instance in Article 77 of the Vienna Convention and Article 7.4.8 of the UNIDROIT Principles for International Commercial Contracts.[62]

The *AIG* tribunal went on to state that such a duty is consistent with the law of Kazakhstan, which "is no different from the rule as to mitigation stated in a leading judgment of the Privy Council," according to which "a claimant cannot recover for 'avoidable loss'."[63] Similarly, the tribunal in *Middle East Cement* justified the existence of such a duty based on a combination of international/transnational law and domestic law:

> The duty to mitigate damages is not expressly mentioned in the BIT. However, this duty can be considered to be part of the General Principles of Law which, in turn, are part of the rules of international law which are applicable in this dispute

60. In investment law, it has been suggested that a principle must at least be found in German, French, English and US law to be qualified as a general principle of law: Stephan W. Schill, "General Principles of Law and International Investment Law," *in International Investment Law: The Sources of Rights and Obligations* 147 (T. Gazzini and E. de Brabandere eds, Brill | Nijhoff, 2012).
61. *Status of South-West Africa*, Separate Opinion of Sir Arnold McNair, *ICJ Report* (1950), p. 148.
62. *AIG Capital Partners, Inc. and CJSC Tema Real Estate Company v. Republic of Kazakhstan* (ICSID Case No. ARB/01/6), Award (October 7, 2003) para. 10.6.4(1).
63. *Ibid.*, para. 10.6.4(2).

according to Art. 42 of the ICSID Convention. The duty to mitigate is also contained in Art. 221 of the Egyptian Civil Code.[64]

Compared to the *AIG* tribunal's express reference to domestic law, the *Clayton/Bilcon* tribunal justified the existence of such a duty on the practice of the ICJ,[65] the United Nations Compensation Commission (UNCC),[66] and other investment tribunals.[67] In *CME v. Czech Republic,* the tribunal found the duty to be applicable as "established general principles in arbitral case law," while referring to a single citation of the treatise written by Fouchard, Gaillard, and Goldman.[68]

[A] Preliminary Issue: Mitigation as Liability or/and Quantum?

As noted in section §17.02[B], some national laws do not provide a clear distinction between contributory fault and the duty to mitigate, even though the two notions are ideally distinct. As some authors suggest, in commercial arbitration, "the effect of lack of mitigation is *similar* to contributory negligence or lack of causality. However, mitigation applies as a duty to be taken by the claimant *after* the breach, whereas contributory negligence is a matter *related to* the breach."[69] In other words, in principle, mitigation concerns quantum while contributory fault concerns liability.

That being said, their effects may not always be similar in investment arbitration practice. In *Yukos*, the tribunal had to deal with the claimants' "questionable" practice and abuse of the respondent's tax regime, which is considered to have partly contributed to the treaty breach. It noted that previous tribunals had proportionally reduced the amount of the award. In *MTD v. Chile,* the damage was reduced by 50% and in *Occidental v. Ecuador* by 25%.[70] The *Yukos* tribunal ultimately decided to reduce the damages by 25%, which in the case meant a reduction of more than USD 16 billion.[71]

In contrast, the argument of mitigation tends to result in a reduction of precise amount. In *EDF v. Argentina,* the tribunal held that the claimants had failed to mitigate their damages in deciding to sell their concession for a mere USD 2 million while negotiations with the government were still on-going. It thus held that the respondent was not liable for the loss of the value of the concession and deducted USD 14 million

64. *Middle East Cement Shipping and Handling Co. S.A. v. Arab Republic of Egypt* (ICSID Case No. ARB/99/6), Award (April 12, 2002), para. 167.
65. *Clayton and Bilcon of Delaware Inc. v. Government of Canada* (PCA Case No. 2009-04), Award on Damages (January 10, 2019) paras. 197–198.
66. *Ibid.*, para. 199.
67. *Ibid.*, paras. 200–201.
68. *CME Czech Republic B.V. v. Czech Republic* (UNCITRAL), Final Award (March 14, 2003), para. 482. The duty is recognized as "one of the most well-established general principles in arbitral case law" and not as a general principle of (domestic) law. *See* P. Fouchard, E. Gaillard and B. Goldman, *Fouchard, Gaillard, Goldman on International Commercial Arbitration* 832, para. 1491 (Kluwer Law International, 1999).
69. Wöss, San Román Rivera, Spiller, and Dellepiane, *supra* n. 55, at 215 (emphases added).
70. *Yukos Universal Limited (Isle of Man) v. The Russian Federation* (PCA Case No. 2005-04/AA227), Final Award (July 18, 2014), para. 1633.
71. *Ibid.*, para. 1637.

from the damages.[72] In *Bridas v. Turkmenistan*, a dispute arising out of a contract applying English law, the claimant refused to operate the joint venture despite express recommendations by the tribunal. As a result, the amount of damages was reduced by USD 50 million.[73] In these cases, contributory fault seems to result in a more substantial decrease in damages than the failure to mitigate.

Furthermore, while international law authorities suggest that mitigation only concerns the calculation of damages,[74] investment tribunals have not followed that rule with rigor. In *Achmea I*, for example, the tribunal held that the claimant's suspension of its operations could be seen as a mitigating act, which would be taken into account both "from the perspective of questions of liability and causation, and from the perspective of the determination of compensation payable."[75]

[B] The Standard of Due Diligence in Mitigation in International Investment Law

As in domestic law, in investor-State arbitration the respondent bears the burden of proving that the claimant had failed to mitigate.[76] While different types of approaches can be identified in domestic laws, it might be difficult to see the one taken by the tribunal in practice. In most cases, the tribunals are willing to delve into the hypothetical scenarios elaborated by the respondent and decide whether they are or are not convinced by it. The mitigation claim would be rejected if the claimant had done their utmost,[77] or if the wrongful act prevented it from doing so,[78] or if the hypothetical

72. *EDF International S.A., SAUR International S.A. and León Participaciones Argentinas S.A. v. Argentine Republic* (ICSID Case No. ARB/03/23), Award (June 11, 2012), para. 1317.
73. *Bridas S.A.P.I.C., et al, v. Government of Turkmenistan* (ICC Case No. 9058/FMS/KGA), Third Partial Award (September 2, 2000), para. 53.
74. *See*, e.g., Stephan Wittich, "Compensation," *in Max Planck Encyclopedias of International Law* para. 21 (Rüdiger Wolfrum ed., 2008) (noting that "[w]hile often called 'duty to mitigate', this is not an enforceable obligation ... the principle of mitigation thereby operates as a basis for the calculation of damages.").
75. *Achmea B.V. v. The Slovak Republic* (PCA Case No. 2008-13), Award (December 7, 2012), para. 320. For other examples, *see* Jawad Ahmad, "Date of Breach, Contributory Fault, and Mitigation of Damages in Investment Arbitration," *in Evolution and Adaptation: The Future of International Arbitration* 922–923 (Jean Engelmayer Kalicki and Mohamed Abdel Raouf eds., Kluwer Law International, 2019).
76. Gabrielle Kaufmann-Kohler, "Compensation Assessment: Perspectives from Investment Arbitration," *in The Law, Economics and Politics of Retaliation in WTO Dispute Settlement* 632 (Chad Philips Bown and Joost Pauwelyn eds., Cambridge University Press, 2010); *AIG Capital Partners, Inc. and CJSC Tema Real Estate Company v. Republic of Kazakhstan* (ICSID Case No. ARB/01/6), Award (October 7, 2003) para. 10.6.4(4).
77. *National Grid P.L.C. v. Argentina Republic* (UNCITRAL), Award (November 3, 2008), para. 273 (finding that the claimant had sold at a best price it could obtain); *CME Czech Republic B.V. v. Czech Republic* (UNCITRAL), Final Award (March 14, 2003), para. 482.
78. *Antoine Abou Lahoud and Leila Bounafeh-Abou Lahoud v. Democratic Republic of the Congo* (ICSID Case No. ARB/10/4), Award (February 7, 2014), para. 628 (noting that "*les Demandeurs n'avaient pas accès à leur équipement et ne pouvaient donc reprendre une activité normale*"); *see also S.D. Myers, Inc. v. Government of Canada* (UNCITRAL), Second Partial Award (October 21, 2002), para. 165.

scenarios proposed by the respondent were not economically feasible.[79] The situation in *P&ID*, where respondents did not advance any hypothetical alternatives, is rather an exception.[80]

Nevertheless, the obiter dicta in some recent cases could provide a rare glimpse into how investment arbitration practitioners deal with the duty to mitigate. It appears that the tribunals are willing to defer to, or will not second-guess, the claimant's business judgments after the wrongful act occurred. In *Magyar Farming v. Hungary*, the respondent appeared to suggest that the claimant could and should have mitigated its loss by growing certain crops on specific parcels of land. The tribunal rejected the argument by noting that it would not "speculate whether the claimants should have exercised a better business judgment."[81]

In *HEP v. Slovenia*, because the tribunal acknowledged the inherent risk of appraising the reasonableness of the acts after many years, it would not second-guess the claimant's decision unless "there is evidence that the decision was unreasonable" or "irrational."[82] In *Unión Fenosa Gas v. Egypt*, the respondent argued that the claimant should have better mitigated its losses by severing its delivery commitments, which forced it to acquire gas elsewhere at a higher price.[83] The majority of the tribunal rejected the argument because it found that "the claimant [cannot] reasonably be required to have effectively closed down its business."[84] The majority of the tribunal even went as far as to comment that "it cannot be forgotten that the claimant's predicament requiring such mitigatory conduct was caused by the respondent's international wrong under the Treaty."[85] For the dissenting arbitrator in *Unión Fenosa Gas*, such a position is hard to understand because "by definition, the question of mitigation never arises at all unless there has been some breach."[86]

These awards thus show a clear preference for the second or third approach.[87] The reason behind this is probably reflected by the *dictum* in *Unión Fenosa Gas* quoted

79. *Middle East Cement Shipping and Handling Co. S.A. v. Arab Republic of Egypt* (ICSID Case No. ARB/99/6), Award (April 12, 2002), para. 168; *Saar Papier Vertriebs GmbH v. Poland* (UNCITRAL), Final Award (October 16, 1996), paras. 99–100 (noting that the alternatives are more costly); *Southern Pacific Properties (Middle East) Limited v. Arab Republic of Egypt* (ICSID Case No. ARB/84/3), Award (May 20, 1992), para. 172 (considering that claimant could not have mitigated its loss by moving to a site that "was totally unsuitable for tourist development."); *Amco Asia Corporation and others v. Indonesia* (ICSID Case No. ARB/81/1). Award in Resubmitted Proceeding (March 31, 1990), para. 168 (considering that the claimant could not have mitigated its loss since it was "virtually impossible to find interested purchasers.")
80. This is potentially due to the respondents' passive defense strategy in *P&ID*.
81. *Magyar Farming Company Ltd, Kintyre Kft and Inicia Zrt v. Hungary* (ICSID Case No. ARB/17/27), Award (November 13, 2019), para. 427. The notion of "business judgment," perhaps borrowed from the famous rule developed under US corporate law, is also invoked by the tribunal in *National Grid, supra* n. 77, para. 273.
82. *Hrvatska Elektroprivreda d.d. v. Republic of Slovenia* (ICSID Case No. ARB/05/24), Award (December 17, 2015), para. 386.
83. *Unión Fenosa Gas, S.A. v. Arab Republic of Egypt* (ICSID Case No. ARB/14/4), Award (August 31, 2018), para. 10.90.
84. *Ibid.*, para. 10.128.
85. *Ibid.*, para. 10.132.
86. *Unión Fenosa Gas, S.A. v. Arab Republic of Egypt* (ICSID Case No. ARB/14/4), Dissenting Opinion of Arbitrator Mark Clodfelter (August 31, 2018), footnote n. 75.
87. *Ibid.* and *Hrvatska Elektroprivreda d.d. v. Republic of Slovenia.*

above. It may be that as in certain domestic legal systems, the tribunal members find it unjust to require specific efforts from the injured party.

A related difficulty to the standard of the duty to mitigate is that of the failure to pursue local or other remedies. The underlying rationale is that the victim should ideally negotiate with the wrongdoer before rushing to court. In *Dunkeld v. Belize*, the tribunal held that the failure to pursue local remedies may be regarded as a failure to mitigate since "local administrative procedures may offer a remedy that appears more rapid or certain than that of an international claim."[88] However, it added that the "duty to make reasonable use of available administrative procedures to reduce losses certainly does not imply that a potential claimant must forego the option of pursuing international remedies."[89] On the facts, the claim was dismissed as the tribunal found that the claimant did, in fact, submitted claims through a local compensation process.[90]

The uncertainty continued in *Clayton/Bilcon v. Canada*, where the respondent argued that since the environmental review on the claimants was flawed, an appeal to Canadian courts would have fully restored the value of claimant's investment.[91] This argument was rejected by the majority because a "[s]uccessful judicial review may not have returned to them the opportunity they lost, given the persisting effects of the NAFTA breach on the ground."[92] While recognizing that "the duty of mitigation under public international law may in principle include recourse to administrative remedies and/or judicial review,"[93] the majority was not willing to impose it on the claimants because "the mitigation requirement must not lead to the imposition of a requirement of exhausting local remedies where there is none provided for in the treaty."[94] The dissenting arbitrator, on the other hand, found that the claimants should have pursued their claim in local courts because, seen from an "informed and dispassionate manner," they actually had strong prospects had they done so.[95]

[C] Reforms and Related Appeal Mechanisms: The Way Forward for More Clarity on the Duty to Mitigate?

The duty to mitigate is always judged by the standard of reasonableness. "Whether the aggrieved party has taken reasonable steps to reduce the loss is a question of fact, not law. What is reasonable depends largely upon the facts of the individual case."[96] This perhaps explains the lack of literature systemically analyzing different determinations

88. *Dunkeld International Investment Ltd. v. The Government of Belize (Number 1)* (PCA Case No. 2010-13), Award (June 28, 2016), para. 197.
89. *Ibid.*, para. 199.
90. *Ibid.*, para. 198.
91. *Clayton/Bilcon v. Canada* (PCA Case No. 2009-04), Award on Damages (January 10, 2019), para. 183.
92. *Ibid.*, para. 216.
93. *Ibid.*, para. 211.
94. *Ibid.*, para. 213.
95. *Clayton/Bilcon v. Canada* (PCA Case No. 2009-04), Concurring Opinion of Professor Bryan Schwartz (January 10, 2019), paras. 19–20.
96. *EDF International S.A., SAUR International S.A. and León Participaciones Argentinas S.A. v. Argentine Republic* (ICSID Case No. ARB/03/23), Award (June 11, 2012), para. 1306; *Bridas*

on the duty to mitigate. The factually oriented nature of the duty to mitigate, however, should not prevent lawyers and tribunals from trying to improve the coherence of their decisions in order to enhance the legitimacy of ISDS.[97] In this sense, the duty to mitigate is not entirely a problem of fact. As shown above, despite the general admission of the standard of "reasonableness," various legal issues can arise, such as that surrounding the standard of proof, the burden of proof, and the distinction between contributory fault and the failure to mitigate. With the obvious lack of an applicable standard and predictability today, counsels for parties can plead and tribunals can take their positions on these issues. If the duty to mitigate can gain the attention in the arbitration community that it deserves with regard to the impact it has, there would be more debates among scholars and practitioners on what type of duty best suits the purpose of ISDS. In the absence of substantial reform, this appears to be the best way forward.

Moreover, with the recent rise of a joint (binding) interpretation mechanism[98] and an investment court,[99] it would be possible and even desirable for them to provide more precision on specific issues, including the duty to mitigate. These mechanisms allow the States and investors to mitigate legal uncertainty when assessing whether to advance their claim/counterclaim. Potential subjects of interpretation can include the approach to take with regard to the duty to mitigate, the distinction between contributory fault and the failure to mitigate, as well as the relationship between local remedies and mitigation. This approach, however, would require consent from both contracting States and would thus involve diplomatic negotiations and political concerns.

Similarly, treaty amendments can be made to clarify the standard of due diligence required to mitigate. While most treaties on investment protection are silent on the issues of liability or causation, one can find exceptions in the model treaties of the US or Canada, which provide that claimants can only receive compensation for "loss or damage by reason of, or arising out of, that breach."[100] When amending existing treaties or negotiating new ones, contracting States can add that tribunals constituted under the treaty can only award "unavoidable" loss. They can also explicitly mention the investor's duty to mitigate or exclude damages arising out of the claimant's aggravating behaviors. The effects of these provisions, however, remain unknown due to the lack of cases interpreting clauses of this kind.

S.A.P.I.C., et al, v. Government of Turkmenistan (ICC Case No. 9058/FMS/KGA), Third Partial Award (September 2, 2000), para. 53.

97. Recent authors have notably criticized tribunals in ISDS of abandoning "crystalline" legal rules: *see*, e.g., Julian Arato, "The Private Law Critique of International Investment Law," 113 American Journal of International Law 1 (2019).
98. *See*, e.g., Art. 40(3) of the ASEAN Comprehensive Investment Agreement (signed on February 26, 2009) and Art. 8.31(3) of the Comprehensive Economic and Trade Agreement (signed on October 30, 2016).
99. *See*, e.g., Art. 12(5) of the EU-Vietnam FTA (signed on October 19, 2018).
100. Article 24(1)(a)(ii) of the 2012 US Model Bilateral Investment Treaty; Art. 22(1) of the 2004 Canadian model Foreign Investment Protection Agreement.

§17.04 CONCLUSION

Amid the backlash against the current ISDS system, nothing sparks more controversy than large damages awards that are not well reasoned. The principle of the duty to mitigate, while undeniably a general principle of law if one refers to transnational law, in fact, comes in all shapes and sizes. The divergence of the principle between common law and civil law systems, as well as that between French law and other systems of civil law, cannot be underestimated. The differences between domestic laws do not reject the duty to mitigate as a general principle. Rather, the differences suggest alternative possible approaches to the application of the same principle, which can be supported by related ideas such as causation, the duty to cooperate (for contracting parties), or good faith.

In investment arbitration, while a wide recognition of the principle appears to exist, some uncertainties persist with regard to the relationship between local remedies and mitigation, as well as the distinction between contributory fault and the failure to mitigate. These are linked to the fact-sensitive character of the reasonableness requirement of the duty to mitigate. Although investor-State tribunals have been sometimes unwilling to strictly enforce the duty to mitigate (with good reasons), this might not always be the case in the future. Following various examples contained in domestic laws, contracting States can modify their treaties or establish institutions interpreting the treaty to tailor the duty to mitigate in the way they see fit. The awareness of tribunals and practitioners with regard to the different types of duty to mitigate also needs to be increased. If the duty to mitigate can gain the attention it deserves, future tribunals can then decide on the types of duty that best fit the purpose of ISDS.

CHAPTER 18

Challenges in Quantifying Damages: Are Damages Getting the Treatment They Deserve by Investor-State Tribunals?

Ahmed Abdel-Hakam[*]

In the past twenty years, there has been an increased awareness of the importance of valuation in international investment disputes. Not only has the number of academic writings on this issue grown but also tribunals have dedicated more attention to calculation and valuation issues in their awards' A study by PricewaterhouseCoopers (PwC) in 2015, analysing ninety-five awards between 1990 and 2015, shows that the number of pages dedicated to explaining the basis for the quantification of damages has risen from eight in pre-2000 decisions to thirty-four pages in 2011–2015. In investment arbitration, tribunals apply a variety of valuation approaches and it is often not clear which tribunal will apply which approach and why. The lack of uniform practice and more foreseeable criteria leads to uncertainty and encourage the claimants to overstate their claims. Against this background, and within the context of investor-State dispute settlement (ISDS) reform, there are questions that need to be addressed: Are arbitrators who are law practitioners or legal academics sufficiently qualified to assess damages? Do arbitrators provide sufficient reasons for their findings on damages? Should new rules obliging arbitrators to provide sufficient reasons for their damages findings be introduced? Would not the ISDS system benefit from a mandatory tribunal-appointed expert to assist the tribunal in their understanding of the quantum and valuation issues? This chapter aims to answer these questions.

* The views expressed herein are those of the author alone, and are not an expression of the views of Eversheds Sutherland International LLP or any of its affiliates, employees or any of the author's or the firm's clients.

§18.01 INTRODUCTION

The question of the amount of damages[1] payable by a State for a breach of its international obligations has always been subject to a heated debate in the international law field. This is the obligation upon the State committing an international wrongful act to repair its breach by way of restitution or, if this is not possible, to pay monetary compensation for the damage incurred.[2] In customary international law, the main areas of debate relate to (a) the appropriate standard of compensation for expropriation; and (b) compensation for lost profits, in particular the applicability of the discounted cash flow (DCF) method of valuation.[3] These two issues have a significant impact upon the quantum of damages awarded to the successful party.

The award of damages and their quantum has always been a source of controversy in investment treaty arbitration. This controversy is best summarised by a United Nations Conference on Trade and Development (UNCTAD) working paper, which stated:

> Another aspect that was raised as warranting consideration by the Working Group was the determination of damages by arbitral Tribunals. In that respect, it was generally felt that concerns about incorrect calculation of damages by Tribunals could be linked to other concerns, for example, concerns about incorrect decisions by arbitral Tribunals and therefore, for the purposes of structuring the work, they could be considered as a sub-topic of those other concerns.[4]

A common perception also exists that there is a lack of a coherent approach to issues pertaining to damages. This situation is thought to lead to an uncertainty within the legal environment and the unpredictability of outcomes of disputes.[5] Some

---

1. Commentators have stated:

> Damages are traditionally understood as a legal remedy available in cases involving an illegal act, including acts contrary to international law. Damages denote the 'duty to pay for the detrimental consequences that the victim of an unlawful act has suffered'. The term 'compensation' had been previously used in international law to refer to the consequences of lawful exercise by States of their sovereign rights, specifically the right to expropriate foreign-owned property. This rigid distinction between 'compensation' and 'damages' has been eroded by the International Law Commission ('ILC'). In the ILC Articles on Responsibility of States for Internationally Wrongful Acts, the term 'compensation' as encompassing consequences of unlawful conduct and thereby changed the terminology of international law.

See S. Ripinsky and K. Williams, *Damages in International Investment Law*, The British Institute of International and Comparative Law (BIICL), 2008, p. 4. Therefore, this chapter uses the terms 'compensation' and 'damages' interchangeably.

2. *The Factory at Chorzow (Germany v. Poland)* (Claim for Indemnity) (Merits), (1928) PCIJ Rep, Ser. A, No. 17, 47.
3. C. McLachlan, L. Shore and M. Weinger, *International Investment Arbitration: Substantive Principles*, 2nd ed. OUP, 2017, p. 414.
4. UNCITRAL, 'Report of Working Group III (Investor-State Dispute Settlement Reform) on the work of its thirty-seventh session (New York, 1–5 April 2019)', UN Doc. No. A/CN.9/970 (9 April 2019); https://uncitral.un.org/en/working_groups/3/Investor-State.
5. S. Ripinsky and K. Williams, *Damages in International Investment Law*, p. 22.

commentators even describe the quantum of damages as 'one of the least understood and unpredictable areas of international investment law'.[6]

This chapter first sets out the scope of an arbitral tribunal's power to award damages. Next, it examines the perceived weaknesses of the current system pursuant to which arbitral tribunals award damages in investment treaty arbitrations. Finally, it proposes a way forward in an attempt to restore faith in the way damages are accorded in investment treaty arbitration.

§18.02 THE SCOPE OF AN ARBITRAL TRIBUNAL'S POWER TO AWARD DAMAGES

In order to properly assess the award of damages in investment arbitration, the proper scope of the tribunal's powers to order compensation to a successful party needs to be determined and considered. The width of such power is determined by the legal basis from which it derives. This section first examines the legal basis for an arbitral tribunal to award damages in an investor-State arbitration and then the extent to which a tribunal is obliged to provide reasons for its award of damages.

[A] Legal Basis for the Tribunal's Power to Award Damages

An arbitral tribunal hearing an investor-State dispute would generally have the power to award damages on four main grounds: (1) international investment agreements (IIAs); (2) customary international law; (3) general principles of law; (4) the body of case law developed by other international tribunals.[7] These sources are relevant as they provide the framework and guiding principles with which the award of damages should comply.

[1] International Investment Agreements

A large number of investor-State disputes are brought pursuant to the dispute resolution provision of the applicable IIA. The relevant IIA is generally the first source of law to be applied by a tribunal to any dispute brought under it. Indeed, a tribunal is required to apply international law according to the terms of the applicable treaty.[8] Three types of provisions with respect to damages can be identified in investment treaties.[9]

The first step is to examine the dispute resolution provision in an IIA. That provision enables investors to bring a claim when they incur damage as a result of a

6. N. Rubins and N.S. Kinsella, *International Investment, Political Risk and Dispute Resolution: A Practitioner's Guide*, Oceana Publications, 2005, 258.
7. S. Ripinsky and K. Williams, *Damages in International Investment Law*, 22.
8. *ADC v. Hungary*, Final Award of 2 October 2006, para. 481.
9. S. Ripinsky and K. Williams, *Damages in International Investment Law*, 22.

breach of one or more of the IIA's substantive obligations. For example, Article 82 of the 2002 Japan-Singapore Economic Partnership Agreement provides:

> For the purpose of this Chapter, an investment dispute is a dispute between a Party and an investor of the other Party that has incurred loss or damage by reason of, or arising out of, an alleged breach of any right conferred by this Chapter with respect to the investments of the investor of that other Party.[10]

Typically, this type of provision simply contains a reference to the incurred damage but does not specify the rules on compensation.

Second, a provision dealing with expropriation is contained in the vast majority of IIAs and provides that the expropriating State shall pay compensation to the investor. For example, Article 4 of the Switzerland-Georgia bilateral investment treaty (BIT) provides:

> Neither of the Contracting Parties shall take, either directly or indirectly, measures of expropriation, nationalization or any other measures having the same nature or the same effect against investments of investors of the other Contracting Party, unless the measures are taken in the public interest, on a non-discriminatory basis, and under due process of law, and provided that provisions be made for effective and adequate compensation. Such compensation shall amount to the market value of the investment expropriated immediately before the expropriatory action was taken or became public knowledge, whichever is earlier. The amount of compensation, interest at a normal commercial rate included, shall be settled in a freely convertible currency and paid without delay to the person entitled thereto without regard to its residence or domicile.[11]

Third, IIAs also generally contain provisions providing for compensation for losses sustained as a result of armed conflicts. For example, Article 4 of the UK-Serbia BIT provides:

> (1) Investors of one Contracting Party whose investments in the territory of the other Contracting Party suffer losses owing to war or other armed conflict, revolution, a state of national emergency, revolt, insurrection or riot in the territory of the latter Contracting Party shall be accorded by the latter Contracting Party treatment, as regards, restitution, indemnification, compensation or other settlement, no less favourable than that which the latter Contracting Party accords to its own investors or to investors of any third State. Resulting payments shall be freely transferable and shall be made without delay.[12]

Thus, although the precise wording of compensation provisions differs from one IIA to another, substantive principles of compensation typically are found only in expropriation clauses. Notably, investment treaties do not contain rules on compensation for damages incurred due to breaches of other substantive obligations such as

10. Article 82 of the 2002 Japan-Singapore Economic Partnership Agreement, https://www.mofa.go.jp/region/asia-paci/singapore/jsepa.html.
11. Switzerland-Georgia BIT, https://investmentpolicy.unctad.org/international-investment-agreements/countries/203/switzerland (accessed on 2 June 2020).
12. UK-Serbia BIT, https://investmentpolicy.unctad.org/international-investment-agreements/countries/221/united-kingdom (accessed on 2 June 2020).

national treatment, fair and equitable treatment or full protection and security. In these situations, awards of damages will be governed by customary international law.

[2] *Customary International Law*

Customary international law is a source to which an arbitral tribunal can have recourse when the applicable IIA does not include such rules or where the relevant treaty provisions are incomplete or vague. While arbitral tribunals recognise the importance of custom as a source of the applicable rule, like most international courts, they face a high evidentiary threshold for establishing the existence and content of the asserted customary rule. In practice, arbitral tribunals will typically turn to three main sources to find the customary rule on compensation.

[a] *ILC's Articles on Responsibility of States for Internationally Wrongful Acts*

First, a tribunal may look to the International Law Commission's ('ILC') Articles on Responsibility of States for Internationally Wrongful Acts ('ILC Articles'). The ILC Articles set out the conditions for a State to be held responsible for wrongful acts or omissions. They deal only with the so-called 'secondary' obligations of a State. These are the obligations that arise as a consequence of a breach by a State of a 'primary' international obligation. The ILC Articles purport to apply to all international obligations, regardless of their source or subject matter.[13] The result is that the ILC Articles form 'a single general regime of State responsibility' in international law, thereby potentially encompassing breaches by States of investment treaty provisions.[14]

The ILC Articles apply to investor-State disputes. Indeed, Article 33(2) of the ILC Articles states: 'This part is without prejudice to any right, arising from the international responsibility of a State, which may accrue directly to any person or entity other than a State.'[15] Article 33(2) was included in the ILC Articles to prevent any reading of Article 33(1) as precluding State responsibility for wrongs committed against private parties.[16] The commentary to Article 33(2) explicitly mentions investors' rights under BITs as one of the examples of State responsibility to non-State entities.[17]

---

13. The relevant ILC Articles that are directly relevant to compensation awards are Arts 31 (reparation); 34 (forms of reparation); 35 (restitution); 36 (compensation); 38 (interest); 39 (contribution to injury).
14. ILC Commentaries to Articles on State Responsibility, commentary to Art. 12, para. 5.
15. ILC Articles, Art. 33(2), https://www.un.org/en/ga/search/view_doc.asp?symbol=A/RES/56/83.
16. Article 33(1) of the ILC Articles provides: 'This Part is without prejudice to any right, arising from the international responsibility of a State, which may accrue directly to any person or entity other than a State.'
17. *See* ILC Commentaries to the Articles on State Responsibility, commentary to Art. 33, para. 4:

> (4) Such possibilities underlie the need for paragraph 2 of article 33. Part Two deals with the secondary obligations of States in relation to cessation and reparation, and those obligations may be owed, inter alia, to one or several States or to the international

In addition, the commentaries to the ILC Articles refer to decisions of the Iran-US Claims Tribunal, human rights courts and bodies and ICSID Tribunals.[18] These references are made despite the fact that in all these cases the claimants were private entities. Indeed, the ILC Articles Commentary notes that 'the rules and principles established by these bodies in assessing compensation can be seen as manifestations of the general principle stated in article 36 [on compensation]'.[19]

Moreover, the Permanent Court of International Justice (PCIJ) noted that the law of State responsibility is relevant in determining the amount of compensation for an injury suffered by a private party. In *Chorzow Factory*, the PCIJ held:

> It is a principle of international law that the reparation of a wrong may consist in an indemnity corresponding to the damage which the nationals of the injured State have suffered as a result of the act which is contrary to international law ... The reparation due by one State to another does not however change its character by reason of the fact that it takes form of an indemnity for the calculation of which the damage suffered by a private person is taken as the measure. The rules of law governing the reparation are the rules of international law in force between the State which has committed a wrongful act and the individual who has suffered damage.[20]

Moreover, in *MTD v. Chile*,[21] the Ad Hoc Annulment Committee suggested that since the ILC Articles cover claims brought by States on behalf of individuals within the framework of diplomatic protection, the same principles apply to claims for treaty breaches brought by individuals. Although to date only the Ad Hoc Annulment Committee in *MTD v. Chile* has briefly addressed the issue of applicability of the ILC Articles in investment disputes, several other tribunals referred to the ILC Articles as embodying international principles that are applicable in the award of damages in the investor-State context.[22]

> community as a whole. In cases where the primary obligation is owed to a non-State entity, it may be that some procedure is available whereby that entity can invoke the responsibility on its own account and without the intermediation of any State. *This is true, for example, under human rights treaties which provide a right of petition to a court or some other body for individuals affected. It is also true in the case of rights under bilateral or regional investment protection agreements.*

(Emphasis added.)

18. *See*, e.g., *ibid.*, commentary to Art. 36 at paras 2, 4 and 6 (citing, *The Gabcíkovo-Nagymaros Project*, ICJ case, p. 81, para. 152; *Velásquez Rodriguez*, Compensatory Damages case, Series C, No. 7 (1989)); *Asian Agricultural Products Limited v. Republic of Sri Lanka*, ICSID Reports (Cambridge University Press, 1997), vol. 4, p. 245 (1990).
19. ILC Commentaries, Commentary to Art. 36, para. 6.
20. *The Factory at Chorzow (Germany v. Poland)* (Claim for Indemnity) (Merits), (1928) PCIJ Rep, Ser A, No 17 27–28.
21. *MTD v. Chile*, Decision on the Application for Annulment of 21 March 2007, para. 99.
22. *See*, e.g., *British Gas v. Argentina*, Final Award of 24 December 2007, paras 426–427; *Siemens v. Argentina*, Award of 6 February 2007, para. 350; *ADC v. Hungary*, Final Award of 2 October 2006, para. 494; *CME v. Czech Republic*, Final Award of 14 March 2003, para. 501; *Nykomb v. Latvia*, Award of 16 December 2003, paras 38–39.

Some commentators have argued that arbitrators give too much authority and influence the ILC articles, and that they refer to them as 'too easily and uncritically'.[23] Other leading authors have suggested that before relying on the ILC Articles, tribunals should probably examine the commentaries and reports for each article shedding light on the practice underlying the rule, the discussions of the ILC and the comments of various governments.[24] As a matter of practice, arbitral tribunals tend to treat the ILC Articles as evidence and as general reflection of international custom.[25] Indeed, the benefit of the ILC Articles is that they provide the rules on State responsibility 'ready for use' by any arbitrator or tribunal. The International Court of Justice (ICJ) has not hesitated to characterise some of the ILC Articles as reflecting customary international law without any additional discussion of why it deems them as such.[26]

[b] *Jurisprudence of International Courts and Tribunals*

A tribunal may also consider decisions of courts and tribunals that have established the content of customary rules. In the area of compensation for damage caused by international wrongs, the most influential decision is that of the PCIJ in *Chorzow Factory*, which held:

> The essential principle contained in the actual notion of an illegal act – a principle which seems to be established by international practice and in particular by the decisions of arbitral Tribunals – is that reparation must, as far as possible, wipe-out all the consequences of the illegal act and re-establish the situation which would, in all probability, have existed if that act had not been committed. Restitution in kind, or, if this is not possible, payment of a sum corresponding to the value which a restitution in kind would bear; the award, if need be, of damages for loss sustained which would not be covered by restitution in kind or payment in place of it – such are the principles which should serve to determine the amount of compensation due for an act contrary to international law.[27]

This judgment recognised the function of reparation in international law and identified, in general terms, the principles of restitution and compensation, which are still authoritative to date.

---

23. D.D. Caron, 'The ILC Articles on State Responsibility: The Paradoxical Relationship between Form and Authority', 96 American J. Int'l L. 867 (2002).
24. *Ibid.*, at 872–873.
25. A complete catalogue of instances of application of the ILC Articles by international courts and Tribunals can be found in S. Olleson, *Impact of the International Law Commission's Articles on Responsibility of States for Internationally Wrongful Acts*, British Institute of International and Comparative Law, 2007).
26. ICJ, *Case Concerning the Application of the Convention on the Prevention and Punishment of the Crime of Genocide (Bosnia and Herzegovina v. Serbia and Montenegro)*, Judgment of 26 February 2007, paras 285, 388, 398, 401 and 407, https://www.icj-cij.org/files/case-related/91/091-20070226-JUD-01-00-EN.pdf (accessed 2 June 2020).
27. *The Factory at Chorzow (Germany v. Poland)* (Claim for Indemnity) (Merits), (1928) PCIJ Rep, Series A, No. 17 (1928) 47.

[c] Resolutions of the UN General Assembly

An arbitral tribunal could also refer to UN General Assembly resolutions. Indeed, resolutions of the UN General Assembly have been accepted as evidence of the consensus of States on a number of legal issues. While the resolutions are not listed under Article 38 of the ICJ Statute as a source of international law, they can be evidence of State practice. Resolutions of the General Assembly are recommendatory and not binding on the UN Member States.[28] However, the practice of the ICJ has been to refer increasingly to the UN General Assembly resolutions as evidence of existing and evolving rules. In its Advisory Opinion in *Nuclear Weapons*, for example, the ICJ noted that:

> The Court notes that General Assembly resolutions, even if they are not binding, may sometimes have normative value. They can, in certain circumstances, provide evidence important for establishing the existence of a rule or the emergence of an *opinio juris*. To establish whether this is true of a given General Assembly resolution, it is necessary to look at its content and the conditions of its adoption; it is also necessary to see whether an *opinio juris* exists as to its normative character. Or a series of resolutions may show the gradual evolution of the *opinio juris* required for the establishment of a new rule.[29]

In *Texaco v. Libya,* General Assembly resolutions were used by an investment tribunal as evidence of custom.[30] This dispute concerned the compensation to be paid by Libya to two US companies on the expropriation of their foreign assets. At issue was the respective customary law status of two General Assembly resolutions. The first, Resolution No. 1803, adopted in 1962, provided that in cases of nationalisation or expropriation 'the owner shall be paid appropriate compensation, in accordance with the rules in force in the State taking such measures in the exercise of its sovereignty and in accordance with international law'.[31]

The second resolution at issue was the Charter of Economic Rights and Duties of 1974. Article 2(2)(C) of the Charter provided that where there has been a nationalisation or expropriation:

> appropriate compensation should be paid by the State adopting such measures, taking into account its relevant laws and regulations and all circumstances that the State considers pertinent. In any case where the question of compensation gives rise to controversy, it shall be settled under the domestic law of the nationalising State and by its Tribunals, unless it is freely and mutually agreed by all States concerned that other peaceful means be sought on the basis of the sovereign equality of States and in accordance with the principle of free choice of means.[32]

---

28. Charter of the United Nations, Arts 10–14.
29. *Legality of the Threat or Use of Nuclear Weapons* [1996] ICJ Rep 226, 254–255, para. 70.
30. *Texaco v. Libya,* Award on the Merits of 10 October 1977, 53 ILR 389.
31. Permanent Sovereignty over Natural Resources, General Assembly resolution 1803 (XVII), New York, 14 December 1962, https://www.un.org/ga/search/view_doc.asp?symbol=A/RES/1803 (XVII).
32. Charter of Economic Rights and Duties of States, General Assembly resolution 3281 (XXIX), New York, 12 December 1974, https://www.un.org/ga/search/view_doc.asp?symbol=a/res/3281 (XXIX).

The critical point of difference between the two resolutions was that Resolution No. 1803 required that compensation be paid according to the principles of international law, while the Charter required only that appropriate compensation should be paid according to the laws of the appropriating State, with no mention of international law. The sole arbitrator in the case was required to determine which of these two resolutions better represented customary international law. While each of the resolutions had been adopted by a significant majority of States, the arbitrator examined the respective voting patterns for each resolution and concluded that the 1974 Charter had not been supported by 'any of the developed countries with market economies which carry on the biggest part of international trade'.[33] He also noted, 'The absence of any connection between the procedure of compensation and international law and the subjection of this procedure solely to municipal law cannot be regarded by this Tribunal except as a *de lege ferenda* formulation, which even appears contra legem in the eyes of many developed countries.'[34]

On these grounds, the arbitrator found that Resolution No. 1803 was the accurate statement of customary international law at that time.[35] Later, Resolution No. 1803 was similarly recognised as an authoritative evidence of custom by the arbitral tribunal in *Kuwait v. Aminol.*[36]

[3] General Principles of Law

The 'general principles of law recognized by civilized nations' is a source of international law serving to fill any possible gaps left by treaty and customary rules. In *LIAMCO v. Libya,* the tribunal defined general principles as follows:

> These general principles are usually embodied in most recognized legal systems, and particularly in Libyan legislation, including its modern codes and Islamic law. They are applied by municipal courts and are mainly referred to in international and arbitral case-law. They, thus, form a compendium of legal precepts and maxims, universally accepted in theory and practice. Instances of such precepts are, inter alia, the principle of the sanctity of property and contracts, the respect of acquired vested rights, the prohibition of unjust enrichment, the obligation of compensation in cases of expropriation and wrongful damage, etc.[37]

International courts and tribunals have also frequently referred to principles of international law. For example, in the *Chorzow Factory* judgment, the PCIJ described the obligation to make reparation in the following terms: 'It is a principle of international law, and even a general conception of law, that any breach of an engagement involves an obligation to make reparation.'[38]

33. *Texaco v. Libya*, Award on the Merits of 10 October 1977, 86 ILR 389.
34. *Ibid.*
35. *Ibid.*
36. *Kuwait v. Aminoil*, Award of 24 March 1982, para. 143.
37. *LIAMCO v. Libya*, Award of 12 April 1977, 1981, 20 ILM, 72.
38. *The Factory at Chorzow (Germany v. Poland)* (Claim for Indemnity) (Merits), (1928) PCIJ Rep, Series A, No. 17 (1928) 29.

Moreover, international tribunals in investor-State disputes have identified a number of general principles of law. These include:

- *Restitutio in integrum* is a primary remedy for international wrongs; it is inapplicable only to the extent that the restoration of the *status quo ante* is impossible.[39]
- Compensation should undo the material harm inflicted by a breach of an international obligation.[40]
- The damages in cases of breaches of contractual obligations should cover only the direct and foreseeable prejudice.[41]
- The claimant carries the burden of proof in respect of the claimed losses; the probative weight of the evidence is for the tribunal to determine; in cases where proof of a fact presents extreme difficulty, a tribunal may be satisfied with less conclusive proof, that is, prima facie evidence.[42]
- Compensation is payable only in respect of harm that is proved to have a sufficient causal link with the provision alleged to have been breached.[43]
- An injured person has a duty to mitigate damages.[44]

These principles of law serve as a helpful framework which allows investor-State tribunals to assess and grant damages.

[4] Body of Case Law of International Tribunals

It is a standard practice for parties to investment disputes and international tribunals to consistently refer to earlier awards.[45] Arbitral tribunals tend to consider previous awards as authoritative or at least persuasive, particularly where they have been well-reasoned and rendered by respected arbitrators, but not as binding on them. In *Saipem v. Bangladesh*, the tribunal took an approach, which is shared by many arbitrators:

> The Tribunal considers that it is not bound by previous decisions. At the same time, it is of the opinion that it must pay due consideration to earlier decisions of international Tribunals. It believes that, subject to compelling contrary grounds, it has a duty to adopt solutions established in a series of consistent cases. It also believes that, subject to the specifics of a given treaty and of the circumstances of the actual case, it has a duty to seek to contribute to the harmonious development

39. *See supra* n. 33, paras 97–109.
40. *Myers v. Canada*, Partial Award of 13 November 2000, para. 315. *See also SwemBalt v. Latvia*, Award of 23 October 2000, para. 38.
41. *Amco v. Indonesia I*, Award on the Merits of 20 November 1984, (1992) 89 ILR 368 para. 268.
42. *Myers v. Canada*, Partial Award of 13 November 2000, para. 316; *AAPL v. Sri Lanka*, Award of 27 June 1990, para. 56.
43. *Ibid.*, para. 316.
44. *Autopista v. Venezuela*, Final Award of 23 September 2003, para. 395.
45. J. Commission, 'Precedent in Investment Treaty Arbitration: The Empirical Backing', 4(5) Transn'l Disp. Mgmt. (2007).

of investment law and thereby to meet the legitimate expectations of the community of States and investors towards certainty of the rule of law.[46]

Further, when it comes to the order in which an arbitral tribunal would apply these sources, a tribunal would first examine the relevant investment treaty. As the tribunal in *ADC v. Hungary* noted, 'There is general authority for the view that a BIT can be considered as a lex specialis whose provisions will prevail over rules of customary international law.'[47] Also, the ILC Articles provide that they 'do not apply where and to the extent that ... the content or implementation of the international responsibility of a State are governed by special rules of international law'.[48]

Tribunals have ruled that where the treaty does not set out rules on compensation that would apply in a specific case, or its provisions are incomplete or vague, the tribunal will refer to international customary law, unless the treaty provides for subsidiary application of a different law, such as the law of the host State. For example, in *MTD v. Chile*, the tribunal held that 'for purposes of Article 42(1) of the Convention, the Parties have agreed to this arbitration under the BIT. This instrument being a treaty, the agreement to arbitrate under the BIT requires the Tribunal to apply international law'.[49]

[B] Are Arbitral Tribunals Obliged to Justify Their Award of Damages?

It is widely accepted that an arbitral tribunal must give reasons for its award. Indeed, many arbitration rules and statutes indicate that for other than consent awards, reasons must be given subject to contrary agreement of the parties.[50] The provision of reasons also supports the entitlement to call for corrections, interpretations and additional awards. This obligation to provide reasons naturally encompasses the obligation to provide reasons underlying the tribunal's decision on the award of damages.

This obligation to justify an award on damages is even more important in light of what leading commentators and practitioners have described as the 'extraordinary power' on the part of investor-State tribunals to discipline States by the imposition of damages awards. For example, in *CME v. Czech Republic*,[51] the tribunal ordered the Czech Republic to pay USD 353 million to the investor. This amount roughly equated to the Czech Republic's entire health-care budget for the relevant year. If adjusted for population size and gross national income, the amount was equivalent to an award of USD 19 billion against the United Kingdom; USD 26 billion against Germany; and USD 131 billion against the US.[52] In practice, awards as large as these are material allocations of public funds, which may have a direct impact beyond the immediate

46. *Saipem v. Bangladesh*, Decision on Jurisdiction and Recommendation on Provisional Measures of 21 March 2007, para. 67.
47. *ADC v. Hungary*, Final Award of 2 October 2006, para. 481.
48. ILC Articles on State Responsibility, Art. 55.
49. See *MTD v. Chile*, Award of 25 May 2004, para. 87.
50. Lord Bingham, 'Reasons and Reasons for Reasons', 4 Arb. Int'l 142–143 (1988).
51. *CME Czech Republic BV v. Czech Republic*, Award on Damages, 14 March 2003.
52. T. Landau, '*Reasons for reasons: The Tribunal's duty in Investor-State Arbitration*', ICCA Congress Series No. 14, Dublin Conference, 2008, Kluwer 2009, p. 196.

parties to the dispute.[53] Thus, there exists the need to rethink the way damages are considered and awarded by arbitral tribunals in the context of investor-State disputes.

§18.03 WEAKNESSES OF THE CURRENT SYSTEM

The perceived weaknesses of the current system of awards of damages should be identified. These include the consistent trend in the increase of the value of claims filed by investors; the perception of lack of reasoning or justification; the perception of unfair or unrealistic compensation; and whether the arbitrators are sufficiently qualified to consider financial valuation models. The assessment of these issues will assist in proposing a way forward in the reform of the way damages are awarded in investor-State arbitration.

[A] Inflation of Claims

A study on damages and costs published in late 2017, which examined 140 publicly available investment treaty awards between 2012 and mid-2017, showed that the mean amount claimed in investment treaty arbitrations from 2013 onwards has increased significantly during that period. The mean amount claimed increased from USD 491.7 million as of the end of 2012 to USD 2.3 billion by 2017. Even excluding the very substantial award in *Yukos*,[54] the mean amount claimed is now USD 1.133 billion. However, these mean figures are distorted by the larger claims, and the median amount claimed from 2013 onwards was a more modest USD 196.4 million (as compared to USD 66.1 million at the end of 2012). Interestingly, despite the increasing size of the average claim, the mean length of proceedings has only increased by around six months, from 3.7 years before the end of 2012 to 4.3 years from 2013 onwards.[55]

In cases since the end of 2012, the mean amount claimed (again excluding *Yukos*) has risen from USD 491 million to USD 1.1 billion. However, this figure masks an interesting discrepancy between claims: those that succeed and those that do not. In cases from 2013 onwards (excluding *Yukos*), the average amount claimed where the claimant was ultimately successful was USD 794 million, compared to USD 1.5 billion in cases where the claimant was unsuccessful. It would appear, therefore, that flawed claims continue to drive up the average amount claimed.[56]

[B] Lack of Sufficient Reasoning

The lack of sufficient reasoning is also an additional perceived weakness in the way tribunals deal with damages. Indeed, an in-depth analysis of damages in investment

53. *Ibid.*
54. In the *Yukos* case, the Russian Federation was ordered to pay approximately USD 50 billion.
55. https://globalarbitrationreview.com/article/1151755/damages-and-costs-in-investment-treaty-arbitration-revisited.
56. *Ibid.*

arbitration carried out by the international accounting firm of PwC has shown that tribunals have taken that concern into consideration by providing more detailed rationale to their damages award. The study shows that tribunals provide more detailed explanations of their approach to damages now than ever before – the number of pages dedicated to damages in awards has increased from an average of eight pages pre-2000 to thirty-four pages in the last five years.[57]

[C] Perception of Unfair and Unrealistic Compensation: The Case of *Tethyan v. Pakistan*

Some arbitral awards, notwithstanding the adequacy of the valuation method used, are the source of intense criticism because of the very high amounts that are awarded to the investor. The most recent case that attracted attention and was subject to heavy commentary in the investment arbitration community is *Tethyan v. Pakistan*.[58] Tethyan was a joint venture between Antofagasta and the Canadian firm Barrick Gold Corporation, which began exploring an area of the Pakistani province of Baluchistan in 2006, discovering what it understood to be one of the world's largest undeveloped copper and gold deposits with a potential life of more than fifty years. However, in 2011, a mining lease application was formally rejected by Baluchistani authorities, and in January 2012 Tethyan turned to arbitration at ICSID under the Australia-Pakistan BIT.

Tethyan alleged that it had conducted extensive feasibility studies and had invested more than USD 220 million in preparing the mine before the Baluchistan government refused to grant the licence in 2011 and the project stalled. In 2017, Pakistan was held to have breached the Australia-Pakistan BIT. Hearings on damages were then held in May 2018, before the proceedings were closed in March 2019, leading to the final July 2019 damages ruling which awarded Tethyan nearly USD 6 billion in damages, including interest.[59] Put into perspective, that amount represented around 2% of Pakistan's GDP, or around 40% of the country's total liquid foreign exchange reserves. The award was not well received either by the Government or by the public opinion of Pakistan. The Attorney General of Pakistan made a statement noting that 'international Tribunals are also urged to consider the implications of their decisions and the impact on development and poverty alleviation'.[60]

57. PwC International Arbitration damages research – 2015, 3, https://www.google.com/url?sa=t&rct=j&q=&esrc=s&source=web&cd=2&ved=2ahUKEwiNiuGalY3oAhXDZxUIHZeWBFUQFjABegQIAhAB&url=https%3A%2F%2Fwww.pwc.com%2Fsg%2Fen%2Fpublications%2Fassets%2Finternational-arbitation-damages-research-2015.pdf&usg=AOvVaw2nFput_nRVXla6M4B_wGLF.
58. *Tethyan Copper Company Pty Limited v. Islamic Republic of Pakistan*, ICSID Case No. ARB/12/1, Award, 12 July 2019.
59. *Ibid.*, at para. 1858.
60. https://www.iareporter.com/articles/pakistan-faces-hefty-loss-in-newly-rendered-icsid-award-in-tethyan-copper-mining-case-core-damages-exceed-4-billion-and-pre-award-interest-adds-another-1-75-billion/.

The tribunal's multi-billion dollar valuation of Tethyan mining project that had not commenced operations drew even more criticism because it contrasted with other contemporaneous mining cases such as *Bear Creek v. Peru*[61] and *South American Silver v. Bolivia,*[62] where projects at very early stages of development were deemed unsuited to a DCF analysis, which is a valuation method used to estimate the value of an investment based on its future cash flows.[63]

Concerning damages, the first question confronting the tribunal was whether the DCF approach to valuation could be applied in the case, and if so, whether a traditional DCF model or the so-called modern DCF model should be applied. The tribunal agreed with Pakistan's legal expert witness that 'fundamental uncertainties' in relation to a project would make a DCF valuation inappropriate. However, the tribunal saw no such uncertainties in the project. A feasibility study had demonstrated the investor's plans for the project, backed by two of the world's largest mining companies, which had already significantly invested in it, the tribunal noted. While some elements of the claimant's proposed DCF model would need adjustment, the tribunal observed, this did not entail any 'fundamental uncertainty' about the project's success.[64]

Thus, a DCF valuation was held to be appropriate for the project. Furthermore, the tribunal pointed to various features of the 'modern DCF' approach[65] that favoured its use in preference to a traditional DCF analysis. In particular, the modern DCF approach attached risk discounts to specific elements of cash flow, rather than applying an overall discount rate to a project's entire cash flow. For the tribunal, this avoided the problem that cash flows far into the future would have almost zero value under the

61. *Bear Creek Mining Corporation v. Republic of Peru,* ICSID Case No. ARB/14/21, Award, 30 November 2017, paras 698–704; https://www.italaw.com/cases/2848.
62. *South American Silver Limited v. Bolivia,* PCA Case No. 2013-15, Award, 22 November 2018, paras 808–823, https://www.italaw.com/cases/2121.
63. A damages publication by FTI defines DCF as follows:

> DCF generally involves quantifying the future cash flows that an asset is expected to generate (whether it be a factory, mine, or parcel of shares in a company). A discount factor (based on a discount rate) is then used to calculate the present value of those cash flows. The purpose of this discounting is to account for the time value of money and the level of risk or uncertainty inherent in the cash flows. Usually, the higher the risk the higher the discount rate.

http://ftiexpertstoronto.com/wp-content/uploads/2019/11/EFC-Canada_IA_Damages-Insights-November-2019.pdf (last accessed on 2 June 2020), 9.
64. *Tethyan Copper Company Pty Limited v. Islamic Republic of Pakistan,* ICSID Case No. ARB/12/1, Award, 12 July 2019, para. 301, https://www.italaw.com/cases/1631.
65. A Damages publication by FTI defines the modern DCF approach as follows:

> Under the 'modern DCF' approach, the forecasted cash flows are reduced by a risk adjustment and then these cash flows are discounted at the 'risk-free' rate. Accordingly, rather than the discount rate encapsulating both the time value of money and cash flow risk, the risk is captured in the cash flows themselves, and only the time value of money is reflected in the discount rate. This approach transfers the challenge of determining the risk premium appropriate to a given expected cash flow, to determining the appropriate risk adjustments in the cash flow forecast itself.

http://ftiexpertstoronto.com/wp-content/uploads/2019/11/EFC-Canada_IA_Damages-Insights-November-2019.pdf (last accessed on 2 June 2020), p. 9.

traditional DCF model, because of the compounding effect of applying a constant discount rate even though risks were roughly constant over time. Moreover, the modern DCF approach used in *Tethyan* took into account the possibility that project managers would respond to changing conditions with appropriate operational decisions.[66] Furthermore, the modern DCF approach used by the tribunal in the same case provided for a distinction between 'systematic' risks to a project (which may have positive or negative effects on the project, such as price fluctuations) and 'asymmetric' risks (which have only negative effects, such as terrorist attacks).[67]

Pakistan objected that the modern DCF approach was not used in the mining industry. However, relying on information from a Canadian mining industry body, the tribunal found that the approach was contemplated. If a hypothetical buyer of the project in 2011 would have used the modern DCF approach, the tribunal said, it should then be applied in valuation here. The tribunal admitted that no prior tribunal had used it, but reasoned that tribunals were also reluctant to use traditional DCF valuations until the practice changed.[68]

In the tribunal's view, the parties' main disagreement was whether TCC's proposed modern DCF model accurately captured all risks in the project, since neither party had offered a traditional DCF valuation, or any usable alternative valuation.[69] As a result, the tribunal agreed to adopt the modern DCF method to be confirmed by reference to any other available data.[70]

Irrespective of whether or not the use of the modern DCF approach was adequate, the very high sums awarded by certain tribunals beg the question whether the parties have full confidence that the tribunal fully appreciates the financial issues attached to the valuation of the project. In other words, do the members of the tribunal have the required qualifications to award such high sums without questioning the methods used?

---

66. *Tethyan Copper Company Pty Limited v. Islamic Republic of Pakistan,* ICSID Case No. ARB/12/1, Award, 12 July 2019, para. 340, https://www.italaw.com/cases/1631.
67. *Ibid.*, para. 346.
68. *Ibid.*, para. 360:

> In any event, however, the Tribunal considers that the absence of investment treaty jurisprudence – affirmative or negative – does not in itself constitute a valid ground for rejecting a valuation method if the Tribunal is otherwise convinced that it is sound to apply it in the present case. As valuation practices for mineral properties develop in the industry itself, the assessment of damages may likewise evolve in investment treaty arbitration. As correctly pointed out by Claimant, the use of the traditional DCF method was even rejected in early jurisprudence but then became more and more common and established for the assessment of damages in investment treaty arbitration. The Tribunal also recalls that the appropriate valuation method can only be selected in the circumstances of each individual case and based on the submissions and evidence brought before the respective tribunal.

69. https://www.iareporter.com/articles/newly-published-damages-award-reveals-that-tethyan-v-pakistan-Tribunal-adopted-modern-dcf-valuation-method/.
70. *Ibid.* The damages award is available at: https://www.italaw.com/sites/default/files/case-documents/italaw10737.pdf. *See* para. 345 of the Damages Award.

[D] Are Arbitrators Well-Equipped to Handle Valuation?

This chapter does not call for an entire overhaul of the way in which arbitral tribunals award damages in investor-State disputes. The objective is rather to break down the different steps of the tribunal's analysis and identify what is the weakest link in the process. Broadly speaking, a tribunal must identify: (a) a breach; (b) an injury; and (c) a causal link between the wrongful act and the injury. Once this three-step identification process is completed ('Pre-quantification Phase'), the tribunal proceeds with quantifying the damage.

A large number of accounting tools are available to an arbitral tribunal to carry out this quantification, and the parties' experts also put forward their own suggested mechanism of quantifying such damage. These include:

- an Income-Based approach, which consists in using methods that convert anticipated economic benefits into a single present value amount (the most famous method and the most popular among tribunals being the DCF method);
- a Market-Based approach, suing methods that compare the business or business interest to similar businesses or business interests; and
- the Asset-Based approach, using methods based on the current market value of assets net of liabilities.[71]

Arbitrators normally are well suited and meet the qualification threshold to conduct the Pre-quantification Phase. However, whether arbitrators, which for the vast majority consist of lawyers and legal academics, are best placed to handle and fully appreciate the adequacy of valuation methods put forward by the parties is an entirely different issue.

Many argue this is precisely why parties appoint experts. The experts' role is to make these damages models intelligible to the members of the tribunal. However, from another perspective, if counsel is allowed to instruct experts to quantify the damages, why are arbitral tribunals not given the possibility to systematically have recourse to their own expert to understand the valuations put forward by the parties? There are a number of ways that may be taken to remedy this problem.

§18.04 PROPOSED WAY FORWARD

In this section, we explore potential avenues for reforming the way damages are awarded in investor-State arbitration. One way is to revise the existing arbitration rules to require that tribunals appoint experts. Another option is to require that appointed arbitrators have the necessary accounting skills to understand the valuation methods to properly assess the damage as is the case for some US court judges who specialise in specific valuation disputes. In parallel, a number of initiatives have been put forward

71. Mark Kantor, *Valuation for Arbitration*, Wolters Kluwer, p. 9.

by some institutions such as the European Commission to tackle the issue of award of damages.

[A] Increase the Use of Tribunal-Appointed Experts

In appropriate cases, arbitrators may employ their own expert. Several of the most popular arbitration rules (such as the ICC,[72] LCIA,[73] SIAC,[74] and HKIAC[75]) authorise the use of tribunal-appointed experts. Some ICSID cases also have witnessed recourse to tribunal-appointed experts.[76] A PwC study on damages in international arbitration[77] noted that where there is a great deal of divergence between experts and/or calculations are highly complex, a tribunal might appoint its own expert to help navigate the differences. The tribunal in *Suez and Vivendi v. Argentina* appointed an independent expert to assist it due to the perceived complexity of the case and the widely differing conclusions reached by the parties' experts.[78] The appointment of an expert by the tribunal can also happen where the tribunal lacks confidence in the evidence given by the parties' experts. In *HEP v. Slovenia*, the tribunal appointed its own expert, partly due to the complexity of the case and partly 'because neither party's experts provided a clear and convincing damages case'.[79]

Although such an appointment is likely to increase costs, it can also help tribunals address issues outside their own expertise when all other approaches have failed. In *HEP v. Slovenia*, the tribunal commented that it had 'benefited significantly'

72. Article 25(4) of the ICC arbitration Rules (2017) provides: 'The arbitral tribunal, after having consulted the parties, may appoint one or more experts, define their terms of reference and receive their reports. At the request of a party, the parties shall be given the opportunity to question at a hearing any such expert.'
73. Article 21.1 of the LCIA Arbitration Rules (2014) provides: 'The Arbitral Tribunal, after consultation with the parties, may appoint one or more experts to report in writing to the Arbitral Tribunal and the parties on specific issues in the arbitration, as identified by the Arbitral Tribunal.'
74. Article 26.1(a) of the SIAC Arbitration Rules (2016) provides: 'Unless otherwise agreed by the parties, the Tribunal may: (a) following consultation with the parties, appoint an expert to report on specific issues.'
75. Article 25.1 of the HKIAC Arbitration Rules (2018) provide:

> To assist it in the assessment of evidence, the arbitral tribunal, after consulting with the parties, may appoint one or more experts. Such expert shall report to the arbitral tribunal, in writing, on specific issues to be determined by the arbitral tribunal. After consulting with the parties, the arbitral tribunal shall establish terms of reference for the expert, and shall communicate a copy of the expert's terms of reference to the parties and HKIAC.

76. The *CMS v. Argentina* Tribunal appointed its own expert for valuation purposes. *See CMS v. Argentina*, ICSID Case No. ARB/01/08, Award, 12 May 2005, paras 418 et seq.; *See also LG&E v. Argentina*, ICSID Case No. ARB/02/01, Award, 25 July 2007, Final Award, para. 6.
77. PwC International Arbitration damages research – 2017, p. 6. https://www.pwc.co.uk/services/forensic-services/disputes/insights/pwc-international-arbitration-damages-research-2017.html.
78. *Suez Sociedad General de Aguas de Barcelona S.A*, and *Vivendi Universal S.A v. The Argentine Republic*, ICSID Case No. ARB/03/19, award dated 9 April 2015.
79. *Hrvatska Elecktroprivreda D.D v. Republic of Slovenia*, ICSID Case No. ARB/05/24, award dated 17 December 2015, paras 174 and 609.

from its expert's insights, 'especially given the vastly differing assessments offered by the party-appointed experts. The tribunal has found Mr Jones' analysis most useful and has to a significant extent followed his recommendation'.[80] However, the cost of a tribunal-appointed expert may be significant. In addition, when an expert is appointed by a tribunal the parties may suspect that the expert will become a de facto the fourth arbitrator. As a result, arbitrators must be careful to ensure that the parties are provided with a full and fair opportunity to be heard.[81] It is also more difficult for the tribunal to dissociate itself from the findings of an expert it has appointed than from the findings of party-appointed experts.[82]

[B] Is the Answer in US Court Litigation? The Example of Appraisal Litigation in the State of Delaware

In combination with the use of tribunal-appointed experts, arbitral tribunals may benefit from considering the practice of US court judges who are heavily involved in complex valuations. This will increase the arbitrators' familiarity with how complex valuations are handled.

The output from US courts about valuation questions has been prolific and is a very valuable resource for valuation-related issues. For example, a leading commentator on valuation noted:

> The Delaware Court of Chancery has developed substantial expertise in valuation matters involving dissenting shareholder appraisal cases and other shareholder valuation disputes. US tax firms similarly have a long record of considering valuation issues. Working inside one of the most complex tax systems in the world, the US tax authorities have built up a body of valuation precedents out of tax disputes in such varied areas such as M&A transactions, spin-offs, recapitalisations and restructurings. US bankruptcy courts, too, have acquired valuation expertise. Bankruptcy courts will, for example, regularly examine complex valuation evidence to decide if a plan of reorganisations properly values the insolvent enterprise for purposes of settling creditor and shareholder claims and interests. Bankruptcy courts also assess the debtor's value to decide if a transfer of assets was made at a time when the debtor company was 'insolvent' and the assets thus subject to recovery.[83]

Taking the example of appraisal litigation in the State of Delaware, the Delaware General Corporation Law provides that if the controlling shares in a public company vote in favour of a merger with another company, then the remaining shareholders are also required to tender their shares to the successful acquirer. Although forced by operation of law to tender their shares, the dissenters may accept the share price offered generally by the acquirer or, in some circumstances, they may instead initiate

80. *Ibid.*, para. 174.
81. M. Kantor, *Valuation for Arbitration*, Wolters Kluwer, p. 305.
82. *Inside the Black Box: How Arbitral Tribunals Operate and Reach Their Decisions*, Edited by B. Berger and M. Schneider, ASA Special Series No. 42, p. 84.
83. M. Kantor, *Valuation for Arbitration*, Wolters Kluwer, p. 5.

'fair value' appraisal proceedings under section 262 of the Delaware General Corporations Law before the Chancery Court in an effort to obtain a higher price. With so many corporations established under Delaware law, it should come as no surprise that Delaware's courts have produced a large body of valuation precedents in dissenting shareholder appraisal cases.[84]

In order to determine fair value, Delaware courts have to 'take into account all relevant factors'. As explained by the Delaware Supreme Court in *Tri-Continental Corp. v. Battye*:

> Market value, asset value, dividends, earning prospects, the nature of the enterprise and any other facts which were known or which could be ascertained as of the date of merger and which throw any light on future prospects of the merged corporation are not only pertinent to an inquiry as to the value of the dissenting stockholders' interest, but must be considered by the agency fixing the value.[85]

However, pursuant to section 262(h), Delaware courts are required to determine the fair value 'exclusive of any element of value arising from the accomplishment or expectation of the merger or consolidation, together with interest, if any, to be paid upon the amount determined to be the fair value'.[86] This means any synergies expected from the merger should be excluded in determining the fair value of the target company, because the appraisal's 'purpose is to compensate dissenting stockholders for what was taken from them'.[87] Commentators, however, have warned arbitrators in commercial and investor-State arbitrations not to be tempted to adopt a similar approach to the one used by Delaware courts because the valuation 'principles in the "fair value" dissenting shareholder cases are occasionally idiosyncratic'. One of the reasons for caution is that Delaware law does not assign the burden of proof to either the petitioner or respondent. Instead, the court must reach an independent valuation of the enterprise.[88]

Although valuation principles developed in one field of legal endeavour should not be adopted into another field without prior careful consideration, the view that the system under which the tribunal reaches its own independent valuation, without for the parties having to quantify their claims, has some merit. First, from a cost perspective, it would cut down the cost of party-appointed experts, which can range from hundreds of thousands to over USD 1 million for each party. Second, this approach could limit the inflationary trend in the value of amounts claimed by investors in investor-State arbitration.

The purpose of taking the example of the Delaware courts is that its findings on valuation are not nearly as contested as the arbitrators' findings on damages. A clear answer to that difference in perception is unclear. However, perhaps by ensuring that

84. *Ibid.*
85. *Tri-Continental Corporation v. Battye*, 74 A.2d 71 (1950) (decision is available at https://law.justia.com/cases/delaware/supreme-court/1950/74-a-2d-71-3.html (accessed on 2 June 2020).
86. Delaware General Corporations Law, s. 262(h).
87. https://corpgov.law.harvard.edu/2019/03/01/appraisal-litigation-in-delaware-trends-in-petitions-and-opinions-2006-2018//.
88. M. Kantor, *Valuation for Arbitration*, Wolters Kluwer, p. 5.

appointed arbitrators have a solid qualification or background in accounting or financial valuation would help alleviate the perceived suspicions about arbitrators' skill and understanding in handling valuation issues. Indeed, when appointing tribunal members, the parties to a dispute often (rightfully so) focus on the legal background of the potential arbitrators and their position with regard to a particular point of law at issue in the dispute. However, little regard often is given to their background in economics or accounting. Moreover, little attention is dedicated to valuation issues during interviews conducted with potential arbitrators.

[C] Institutional Proposals for Reform

Some international organisations have taken the opportunity of discussions surrounding the revision of existing multilateral investment treaties to propose the introduction of new and more precise rules governing the award of damages in investor-State arbitration. For example, on 27 May 2020, the European Union ('EU') published its proposal for the modernisation of the Energy Charter Treaty (ECT).[89]

In its proposed draft revised treaty, the EU introduced a new article entitled 'Valuation of Damages'. The new article provides for a number of criteria that would serve as a framework that would govern the valuation of damages in disputes heard by arbitral tribunals constituted under the newly revised ECT. That new article reads:

> 1. Monetary damages shall not be greater than the loss suffered by the Investor as a result of the breach of the provisions referred to in Part III, reduced by any prior damages or compensation already provided by the Contracting Party concerned.
> 2. The tribunal shall not award punitive damages.
> 3. Valuation criteria shall be based on internationally recognised principles and norms.
>
> [Note: The EU reserves the right to propose more detailed rules on valuation at a later stage.][90]

This is a welcome initiative as it will provide certainty to the parties over the way tribunals will valuate damages and will contribute to strengthening the legitimacy of investor-State tribunals in awarding damages.

Moreover, even if such an initiative does not materialise in the newly revised and adopted ECT, investors and their contractual counterparties at a governmental level, or even States when negotiating new bilateral investment treaties (or when revising old ones), are encouraged to pay particular attention to the drafting of the dispute resolution provision or any other substantial provision governing compensation, so that the valuation methods and criteria that the tribunal should use are clearly set out. This will ensure that should a dispute arise, parties will have a clear view as to how damages will be evaluated.

---

89. The EU's proposal can be accessed at https://trade.ec.europa.eu/doclib/docs/2020/may/tradoc_158754.pdf (accessed on 2 June 2020).
90. *Ibid.*, p. 20.

§18.05 CONCLUSION

Damages in investor-State disputes are often the source of heated discussions and commentary and trigger a backlash in the public opinion of States, which are sometimes ordered to pay significant amounts of the taxpayers' money. However, the attention paid to the reasons underlying damage quantification has significantly increased over the past ten years, and arbitral tribunals spend more time explaining the underlying rationale to their awards on damages. For example, in a 2016 award issued in *Copper Mesa Mining v. Ecuador*, a United Nations Commission on International Trade Law (UNCITRAL) Tribunal rejected several valuation methodologies from the experts as being 'too uncertain, subjective and dependent on contingencies'.[91] While the tribunal ultimately adopted a valuation method presented by the claimant's expert, it assessed compensation with 'extreme caution'.[92] Also, another ICSID Tribunal issued an award against Tanzania Electric Supply Company in favour of Standard Chartered Bank after completely rejecting the experts' calculations for a new tariff. In its reasoning, the tribunal criticised the parties for disregarding the tribunal's order to ignore any new assumptions and ruled that neither of the experts had focused on the principal issue relating to the tariff. The tribunal went on to make its own estimate.[93]

In addition, one should not assume that tribunals automatically award damages whenever a breach is found. A comprehensive research has found that in numerous cases, tribunals did not award damages despite having found a breach by the host state.[94] According to this study, this mostly occurred in four different situations: (i) the absence of a causal link between the breach and damages;[95] (ii) what the author of the publication calls 'aborted tenders during which the winner ended up not acquiring the company';[96] (iii) losses are attributable to the claimant's actions;[97] and (iv) wrong counterfactual.[98]

This improvement has not been enough to alleviate the concern about the credibility or the adequacy of the arbitrators' qualifications to consider complex

91. *Copper Mesa Mining Corporation v. Republic of Ecuador*, PCA No. 2012-2, Award, para. 7.24.
92. *Ibid.*
93. PwC International Arbitration damages research – 2017, p. 4. https://www.pwc.co.uk/services/forensic-services/disputes/insights/pwc-international-arbitration-damages-research-2017.html.
94. J. Alberro, 'Liability Yes; Damages No. Consolation without Monetary Compensation: When Tribunals Rule for Claimant on the Merits and Award No Damages', Transnational Dispute Management (TDM) (September 2019).
95. *Ibid.*, at 3. *See Cervin Investissements S.A. y Rhone Investissements S.A. v. República de Costa Rica* (ICSID Case No. ARB/13/2), paras 699–703; *Biwater Gauff (Tanzania) Ltd. v. United Republic of Tanzania* (ICSID Case No. ARB/05/22), para. 805; *MNSS B.V. and Recupero Credito Acciaio N.V. v. Montenegro* (ICSID Case No. ARB (AF)/12/8), para. 356; *Rompetrol Group N.V. v. Romania* (ICSID Case No. ARB/06/3), p. 163; *Mohammad Ammar Al-Bahloul v. The Republic of Tajikistan* (AISCC Case No. V 064/2008), Final Award, paras 98–99.
96. *Ibid. See Luigiterzo Bosca v. The Republic of Lithuania* (PCA Case No. 2011-05), para. 300.
97. *See Urbaser S.A. and Consorcio de Aguas Bilbao Bizkaia, Bilbao Biskaia Partzuergoa v. The Argentine Republic* (ICSID Case No. ARB/07/26), paras 845–847; *Hesham Talaat M. Al Warraq v. The Republic of Indonesia, Ad Hoc* UNCITRAL, para. 645.
98. *AES Corporation and Tau Power B.V. v. Republic of Kazakhstan* (ICSID Case No. ARB/10/16), paras 467–469.

accounting and valuation issues. In order to address this concern, there are no revolutionary ideas in which the award of damages could be overhauled. That said, the trend in the way arbitral tribunals handle damages is encouraging. Doing more of what has already been done would significantly increase trust in the ISDS system. That means the use of tribunal-appointed experts should be incentivised or even imposed for claims, which are above a certain value. Parties should be mindful of appointing arbitrators who have a solid accounting/valuation background. Finally and most importantly, when entering into contracts with foreign investors or when negotiating the entry into force of IIAs, States should ensure that the dispute resolution provision or any other substantial provision calling for compensation states very clearly what are the valuation methods and process that the tribunal should use, and which should be excluded from the tribunal's mandate. This will ensure that the parties have maximum control over the tribunal's consideration of potential claims and avoid bad surprises and increased burdens on States' budgets and taxpayer's money.

CHAPTER 19

Improving Post-award Efficiency: Proposed Reforms to the ICSID Annulment Process

Ankita Ritwik & Marryum Kahloon[*]

Awards rendered under the International Centre for Settlement of Investment Disputes (ICSID) Convention are presumed to be binding and final without any right to an appeal. Yet losing parties have often tried to use the annulment process under the ICSID Convention, generally reserved for egregious procedural violations during the conduct of the arbitration, as an automatic appeal of the award. This chapter examines the increased utilization of the ICSID annulment process by unsuccessful parties to prolong and delay enforcement of adverse awards. In particular, this chapter assesses the significant time some ad hoc committees have taken to decide whether to terminate or to continue automatic provisional stays of enforcement. This in turn has caused delays and confusion in parallel domestic enforcement proceedings, undermining the post-award efficiency contemplated by the drafters of the ICSID Convention. This chapter concludes with proposals to enhance post-award efficiency under the ICSID Convention.

§19.01 INTRODUCTION

Article 53(1) of the Convention on the Settlement of Investment Disputes between States and Nationals of Other States (ICSID Convention) enshrines the finality of an ICSID award. The ICSID Convention provides narrow, limited remedies once an award

* The authors would like to thank Jeffrey M. Sullivan for his guidance, and support from Katherine M. Davis in drafting this chapter. All views expressed herein are their own and do not represent the views of Gibson, Dunn & Crutcher LLP or any other entity or organization.

is issued, including that of annulment,[1] but expressly forbids any appeal.[2] Nevertheless, losing parties increasingly attempt to treat the annulment process as an automatic right of appeal, delaying near-inevitable award enforcement for years.[3] Of ICSID awards rendered since 2011, annulment was sought in almost 40% of the cases.[4] Yet since 1966, annulment has been granted, in part or in full, in only eighteen cases.[5] Thus, annulment processes generally increase the length of the overall proceedings and delay enforcement of the award.

This chapter examines disputing parties' application of post-award remedies in light of the ICSID Convention's overarching goals. Section §19.02 summarizes the ICSID post-award regime. Section §19.03 describes some of the contemporary issues faced by the system. Finally, Section §19.04 outlines some options for reforming the post-award regime under the ICSID Convention. This chapter concludes that some parties have used the annulment mechanism to avoid or delay enforcement rather than to redress genuine misgivings with the conduct of the arbitration. In order to preserve the integrity of the ICSID system, and the intended final and binding nature of awards, this chapter recommends a combination of reforms to the ICSID Arbitration Rules as well as the potential use of alternative post-award procedures.

§19.02 OVERVIEW OF THE POST-AWARD REGIME

Even within the investor-state-dispute settlement system, ICSID's finality and self-contained processes are unique. ICSID awards are treated as "binding," "final judgment[s]" that are not "subject to any appeal or to any other remedy except those provided for in th[e] Convention."[6] These limited remedies are listed in Articles 49–52 of the ICSID Convention and include supplementation, rectification, interpretation, revision, and annulment.

[A] Supplementation, Rectification, Interpretation, and Revision

Under Article 49(2), a party may request that a tribunal provides a supplementary decision on "any question which it had omitted to decide in the award" within forty-five days of rendering the award. Considering an application for annulment of a supplementary decision, in *Amco Asia Corporation and others v. Republic of Indonesia*, the ad hoc committee opined that the procedure "appears to offer a remedy merely for

1. *See* ICSID Convention Art. 52.
2. ICSID Convention, Art. 53(1). *See also* Aron Broches, *Awards Rendered Pursuant to the ICSID Convention: Binding Force, Finality, Recognition, Enforcement, Execution*, 2(2) ICSID Review – Foreign Investment Law Journal 287, 288–298 (1987).
3. Adam Raniv, *A Few Steps to a Faster ICSID*, 8(5) Global Arb. Rev. 23, 26 (2013) ("between mid-2007 and mid-2012, the average annulment proceeding took 26 months from registration to decision.").
4. *See* ICSID, *The ICSID Caseload – Statistics: Issue 2019-2* (June 30, 2019), p. 16, https://icsid.worldbank.org/en/Documents/ICSID_Web_Stats_2019-2_(English).pdf.
5. *See* the Annex to this chapter, "Decisions on Annulment."
6. ICSID Convention, Arts. 53(1), 54(1).

unintentional omissions to decide 'any question'."[7] Although, "it may be sagely assumed that arbitrators will strive in their award to express clearly at least the main reasons on which the award rests[,] [a]ny omissions of relatively minor points may be repaired pursuant to Article 49(2) by simply inserting the tribunal's conclusions thereof in the award."[8] However, "the main reasoning of the award [must remain] unaffected by such insertion."[9] Similarly, considering a request for a supplementary decision, the tribunal in *LG&E Energy Corp., LG&E Capital Corp. and LG&E International Inc. v. Argentine Republic* confirmed that the "supplementation process is not a mechanism by which parties can continue proceedings on the merits or seek a remedy that calls into question the validity of the Tribunal's decision."[10] Several tribunals have refused to grant supplementary reasons on this basis.[11] Where a request for a supplementary decision has been granted, tribunals have recognized that supplementary decisions are intended to correct a minor oversight or error. For example, in *Pac Rim Cayman LLC. v. Republic of El Salvador*, the tribunal recognized that it made an "inadvertent error" by failing to order post-award interest on El Salvador's legal costs, and accordingly corrected its error in an order granting El Salvador's request for a supplementary decision.[12]

Similarly, Article 49(2) also permits parties to request a rectification of the award, asking the tribunal "to rectify any clerical, arithmetical or similar error in the award" within forty-five days of rendering the award. While "a supplemental decision is discretionary ... rectification of an error is obligatory."[13] Examples of rectification include correcting an error in the listing of counsel in the award[14] and correcting arithmetical errors in the calculation of quantum of damages.[15] In the rectification decision in *Compañía de Aguas del Aconquija S.A. and Vivendi Universal S.A. v. Argentine Republic*, the tribunal substituted "Claimant" for "Respondent" and deleted

7. *Amco Asia Corporation and others v. Republic of Indonesia*, ICSID Case No. ARB/81/1, Decision on the Application for Annulment, May 16, 1986, para. 34.
8. *Ibid.*
9. *Ibid.*
10. *LG&E Energy Corp., LG&E Capital Corp. and LG&E International Inc. v. Argentine Republic*, ICSID Case No. ARB/02/1, Decision on Claimants' Request for Supplementary Decision, July 8, 2008, para. 16.
11. *Ibid.*, paras. 13–18; *See also, e.g., Enron Creditors Recovery Corporation (formerly Enron Corporation) and Ponderosa Assets, L.P. v. Argentine Republic*, ICSID Case No. ARB/01/3, Decision on Claimants' Request for Rectification and/or Supplementary Decision of the Award, October 3, 2007, para. 56; *Railroad Development Corporation v. Republic of Guatemala*, ICSID Case No. ARB/07/23, Decision on Claimant Request for Supplementation and Rectification of the Award, January 18, 2013, para. 42.
12. *Pac Rim Cayman LLC. v. Republic of El Salvador*, ICSID Case No. ARB/09/12, Decision on the Respondent Request for a Supplementary Decision, March 28, 2017, paras. 1.17–1.19.
13. Christoph H. Schreuer, Loretta Malintoppi, August Reinisch and Anthony Sinclair, *The ICSID Convention: A Commentary* (2d ed. 2009), p. 853, para. 39.
14. *See, e.g., Hussein Nuaman Soufraki v. United Arab Emirates*, ICSID Case No. ARB/02/7, Rectification of the Decision of the ad hoc Committee on the Application for Annulment of Mr. Soufraki, August 13, 2007; *Noble Ventures, Inc. v. Romania*, ICSID Case No. ARB/01/11, Rectification of Award, May 19, 2006.
15. *See, e.g., Railroad Development Corporation (RDC) v. Republic of Guatemala*, ICSID Case No. ARB/07/23, Decision regarding the Claimant's Request for a Supplementary Decision and Rectification of the Award, January 18, 2013, para. 43.

the words "and neither party disputes" from its summary of a point of law, noting that the respondent had in fact argued the points in question and had not formally abandoned those arguments.[16] More recently, in *ConocoPhillips Petrozuata B.V., ConocoPhillips Hamaca B.V. and ConocoPhillips Gulf of Paria B.V. v. Bolivarian Republic of Venezuela*, the tribunal considered an application for rectification from Venezuela that raised three arithmetical issues in the tribunal's award.[17] The tribunal held pursuant to Article 49(2) that "in case the requesting party has correctly identified a clerical or arithmetical error in an amount, it is the Tribunal's duty not only to correct the error invoked by the requesting party but other errors in the same amount, so that all erroneous components of the Award related to the same amount are corrected."[18]

Under Article 50, parties can request interpretation of the award if a dispute arises "as to the meaning or scope of an award." Considering an application for interpretation by the claimant, the tribunal in *Wena Hotels Ltd. v. Arab Republic of Egypt*, held that "[t]he existence of a dispute as to the meaning or scope of an award requires that the dispute is sufficiently concrete to be susceptible of a specific request for interpretation."[19] Therefore, the parties need to "have actually exposed their divergence of views on definite points in relation to the award's meaning or scope" and "general complaints about the award's lack of clarity do not suffice."[20] A request for interpretation can also only relate to an award's operative section:[21] "the dispute [forming the basis of the request for interpretation] must at least have some practical relevance to the award's implementation; mere theoretical discussions about the award's meaning or scope are not sufficient."[22]

Finally, under Article 51, parties can request alteration of the award on the basis of previously unknown facts "of such a nature as decisively to affect the award." The new fact must have been unknown to the tribunal and the applicant party at the time the award was rendered, and this lack of knowledge must not be attributable to negligence. Furthermore, the application must be made within ninety days of discovery of the fact and, at latest, within three years after the date the award was rendered.

All of these post-award remedies may be granted by the tribunal that rendered the award.[23] If that tribunal cannot be reconstituted, the parties must constitute a new tribunal to decide on the application.[24] Once a final award is rendered, either party may initiate its enforcement notwithstanding the option to pursue these limited remedies

16. *See Compañía de Aguas del Aconquija S.A. and Vivendi Universal S.A. v. Argentine Republic*, ICSID Case No. ARB/97/3, Decision of the ad hoc Committee on the Request for Supplementation and Rectification of its Decision Concerning Annulment of the Award, May 28, 2003.
17. *ConocoPhillips Petrozuata B.V., ConocoPhillips Hamaca B.V. and ConocoPhillips Gulf of Paria B.V. v. Bolivarian Republic of Venezuela*, ICSID Case No. ARB/07/30, Decision on the Rectification of the Award, August 29, 2019, para. 28.
18. *Ibid.*, para. 30.
19. *Wena Hotels Ltd. v. Arab Republic of Egypt*, ICSID Case No. ARB/98/4, Decision on the Application by Wena Hotels Ltd. for Interpretation of the Arbitral Award, October 31, 2005, para. 81.
20. *Ibid.*
21. *See ibid.*, para. 82.
22. *Ibid.*, para. 35.
23. ICSID Arbitration Rules 49(2), 51(1).
24. *Ibid.*, Rule 51(3).

under the ICSID Convention. Nonetheless, a party can request a stay of enforcement of the award in any application for interpretation or revision, and the tribunal retains discretion to stay enforcement pending resolution of these remedial proceedings.[25]

[B] Annulment

Despite their long-standing availability, shorter duration and arguably lower cost, parties have only sparingly applied for these post-award remedies, perhaps because of their narrow scope of review. Instead, parties have frequently opted to apply for annulment of the award before a separately constituted ad hoc committee by ICSID. Article 52(1) articulates the five narrow annulment grounds provided by the ICSID Convention:

> Either party may request annulment of the award by an application in writing addressed to the Secretary-General on one or more of the following grounds:
>
> (a) that the Tribunal was not properly constituted;
> (b) that the Tribunal has manifestly exceeded its powers;
> (c) that there was corruption on the part of a member of the Tribunal;
> (d) that there has been a serious departure from a fundamental rule of procedure; or
> (e) that the award has failed to state the reasons on which it is based.

Parties may challenge the proper constitution of the tribunal on annulment on the basis that challenges and conflicts of interest were not satisfactorily addressed in the underlying arbitration. However, in order for this ground to be admissible, the applicant party must demonstrate that all available remedies were exhausted during the underlying proceeding. Without this limitation, "a party aware of a defect in the tribunal's composition could await the outcome of the proceedings in order to attack an unfavourable award on this ground."[26]

Ad hoc committees have held that tribunals had committed a manifest excess of powers in three circumstances: (i) when the tribunal exceeded its jurisdiction;[27] (ii) when the tribunal did not exercise jurisdiction that it had;[28] and (iii) when the tribunal

25. ICSID Convention, Arts. 50(2), 51(4); ICSID Arbitration Rule 54.
26. Christoph H. Schreuer, Loretta Malintoppi, August Reinisch and Anthony Sinclair, *The ICSID Convention: A Commentary* (2d ed. 2009), p. 935, para. 122.
27. *See Patrick Mitchell v. Democratic Republic of the Congo*, ICSID Case No. ARB/99/7, Decision on Annulment, November 1, 2006; *Occidental Petroleum Corporation and Occidental Exploration and Production Company v. Republic of Ecuador*, ICSID Case No. ARB/06/11, Decision on Annulment, November 2, 2015; *RSM Production Corporation v. Saint Lucia*, ICSID Case No. ARB/12/10, Decision on Annulment, April 29, 2019.
28. *See Compañía de Aguas del Aconquija S.A. and Vivendi Universal S.A. v. Argentine Republic*, ICSID Case No. ARB/97/3, Decision on Annulment, July 3, 2002; *Malaysian Historical Salvors, SDN, BHD v. Malaysia*, ICSID Case No. ARB/05/10, Decision on Annulment, April 16, 2009; *Helnan International Hotels A/S v. Arab Republic of Egypt*, ICSID Case No. ARB/05/19, Decision on Annulment, June 14, 2010.

did not apply the proper law.[29] An excess of power will be "manifest" when it is "textually obvious and substantively serious."[30]

In assessing whether an exercise or non-exercise of jurisdiction was an excess of power, ad hoc committees do not engage in a de novo review, but rather have assessed whether the interpretation adopted by the tribunal was "tenable."[31] Ad hoc committees have also distinguished between the non-application of the proper law, which is a basis for annulment, and the erroneous application of the proper law, which is not a basis for annulment.[32] Non-application occurs when the tribunal "has failed altogether to apply the applicable law"[33] or when the tribunal has applied a law other than the applicable law (e.g., customary international law instead of the relevant bilateral investment treaty (BIT) provision).[34] Ad hoc committees have suggested "the possibility that a manifest error of law may, in an exceptional situation, be of such egregious nature as to amount to a manifest excess of powers."[35] However, in other cases, despite finding that the tribunal committed "a manifest error of law," the ad hoc committee refused to annul as "[n]otwithstanding the identified errors and lacunas in the Award, it is the case in the end that the Tribunal applied [the provisions of the Bilateral Investment

29. *See Klöckner Industrie-Anlagen GmbH and others v. United Republic of Cameroon and Société Camerounaise des Engrais,* ICSID Case No. ARB/81/2, Decision on Annulment, May 3, 1985; *Amco Asia Corporation and others v. Republic of Indonesia,* ICSID Case No. ARB/81/1, Decision on the Application for Annulment, May 16, 1986; *Sempra Energy International v. Argentine Republic,* ICSID Case No. ARB/02/16, Decision on Annulment, June 29, 2010; *Enron Creditors Recovery Corporation v. Argentine Republic,* ICSID Case No. ARB/01/3, Decision on Annulment, July 30, 2010; *Venezuela Holdings B.V. and others v. Bolivarian Republic of Venezuela,* ICSID Case No. ARB/07/27, Decision on Annulment, March 9, 2017 ("Venezuela Holdings").
30. *Hussein Nuaman Soufraki v. United Arab Emirates,* ICSID Case No. ARB/02/7, Decision on Annulment, June 5, 2007, para. 40. However, ad hoc committees have recognized that "'manifest' does not prevent that in some cases an extensive argumentation and analysis may be required to prove that the misuse of powers has in fact occurred." *Occidental Petroleum Corporation and Occidental Exploration and Production Company v. Republic of Ecuador,* ICSID Case No. ARB/06/11, Decision on Annulment, November 2, 2015, para. 59.
31. *See Klöckner Industrie-Anlagen GmbH and others v. United Republic of Cameroon and Société Camerounaise des Engrais,* ICSID Case No. ARB/81/2, Decision on Annulment, paras. 11–16, 52(e); *Helnan International Hotels A/S v. Arab Republic of Egypt,* ICSID Case No. ARB/05/19, Decision on Annulment, June 14, 2010, para. 55; *Fraport AG Frankfurt Airport Services Worldwide v. Republic of the Philippines,* ICSID Case No. ARB/03/25, Decision on Annulment, December 23, 2010, paras. 44, 112; *Víctor Pey Casado and President Allende Foundation v. Republic of Chile,* ICSID Case No. ARB/98/2, Decision on Annulment, December 18, 2012, para. 70; *TECO Guatemala Holdings, LLC v. Republic of Guatemala,* ICSID Case No. ARB/10/23, Decision on Annulment, April 5, 2016, paras. 78, 222.
32. *See Enron Creditors Recovery Corporation v. Argentine Republic,* ICSID Case No. ARB/01/3, Decision on Annulment, July 30, 2010, para. 67; *Tidewater Investment SRL and Tidewater Caribe, C.A. v. Bolivarian Republic of Venezuela,* ICSID Case No. ARB/10/5, Decision on Annulment, December 27, 2016, paras. 128–29.
33. *Sempra Energy International v. Argentine Republic,* ICSID Case No. ARB/02/16, Decision on Annulment, June 29, 2010, para. 165. *See also Enron Creditors Recovery Corporation v. Argentine Republic,* ICSID Case No. ARB/01/3, Decision on Annulment, July 30, 2010, paras. 361–77.
34. *See Venezuela Holdings,* paras. 175–184.
35. *Sempra Energy International v. Argentine Republic,* ICSID Case No. ARB/02/16, Decision on Annulment, June 29, 2010, para. 164. *See also Amco Asia Corporation and others v. Republic of Indonesia,* ICSID Case No. ARB/81/1, Resubmission, Decision on Annulment, December 3, 1992, para. 7.19.

Treaty giving rise to the arbitration]. Although applying it cryptically and defectively, it applied it. There is accordingly no manifest excess of powers."[36]

Parties may challenge an award on the basis of alleged corruption by a tribunal member. However, the "fact of corruption must be established and not inferred in order to constitute a ground for annulment. Corruption would be improper conduct by an arbitrator induced by personal gain."[37] To date, no annulment applications have been successful on this ground.

Ad hoc committees have held that tribunals have failed to state reasons in three circumstances: (i) where there is an absence of reasons;[38] (ii) where reasons proffered are contradictory;[39] and (iii) where there has been a failure to deal with questions.[40] The prevailing standard is that "the requirement to state reasons is satisfied as long as the award enables one to follow how the tribunal proceeded from Point A, to Point B, and eventually to its conclusion, even if it made an error of fact or of law."[41] The tribunal's reasons "may be implicit in the considerations and conclusions contained in the award, provided they can be reasonably inferred from the terms used in the decision."[42] However, an absence of reasons exists if the reasons provided by a tribunal are frivolous or contradictory.[43] Reasoning is frivolous if "manifestly irrelevant and

---

36. *CMS Gas Transmission Company v. Argentine Republic,* ICSID Case No. ARB/01/8, Decision on Annulment, September 25, 2007, paras. 135-136.
37. Christoph H. Schreuer, Loretta Malintoppi, August Reinisch and Anthony Sinclair, *The ICSID Convention: A Commentary* (2d ed. 2009), p. 978, para. 273.
38. *See Klöckner Industrie-Anlagen GmbH and others v. United Republic of Cameroon and Société Camerounaise des Engrais,* ICSID Case No. ARB/81/2, Decision on Annulment; *Patrick Mitchell v. Democratic Republic of the Congo,* ICSID Case No. ARB/99/7, Decision on Annulment, November 1, 2006; *CMS Gas Transmission Company v. Argentine Republic,* ICSID Case No. ARB/01/8, Decision on Annulment, September 25, 2007; *Enron Creditors Recovery Corporation v. Argentine Republic,* ICSID Case No. ARB/01/3, Decision on Annulment, July 30, 2010; *TECO Guatemala Holdings, LLC v. Republic of Guatemala,* ICSID Case No. ARB/10/23, Decision on Annulment, April 5, 2016.
39. *See Amco Asia Corporation and others v. Republic of Indonesia,* ICSID Case No. ARB/81/1, Decision on the Application for Annulment, May 16, 1986; *Maritime International Nominees Establishment v. Republic of Guinea,* ICSID Case No. ARB/84/4, Decision on Annulment, December 22, 1989; *Víctor Pey Casado and President Allende Foundation v. Republic of Chile,* ICSID Case No. ARB/98/2, Decision on Annulment; *Tidewater Investment SRL and Tidewater Caribe, C.A. v. Bolivarian Republic of Venezuela,* ICSID Case No. ARB/10/5, Decision on Annulment, December 27, 2016.
40. *See Klöckner Industrie-Anlagen GmbH and others v. United Republic of Cameroon and Société Camerounaise des Engrais,* ICSID Case No. ARB/81/2, Decision on Annulment; *Maritime International Nominees Establishment v. Republic of Guinea,* ICSID Case No. ARB/84/4, Decision on Annulment, December 22, 1989.
41. *Maritime International Nominees Establishment v. Republic of Guinea,* ICSID Case No. ARB/84/4, Decision on Annulment, December 22, 1989, para. 5.09, cited by *Enron Creditors Recovery Corporation v. Argentine Republic,* ICSID Case No. ARB/01/3, Decision on Annulment, July 30, 2010, para. 74; *Occidental Petroleum Corporation and Occidental Exploration and Production Company v. Republic of Ecuador,* ICSID Case No. ARB/06/11, Decision on Annulment, November 2, 2015, para. 64; *TECO Guatemala Holdings, LLC v. Republic of Guatemala,* ICSID Case No. ARB/10/23, Decision on Annulment, April 5, 2016, para. 87.
42. *Wena Hotels Ltd. v. Arab Republic of Egypt,* ICSID Case No. ARB/98/4, Decision on Annulment, February 5, 2002, para. 81.
43. *See Maritime International Nominees Establishment v. Republic of Guinea,* ICSID Case No. ARB/84/4, Decision on Annulment, December 22, 1989, para. 5.09.

known to be so to the tribunal," and contradictory if it "cancel[s] each other and will not enable the reader to understand the tribunal's motives."[44]

Ad hoc committees have held that tribunals have seriously departed from a fundamental rule of procedure by violating a party's right to be heard.[45] The focus of this ground is "on the manner in which the Tribunal proceeded, not on the content of its decision."[46] To succeed, an applicant must: (i) identify the fundamental rule of procedure that has not been complied with; and (ii) establish that the departure was serious in that it (a) may have caused the tribunal to reach a substantially different result, or (b) would deprive a party of the benefit of the rule thus impacting the proceedings.[47]

These grounds make clear that an ICSID annulment proceeding is not an appeal. Indeed, "annulment is, or should be, concerned only with the legitimacy of the process of decision and not with its substantive correctness."[48] While independent of the tribunal, the ad hoc committee is composed by and functions within the ICSID system (as opposed, for instance, to an appeal to a separate judicial body such as the International Court of Justice), and further emphasizes the self-contained nature of ICSID processes.[49] As one ad hoc committee noted, an annulment proceeding "in no way consists of a means of appealing or otherwise revising the merits of the decision

---

44. *See Occidental Petroleum Corporation and Occidental Exploration and Production Company v. Republic of Ecuador,* ICSID Case No. ARB/06/11, Decision on Annulment, November 2, 2015, para. 65. However, as the ad hoc committee in *Vivendi I* observed, "tribunals must often struggle to balance conflicting considerations, and an ad hoc committee should be careful not to discern contradiction when what is actually expressed in a tribunal's reasons could more truly be said to be but a reflection of such conflicting considerations." *Compañía de Aguas del Aconquija S.A. and Vivendi Universal S.A. v. Argentine Republic,* ICSID Case No. ARB/97/3, Decision on Annulment, July 3, 2002, para. 65. *See also TECO Guatemala Holdings, LLC v. Republic of Guatemala,* ICSID Case No. ARB/10/23, Decision on Annulment, April 5, 2016, para. 101.
45. *See Amco Asia Corporation and others v. Republic of Indonesia,* ICSID Case No. ARB/81/1, Resubmission, Decision on Annulment, December 3, 1992; *Fraport AG Frankfurt Airport Services Worldwide v. Republic of the Philippines,* ICSID Case No. ARB/03/25, Decision on Annulment, December 23, 2010; *Víctor Pey Casado and President Allende Foundation v. Republic of Chile,* ICSID Case No. ARB/98/2, Decision on Annulment; *TECO Guatemala Holdings, LLC v. Republic of Guatemala,* ICSID Case No. ARB/10/23, Decision on Annulment, April 5, 2016.
46. *Compañía de Aguas del Aconquija S.A. and Vivendi Universal S.A. v. Argentine Republic,* ICSID Case No. ARB/97/3, Decision on Annulment, July 3, 2002, para. 83.
47. *See Víctor Pey Casado and President Allende Foundation v. Republic of Chile,* ICSID Case No. ARB/98/2, Decision on Annulment, paras. 72–82.
48. Christoph Schreuer, *Foreword, in Annulment under the ICSID Convention* (R.D. Bishop and S.M. Marchili eds., 2012).
49. *Annulment under the ICSID Convention* 15 (R.D. Bishop and S.M. Marchili eds., 2012). *See also* Aron Broches, *Awards Rendered Pursuant to the ICSID Convention: Binding Force, Finality, Recognition, Enforcement, Execution,* 2(2) ICSID Review – Foreign Investment Law Journal 287, 290 (1987) (noting that the International Law Commission contemplated submission to the International Court of Justice when drafting the predecessor to the ICSID Convention, the Revised Draft on Arbitral Procedure, but this was ultimately excluded by the drafters of the Convention as the International Court of Justice's statute limits it to adjudicating inter-State disputes).

subject to supplementation or rectification. Those sorts of proceedings are simply not provided for in the ICSID system."[50]

§19.03 CONTEMPORARY ISSUES

Losing parties routinely seek annulment.[51] Of 228 ICSID awards rendered between 1966 and 2016, applications for annulment were filed in 90 cases.[52] This trend is only increasing.[53] According to some commentators, annulment applications often employ "inflationary," "shrapnel tactics," indicating an intent to do away with the award by any means possible, rather than expressing a pointed grievance with the process.[54] Christoph Schreuer, for example, notes that of Article 52(1)'s five grounds for annulment, three grounds (manifest excess of powers, serious departure from a fundamental rule of procedure, and failure to state reasons) "are invoked in virtually every request for annulment."[55]

Although annulments have been frequently sought, they have been rarely granted. Of all the annulment applications to date, only eighteen have been granted, of which only six have been granted in full.[56] Thus, most ad hoc committees appear to recognize the limited scope of their review and accordingly deny applications that do not rise to the threshold set by Article 52(1). Annulment applications nevertheless can lead to increased delays in the arbitration process, undermining the intent of the ICSID process that underscores the finality of the award. Moreover, enforcement of the award can suffer from significant delays during the pendency of annulment proceedings.

[A] Annulment-Related Delays

The post-award remedies process, and in particular annulment proceedings, can be a sometimes-serious source of delay. This arguably undermines the principle of finality of the award, which underpins the ICSID Convention. Delays can be a result of problems constituting the ad hoc committee, prolonged stay proceedings, "guerilla tactics" employed by parties, and other sources of delay inherent in the annulment process itself. Under the current ICSID Arbitration Rules, there is no prescribed time limit to constitute ICSID ad hoc committees. According to ICSID's 2016 background

50. *Compañía de Aguas del Aconquija S.A. v. Argentine Republic,* ICSID Case No. ARB/97/3, 2 Decision of the Ad Hoc Committee on the Request for Supplementation and Rectification of Its Decision Concerning Annulment of the Award, May 28, 2003, para. 11.
51. Christoph Schreuer, *From ICSID Annulment to Appeal: Halfway Down the Slippery Slope,* 10 Law and Practice of International Courts and Tribunals 211, 213 (2011).
52. *See* ICSID, *Updated Background Paper on Annulment for the Administrative Council of ICSID,* para. 31 (May 5, 2016), https://icsid.worldbank.org/en/Documents/resources/Background%20Paper%20on%20Annulment%20April%202016%20ENG.pdf.
53. *See* ICSID, *The ICSID Caseload – Statistics: Issue 2019-2* (June 30, 2019), p. 16, https://icsid.worldbank.org/en/Documents/ICSID_Web_Stats_2019-2_(English).pdf.
54. Christoph Schreuer, *From ICSID Annulment to Appeal: Halfway Down the Slippery Slope,* 10 Law and Practice of International Courts and Tribunals 211, 214 (2011).
55. *Ibid.*
56. *See* Annex, "Decisions on Annulment."

paper, it takes approximately 56 days on average to constitute the ad hoc committee.[57] A more recent analysis of ICSID's annulment cases, contained in the annex to this chapter, reveals that the average is now closer to 70 days. The variance, however, is broad, ranging from as little as 20 days[58] to as many as 229 days.[59]

The swift constitution of the ad hoc committee becomes particularly important in cases where the parties have requested a stay of enforcement with their annulment applications. In this circumstance, under Article 52(5) of the ICSID Convention,[60] the enforcement of the award is automatically stayed until the ad hoc committee is constituted and can determine if the stay should be continued. Either party may request an expedited ruling on the stay, in which case the ad hoc committee must decide whether to continue the stay of enforcement within thirty days of its constitution.[61] Crucially, the ICSID Convention requires the ad hoc committee to be constituted before it can resolve any dispute over the stay. There are no emergency appointment procedures that would enable the stay to be removed pending ad hoc committee constitution. This not only prejudices the award recipient by delaying enforcement but may also allow the party applying for a stay to engage in asset dissipation in an attempt to make themselves judgment proof.

A notable example is *Border Timbers Limited, Border Timbers International (Private) Limited and Hangani Development Co. (Private) Limited v. Republic of Zimbabwe*. In this case, Zimbabwe filed annulment applications and requests for stays of enforcement in two joined cases on 21 October 2015.[62] The ad hoc committee was constituted on 21 December 2015, and the timetable for the annulment proceedings was determined in February 2016.[63] Briefings on the stay of enforcement were filed from April 2016 through July 2016, and amidst deep disagreement on the nature of ICSID's pertinent rules, the ad hoc committee held a joint hearing on the stay of enforcement in December 2016.[64] The ad hoc committee ultimately issued its decision on 24 April 2017, rejecting Zimbabwe's request for a stay of enforcement.[65] Thus, it

57. *See* ICSID, *Updated Background Paper on Annulment for the Administrative Council of ICSID*, para. 42 (May 5, 2016), https://icsid.worldbank.org/en/Documents/resources/Background%20Paper%20on%20Annulment%20April%202016%20ENG.pdf.
58. *See Standard Chartered Bank (Hong Kong) Limited v. Tanzania Electric Supply Company Limited*, ICSID Case No. ARB/10/20, Decision on Annulment, August 22, 2018.
59. *See Sempra Energy International v. Argentine Republic*, ICSID Case No. ARB/02/16, Decision on Annulment, June 29, 2010.
60. *See also* ICSID Arbitration Rule 54(1).
61. *See* ICSID Arbitration Rule 54(2) ("If an application for the revision or annulment of an award contains a request for a stay of its enforcement, the Secretary-General shall, together with the notice of registration, inform both parties of the provisional stay of the award. As soon as the Tribunal or Committee is constituted it shall, if either party requests, rule within 30 days on whether such stay should be continued; unless it decides to continue the stay, it shall automatically be terminated."). *See also* ICSID Regulations and Rules, 1968, Doc. ICSID/4/Rev. 1 (explanatory note).
62. *Border Timbers Limited, Border Timbers International (Private) Limited and Hangani Development Co. (Private) Limited v. Republic of Zimbabwe*, ICSID Case No. ARB/10/25, Decision on Stay of Enforcement of the Award, April 24, 2017, para. 1.
63. *Ibid.*, paras. 3–4.
64. *Ibid.*, paras. 6–17.
65. *Ibid.*, paras. 80, 92.

took eighteen months from the filing of the annulment application to receive a decision on whether to continue the provisional stay of enforcement.

The annex shows that the average number of days to resolve a stay application is 233 days (i.e., more than 7 months), despite the suggestion in ICSID Arbitration Rule 54(2) that such applications should be resolved within 30 days. Further to that, the average time to resolve an annulment application is 773 days, or over 2 years. These timelines do not reflect a swift, efficient annulment process.

[B] Impact on Enforcement

Exacerbated procedural delays in annulment prolong not only ICSID-level proceedings but domestic enforcement proceedings as well. According to Professor Schreuer, "annulment proceedings that are not accompanied by a stay of enforcement ... are neither a justification for non-compliance with the award nor a basis for domestic courts to withhold recognition or refuse enforcement."[66] "The fact alone that annulment proceedings are pending has no suspensive effect."[67] Instead, "if the [ad hoc] committee ... declines to continue or to grant a stay, the award is fully binding and enforceable."[68] Critically, the decision on whether to stay enforcement rests with the ad hoc committee, which must resolve the question based on the terms of the ICSID Convention. This mechanism is markedly different from the enforcement of non-ICSID arbitral awards. The Convention on the Recognition and Enforcement of Foreign Arbitral Awards (New York Convention), for instance, allows domestic courts to determine whether to stay enforcement pending proceedings to "se[t] aside" an award.[69]

Courts have accordingly enforced awards that are not suspended by a stay.[70] For example, in *Infrastructure Services Luxembourg S.A.R.L v. Kingdom of Spain*, the Federal Court of Australia, after earlier ordering a stay on proceedings as a result of a provisional stay pursuant to the Secretary-General's orders under Article 52(5) of the ICSID Convention,[71] lifted the stay on proceedings in Australia once the ICSID ad hoc committee discontinued the stay of enforcement.[72]

---

66. Christoph H. Schreuer, Loretta Malintoppi, August Reinisch and Anthony Sinclair, *The ICSID Convention: A Commentary* (2d ed. 2009), para. 581.
67. *Ibid.*
68. *Ibid.*
69. Convention on the Recognition and Enforcement of Foreign Arbitral Awards, Art. VI; ICSID Convention, Art. 52.
70. *Cf. Maritime International Nominees Establishment v. Republic of Guinea*, ICSID Case No. ARB/84/4, Interim Order 1, August 12, 1988, para. 10 ("although the Convention does not explicitly so provide, it seems clear that suspension of a party's obligation to abide by and comply with the award necessarily carries with it suspension of a Contracting State's obligation (and for that matter its authority) to enforce the Award, even though during the pendency of the Committee's examination of the application for annulment the validity of the Award remains unaffected").
71. *See Infrastructure Services Luxembourg S.A.R.L v. Kingdom of Spain* [2019] FCA 1220 (August 1, 2019).
72. *See Eiser Infrastructure Ltd v. Kingdom of Spain* [2020] FCA 157 (February 24, 2020), paras. 33–34.

A lack of clarity over the effect of the annulment process on the validity of awards has, however, led some courts to suspend enforcement on the basis of continuing enforcement proceedings. This can often derive from misplaced analogizing between annulment and domestic appeals proceedings where stays of enforcement are automatic during the pendency on an appeal. For example, in *Masdar Solar & Wind Cooperatief U.A. v. Kingdom of Spain*, the U.S. District Court for the District of Columbia entered a stay of enforcement "pending the opinion of ... ICSID regarding Spain's petition to annul."[73] The District Court relied on the mistaken assumption that "ICSID's temporary stay ... will persist until the termination of the annulment proceedings."[74] Some courts have even refused to lift the stay on domestic proceedings despite the ad hoc committee having lifted the stay, in direct contravention of the language and purpose of the ICSID Convention.[75] In *OI European Group BV v. Bolivarian Republic of Venezuela*, for example, the U.S. District Court for the District of Columbia granted a stay of enforcement even after the ad hoc committee lifted the provisional stay.[76] In a minute order without citation, the court offered:

> Given the pendency of proceedings to annul the very award the Court is being asked to enforce, the Court is persuaded, in an exercise of its judgment, after weighing the competing interests involved, ... that the matter should be stayed, and that the circumstances should be reviewed with regularity to avoid an unduly lengthy or indefinite stay.[77]

Overall, undermining the finality of the award undermines the purpose and scope of the ICSID Convention to create a "complete, exclusive and closed jurisdictional system, insulated from national law."[78] Undermining these advantages could undermine the legitimacy of the process. Indeed, disputing parties may prefer to turn to commercial arbitration, or diplomatic protection, if the perceived benefits of ICSID arbitration are no longer available to them.

73. *Masdar Solar & Wind Cooperatief U.A. v. Kingdom of Spain*, 1:18-cv-2254, ECF No. 28, 1, (D.D.C., September 18, 2019).
74. *Ibid.*, 9.
75. *Cf.* Aron Broches, *Awards Rendered Pursuant to the ICSID Convention: Binding Force, Finality, Recognition, Enforcement, Execution*, 2(2) ICSID Review – Foreign Investment Law Journal 287, 294 ("Although the Convention does not explicitly so provide, a *stay of enforcement* necessarily carries with it a *suspension of recognition* of the award which means that to the extent of such a stay the award may not be relied upon as a final decision.").
76. *OI European Group BV v. Bolivarian Republic of Venezuela*, 1:16-cv-1533, Minute Order (D.D.C., December 21, 2017).
77. *Ibid.*
78. Aron Broches, *Awards Rendered Pursuant to the ICSID Convention: Binding Force, Finality, Recognition, Enforcement, Execution*, 2(2) ICSID Review – Foreign Investment Law Journal 287, 288. *See also Compañiá de Aguas del Aconquija S.A. and Vivendi Universal S.A. v. Argentine Republic*, ICSID Case No. ARB/97/3, Decision on the Argentine Republic's Request for a Continued Stay of Enforcement of the Award (ICSID Rule 54), November 4, 2008, para. 34 ("Consequently, whenever the stay of enforcement comes to an end ... the '*binding*' inherent character of the '*award*' becomes mandatory without any need or requirement for any other action to be undertaken. This rule constitutes a cardinal pivot upon which the entire structure of the ICSID system is based.").

§19.04 ENHANCING POST-AWARD EFFICIENCY

There has been significant debate on whether and how to reform the investor-State Dispute Settlement ("ISDS") system. Some commentators have argued that there is a need to move away from current arbitral mechanisms, such as ICSID and bilateral investment treaties toward a multilateral investment treaty or an investment court to resolve disputes that touch on issues of public interest and State sovereignty.[79] Others have argued that while no system is perfect, there are piecemeal reforms that can ameliorate shortcomings in the ISDS system, and there is no need to overhaul existing mechanisms in favor of a standing investment court.[80] Whatever the best path forward, improving the efficiency of the post-award process ought to be a common goal. States can be assured that the matter has been resolved with finality. And successful parties can enforce their awards without unnecessary delay and follow-on litigation.

[A] Encourage Use of Post-award Remedies Other Than Annulment under the ICSID Convention

As discussed in §19.02, while there are a number of post-award remedies available under the ICSID Convention, applicants tend to disproportionately favor annulment. It may be, however, that other post-award remedies may better address many of the applicants' grievances with the award. This would, at minimum, eliminate an often-lengthy ad hoc committee constitution process. For example, annulment applications routinely allege flaws with the tribunal's reasoning and assert that these constitute a "failure to state reasons" under Article 52(1)(e). Submitting a request for a supplemental decision under Article 49(2) or interpretation under Article 50 to remedy unclear reasoning or a failure to deal with questions could act as a substitute for an annulment application in some contexts.[81] Notably, the applicant for such a request could be the

79. *See, e.g.*, Christian Tietje and Freya Baetens, *The Impact of Investor-State-Dispute Settlement (ISDS) in the Transatlantic Trade and Investment Partnership* (2014), https://www.senate.nl/9370000/1/j4nvgs5kjg27kof_j9vvkfvj6b325az/vjn8fj4hhtzc (study prepared for the Minister for Foreign Trade & Development Cooperation, Ministry of Foreign Affairs, the Netherlands); Freya Baetens, *The European Union's Proposed Investment Court System: Addressing Criticisms of Investor-State Arbitration While Raising New Challenge*, 43(4) Legal Issues of Economic Integration 367 (2016); David M. Howard, *Creating Consistency through a World Investment Court*, 41 Fordham Int'l L.J. 1 (2017).
80. *See, e.g.*, Luis González García, *Making Impossible Investor-State Reform Possible, in Reshaping the Investor-State Dispute Settlement System* 424 (Jean E. Kalicki and Anna Joubin-Bret eds., 2015); Leon E. Trakman, *The ICSID Under Siege*, 45 Cornell Int'l L.J. 603 (2013).
81. *See Enron Creditors Recovery Corporation v. Argentine Republic*, ICSID Case No. ARB/01/3, Decision on Annulment, July 30, 2010, para. 73 ("Furthermore, even in cases where a tribunal has failed to deal with a question submitted to it, the appropriate remedy may not be an application for annulment, but rather, an application to the tribunal for a supplementary decision, pursuant to Article 49(2) of the ICSID Convention."). *Cf. Maritime International Nominees Establishment v. Republic of Guinea*, ICSID Case No. ARB/84/4, Decision on Annulment, December 22, 1989, para. 5.13 ("Guinea's complaint against the Award falls into a different category. Article 49(2) would not have provided a remedy for the Awards failure to deal with questions submitted by Guinea to the Tribunal. The defect complained of by Guinea could not have been cured by supplementing the Award, but would have required in effect that it be

successful party, who may choose to preemptively clarify gaps in reasoning in the award to circumvent the risk of potentially lengthy annulment proceedings.

The risk of encouraging usage of other post-award remedies is that these may also be employed as yet another delay tactic by a party dissatisfied with the award, who may nonetheless plan to eventually apply to annul the award in order to delay or prolong enforcement. Furthermore, usage of other post-award remedies does not necessarily preclude a party from applying for a stay of enforcement.[82] For example, in the recently concluded case of *Victor Pey Casado and President Allende Foundation v. Republic of Chile*, it took almost twenty-two years to obtain an award that was final and binding.[83] The request for arbitration was registered in April 1998, and in addition to the original arbitration, the proceedings included two annulment proceedings (with corollary stay applications), a revision proceeding (also with a corollary stay application), a supplementary decision proceeding, a resubmission proceeding, an interpretation proceeding, and a rectification proceeding.

Further clarity in the ICSID Arbitration Rules and developments in jurisprudence may help mitigate these concerns. For example, unsuccessful applications of post-award remedies could be more strictly scrutinized by ad hoc committees, particularly if the applicant is using the annulment proceeding to reargue grievances already advanced in another post-award proceeding, thus attempting a second bite at the apple.

[B] Impose and Enforce Time Limits on the Annulment Process

While some time limits already exist in the ICSID Arbitration Rules, there is scope to further define deadlines within which the annulment process must operate. As noted in §19.04[A], delay in the constitution of the ad hoc committee can have significant knock-on effects by postponing not just resolution of the annulment application but also whether domestic enforcement of the award should be stayed pending resolution of the annulment proceedings. Therefore, imposing time limits for ad hoc committee constitution could improve efficiency of the entire process. This would include not just a deadline by which ICSID must appoint ad hoc committee members, but also deadlines by when parties must submit any comments, including challenges. If a committee member is challenged, the challenge process must also have time limits.

In addition to ad hoc committee constitution, incorporation of time limits on other aspects of the procedure could also be helpful. These include, to name a few, a timeline by when the ad hoc committee must hold the first procedural session, issue the first procedural order and timetable, receive submissions, hold the hearing, and issue the decision. The most recent version of the proposed ICSID rule amendments seeks to

---

reconsidered in the light of the Tribunal's decision on the 'omitted' question. The Committee accepts that in such a case failure to deal with a question may render the award unintelligible and thus subject to annulment for failure to state reasons").

82. *See supra* §19.02[A].

83. *See Victor Pey Casado and President Allende Foundation v. Republic of Chile*, ICSID Case No. ARB/98/2.

increase the expediency of annulment proceedings by permitting the ongoing application of the first procedural order from the underlying arbitration, limiting written submissions to two rounds of pleadings, and making a hearing optional.[84]

Given the urgency of the issue of a stay on enforcement, ad hoc committees should also have strict timelines to resolve whether to lift or continue a provisional stay triggered by an annulment application. While ICSID Arbitration Rule 54(2) calls for ad hoc committees to rule on the matter within thirty days of their constitution, this deadline has been rarely observed.[85] This is likely because ad hoc committees seek pleadings on the issue from the parties. Moreover, Rule 54(2) has been some source of confusion, given its awkward phrasing. The rule provides:

> If an application for the revision or annulment of an award contains a request for a stay of its enforcement, the Secretary-General shall, together with the notice of registration, inform both parties of the provisional stay of the award. As soon as the Tribunal or Committee is constituted it shall, if either party requests, *rule within 30 days on whether such stay should be continued*; unless it decides to continue the stay, it shall automatically be terminated.[86]

In *Tenaris S.A. and Talta - Trading e Marketing Sociedade Unipessoal Lda. v. Bolivarian Republic of Venezuela I*, the ad hoc committee opined, "[p]ursuant to Rule 54(2), this provisional stay shall automatically be terminated unless the committee decides to continue the stay."[87] Other ad hoc committees have ignored the thirty-day deadline and instead decided to continue the stay until the ad hoc committee has had a chance to consider the parties' submissions on the matter and make a final determination.[88] While the intent of the rule is clear, ad hoc committees have frequently relied on a perceived ambiguity to ignore that intent. The most recent version of the proposed ICSID rule amendments sticks with the thirty-day deadline but also clarifies it, providing that the Secretary-General can fix time limits for written submissions on any request for a stay to allow the ad hoc committee to "consider the request promptly upon its constitution."[89] Following its constitution, the tribunal is obliged to issue a decision within thirty days after the later of: (i) its date of constitution; (ii) the last written submission on the request; or (iii) the last oral submission on the request.[90] While any clarification is welcome, setting deadlines on the stay applications and limits on the rounds of pleadings can help limit provisional

84. *See* ICSID, *Working Paper 4: Proposals for Amendment of the ICSID Rules*, Rule 72 (February 2020) https://icsid.worldbank.org/en/Documents/WP_4_Vol_1_En.pdf.
85. *See* Annex, "Decisions on Annulment."
86. ICSID Arbitration Rule 54(2) (emphasis added).
87. *Tenaris S.A. and Talta - Trading e Marketing Sociedade Unipessoal Lda. v. Bolivarian Republic of Venezuela I*, ICSID Case No. ARB 11/26, Decision on the Request to Maintain the Stay of Enforcement of the Award, March 24, 2017, para. 81.
88. *See, e.g., Continental Casualty Company v. Argentine Republic*, ICSID Case No. ARB/03/9, Decision on Argentina's Application for a Stay of Enforcement of the Award, October 23, 2009; *SGS Société Générale de Surveillance S.A. v. Republic of Paraguay*, ICSID Case No. ARB/07/29, March 22, 2013.
89. *See* ICSID, *Working Paper 4: Proposals for Amendment of the ICSID Rules*, Rule 73(3)(c) (February 2020) https://icsid.worldbank.org/en/Documents/WP_4_Vol_1_En.pdf.
90. *See ibid.*

stays on enforcement and ensure that award recipients can enforce their rights in a timely manner.

[C] Socialize the Limited Scope of Post-award Remedies

Perhaps the simplest path to a clearer, more reliable future for ICSID award enforcement is greater clarity on the exceptional and limited scope of post-award remedies. Amendments to the ICSID Arbitration Rules could help memorialize the limited scope of ad hoc committee review.

Some ad hoc committees well understand and respect their limited role.[91] However, according to some commentators like Schreuer, "[i]t has become common for ad hoc committees to offer gratuitous advice and criticism. Even if the award survives, the criticism may act as a consolation prize to the losing party. At the same time this makes compliance with the award more difficult."[92] Other commentators note that some ad hoc committees "have succumbed to the temptation to cross [the] boundary" from annulment to reviewing the merits, even while agreeing theoretically that they were not assembled to re-assess merits.[93] As others have already stated, the simplest and most potent reform to the ICSID process is to "refocus on refining the application of the annulment standards and ensuring through debate and training that members of annulment committees are aware of the scope and limits of their powers."[94]

Moreover, while resources such as ICSID's Background Paper on Annulment, exist for annulment proceedings, few such resources are available for other post-award remedies. Similarly, additional guidance on stay proceedings would be welcome. At least one ad hoc committee has lamented the Explanatory Notes' exclusions omissions regarding stays of enforcement amidst annulment proceedings.[95] For example, there is

91. *See Annulment under the ICSID Convention* 25 (R.D. Bishop and S.M. Marchili eds., 2012).
92. Christoph Schreuer, *From ICSID Annulment to Appeal: Halfway Down the Slippery Slope*, 10 Law and Practice of International Courts and Tribunals 211, 225 (2011).
93. *Annulment under the ICSID Convention* 25 (R.D. Bishop and S.M. Marchili eds., 2012). *See also* Christoph Schreuer, *From ICSID Annulment to Appeal: Halfway Down the Slippery Slope*, 10 Law and Practice of International Courts and Tribunals 211, 222 (2011) ("Some of the recent decisions indicate that ad hoc committees have an extremely wide perception of their functions.").
94. *Annulment under the ICSID Convention* 274 (R.D. Bishop and S.M. Marchili eds., 2012).
95. *See Border Timbers Limited, Border Timbers International (Private) Limited and Hangani Development Co. (Private) Limited v. Republic of Zimbabwe*, ICSID Case No. ARB/10/25, Decision on Stay of Enforcement of the Award, April 24, 2017, para. 92 ("neither the ICSID Convention nor the ICSID Arbitration Rules specifically address the issue as to when the provisional stay of enforcement takes effect.").

some disagreement as to whether a grant of a stay of enforcement is "almost automatic,"[96] granted "absent unusual circumstances,"[97] or "exceptional."[98]

As of April 2020, parties applied for a stay of enforcement in 67% of concluded annulment proceedings. Among fifty-one requests for stays of enforcement, forty were granted (i.e., 78% of requests). In 76% of cases where the ad hoc committee granted a continuation of the provisional stay, it ultimately rejected annulment.[99] There is, however, a downward trend and ad hoc committees are granting stays of enforcement in fewer cases. In concluded annulment proceedings registered since 2015, applications for stays of enforcement were requested in fifteen cases but only granted in seven cases (i.e., 47% of requests).[100]

Given the frequency with which ad hoc committees are asked to consider whether to continue a stay of enforcement, and the concomitant implications for award creditors, more guidance on this matter would greatly aid not just stay proceedings before ad hoc committees but also concurrent stay proceedings before domestic courts adjudicating enforcement of awards.

[D] Use of ICSID Arbitration Rule 41(5)

ICSID Arbitration Rule 41(5) was introduced in 2006 as part of the most recent amendment of the ICSID Arbitration Rules. Rule 41(5) was introduced in response to a call by many frustrated States that they were being inundated by meritless claims. The rule authorizes a tribunal to reject a claim that is "manifestly without legal merit." Some commentators have observed that the rule is fashioned after the civil procedural rule in U.S. Federal Courts, known as Rule 12(b)(6), which allows courts to dismiss applications for failure to state a claim on which relief can be granted. Its goal has been to weed out frivolous and "facially" invalid claims to avoid unnecessary and expensive dispute resolution processes. Rule 41(5) provides in full:

> Unless the parties have agreed to another expedited procedure for making preliminary objections, a party may, no later than 30 days after the constitution of the Tribunal, and in any event before the first session of the Tribunal, file an objection that a claim is manifestly without legal merit. The party shall specify as precisely as possible the basis for the objection. The Tribunal, after giving the parties the opportunity to present their observations on the objection, shall, at its

96. *Victor Pey Casado and President Allende Foundation v. Republic of Chile*, ICSID Case No. ARB/98/2, Decision on the Republic of Chile's Application for a Stay of Enforcement of the Award, May 5, 2010, para. 25.
97. *Tenaris S.A. and Talta – Trading e Marketing Sociedade Unipessoal Lda. v. Bolivarian Republic of Venezuela I*, ICSID Case No. ARB 11/26, Decision on the Request to Maintain the Stay of Enforcement of the Award, March 24, 2017, paras. 73–74.
98. *Tenaris S.A. and Talta – Trading e Marketing Sociedade Unipessoal Lda. v. Bolivarian Republic of Venezuela*, ICSID Case No. ARB/12/23, Decision on Venezuela's Request for the Continued Stay of Enforcement of the Award, February 23, 2018, para. 90.
99. *See* Annex, "Decisions on Annulment."
100. *See ibid.*

> first session or promptly thereafter, notify the parties of its decision on the objection. The decision of the Tribunal shall be without prejudice to the right of a party to file an objection pursuant to paragraph (1) or to object, in the course of the proceeding, that a claim lacks legal merit.

While States have frequently, and increasingly, used Rule 41(5) in arbitration proceedings, respondents to annulment applications have used it more sparingly. This is curious, given that applications for annulment have only been partly or fully successful in a minority of cases.[101] Yet parties responding to annulment applications have made Rule 41(5) applications only three times, out of more than 100 registered annulment applications. All three applications were rejected.[102] Given the small sample size, however, this may not accurately reflect the true potential of Rule 41(5) in warding off frivolous applications.

As expressed by the tribunal in *RSM Production Corporation v. Grenada*, Rule 41(5) addresses legal and not factual impediments to claims.[103] Indeed, the *Eskosol v. Italy* tribunal opined that "the Rule 41(5) procedure is not intended, nor should it be used, as the mechanism to address complicated, difficult or unsettled issues of law."[104] Since a review of an annulment application arguably involves only a review of threshold legal questions, not a review of the merits of the award, it could be well-suited to the Rule 41(5) process. For example, if an applicant has only alleged that the tribunal committed various errors in its review of the facts and application of the law, the ad hoc committee may well decide that the claim is manifest without legal merit since it is unreviewable under the narrow Article 52(1) grounds.

§19.05 CONCLUSION

The ICSID Convention enshrines the finality of an award and makes it immediately enforceable. Only in exceptional circumstances can award's finality be disturbed. However, in practice, the exceptional post-award remedy of annulment is being utilized with increased frequency. Delays in the resolution of annulment proceedings, underutilization of post-award remedies other than annulment, and ambiguities on the applicable standards governing stays of enforcement have arguably undermined the efficiency of the ICSID system. Maintaining the credibility of the ICSID system requires reforms that will enhance post-award efficiency. Efficiency could be enhanced by a

101. *See ibid.*
102. *See Ioan Micula, Viorel Micula and others v. Romania*, ICSID Case No. ARB/05/20, Decision on the applicable arbitration rules and on the preliminary objections filed by the Respondents on Annulment, June 25, 2014; *Elsamex, S.A. v. Republic of Honduras*, ICSID Case No. ARB/09/4, Decision on Elsamex S.A.'s Preliminary Objections, January 7, 2014; *Venoklim Holding B.V. v. Bolivarian Republic of Venezuela*, ICSID Case No. ARB/12/22, Decision on Respondent's Preliminary Objections pursuant to ICSID Arbitration Rule 41(5), March 8, 2016.
103. *RSM Production Corporation v. Grenada*, ICSID Case No. ARB/10/6, Award, December 10, 2010. paras. 4.2.1, 6.1.
104. *Eskosol S.p.A. in liquidazione v. Italian Republic*, ICSID Case No. ARB/15/50, Decision on Respondent's Application under Rule 41(5), March 20, 2017, para. 41.

combination of using existing tools within the ICSID Convention, such as other post-award remedies and Rule 41(5), as well as structural reform, such as amendments to the ICISD Rules. Additionally, greater socialization of the rules among decision makers through, *inter alia*, the development of specific guidance on post-award remedies can help ensure greater compliance with the terms of the ICSID Convention.

ANNEX DECISIONS ON ANNULMENT[105]

Case Name	Annulment Application Registration	Committee Constituted	Days To Constitute Committee	Stay Decision	Outcome of Stay Application	Days to Resolve Stay Application[106]	Annulment Decision	Days from Registration to Decision	Outcome Of Annulment Application
Klöckner Industrie-Anlagen GmbH and others v. United Republic of Cameroon and Société Camerounaise des Engrais (ICSID Case No. ARB/81/2)	16 February 1984	19 March 1984	32	N/A	N/A	N/A	3 May 1985	442	Annulled in full
Amco Asia Corporation and others v. Republic of Indonesia (ICSID Case No. ARB/81/1)	27 March 1985	22 April 1985	26	17 May 1985	Granted – security	51	16 May 1986	415	Annulled in full

105. Current as of April 15, 2020.
106. This has been calculated from the date that the annulment application is registered and a provisional stay of enforcement comes into effect.

Maritime International Nominees Establishment v. Republic of Guinea (ICSID Case No. ARB/84/4)	30 March 1988	29 April 1988	30	12 August 1988	Granted – no security or undertaking	135	22 December 1989	632	Annulled in part
Klöckner Industrie-Anlagen GmbH and others v. United Republic of Cameroon and Société Camerounaise des Engrais (ICSID Case No. ARB/81/2) (Resubmission)	1 July 1988	8 July 1988	7	N/A	N/A	N/A	17 May 1990	685	Annulment rejected
Amco Asia Corporation and others v. Republic of Indonesia (ICSID Case No. ARB/81/1-Resubmission)	18 October 1990	30 January 1991	104	2 March 1991	Granted – security	135	17 December 1992	791	Annulment rejected (Supplemental Decision and Rectification annulled)
Wena Hotels Limited v. Arab Republic of Egypt (ICSID Case No. ARB/98/4)	24 January 2001	6 March 2001	41	5 April 2001	Granted – security	71	5 February 2002	377	Annulment rejected

Case Name	Annulment Application Registration	Committee Constituted	Days To Constitute Committee	Stay Decision	Outcome of Stay Application	Days to Resolve Stay Application	Annulment Decision	Days from Registration to Decision	Outcome Of Annulment Application
Compañía de Aguas del Aconquija S.A. and Vivendi Universal S.A. v. Argentine Republic (ICSID Case No ARB/97/3)	23 March 2001	18 May 2001	56	N/A	N/A	N/A	3 July 2002	467	Annulled in part
CDC Group plc v. Republic of Seychelles (ICSID Case No. ARB/02/14)	30 April 2004	28 May 2004	28	14 July 2004	Granted – security	75	29 June 2005	425	Annulment rejected
Consortium R.F.C.C. v. Kingdom of Morocco (ICSID Case No. ARB/00/6)	30 April 2004	8 June 2004	39	N/A	N/A	N/A	18 January 2006	628	Annulment rejected
Patrick Mitchell v. Democratic Republic of the Congo (ICSID Case No. ARB/99/7)	15 July 2004	24 August 2004	40	30 November 2004	Granted – no security or undertaking	138	1 November 2006	839	Annulled in full

Repsol YPF Ecuador S.A. v. Empresa Estatal Petróleos del Ecuador (Petroecuador ICSID Case No. ARB/01/10)	15 July 2004	14 September 2004	61	22 December 2005	Granted – security	525	8 January 2007	907	Annulment rejected
MTD Equity Sdn. Bhd. and MTD Chile S.A. v. Republic of Chile (ICSID Case No. ARB/01/7)	30 September 2004	18 January 2005	110	1 June 2005	Granted – no security or undertaking	244	21 March 2007	902	Annulment rejected
Hussein Nuaman Soufraki v. United Arab Emirates (ICSID Case No. ARB/02/7)	12 November 2004	18 January 2005	67	N/A	N/A	N/A	5 June 2007	935	Annulment rejected
Industria Nacional de Alimentos, S.A. and Indalsa Perú, S.A. (formerly Empresas Lucchetti, S.A. and Lucchetti Perú, S.A.) v. Republic of Peru (ICSID Case No. ARB/03/4)	1 July 2005	17 November 2005	139	N/A	N/A	N/A	5 September 2007	796	Annulment rejected

Case Name	Annulment Application Registration	Committee Constituted	Days To Constitute Committee	Stay Decision	Outcome of Stay Application	Days to Resolve Stay Application	Annulment Decision	Days from Registration to Decision	Outcome Of Annulment Application
CMS Gas Transmission Company v. Argentine Republic (ICSID Case No. ARB/01/8)	27 September 2005	18 April 2006	203	1 September 2006	Granted – undertaking	339	25 September 2007	728	Annulled in part
Malaysian Historical Salvors, SDN, BHD v. Malaysia (ICSID Case No. ARB/05/10)	17 September 2007	30 October 2007	43	N/A	N/A	N/A	16 April 2009	577	Annulled in full
Azurix Corp. v. Argentine Republic (ICSID Case No. ARB/01/12)	11 December 2006	14 June 2007	185	28 December 2007	Granted – no security or undertaking	382	1 September 2009	995	Annulment rejected
M.C.I. Power Group, L.C. and New Turbine, Inc. v. Republic of Ecuador (ICSID Case No. ARB/03/6)	6 December 2007	7 April 2008	123	N/A	N/A	N/A	19 October 2009	683	Annulment rejected

Rumeli Telekom A.S. and Telsim Mobil Telekomunikasyon Hizmetleri A.S. v. Republic of Kazakhstan (ICSID Case No. ARB/05/16)	7 November 2008	12 December 2008	35	19 March 2009	Granted – undertaking	132	25 March 2010	503	Annulment rejected
Compagnie d'Exploitation du Chemin de Fer Transgabonais v. Gabonese Republic (ICSID Case No. ARB/04/05)	10 July 2008	21 October 2008	103	13 March 2009	Granted – undertaking	246	10 May 2010	669	Annulment rejected
Helnan International Hotels A/S v. Arab Republic of Egypt (ICSID Case No. ARB/05/19)	10 November 2008	22 December 2008	42	N/A	N/A	N/A	14 June 2010	581	Annulled in part
Sempra Energy International v. Argentine Republic (ICSID Case No. ARB/02/16)	30 January 2008	15 September 2008	229	5 March 2009	Granted – security	400	29 June 2010	881	Annulled in full

Case Name	Annulment Application Registration	Committee Constituted	Days To Constitute Committee	Stay Decision	Outcome of Stay Application	Days to Resolve Stay Application	Annulment Decision	Days from Registration to Decision	Outcome Of Annulment Application
Enron Creditors Recovery Corporation v. Argentine Republic (ICSID Case No. ARB/01/3)	7 March 2008	22 May 2008	76	7 October 2008	Granted – no security or undertaking	92	30 July 2010	875	Annulled in part
Compañía de Aguas del Aconquija S.A. and Vivendi Universal S.A. v. Argentine Republic (ICSID Case No. ARB/97/3) (Resubmission)	19 December 2007	22 May 2008	155	4 November 2008	Granted – undertaking	321	10 August 2010	965	Annulment rejected
Sociedad Anónima Eduardo Vieira v. Republic of Chile (ICSID Case No. ARB/04/7)	24 January 2008	1 May 2008	98	N/A	N/A	N/A	10 December 2010	1051	Annulment rejected

Fraport AG Frankfurt Airport Services Worldwide v. Republic of the Philippines (ICSID Case No. ARB/03/25)	8 January 2008	14 April 2008	97	N/A	N/A	N/A	23 December 2010	1080	Annulled in full
Duke Energy International Peru Investments No. 1 Ltd. v. Republic of Peru (ICSID Case No. ARB/03/28)	24 December 2008	4 March 2009	70	23 June 2009	Granted – undertaking	181	1 March 2011	797	Annulment rejected
Togo Electricité and GDF-Suez Energie Services v. Republic of Togo (ICSID Case No. ARB/06/7)	4 November 2010	22 November 2010	18	31 January 2011	Granted – no security or undertaking	88	6 September 2011	306	Annulment rejected
Continental Casualty Company v. Argentine Republic (ICSID Case No. ARB/03/9)	14 January 2009	19 March 2009	64	23 October 2009	Granted – no security or undertaking	140	16 September 2011	975	Annulment rejected

Case Name	Annulment Application Registration	Committee Constituted	Days To Constitute Committee	Stay Decision	Outcome of Stay Application	Days to Resolve Stay Application	Annulment Decision	Days from Registration to Decision	Outcome Of Annulment Application
AES Summit Generation Limited and AES-Tisza Erömü Kft. v. Republic of Hungary (ICSID Case No. ARB/07/22)	28 January 2011	21 March 2011	52	N/A	N/A	N/A	29 June 2012	518	Annulment rejected
Víctor Pey Casado and President Allende Foundation v. Republic of Chile (ICSID Case No ARB/98/2)	6 July 2009	22 December 2009	169	7 May 2010	Granted – no security or undertaking	112	18 December 2012	1261	Annulled in part
RSM Production Corporation v. Central African Republic (ICSID Case No. ARB/07/2)	21 November 2011	20 December 2011	29	29 March 2012	Rejected	129	20 January 2013	426	Annulment rejected
Libananco Holdings Co. Limited v. Republic of Turkey (ICSID Case No. ARB/06/8)	20 December 2011	14 February 2012	56	7 May 2012	Granted – no security or undertaking	139	22 May 2013	519	Annulment rejected

Malicorp Limited v. Arab Republic of Egypt (ICSID Case No. ARB/8/18)	13 June 2011	8 July 2011	25	N/A	N/A	N/A	3 July 2013	751	Annulment rejected
Joseph C. Lemire v. Ukraine (ICSID Case No. ARB/06/18)	27 July 2011	7 October 2011	72	14 February 2012	Granted – security	202	8 July 2013	712	Annulment rejected
Impregilo S.p.A. v. Argentine Republic (ICSID Case No. ARB/07/17)	25 October 2011	30 January 2012	97	N/A	No decision made. Provisional stay continued throughout annulment proceeding.	822	24 January 2014	822	Annulment rejected
Caratube International Oil Company LLP v. Republic of Kazakhstan (ICSID Case No. ARB/08/12)	5 October 2012	12 November 2012	38	14 March 2013	Granted – no security or undertaking	160	24 February 2014	507	Annulment rejected
SGS Société Générale de Surveillance S.A. v. Republic of Paraguay (ICSID Case No. ARB/07/29)	8 June 2012	27 July 2012	49	22 March 2013	Rejected	287	19 May 2014	710	Annulment rejected

Case Name	Annulment Application Registration	Committee Constituted	Days To Constitute Committee	Stay Decision	Outcome of Stay Application	Days to Resolve Stay Application	Annulment Decision	Days from Registration to Decision	Outcome Of Annulment Application
Alapli Elektrik B.V. v. Republic of Turkey (ICSID Case No. ARB/08/13)	16 November 2012	12 December 2012	26	N/A	N/A	N/A	10 July 2014	601	Annulment rejected
El Paso Energy International Company v. Argentine Republic (ICSID Case No. ARB/03/15)	7 March 2012	22 May 2012	76	14 November 2012	Granted – no security or undertaking	252	22 September 2014	929	Annulment rejected
Daimler Financial Services AG v. Argentine Republic (ICSID Case No. ARB/05/1)	27 December 2012	7 March 2013	70	N/A	N/A	N/A	7 January 2015	741	Annulment rejected
Iberdrola Energía, S.A. v. Republic of Guatemala (ICSID Case No. ARB/09/5)	18 December 2012	15 February 2013	59	28 October 2013	Stay and security agreed by the parties	314	13 January 2015	756	Annulment rejected
Tza Yap Shum v. Republic of Peru (ICSID Case No. ARB/07/6)	9 November 2011	11 January 2012	63	N/A	N/A	N/A	12 February 2015	1191	Annulment rejected

Kiliç İnşaat İ thalat İhracat Sanayi ve Ticaret Anonim Şirketi v. Turkmenistan (ICSID Case No. ARB/10/1)	27 January 2014	3 March 2014	35	5 June 2014	Granted – security	64	14 July 2015	533	Annulment rejected
Occidental Petroleum Corporation and Occidental Exploration and Production Company v. Republic of Ecuador (ICSID Case No. ARB/06/11)	11 October 2012	18 January 2013	99	9/30/2013 & 9/23/2014	Granted – no security or undertaking	N/A	2 November 2015	1117	Annulled in part
Tulip Real Estate and Development Netherlands B.V. v. Republic of Turkey (ICSID Case No. ARB/11/28)	14 July 2014	26 August 2014	43	N/A	N/A	N/A	30 December 2015	534	Annulment rejected
Adem Dogan v. Turkmenistan (ICSID Case No. ARB/09/9)	28 August 2014	30 September 2014	33	24 November 2014	Granted – security	88	15 January 2016	505	Annulment rejected

Case Name	Annulment Application Registration	Committee Constituted	Days To Constitute Committee	Stay Decision	Outcome of Stay Application	Days to Resolve Stay Application	Annulment Decision	Days from Registration to Decision	Outcome Of Annulment Application
Total S.A. v. Argentine Republic (ICSID Case No. ARB/04/1)	2 April 2014	27 May 2014	55	4 December 2014	Rejected	246	1 February 2016	670	Annulment rejected
EDF International S.A. SAUR International S.A. and Leon Participaciones Argentinas S.A. v. Argentine Republic (ICSID Case No. ARB/03/23)	11 October 2012	2 January 2013	83	18 July 2013	Granted – undertaking	280	5 February 2016	1212	Annulment rejected
Ioan Micula, Viorel Micula and others v. Romania (ICSID Case No. ARB/05/20)	18 April 2014	12 May 2014	24	7 August 2014	Granted – undertaking	111	26 February 2016	679	Annulment rejected
Antoine Abou Lahoud and Leila Bounafeh-Abou Lahoud v. Democratic Republic of the Congo (ICSID Case No. ARB/10/4)	19 June 2014	18 July 2014	29	30 September 2014	Granted – security	103	29 March 2016	649	Annulment rejected

TECO Guatemala Holdings, LLC v. Republic of Guatemala (ICSID Case No. ARB/10/23)	22 April 2014	29 May 2014	37	10 February 2015	Granted – no security or undertaking	294	5 April 2016	714	Annulled in part
Poštová banka, a.s. and ISTROKAPITAL SE v. Hellenic Republic (ICSID Case No. ARB/13/8)	5 August 2015	2 September 2015	28	N/A	N/A	N/A	29 September 2016	421	Annulment rejected
SAUR International v. Argentine Republic (ICSID Case No. ARB/04/4)	22 September 2014	7 January 2015	107	1 March 2016	Granted – security (stay later lifted on 1 April 2016 when undertaking not provided by respondent)	526	19 December 2016	819	Annulment rejected

Case Name	Annulment Application Registration	Committee Constituted	Days To Constitute Committee	Stay Decision	Outcome of Stay Application	Days to Resolve Stay Application	Annulment Decision	Days from Registration to Decision	Outcome Of Annulment Application
Tidewater Investment SRL and Tidewater Caribe, C.A. v. Bolivarian Republic of Venezuela (ICSID Case No. ARB/10/5)	16 July 2015	9 September 2015	55	29 February 2016	Granted in part – no security or undertaking	228	27 December 2016	530	Annulled in part
Venezuela Holdings B.V. and others v. Bolivarian Republic of Venezuela (ICSID Case No. ARB/07/27)	9 February 2015	8 May 2015	88	17 September 2015	Granted – undertaking	220	9 March 2017	759	Annulled in part
Suez, Sociedad General de Aguas de Barcelona S.A. and Vivendi Universal S.A v. Argentine Republic (ICSID Case No. ARB/03/19)	21 August 2015	23 October 2015	63	7 June 2016	Rejected	291	5 May 2017	623	Annulment rejected

Gambrinus, Corp. v. Bolivarian Republic of Venezuela (ICSID Case No. ARB/11/31)	16 October 2015	15 January 2016	91	N/A	N/A	N/A	3 October 2017	718	Annulment rejected
Venoklim Holding B.V. v. Bolivarian Republic of Venezuela (ICSID Case No. ARB/12/22)	6 August 2015	23 September 2015	48	N/A	N/A	N/A	2 February 2018	911	Annulment rejected
Tenaris S.A. and Talta – Trading e Marketing Sociedade Unipessoal Lda. v. Bolivarian Republic of Venezuela (ICSID Case No. ARB/11/26)	26 September 2016	27 December 2016	92	24 March 2017	Rejected	179	8 August 2018	681	Unknown

Case Name	Annulment Application Registration	Committee Constituted	Days To Constitute Committee	Stay Decision	Outcome of Stay Application	Days to Resolve Stay Application	Annulment Decision	Days from Registration to Decision	Outcome Of Annulment Application
Standard Chartered Bank (Hong Kong) Limited v. Tanzania Electric Supply Company Limited (ICSID Case No. ARB/10/20)	13 January 2017	2 February 2017	20	12 April 2017	Granted – security (stay later lifted on 25 May 2017 when undertaking not provided by respondent)	89	22 August 2018	586	Annulment rejected
Bernhard von Pezold and others v. Republic of Zimbabwe (ICSID Case No. ARB/10/15) and Border Timbers Limited and others v. Republic of Zimbabwe (ICSID Case No. ARB/10/25)	2 November 2015	21 December 2015	49	24 April 2017	Rejected	539	21 November 2018	1115	Annulment rejected

OI European Group B.V. v. Bolivarian Republic of Venezuela (ICSID Case No. ARB/11/25)	17 July 2015	13 October 2015	88	4 April 2016	Rejected	262	6 December 2018	1238	Annulment rejected
Suez, Sociedad General de Aguas de Barcelona S.A. and Interagua Servicios Integrales de Agua S.A. v. Argentine Republic (ICSID Case No. ARB/03/17)	21 September 2016	15 December 2016	85	21 June 2017	Rejected	273	14 December 2018	814	Annulment rejected
Tenaris S.A. and Talta – Trading e Marketing Sociedade Unipessoal Lda. v. Bolivarian Republic of Venezuela (ICSID Case No. ARB/12/23)	18 April 2017	17 October 2017	182	23 February 2018	Rejected	311	28 December 2018	619	Annulment rejected

Case Name	Annulment Application Registration	Committee Constituted	Days To Constitute Committee	Stay Decision	Outcome of Stay Application	Days to Resolve Stay Application	Annulment Decision	Days from Registration to Decision	Outcome Of Annulment Application
Churchill Mining Plc and Planet Mining Pty Ltd v. Republic of Indonesia (ICSID Case No. ARB/12/40 and 12/14)	11 April 2017	15 May 2017	34	27 June 2017	Granted – security	77	18 March 2019	706	Annulment rejected
Flughafen Zürich A.G. y Gestión e Ingeniería IDC S.A. v. República Bolivariana de Venezuela (ICSID Case No. ARB/10/19)	27 March 2015	24 August 2015	150	11 March 2016	Granted – security	350	15 April 2019	1480	Annulment rejected
Vestey Group Ltd v. Bolivarian Republic of Venezuela (ICSID Case No. ARB/06/4)	16 August 2016	8 November 2016	84	18 October 2017	Rejected	428	26 April 2019	983	Annulment rejected

RSM Production Corporation v. Saint Lucia (ICSID Case No. ARB/12/10)	21 November 2016	4 January 2017	44	N/A	N/A	N/A	29 April 2019	889	Annulled in part
Mobil Exploration and Development Argentina Inc. Suc. Argentina and Mobil Argentina S.A. v. Argentine Republic (ICSID Case No. ARB/04/16)	29 June 2016	18 August 2016	50	18 January 2017	Granted – no security or undertaking	203	8 May 2019	1043	Annulment rejected
Teinver S.A., Transportes de Cercanías S.A. and Autobuses Urbanos del Sur S.A. v. Argentine Republic (ICSID Case No. ARB/09/1)	22 November 2017	21 December 2017	29	Unknown	Unknown	N/A	29 May 2019	553	Annulment rejected

Case Name	Annulment Application Registration	Committee Constituted	Days To Constitute Committee	Stay Decision	Outcome of Stay Application	Days to Resolve Stay Application	Annulment Decision	Days from Registration to Decision	Outcome Of Annulment Application
Highbury International AVV and Ramstein Trading Inc. v. Bolivarian Republic of Venezuela (ICSID Case No. ARB/11/1)	10 January 2014	6 March 2014	55	N/A	N/A	N/A	8 September 2019	2067	Annulment rejected
Capital Financial Holdings Luxembourg S.A. v. Republic of Cameroon (ICSID Case No. ARB/15/18)	31 October 2017	11 January 2018	72	N/A	N/A	N/A	25 October 2019	724	Annulment rejected
Fábrica de Vidrios Los Andes, C.A. and Owens-Illinois de Venezuela, C.A. v. República Bolivariana de Venezuela (ICSID Case No. ARB/12/21)	16 March 2018	23 April 2018	38	N/A	N/A	N/A	22 November 2019	616	Annulment rejected

Víctor Pey Casado and President Allende Foundation v. Republic of Chile (ICSID Case No. ARB/98/2) (Resubmission)	25 October 2017	20 December 2017	56	15 March 2018	Granted – no security or undertaking	141	8 January 2020	805	Annulment rejected
Blusun S.A., Jean-Pierre Lecorcier and Michael Stein v. Italian Republic (ICSID Case No. ARB/14/3)	2 May 2017	20 June 2017	49	N/A	N/A	N/A	13 April 2020	1077	Annulment rejected

CHAPTER 20

Enforcement of Investment Court Decisions under the New York Convention: A Search for Defining Elements

Brian McGarry[*]

This chapter explores whether a decision rendered by an international investment court or similar body would be enforceable in the courts of third States as a 'foreign arbitral award', pursuant to the 1958 New York Convention on the Recognition and Enforcement of Foreign Arbitral Awards. After asserting the premise that an investment court would be harmonious with States' existing obligations under the Convention on the Settlement of Investment Disputes between States and Nationals of Other States (ICSID Convention), this chapter reviews salient aspects of the New York Convention's *travaux préparatoires*, and its use to enforce the decisions of bodies that challenge assumptions concerning what features make an award 'foreign' and 'arbitral'. The chapter then charts a new path by gauging the meaning of 'arbitration' in international economic law, in light of its widely ratified usage decades later in the distinctive arbitral procedures of the World Trade Organization (WTO). Drawing from this variety of contexts, the chapter concludes by linking the interim arbitration mechanism adopted by some WTO members in April 2020 to the institutional body that may yet emerge from UN Commission on International Trade Law (UNCITRAL) negotiations on the reform of investor-State dispute settlement (ISDS).

* The author thanks Ms Elena Murashko for her valuable assistance in researching sections of this chapter.

§20.01 INTRODUCTION

The prospect of institutional reforms to ISDS has raised questions regarding the legality of specific reforms in relation to States' obligations within the prevailing ISDS framework. These hypothetical questions became relevant in July 2017, when members of the UNCITRAL placed ISDS reform on the organization's formal agenda.[1] Some members have contemporaneously forged permanent institutional dispute settlement reforms in this field, such as those found in provisions of the recent Canada-EU Comprehensive Economic and Trade Agreement[2] and EU-Vietnam Free Trade Agreement[3] establishing a standing tribunal and a separate appeals chamber.

As of September 2020, UNCITRAL continues to discuss a number of proposals from members concerning the nature of any forthcoming institutional reform to ISDS. Some members have proposed a standing body with a built-in appellate tier,[4] or the maintenance of investor-State arbitration with an appellate mechanism superimposed upon it.[5] These two approaches have indeed been a principal focus of the broader debate on how best to conduct ISDS at the international level in a manner that retains the current direct right of access for individuals.[6] However, these approaches have been considered in tandem with proposals to strengthen complementary channels, such as non-binding conciliation[7] and inter-State dispute resolution.[8]

While the possibility of an appellate mechanism constitutes a less radical departure from the status quo than would the creation of an exclusively court-based ISDS process, it has raised more critical questions regarding the modification and potential breach of existing ISDS treaties. One such question is whether this mechanism would be compatible with States' rights and obligations under the ICSID Convention. While scholarly opinion on this matter has been somewhat divided,[9] the

1. *See UNCITRAL to Consider Possible Reform of Investor-State Dispute Settlement*, UN Information Service, UNIS/L/250 (14 July 2017).
2. *See* Comprehensive Economic and Trade Agreement between Canada and the European Union (Canada-EU) (Brussels, 30 October 2016), 2017 OJ L11 23, provisionally entered into force 21 September 2017, Art. 8.29.
3. *See* Free Trade Agreement between the European Union and the Socialist Republic of Vietnam (EU-Vietnam) (Hanoi, 30 June 2019), Ch. 8.
4. *See*, e.g., UNCITRAL, 'Possible reform of investor-State dispute settlement (ISDS). Multilateral instrument on ISDS reform. Note by the Secretariat', A/CN.9/WG.III/WP.194 (16 January 2020), para. 9 (citing the Submission from the European Union and its Member States, A/CN.9/WG.III/WP.159/Add.1).
5. *See ibid.* A/CN.9/WG.III/WP.194, para. 18.
6. *See*, e.g., Gabrielle Kaufmann-Kohler and Michele Potestà, *Can the Mauritius Convention Serve as a Model for the Reform of Investor-State Arbitration in Connection with the Introduction of a Permanent Investment Tribunal or an Appeal Mechanism*, CTR Int'l Disp. Sett. (2016), 16–17.
7. *See*, e.g., UNCITRAL, 'Possible reform of investor-State dispute settlement (ISDS). Dispute prevention and mitigation – Means of alternative dispute resolution. Note by the Secretariat', A/CN.9/WG.III/WP.190 (15 January 2020), paras 29, 46 (citing the Submission from the Government of Indonesia, A/CN.9/WG.III/WP.156, para. 15).
8. *Ibid.*, at para. 24 (citing Submission from the Government of Brazil (A/CN.9/WG.III/WP.171, para. 5); Submission from the Government of South Africa (A/CN.9/WG.III/WP.176, para. 47); Submission from the Government of the Republic of Korea (A/CN.9/WG.III/WP.179, 5)).
9. *See*, e.g., Jansen N. Calamita, *The (In)Compatibility of Appellate Mechanisms with Existing Instruments of the Investment Treaty Regime*, 18 J. World Inv. & Trade 585, 605–613 (2017).

text and *travaux préparatoires* of Article 41 of the 1969 Vienna Convention on the Law of Treaties (embodying a customary rule for modification of multilateral treaties *inter se*) permit ICSID members to carve out the Annulment Committee provisions of that treaty in favour of submitting arbitrated decisions to a standing appellate mechanism.[10] This could be fulfilled by establishing an 'opt-in' protocol treaty in a manner similar to the 2014 Mauritius Transparency Convention vis-à-vis UNCITRAL transparency rules in ISDS, or the Organisation for Economic Co-operation and Development's 2017 adoption of a multilateral convention for amending bilateral tax treaties.[11] Irrespective of the means of treaty amendment, however, the investment court that may emerge from the UNCITRAL reform process appears to be harmonious with States' existing obligations under the ICSID Convention.

Based on this premise, this chapter explores a potentially thornier question facing UNCITRAL negotiators: whether a decision rendered by an international investment court or similar body would be subject to enforcement in the courts of third States as a 'foreign arbitral award', pursuant to the 1958 New York Convention on the Recognition and Enforcement of Foreign Arbitral Awards (NYC). In this respect, the chapter examines the meaning of this treaty term, in light of its *travaux préparatoires* and its distinctive role in the practice of the Iran-US Claims Tribunal (IUSCT). The chapter then compares these findings to WTO proceedings which are referred to as arbitration, but which nevertheless test assumptions about the critical components of arbitral process. It thereafter concludes by placing the ISDS reform project in the context of contemporary arbitral innovations in other regimes of international economic law.

§20.02 ENFORCEMENT AND THE TERMS OF THE NEW YORK CONVENTION

This section first considers the significance of jurisdictional seat to the 'foreign' character of awards enforceable under the NYC, a widely ratified treaty seen as critically important to the effectiveness of international arbitration.[12] In doing so, it assesses enforcement under the terms of the Convention with an eye towards their application to investment court decisions in a decentralized (i.e., national court-based)

10. *See*, e.g., Brian McGarry and Josef Ostransky, *Is the Law of Treaties an Obstacle or a Conduit for the Reform of Investor-State Dispute Settlement?*, 32 Emory Int'l L.R. 1001 (2017). While Art. 4 of the 1969 Vienna Convention confirms its non-retroactivity (and thus that it is not formally applicable to the 1965 ICSID Convention, much of the Convention has been found to codify extant customary international law.
11. *See* the discussion in Colin M. Brown, 'A Multilateral Mechanism for the Settlement of Investment Disputes: Some Preliminary Remarks', 32(3) ICSID Rev. 673, 685 (2017) (referencing the Multilateral Convention to Implement Tax Related Measures to Prevent Base Erosion and Profit Shifting).
12. Finding only Arts II, V and VII to be 'critically important', *see* V.V. Veeder, *Is There a Need to Revise the New York Convention: Key note speech*, Int'l Arb. Instit. (Dijon, 12–14 September 2008), 184. Some States have directly incorporated the NYC into national laws. *See also* 9 USC §§201, et seq. *See further* John A. Spanogle, *The Enforcement of Foreign Arbitral Awards in the U.S. – A Matter of Federal Law*, 13 U.S.-Mex. L.J. 97, 97 (2005).

system. A system instead modelled on the ICSID Convention would include a self-contained enforcement regime, removing the need to institute enforcement proceedings before asset-state courts. Moreover, an institutional ISDS reform based on the ICSID model would presumably establish a two-tiered structure with statutory authority to review decisions, as with the ICSID Annulment Committee.[13] In order to assess the roles of permanence and privity to the enforcement of investment court awards before national courts, this section thereafter considers the importance of features such as party appointment of arbitrators - and bilateral autonomy generally - to the definition of the 'arbitral award' in the NYC's *travaux préparatoires*.

[A] Requirement of a 'Foreign' Award

The NYC was drafted against the backdrop of the 1927 Geneva Convention on the Execution of Foreign Arbitral Awards. The International Chamber of Commerce (ICC), which initiated the drafting process, considered the Geneva Convention's main defect to be that it provided for the enforcement of only those awards that were strictly in accordance with the procedural law of the country where the arbitration took place. The ICC's 1953 draft convention introduced for this reason the primacy of procedural law that the parties import through mutual agreement, which would be reflected five years later in the NYC.[14]

The NYC drafting committee decided not to include a requirement found in the Geneva Convention that the arbitral award must have been made between persons who are subject to the jurisdiction of one of the Contracting States. This exclusion was justified largely on the premise that the expression was too vague to be predictably interpreted in different countries.[15] Notably, the Geneva Convention also required that an award had become 'final' in the country in whose territory it was issued. This led to situations of double exequatur, wherein a successful party would be in practice required to obtain enforcement authorization by courts in both the country of origin and the country of assets. The drafters of the NYC sought to improve upon this cumbersome situation by deleting 'final' in favour of Article V(1)(e)'s condition that an award has become 'binding' upon the parties.[16]

The Convention would not take up the ICC's proposal for a truly international conception of arbitration, rejecting reference to 'international awards' in favour of the treaty title's reference to 'foreign arbitral awards'.[17] Article I(1) states:

13. *See* ICSID Convention, Art. 52.
14. *See* NYC, Art. V(1)(d).
15. UN Economic and Social Council, 'Report of the Committee on the Enforcement of International Arbitral Awards', E/27C4: E/AC.42/4/Rev.1 (18 March 1955), para. 23.
16. *See* Albert Jan van den Berg, *New York Convention of 1958: Refusals of Enforcement*, 18(2) ICC Int'l Ct Arb. Bull. 1, 14 (2007). On the binding character of awards in relation to the prospect of subsequent challenge before another arbitral body, *see* further *La Société Diag v. The Czech Republic*, 12-29.112 (Fr. Court of Cassation), 5 March 2014; Federal Court of Germany, 18 January 1990, III ZR 269/88.
17. *See* van den Berg, *supra* n. 16, at 11.

> This Convention shall apply to the recognition and enforcement of arbitral awards *made in the territory of a State* other than the State where the recognition and enforcement of such awards are sought, and arising out of differences between persons, whether physical or legal. It shall also apply to arbitral awards *not considered as domestic awards* in the State where their recognition and enforcement are sought. (Emphasis added)

Different national delegations brought distinct understandings of the foreign or international character of arbitral awards to these negotiations. Some considered that the effectiveness of the Convention would depend upon providing a definition for the term 'foreign arbitral award',[18] while others contended that the Geneva Convention had operated adequately without entering into the risks of defining 'foreign'-ness in this respect.[19] Some defined a 'foreign' award as any award not rendered within their own national territory.[20] Others considered that this requires that the award has been rendered under the jurisdiction of one of the Contracting States,[21] and that the draft text as formulated was too vague as to whether it might also require enforcement of awards rendered in cases where neither party was under the jurisdiction of a Contracting State.[22] A joint proposal from eight European delegations suggested that foreign awards simply be defined as 'other than those considered as domestic in the country in which they are relied upon'.[23] This in particular accommodated the views of some States that 'foreign'-ness had more to do with the parties' choice of law than the physical territory in which an award was concluded.[24] Some delegations further suggested that this be accompanied with a clause expressly permitting a State to declare upon signing that its reciprocal recognition only applies to awards that are considered to be 'commercial' under its national law.[25]

---

18. *See*, for example, the views of Sweden in UN Economic and Social Council, Committee on the Enforcement of International Arbitral Awards, 'First Session. Summary Record of the Second Meeting', E/AC.42/SR.2 (2 March 1955), 9–10.
19. *See*, e.g., *ibid.* (views of the USSR), at 10.
20. *See*, e.g., *ibid.* (views of the UK).
21. *See*, for example, views of Hungary in UN Economic and Social Council, 'Recognition and Enforcement of Foreign Awards. Comments by Governments on the draft Convention on the Recognition and Enforcement of Foreign Arbitral Awards', E/2822/Add.5 (13 April 1956), 1.
22. *See*, e.g., *ibid.*, at 3 (views of Norway). *See also* the variant phrasing proposed in the UN Economic and Social Council, Conference on International Commercial Arbitration, 'Consideration of the Draft Convention on the Recognition and Enforcement of Foreign Arbitral Awards (Item 4 on the Agenda). Pakistan: amendments to draft Convention', E/CONF.26/L.16 (26 May 1958) (amendments to Arts. 1, 3, 4, 6, 12, and suggestion of an additional article).
23. *See*, for example, the 'European' proposal in UN Economic and Social Council, Conference on International Commercial Arbitration, 'Consideration of the Draft Convention on the Recognition and Enforcement of Foreign Arbitral Awards (Item 4 on the Agenda). Austria, Belgium, Federal Republic of Germany, France, Italy, Netherlands, Sweden, Switzerland: amendment to Article 1', E/CONF.26/L.6 (22 May 1958). *See also ibid.*, E/CONF.26/L.13 (Italy: amendment to Art. 1); E/CONF.26/L.29 (Yugoslavia: amendment to Art. 1).
24. *See*, for example, the views of France in UN Economic and Social Council, Conference on International Commercial Arbitration, 'Summary Record of the Fifth Meeting', E/COHF.26/SR.5 (12 September 1958), 8–9. *See also ibid.* (comments of Norway).
25. *See* UN Economic and Social Council, Conference on International Commercial Arbitration, 'Consideration of the Draft Convention on the Recognition and Enforcement of Foreign Arbitral Awards (Item 4 on the Agenda). United Kingdom: amendments to the draft Convention',

This definition advanced in the joint European proposal – and generally reflected in the adopted text of the Convention – also accommodated some States' embrace of the concept of delocalized, a-national awards. While some delegations considered it 'unthinkable that the will of the parties should create a novum', devoid of reference to positive rules of national or international law,[26] others considered that this touched upon the critical difference between a judgment and an award, observing that the Convention's potential to improve upon its 1927 predecessor was possible 'only to the extent that international arbitral awards are made more independent of the law of the country in which the arbitration takes place'.[27]

Taking these negotiations into account, the ICC Secretary-General surmised that the new Convention should also apply to arbitral awards rendered in the territory of the State in which the award is being enforced, provided that the dispute submitted to arbitration arose between parties domiciled (or having their main establishments) in the territories of different States.[28] These discussions also determined that the scope of the application of the Convention should be further extended to a third class of arbitral awards, comprising all arbitral awards 'made in disputes involving legal relationships implemented in the whole or in part in the territories of different states', irrespective of whether or not such awards were rendered abroad, and regardless of the domicile of the parties between which arbitration took place.[29]

On this basis, one may query whether the decisions of an international investment court or appellate mechanism would meet the territorial requirements for enforcement under the Convention (i.e., in a decentralized system reliant upon national courts' review and recognition of these decisions). As noted, the Convention applies to 'foreign' awards and those 'not considered as domestic awards in the State

E/CONF.26/L.7 (22 May 1958) (amendment to Art. I(2)). The drafting committee also considered whether the Convention should be more generally limited to arbitral awards arising out of commercial disputes, as was envisaged in the ICC draft. While in some countries the word 'commercial' and *commerçant* has a clear legal meaning, the law of other countries does not specifically differentiate between civil and commercial matters. For this reason, the Committee decided not to include any qualification in paragraph 1 of Art. I. *See* UN Economic and Social Council, 'Report of the Committee on the Enforcement of International Arbitral Awards', E/2704 E/AC.42/4/Rev.1 (18 March 1955), para. 26.

26. *See*, for example, the comments of Luxembourg in UN Economic and Social Council, Committee on the Enforcement of International Arbitral Awards, 'Comments received from Governments regarding the Draft Convention on the Enforcement of International Arbitral Awards', E/AC.42/1 (21 January 1955), 5–6. *See also* the comments of Germany in UN Economic and Social Council, 'Recognition and Enforcement of Foreign Arbitral Awards. Report by the Secretary-General', Twenty-first session, Item 8, E/2822 (31 January 1956), 5–7 (observing *inter alia* that '[t]here is no such thing as an arbitral procedure that is completely divorced from some municipal procedural law').
27. *See*, e.g., *ibid.* (comments of Switzerland in Report by the Secretary-General), at 8–9.
28. *See* UN Economic and Social Council, Conference on International Commercial Arbitration, 'Comments on the Draft Convention on the Recognition and Enforcement of Foreign Arbitral Awards. Note by the Secretary-General', E/CONF.26/2 (6 March 1958), 2 (acknowledging the views of Switzerland and the ICC).
29. *Ibid.*

where their recognition and enforcement are sought'.[30] Subjecting these new institutional proceedings to a domestic *lex arbitri* would meet this requirement.[31] In a system based instead on the self-contained ICSID regime (creating an a-national procedural forum), the practice of national courts applying the New York Convention and the enforcement of ICSID awards in non-ICSID states in particular suggests that the decisions of an international investment court or appellate mechanism would satisfy the Convention's 'non-domestic' requirement.[32]

Similar questions have recently arisen as concerns the practice of bodies with structural links to a prospective international investment court. For example, the 1980 Unified Agreement for the Investment of Arab Capital in the Arab States established the Arab Investment Court, a second instance after a traditional arbitration mechanism, which has as of September 2020 given rise to only two cases, with one of these being discontinued.[33] The other award, *Al-Kharafi v. Libya*, led to multiple enforcement proceedings before being annulled by the Cairo Court of Appeals in June 2020, which ascribed certain a-national characteristics to the decisions of the Arab Investment Court despite having its legal seat in the same country.[34]

Another body with a potentially relevant institutional structure, the IUSCT, an institution with judges seated in The Hague, has issued decisions that have been subject to notable scrutiny under the NYC, at times in tandem with an analysis as to whether there was a satisfactory agreement in writing between the parties.[35] Whereas the English Court of Appeals in *Dallal* observed in obiter dicta that Dutch law in force at the time did not recognize the validity of the arbitration agreement underlying an

30. NYC, Art. I(1). *See also* Art. I(3) (permitting Contracting Parties, on the basis of reciprocity, to file reservations to the Convention which declare that they will only recognize awards rendered 'in the territory of another Contracting State'). *See further Societe Europeenne d'Etudes et d'Enterprises v. Socialist Federal Republic of Yugoslavia*, HR [Hoge Raad der Nederlanden] NJ 74, 361 (1974).
31. *See also* Kaufmann-Kohler and Potestà, *supra* n. 6, at paras 156–157. On the significance of the parties' chosen seat over the physical place of arbitration, *see also* Gary Born, *International Commercial Arbitration* (Kluwer 2d ed. 2014), 2943–2948.
32. *See* UNCITRAL, *UNCITRAL Secretariat Guide on the Convention and Enforcement of Foreign Arbitral Awards*, paras 58–64. *See generally* Giuliana Cane, *The Enforcement of ICSID Awards: Revolutionary or Ineffective?*, 15(3–4) Amer. Rev. Int'l Arb. 439.
33. *See* UN Conference on Trade and Development, Investment Policy Hub, Investment Dispute Settlement Navigator, https://investmentpolicy.unctad.org/investment-dispute-settlement. *See also* Walid Ben Hamida, *The First Investment Court Decision*, 7 J. World Inv. & Trade 699 (2006).
34. *See Mohamed Abdulmohsen Al-Kharafi & Sons Co. v. Libya and others*, Cairo Court of Appeal Decision, Arabic and English translation, 3 June 2020, unofficial English translation at https://jusmundi.com/en/document/decision/en-mohamed-abdulmohsen-al-kharafi-sons-co-v-libya-and-others-judgment-of-the-cairo-court-of-appeal-unofficial-english-translation-wednesday-3rd-june-2020#decision_11421 (characterizing the Egyptian courts' review of the underlying award as finding that the Arab Investment Court 'is an independent special regional judicial body that is not related to the national procedural systems including any national arbitration system'). *Cf.* Unified Agreement for the Investment of Arab Capital in the Arab States, Art. 28(5).
35. *See Ministry of Defense of the Islamic Republic of Iran v. Gould International Inc. and others*, U.S. C.D. Cal., Decision of 14 January 1988, published in XIV YB Comm. Arb. 763 et seq. (1989), 763, et seq.; *Gould Inc., Gould Marketing v. Hoffman Export Corporation, Gould International, Inc. v. Ministry of Defense of the Islamic Republic of Iran*, 887 F.2d 1357 (9th Cir. 1989).

award of the Iran-US Tribunal,[36] the US 9th Circuit Court of Appeals in *Gould* considered that enforcement under the New York Convention did not require that an award be made 'under a national law'.[37] The Court in *Gould* thus expressly addressed the territoriality and consensual requirements of the New York Convention, while implicitly acknowledging that the Tribunal falls within the scope of 'arbitral' bodies. This is notable because of certain institutional features of the IUSCT, such as the inability of parties to appoint arbitrators – an issue raised by neither party in *Gould*.[38]

[B] Requirement of an 'Agreement in Writing'

A standing investment court would appear to qualify as a 'permanent arbitral body' within the meaning of the NYC. Article I(2) of the Convention states:

> The term 'arbitral awards' shall include not only awards made by arbitrators appointed for each case but also those made by *permanent arbitral bodies* to which the parties have submitted.

Some national courts have supported this point when enforcing decisions of the IUSCT,[39] a body established by the 1981 Algiers Accords as an exclusive forum for nationals' claims falling within its subject matter and temporal jurisdiction. During the drafting of the NYC, some delegations considered the critical difference between awards and judgments to be one of the parties' consent (regardless of the type of

36. *See Dallal v. Bank Mellat* [1986] QB 441 (C.A.), pp. 455, 461. The Court of Appeals in *Dallal* observed that the Algiers Accords do not qualify as an 'agreement in writing' under the NYC. The Court found dispositive that even if the US government had lacked authority to enter into an enforceable 'agreement in writing' on behalf of its nationals, the applicant's filing of a claim before the IUSCT subsequently 'ratified' these actions. *See also Dames & Moore v. Regan*, 453 U.S. 654, 656–657, 679–680, 686–688 (1981); *In re Islamic Republic of Iran Terrorism Litigation*, 659 F. Supp. 2d 31, 51 (D.D.C. 2009); *United States v. Pink*, 315 U.S. 203, 240 (1942), at p. 240; Kaufmann-Kohler and Potestà, *supra* n. 7, at paras 95, 102.
37. *See Gould*, Court of Appeals, *supra* n. 35, at 1365 (agreeing with the District Court regarding the applicability of the New York Convention). *See also Iran Aircraft Industries v. Iran Helicopter Support, Renewal Company v. Avco Corporation*, 980 F.2d 141 (2d Cir. 1992) (agreeing that the NYC was applicable, but refusing enforcement of the award pursuant to Art. V(1)(b) of the Convention). On other aspects in which the significance of national law may be minimized during NYC enforcement proceedings, *see* China International Economic and Trade Arbitration Commission, Okayama District Court, Civil Section II, 14 July 1993, Case No. Hei 4 (Wa) 8, *Zhe-jiang Provincial Light Industrial Products Import & Export Corp. v. Takeyari K.K.*, YCA, Vol. 22 (1997), 744–747.
38. *Cf.* Similar treatments of the claimant's initiation of IUSCT proceedings as effectively waiving any right to subsequently object to the consensual basis of the Tribunal's jurisdiction, in *Dallal*, *supra* n. 36, 152; *Gould*, District Court, *supra* n. 35, at 765. *See also* David D. Caron, *The Nature of the Iran-United States Claims Tribunal and the Evolving Structure of International Dispute Resolution*, 84 Am. J Int'l L. 104, 148 (1990).
39. *See Gould*, District Court, *supra* n. 35, at 765 ('The [New York] Convention certainly is applicable to the claim here in that the Tribunal is a permanent arbitral body, the dispute involved legal persons and a commercial relationship, and the decision was rendered in the territory of a Contracting State.'). *See also Gould*, Court of Appeals, *supra* n. 35, at 1362 (noting in the context of enforcement requirements that '[t]he Convention defines "arbitral awards" to include those "made by permanent arbitral bodies"').

forum).[40] As reflected in Article I(2), the Committee understood the expression 'arbitral awards' to include awards made by arbitral bodies appointed for each case (whether selected by the parties or by an organization), as well as awards made by *permanent* arbitral bodies.[41]

A standing investment court or appellate mechanism would also satisfy the requirements of Article II(1) of the Convention, which states:

> Each Contracting State shall recognize an agreement in writing under which the parties undertake to submit to arbitration all or any differences which have arisen or which may arise between them in respect of a defined legal relationship, whether contractual or not, concerning a subject matter capable of settlement by arbitration.

Article II(2) further defines an 'agreement in writing' to include 'an arbitral clause in a contract or an arbitration agreement, signed by the parties or contained in an exchange of letters or telegrams'. The reference to 'telegrams' is a fairly classic example of a term which requires evolutionary interpretation to preserve its effectiveness. This may be seen, in turn, to lend support to commentators who characterize an international investment court as a 'permanent arbitral body' by evolutionarily interpreting this term in Article I(2), taking into account developments in international law and arbitration over the six decades since the Convention's adoption.[42]

An institutional body to which the parties do not directly consent, or which they may be legally required to use, differs from traditional depictions of arbitration as arising from an agreement made directly between disputing parties. Yet many international investment agreements confirm that arbitration without privity (i.e., the investor's acceptance, by initiating proceedings, of the host State's treaty-based offer to arbitrate) satisfies Article II(1)'s 'agreement in writing' requirement.[43] Some national courts have recognized this as well in NYC enforcement proceedings for non-ICSID investment awards.[44]

---

40. *See*, for example, the views of Belgium and Sweden in UN Economic and Social Council, Committee on the Enforcement of International Arbitral Awards, 'First Session. Summary Record of the Third Meeting', E/AC.42/SR.3 (23 March 1955), at 6.
41. *See also ibid.*, at 5 (views of the USSR), Point 2 of the USSR's proposed amendment at E/AC.42/L.2, and the remarks of the Chairman at UN Economic and Social Council, Committee on the Enforcement of International Arbitral Awards, 'First Session. Summary Record of the Third Meeting', E/AC.42/SR.3 (23 March 1955), 4. *See also* UN Economic and Social Council, 'Report of the Committee on the Enforcement of International Arbitral Awards', E/27C4: E/AC.42/4/Rev.1 (18 March 1955), para. 25.
42. *See* Kaufmann-Kohler and Potestà, *supra* n. 6, at paras 154, 159. To those commonly cited economic instruments may be added the 1982 UN Convention on the Law of the Sea, which achieved the difficult task of creating a mechanism for unilaterally instituted arbitration in the compromissory clause of a widely ratified treaty. *See* UN Convention on the Law of the Sea (Montego Bay, 10 December 1982), 1833 UNTS 3, Art. 287.
43. *See*, e.g., Art. 25(5)(b) of the 1991 Energy Charter Treaty; Art. 25(2)(b) of the 2012 US Model BIT; Art. 28(2)(b) of the 2004 Canada Model BIT. In respect of permanent tribunals, *see* Comprehensive Economic and Trade Agreement, *supra* n. 2, Art. 8.25(2)(b); EU-Vietnam Free Trade Agreement, *supra* n. 3, Art. 10(4)(b).
44. *See Occidental Exploration & Production Company v. Republic of Ecuador* [2005] EWCA Civ. 1116, at para. 32; *Republic of Ecuador v. Chevron Corp.*, 6338 F.3d 384, 392-393 (2d Cir. 2011); *Werner Schneider v. The Kingdom of Thailand*, 688 F.3d 68, 72-73 (2d Cir. 2012).

A point of consensus that emerged during the 1953 debates at the ICC is that arbitration is fundamentally voluntary, and therefore 'must be based on an agreement between the parties'.[45] The term 'voluntary' survived in the draft text as late as 9 June 1958, one day before the Convention was opened for signature. The draft text was codified verbatim in Article I(2), except for the draft's reference to permanent bodies 'to which the parties have *voluntarily* submitted'.[46]

Some delegates to the conference in New York considered the term redundant,[47] while others had previously stated that its inclusion would be impractical.[48] Some delegates considered that a decision in a proceeding to which the parties had not directly consented would be a judgment, rather than an arbitral award as commonly understood.[49] A proposal to delete 'voluntarily' from the text of Article I(2) was thus approved on the eve of the Convention's adoption.[50]

The adopted text would ultimately not take up the recommendations of some members for greater clarity on the character of arbitral awards. Some delegates considered that defining 'arbitral award' and 'arbitration proceedings' with specificity would 'not only be in conformity with the usual international practice, but it would also provide a more practical basis for the Convention'.[51] Indeed, some of the same delegations who would successfully propose omitting 'voluntarily' in Article I(2) had unsuccessfully lobbied for the inclusion of a more complete definition for 'arbitral award' in the same provision.[52] Ultimately, more importance was attached to the

45. ICC, Report and Preliminary Draft Convention adopted by the Committee on International Commercial Arbitration at its meeting of 13 March 1953, republished in 9 Int'l Ct Arb. Bull. 1998, 10.
46. *See* UN Economic and Social Council, 'Text of the Convention as provisionally approved by the Drafting Committee', E/CONF.26/8 (9 June 1958); UN Economic and Social Council, 'Summary Record of the Twenty-Third Meeting-Consideration of other possible measures for increasing the effectiveness of arbitration in the settlement of private law disputes', E/CONF.26/SR23 (emphasis added). Viewing Art. I(2) as superfluous, *see* Pieter Sanders, *Commentary on UNCITRAL Arbitration Rules*, 1 YB Comm. Arb. 207 (1976).
47. *See* the delegate of Argentina raising this point in UN Economic and Social Council, Conference on International Commercial Arbitration, 'Summary Record of the Twenty-Third Meeting', E/CONF.26/SR.23 (12 September 1958). *See also* UN Economic and Social Council, Conference on International Commercial Arbitration, 'Consideration of Other Measures for Increasing the Effectiveness of Arbitration in the Settlement of Private Law Disputes (Item 5 on the Agenda). Report of the Committee on Other Measures', E/CONF.26/L.60 (6 June 1958).
48. *See* the comments of Austria in UN Economic and Social Council, 'Recognition and Enforcement of Foreign Arbitral Awards. Report by the Secretary-General', Twenty-first session, Item 8, E/2822 (31 January 1956), 10 (considering that the absence of definition regarding 'arbitral award' implies that 'it will depend on the law of the state in which it is to be enforced whether a particular decision is to be regarded as an arbitral award').
49. *See* the delegate of Sweden raising this point in UN Economic and Social Council, Committee on the Enforcement of International Arbitral Awards, 'First Session. Summary Record of the Third Meeting', E/AC.42/SR.3 (23 March 1955).
50. *See* the delegate of Israel making this proposal in Summary Record of Twenty-Third Meeting, *supra* n. 47, at 6.
51. *See* the delegate of Pakistan at UN Economic and Social Council, Conference on International Commercial Arbitration, 'Summary Record of the Sixth Meeting', E/CONF.26/SR.6 (12 September 1958), 5-6.
52. *See* the comment of Israel in UN Economic and Social Council, Conference on International Commercial Arbitration, 'Consideration of the Draft Convention on the Recognition and Enforcement of Foreign Arbitral Awards (Item 4 of the Agenda)', E/CONF.26/L.18 (26 May

inclusion of the reference to permanent bodies in this provision[53] (as discussed above), which some delegations lobbied to retain so as to leave 'no room for misunderstanding' that the treaty encompassed 'permanent arbitral bodies'.[54]

§20.03 COMPARISON TO WTO ARBITRATION

Given that national courts have characterized in different ways the 'arbitral award' and 'agreement between the parties' criteria of NYC enforcement, and noting as well the possibility for distinguishing the systemic elements of any prospective ISDS institution with entities such as the IUSCT, it is worth considering the treatment of the requirements of 'arbitration' in other dispute settlement systems. Particularly relevant in this respect is the WTO, given its broad ratification by 164 members, its outgrowth from the 1944 Bretton Woods Conference in a manner similar to ICSID, and the distinct characteristics of its Dispute Settlement Understanding (DSU). These include substantial multilateral participation, exclusive and automatic jurisdiction, and a two-tiered institutional structure.

Commentators have noted a tendency to frame arbitration as an *alternative* supplement to mandatory dispute settlement systems, and have emphasized defining characteristics such as choice of arbitrators and arbitral procedure, as well as acceptance of binding effect.[55] Others have specifically asserted the enforceability of WTO arbitration awards for compensation under the NYC.[56] As discussed next, the evolution of arbitration within the WTO system includes '"*sui generis*" forms of arbitration'[57] that suggest 'an overall incoherency in the concept of arbitration'.[58]

1958) (defining this as 'an award made by an arbitral body, whether permanent or constituted for any particular case, in pursuance of an agreement [in writing] by which the parties named in the award have voluntarily submitted to the arbitration by such arbitral body of any existing or future disputes between them [in any matter susceptible of arbitration]').

53. *See* proposal of Czechoslovakia in UN Economic and Social Council, Conference on International Commercial Arbitration, 'Consideration of the Draft Convention on the Recognition and Enforcement of Foreign Arbitral Awards (Item 4 of the Agenda)', E/CONF.26/L.10 (22 May 1958).
54. *See* the comment of Ceylon in UN Economic and Social Council, Conference on International Commercial Arbitration, 'Summary Record of the Eighth Meeting', E/CONF.26/SR.8 (12 September 1958), 7.
55. *See* in the WTO context addressed in this section, *WTO: Institutions and Dispute Settlement* 567–571 (Rüdiger Wolfrum, Peter-Tobias Stoll, Karen Kaiser eds, 2006); David Jacyk, *The Integration of Article 25 Arbitration in WTO Dispute Settlement: The Past, Present and Future*, 11 Austl. Int'l L.J. 238–239 (2008) (emphasizing as well that an arbitral tribunal is constituted to hear one particular case only); Ernst-Ulrich Petersmann and Meinhard Hilf, 'Strengthening the GATT Dispute Settlement System: On the Use of Arbitration in GATT', in *The New GATT Round of Multilateral Trade Negotiations* 323, 337 (Ernst-Ulrich Petersmann and Meinhard Hilf eds, 1988).
56. *See*, e.g., William J. Davey, *The WTO Dispute Settlement System: Dealing with Success* 11, 24 (Julian Chaisse and Tsai-yu Lin eds, 2016).
57. *See* Laurence Boisson de Chazournes, *L'Arbitrage A L'OMC*, 949 Revue de l'arbitrage 95 (2003).
58. *See* David Jacyk, *The Integration of Article 25 Arbitration in WTO Dispute Settlement: The Past, Present and Future*, 11 Austl. Int'l L.J. 250 (2008).

[A] Systemic Considerations

The WTO DSU provides for two types of procedure that it labels as arbitration. One of these may arise after an Appellate Body decision and consists solely of clarifying the duration of a 'reasonable period of time', under DSU Article 21.3(c), or the appropriate level of suspension of concessions, under DSU Article 22.6, for compliance with the decision. These *implementation* arbitrations are conducted by individuals assigned by the WTO Director-General, and result in decisions that are binding for the parties.[59] The other type of procedure, as seen in DSU Article 25, is *alternative* arbitration, whereby parties can agree to expeditiously resolve the dispute through arbitration instead of 'mainstream' WTO proceedings.[60] As in ad hoc arbitration, the specific procedural aspects, including choice of arbitrator, are left to the parties.

Quite distinct from traditional arbitration, however, awards under both types of procedure remain enforceable under the institutional implementation provisions of the DSU. The fact that a proceeding is administered under the auspices of an institution certainly does not affect its status as 'arbitration', e.g., awards issued by the Permanent Court of Arbitration (PCA). However, it appears that a principal reason why the expeditious arbitration procedure is referred to as 'within the WTO', as opposed to arbitration by parties' agreement, e.g., *Softwood Lumber*, or by WTO-authorized waiver, e.g., *EC – Bananas III*, is that compliance with the resulting award is expressly subject to the same WTO supervisory proceedings as Appellate Body reports.

The drafting context of WTO arbitration notably predates the Uruguay Round. While the 1948 Havana Charter[61] would provide for the possibility of recourse to arbitration, the agreement salvaged from that failed experiment – the General Agreement on Tariffs and Trade 1947 (GATT) – did not explicitly provide for arbitration.[62] This omission appears to have been deliberate, because the GATT's dispute settlement provision tracks much of the wording found in the Havana Charter, with the notable exception of this reference to arbitration.[63] In 1979, several improvements were adopted during the Tokyo Round of GATT negotiations. While these included a mechanism for 'the settlement of disputes through resort to good offices and to conciliation', arbitration was again omitted.[64]

59. *A Handbook on the WTO Dispute Settlement System* 25 (2004).
60. Award of the Arbitrators, *US – Section 110(5) Copyright Act* (Art. 25), WT/DS160/ARB25/1 (9 November 2001) para. 2.3.
61. Havana Charter for an International Trade Organization, 24 March 1948, CTS No. 32, 3; UN Doc. E/CONF.2/78 (1948), Art. 93.
62. GATT Secretariat, Group of Negotiations on Goods, Negotiating Group on Dispute Settlement, 'Summary and Comparative Analysis of Proposals for Negotiations', MTN.GNG/NG13/W/14 (3 November 1987), para. 75.
63. *See* Valerie Hughes, 'Arbitration within WTO', in *The WTO Dispute Settlement System 1995–2003* 76 (Federico Ortino and Ernst-Ulrich Petersmann eds, 2004).
64. *Ibid.*, at 77.

Only during the Uruguay Round did several states submit proposals[65] providing for the resolution of disputes through arbitration.[66] These proposals served in part to address one of the GATT's key problems: the requirement that panel reports be adopted by consensus decision in the GATT Council, where a losing party could unilaterally block the adoption of the report and avoid compliance.[67] In particular, the US proposed arbitration 'as an alternative means of dispute settlement for defined classes of cases, or by prior agreement of the disputing parties on an ad hoc basis'.[68] The US delegation further argued that since all GATT disputes are subject to the same procedures, 'issues that should be relatively simply and easily settled are taking too long and becoming too political because of procedures and practices designed for harder cases'.[69] In so doing, it characterized 'binding arbitration' as a process wherein '[the] arbitrators' decision would not require approval by the GATT Council'.[70] While some delegations expressed caution[71] as to the strength of the US analogy between commercial contract arbitration and decision-making under the GATT,[72] several others voiced their support for arbitration of disputes of a 'factual' nature,[73] or support for non-mandatory arbitration in general.[74]

While these discussions revealed an intention to explore arbitration within an institutional context, they also demonstrated uncertainty as to how arbitration was distinguishable from the panel system, and thus as to its place within the GATT system.[75] Thereafter, the GATT Secretariat prepared a note on 'Concept, forms and

65. Improved Dispute Settlement: Elements For Consideration. Discussion Paper Prepared by United States Delegation, GATT Doc. No. MTN.GNG/NG13/W/6 (25 June 1987); Communication from Switzerland, GATT Doc. No. MTN.GNG/NG13/W/8 (18 September 1987); Communication from the Nordic Countries, GATT Doc No. MTN.GNG/NG13/W/10 (18 September 1987); Communication from the EEC, GATT Doc. No. MTN.GNG/NG13/W/12 (24 September 1987), Communication from Canada, GATT Doc. No. MTN.GNG/NG13/W/13 (24 September 1987); Communication from Korea, GATT Doc. No. MTN.GNG/NG13/W/19 (20 November 1987).
66. *WTO: Institutions and Dispute Settlement* 567 (Rüdiger Wolfrum, Peter-Tobias Stoll and Karen Kaiser eds, 2006).
67. *See* Jens Hillebrand Pohl, 'Blueprint for a Plurilateral WTO Arbitration Agreement under Article 25 of the Dispute Settlement Understanding', in *Restoring Trust in Trade: Liber Amicorum in Honour of Peter Van den Bossche* 4-5 (Denise Prévost, Iveta Alexovicova and Jens Hillebrand Pohl eds, 2018).
68. 1987 US Discussion Paper, *supra* n. 65, at 2.
69. *Ibid.*
70. *Ibid.*
71. *See* Nordic countries' proposal, MTN.GNG/NG13/W/10. *See also* Proposals summarized, MTN.GNG/NG13/W/14 (3 November 1987) paras 72-74.
72. *See* 1987 US Discussion Paper, *supra* n. 65, at 2 ('Arbitration is a widespread and common form of dispute settlement in international trade. Many commodity and transportation contracts between firms normally provide for impartial arbitration by specialists in those fields. Arbitration provisions may also be found in a number of bilateral intergovernmental trade agreements and in air transport agreements').
73. *See* Hughes, *supra* n. 63, at 77 (*citing* the EEC's proposal, MTN.GNG/NG13/W/12 (24 September 1987). *See also* Korea's proposal), MTN.GNG/NG13/W/19 (20 November 1987) 2.
74. *See* Switzerland's proposal, MTN.GNG/NG13/W/8. *See also* Communication from Canada, GATT Doc. No. MTN.GNG/NG13/W/13 (24 September 1987).
75. *See* David Jacyk, *The Integration of Article 25 Arbitration in WTO Dispute Settlement: The Past, Present and Future*, 11 Austl. Int'l L.J. 246 (2008).

effects of arbitration' for the Uruguay Round's Negotiating Group on Dispute Settlement. Contrasting arbitration with both diplomatic and judicial settlement, the Secretariat defined it as 'the process of resolving disputes on the basis of respect for law through decisions binding upon the disputant parties by arbitrators appointed by the parties to hear a particular case submitted by the parties'.[76] In particular, the Secretariat observed that '[a]rbitration presupposes (A) an agreement among the parties to the dispute, which (B) defines the form of arbitration, (C) the selection of arbitrators, (D) the terms of reference, (E) the basis of the decision, and (F) the effect of the award'.[77] The Secretariat also highlighted the 1907 Hague Convention for the Pacific Settlement of International Disputes (one of the founding treaties of the PCA), noting that Article 84(2) of that convention provides third states with the right to intervene in a pending arbitration if it concerns the interpretation of a treaty to which they are parties.[78] Yet several members appeared more concerned that awards would not prejudice the rights of dormant third parties, irrespective of any such opportunity to participate in the underlying arbitration.[79]

Indeed, the negotiating record provides little evidence that GATT members shared a common understanding of Article 25 procedure beyond the skeletal text of that provision. To the contrary, the *travaux préparatoires* suggests that members deliberately opted to avoid providing further detail regarding the form and nature of arbitration.[80] Arbitration was first incorporated in this manner in the 1989 Montreal Rules, which applied provisionally until the end of the Uruguay Round, and which would closely resemble Article 25 of the DSU.[81]

Some delegates during early phases of these negotiations considered that parties could authorize a GATT arbitration tribunal to exceed a purely fact-finding mandate.[82] This would seem to have presciently foretold the establishment of Articles 21 and 22 arbitration under the DSU, insofar as those fact-finding arbitrations can be instituted unilaterally by either party.[83] The formalization of Articles 21.3 and 22.6 of the DSU

---

76. Negotiating Group on Dispute Settlement, Concept, Forms and Effect of Arbitration, Note by the Secretariat, MTN.GNG/NG13/W/20 (22 February 1988) 3. *See also* discussion of the 1963 'chicken panel' precedent at *ibid.*, at 9.
77. *Ibid.*, at 3–4.
78. *Ibid*, at 5.
79. For example, communication from the EEC, MTN.GNG/NG13/W/22 (2 March 1988) 4. Indeed, some scholars consider that the Art. 25's historical unpopularity can be partly explained by the multilateral, rather than bilateral, nature of WTO disputes. *See*, e.g., Hughes, *supra* n. 64, at 85.
80. *See* Jens Hillebrand Pohl, 'Blueprint for a Plurilateral WTO Arbitration Agreement Under Article 25 of the Dispute Settlement Understanding' in *Restoring Trust in Trade: Liber Amicorum in Honour of Peter Van den Bossche* (Denise Prévost, Iveta Alexovicova and Jens Hillebrand Pohl eds, 2018), 5.
81. *See* Trade Negotiations Committee Meeting at Ministerial Level, Montreal, December1988, GATT Doc. No. MTN.TNC/7(MIN) (9 December 1988); *WTO: Institutions and Dispute Settlement* 567 (Rüdiger Wolfrum, Peter-Tobias Stoll and Karen Kaiser eds, 2006); *see also* Hughes, *supra* n. 63, at 78–80; David Palmeter and Petros C. Mavroidis, *Dispute Settlement in the World Trade Organization: Practice and Procedure* (2004), 10.
82. *See* Communication from Japan, MTN.GNG/NG13/W/21 (1 March 1988).
83. Comparison of Existing Texts And Proposals For Improvements to the GATT Dispute Settlement System, MTN.GNG/NG13/W/29 (8 August 1988).

would occur after discussion of initial texts and proposals,[84] with subsequent communications suggesting as well the role of the Director-General in the appointment of arbitrators under those provisions.[85] While arbitration was not embraced by all members as a means to rectify problems of implementation and retaliation,[86] the Chairman of the negotiations observed that with regard to the question of implementation and determination of a reasonable period of time, '[t]he need for *rapid completion* of the dispute settlement process, including implementation, is *stressed by all delegations*, with some delegates giving particular emphasis to the need for quick action in the context of perishable goods'.[87] Within a matter of months, these provisions concerning binding arbitration procedures would appear in the Uruguay Round's final draft text on dispute settlement.[88]

[B] Specific Forms of WTO Arbitration

WTO arbitrators have observed that DSU Article 25 reflects arbitration's general consistency with the object and purpose of the DSU, as '[a]rbitration is likely to contribute to the prompt settlement of a dispute between Members' and 'strengthens the dispute resolution system by complementing negotiation under Article 22.2'.[89] Importantly for its characterization as an *alternative* form of dispute settlement, arbitration is framed in Article 25 as consensual, as opposed to compulsory adjudication through panel or Appellate Body proceedings.[90]

In terms of choice of procedural rules and selection of arbitrators, Article 25.2 of the DSU provides that parties are free to depart from standard DSU procedures and to agree on rules they deem appropriate for the arbitration. Third parties may participate 'only with the agreement' of the parties to the arbitration.[91] Unlike the other forms of WTO arbitration discussed below, Article 25 does not enable the Director-General to appoint arbitrators – this remains subject to the parties' mutual agreement.[92] Arbitration awards under Article 25 are not appealable but can be enforced through the same

84. *See* Communication by the USA, MTN.GNG/NG13/W/40 (6 April 1990), 6–7. *See also* Statement by the Spokesman of the European Community, MTN.GNG/NG13/W/44 (19 July 1990), 2.
85. *See* Communication from Canada, MTN.GNG/NG13/W/41 (28 June 1990), 4.
86. *See* Communication from Mexico, MTN.GNG/NG13/W/42 (12 July 1990).
87. Report by the Chairman, MTN.GNG/NG13/W/43 (18 July 1990) 2–3 (emphasis added).
88. Draft text on dispute settlement, MTN.GNG/NG13/W/45 (21 September 1990).
89. Award of the Arbitrators, *US – Section 110(5) Copyright Act* (Art. 25), WT/DS160/ARB25/1 (9 November 2001) paras 2.4–2.7.
90. Analytical Index, DSU – Art. 25 (Jurisprudence) p. 6 *citing* Appellate Body Reports, *US/Canada – Continued Suspension*, para. 340.
91. *A Handbook on the WTO Dispute Settlement System* 96 (2004).
92. Article 25 arbitration remains within the parties' overall control to commence, without need to more than notify that decision to the supervisory WTO DSB, thus making it 'incumbent on the Arbitrators themselves to ensure that [Art. 25] is applied in accordance with the rules and principles governing the WTO system'. Analytical Index, DSU – Art. 25 (Jurisprudence) 2 *citing* Award of the Arbitrators, *US – Section 110(5) Copyright Act (Article 25)*, para. 2.1. On the role of third parties in this context, *see* further Jens Hillebrand Pohl, 'Blueprint for a Plurilateral WTO Arbitration Agreement Under Article 25 of the Dispute Settlement Understanding', in *Restoring Trust in Trade: Liber Amicorum in Honour of Peter Van den Bossche* 8 (Denise Prévost, Iveta Alexovicova and Jens Hillebrand Pohl eds, 2018).

DSU mechanisms as traditional WTO decisions (including the other form of arbitration discussed below).[93]

In only one dispute thus far have the parties resorted to arbitration under Article 25. For this reason, the arbitrators in *US – §110(5) of the US Copyright Act* considered some questions of first impression, including whether the arbitration was even permissible under Article 25, given that this provision envisages arbitration as an 'alternative' to the dispute settlement procedures laid out elsewhere in the DSU, whereas the parties had asked the arbitrators to determine questions concerning the level of nullification or impairment of benefits in the implementation of an already-adopted panel report.[94] The arbitrators found that it was permitted to proceed because Article 25 proceedings are based upon the consent of the parties, and as such consent embraced the determination of the scope of the dispute.[95] Arbitration was used in this manner to resolve a specific aspect of the dispute, rather than the full dispute as originally submitted to the panel.[96] In so doing, the arbitrators affirmed the principle of *compétence de la compétence* in this novel context.[97]

In terms of the power to seek information or investigate factual issues, Article 14 of the DSU provides for a panel's 'right to seek information and technical advice from any individual or body which it deems appropriate', and permits panels to 'consult experts to obtain their opinion on certain aspects of the matter'. This power appears to apply to Article 25 arbitration by analogy. In *US – Section 110(5) Copyright Act*, the arbitrators decided to seek additional information from US collective management organizations, although in the end they decided not to use the information submitted.[98]

Turning to *implementation* arbitration, DSU Article 21.3 provides that when immediate compliance with a panel or Appellate Body report is not possible, the concerned WTO member shall have a 'reasonable period of time' to implement the WTO Dispute Settlement Body's (DSB) rulings and recommendations. The 'reasonable period of time' may be 'the period of time proposed by the Member concerned, provided that such period is approved by the DSB' or 'a period of time mutually agreed by the parties to the dispute'. If neither of these two options is possible, Article 21.3(c) provides that the 'reasonable period of time' shall be 'a period of time determined through binding arbitration'.[99]

---

93. *A Handbook on the WTO Dispute Settlement System* 24 (2004).
94. *Dispute Settlement without recourse to Panels and the Appellate Body*, WTO, https://www.wto.org/english/tratop_e/dispu_e/disp_settlement_cbt_e/c8s2p1_e.htm.
95. *WTO: Institutions and Dispute Settlement* 569 (Rüdiger Wolfrum, Peter-Tobias Stoll, Karen Kaiser eds, 2006).
96. *See* Matthew Weiniger and Akshay Sewlikar, *Arbitrating WTO Disputes*, Kluwer Arbitration Blog (3 July 2018), http://arbitrationblog.kluwerarbitration.com/2018/07/03/arbitrating-wto-disputes/.
97. Analytical Index, DSU – Art. 25 (Jurisprudence) 2 *citing* Award of the Arbitrators, *US – Section 110(5) Copyright Act* (Art. 25), para. 2.1.
98. Award of the Arbitrators, *US – Section 110(5) Copyright Act* (Art. 25), WT/DS160/ARB25/1 (9 November 2001) para. 1.10.
99. *Arbitrations under Article 21.3(c) of the DSU*, WTO https://www.wto.org/english/tratop_e/dispu_e/arbitrations_e.htm.

Unlike under Article 25, Article 21 arbitration does not proceed on the basis of mutual agreement at that time, but rather as a default procedure.[100] While consent to implementation arbitration is thus grounded in the act of becoming Contracting Parties to the DSU (i.e., through a treaty compromissory clause, rather than through a special agreement at the time of the dispute), the 'arbitration process can also be subsequently modified by mutual agreement of the parties in dispute' if they do agree on this point.[101] This form of arbitration has been similarly described as a 'residual' means of dispute settlement. The arbitrator in this sense 'comes across as the "executive arm" of a panel and the Appellate Body'.[102]

Article 21 arbitrators are selected by the parties to the arbitration or, if they cannot agree on an arbitrator, the Director-General appoints the arbitrator. An arbitrator can be an individual or a group of individuals.[103] Thus far, every arbitration under Article 21 has been conducted by an Appellate Body member acting in his or her individual capacity.[104] At the same time, the DSU does not provide for any guidelines as to the professional requirements for serving as an Article 21 arbitrator.[105]

The role of arbitration under Article 21 has become clarified through the thirty-two disputes (as of 30 June 2019) where an arbitrator has determined the reasonable period of time.[106] This includes clarification that the mandate of an arbitrator is limited 'to determin[ing] the time period within which the implementing Member must comply with the recommendations and rulings of the DSB'.[107] However, the mandate does not include suggesting means of implementation.[108] As arbitrators have stressed, they focus 'on the *when*, not the *what*'.[109] Furthermore, arbitrators are bound 'by the factual findings and the legal judgments that form the basis of the Panel and the Appellate Body Reports that have been adopted as recommendations and

100. *See* Hughes, *supra* n. 64, at 82.
101. Shin-yi Peng, *Determination of Reasonable Period of Time: Dispute Settlement of the World Trade Organization*, Max Planck Encyclopedias of International Law (2019). para. 6.
102. Laurence Boisson de Chazournes, 'Arbitration at the WTO: A Terra Incognita to Be Further Explored', in *Law in the Service of Human Dignity: Essays in Honour of Florentino Feliciano* (Steve Charnovitz, Debra P. Steger and Peter Van den Bossche, eds, 2005), 188, 192.
103. *A Handbook on the WTO Dispute Settlement System* 77 (2004).
104. *Arbitrations under Article 21.3(c) of the DSU*, WTO https://www.wto.org/english/tratop_e/dispu_e/arbitrations_e.htm.
105. *See* Peter Van den Bossche, *The Law and Policy of the World Trade Organization* 278 (2005). *See also* Shin-yi Peng, *Determination of Reasonable Period of Time: Dispute Settlement of the World Trade Organization*, Max Planck Encyclopedias of International Law (2019), para. 43.
106. This does not include cases where the parties managed to reach an agreement about time period themselves although an arbitrator was appointed. *See* 'Table of Cases' at *Arbitrations under Article 21.3(c) of the DSU*, WTO https://www.wto.org/english/tratop_e/dispu_e/arbitrations_e.htm. *See further* WTO Analytical Index, DSU – Art. 21 (Jurisprudence), p. 14 (updated 30 June 2019).
107. *See*, e.g., Award of the Arbitrator Simon Farbenbloom in *United States – Anti-Dumping Methodologies (China)*, WT/DS471/RPT, p. 8.
108. Analytical Index, DSU – Art. 21 (Jurisprudence) p. 16 (*citing* Award of the Arbitrator, *EC – Hormones* (Art. 21.3(c)), para. 38).
109. Analytical Index, DSU – Art. 21 (Jurisprudence) p. 17 (*citing* Award of the Arbitrator, *EC – Chicken Cuts* (Art. 21.3(c)), para. 49).

rulings by the DSB'.[110] As for the participation of other WTO members in these proceedings, it has been clear since *Japan – Alcoholic Beverages II* that '[a]ll the original parties to the dispute could participate in the arbitration process', even though only the US had requested binding arbitration under this provision.[111]

The other variety of implementation arbitration is found in DSU Article 22, which enables the complainant to request the DSB to suspend concessions or grant other remedies if parties cannot agree on mutually acceptable levels of suspension. According to Article 22.6, if the respondent 'objects to the level of suspension proposed, or claims that [complainant did not follow] the principles and procedures set forth in [relevant DSU provisions], the matter shall be referred to arbitration'.[112]

Article 22 explicitly provides that arbitration shall be carried out by the original panel, if members are available, or by an arbitrator appointed by the Director-General. As of 30 June 2019, all of the fifteen arbitrations under Article 22 have been referred to the original panel, except for two cases.[113] This provision thus demonstrates the value its drafters placed on knowledge of the original dispute, as a relevant asset for effectively completing the arbitrators' task.[114] The parties must accept the arbitrator's decision as final and not seek a second arbitration.[115]

In many instances, Article 22 arbitrations have adapted working procedures based on the text of the DSU, through which 'the Arbitrator will meet in closed session; the deliberations of the Arbitrator and the documents submitted to it shall be kept confidential'.[116] As for the participation of other WTO members in proceedings, in *EC – Hormones*, involving two parallel proceedings, one initiated by Canada and one by the US against the EC, the arbitrator granted third-party rights to the US and Canada based on a rule that arbitrators have discretion to decide on procedural matters not regulated in the DSU in accordance with due process.[117] At the same time, in *EC –*

110. Analytical Index, DSU – Art. 21 (Jurisprudence) p. 17) *citing* Award of the Arbitrator, *EC – Chicken Cuts* (Art. 21.3(c)), para. 59).
111. Award of the Arbitrator, *Japan – Alcoholic Beverages II*, WT/DS8/15, WT/DS10/15, WT/DS11/13 (14 February 1997) Art. 21.3(c), para. 3.
112. *See* Carlo Cantore and Petros Mavroidis, *Arbitration on the Level of Retaliation: Dispute Settlement of the World Trade Organization*, Max Planck Encyclopedias of International Law (2018), para. 19 ('The simple objection by the losing party should be sufficient to trigger the arbitration procedures envisaged under Article 22.6 DSU'); Analytical Index, DSU – Art. 22 (Jurisprudence), p. 26 (*citing* Decision by the Arbitrators, *EC – Bananas III* (Ecuador) (Art. 22.6 – EC), para. 11).
113. Analytical Index, DSU – Art. 22 (Jurisprudence) pp. 20, 23 (updated 30 June 2019).
114. *WTO: Institutions and Dispute Settlement* 549 (Rüdiger Wolfrum, Peter-Tobias Stoll and Karen Kaiser eds, 2006).
115. *A Handbook on the WTO Dispute Settlement System* 84 (2004). The DSB does not have to adopt the decision. Carlo Cantore and Petros Mavroidis, *Arbitration on the Level of Retaliation: Dispute Settlement of the World Trade Organization*, Max Planck Encyclopedias of International Law (2018), para. 65.
116. *See US – Offset Act (Byrd Amendment) (22.6)*, WT/DS217/ARB/BRA (31 August 2004) Annex A, 49; Analytical Index, DSU – Art. 22 (Jurisprudence) 21–22.
117. Analytical Index, DSU – Art. 22 (Jurisprudence), 19 *citing* Decision by the Arbitrator, *EC – Hormones* (US) (Art. 22.6 – EC), para. 7; decision by the Arbitrator, *EC – Hormones* (Canada) (Art. 22.6 – EC), para. 7. In *EC – Hormones*, the Arbitrator granted third-party rights to the United States and Canada respectively in parallel Art. 22.6 proceedings initiated against the other by the European Communities. *EC – Hormones (US)* (Art. 22.6 – EC) and *EC – Hormones*

Bananas III (US), Ecuador requested third-party status. However, the arbitrator (applying Article 10 of the DSU by analogy) decided that 'in light of the absence of provisions for third-party status under Article 22 of the DSU and given that we do not believe that Ecuador's rights will be affected by this proceeding, we declined Ecuador's request'.[118] This is in contrast with Article 25 arbitration, which explicitly provides that 'other members may become party to an arbitration proceeding only upon the agreement of the parties [to the dispute]'.

§20.04 CONCLUSIONS

Viewed as relevant context for treaty interpretation, the 1940s GATT, 1950s NYC, 1960s ICSID Convention, and 1990s WTO negotiating conferences reflect a continuum of understanding in international economic law as to the meaning of the key terms of international arbitration. The use of 'arbitration' to signal fundamentally different concepts in these instruments recalls that without a self-contained enforcement regime, national courts will inevitably be called upon to assess the character of investment court decisions under the NYC.

For instance, the DSU only recognizes arbitrations which are notified to the DSB, and the implementation of every such award is subject to institutional oversight. Alternative and implementation arbitration within the WTO system have moreover been interpreted differently in regards to party autonomy to restrict third-party participation: an express opportunity for third-party members to intervene during panel proceedings; a clear bar against third-party intervention without party consent during Article 25 arbitrations; and case law under Articles 21 and 22 relying at times on an implied right of the arbitrator to admit third-party participation in these proceedings. All these models also differ in terms of the requirement of parties' consent for the determination of procedures, and the possibility for parties to select arbitrators and mutually adjust the scope of issues addressed in the award.

In light of these distinctions, delegations during the Uruguay Round appear to have characterized all forms of WTO arbitration in terms of their expeditious objective and res judicata character. This explains as well the default settings of implementation arbitration, such as the appointment of the original panelists as arbitrators in Article 22 proceedings to achieve a timely settlement of technical questions closely linked with the 'main' case. The other principal commonality among these procedures is party's consent. While WTO practice includes forms of arbitration often framed as sui generis,

---

(Canada) (Art. 22.6 - EC) (noting that the DSU 'give[s] the arbitrators discretion to decide on procedural matters not regulated in the DSU ... in accordance with due process', and 'leave[s] panels a margin of discretion to deal, always in accordance with due process, with specific situations that may arise in a particular case and that are not explicitly regulated'). Art. 12.1 of the DSU further states that panels shall follow the pre-established Working Procedures in Appendix 3 'unless the panel decides otherwise after consulting the parties to the dispute'. *See European Communities – Measures Concerning Meat and Meat Products (Hormones) (US) (22.6 - EC)*, DS26, Decision by the Arbitrator, para. 7, n. 5.

118. Analytical Index, DSU - Art. 22 (Jurisprudence), p. 18, *citing* Decision by the Arbitrator, *EC – Bananas III* (US) (Art. 22.6 - EC), para. 2.8.

unilaterally instituted arbitration under DSU Article 21 or 22 is nevertheless consensual in light of the parties' statutory consent to unilaterally instituted proceedings incidental to the main case.[119]

The experience of the IUSCT is particularly relevant in this light, as the model of arbitration without privity found there is akin to what might be more expected of an international investment court more so than the WTO model, where all disputing parties are also contracting parties. National court enforcement of IUSCT decisions under the NYC also provides support for those who assume an international investment court to be a 'permanent arbitral body' within the meaning of Article I(2) of the Convention.

Subjecting a prospective investment court's proceedings to a domestic *lex arbitri* would satisfy the territoriality requirements of the NYC. In a system instead based on the self-contained ICSID regime – creating an a-national procedural forum – this matter only arises as to the enforcement of such decisions in the courts of non-Member States. The practice of national courts applying the NYC and the enforcement of ICSID awards in non-ICSID states in particular suggests that the decisions of an international investment court or appellate mechanism would satisfy the Convention's 'non-domestic' requirement.

In addition to informing the meaning of arbitration, the broad ratification of different meanings of the same term during fifty years of economic liberalization treaties highlights current initiatives that are developing contemporaneously with the ISDS reform project. In light of the crisis that resulted in the WTO Appellate Body's de facto suspension in December 2019, the EU concluded several agreements with WTO members in order to preserve the dispute settlement system.[120] These arrangements were based on Article 25 of the DSU, yet aimed to replicate 'as closely as possible all substantive and procedural aspects as well as the practice of Appellate Review pursuant to Article 17 of the DSU'.[121] Subsequently, nineteen WTO members concluded the Multi-Party Interim Arbitration Arrangement, which entered into force on 30 April 2020,[122] and which became available to its twenty-four members upon constituting a pool of arbitrators on 31 July 2020.[123]

While this text diverges in some respects from those bilateral instruments, such as by not relying upon former Appellate Body members, it too seeks to use arbitration under Article 25 of the DSU to fill the lacuna left by the Appellate Body's current

119. Elaborating upon 'incidental' proceedings in a general sense by reference to ICJ practice, *see* further *The Law and Practice of the International Court, 1920–2005* (Shabtai Rosenne and Yael Ronen eds, 2006), 578, et seq.

120. *Trade: EU and 16 WTO members agree to work together on an interim appeal arbitration arrangement*, European Commission (24 January 2020), https://ec.europa.eu/commission/presscorner/detail/en/IP_20_113.

121. *See*, e.g., Interim Appeal Arbitration Pursuant to Art. 25 of the DSU (EU-Nor.) (Brussels, 21 October 2019), paras 2, 3 (providing that appeals would be heard by former Appellate Body members to be selected by the Director-General).

122. *Multi-Party Interim Appeal Arbitration Arrangement Pursuant to Article 25 of the DSU*, WTO (30 April 2020), JOB/DSB/1/Add.12.

123. *Statement on a Mechanism for Developing, Documenting and Sharing Practices and Procedures in the Conduct of WTO Disputes*, WTO (3 August 2020), JOB/DSB/1/Add.12/Suppl.5.

dysfunction, rather than to serve as a true 'alternative' thereto. In this light, the ISDS reform project currently underway at UNCITRAL is part of larger institutional upheaval in international economic law. The arbitral innovations arising out of both regimes demonstrate the importance attached to access to justice in the international trade and investment fields. But at the same time, they recall that the effectiveness of these systems depends upon prior analysis as to what form of treaty-based enforcement system would suit the nature of a particular institution.

Index

B

J

www.ingramcontent.com/pod-product-compliance
Lightning Source LLC
LaVergne TN
LVHW020647300926
849161LV00004B/848